DMI	Desktop Management Interface
DMTF	Desktop Management Task Force
DOCS	Data Over Cable System
DOCSIS	Data Over Cable System Interface Specifications
DTE	Data Terminating Equipment
DSL	Digital Subscriber Line
DSLAM	Digital Subscriber Line Access Multiplexer
EGP	External Gateway Protocol
EIA	Electrical Industries Association
ELAN	Emulated Local Area Network
FDDI	Fiber Distributed Data Interface
FSK	Frequency Shift Keying
FTAM	File Transfer and Access Management
FTP	File Transfer Protocol
FTTN	Fiber cable To The Neighborhood
GDMO	Guidelines for Definition of Managed Objects
HDSL	High data rate Digital Subscriber Line
HFC	Hybrid Fiber Coaxial cable
HMAC	Hashed Message Access Code
HTTP	Hypertext Transport Protocol
IAB	Internet Advisory Board
IANA	Internet Assigned Numbers Authority
ICI	Interface Control Information
ICMP	Internet Control Message Protocol
IEEE	Institute of Electrical and Electronic Engineers
IETF	Internet Engineering Task Force
IGP	Internal Gateway Protocol
ILMI	Integrated Local Management Interface
IP	Internet Protocol
IRTF	Internet Research Task Force
ISDN	Integrated Services Digital Network
ISO	International Organization for Standardization
ITU	International Telecommunications Union
ITU-T	ITU - Telecommunications Sector
JDMK	Java Dynamic Management Kit
JMAPI	Java Management Application Interface
JMX	Java Management Extensions
LAN	Local Area Network
LANE	Local Area Network Emulation
LLC	Logical Link Control
LMDS	Local Multipoint Distribution

NETWORK MANAGEMENT

Principles and Practice

NETWORK MANAGEMENT

Principles and Practice

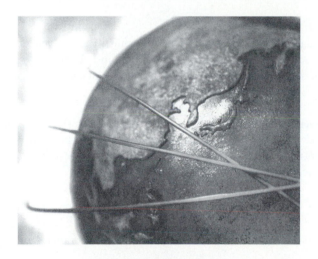

Mani Subramanian

Georgia Institute of Technology

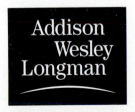

An imprint of Addison Wesley Longman, Inc

Reading, Massachusetts • Menlo Park, California
New York • Harlow, England • Don Mills, Ontario
Sydney • Mexico City • Madrid • Amsterdam

Senior Acquisitions Editor: Susan Hartman
Project Editor: Katherine Harutunian
Production Supervisor: Pat Mahtani
Composition: Northeast Compositors, Inc.
Manufacturing: Tim McDonald
Cover Design: S. Heiser, Night & Day Design
Interior Design: Joyce Cosentino

Access the latest information about Addison-Wesley titles from our World Wide Web site at http://www.awlonline.com

Many of the designations used by manufacturers and sellers to distinguish their products are claimed as trademarks. Where those designations appear in this book, and Addison-Wesley was aware of a trademark claim, the designations have been printed in initial caps or all caps. In addition, a list of known trademarks follows the appendixes.

The programs and applications presented in this book have been included for their instructional value. They have been tested with care but are not guaranteed for any purpose. The publisher does not offer any warranties or representations, nor does it accept any liabilities with respect to the programs or applications.

Library of Congress Cataloging-in-Publication Data

Subramanian, Mani.
    Network management: An introduction to principals and practice / Mani Subramanian.
        p. cm.
    Includes bibliographical references and index.
    ISBN 0-201-35742-9
    1. Computer networks—Management.   I. Title.
    TK5105.5 .S83 2000
    004.6—dc21   99-047374
                                                        CIP

2 3 4 5 6 7 8 9 10-MA-03

Dedicated with affection

and namaskarams to
Appa Mahadevan
Amma Kalyani

and deepest love to
Ruth Subramanian

PREFACE

Changing Role of Network Management in Academia

Imagine that you are leading a group of engineers who are developing application software to provide a sophisticated network printing service for high-speed plotters. Picture further that the LAN being used to develop the software is so unstable and that they are so frustrated they come to you complaining about the unsatisfactory information technology (IT) services each time the network goes down. The IT manager and the engineers both think that the cause of the problem belongs to the other. In this real-world situation both parties, who are closely related to networking in their daily activities, do not have a handle on the source of the problem. Neither was to blame because they were not knowledgeable about networking tools and network management, but you have been called upon to sort it out.

It is not uncommon to observe this lack of practical knowledge in bright young graduates (or even the more experienced ones), who have specialized in networking and telecommunications, when they enter the work environment. It is obvious that making network management a part of the academic curriculum is a necessity to remedy this deficiency. In this book we aim to give you the background you will need to attack the problems such as the one just posed.

According to a Data Quest report in *Information Week,* April 1998, the value of information technology services is expected to double in 5 years, reaching $622 billion by 2002. Hardly an organization, public or private, functions today without the deployment of LANs in its networking environment. The Internet is expanding at such a rate that Webphones will be in many homes within the next decade. These devices will have to be managed from the centralized network operation center of a service provider.

The technical aspects of network, systems, and applications management in information technology services have so far been the responsibility of telecommunications and networking industries and standards bodies. Academia participates peripherally in the work of standards bodies by setting up protocol standards. The proliferating use of the Internet and the emerging technology of network computers and Webphones have spurred a scientific approach to network management that includes academic research.

Rationale for a Textbook on Network Management

The first step in starting a network management program is to introduce a course on network management. Although the available books I surveyed for use as a textbook that satisfied quarter/semester course requirements were good professional books, none met the needs of a textbook for my course. The reason is that most people learn network management on the job; hence network management books were oriented toward the professional, covering a narrow field in depth. A textbook on network management was sorely needed.

This book covers management principles, practices, and technologies for managing networks, systems, applications, and services. A balance between theoretical background and the practical aspects of network management is maintained. The treatment of practical aspects includes real-world examples. If "a picture is worth a thousand words," this book contains more than a million words! Just as a programming course requires hands-on exercises, so should a network management course, and we provide them.

About the Contents

This book is divided into three parts. Part I deals with background material on networking and networking technologies. Part II addresses network management architectures and protocols. Part III focuses on tools and systems for monitoring and managing networks, systems, applications, and services. The book concludes with a discussion of the latest in management technology, Web-based management.

Part I consists of Chapters 1 and 2. Chapter 1 presents an overview of networking and network management. It is intended not only to provide background and top-down information, but also as a motivation for the student. Chapter 2 reviews networking technology, with a slant on its management aspects. The course for which this textbook is intended is based on the assumption that the student has had a quarter or semester of data communications. Chapter 2 can be either skipped or covered in parts by the instructor. Relevant sections of it could also be used when dealing with subjects in Parts II and III.

Chapters 3–11 form Part II. Basic foundations of standards, models, and language, which are needed to build various network management architectures and protocols, are covered in Chapter 3. SNMP-based protocols that manage TCP/IP networks are covered in Chapters 4–8. Chapters 4 and 5 are devoted to learning the concepts and use of SNMP (version 1) in network management. Chapters 6 and 7 deal with the additional specifications defined in SNMP versions 2 and 3. Chapter 8 extends network management to the use of remote monitoring capabilities.

The demarcation of telecommunications and computer communication is becoming increasingly fuzzy in broadband communications. The impact of ATM technology on broadband network management is dealt with in Chapter 9. Chapter 10 addresses access networks in broadband services to the home and management of emerging access technologies. Chapter 11 extends management concepts to cover the broader aspects of network management from managing network elements to business management, as addressed in the Telecommunications Management Network (TMN).

In Part III, Chapter 12 discusses networking and network management tools. The architecture and features of some of the widely used network and system management systems are also covered. The knowledge gained of management tools and systems—as well as the principles covered in Part II—is applied to practical applications in managing fault, configuration, performance, security, and accounting, which forms the contents of Chapter 13. The impact of emerging technologies in Web-based management and its influence on distributed network management is addressed in Chapter 14.

Suggestions for Course Syllabus

The contents of the book are more than can be covered in a semester course. We have indicated the dependencies on the contents of the various chapters in Figure P.1 to help the instructor select appropriate material to cover in a dedicated network management course or as a part of a data communications course. A project to accompany the course is recommended and suggestions are given in Appendix B.

For a graduate course with students having a strong background in networking, the review of network technology in Chapter 2 may be bypassed. For a general course on SNMP management of network elements, Chapters 3–5, followed by Chapter 8 on RMON are suggested. Chapters 12 and 13 apply the principles introduced to practical aspects of network management.

For an advanced treatment of SNMP management, Chapters 6 and 7, covering SNMPv2 and SNMPv3, may be used. If telecommunications is emphasized (which is more likely in computer engineering schools), the instructor may include ATM management (Chapter 9) and TMN (Chapter 11).

Finally, if the school has a network management research program, the management applications in Chapter 13 should be dealt with in depth. In addition, adequate treatment of Web-based active and distributed network management is suggested.

To the Instructor

This textbook is for use in senior-level undergraduate or graduate level courses. Although a chapter is devoted to the review of network technology, we assume that the student has taken a prerequisite course in either data or telecommunication networks or has equivalent knowledge.

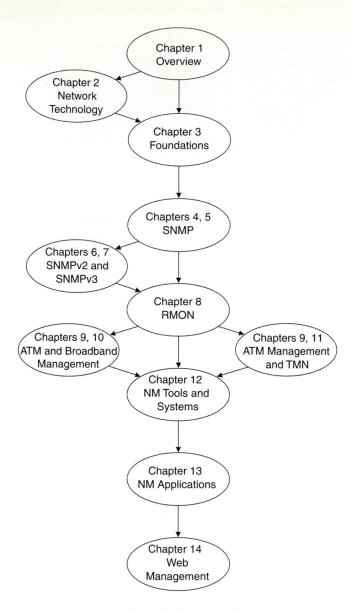

Figure P.1   Figure Title

Online Supplements: A Web site provides a solutions manual for the exercises at the end of the chapters. It is available only for the instructors through your Addison Wesley Longman sales representative or by sending an e-mail message to aw.cse@awl.com. Please also watch for visual aids for teaching that would be accessible on the Web site. These aids are PowerPoint presentations for each chapter, with key figures and bullet-point notes.

To the Student

The book is written as a textbook to be used for a course on network management. Additional information is provided in the book that can serve as a reference book for you. The basic information presented, along with the references, serve as a springboard for access to additional details on numerous specialized network management topics.

You are exposed to current network management technology and commercial products. Upon completing a course using this book, you could either enter industry with adequate network management knowledge or pursue further study and research in graduate school. An encouraging sign is that enterprises dealing in network management solutions have recently started supporting network management programs at institutions of higher learning.

The book is also geared toward self-motivated engineers in the industry who are eager to learn network management. If an engineer has access to network resources, many of the hands-on exercises could be practiced. At a minimum, it provides enough tools and knowledge for the frustrated worker who cannot access network resources and doesn't know why.

Grateful Acknowledgements

The major impetus for this book has come from students during three course offerings. It has been reviewed at various levels and to various depths by many students. Some of the student project reports have been an inducement to include new material. My gratitude goes to Sidharth Bajaj, Kasyapa Balemarthy, Liang Chu, Lenitra Clay, Minaxi Gupta, Azita Miahnari, and David Montgomery for their review and suggestions. Brandon Rhodes and Oleg Kolesnikov provided interesting practical exercises to be included in the book.

Many reviewers' comments and suggestions have contributed to the richness of the book's contents. I owe special gratitude to Lundy Lewis, who has made numerous and specific suggestions for improvement. With the ever-changing technology, I thank Subodh Bapat who pointed me to the latest in Web-based management. Nouri Soued, who used the early manuscript to teach his class and gave me feedback, is also acknowledged. I want to express my appreciation to Professor Y. Yemini for getting me started right in my first attempt to write a textbook. I would also like to thank the following for reviewing the manuscript and making constructive suggestions: Bruce S. Elenbogen, Melody Moh, Richard Newman, Kihong Park, Adarsh Sethi, Raymond A. Vigeant, Alfred C. Weaver, Brit Williams, and Taieb B. Znati.

The results of the interviews described in Chapter 1 generated positive feedback from reviewers and students, and I thank the following for consenting to be interviewed: Cas D'Angelo, Ron Hutchins, Dave Miller, John Mize, and John Mullin. Some of the case histories were provided by Rob Beverly, Ron Hutchins, and Dave Miller.

I would like to add more interesting projects to Appendix B.9. If students/instructors have suggestions, I would appreciate hearing (manis@cc.gatech.edu).

My thanks go to Susan Hartman (Acquisitions Editor), Katherine Harutunian (Project Editor), and Patricia Mahtani (Production Supervisor), all of Addison Wesley Longman for their ever-willing cooperation in seeing this project through its successful conclusion.

This book would not have the seen daylight without the multitude of help and personal sacrifice of my wife, Ruth. She has contributed to the book by inputting revisions, acting as the local copy editor, and being production manager of manuscripts at home. Thank you, Ruth.

Mani Subramanian
(Mä′ne Sū brä män′ e än)

CONTENTS

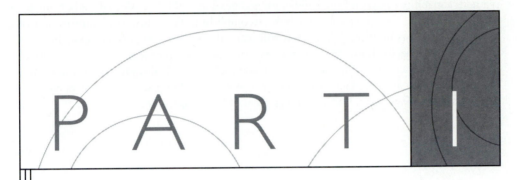

PART I

Background

Chapter 1 presents an overview of computer, or data, communications and network management. As a broad review of networking and network management, it starts with an analogy of the telephone network, which has achieved high quality and reliability. You will learn the relationship between data communications and telecommunications, and that the distinction between the two is slowly disappearing. The influence of desktop computing and distributed computing environments based on client/server architecture has revolutionized computer communication. Internet is a worldwide fabric and you will learn to appreciate how information travels across it around the globe. The basics of communication protocols and architecture are presented along with the various standards.

Components of network management are described, complemented by interviews with network managers, whose experiences emphasize the need for network management. Also described is the role of a network operations center in managing the network efficiently from a central location using network and system management solutions.

Chapter 2 focuses on network technology. You may skip this chapter if you are fairly familiar with the practical aspects of networking. If you understand principles of data communication, this chapter will help you appreciate the technological aspects of it. You will learn how various topologies are implemented in local area networks (LANs) and wide area networks (WANs). Basics of the Ethernet, Token Ring, and FDDI LANs are described from a practical point of view. Of these, Ethernet and FDDI are the two most widely deployed LANs in narrow-band networks today. LAN evolution from basic Ethernet to Gigabit Ethernet with half- and full-duplex configurations is presented. Switched Ethernet adds capability to expand the bandwidth and flexibility of LAN. Virtual LAN is implemented using the Switched Ethernet hub, accomplishing flexibility in administration of workstations across multiple LANs. You will learn the various network components that need to be managed—hubs, bridges, routers, gateways, and protocol converters. A brief review of wide-area networking and transmission technology is also presented. Broadband technology is briefly described in this chapter, but a detailed discussion of it appears in Chapters 9 and 10, which addresses management of broadband service.

CHAPTER I

*Data Communications and Network
Management Overview*

This chapter demonstrates the necessity of network and system management in providing information technology services. We start with the history of computer communication, walk you through some real-world case histories, and then present an overview of network and system management.

The telephone system is known to be very reliable and dependable. One can make a telephone call from anywhere to anywhere at any time of the day and be reasonably sure that the connection will be made and the quality of connection will be good. This is partly due to the efficient management of the telephone network. Section 1.1 discusses successful management of the telephone network by using operation support systems.

Computer communication initially used the telephone network to carry digital data. There was a clear demarcation between the traditional telecommunication network and computer communication network. The evolution of early computer communication networks is treated in Section 1.2.

Computer communication technology radically changed with the advent of desktop computing power and distributed computing environments using local-area networks as described in Section 1.3. Global communication via the Internet became a reality with the introduction of TCP/IP–based networks. Section 1.4 describes the Internet, followed by a discussion in Section 1.5 on the importance of communication protocols and standards.

Sections 1.6 and 1.7 present case histories that tell the "war stories" of information technology managers and the challenges they face in today's computer and telecommunication environment. The interviews with them emphasize the importance of network and system management tools. Section 1.8 describes network management that comprises operations, administration, maintenance, and provisioning. Three groups perform these functions: Engineering, Operations, and Installation and Maintenance (I&M). Section 1.9 focuses on the network management system and the relationships among its various components. Besides the network components, the application system resources also need to be managed. This is the subject of Section 1.10.

Network management technology is still in an evolutionary mode as the network and software technology advance. The future directions of network management technology form the content of Section 1.11.

1.1   Analogy of Telephone Network Management

The need for data or computer communication network management is best illustrated by an analogy of telephone network management. The high degree of reliability of the telephone network is evidenced by the following illustration. We can pick up a telephone, call anybody, anytime, anywhere in the world, and be almost sure to be connected to the destination. The telephone network is reliable and dependable, and the quality and speed of connection is good, especially if it is a domestic call in the United States. It is reliable because it almost always provides the vocal communication that we expect. It is dependable because we can be fairly sure it will work when we need it, especially for emergency calls (i.e., 911) and in military defense situations. The quality of service is generally good, and we can have a conversation across the world with the same clarity that we have when we call our neighbor.

The reason for such reliability, dependability, and quality is more than the careful planning, design, and implementation of a good telephone network using good and reliable components. The key is the management and operations of the network. Much of the management of the network is so well automated that it becomes part of the operations. Let us look first at the telephone network architecture and then at some of the operations support systems that manage it.

The architecture of the telephone network is hierarchical, as shown in Figure 1.1 [AT&T 1977]. There are five levels of network switches and three types of trunks that connect these switches. A *trunk* is a logical link between two switches that may traverse

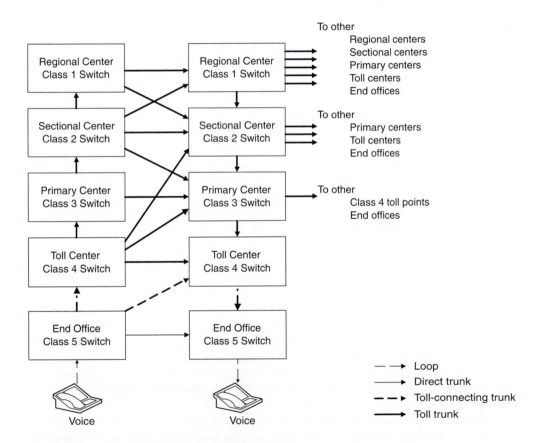

Figure 1.1   Telephone Network Model

one or more physical links. The end office (class 5), the lowest in the hierarchy, is the local switching office. The customer's telephone, or PBX (private branch exchange), which is a switch on the customer premises, is connected to the end office via a dedicated link called a loop. The other four levels of switches (class 4 through class 1) are toll switches that carry toll (long-distance) calls. The direct distance dialing (DDD) network, which enables us to dial the far-end telephone without an operator's assistance, comprises three transmission trunks. A direct trunk connects two end offices, a toll-connecting trunk connects an end office to any toll office, and a toll (internal) trunk connects any two toll offices.

From the local class 5 office to the called party's class 5 office, there are multiple routes. A circuit connection is set up either directly using a local trunk or via the higher level switches and routes. Primary and secondary routes are already programmed into the switch. If the primary route is broken or the facilities over the primary route are filled to capacity, an alternative route is automatically assigned. For example, on Mother's Day, which is the busiest telephone-traffic day of the year, a call to the neighboring town could travel clear across the country and back, if that's the route where adequate bandwidth is available. Let's remember that there is a three-hour time difference between the two coasts in the United States, and the traffic starts three hours later on the West Coast than on the East Coast.

Operations support systems ensure the quality of service in the telephone network. They constantly monitor the various parameters of the network. For example, to ensure that there is adequate bandwidth to carry the traffic over the facilities, a traffic measurement system constantly measures traffic over the switch appearances. The measurements are analyzed to help in facility planning, and they provide real-time input to a network management system when there is excessive blocking (traffic over the capacity of the trunk group) in any link.

The quality of the call, measured in terms of a signal-to-noise (S/N) ratio, is measured regularly by a trunk maintenance system. This system accesses all the trunks in an office during the night and does a loop-back test to the far end. The results are analyzed in the morning and corrective actions are taken as necessary. For example, if the S/N ratio of a trunk is below the established acceptable level, the trunk is removed from service before the customer experiences poor performance by seizing that trunk.

For a given region, there is a network operations center (NOC) where the global status of the network is monitored. The traffic patterns are observed constantly and corrective operations are taken, if needed, in real time. The NOC is the nerve center of telephone network operations.

It is worth noting that the telephone network is managed from the users' perspective, not that of the system or service provider, even though the objectives of both are the same. However, with emphasis on the users' point of view, the first objective in operations is restoration of service, and then the quality and economy of service. Thus, isolation of the problem and providing alternative means of service, by either manual or automated means, become more important than fixing the problem.

To manage a network remotely, that is, to monitor and control the network components from a central location, network management functions need to be considered in building the components of the network. In that sense, network component designs should include the network management functions as part of their requirements and specifications.

The computer communication network, however, has not matured to the same extent as the telephone network. The data communications technology is still evolving and is merging with telephone technology. Besides, computer and modern telecommunication networks are more complicated than plain old telephone service (POTS). The management and operations of these networks are still being developed. Further, the telephone industry all over the world, and in the United States in particular, has been monopolistic and thus single-vendor oriented. This is no longer true since the passing of the federal Telecommunications Act of 1996 [Clinton 1996]. In contrast, computer communications started as a private industry and hence is multivendor oriented. Unfortunately this has produced enormous problems to users because the network components supplied by different vendors cannot always communicate. Dealing with these problems is the responsibility of the network or information systems manager, who is charged with keeping the service alive all the time. This situation has been recognized by the various industrial and standards groups, who are actively seeking solutions.

1.2   Data (Computer) and Telecommunication Network

Network communications technology deals with the theories of electrical engineering, computer engineering, and computer science and their application to all types of communications over networks. It also addresses accessing of databases and applications remotely over local-area networks, as well as over switched and private lines. A basic network can be viewed as interconnected nodes and links, as shown in Figure 1.2. A link carries information from one node to another that is directly connected to it. A node behaves as an end (terminating or originating) node, or an intermediate node, or both. If the node behaves as an end node, information either originates or terminates there. An intermediate node redirects the information from one link to another. End-office nodes (see Figure 1.1) behave as end nodes. A node can drop and add information channels and at the same time switch information transparently between two links. Each end node has a connection to a user interface, if the information originates or terminates there. This interface could use any type of equipment—audio, video, or data terminating equipment (DTE). A DTE is any equipment that generates or accepts digital data.

Data can be transmitted in either analog or digital format. The analog data is sent either as base band (e.g., voice data from the switching office to the customer premises) or on top of a carrier (e.g., cable TV). Digital data is generated either directly by the user equipment (e.g., computer terminal) or as analog data and converted to digital data (e.g., Integrated Services Digital Network, ISDN, connection to customer premises). The latter scenario of ability to handle integrated digital and analog signals is becoming extremely important as the popularity of multimedia broadband services grows. The management considerations associated with broadband services are also very challenging, as we will see in Chapters 9 and 10. Long-distance data transmission today is mostly digital due to its superior price and performance.

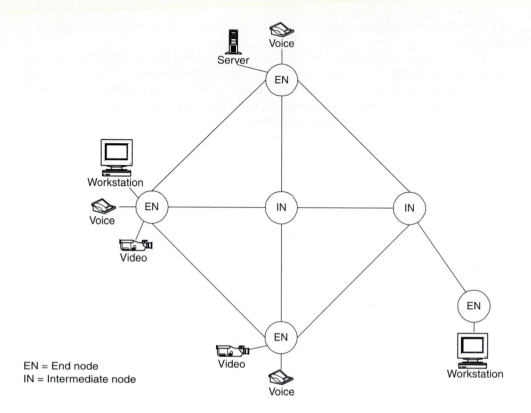

Figure 1.2   Logical Network Model

Data are sent from the originating to the terminating node via a direct link, or via a tandem of links and intermediate nodes. The data can be transmitted in one of three modes: circuit switched, message switched, or packet switched. In the circuit-switched mode, a physical circuit is established between the originating and terminating ends before the data is transmitted. The circuit is disconnected after completion of transmission.

In message-switched and packet-switched modes, the data is broken into packets and each packet is enveloped with the destination and originating addresses. Message-switched mode is used to send long messages, such as e-mail. Packet-switched mode is used to transmit small packets used in applications such as interactive communication. The bridges and routers open each packet to find the destination address and switch the data to the appropriate output links. The path between the two ends may change during transmission of a message because each packet may take a different route. The packets are reassembled in the right order at the receiving end. The main difference between message switching and packet switching is that in the former the data is stored by the system and then retrieved by the user at a later time (e.g., e-mail). In packet-switched mode, the packets are fragmented and reassembled in almost real time. They are stored in the system only long enough to receive all the packets in the message. In Europe, the X.25 packet-switched network is used extensively in the Public-Switched Data Network (PSDN).

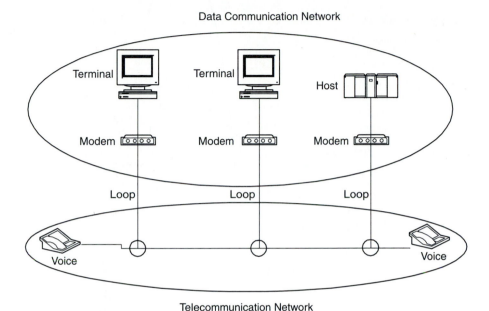

Figure 1.3   Data and Telecommunication Networks

Network communications are classified as either telecommunications or data communications. This classification is based on historical evolution. The telephone network, which came into existence first, was known as a **telecommunication network**. It is a circuit-switched network that is structured as a public network accessible by any user. The telephone network in Figure 1.1 represents a telecommunication network. The organization that provides this service is called a telecommunication service provider (e.g., AT&T, BellSouth, British Telecom, etc.).

With the advent of computers, the term **data communication network** came into vogue. It is also sometimes called computer communication network. The telecommunications infrastructure was and is still used for data communications. Figure 1.3 shows an early configuration of terminal-to-host and host-to-host communications, and the interface of data and telecommunication networks. To interface, a terminal or host connected to an end-office switch communicates with the host connected to another end-office switch by modems at each end. Modems transfer the information from digital to analog at source (telephone networks carried analog signals) and back to digital at destination.

Figure 1.4 shows a corporate, or enterprise, environment in the interim stage of the evolution of data and telephone communications. A number of telephones and computer terminals at various corporate sites are connected by the telecommunication network. The telephones are connected locally by a local (onsite) switch, PBX, which interfaces to

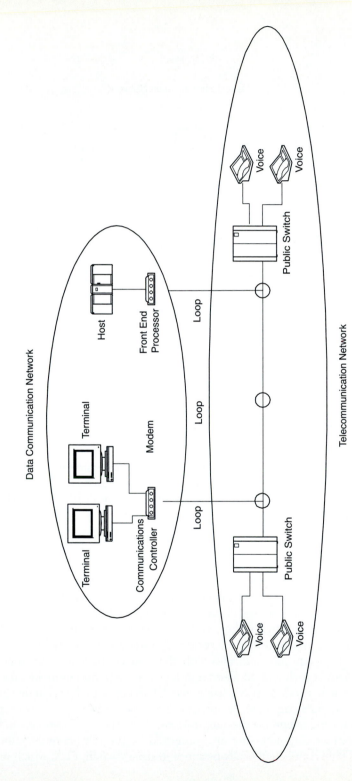

Figure 1.4   Interim Corporate Data and Telecommunication Networks

the telephone network. The computer terminals are connected to an onsite communication controller, which manages the local terminals and provides a single interface to the telephone network. There are many devices available to serve as communications controllers, such as multiplexers or IBM's cluster controller.

In the above corporate environment, the computer terminals communicate directly with the host. This communication system architecture is expensive and inefficient because the user has to pay for the data traffic over the public or leased telecommunications line. Besides, there is time delay in transmission. To reduce the cost and improve the performance, the computer terminals can communicate with a local communications processor, which can then communicate with remote hosts. Processor-to-processor communications over the telecommunications lines take less time and therefore are less expensive. This type of hierarchical communications architecture was developed by IBM for data communication control network. This development led to IBM's well-known Systems Network Architecture (SNA), shown in Figure 1.5, where the host is connected to the terminals via the communications controllers and cluster controllers. Cluster

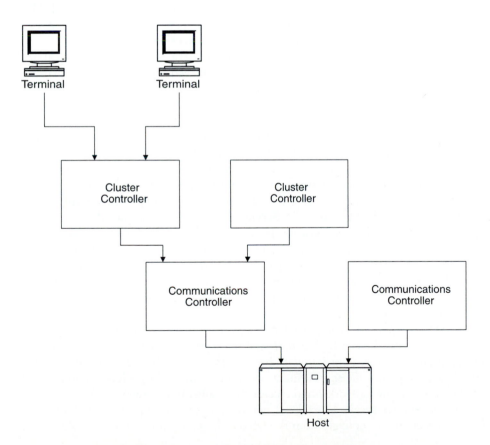

Figure 1.5   IBM Systems Network Architecture Model

controllers manage the DTEs at the peripheral nodes; and the communication controllers manage the traffic at the subnetwork levels.

Desktop computers and local-area networks (LANs) revolutionized data communication because desktop computers could communicate with each other over the LAN. This possibility led to a distributed computing environment (DCE), which is discussed in the next section.

1.3   Distributed Computing Environments

Figure 1.6 shows a LAN with hosts and workstations, which are workstations with processing power and not just dumb terminals as described in the previous section. Any workstation can communicate with any host on the LAN; depending on the type of LAN, there can be a large number of workstations and hosts. DTEs (any digital terminal equipment that generates and processes digital data) connected to different LANs that are geographically far apart can communicate via a telecommunication network, either public or private switched. The system of links that connect remote LANs is called wide-area network (WAN). A LAN is physically connected to a WAN link by a bridge or router at each end, as shown in Figure 1.6(b). We'll discuss the types of LANs and WANs in Chapter 2. First, we want to bring out two important aspects of **distributed computing environments** (DCEs).

The first aspect is the question of whether the different platforms and applications running on DCEs have the ability to communicate with each other. Proprietary interface between platforms and processes was implemented by telecommunication service providers and computer vendors to communicate autonomously within each of their networks. For example, Bell Systems, a monopolistic telecommunication service provider, and IBM, the largest computer vendor, established transmission, switching, and interface standards and manufactured their own communications equipment to meet them. They made significant research contributions to the standards bodies to make such specifications the industry standards. They also published specifications to indicate how equipment on the customer premises interfaces cleanly with the network. For example, Bell Systems published specifications for their Customer Service Unit (CSU) to ensure that customers' equipment interfaced with the network. However, as the telecommunications industry rapidly grew, national and international standards needed to be established to make communication possible between equipment provided by various vendors. Protocols and database standards for handshaking and information exchange are discussed in the following sections. For now, we'll assume that the different processors and the processes running on them can communicate.

The second important aspect of a distributed computing environment is the ability of the processors attached to LANs to do multiple functions. They could continue, as dumb terminals did, to request a host to perform the functions and return the results. Or, they could request some special functions to be performed by a host—and it could be any processor in the network—and receive the results. In this scenario, the processor that requests a service is called the client, and the processor that provides the service is called the server. Such a configuration is termed a client/server environment. Although

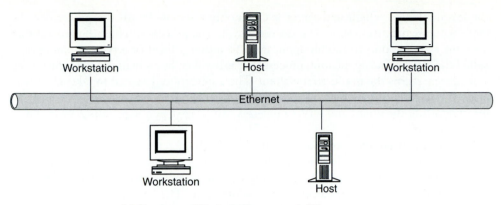

(a) Hosts and Workstations on a LAN

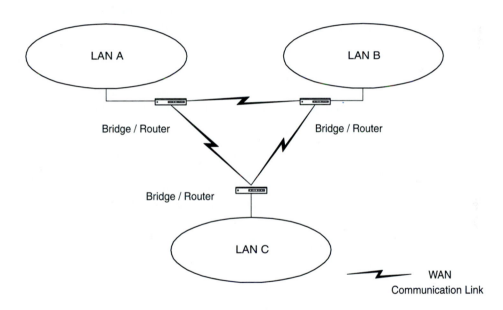

(b) Remote LANs connected by a WAN

Figure 1.6   A Distributed Computing Environment with LANs and WANs

the terminology of client and server is commonly associated with the processors, the more accurate definition should be associated with the processes. Thus, the process that initiates a transaction to run an application in either a local or a remote processor is called the client. The application process that is invoked by a client is called the server. The server returns the results to the client. The application designed to take advantage of such a capability in a network is called a client/server architecture. With such an interpretation, the client and server processes can coexist in one processor or in different processors.

We will now go into some detail on the salient characteristics and features of client/server architecture and models, because they are very pertinent to network management applications and architecture. There is apt to be confusion between which is a client and which is a server in distributed computing architecture. The best way to distinguish the two is to remember that the client initiates the request and the server responds. A simple client/server model is shown in Figure 1.7.

The client initiates a request to the server and waits. The server executes the process to provide the requested service and sends the results to the client. It is worth noting that the client cannot initiate a process in the server. Thus, the process should have already been started in the server and be waiting for requests to be processed.

A real-world analogy to the client/server operation is a post office. The clerk behind the counter is ready and waiting for a client. She is a server. When a customer walks in and initiates a transaction, for example ordering stamps, the clerk responds. The customer is the client. After the clerk gives the stamps to the customer (i.e., she has delivered the results), the customer leaves and the clerk, as a server, goes into a waiting mode until the next client initiates a transaction.

As with any system, delays and breakdowns of communication need to be considered in this model. The server may be providing the service to many clients that are connected to it on a LAN, as shown in Figure 1.8(a). Each client's request is normally processed by the server according to the FIFO rule—first in first out. This delay could be minimized,

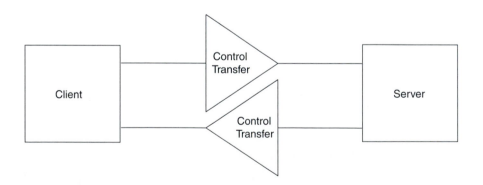

Figure 1.7   A Simple Client/Server Model

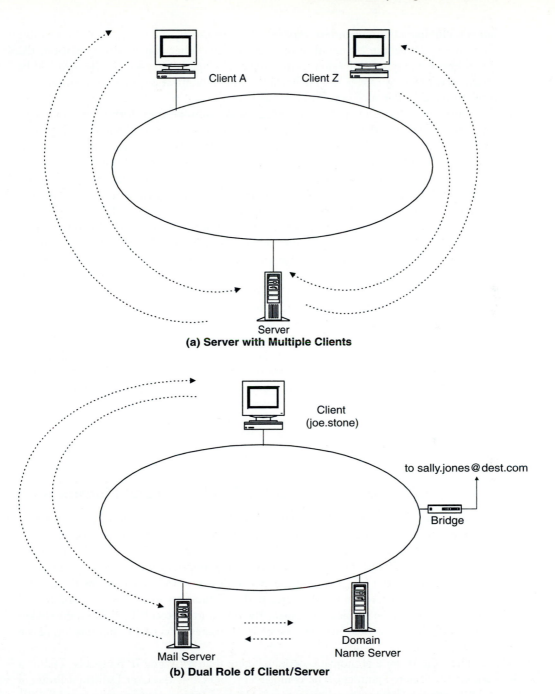

(a) Server with Multiple Clients

(b) Dual Role of Client/Server

Figure 1.8   **A Model of a Client/Server Network in a Distributed Computing Environment**

but not eliminated, by concurrent processing of requests by the server. It is also possible that, due to either the communication link or some other abnormal termination, the server may never return the result to the client. The application on the client should be programmed to take care of such deficiencies in communication, by re-requesting if no results are received in a certain period of time.

Since the client and application processes are running in a distributed computing environment, each of them can be designed to execute a specific function efficiently. Further, the functions may be under the jurisdiction of different departments in an organization. For example (see Figure 1.8b), joe.stone (Joe Stone's user id) using a client in a network sends a message to sally.jones@dest.com (Sally Jones's user id) on the network. The message first goes to the mail server on the network. Before it can process the request, the mail server needs to know the network address of sally.jones, which is dest.com. Therefore, it makes a request to the domain name server (DNS) on the network for the routing information for the address of dest.com. When it receives that information, it sends out joe.stone's message via the bridge to the network. It then sends a message to joe.stone on the client stating that the message has been sent (or not sent because dest.com address does not exist in the domain name server). In this example, the mail server behaves both as a server and as a client. The three processes in this scenario, namely the client, the mail server, and the domain name server, are considered cooperative computing processes and may be running in three separate platforms on remote LANs connected by a WAN. The communication between these processes is called peer-to-peer communication. We will soon learn how network management fits into such a model and manages components on the network that perform cooperative computing using peer-to-peer communication. However, before we pursue that, let's first look at a new dimension of the distributed computing environment that has caused networking to mushroom into the Internet.

1.4   TCP/IP–Based Networks: The Internet and Intranets

Transmission Control Protocol/Internet Protocol (TCP/IP) is a suite of protocols that enable networks to be interconnected. TCP/IP forms the basic foundation of the Internet. The architecture and protocols are discussed in detail in Section 1.5. We will briefly describe the role TCP/IP plays in the Internet. The nodes in the network use network protocol, IP, to route packets. IP is a connectionless protocol. That means there is no guarantee that the packet will be delivered to the destination node. However, end-to-end communication can be guaranteed by using the transport protocol, TCP. Thus, if a packet is lost by IP, the acknowledgment process of TCP ensures successful retransmission of the packet.

The TCP/IP suite of protocols contains more than TCP and IP protocols. TCP is a connection-oriented protocol. The complement to TCP is the User Datagram Protocol (UDP), which is a connectionless protocol. Much of Internet traffic really uses UDP/IP, because of the reliability of data transmission. For example, e-mail and management messages are connectionless transmissions.

The Internet is a network of networks. Just as we can use the telephone to communicate over the telecommunication network from anywhere to anywhere in the world today, we can now use the computer network to communicate worldwide via e-mail. We looked at the example of Joe Stone sending a message to Sally Jones in the previous section, Figure 1.8(b). Let's expand that example and visualize that Joe Stone, who is in the College of Computing building at the Georgia Institute of Technology, is sending an e-mail to Sally Jones, who is at a residence in Australia and is connected to the Internet via the service provider ostrich.com. Similar to a unique telephone number that each station has in the telephone world, each person has a unique address in the computer communication network. Joe's e-mail address is **joe@cc.gatech.edu** and Sally's address is **sally@ostrich.com.au**.

Figure 1.9 shows an Internet configuration for our scenario. Assume Joe is at Workstation A on LAN A sending the e-mail to Sally at Workstation Z that is "teleconnected" to her Internet service provider's e-mail server on LAN Z. The two servers shown on LAN A are mail server and domain name server (DNS). We should note that the servers do not have to be on the same LAN as the sender's LAN, as shown in Figure 1.9. The two servers cooperatively transmit the e-mail message to LAN C on the computer network made up of bridges and routers. The link between LAN A and LAN C could be a WAN. The information is transported exclusively based on TCP/IP–based protocols. We will explain TCP/IP protocol in Section 1.5.2.

Information from LAN C progresses via gateways and WANs to the computer communications network in Australia, as shown in Figure 1.9. The WAN network in Figure 1.9 is composed of a series of networks, not all necessarily using TCP/IP. Gateways between them serve as the interfaces between dissimilar and independent, autonomous, networks and perform many functions including protocol conversions. Autonomous networks have little knowledge of each other's attributes, configurations, and addresses and yet communication is automatically facilitated by a hierarchy of Internet servers along the path.

Joe's e-mail message finally reaches the e-mail server on LAN Z in Australia and is stored there until Sally retrieves it via her Internet link with the Internet service provider's server. In fact, e-mail messages are transmitted by a "store-and-forward" scheme all along the path. (In addition, the final stage in the Internet link uses a TCP/IP suite of protocol.)

Thus, via the Internet, any user can communicate with any other user in any part of the world as long as both are connected to a network that is part of the Internet. Because of this great advantage, Internet users are currently doubling in population each year. This has also revolutionized the software interface-providing capabilities, like Web pages, so users can gather information about any Web user in the world instantly through the Internet.

Another perspective of the Internet is to view it as a layered architecture, as shown in Figure 1.10. The architecture shows the global Internet as concentric layers of workstations, LANs, and WANs interconnected by fabrics of medium access controls (MACs), switches, and gateways. The workstations belong to the user plane, the LANs to the LAN plane, and WANs to the WAN plane. The interfaces are defined as the fabrics. MAC

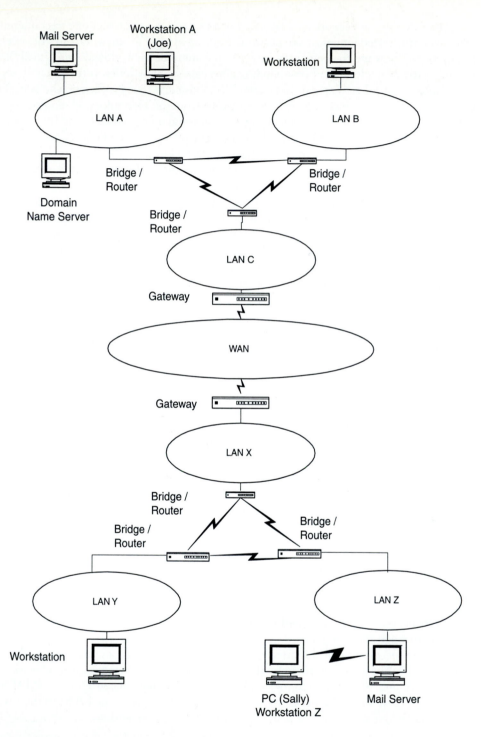

Figure 1.9   Internet Configuration

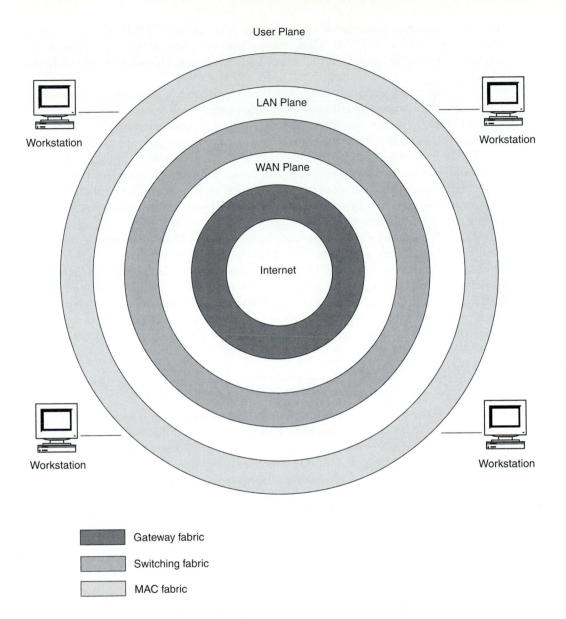

Figure 1.10   Internet Fabric Model

fabric interfaces the user plane and the LAN plane. The LAN and WAN planes interface through switching fabric. The WANs in the WAN plane interface via the gateway fabric.

The user's workstation interfaces to a LAN via a medium access control (MAC), which is explained in Chapter 2. LANs interface to a WAN by a switching fabric of bridges, routers, and switches. Each WAN can be considered an autonomous network, and hence needs a gateway to communicate with another WAN. Gateway fabric interconnects different WANs. Thus, a single Internet plane at the core of the model multiplies into millions and millions of users in the user plane, with virtually no limits in sight.

Communication between two users in the user plane (i.e., a logical link connection on the user plane) takes the following path. The physical path traverses the MAC fabric, the LAN plane, the switching fabric, the WAN plane, and the gateway fabric to the core and then returns to the user plane going through all the planes and interface fabrics.

The huge success of Internet technology has spawned intranet technology. The main distinction between the two is similar to that between private- and public-switched networks. An intranet is a private network and access to it is controlled by the enterprise that owns it, whereas the Internet is public. We will learn how to accomplish a secured private network using a firewall in Chapter 13.

The impact of the Internet in networking is enormous. How do we manage the Internet? For example, if the e-mail does not reach the destination, how do we detect where the communication broke down? How do we take advantage of Internet capabilities to implement network management? We have not yet defined network management and how it fits into a client/server environment. However, before we define network management, let us briefly look at the protocols and protocol architecture, that enable communication between components on the network.

1.5   Communications Protocols and Standards

Consider a fax machine and a modem bought from a local store successfully sending a message to a modem and fax machine anywhere in the world, even though each fax machine and modem were manufactured by local vendors. Likewise, isn't it a technological miracle that two computers in different places anywhere in the world can transmit messages to each other as long as both are connected to the Internet? Although fax and Internet technologies have been in existence for decades, only recently has their use surged to be a universal service. The key to practical success of these and other such technologies is the interoperability of the two end devices. More and more vendors in more and more countries have recognized that in this world of shrinking cyberspace and advancing modern communication technology, interoperability is the key to the success of their businesses.

Universal interoperability is achieved when all participants agree to establish common operational procedures. In communications lingo, commonality can be interpreted as standards and procedures as protocols. Let's consider the scenario of Joe sending e-mail from the Georgia Institute of Technology (GIT) in Atlanta to a colleague in Japanese Telecommunications Company (JTC) in Tokyo. Joe composes the message on his computer terminal and sends it to his colleague (yoho@jtc.com.jp). Joe's message with his user id (joe@cc.gatech.edu) and IP address (169.111.103.44) goes through several changes before it is transmitted on the physical LAN medium at GIT. The message goes to GIT's College of Computing (cc)'s e-mail server, which obtains the IP address of the destination and sends the message out on the Internet. The message traverses several nodes and links and arrives at the post office box of Yoho's mail server at JTC. She establishes a session in her computer and gets the complete message that Joe transmitted. In this scenario Joe's message is wrapped with several layers of control information at various times and is broken down into packet units and reassembled at the destination. All these steps happen each time an e-mail is sent without loss or error in the message, as a result of standardization and modular (layered) architecture of data communication protocols. As we will soon learn in this section, the popularity of the Internet as a peer-to-peer network has been made possible by the peer-to-peer protocol TCP/IP (Transmission Control Protocol/ Internet Protocol) suite.

Architecture can be defined as the basic structure of a system that shows its functional components and the relationships among them. Thus, communication architecture describes the functional components of a communication network, as well as the operational interfaces among them. The operational procedures—both intra- and inter-modules—are specified in terms of protocols. Just as human communication is possible when people speak a common language, standardized communication protocols make interfaces possible for the service provider and the service user. If different vendors of a system's components implement the same standards, then communication between their different components can be universal. Standardization of protocols involves agreement in the physical characteristics and operational procedures of communication equipment that performs similar functions. Thus, looking at our example, all fax machines are able to communicate with each other because all vendors have implemented the standards recommended by the International Telecommunication Union (ITU). Similarly, e-mail exchange across the world is possible because most vendors have adopted the standard Simple Mail Transport Protocol (SMTP) in their software. However, there are e-mail software packages that have not implemented SMTP, and their users have to install a gateway to those systems to convert back and forth between SMTP and the vendor-specific proprietary protocol. For example, IBM Lotus uses cc:mail protocol and any network that uses cc:mail has to implement a gateway to send e-mail over the Internet. We will now look at the details of communication architecture.

1.5.1   Communication Architectures

Communication between users (human beings who use a system) and applications (programs that run in a system) occurs at various levels. They can communicate at the application level, the highest level of communication architecture. Or, they can exchange information at the lowest level, the physical medium. Each system can be divided into two broad sets of communication layers. The top set of layers consists of the application layers and the bottom set of the transport layers. The users—and users include application programs—interface with the application-level layer and the communication equipment interfaces with the physical medium. The basic communication architecture is shown in Figure 1.11. In Figure 1.11(a), the two end systems associated with the two end nodes communicate directly. Direct communication occurs between the corresponding cooperating layers of each system. Thus transport layers can exchange information, and so can the application layers and the users.

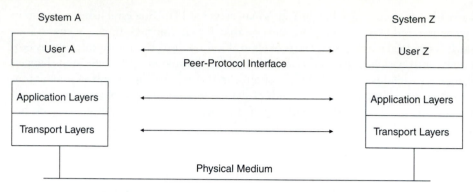

(a) Direct Communication between End Systems

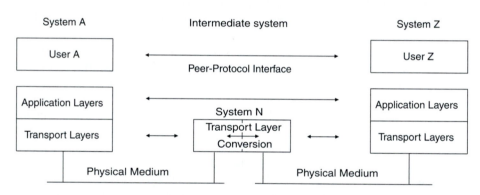

(b) Communication between End Systems via an Intermediate System

Figure 1.11   Basic Communication Architecture

For example, a hearing-impaired person, accompanied by an interpreter, attended one of my classes. As I lectured, the interpreter translated it to sign language for the student. If the student had a question, the interpreter translated the information from sign language to spoken English for the class and me. In this illustration, the hearing-impaired student and I are at the application layer. The interpreter did the protocol conversion at the application-layer level. The transport layer is the aural and visual media.

Figure 1.11(b) shows the end systems communicating via an intermediate system N, which enables the use of different physical media for the two end systems. System N converts the transport-layer information into the appropriate protocols. Thus, system A could be on a copper-wire LAN and system Z could be on a fiber-optic cable.

Various professional organizations propose, deliberate, and establish standards. One of these organizations is the renowned International Standards Organization (ISO). The ISO has developed a highly modular, or layered, architecture for communication proto-

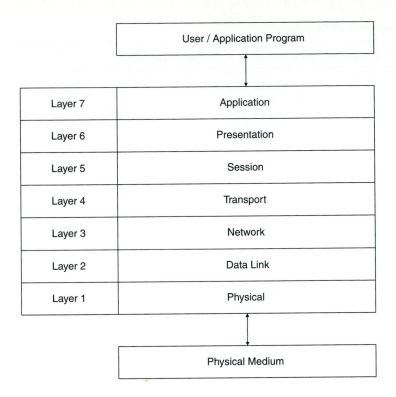

Figure 1.12   The OSI Protocol Layers

cols that is called the Open Systems Interconnection (OSI) Reference Model, published as OSI RM—ISO 7498. This model was developed based on the premise that the different layers of protocol provide different services, and that each layer can communicate with only its own neighboring level. Two systems can communicate on a peer-to-peer level, that is, at the same level of the protocol. The OSI protocol architecture is shown in Figure 1.12. Table 1.1 describes the salient features of and services provided by each of the seven layers. Layers 1 through 4 are the transport system protocol layers; and layers 5, 6, and 7 are application support protocol layers.

   OSI protocol architecture truly enables building systems with open interfaces so that networks using systems from different vendors are interoperable. Figure 1.13 expands the basic communication architecture shown in Figure 1.11 to an OSI model. Figure 1.13(a) is a direct end-to-end communication model. The corresponding layers in the two systems communicate on a peer-to-peer protocol interface associated with those layers. In Figure 1.13(b), the end systems communicate by going through an intermediate node/system. Again, notice that the physical media connected to the end systems could be different. The intermediate system is involved only up to the first three layers in the process. Layers 4 through 7 are not involved in the intermediate system. This is analogous to a mail container with letters enclosed in envelopes being transported from one town to another town anywhere in the world. It does not matter what network of intermediate cities (nodes) it goes

Table 1.1   OSI Layers and Services

Layer No.	Layer Name	Salient services provided by the layer
1	Physical	• Transfers to and gathers from the physical medium raw bit data • Handles physical and electrical interfaces to the transmission medium
2	Data link	• Consists of two sublayers: Logical link control (LLC) and media access control (MAC) • LLC: Formats the data to go on the medium; performs error control and flow control • MAC: Controls data transfer to and from LAN; resolves conflicts with other data on LAN
3	Network	• Forms the switching/routing layer of the network
4	Transport	• Multiplexes and de-multiplexes messages from applications • Acts as a transparent layer to applications and thus isolates them from the transport system layers • Makes and breaks connections for connection-oriented communications • Controls flow of data in both directions
5	Session	• Establishes and clears sessions for applications, and thus minimizes loss of data during large data exchange
6	Presentation	• Provides a set of standard protocols so that the display would be transparent to syntax of the application • Data encryption and decryption
7	Application	• Provides application-specific protocols for each application and each transport protocol system

through, or what network of transportation media—surface, air, or water—it takes to get to the destination. The letters in envelopes and the contents of packages are untouched at the transfer points and are handled only by the sender and receiver, that is, user applications.

The message in each layer is contained in message units called protocol data units (PDUs), which consist of two parts—protocol control information (PCI) and user data (UD). PCI contains header information about the layer. UD contains the data that the layer, acting as a service provider, receives from or transmits to the upper layer/service user layer. The PDU communication model between two systems A and Z, including the users at the top and the transmission medium at the bottom of the PDU layers, is shown in Figure 1.14. As you can see in Figure 1.14, the size of the PDU increases as it goes toward lower layers. If the size of the PDU exceeds the maximum size of layers specifications, it is fragmented into multiple packets. Thus, a single application-layer PDU could multiply into several physical PDUs.

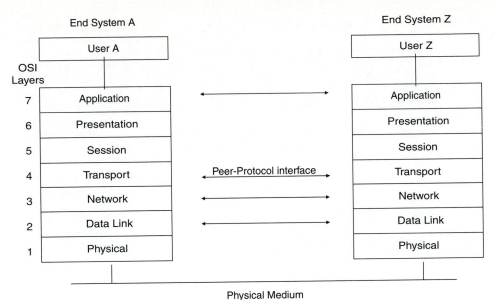

(a) **Direct Communication between End Systems**

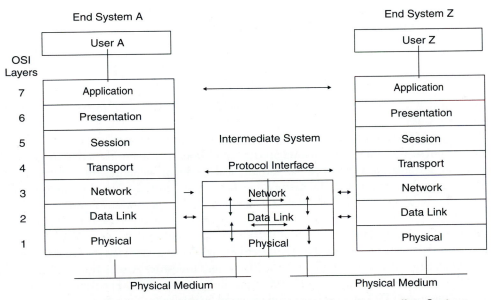

(b) **Communication between End Systems via an Intermediate System**

Figure 1.13   OSI Communication Architecture

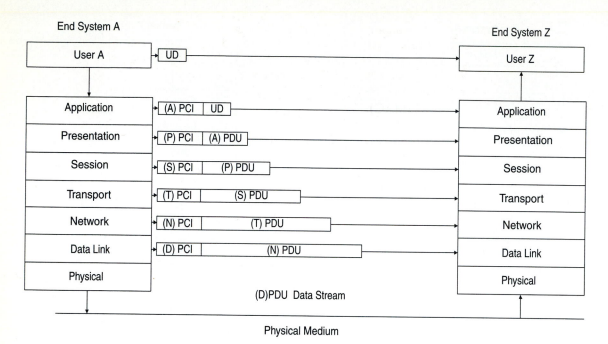

Figure 1.14   PDU Communication Model between End Systems

1.5.2   Protocol Layers and Services

We will now go into some detail regarding the services provided by the seven layers of OSI protocols.

Layer 1, the physical layer, is responsible for physically placing the electrical signal on the physical medium and picking up the signal from it. It controls and manages the physical and electrical interfaces to the physical medium, including the connector or transceiver. The physical medium could be copper (e.g., in the form of twisted pair or coaxial cable), optical fiber, or wireless media (e.g., radio, microwave, or infrared). The signal could be either analog or digital. There are various protocol standards for physical-layer interface, depending on the transmission medium and type of signal. Two classes of standards have been established by the International Telecommunications Union—Telecommunications Sector (ITU-T) and the Electronics Industries Association (EIA).

Layer 2 is the data link control layer, or data link layer for short. The data communication between two DTEs is controlled and managed by this layer. Note that in contrast to a byte-oriented transmission across a computer bus, the data communication is a serial-bit–oriented stream. The data link layer needs to do basic functions: first, establish and clear the link, and second, transmit the data. In addition to these functions, it does error control and data compression. Flow control on the data link layer is done on a hop-to-hop basis.

For point-to-point communication using a dedicated facility, like the loop link from a customer's telephone to the telephone company's switching office, the data link control is simple and straightforward to implement. However, if the DTE is connected to a LAN or a multidrop telephone line (i.e., a multipoint network of shared transmission media that is accessed simultaneously by many users), then the data link control becomes more complex. In the case of a multidrop line, the switching office controls access to the medium. A LAN is a distributed environment and thus the access control is distributed. In the OSI layered model, the data link layer is divided into two sublayers—logical link control (LLC) and media access control (MAC). This is shown in Figure 1.15. The lower MAC layer controls the access and transmittal of data to the physical layer in an algorithmic manner. There are two basic forms of LANs. Ethernet LAN is a bus type and the media is accessed using a distributed probabilistic algorithm, Carrier Sense Multiple Access with Collision Detection (CSMA/CD). The second type of LAN is a ring type used in token ring (TR) and Fiber Distributed Data Interface (FDDI). A deterministic token-passing algorithm is used in this case. LLC performs the link management and data transfer. LAN operation is explained in Chapter 2.

The network layer is the third layer in the OSI protocol stack. It controls and manages the switching fabric of the network. It provides both connectionless network service (CLNS) and connection-oriented network service (CONS). The former is used when the lower layers are highly reliable, such as LANs and bridges, as well as when the messages are short. CONS is the method for transmitting long messages, such as file transfer. It is also used when the transmission medium is not reliable. It subdivides the transport PDUs into frames of appropriate size based on the transmission parameters. The destination address of each packet is read in both CLNS and CONS at the network layer and routed on the appropriate links.

A router, or a routing bridge, at the nodes of a network performs the function of routing and switching the data. Any subnetwork of the node is under the control of that router. The subnetwork(s) can be anything from a simple single-segment LAN to complex subnetworks operating under a proprietary protocol. The OSI architectural model handles this by dividing the network layer into three sublayers as shown in Figure 1.16. The top sublayer is the Subnetwork-Independent Convergence Protocol (SNICP) that interfaces to the transport layer. The Internet communicates between nodes using an Internet address and the SNICP. The nodes in turn communicate with subnetworks using the Subnetwork-Dependent Convergence Protocol (SNDCP), which depends on the subnetwork protocol and could be any proprietary protocol. In such a situation, the SNDCP communicates with its data link layer via the third network sublayer, the Subnetwork-Dependent Access Protocol (SNDAP).

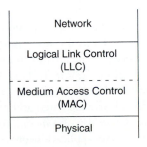

Figure 1.15   The Sublayer Structure of a Data Link Protocol Layer

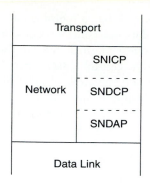

SNICP = Subnetwork Independent Convergence Protocol
SNDCP = Subnetwork Dependent Convergence Protocol
SNDAP = Subnetwork Dependent Adapter Protocol

Figure 1.16   The Sublayer Structure of a Network Protocol Layer

This subnetwork architecture separates layers 4 through 7 from the subnetwork dependencies. It also enables communication between a DTE on the Internet and a DTE on a subnetwork node. This is shown in Figure 1.17. Figure 1.17(a) depicts the network configuration in which DTE-A connected to end node A communicates with DTE-N1 connected to subnetwork node N1 via the intermediate system gateway node N. Figure 1.17(b) describes the path of communication through different protocol layers from the originating end system to the terminating end system via the intermediate node gateway. The formats of the PDUs are identical in all three systems at SNICP layer and levels above.

The most used network protocol is Internet Protocol (IP) and has been popularized by the Internet. It is part of the Internet suite of Transmission Control Protocol and Internet Protocol (TCP/IP) and is a connectionless network service protocol. In OSI terminology, it is called ISO-IP or ISO CLNP. A connection-oriented OSI protocol is X.25 PLP, a packet layer protocol.

The transport layer is the fourth layer of OSI protocol. It multiplexes the user data provided by the application layers and passes the packets to the network layer. Its service is independent of the network on which the packets are transmitted. The transport layer can be connectionless or connection oriented and is implemented in both Internet and OSI protocols. As mentioned earlier, TCP is a component of the Internet protocol suite and is connection oriented. The connectionless transport protocol in the TCP/IP suite is called User Datagram Protocol (UDP). Flow control is also implemented in transport layers and functions as a data rate manager between the application programs and the network layer. ISO has five transport-layer specifications, TP0 to TP4. TP4 is analogous to TCP.

Layers 5 through 7 are application-layer protocols. Except in the OSI Reference Model, the three application layers are not clearly separated and independent. Let us look at each layer as if they were independent, like in the OSI model, to understand their specific functions and the services they provide. An application process communicates with another application process during a session. The session-layer services establish the communication at the beginning of the session, monitor, synchronize, and error-correct the information

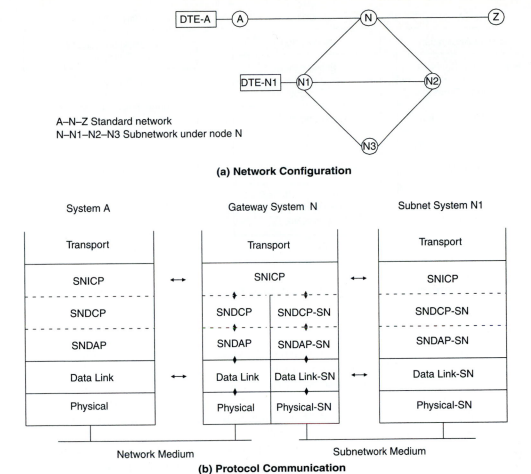

(a) Network Configuration

(b) Protocol Communication

Figure 1.17   Gateway Communication to a Proprietary Subnetwork

exchanged during the session, and then release the logical link at the end of the session. The session layer is very strongly related to the presentation layer, which is the medium of presentation of the message's context to the user or application program. In that sense, the presentation layer is a context-sensitive layer. It can be interpreted as the common language and image that the users at both end systems use and understand—the shared semantics of the two end users. A common syntax that is used for semantics is Abstract Syntax Notation Number One (ASN.1). Although the primary function of the presentation layer is conversion of syntax, data encryption and data compression are also generally done in that layer.

The top and seventh protocol layer is the application layer. The application process interfaces with the application support processes that are provided by this layer. Like the other two layers in the set of application layers (session and presentation), the application layer is strongly coupled with the rest of the application layers. In the OSI Reference Model, one can separate these processes from the presentation and session layers, but in

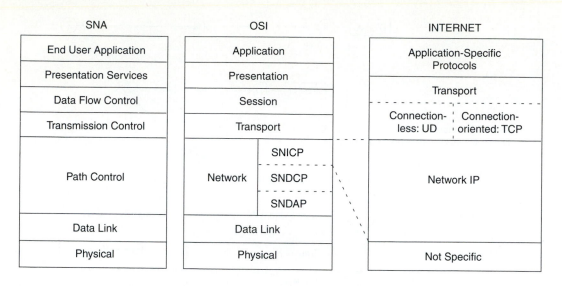

Figure 1.18   Comparison of SNA, OSI, and Internet Protocol Layer Models

other models, there is no clear distinction of the functions. Figure 1.18 presents a comparison of the SNA, OSI, and Internet models.

The Internet model does not specify the two lower layers, although it is obvious that they use distributed LAN and WAN configurations. The transport and network layers form the suite of TCP/IP protocols that we mentioned earlier. The application layers are combined into application-specific protocols.

We do not discuss the SNA protocol in detail in this book. However, it is good to be familiar with that structure because significant corporate data on networks today are believed to reside in legacy systems using the mainframe architecture. The SNA model has a one-to-one comparison with the OSI model, and has seven protocol layers. In fact, the SNA layered structure of IBM triggered the rest of the industry to generate an industry standard that all vendors can use.

In the seven-layered SNA model, the physical, data link, and application layers have one-to-one correspondence with the OSI layers. However, the OSI Reference Model layers 3 (network), 4 (transport), 5 (session), and 6 (presentation) are structured differently in the SNA model. The path control layer in the SNA model is similar to the OSI network layer, but it overlaps a little with the OSI transport functions. Much of the SNA transport- and session-layer functions equivalent to those of the OSI model are done in the data flow control and transmission control layers. The combination of these two services is also called the SNA transmission subsystem. The presentation services, which are known as SNA high-level services, combine the presentation services and functions with some of the session control functions.

Figure 1.19 compares four common application-specific protocols in the OSI and Internet models. There are more OSI application-specific protocols, which we do not discuss here. All application-specific protocol services in OSI are sandwiched between the

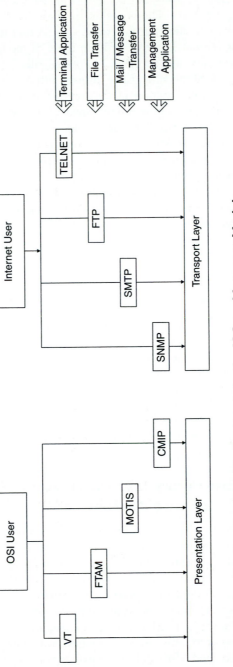

Figure 1.19   Application-Specific Protocols in the ISO and Internet Models

user and presentation layers. In the Internet model, they are sandwiched between the user and the transport layers. The boxes on the right-hand side of Figure 1.19 describe the comparable services offered in the two models. A user interfaces with a host at a remote terminal using Virtual Terminal (VT) in the OSI model and TELNET in the Internet model. File transfers are accomplished using File Transfer Access and Management (FTAM) in the OSI model and File Transfer Protocol (FTP) in the Internet. The most common mail service function in the Internet is the Simple Mail Transport Protocol (SMTP). A similar protocol in the OSI model is the Message-Oriented Text Interchange Standard (MOTIS). Network management is accomplished using Common Management Information Protocol (CMIP) in the OSI model and Simple Network Management Protocol (SNMP) in the Internet. We discuss extensively the details of SNMP in this book. CMIP is discussed briefly in Appendix A for completeness. However, it is important to understand the overall picture of the protocol layers and other application protocols to appreciate the network management functions that are accomplished using the network management protocols.

1.6   Case Histories of Networking and Management

Network management is more than just managing the network. In professional organizations it is referred to as OAM&P (operations, administration, maintenance, and provisioning). Of course, networking and network management existed before network management became a formalized discipline. As one information technology (IT) manager commented, the configuration and use of a network management system (NMS) formalizes what a network administrator would have otherwise done. The network administration "war stories" in the next two subsections illustrate that network management (especially without proper tools) could present a challenge to IT managers.

1.6.1   Case History 1: The Importance of Topology ("The Case of the Footprint")

A stable corporate network consisting of several minicomputers and about 100 desktop workstations and personal computers suddenly started "crashing" frequently. How often have we heard a network coming down without an apparent reason? Here is how one Vice President of Information Systems describes an incident.

Part of the network went down in the engineering area one morning. Since there were a whole series of users and at that time we were not using a star (hub) topology, but rather the old-fashioned serial topology (where all the users were daisy chained to the coaxial cable, or coax), we suspected a break in the chain, probably at a transceiver tap. Lacking sophisticated NMS tools, Information System personnel started walking the hallways and asking the users if anyone had just been doing anything out of the ordinary which might have broken the chain and caused the problem.

The guys came back and reported that no one had said that they had "done anything." So I (VP) started back down the halls with the guys and peeked into each office. Finally, I stopped and said, "Let's look up in the ceiling here." Sure enough, we found a transceiver that someone had been fooling with and that was not connected properly; it had caused the break. Once connected, the network segment came back up.

The guys asked, "Why did you say, 'try here,' particularly since the engineer in that office claimed ignorance?" I calmly pointed to a dusty sneaker footprint on the engineer's desk and the ceiling tile that was ajar above the desk and said, "You need to use all the diagnostic tools at your disposal!"

1.6.2   Case History 2: Filtering Does Not Reduce Load on Node

This case illustrates several issues related to network design, configuration, and maintenance. An autonomous group in a medium-sized corporation consisted of fifty personnel, all with personal computers or workstations. The entire group was on a single Ethernet LAN segment connected to one port of a six-port bridge. The single logical segment consisted of five physical segments connected by four repeaters. The topology was a bus configuration and the cable drop to the desktop was with a coax T. Most of the activities of the group were internal to the segment, as were the servers, except the mail server, which was common to the entire corporation. Thus, most of the traffic was internal to the LAN segment, except for e-mail and backup operations, which went across the bridge. This is shown in Figure 1.20(a).

As the volume of activities increased, the network segment would go down frequently. Initially, the problem was attributed to people disturbing the cable or to the failure of repeaters because only one group's segment went down. After unsuccessful attempts to cure the problem by replacing cables and repeaters, the attention turned to the volume of Ethernet traffic and the impact that it had on the bridge.

Every packet generated in the segment is opened by the bridge to check whether it is local traffic (the packet is intended for another host in the segment), or external traffic (the packet is intended for a host external to the segment). Thus, every packet had to be analyzed for filtering, which caused a heavy load on the port interface card, especially during heavy data bursts such as code compilation. Every time the network went down, the bridge had to be reset. This involved all the hosts in the segment going down and when the bridge came up, it needed to acquire all the addresses for routing purposes. The cause of the problem was guessed to be the overload on the bridge port, and hence the LAN segment was split into two and used two ports of the bridge as shown in Figure 1.20(b). This decreased the rate of failure from two per day to two per week. The problem was eliminated when the group moved to a new building and the network was reconfigured using a hub topology with cat-5 twisted-pair cable (cheaper than coaxial cable). It was the same traffic and same 10-Mbps Ethernet LAN. However, separating the four administrative subgroups into different LAN segments and interconnecting the workstations in each LAN by star topology using hubs made the difference. The final configuration is shown in Figure 1.20(c), where all three hubs and the bridge are in a central place.

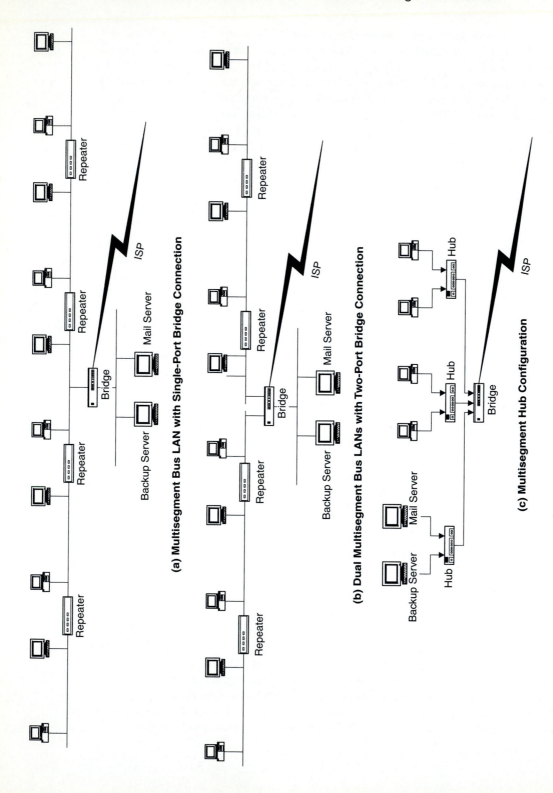

(a) Multisegment Bus LAN with Single-Port Bridge Connection

(b) Dual Multisegment Bus LANs with Two-Port Bridge Connection

(c) Multisegment Hub Configuration

Figure 1.20   The Evolution of a Network Configuration

1.6.3   Some Common Network Problems

The most common and serious problems of networks are connectivity failures, which are in the category of fault management. *Fault* is generally interpreted to mean failures in accessing networks and systems by the users. The network failure is caused more often by a node failure than by failure of passive links (except when one is cut off by a construction crew). Even the node failures are more often limited to specific interface failures. When this happens, all the downstream systems from that interface are inaccessible. Such failures are associated with the network interface card, which needs replacement, or with the node equipment, which needs resetting, as mentioned in Case History 2 in Section 1.6.2.

The node failures manifest as connectivity failures to the user. There are networking tools available to the manager to localize the fault, as we will learn in Chapter 12 on Network Management Systems and Tools.

Another cause of network connectivity failure is procedural, but very common. Network connectivity is based on IP address, which is a logical address assigned by the network administrator. The IP address is uniquely associated with a physical MAC address of the network component. However, mistakes are made in assigning duplicate IP addresses, especially in an enterprise environment with many system administrators.

A host or system interface problem in a shared medium can bring the entire segment down, sometimes intermittently, as in Case History 1 in Section 1.6.1. It could be a nightmare for the network manager to isolate the problem without causing interruption in service. A network manager uses intuitive knowledge to look for patterns such as a change in configuration, the addition of equipment, or a new facility.

The intermittent problems could also occur as a result of traffic overload, which could cause packets to be lost. Sometimes, the management system indicates failures, when in actuality, data traffic is flowing normally. Performance-monitoring tools could be useful in tracking such problems.

Power hits could reset network component configuration, causing network failure. The network has a permanent configuration (default) and a dynamic configuration (runtime) and thus a power hit could change the configuration.

Finally, there is the nonproblem, which really means that the cause of failure is a mystery. There is nothing that a network manager can do except turn the system off and then on. Bingo! The problem is resolved.

A performance problem could manifest as a network delay and is an annoyance to the network manager. He or she needs to separate the network delay from the application program or application processes delay, then convince the user and the person responsible for the application to rectify the situation.

With the ever-increasing size of networks and the connectivity to the Internet, security violation is a frequent problem. This is more a matter of policy than a technical issue, which we address in Chapter 13 when we discuss security management.

1.7   Challenges of Information Technology Managers

Managing a corporate network is becoming harder as such networks become larger and more complex. When we talk about network management, it includes not only the components that transport information in the network, but also systems that generate the traffic in the network. What use is a computer network if there are no systems in the network to provide service to the users? The systems could be client hosts, or database servers, or file servers, or mail servers. In the client/server environment, the network control is no longer centralized, but distributed, as was illustrated in the previous section. The computer and telecommunication networks are slowly merging in function; and the information technology manager needs to maintain both types of networks. Thus, the functions of data communications and telecommunication have been merged as the responsibility of the information technology manager. With the explosion of information storage and transfer in the modern information era, management of information is also the responsibility of the IT manager. The title of Chief Technical Officer (CTO) has changed to Chief Information Officer (CIO). For example, the IT manager must control and monitor access to information—both who has access and to what information; that is, the authentication and authorization issues of security management. The corporate network needs to be secured for privacy and content, using firewalls and encryption. The technology is moving fast and the corporate growth is enormous, and a CIO has to keep up with the new technologies and the responsibility for financial investment that the corporation has made. This amounts to millions of dollars, and the success or failure of a manager's guess—not choice—could make or break the CIO's job. Notice that the word *guess* was used instead of *choice*, because it is not always clear which of the options are dead ends, and should be avoided. Since they are not obvious, the IT manager needs to make provisions for contingencies to change direction when the IT industry does.

A good example of indeterminacy in the fast-moving technology industry is the competition between the two technologies of Ethernet and ATM in the desktop market. ATM was predicted to be the way to go a few years ago. However, its dominance has not been realized because of the enhanced capability of Ethernet. The ATM speed is 150 Mbps, larger than regular Ethernet at 10 Mbps and Fast Ethernet at 100 Mbps. But as of now, the development of 1 Gbps Ethernet seems to be more economical, further delaying the implementation of ATM to desktop.

Perspectives of Network Managers

In order to present the challenges that IT managers face, we interviewed several of them. They face network administration and management problems day in and day out. These are the folks who carry a beeper with them all the time because most of the corporate networks run 24–7, that is, 24 hours a day and 7 days a week! The following compilation of the questions and their answers indicate the complexity of managing a network. Notice that it is not just a technical function, as Case History 1 exemplifies. Also, even use of the best network management system does not solve the problems associated with building and maintaining a network, but it is a necessary tool. Thus, learning network management involves more than understanding networks and network management protocols.

General

- People expect all networks to be like telephone networks.
- Network reliability equal to telephone reliability is unrealizable. The telephone network was monopolistic and had expensive redundancy. Data network is ad

hoc, decentralized, has loosely specified interfaces, and has dynamic routing. Thus, it is more flexible than a telephone network, though less reliable. The latest user satisfaction for an ISP is 16 percent and the ISPs are still growing.

- Some of the data communications are non-real time such as execution of instructions like Mars Rover. Thus, when a problem is detected it is too late to fix it.

1. **What are your top challenges in managing the network?**
   - Staying abreast of the rapid advance of technology, depending on trade journals, vendor product info, and conversations with colleagues
   - Analyzing problems, which requires intuition and skill
   - Anticipating customers' demands
   - Acquiring resources
   - Sustainable network that is scaleable and maintainable (had thick Ethernet three years ago, now it is hub with twisted pair)
   - Managing the client/server environment
   - Networking with emerging technology as part of continuing education
   - Collaborative research between academic institutions and industry
   - Maintaining reliability; that is, making changes, upgrades, and such without disrupting the network and affecting business
   - Diagnosing problems or outages in a nondisruptive manner (without impacting other users on the network)
   - Estimating the value of a technology transition (e.g., Would the business benefit from upgrading some or all users to switched 10MB Ethernet to their desktop? Should we upgrade our link to our ISP from 384K to 768K or to a full T1?)
   - Maintaining a secure firewall between the internal network and the Internet while gaining the value of the information and services available from the Internet
   - Determining responsibility for outages to the WAN (which piece broke—our interface, the local loop, or the long-distance portion?); coordinating telephone company repair efforts
   - Keeping the topology as simple as possible within the confines of the technology in order to reduce administrative effort and chance for mistakes (e.g., Is introducing a router and thus having to create several subnetworks with different IP addresses worth the costs, or can we stay flat and still get the performance we need?)

2. **Which elements of managing your network require most of your time? What percentage of time do you spend on maintenance compared to growth?**
   - Configuring the management system itself
   - Expanding the network
   - Gathering and analyzing statistics for presentation to upper management

- Traditional maintenance 30%(Manager of Organization X)
    Mandatory maintenance   40%
    Growth   30%
- Growth   50%(Manager of Organization Y)
    Maintenance   50%

3. **How did you or would you manage your network without an NMS?**

- Reactively, not proactively; firefighting
- Troubleshooting tools (e.g., sniffer)
- Home-grown systems
- Managed the network in the spare time after installation
- Human intuition
- Rely on consultant advice and technical information for growth decisions

4. **Do you need an NMS? If so, why?**

- Yes, for proactive management of the network
- Yes, to verify customer configuration
- Yes, to diagnose problems
- Yes, to provide statistics on performance
- Yes, to help remove bottlenecks
- Yes, because an NMS formalizes the manual practice of network management
- Yes, because NMS products reflect the practices of the company that develops them
- Yes, but remember NMS does not solve problems, people do
- Yes, but a low-end NMS is adequate
- Yes, the configuration and operation of NMS reflects the person who sets it up
- Yes, to see the trend in growth

5. **How would you use NMS and why?**

- Save time and use human resources effectively
- Saved time goes into improving network management
- Turn-around time for problem resolution smaller
- Monitor the status and performance of the network
- Gather statistics to improve OAM&P
- Document events for auditing purposes
- Troubleshooting
- Remove constraints and bottlenecks
- Fault isolation
- I would expect the NMS to help me evaluate load on network segments and pinpoint failures

6. **What does a network failure cost the user?**

    (Note: The answers to this question are qualitative and of general nature)

    - There are tangible and intangible losses
    - The losses of academic and research (A&R) laboratories differ from the losses of business corporations. A&R labs need high technology and tolerate low reliability. Businesses accept lower and proven technology but require high reliability. (For example, Mead Data counts profit looking at the "Tot Board.")
    - The cost is a function of the dependence of the business upon shared data. If we have a general network failure, our ability to conduct business is severely impacted because we cannot get access to the data.

7. **What are your expectations of a newly graduated student with networking as area of specialization?**

    - Prefer to hire candidates with networking experience
    - Need to be familiar with protocols
    - Possess the drive to understand and to envision
    - Be a self-starter
    - Lab experience at school is essential
    - Knowledge of basic networking
    - Know the differences between system, applications, and network
    - Technical: knowledge foundations, applications, tools, utilities, and so forth
    - Be technically current with the common protocols, wiring topologies, and common network equipment
    - Be professional, have more than just technical skill
    - Know how to succeed in commercial organizations
    - Recognize the importance of customer service, and see IT as the service provider
    - Know how to stay ahead of demand curve
    - Possess personal communication skills
    - Be cost conscious
    - Have a sense of business risk reduction. The prime goal is to provide service in the pursuit of a robust, stable network environment. New graduates need to confine "experiments" and "tinkering" to evenings and weekends so that if their actions crash the network or create a problem, the business impact is minimized. I fight this same educational battle with my server administrators and even my desktop support personnel. Initially, they are not sensitive to the dangers of trying things during the day when people are working. Several of our worst breakdowns occurred because a member of the Information System Team was trying out new software or a new utility or doing something similarly risky during the business day without comprehending the risk if their activity dumped the system or network.

In the next two sections, we briefly introduce the subject of network management functions and systems.

1.8   Network Management: Goals, Organization, and Functions

Network management can be defined as **OAM&P** (operations, administration, maintenance, and provisioning) of network and services. The operations group is concerned with daily operations in providing network services. Network administration is concerned with establishing and administering the overall goals, policies, and procedures of network management. The installation and maintenance group handles functions that include both installation and repairs of facilities and equipment. Provisioning involves network planning and circuit provisioning, traditionally handled by the engineering or provisioning department. We will describe each of these functions in this section. Although we continue to use the terminology of network management, this addresses in the modern enterprise environment all of information technology and information technology services.

1.8.1   Goal of Network Management

The goal of network management is to ensure that the users of a network receive the information technology services with the quality of service that they expect. Toward meeting this goal, management should establish policy to either formally or informally contract a Service Level Agreement with the users. For example, operation-critical servers such as e-mail and Web servers, as well as networks involving activities that cannot be interrupted, would require 24-7 (24 hours, 7 days-a-week) service and would be contracted as such. Other non-critical networks and systems could be contracted for 8-5 (8 hours Monday through Friday) maintenance.

From a business administration point of view, network management involves strategic and tactical planning of the engineering, operations, and maintenance of a network and network services for current and future needs at minimum overall cost. Well-established communication and interaction among the various groups is necessary to perform these functions.

Figure 1.21 presents a top-down view of network management functions. It comprises three major groups: (1) network provisioning, (2) network operations, and (3) network installation and maintenance (I&M). It is useful to consider the different functions as belonging to specific administrative groups, although there are other ways of assigning responsibilities based on organizational structure. Network provisioning is the primary responsibility of the engineering group; and network I&M is the primary responsibility of the plant facilities group. The interactions among the groups are shown in Figure 1.22. The normal daily operations are the function of the network operations group, which controls and administers a network operations center (NOC), the nerve center of network management operations. The functions of the NOC are concerned primarily with network operations; its secondary responsibilities are network provisioning and network I&M.

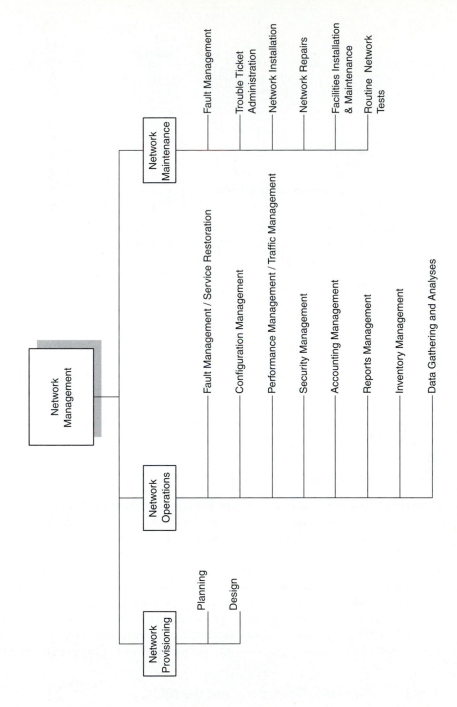

Figure 1.21   Network Management Functional Groupings

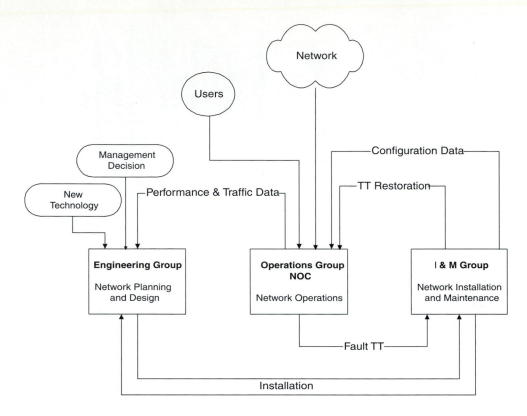

Figure 1.22   Network Management Functional Flowchart

1.8.2   Network Provisioning

Network provisioning consists of network planning and design and is the responsibility of the engineering group. The engineering group keeps track of new technologies and introduces them as needed. Determination of what is needed and when is made through analysis of the traffic and performance data provided by the network operations. Modifications to network provisioning may also be initiated by management decisions. Planning and efficient use of equipment can be achieved with good inventory management of modifications of network configuration by the network-provisioning group.

Network management tools are helpful to the engineering group in gathering statistics and studying the trends of traffic patterns for planning purposes. Automated operations systems help in the design of circuits and measurement of the performance tune-up.

1.8.3   Network Operations and the NOC

The functions of network operations, listed in Figure 1.21, are administered by the **network operations center** (NOC). They are concerned with daily operations of the network and providing network services. ISO has defined five OSI network management applications: fault, configuration, performance, security, and account management. The NOC is also responsible for gathering statistics and generating reports for management, system support, and users. A network management system and tools are a necessity for NOC operations. They are used in the various management applications as described below.

Fault Management/Service Restoration: Whenever there is a service failure, it is NOC's responsibility to restore service as soon as possible. This involves detection and isolation of the problem that caused the failure, and restoration of the service. In several failure situations, the network will do this automatically. This network feature is called self-healing. In other situations, an NMS can detect failures of components and indicate them with appropriate alarms. Restoration of service does not include fixing the cause of the problem. That responsibility to fix the problem usually rests with the I&M group. A trouble ticket is generated manually by a source engineer at NOC using a trouble-ticket system or automatically generated by an NMS. The information on the trouble ticket includes a tracking number assigned by the system, time at which problem occurred, the nature of the problem, affected user, any SLA contracted with the customer, the responsible group or engineer to resolve the problem and who generated the trouble ticket. It would be forwarded to the I&M group who would fix the problem and fill in the details of resolution before closing the trouble ticket. The tracking of a trouble involves several groups and the administration of it generally belongs to the network maintenance group.

Trouble Ticket Administration: Trouble ticket administration is the administrative part of fault management and is used to track problems in the network. All problems, including nonproblems, are to be tracked until resolved. Periodic analysis of the data, which is maintained in a database, establishes patterns of the problems for follow-up action. There are automatic systems that track troubles from the automatic generation of a trouble ticket by a network management system to the resolution of the problem.

Configuration Management: There are three configurations of the network. One is the static configuration and is the permanent configuration of the network. The static configuration is one that would come up if the network is started from idle status. However, it is likely that the current running configuration is different from that of the permanent configuration. The second configuration of a network, then, is the current running configuration. The third configuration is the planned configuration of the future when the configuration data will change as the network is changed. This information is useful for planning and inventory management. The configuration data is gathered automatically as much as possible, and is stored by network management systems.

The NOC has a display that reflects the dynamic configuration of the network and its status. The status of the network is displayed by a network management system and indicates any failure of its components, as well as the traffic pattern and performance. Any configuration changes made to relieve temporary congestion in traffic are made by the NOC and are reflected in the dynamic display at the NOC.

Security Management can cover a very broad range of security, which includes physically securing the network, as well as controlling access to the network by the users. Access privilege to application software is not the responsibility of the NOC unless the application is either owned or maintained by the NOC. A security database is established and maintained by the NOC for access to the network and network information. Other aspects of security management, such as firewalls and cryptography, are introduced later in this chapter in Section 1.11.

Performance Management: The NOC gathers data and keeps them up to date in order to perform some of the above functions, as well as to tune the network for optimum performance. The network statistics include data on traffic, network availability, and network delay. The traffic data can be captured based on volume of traffic in the various segments of the network. It can also be obtained based on different applications such as Web traffic, e-mail, and network news, or based on transport protocols at various layers such as TCP, UDP, IP, IPX, Ethernet, Token Ring, FDDI, and so on. Traffic statistics are helpful in detecting trends and planning future needs. Performance data on availability and delay is useful for tuning the network to increase the reliability and to improve its response time.

Accounting Management: The NOC administers costs and allocates the use of the network. Metrics are established to measure the usage of resources and services.

Since the network consists of components manufactured by multiple vendors, commonality in the definition and relationship of component attributes is needed. This is defined by the Management Information Base (MIB), which we discuss in Chapter 4. Some of the data acquisition has to be manual (because of legacy systems), but most of the data can and should be acquired in an automated mode. SNMP, the Internet management protocol, is the most popular protocol to acquire the data automatically using protocol and performance-analyzing tools.

Part of implementing the above standards includes ensuring that adequate reports are generated and distributed to the relevant personnel. There are, in general, three classes of reports: systems, management, and user. System reports are needed for network operations to track the activities. Management reports go to the management of the network management group to keep them informed about the activities and performance of the NOC and the network. The user reports are distributed to the users on a periodic basis to let them know the status of network performance.

1.8.4   Network Installation and Maintenance

The network I&M group takes care of all installation and maintenance of equipment and cables. This group is the service arm of the engineering group for installation and fixing troubles for network operations. The I&M group works closely with the Help Desk in responding to the problems reported from the field.

Having encountered network management from the perspectives of operations, administration, maintenance, and provisioning, let us next consider how a network of systems is managed.

1.9   Network and System Management

We need to distinguish at the onset the difference between network management and system management. Remember that a user may not make that distinction when he or she cannot access an application on a server from a client application in his or her workstation. This could be due to a problem in the application program or due to a transport problem from the client's workstation to the server platform. The former is a system problem and falls under the category of system management. The latter is a connectivity problem and falls under network management. We can generalize system management as the management of systems and system resources in the network. Network management is concerned with network resources such as hubs, switches, bridges, routers, and gateways, and the connectivity among them via a network. It also addresses end-to-end connectivity between any two processors (not application processes) in the network.

As we saw in Section 1.1, a network consists of network components and their interconnections. The vendor who manufactures a network component or set of network components is best qualified to develop a network management system for that product or set of products. This involves getting the data from each instance of a component in the network to one or more centralized locations and displaying its status on a network management system. For example, failure of a bridge would set up an alarm in the network management system to alert the operations personnel of the failure. This would enable the operations personnel to follow up on the problem and restore the service, even before the user calls in a complaint.

As we mentioned, each type of component is managed most efficiently by the respective management system. A network management system manages all the components that are connected to a network. Again, it is relatively simple for a vendor to develop a network management system to manage a network of components it produced. However, a user, such as a global corporation, buys components from different vendors and the information systems manager of the corporation has the responsibility to maintain the network of all vendor components. This might require installation of multiple network management systems for an enterprise, or a network management system that can manage multiple vendor components. Thus, a common management system, as well as the integration of different management systems and their interoperability, has played a major role in the network management arena in the past decade. Professional organizations and industrial communities have been establishing standards for this purpose, which are still evolving. The two major standards are the Internet and the OSI standards. We will look at the former in detail in this book.

A network management dumbbell architecture for interoperability is shown in Figure 1.23(a) where vendor systems A and B exchange common management messages. The messages consist of management information data (e.g., the type, id, and status of managed objects) and management controls (e.g., setting and changing the configuration of an object). The protocols and services associated with the dumbbell architecture are presented in Figure 1.23(b). Application services are the management-related applications such as fault and configuration management. The management protocols are CMIP for the OSI model and SNMP for the Internet model. Transport protocols are the first four layers of the OSI model and TCP/IP over any of the first two layers of the seven-layer OSI model.

Figure 1.24 models a hierarchical configuration of two network agents monitoring two sets of managed objects. A network management system (NMS) is at the top of the hierarchy. Each network agent monitors its respective objects. Either in response to a polled query from the NMS or triggered by a local alarm, the agent communicates the relevant data to the NMS.

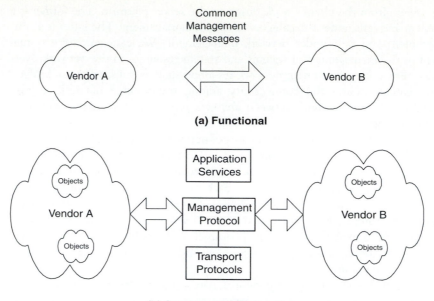

Figure 1.23   **Network Management Dumbbell Architecture**

Peer networks can communicate network management messages and controls to each other, as shown in Figure 1.25. An example where such a configuration could be implemented would be two NMSs associated with two telecommunication networks belonging to two network service providers, for example, an interexchange carrier and a

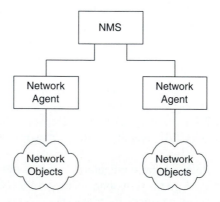

Figure 1.24   **Network Management Components**

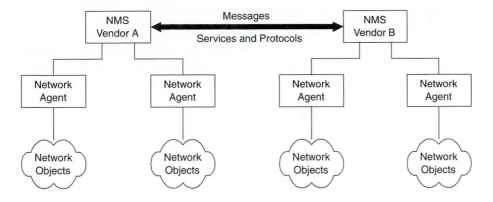

Figure 1.25   Network Management Interoperability

local access provider. As the two NMSs communicate, each NMS can superimpose the data from the other and present an integrated picture to the network administrator.

We want to make one final note before we leave this section. Some of the issues associated with the management of a telecommunication network by the telecommunication service providers are unique and involve more than just the management of networks. This has given birth to the Telecommunication Management Network (TMN) framework and related standards. We'll address these in Chapter 11.

As we said at the beginning of this section, a network management system primarily manages the networks that transport information. However, from a user's perspective, networks are means to an end, namely to have access to information across the networks. Thus, the user's needs require a way to manage the total network, system resources, and applications that run on systems. The applications could be specific user applications, or general-purpose servers such as file servers, database servers, and domain name servers. Software products have been developed recently to address such systemwide solutions.

An IT manager is interested in more than managing networks, systems, and applications. He or she would like to automate other functions such as backup of databases and programs, downloading of software updates from a central location, and a host of other support functions. These functions are required to run an IT operation efficiently and in a cost-effective manner.

Another area of system management is logging and archiving events, the need for which is illustrated by a case history. A system's performance during the normally low activity time at night was poor. Further probing of the system resources indicated that the system was busy with processes being executed from outside the institution. The system had been "compromised," that is, it had been broken into. The intruder could manipulate the normal system resource tools so as to hide the intruding programs. The intruder was finally discovered from the archival system log.

Solutions to the total information technology services are being offered now by commercial vendors. We discuss them along with network and system management tools in Chapter 12.

1.10   Network Management System Platform

Network management systems and tools are available in various platforms—hardware and operating system. The popular high-end systems are housed either on SUN or HP UNIX-based workstations. Some of them run on Windows NT-based PCs also. The low-end network management systems run either on Windows 95/98 or Windows NT.

Common troubleshooting and monitoring of network element parameters could be done by using simple networking and network management tools. These are part of TCP/IP stack. For example, network connectivity could be tested using the *ping* command in UNIX (*traceroute*) and Windows NT (*tracert*)–based system. We discuss network management systems and tools in detail in Chapter 12.

1.11   Current Status and Future of Network Management

The current network management systems are based on the SNMP protocol. Most of the commercial network components have embedded SNMP agents. Because of the universality of the Internet with TCP/IP protocol, the transport of management information for SNMP management, which is TCP/IP–based, is resolved automatically. In addition, most of the popular host operating systems come with the TCP/IP suite and thus are amenable to SNMP management.

The current network management systems, however, suffer from several limitations. They need a dedicated NMS monitoring station, which must be on a specific type of platform. Access to an NMS from remote locations is accomplished by using ad hoc schemes such as X-host application in UNIX-based NMS. This permits the export of the presentation and running the NMS from a remote workstation. However, the remote workstation also needs to be a UNIX platform.

Another limit of an SNMP-based management system is that the values of the managed objects should be defined as scalar values. The OSI-based management protocol, CMIP, is object-oriented. However, it has so far not been successful due to the complexity of specifications of managed objects, and the enormous memory required to handle CMIP stacks in workstations.

The SNMP–based management is a polling-based system. In other words, NMS polls each agent as to its status, or for any data that it needs for network management. Only a small set of transactions is initiated by a management agent to an NMS, as alarms. To detect a fault quickly, or to obtain good statistics, more frequent polling of agents needs to be done by the NMS, which adds to the basic network traffic. An alternative solution to this problem is deployment of remote monitors, as discussed in Chapter 8. However, this solution is expensive.

Most of the above constraints in SNMP–based management have been overcome by the emerging Web-based management, discussed in Chapter 14. In this scheme, management software could be embedded in network components, for example as Java applets. These applets could then communicate the management information to a Web-based

NMS server without being polled. The NMS could be monitored from any Web browser from any location.

A Web-based system is platform-independent for the management software using Java language in the managed components, for the Web-based NMS server, as well as for Web-browser monitors. Further, the information is transmitted mostly in one direction—from managed element to the NMS, and only as needed. This reduces the network management traffic significantly.

Object-oriented technology is reaching a mature stage and the hardware capacity to handle object-oriented stacks is now commercially available. The price of hardware has plummeted in the last year. Thus, object-oriented network management is being reconsidered. This has potential application in Telecommunications Management Network discussed in Chapter 11.

We will discuss two potential Web-based management schemes in Chapter 14. They are Java-based JMX (Java Management Extensions) developed by Sun, and WBEM (Web-Based Enterprise Management) based on the Common Information Model developed by Microsoft.

Information technology itself is exploding, and this gives rise to new challenges for expanding the horizon of network management. The transport of voice, video, and data is integrated in broadband multimedia services. The broadband multimedia service is based on ATM SONET wide-area network and several emerging access technologies such as HFC (hybrid fiber coax) and ADSL (Asymmetric Digital Subscriber Loop). Quality of service (QoS) in integrated services is important. Managing these new service offerings form the content of Chapter 10.

Another re-emerging technology on the horizon for network management is wireless technology. This is being deployed widely for WAN, mobile, and broadband access services. Very little work on management of this technology has been done yet.

An active network, which is the direction of the next-generation network, would include embedded network management applications. Besides the advancement of research and development in network management in standards, protocols, methodology, and new technology, there is considerable activity in management applications, which form the topic of Chapter 13. Of particular significance are event-correlation technology in fault management, and secured network and communication in security management. The recent efforts on policy-based management and service level management are also briefly covered.

A single failure in a network can cause multiple symptoms and manifest itself in multiple locations. The fault can propagate in space and time across the network. Several methods are being researched to find the root of a problem. We discuss some of these methods, such as artificial intelligence, algorithmic schemes, and a finite state machine in Chapter 13.

With the proliferation of the Internet, securing networks and communication has become extremely important. Existing management standards do not go far enough in this. However, security management has taken on the role of a special topic in network management. Topics of high interest in this field are firewalls that establish secure networks, and cryptography that ensure secure communication. We address these issues in Chapter 13.

Summary

We presented in this chapter an overview of data and telecommunication networks and how these networks are managed. The telephone network was shown as a model to be followed in accomplishing a reliable, dependable, and quality data communication network. We explained the difference between data communication and telecommunication networks, although this distinction is fast disappearing. The desktop processors and LAN technology have contributed to the client/server distributed computing environment, which has changed the direction of data communication. We briefly talked about the Internet and intranets in today's environment. Adoption of standards has played a significant part in the popularity of the Internet. The OSI and Internet protocols are very important in data communication today. Their relationship to the SNA protocol is identified.

We have presented some practical day-to-day experiences of network managers, including "war stories" to highlight the importance of network management. We saw a bird's-eye view of network management, and described how network components and networks are managed by network management systems. We extended the concept of network management to managing networks and systems and all of IT services. IT management is undergoing changes due to advancement in software and information technology. Possible future directions in network management technology were addressed at the end of the chapter.

Exercises

Note for exercises 1 through 4: It is important that a network administrator be familiar with both the protocols employed in the network and the tools with which its operation can be investigated. Several tools are fundamental for administration of an IP network; the most important are *ping, nslookup,* and *traceroute.* These commands should be available on UNIX platforms. You may get the syntax of their usage by logging into a UNIX system and accessing the on-line manual by invoking the command *man commandname.* Similar tools or commands are available in Windows 95/NT machines (*ping, tracert, nslookup* either built in or via external software) connected to the Internet. Exercises 1 through 7 will help you become familiar with exploring a network. You should be able to complete all of these exercises with the three tools just mentioned, by knowing how to telnet to nic.internic.net to do a *whois* query, and through research on the Web.

While doing these exercises, if you have a problem reaching the destination host, you may use any other equivalent destination site. It is important for you to learn to use the tools and interpret the results.

1. Who is the primary Internet service provider (ISP) for your institution? Find one other institution that is served by the same ISP by using traceroute. (*Hint:* For the Georgia Institute of Technology, try University of Arizona, University of North Carolina, and MIT).

2. The educational institutions of Georgia are connected by a network. Discover that network by tracing the route from the Georgia Institute of Technology to the

University of Georgia. (This exercise can be adapted to the network of a local institution.)

3. Draw the route, identifying each node, for the following data obtained using the trace-routing tool. What is the average time a packet takes to travel from the noc2 host to the *netman* host?

noc2% traceroute netman.cc.gatech.edu

traceroute to netman.cc.gatech.edu (130.207.8.31), 30 hops max, 40 byte packets

main-rtr.gcatt.gatech.edu (199.77.147.1) 1.045 ms 1.012 ms 0.971 ms

130.207.251.2 (130.207.251.2) 2.198 ms 1.404 ms 1.837 ms

netman.cc.gatech.edu (130.207.8.31) 3.528 ms 1.671 ms 1.602 ms

4. Between which two hosts on the route between your site and www.president.lv is the largest geographic distance probably traversed? Support your answer with evidence.

5. Ping ns1.bangla.net in this exercise. State what data you gathered and how it determined your conclusion.

   a. Measure the percentage of packets lost between a host at your site and the machine ns1.bangla.net, and record the time of your measurement.
   b. Determine where along the route to ns1.bangla.net the packets are getting lost.

6. For each host on the route between Tech and ns1.bangla.net, determine the name of the administrative contact responsible for it (use the *whois* command from your UNIX system or from nic.internet.net). List these names alongside the hosts. If you can't find an administrative contact for some of the hosts, then at least state what you did find.

7. You can discover the hosts in your subnetwork by using the ping command with your network IP address and host address of decimal 255. Discover all the hosts in the subnetwork that you are logged on.

8. In Exercise 5, identify the gateway from your subnetwork to others.

9. Identify the hosts in the neighboring subnetworks and draw the configuration of interconnected subnetworks.

10. The e-mail system is based on client/server architecture. Send an e-mail to a wrong node address (for example, misspelling the remote node address). Explain the error message(s) that you get and the servers that sent them.

11. Send an e-mail to a remote site with a wrong userid, but correct node address. Explain the error message(s) that you get and the servers that sent them.

12. Explain the decimal notation in representing the classes of IPv4 addresses. Give an example for each class.

13. You are given a class B IP address of 145.45.x.y for your network node. As a network engineer, you are asked to configure your network for 126 subnets (Remember that 0 and 1 are reserved).

   a. How would you configure your address for subnets and hosts?

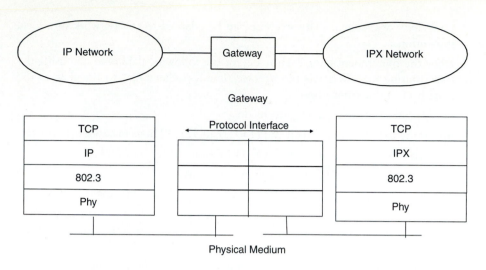

Figure 1.26   Exercise 14

    b. What is the maximum number of hosts that each subnet can accommodate?

14. An IP network is connected to a Novell IPX network via a gateway as shown in Figure 1.26. Draw the protocol layers of the gateway.

15. MBI Corporation uses cc:mail, which is not Internet standard. The company also uses Novell LAN. Novell has Internet Exchange Protocol, IPX (connectionless datagram service) as its equivalent to Internet TCP/IP. As you know well, most of the global e-mail traffic on the Internet uses SNMP as the mail protocol. Figure 1.27 shows the high-level configuration of the two networks connected through a gateway. Fill in the protocol layers of the gateway.

16. Picture a scenario where you are downloading a file from a server located in Europe, which has an X.25 protocol based on the OSI Reference Model. Its physical medium interface is X.21. Your client machine is connected to the Internet with Ethernet as the physical medium.

    a. Draw the details of the communications network in Figure 1.28(a) using bridges, routers, and a gateway between the server and client.

    b. Complete the protocol architecture in Figure 1.28(b) for the intermediate gateway system.

17. As a network engineer in an NOC, you are following up on the following two trouble tickets. You do not have a network management system and you have to use the basic network tools to validate the problems before you can resolve them. Please explain what tools you would use in each case and how it would validate the customer's complaint.

    a. Trouble Ticket 100: Customer says that periodically the messages he receives are missing some characters.

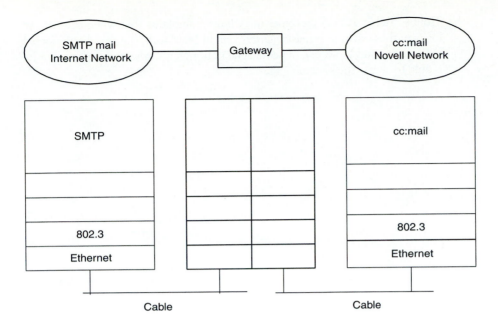

Figure 1.27   Exercise 15

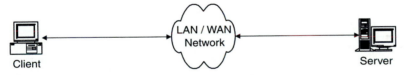

(a) Communication Network between Client and Server

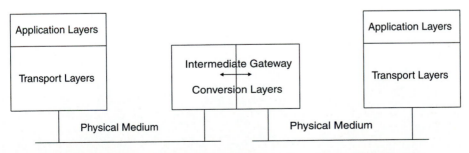

(b) Communication between End Systems via an Intermediate System

Figure 1.28   Exercise 16

b. Trouble Ticket 101: A customer in Atlanta complains that when she tries to log into the system *server.headquarters.com* in New York, she gets disconnected with a time-out. However, her colleague in her New York office reports that he is able to access the system.

CHAPTER 2

Review of Computer Network Technology

In Chapter 1 we learned that a network comprises nodes and links. Nodes are switches, bridges, routers, or gateways. Links are either LANs (local area networks) or WANs (wide area networks). In this chapter we review these components from the perspectives of concept, technology, and management.

Section 2.1 presents the various network topologies of LANs and WANs. The LAN technology has been evolving rapidly. In Section 2.2 we start with the basic Ethernet, and then traverse the development of Ethernet, Fast Ethernet, Gigabit Ethernet, and Switched Ethernet. Token Ring is a commonly used LAN in the IBM mainframe environment. Fiber-optic technology uses Token Ring architecture to develop the Fiber Distributed Data Interface (FDDI). The bandwidth usage of facilities over which LANs are implemented has been increased significantly by the development of virtual LANs (VLANs).

Section 2.3 presents network node components, starting with the implementation of a LAN as a discrete component, a hub. LANs are interconnected by bridges. Bridged network is made up of remote bridges in a tree topology. LANs can also be connected in a mesh WAN topology using routers as nodal components. Autonomous WANs with diverse networking protocols are connected with gateways that do protocol conversion at network layers and above. Half-bridge/half-router configurations are used for Internet point-to-point communication links. The discussion of Section 2.3 ends with switches and the part they play in WAN topology. Section 2.4 briefly discusses wide area networks, the telecommunication networks that computer (or data) communication traverse over long distances.

Section 2.5 addresses transmission technology, which comprises wired and wireless technology that transports information over LANs and WANs. The mode of transmission can be either analog or digital; a message can be transmitted in either mode, or part of the way in analog mode and the rest in digital. This becomes especially true in broadband multimedia services where the data, voice, and video are integrated into a common service, ISDN (Integrated Services Digital Network). ISDN, a hybrid technology, is introduced in this chapter for completeness in Section 2.6, but discussed in detail in Chapter 9.

2.1   Network Topology

A LAN is a shared medium that serves many DTEs (data terminal equipment) located in close proximity, such as in one building. LANs could also be deployed in a campus environment to connect equipment in many buildings.

Three topologies are associated with LANs: bus, ring, and star. A fourth pseudotopology combines star topology with either of the other two, to form a hub configuration. Hubs play an important role in networking and we'll review the various hub configurations in Section 2.3.1.

The LAN topology depicts the configuration of connections among DTEs. Different protocols are used in different topological configurations. Bus architecture is implemented in LANs that use the Ethernet protocol. Token ring and FDDI configurations use ring topology. Star topology is used in cabling infrastructure and is ideal for hub implementation.

WANs are configured with either mesh or tree topology. Mesh topology is the most common form for Internet routing. Tree topology is employed in networks that use brouters, which are bridged routers that do the routing at OSI layer 2.

The three LAN topologies and the hub configuration are shown in Figure 2.1. In the **bus topology**, in Figure 2.1(a), all DTEs are on a shared bus and have equal access to the LAN. However, only one DTE can have control at a time. A randomization algorithm determines which DTE has control of the LAN at any given time. This topology is used in Ethernet LANs and broadband network configurations. Because collisions occur when more than one station tries to seize the LAN at or about the same time, the bus LAN usually functions at much less than full efficiency.

Figure 2.1(b) shows the **ring topology**, which was popularized by IBM's Token Ring LAN. In this topology, each active DTE connected to the ring takes a turn in sending information to another DTE in the ring, which is either a receiving host or a gateway to an external network. At the time a DTE communicates over the ring, it is in control of the ring and the control is managed by a token-passing system. The DTE holds on to the token while it's sending data and releases the token to its downstream neighbor when its turn is finished. Thus, the process in this topology is deterministic and the LAN operates at almost full bandwidth efficiency.

Figure 2.1(c) represents a **star topology** that was once used in a star LAN; however, it is now used in a hybrid mode, as discussed in the next paragraph. In the star topology, all DTEs are connected to a central node and interconnected in one of two modes. They can be connected in a broadcast configuration so that all DTEs receive data transmitted by a DTE. This would be similar to bus topology. In the second configuration, the DTEs are connected to the central node, but are interconnected selectively as pairs. In this situation, multiple conversations can occur concurrently among various DTEs.

As mentioned earlier, **hub** configuration uses star topology in combination with either a bus or token ring topology. The hub configurations shown in Figure 2.1(d) are the most popular LAN implementation in a corporate environment. They are a hybrid of Figure 21(c) and either Figure 21(a) or Figure 21(b). The DTEs are connected electronically (electronic connection not explicitly shown in the figure) at the central node in either a bus or a ring topology. If they are interconnected in a broadcast configuration for an Ethernet LAN, it is called an Ethernet hub. If the DTEs are connected in a ring topology for use with a token ring LAN, the configuration is called a token ring hub.

A WAN differs from a LAN in that a WAN links networks that are geographically separated by long distance. Typically, the WAN link interconnects nodes made of switches, bridges, and routers.

WANs are connected in either a mesh topology or a tree topology, as shown in Figure 2.2. **Mesh topology**, shown in Figure 2.2(a), provides multiple paths between nodes (N). Thus, a message between N1 and N6 may traverse the paths N1-N2-N5-N6, N1-N3-N5-N6, N1-N2-N3-N5-N6, N1-N3-N2-N5-N6, N1-N4-N5-N6, N1-N4-N3-N5-N6, and

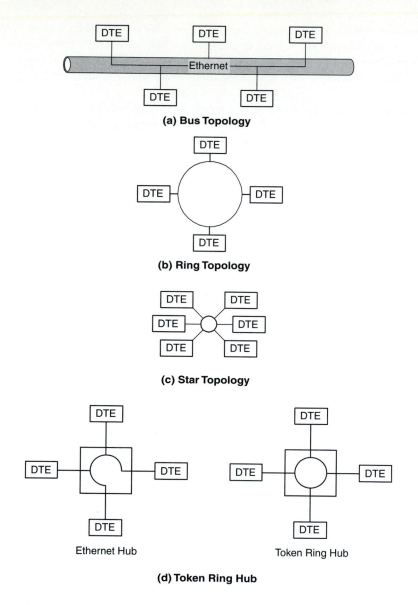

Figure 2.1   LAN Topologies

N1-N3-N4-N5-N6. This allows the packets of one message to traverse different paths, thus balancing the traffic load. It also provides redundancy for reliability of service. However, a broadcast message from N1 to all other nodes will be rebroadcast by neighboring nodes N2, N3, and N4 to all other nodes. This could cause flooding on the network and looping of packets, which need to be addressed carefully. Flooding occurs when a node retransmits the same packet to all other nodes and looping occurs when one packet goes

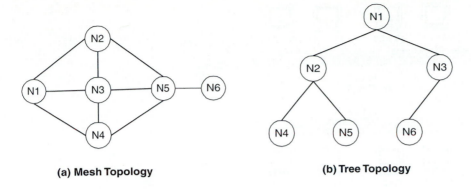

(a) Mesh Topology   (b) Tree Topology

Figure 2.2   WAN Topologies

around the nodes in a loop, such as on the paths N2-N3-N1-N2 or N4-N3-N2-N1-N4. A mesh topology is usually implemented with switches and routers.

A **tree topology**, shown in Figure 2.2(b), is a hierarchical architecture. The tree structure starts with a node, called the header node, and branches out to other nodes. There can be no closed loops in the network; paths between nodes may be longer in a tree than in a mesh topology. For example, to go from N4 to N6 a packet has to travel to the top of the hierarchy N1 and then down to N6. Its path would be N4-N2-N1-N3-N6. Tree topology is simpler to implement than mesh topology, and it usually uses bridges at the OSI data link layer.

2.2   Local Area Networks

Two types of local-area networks (LANs) are widely deployed, bus based and ring based. The most common bus-based LAN is an Ethernet. The ring-based LANs are Token Ring and Fiber Distributed Data Interface (FDDI).

A representation of a campus network with different LANs is shown in Figure 2.3. The backbone of the campus network is an FDDI ring 10.10.0.0. The notation of the fourth decimal position being 0 is used to represent the network address. The Ethernet LAN (10.1.2.0) is connected to the backbone via a router. The workstations on this LAN have the fourth decimal position in their IP addresses from 2 to 5. The IP address 10.1.2.1 and 10.1.2.6 are the interface addresses to the router and bridge.

The second Ethernet LAN (10.1.1.0) is connected to the first Ethernet (10.1.2.0) with a bridge. The IP addresses 10.1.1.2 to 10.1.2.5 are interfaces to the workstations and the IP address 10.1.1.1 is the interface to the bridge. Notice that all external traffic from the 10.1.1.0 Ethernet has to traverse the 10.1.2.0 Ethernet LAN. The 10.2.1.0 is a token-ring LAN connected to the backbone FDDI ring via a router. The two other LANs that are connected to the backbone are ATM ELAN (10.4.1.0) via a router and an Ethernet LAN (10.3.1.0) via two half-routers. The two half-routers are connected via a dial-up link. We will review the LANs in this section and the network node components in Section 2.3.

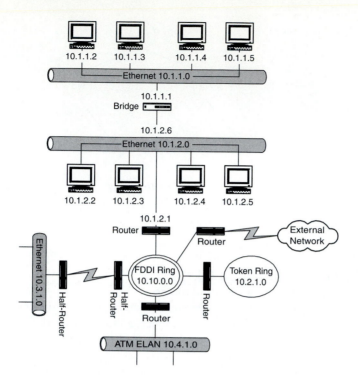

Figure 2.3   A Campus Network of LANs

2.2.1   Ethernet

An **Ethernet** uses a bus architecture that has Carrier Sense Multiple Access with Collision Detection (CSMA/CD). The DTEs are all connected to the same bus and transmit data in a multiple-access mode. In other words, several DTEs can start transmitting frames at the same time. A frame comprises the user data encapsulated with a header that contains the source and destination addresses. A DTE starts transmitting when there is no carrier sensed on the bus. The transmitted signal travels in both directions on the physical medium. While transmitting, if a collision with another frame is detected, the DTE stops transmitting and attempts again after a certain period. Thus, the mode of transmission is a broadcast type with probabilistic collision of the signal.

A good analogy to understand the collision phenomenon is to envision a hollow pipe with holes all along it. Each hole represents a station, where there could be a person. The ends of the pipe are sealed and do not reflect sound. Let us suppose Joe starts speaking at a hole near one end of the pipe. He makes sure that he does not hear anybody speaking before he starts (carrier sensing). Once he starts talking, he has to make sure that nobody else starts talking until he finishes. He does this by continuing to talk and at the same time listening for other messages on the pipe. If he hears nobody else, then there is no collision. If he hears somebody else, and then his message collides with another person's message, they both have to start again. The longest time that Joe has to wait is for a voice to reach him from a person speaking at a hole near the other end of the pipe; and that

Table 2.1   Ethernet LAN Topology Limits

Type	Description	Segment Length	Drop Cable Length
10Base2	Thin coax (0.25")	200 meters	Not allowed
10Base5	Thick coax (0.4")	500 meters	Twisted pair: 50 meters
10Base-T	Hub topology	N/A	Twisted pair: 100 meters
10Base-F	Hub topology	N/A	2 km fiber cable

person starts speaking just before Joe's voice reaches him. From this analogy, we can calculate that the minimum duration of time that Joe has to keep talking to ensure that there is no collision is the round-trip propagation time of his voice along the length of the pipe. Thus, there is a minimum frame size for Ethernet packets, which is 64 bytes. In Exercise 1 at the end of this chapter, we ask you to prove this.

The Institute of Electrical and Electronic Engineers (IEEE) and the International Standards Organization (ISO) have developed standards for an Ethernet second layer, MAC. They are IEEE 802.3 and ISO 8802.3, respectively. According to the standards, a physical coaxial segment can be a maximum of 500 meters, and there can be a maximum of 100 DTEs connected to it. A maximum of five segments can be connected with four repeaters to form one Ethernet LAN. However, if there are branches in the LAN, as in a tree structure, then any one total Ethernet segment should obey the above rule.

The data rate on an Ethernet bus is normally 10 Mbps (million bits per second). When the traffic on the bus reaches between 40 percent and 70 percent of the maximum data rate of 10 Mbps, depending on the packet size, the performance degrades significantly because there is an increased collision rate. The bus medium can either be thick (0.4" diameter, but this is no longer deployed) or thin (0.25" diameter) coaxial cable; and DTEs are tapped on to the bus in a T-connection. The maximum segment lengths for LANs depend on the medium, as listed in Table 2.1. There is also a limit on the length of drop cable, which is the cable from the LAN tap to the connector on the DTE's network interface card (NIC); these limits are also shown in Table 2.1. As the table shows, the original segment length defined for 10Base5 determined the minimum packet size of 64 bytes. However, with different configurations (10Base2, 10Base5, 10Base-T, and 10Base-F) the maximum lengths of segments and drop cables vary based on the medium. However, the minimum packet size is still 64 bytes.

Ethernet LANs are configured by running the coaxial cable around the DTEs and tapping each DTE on to the cable. This configuration could make it difficult for a manager to track a faulty DTE. It is also difficult to isolate a DTE that puts heavy loads on the LAN, or a killer DTE that brings the network down frequently. Sometimes the maximum length of an Ethernet LAN exceeds the allowable limit, and the network crashes intermittently at the limit length. It could also have an intermittent problem when the traffic on the LAN exceeds the threshold. These problems can be minimized by setting up the Ethernet LAN in a hub configuration, as shown in Figure 2.1(d), where all DTE links are brought to a hub in a central wiring closet and connected to a dedicated port of the hub. The DTEs are connected inside the hub in an Ethernet configuration with active electronics, namely, a repeater that amplifies the signal. In this configuration, problems associated with a DTE can be isolated to a port and resolved fairly quickly and easily.

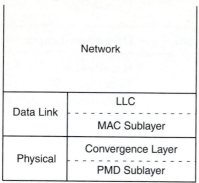

LLC = Logical link control
MAC = Medium access control
PMD = Physical medium dependent

Figure 2.4   100Base-T Fast Ethernet Protocol Architecture

2.2.2   Fast Ethernet

The hub technology described above led to the development of **Fast Ethernet** technology. Fast Ethernet operates at a data rate of 100 Mbps on an unshielded twisted-pair (UTP) cable and is called 100Base-T. The maximum length from the hub to the DTE is specified as 100 meters, or 200 meters round trip. This produces a maximum path delay, which is the delay between two DTEs of 400 meters, plus the repeater delay of one repeater instead of four repeaters. This is less than one-tenth the delay in straight Ethernet MAC specifications (5,000 meters) with four repeaters. Thus, the speed can be increased ten times from 10 Mbps to 100 Mbps. However, to be consistent with the IEEE 802.3 standard, an additional sublayer, a convergence layer, needs to be introduced in the physical layer above the physical medium-dependent (PMD) sublayer (similar to what we saw in the OSI network layer in Chapter 1). This is shown in Figure 2.4. The physical medium should be capable of carrying 100 Mbps of data over the maximum length of the drop cable, which is 100 meters. Category 3 UTP cannot carry data at such a high rate. Therefore, four pairs of UTP cables are used to distribute the data, each pair carrying 25 Mbps. The term for this is 100Base-T4, that is, 100 Mbps of data carried over four twisted-pair cables. This limitation could be overcome by using two pairs of category 5 UTP in full-duplex mode configuration, which we will discuss in Section 2.2.4. The minimum packet size of 64 bytes is maintained for Fast Ethernet.

2.2.3   Gigabit Ethernet

With the successes of Ethernet and fiber-optic communications, the logical evolution in Ethernet technology led to the development of the **Gigabit Ethernet**, which is an Ethernet that operates at 1 Gbps (gigabit per second). The cost performance of Gigabit Ethernet outweighs FDDI and ATM (asynchronous transfer mode) in providing data to the desktop, leveraging on an existing Ethernet. We will learn about the FDDI and ATM later in this chapter in Sections 2.2.8 and 2.6. Gigabit Ethernet is one hundred times the speed of regular Ethernet, ten times that of Fast Ethernet, and faster than FDDI operating at 150 Mbps.

Along with the development of Gigabit Ethernet, a parallel task was undertaken to double the bandwidth of Ethernets by full-duplex operation. We have so far considered only half-duplex operation in the CSMA/CD scheme. We first describe Gigabit Ethernet in CSMA/CD half-duplex mode in this section and consider the full-duplex mode for all types of Ethernet in the following subsection.

An approach similar to that of Fast Ethernet was taken to make Gigabit Ethernet compatible with the existing Ethernet network. The IEEE 802.3z protocol, whose architecture is shown in Figure 2.5, maintains the data link layer components, logical link control (LLC) and the media access control (MAC), and modifies the physical layer. The physical-layer architecture combines the physical interface of the high-speed FibreChannel (developed for fiber-optic communication) with that of the IEEE 802.3 Ethernet frame format. It consists of four sublayers: physical medium dependent (PMD), physical medium attachment (PMA), convergence, and reconciliation, which interfaces with the MAC layer.

The Gigabit Ethernet specification initially permits the use of three physical media. They are long-wave laser over single-mode and multimode fiber, called 1000BASE-LX; short-wave laser over multimode fiber, called 1000BASE-SX; and balanced shielded 150-ohm copper cable 1000BASE-CX. Another IEEE committee is examining the use of UTP cable for Gigabit Ethernet transmission, called 1000BASE-T.

Both short-wave (780 nanometer, light frequency) and long-wave (1300 nanometer, near-infrared frequency) lasers are specified to be transmitted over multimode fiber, whereas only long-wave laser specification addresses transmission over single-mode fiber. There is no

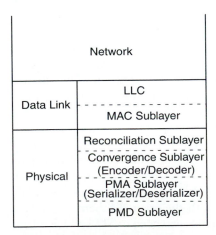

LLC = Logical link control
MAC = Medium access control
PMA = Physical medium attachment
PMD = Physical medium dependent

Figure 2.5   IEEE 802.3z Gigabit Ethernet Protocol Architecture

Table 2.2   Gigabit Ethernet Topology Limits

	9-Micron Single-Mode	50-Micron Single-Mode	50-Micron Multimode	62.5-Micron Multimode	Balanced Shielded Cable	UTP Cable
1000BASE-LX	10 km	3 km	550 m	440 m	—	—
1000BASE-SX	—		550 m	260 m	—	—
1000BASE-CX	—		—	—	25 m	—
1000BASE-T	—		—	—	—	100 m

support for short-wave laser transmission over single-mode fiber, because of its cost. Long-wave laser transmission over single-mode fiber (1300-nanometer laser over 9-micron fiber) can be used up to a distance of ten kilometers, whereas the multimode fiber typically extends up to two kilometers. The commercially available multimode fibers are 50 microns and 62.5 microns in diameter with fiber connectors that can be plugged into equipment.

Balanced shielded 150-ohm copper cable is a new specification with a DB-9 connector. This is specified for up to 25 meters (round-trip of 50 meters). Specifications to use UTP category 5 (cat-5) cable are in the offing to go up to 100 meters for drop length. Table 2.2 summarizes the various combinations of media, modes, and drop lengths (one-way).

In Figure 2.5, the physical medium attachment (PMA) is a serializer/deserializer that handles multiple encoding schemes of the upper convergence layer. The encoding schemes of optical (8B/10B) and copper media in the convergence layer are different. The reconciliation layer is a Media-Independent Interface (MII) between the physical media and the MAC layer of the data link control layer.

An added complication of going to 1 Gbps speed is the minimum frame size. Original Ethernet specifications, based on 2500 meters in length with four repeaters, each producing delays of approximately 5 microseconds and carrying data at 10 Mbps, required a minimum 64-byte frame, shown in Figure 2.6(a) to detect any collision. The time to accommodate the 64-byte frame is the slot time, which is 51.2 microseconds. An idle time of 96 bits was allowed between frames. This is shown in Figure 2.6(b). Fast Ethernet with a 100-meter drop, a 100-Mbps data rate, and one repeater (minimum time each packet needs to traverse in a hub configuration) would take a little longer than 5 microseconds. Thus, a slot time of 5.12 microseconds with a 64-byte minimum frame meets the minimum 64-byte slot size, as shown in Figure 2.6(c), to be compatible with the original Ethernet specifications. The round-trip delay in Gigabit Ethernet is determined primarily by the repeater delay. To be backward compatible with the original Ethernet specifications based on CSMA/CD, the minimum packet size was extended to 512 bytes, but kept the minimum frame size of 64 bytes. For small frames, a carrier extension was allowed, as shown in Figure 2.6(d), to increase the number of bytes in a slot to 512 bytes corresponding to 4.096 microseconds.

An additional modification was made to Gigabit Ethernet specifications to permit bursts of frames to be transmitted by a single station. This is called packet bursting,

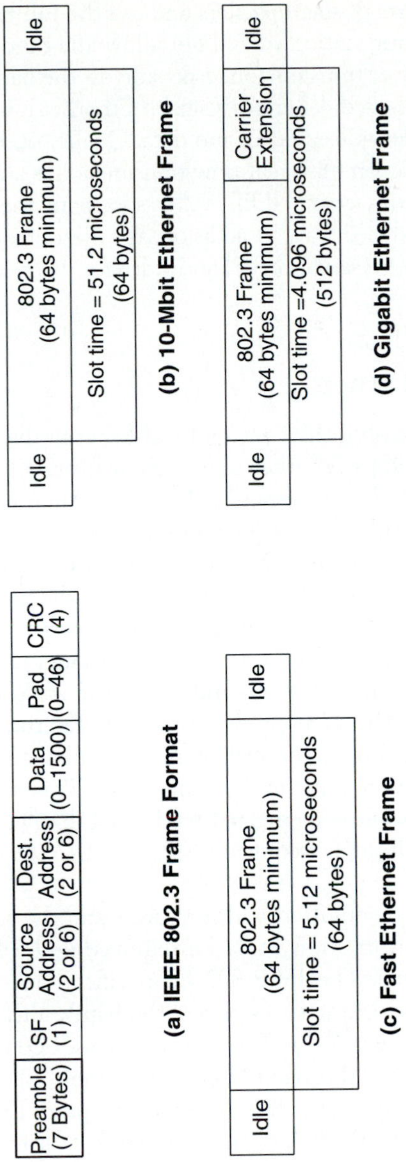

Preamble (7 Bytes)	SF (1)	Source Address (2 or 6)	Dest. Address (2 or 6)	Data (0–1500)	Pad (0–46)	CRC (4)

(a) IEEE 802.3 Frame Format

Idle	802.3 Frame (64 bytes minimum)	Idle

Slot time = 51.2 microseconds (64 bytes)

(b) 10-Mbit Ethernet Frame

Idle	802.3 Frame (64 bytes minimum)	Idle

Slot time = 5.12 microseconds (64 bytes)

(c) Fast Ethernet Frame

Idle	802.3 Frame (64 bytes minimum)	Carrier Extension	Idle

Slot time = 4.096 microseconds (512 bytes)

(d) Gigabit Ethernet Frame

Figure 2.6   Ethernet Formats and 802.3 Frame

whereby devices can send bursts of small packets and use the full bandwidth capacity. In such a situation, the transmitting station should not allow idle time between frames. This feature improves the efficiency of transmission, especially in the backbone configuration.

With the capability of increased data rates, Gigabit Ethernet has the potential to carry multimedia service that includes voice, video, and data. Quality of service (QoS) that can establish priority of service to accomplish real-time transmission is an essential requirement for implementation of multimedia service. IEEE 802.1p specifying the class of service (CoS) meets this requirement in a limited way. In addition, the Resource Reservation Protocol (RSVP) can be used for advance reservation of bandwidth for this purpose.

2.2.4   Full-Duplex Ethernets

We have so far discussed increasing the bandwidth of Ethernet by two orders of magnitude by migrating from a 10-Mbps Ethernet to a Gigabit Ethernet. We will now discuss how the data rates of Ethernet, Fast Ethernet, and Gigabit Ethernet could be doubled by migrating from half-duplex to full-duplex configuration.

As we mentioned in the previous subsection, CSMA/CD configuration is a half-duplex operation. This means that the signal could traverse the cable only in one direction at a time to avoid collision with another signal. In Section 2.2.1, we gave the analogy of speaking into a hollow pipe to demonstrate the collision. Let's extend that analogy to the case where there are two hollow pipes and the sound is allowed to travel only in one direction. One pipe carries the sound in one direction, and the other in the opposite direction. In this case, each person can be speaking on one pipe and receiving a message from somebody else on the other pipe at the same time. This analogy applies to the switched LAN where each station is connected to the hub by two pairs of drop cables. This is the basic concept of full-duplex configuration. CSMA/CD does not apply in this configuration.

With an active LAN implementation with repeaters and the sophistication of electronics in a hub, CSMA/CD restriction could be removed and a hub with full-duplex operation could be implemented. The IEEE 802.3x specifications, shown in Figure 2.7, were developed for this purpose. Using this scheme, the bandwidth could be doubled for each type of Ethernet configuration. Thus, Ethernet full-duplex configuration could handle 20 Mbps; Fast Ethernet, 200 Mbps; and Gigabit Ethernet, 2000 Mbps. This feature can be turned on or off in configuring the hub. For point-to-point links, an optional flow-control feature specified in IEEE 802.3x can be exercised so that the receiver can send a "pause frame" to the transmitter to relieve congestion.

Because of the 802.3x protocol extension, the notation for Ethernet type is modified with an "x" extension. Thus, 10Base-T, 100Base-T, 100Base-F are modified to be 10Base-Tx, 100Base-Tx, and 100Base-Fx. The Gigabit Ethernet types are already denoted ending in x, the option being set to either full- or half-duplex.

To be compatible with original Ethernet with CSMA/CD, the limitations in Gigabit Ethernet implementation are removed in full-duplex configurations. Thus, the carrier extension, slot time extension, and packet bursting are not applicable. The Ethernet 96-bit interface gap (idle time between frames) and 64-byte minimum packet size still apply.

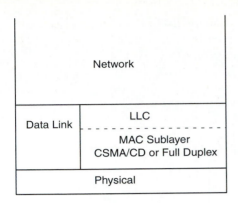

Figure 2.7   IEEE 802.3x Protocol Architecture

2.2.5   Switched Ethernet

Another outcome of hub technology is the **switched Ethernet**. Instead of just broadcast inside the hub, the packets are opened by a switch to see the destination address and passed through to the appropriate destination port. The switched hub can be implemented as a learning device by reading the source address and thus building a routing table to speed up the process. Pairs of DTEs can communicate in parallel as long as they are different DTE pairs and consequently, multiples of 10-Mbps channels can traverse the Ethernet hub at the same time. This is shown in Figure 2.8. There will, however, be a collision if a DTE receives packets from two other DTEs simultaneously.

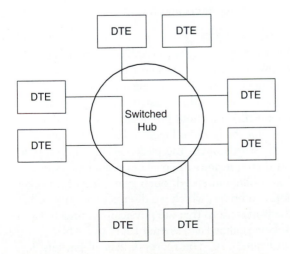

Figure 2.8   A Switched Ethernet Hub

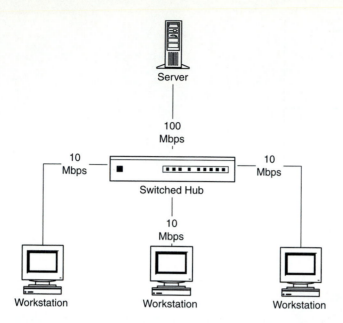

Figure 2.9   A Switched Hub in Client/Server Configuration

Not all the ports in a switched hub have to operate at the same data rate. A typical arrangement is for one port to operate at a high data rate and be connected to a server DTE, with other ports connected to client DTEs. A switched hub in a client/server configuration is shown in Figure 2.9, with the server operating at 100 Mbps and the clients at 10 Mbps.

2.2.6   Virtual LANs

Another advantage of a switched Ethernet is the capability to establish virtual networking. In a network management system, any port can be assigned to any LAN and thus LAN configurations can be changed without physically moving the equipment. For example, in a corporate environment, this capability allows assignment of personnel to different administrative groups that share one LAN without physically moving anyone.

As an illustration, the MAC addresses for the hosts in Figure 2.10 could be assigned to two LANs. When switching occurs, the switch opens the packet received on a port, reads the OSI layer-2 MAC address, and then transmits the packet on another port that may be connected to a different LAN at a different speed. Such switching of a packet from one LAN to another is the function of a bridge, which we discuss in Section 2.3.2. However, it is worth noting here that the workstations that are physically connected to a switched hub belong to two LANs, each being defined as a **virtual LAN** (VLAN).

The concept of VLANs is shown in Figure 2.10. The router directs all packets destined for subnets 200.100.150.1 and 200.100.160.1 to the same port on the router. They arrive at the switched hub and are routed to DTEs 1 through 5. Each of the five DTEs

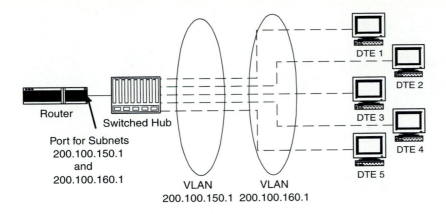

Figure 2.10   Virtual LANs

shown in the figure could be assigned an IP address belonging to either 200.100.150.1 or 200.100.160.1 and thus will be intermingled in the two VLANs. If DTE 1 and DTE 3 both belong to 200.100.150.1 VLAN, then traffic emanating from DTE 1 destined for DTE 3 would be switched within the same VLAN. If DTE 1 is assigned an IP address 200.100.150.2 and DTE 3 is assigned an address 200.100.160.2, they belong to different VLANs. The MAC addresses remaining fixed (they are assigned in the factory), the packet now is switched between the two VLANs.

We will address VLANs again when we deal with ATM LANs in Chapter 9. The management of VLANs can become difficult because the relationship between the logical and physical topologies is not obvious. We will discuss this in Chapter 13.

2.2.7   Token Ring

A **token-ring** LAN uses ring topology and is specified by IEEE 802.5 protocol. There is no limit to segment length as there is for Ethernet LANs. All DTEs are connected in a serial fashion in a ring, as shown in Figure 2.11.

A token is passed around in a unidirectional mode (counterclockwise in Figure 2.11); the DTE that has the token is in control of the LAN. Let us consider in Figure 2.11 a situation where DTE 4 has just completed transmission of a message and has released the token. DTE 1 is waiting to pass a message to DTE 3. As soon as the token is received, DTE 1 holds on to the token and transmits its message to DTE 3. The message has the source and destination addresses. As it travels around the ring, DTE 2 looks at the destination address and does not pick up the message. DTE 3 examines the destination address, and realizes that the message is for itself. It then picks up the message and retransmits it with an acknowledgment marked in the trailer of the message format. The frame goes around to DTE 1 with DTE 4 just passing the message through. Recognizing that the message has been received, DTE 1 releases the control token and now DTE 2 has a chance to send a message. If the message was not accepted by DTE 3 for any reason, such as a corrupt message, then the message trailer is so marked and appropriate action is taken by DTE 1.

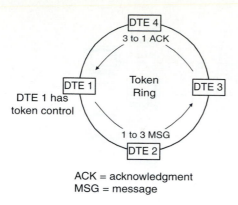

ACK = acknowledgment
MSG = message

Figure 2.11   A Token Ring LAN

As you can see, in the token-ring LAN, MAC is deterministic, in contrast to the probabilistic nature of an Ethernet LAN. The standards that specify a token ring's MAC are IEEE 802.5 and ISO 8803.5. This is a good configuration for heavily loaded networks.

The maximum size of a frame is not limited by the 802.5 standard. However, in order that no one station monopolizes the ring, maximum token-holding time by any station is configured, which determines the maximum frame size. The minimum frame size is the size of the token. The ring should be long enough to accommodate the entire token; otherwise, the token starts wrapping itself around and all the stations are in idle mode.

Because of the serial configuration, it is important that any failure of a DTE, or turning off a DTE, should not halt the operation of the LAN. One scheme to prevent this failure is to design the token-ring network interface card to create a short whenever there is a failure or a DTE is turned off. This is analogous to serially connected Christmas tree lights. When one bulb burns out, the bulb shorts the connection so that the rest of the lights continue to be lit.

If there is a break in the link segment of the ring, then the downstream DTE sends a beacon to the others indicating a failure. For example, if the link between DTE 4 and DTE 1 breaks, DTE 1 will send the beacon. The problem has to be rectified manually.

The ring failure can be resolved permanently by a dual-ring configuration, where the second ring is redundant. This is shown in Figure 2.12(a). Let us assume that the normal mode of operation is along the inner ring and the token is going around in the counterclockwise direction. The outer ring is the redundant ring and acts as backup. Figure 2.12(b) shows the situation where DTE 1 has failed. DTE 2 does not receive a signal from DTE 1. DTE 2 will send a beacon. Under this condition, DTE 2 and DTE 4 go into loop-back condition. DTE 4 receives the token on the inner ring and forwards it on the outer ring to DTE 3. DTE 2 receives the token on the outer ring and forwards it on the inner ring.

Figure 2.12(c) shows the situation where the section of the ring between DTE 4 and DTE 1 is broken. DTE 1 sends a beacon. DTE 4 and DTE 1 perform the loop-backs and the continuity of the rings among all four stations is established using both the inner and outer rings.

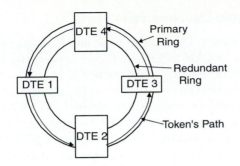

(a) Dual-Ring Management of a Token Ring

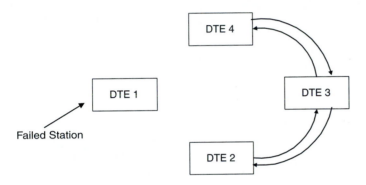

(b) Isolation of a Token-Ring DTE

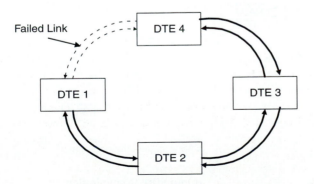

(c) Isolation of a Token-Ring Segment

Figure 2.12   **Dual-Ring Configurations of a Token-Ring**

2.2.8   Fiber Distributed Data Interface

Fiber Distributed Data Interface (FDDI) LANs came into being to take advantage of fiber-optic transmission media for LAN technology. It operates at a data rate of 100 Mbps and can include up to 500 DTEs in a single segment of 100 km without repeaters. The separation between neighboring stations on the cable can be up to 2 km. Fiber-optic cable has low noise interference compared to copper cable, and hence FDDI is ideally suited for campus backbone network. As mentioned earlier, FDDI is configured as a ring topology and has a token for medium access control. Thus, it follows the IEEE 802.5 token-ring standard, but with some significant differences. It is adopted as an international standard by ISO 9314 and ANSI (American National Standards Institute) H3T9.5.

Figure 2.13(a) shows the network configurations of FDDI, which is usually implemented as two rings (primary and secondary) for high reliability. A station can be

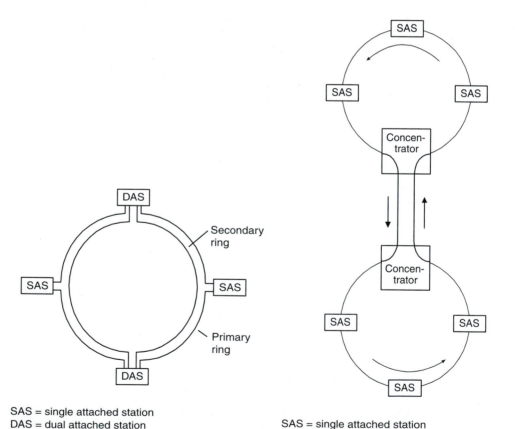

SAS = single attached station
DAS = dual attached station

**(a) Configuration of a Dual-Ring
    FDDI Network**

SAS = single attached station

**(b) An FDDI Configuration
    with Concentrators**

Figure 2.13   FDDI Configurations

connected to the dual-ring FDDI network either as a single attached station (SAS) to the primary ring or as a dual attached station (DAS) to both rings. A hierarchical topology can be created using concentrators as shown in Figure 2.13(b). Concentrators permit attachment of only SASs, but are economical for wiring and expansion of FDDI networks.

Although the topology of FDDI is similar to Token Ring, the algorithm that controls token passing is different. In Token Ring, only one DTE uses the ring at any given time, whereas in FDDI there can be many frames traversing the ring with communication between multiple pairs of stations.

2.3   Network Node Components

A network node is a component at either end of a network link, such as a hub or router. It is also a device that connects two networks, such as a bridge connecting two LANs or a gateway connecting two autonomous networks. The network nodes are hubs, switches, bridges, routers, and gateways, and combinations such as brouters (bridged routers) and switched hubs. A DTE is not considered a node; however, a workstation that has two network interface cards connecting to two LANs is a bridge and is considered a node. Hubs are platforms that house one or more functions. Switches now use solid-state devices. The progress in solid-state technology has contributed to the advancement of switching technology that includes ATM switches. The other network nodes are smart switches with built-in intelligence of various degrees.

In a simplistic view, a node can be looked at as a switch, a bridge, a router, or a gateway. The basic concepts of the four primary nodal components are shown in Figure 2.14. Figure 2.14(a) shows a switch, the inputs and outputs are of the same format. For example, if the input format is in ATM format, the output is also in ATM format. The switch can be used to switch both analog and digital data. When a switch is used in the analog mode, a call is set up first (i.e., connection through the switch is made), and then the data is passed through insensitive to the content of the information. When it is used in digital mode, it is used as a packet switch. Each input packet is looked at and then switched to the appropriate output port based on the content.

A bridge can be viewed as an intelligent packet switch at the data link layer and is shown in Figure 2.14(b). Besides switching the input packets to the appropriate output ports, it can filter those packets as well. This function is useful for connecting two local area networks. If the traffic is pertinent to the local-area network only, it is filtered out. If it is to be delivered outside of the local-area network where it was generated, then it is switched through the bridge. An intelligent bridge can learn over time; for example, it can learn which packets should be delivered to which ports. The input and output protocols, in practice, are usually the same for all bridges. However, some bridges can also do protocol conversion, as we will learn in Section 2.3.2.

Not only can a router perform all the functions of a switch and a bridge, but it can also route packets to the appropriate ports in the correct direction of their destinations. It functions at the network layer. Thus, in Figure 2.14(c), input packets from a node in an

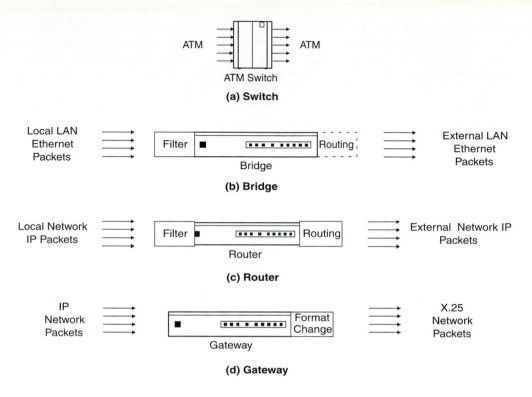

Figure 2.14   Basic Network Nodes

IP (Internet Protocol) network are sent out as IP packets to a node in either the same or some other network.

Not all networks use the same protocol, so a gateway is used to convert one protocol format to another protocol format. Figure 2.14(d) shows a gateway between an IP network and an X.25 network.

2.3.1   Hubs

Figure 2.15 shows the role of the various components in a network. The router, gateway, and half-router function at the network layer and perform the function of routing packets. The bridges, local and remote, operate at the data link layer and connect two LANs. The hubs are used to build LANs, as we learned in the previous section. The ATM switch is a hybrid component. It makes connections at the physical layer, but acts as a sublayer under the data link layer and is deployed as an emulated LAN (ELAN), among other applications. We will review the various network components in this section.

As we mentioned earlier, a **hub** is a platform with multiple ports. It has a processor on interface cards on one or more ports. A hub is implemented to perform some specific

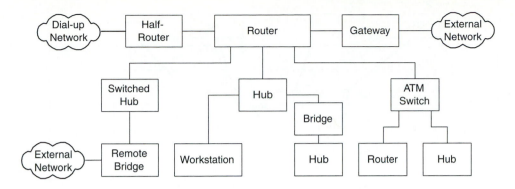

Figure 2.15   Networked Components

functions or combination of functions. For example, it could house a simple LAN, or multiple LAN segments. It can do switching functions and thus act as a switched LAN. When it switches between LANs, it performs a bridge function. In this section, we consider hubs used to implement LANs.

Hubs can be looked at as active LANs—DTEs connected with repeaters in a LAN configuration. The limitations of length and number of stations that are imposed on LANs are overcome by "homing" the wiring from the DTEs to the hub in the wiring closet and connecting them in the desired topology. The only limitation is the drop length from the hub to the station, such as the 100-meter maximum length in Ethernet configuration. There is usually a patch panel in the wiring closet that enables any DTE to be connected to any port of the hub. Stacking hubs and daisy-chaining them can increase the number of ports. Figure 2.16(a) shows a hub configuration where the DTEs are connected to the hub through a patch panel. By connecting any hub port to any jack in the patch panel, DTE configurations can be changed from a centrally located hub. Further, any DTE could be disconnected easily from the LAN for troubleshooting without impacting the operation of other stations.

Hubs can be stacked to increase the number of ports, as shown in the stacked hub configuration in Figure 2.16(b). Stacked hubs have a common backplane. Thus, stacking hubs is equivalent to increasing the number of ports in a hub. For example, two 16-port hubs will behave as a 32-port hub.

2.3.2   Bridges

Bridges are used to connect LANs. Three types of local bridge connecting two LANs are shown in Figure 2.17. Figure 2.17(a) shows a simple bridge configuration connecting two Ethernet LANs. This configuration can be looked at as two LANs connected by a repeater, except that all the traffic among DTEs in one LAN does not go over to the other LAN. The only traffic that is exchanged between the two LANs via the bridge is that which requires inter-LAN communication. Figure 2.17(b) shows three LANs connected

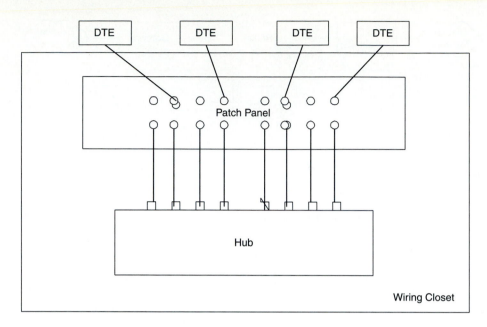

(a) A Hub Configuration

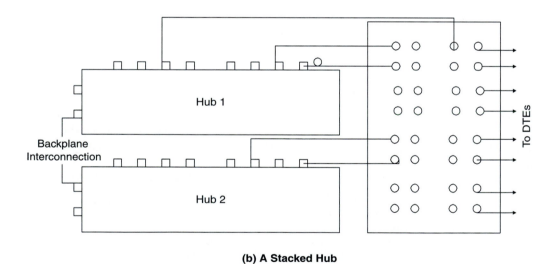

(b) A Stacked Hub

Figure 2.16   Hub Configurations

by a multiport bridge. In this case, the bridge opens the packet, reads the MAC address, and switches the packet to the appropriate port to the pathway of the destination address. Usually the bridge is a self-learning bridge. To transmit packets, it looks at all the packets that are received and records in a table the source addresses and the ports where they

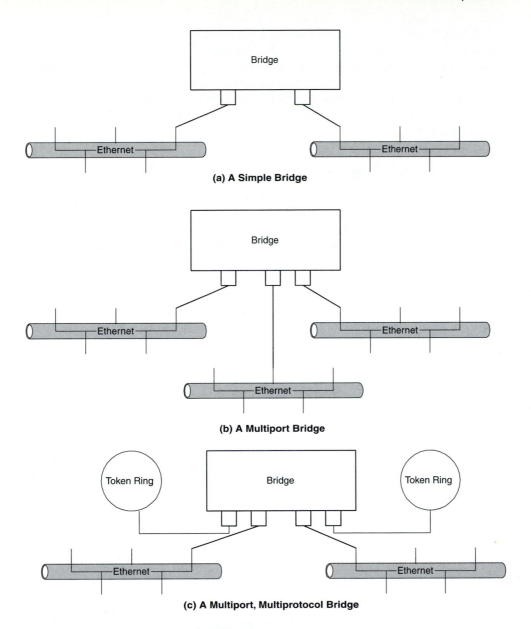

(a) A Simple Bridge

(b) A Multiport Bridge

(c) A Multiport, Multiprotocol Bridge

Figure 2.17   Local Bridge Configurations

were received. If a destination address is not in the table, the bridge does a flooding on all ports and discovers the correct port to add to the table. The table is periodically (less than a few minutes) purged of inactive addresses.

A bridge switches data packets between LANs; to accomplish this, it has a store-and-forward capability. Local bridges are usually developed as a single protocol device, and have the primary features of switching and filtering out the intra-LAN traffic. However, because of the store-and-forward capability in a bridge, additional features could be incorporated to convert protocol. Figure 2.17(c) shows a multiport, multiprotocol bridge configuration that connects Ethernet and token-ring LANs. The protocol conversion is done at OSI layer 2.

2.3.3   Remote Bridges

Figure 2.17 shows bridges in local LAN configurations where the LANs are brought to a centralized wiring closet and connected via a bridge. Figure 2.18 shows a remote bridge configuration, where two bridges at remote locations are linked via a WAN. WAN architecture mostly uses routers. However, using remote bridges and leased dedicated telecommunication links, we can connect remote LANs.

LANs can be connected with bridges that have been networked using either tree topology or mesh topology. Bridged networks operate at the data link layer. Bridged networks use two network-routing algorithms: a spanning tree algorithm for bridging Ethernet LANs and a source routing algorithm for bridging token-ring LANs.

2.3.4   Transparent Bridges

Figure 2.19 shows four LANs networked using three bridges in a tree topology. Each bridge has knowledge only of its neighbor and is transparent to other bridges and LANs, as described below, hence the name **transparent bridge**.

The transparent bridge uses a routing algorithm called a **spanning tree algorithm**. A spanning tree algorithm builds and stores a table of ports associated with destination

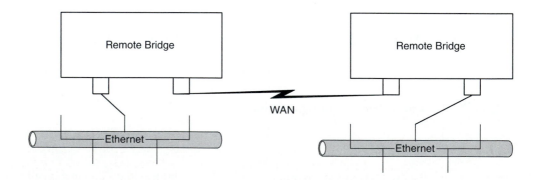

Figure 2.18   A Remote Bridge Configuration

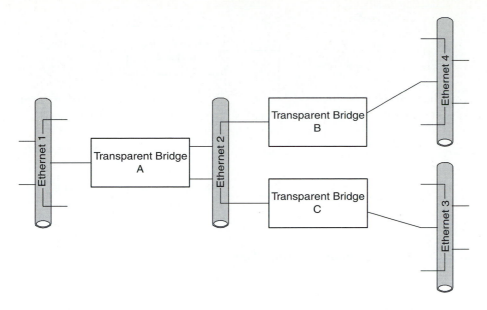

Figure 2.19   A Transparent Bridge Network

addresses. When a packet arrives, the bridge sends the packet on the port to its destination. The bridge has no knowledge of the destination LAN; it only has knowledge of the neighboring node responsible for that destination address.

A transparent bridge learns the routing information by a backward learning process. That is, when a packet arrives at a port, it notes the source address of the packet and associates that address with that port in its routing table. It then forwards the packet to the port associated with its destination. If the destination address is not in its routing table, a transparent bridge does a broadcast message to acquire the address.

As shown in Figure 2.19, a transparent bridged network uses tree topology, which means that there are no closed loops. One of the nodes acts as the header node, which is transparent bridge A in the figure. Although there may be more than one physical path between two LANs, the spanning tree algorithm eliminates all but one link during the operation. For example, if transparent bridge B had links to both Ethernet 3 and Ethernet 4, then that would form a closed loop, Ethernet 3 - transparent bridge B - Ethernet 2 - transparent bridge C - Ethernet 3. The spanning tree algorithm would prevent transparent bridge B from sending or receiving packets on its link to Ethernet 3.

Let us track a message from a host attached to LAN 3 to LAN 4. It takes the path all the way up the tree to the header bridge A, and then traverses down the other half of the tree to LAN 4. Thus, the header bridge normally needs to handle more traffic than other nodes. Referring to Figure 2.2(b), this will be equivalent to a message going from N4 (LAN3) to N6 (LAN4) traversing bridges N2 (C), N1 (A), and N3 (B).

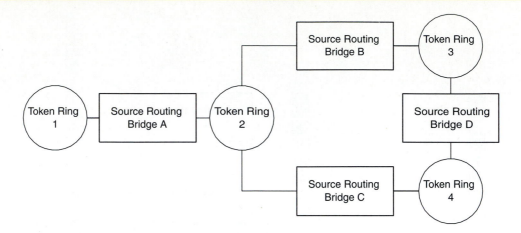

Figure 2.20   A Source Routing Bridge Network

2.3.5   Source Routing Bridges

A **source routing bridge** is used to network token-ring LANs, as shown in Figure 2.20. In the source routing algorithm used in a bridged token-ring network, the source is aware of the entire path to the destination. In addition to the destination address, the source inserts in the packet the route that the packet should take. Thus, the intermediate nodes make no decision as to the path that the packet takes. This is the reason that the token-ring bridge is called source routing bridge. The routing table can be stored either centrally on a server or in each source routing bridge. The route is determined by broadcast packets flooding the entire network.

In comparing source routing bridges and transparent bridges, we find that the latter is more robust and reliable, whereas the former is faster. Thus, changes in the network (e.g., additions or deletions of hosts, failures), are tracked easier in transparent bridge networks than in source routing bridge networks. In networks with source routing bridges, the entire routing table has to be rediscovered, which is a heavy resource-consumption process.

Bridges are used for special-purpose networks and have several limitations. Due to the dissimilarities of routing algorithms, communication between media using different protocols becomes difficult, for example between Ethernet and Token Ring or FDDI. Besides, the routing algorithms are difficult to create and to maintain. Routers, which operate at the network layer, are designed for routing and hence are better suited for this purpose. Routers and gateways can route packets between different media and different networks (using different network protocols) in a transparent manner. We will now discuss the role of routers in networking.

2.3.6   Routers

Routers and gateways form the backbone of networking. Although we have shown alternative ways—sometimes cheaper and a short cut to establish enterprise networking—the clean approach to establishing computer networks is with the use of routers.

A router, as the name indicates, routes packets through the network. Each router in a computer network has some knowledge of the possible routes that a data packet could take to go from the source to the destination. It has the high-level data on the best overall route, as well as detailed local data on the best path for the next hop in the link. This is built into a routing table that it periodically updates and stores in its database. The router employs a broadcast scheme using ARP (Address Resolution Protocol) to determine the ports associated with destination addresses. The router may also read the contents of a data packet arriving at a given port to determine its source and destination address, as well as the type of data and the time it was received. Then, using the routing table, it intelligently routes the packet to one or more output ports toward its destination address. The output goes to a single port if it is a data packet going between a source and a destination; the output is directed to multiple ports if it is a broadcast or multicast packet. Figure 2.21 shows a router configuration with protocol architecture. Notice that network layers have the same protocols (IP). However, the data link layer protocol (DP) and the physical layer protocol (Phy), as well as the physical media 1 and 2, could be different.

Routers permit loops in their topology and thus are more universal than bridges. Loops enable load balancing of traffic as well as self-healing of the network in the case of a link or router failure. Routers have various algorithms to optimize load balancing of traffic and economize on cost. Of several routing algorithms, open shortest path first (OSPF) is the most widely used. In this algorithm, each router broadcasts routes and request packets on the links that it is connected to. The other routers in the network acknowledge the

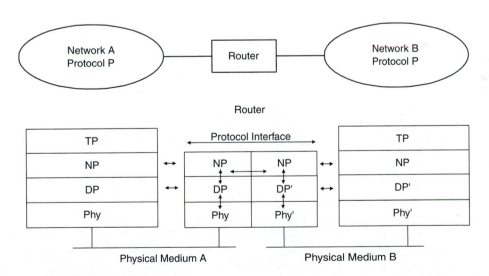

TP = Transport protocol
NP = Network protocol
DP, DP' = Data link protocols
Phy, Phy' = Physical layer protocols

Figure 2.21   A Router Configuration

request and repeat the process. Thus, a distributed routing database is built using an algorithm for the shortest path and is kept updated whenever there is a change in the network configuration.

Network managers can build routing tables to optimize their network's performance with respect to several parameters, such as cost, route, delay, bandwidth, and so on. The performance (throughput and delay) of a bridged network is better than that of a router network because routers have the additional network layer. Hence, bridged networks are used in some special applications where speed is of importance. However, routers are specifically designed based on a network layer, whose main purpose is for ranking (i.e., carrying packets from the source node to the destination node). Thus, degradation in performance using routers over bridges is worth the price for the far-reaching benefits we achieve. For example, the main mission of the Internet protocol (IP) is to ensure that the packets are delivered to the correct destination, and not even worry about the integrity of the data. That is left to the other layers.

2.3.7   Gateways and Protocol Converters

A **gateway** connects two autonomous networks, each of which is self-contained in all aspects—routing algorithms, protocol, domain name servers, and network administration procedures and policies. When such an autonomous network communicates with another autonomous network, it traverses a gateway, as shown in Figure 2.22. Generally, the protocol conversion is done at the network layer, as shown in the figure.

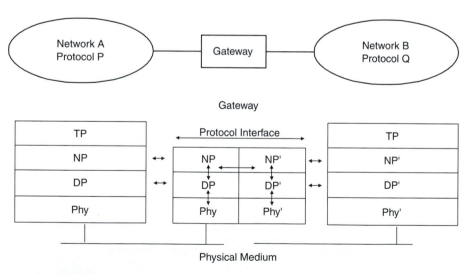

TP = Transport protocol
NP, NP' = Network protocols
DP, DP' = Data link protocols
Phy, Phy' = Physical layer protocols

Figure 2.22   A Gateway Configuration

Since the protocol conversion for a gateway is done at the network layer level, it could generally be combined with routing function. Thus, a router with protocol conversion could also be considered a gateway. Node N in Figure 1.17 that connects an IP network with a proprietary subnetwork is an example of this. Node N not only does the protocol conversion, but it also has the routing table that contains information on both networks. In this scheme, Node N would have an IP address, but nodes N1, N2, and N3 may follow a proprietary addressing scheme.

A protocol converter, as shown in Figure 2.23, does the protocol conversion at the application layer. A protocol converter used to be distinguished from a gateway, but this is no longer the case. *Gateway* is the generic term currently in vogue. For example, let us consider a company that uses the cc:mail system developed by IBM/Lotus Corporation. When a person using cc:mail wants to send a message via the Internet to a person using SMTP, a protocol converter (gateway) converts cc:mail protocol to SMTP. Note that a company could be using IP as the network protocol and cc:mail as the e-mail software system.

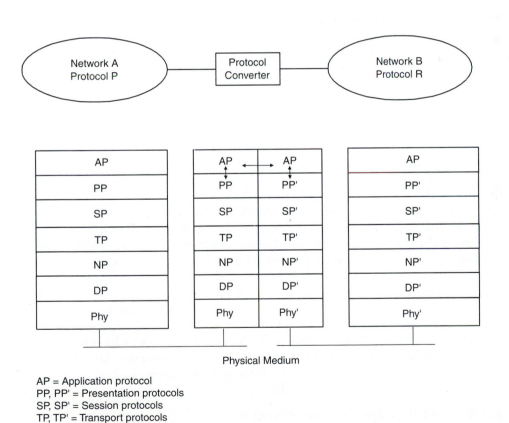

AP = Application protocol
PP, PP' = Presentation protocols
SP, SP' = Session protocols
TP, TP' = Transport protocols
NP, NP' = Network protocols
DP, DP' = Data link protocols
Phy, Phy' = Physical layer protocols

Figure 2.23   Configuration of a Protocol Converter

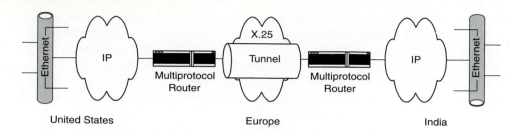

Figure 2.24   Tunneling Using Multiprotocol Routers

2.3.8   Multiprotocol Routers and Tunneling

An alternative to the use of gateways to communicate between autonomous networks is tunneling using multiprotocol router. *Tunneling* is generally used when the source and destination stations are on similar networks, but the data has to traverse intermediate network systems, which may be using different protocols. In this case, the data frame does not go through a protocol conversion in the intermediate networks, but is encapsulated and "**tunneled**" through as pass-through traffic.

Figure 2.24 shows communications between two Ethernet LANs on IP networks. One of them could be in the United States and the other in India. However, the data has to go through Europe, which is on an X.25 packet-switching data network. The multiprotocol router at the near end encapsulates the IP packet in an X.25 frame and transmits it to the far-end multiprotocol router. The far-end multiprotocol router de-encapsulates the frame and routes it as an IP packet again. The path through Europe behaves very similar to a serial link.

Another application for tunneling is to enable a station with an IP address belonging to a LAN to communicate with another LAN in a distant location, but from a location other than the sender's LAN. This would be the situation if the station were a portable PC and a traveling person needed to communicate from a foreign location. Let us picture the scenario where Joe wants to communicate from Seattle in the northwestern United States to Sally at Los Angeles in the southwestern United States. Joe's PC belongs to a network domain in New York, which is on the East Coast of the United States. His initial message is routed from his PC to the server of the LAN that the station belongs to, in this case New York. The server, recognizing that the station is currently outside of its domain, locates the foreign agent who handles the area where Joe is and informs Joe and the foreign agent. From then on, the sender "tunnels" the packets directly to the user via the foreign agent.

2.3.9   Half-Bridge Configuration of Routers

There are situations where it is desirable to have point-to-point communication. For example, when a residential station communicates with an Internet Service Provider, Point-to-Point Protocol (PPP) could be used. It provides a standard method for multi-

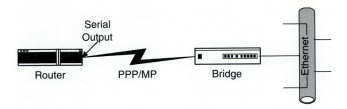

Figure 2.25 Configuration of a Half-Bridge

protocol datagrams over point-to-point links. This method of communication has been extended to PPP Multilink Protocol (MP). Using MP, datagrams can be split, sequenced, transmitted over multiple parallel links, and recombined to construct the original message. MP increases the bandwidth and efficiency of point-to-point link communication.

With the expanding universe of the Internet, small corporations as well as small Internet Service Providers (ISPs) would like to establish dial-up serial links. They require connections to the Internet from their local LANs only when they need them. Typically, they do not need permanent dedicated links. A number of proprietary PPP protocols are currently in use. The most common one is SLIP (Serial Link Internet Protocol) for UNIX. The Internet Engineering Task Force (IETF) has standardized Internet data link layer protocol to be used with point-to-point links. **Half-bridge** provides a method to connect a LAN via a bridge to a router.

Figure 2.25 shows a half-bridge configuration. The router port connecting to the bridge is configured as a serial interface to the PPP half-bridge. The interface functions as a virtual node on the Ethernet subnetwork on the bridge. The serial interface has an IP address associated with the Ethernet subnetwork. Thus, if the Ethernet subnetwork address is 155.55.123.1, the serial interface on the router could be assigned an IP address 155.55.123.5.

When a packet destined to the Ethernet arrives at the router, it is converted to Ethernet packets, encapsulated in PPP frames, and sent on the Ethernet bridge link. In the reverse direction, the Ethernet packets encapsulated in PPP frames are extracted by the router, which converts them to IP packets, and routes them on the Internet.

2.3.10 Switches

It would have been logical for us to start reviewing the switch component before we discussed bridges and routers as network components. However, we have chosen to delay its discussion until now for a good reason: It logically flows into discussing wide area networks.

Switches operate at the physical layer of the OSI Reference Model that we discussed in Chapter 1. In Section 2.3, we described a switch as a component that makes a physical connection between the input and output ports and that the bits and bytes come in and go out exactly the same way. Bridges and routers use the switching function when they route packets.

Most switching technology is based on solid-state technology, and the speed of switching is getting faster and faster. This technology enables networks to achieve a digital rate of gigabits per second. The performance of a network is determined by how fast we can switch and multiplex data using switches (and consequently routers and bridges). More important, end-to-end performance of the network depends on the speed, latency (delay), and latency variation in transporting data from source to destination. Voice, video, and data have different quality-of-service requirements, which determine the types of end-to-end circuits that are established using switches.

The switching functions accomplished in establishing circuits can be classified into circuit switching and packet switching, depending on how they are used. Telephone communication uses circuit switching. A physical path from end-to-end is established prior to talking; this is termed call setup. During the actual telephone conversation, the path remains connected whether there is a conversation actually happening or not. That is, the allocated bandwidth for the path is wasted during the idle time of the conversation. Thus, when you are on the telephone and the other party gives you a telephone number, you may say, "Please wait while I get a paper and pencil to write." The facilities remain idle during that time and could have been used by others. A "nailed-up circuit," where a permanent path is established for the session, is good for voice and video communications where latency and latency variations are intolerable.

Computer traffic is bursty in nature and lends itself more to packet switching than circuit switching. It would be a waste of bandwidth to use circuit switching for computer data networks. Packet switching uses the facilities and, hence, the bandwidth more efficiently. Data is framed into packets and each packet is switched independently. Data from multiple sources is multiplexed and thus the available bandwidth is shared.

Packet switching is used in routers. The maximum size of the packet is limited to make the router efficient. The packet sizes can vary from source to source, as well as from the same source. The message from a single source is divided into multiple packets and transmitted over the network to the destination. Each packet may take a different path from source to destination so that the packets arrive out of sequence. Thus, the message has to be reordered at the destination. This type of transmission is termed datagram service and is shown in Figure 2.26(a). The message from DTE A has been split into three packets. Packets 1 and 3 take the path A-B-D, and packet 2 travels the path A-C-B-D. Packets 1 and 3 arrive at DTE Z before packet 2, so the three packets have to be reassembled in the correct order.

It is desirable in many situations, such as in broadband service using ATM (discussed in Section 2.6), to have all the packets from a given source to a given destination take the same path. This is analogous to circuit switching in that the path is fixed for the entire session. The concept of "session" is the same as in circuit switching. During call setup, a virtual path/virtual circuit is set up between the source and destination and a "virtual circuit identification" (one for each hop) is associated with the channel carrying the traffic. The path and circuit identifications are called virtual because they resemble the operation in circuit switching, but differ in that the connection is not physical. Figure 2.26(b) shows the virtual circuit path for the same message as in Figure 2.26(a) to travel from DTE A to DTE Z. In this situation the packets arrive in the

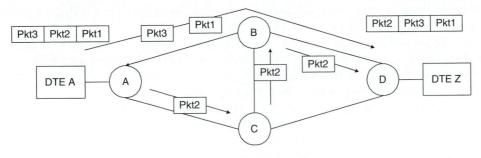

(a) Configuration of a Datagram

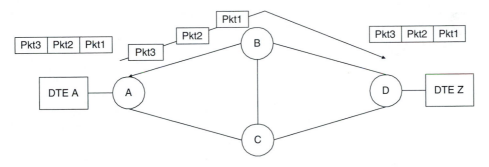

(b) Configuration of a Virtual Circuit

Figure 2.26   Packet-Switching Configurations

correct order at DTE Z. Although the initial call setup is an overhead (a significant delay), subsequent data transmission is faster than in datagram service. We discuss in more detail the virtual path/virtual circuit configuration in asynchronous transfer mode in Chapter 9.

Circuit and packet switching are applicable to wide-area networks, which we will review now.

2.4   Wide-Area Networks

The main difference between a wide-area network (WAN) and a local-area network (LAN) is the geographical separation between sources and destinations. If the end stations are within a building or campus of buildings, the network is considered a LAN with a possible high-speed backbone LAN, such as FDDI or ATM.

As we saw in Chapter 1, computer communication network rides on top of the telecommunications network, which is a wide area network. Although most of the telephone and video communications traversing the WAN are circuit switched, the data traffic generated by computer communications is packet switched.

Virtual circuits can be established on a session basis or on a permanent basis. The former are called switched virtual circuits (SVCs) and the latter are permanent virtual circuits (PVCs). Geographically distributed organizations often lease PVCs from public service providers to handle large amounts of traffic. Otherwise, SVC service is used, often provided by public telecommunication service providers. However, some private corporations use their own switches and leased lines from public service providers to set up large corporate data networks.

From a network management perspective, we can partition a WAN into two sections and analyze the components and services that need to be managed in each. The two end sections of a WAN are the subscriber loops, where the information flows from the central offices of the service provider(s) to the customer premises, and the transmission between switching offices.

The subscriber loop sections could be either passive, such as dedicated pairs of wires from the central office to the customer premises, or active links such as coaxial cable interspersed with amplifiers to boost the signal along the way. In either case, a digital subscriber loop (DSL) terminates in a network interface unit (NIU) at the customer premises. Examples of NIUs are Channel Service Units (CSUs) for DSL interfaces with analog equipment at a customer premises, and Digital Service Units (DSUs) for DSL interfaces with digital equipment. The responsibility of the service provider is providing the service up to the NIU. Thus, the components that need to be managed are the NIUs and the active components on the loop transmission line.

The transmission section consists of link transmission facilities and nodal components. These are between central offices in public-switched networks and between the routers of service providers in private networks. We have looked at nodal components already. We will now consider transmission media and modes of LANs and WANs.

2.5   Transmission Technology

Transmission technology deals with transmission media and modes. We will look at transmission media first and then transmission modes.

The transmission medium consists of the link that carries the data between two physical systems. There is a coupling mechanism, a transceiver (denoting transmitter and receiver), that delivers to and receives data from the medium. The transmission media can be classified broadly into wired and wireless media. Information is transported via physical transmission facilities, such as wires and optical fiber, or via wireless media using technology like radio frequencies, infrared, and light waves. In wired media information is transmitted from point to point, whereas in wireless media it is generally done on a broadcast basis.

Both wired and wireless transmissions are used for LANs and WANs. The physical connection and the electronics of the transceiver play an important part in a LAN, because they determine the speed and accuracy of information transmitted on to and received from the various transmission media. We observed that the bandwidth of all types of Ethernet LANs could be doubled by changing from simplex to duplex configuration. In fact, advancement of new technologies depends on the enhancements to existing ones. For example, progress of the new technology ATM (asynchronous transfer mode) to the desktop has been slowed by several years because of Ethernet technology's increased ability to handle large bandwidth (in gigabits per second) to the desktop. We also saw in Section 2.3.1 that hub technology has increased the throughput of many stations on a LAN.

Wireless LAN technology has so far found only limited use. However, wireless technology is used very extensively for mobile communication, satellite transmission, and television access in rural areas.

2.5.1   Wired Transmission

Wired transmission technology uses three media: coaxial cable, twisted-pair cable, and optical fiber. The key parameters to consider in choosing the transmission medium are the following: loss of signal, sensitivity to environmental noise sources (such as cross talk and spurious radio frequency signals generated by appliances), bandwidth handling capability, and transmission delay. The selection of the medium is also determined by the type of stations on the medium and their access control mechanism. We listed the limitations and capabilities of the various LAN media for Ethernet LAN in Tables 2.1 and 2.2.

There are two types of coaxial cables, thick and thin. Thick cable is 0.4 cm in diameter and is not used any more. Thin coaxial cable is 0.25 cm in diameter and is present in legacy systems or small LANs, where it can be installed economically without a hub.

Twisted-pair cable, a pair of wires twisted, is available as unshielded twisted pair (UTP) and shielded twisted pair (STP). The gauge of the wire and the type of twist determine the quality of transmission. Obviously, STP cable reduces the interference of radio frequency noise better than UTP cable. Most of the twisted-pair cable used in LANs is category 5 (cat-5) UTP. With cat-5 cable, the drop length for an IEEE 802.3 LAN (see Table 2.1) can be extended from 100 to 150 meters.

The fiber-optic medium provides the best quality transmission. Of course, it is the most expensive. However, it is economical when LANs need to be networked in a campus environment or a building with multiple stories. As shown in Tables 2.1 and 2.2, the point-to-point drop cable for an Ethernet LAN could be as long as 2 km, and in Gigabit Ethernet, we can extend it up to 9 km.

It is worth noting the importance of cabling in geographically placing network components. As we all know, implementers always try to stretch the limits of specifications or economize in the installation process. For example, the maximum distance for a cat-3 cable is 100 meters. Instead of cabling all workstations using cat-5 and optical fibers to a central location where patch panels and hubs are collocated, hubs could be distributed to use only cat-3 cable and thus economize in cabling costs. However, there is a price to pay in operations and maintenance for this approach, because the hubs could not be shared and it takes much longer to restore service when a remote hub fails.

Wired WAN media comprises bundles of twisted pairs (such as in T1 and loop facilities), coaxial cable for analog transmission (for example N1), and optical fiber (underwater sea cable).

2.5.2   Wireless Transmission Media

Wireless media are used in wireless LANs, as well as in mobile and satellite communications.

Wireless LAN is in its early stage of use, for example, in a factory floor environment. The floor supervisor does not have access to a phone and needs to communicate to a central station for controlling processes and for administrative purposes. The input uses a hand-held portable communication device or a computer with a wireless antenna. Wireless LAN technology focuses primarily on transmitting data from portable stations to a wired LAN access point by radio frequency, infrared, or optical transmission. Since the range of transmission is limited for all these, they all function within a given region, or cell. If the portable station is a moving target, then the signal has to be handed from one cell to another cell.

Two fast-growing segments of wireless technology in the non–LAN environment are of interest for data communication: Personal Communication Services (PCS) and digital cellular services [Littwin A]. Both of these are based on cell-based technology. The data is transmitted by wireless to local cell antennas, then it goes to the central location by wired network. PCS is all-digital technology. It operates at lower power (100 watts) and antennas are more closely spaced (1/2 to 1 mile). The digital cellular technology, although analog, carries digitized signal. It needs higher power antennas, which are farther apart (several miles).

Another area of wireless technology is broadband multimedia services [IEEE Com, January 1997]. The multimedia is transmitted using satellite wireless technology from a central office to the customer's premises. The return path is via telephone lines.

2.5.3   Transmission Modes

The data transmission mode can be either digital or analog. Narrow-band LAN technology uses the digital mode of transmission. Broadband and WAN technologies employ both analog and digital modes of transmission. In analog transmission mode, information can be transmitted in either baseband or on a carrier.

In a physical medium, digital transmission is a series of ones and zeros. A physical medium is shared by multiple sources to transport information to multiple destinations. The distinction between various transmission technologies is the method of coding information between pairs of end-users to share the same medium. They should be multiplexed and de-multiplexed efficiently at the nodes to keep the delay as brief and as constant as possible, as well as for high throughput.

Figure 2.27 shows three basic modes of transmission. They are TDM (Time Division Multiplexing) transmission, packet transmission, and cell transmission. T1 is the early implementation of TDM digital transmission in the United States by Bell Systems. Figure 2.27(a) shows TDM transmission of a T1 carrier, which carries 24 voice channels. The T1 carrier has a data rate of 1.544 Mbps and is equally divided among 24 voice channels, each with a bandwidth of 64 kbps. The top of Figure 2.27(a) shows that the 1.544 Mbps transmission "pipe" is divided into 24 small dedicated pipes distributed among the 24 channels. The bottom of the figure shows the multiplexing of the 24 channels as a bit stream on the physical medium. They are multiplexed cyclically from Channel 1 through Channel 24. The maximum bandwidth available for each channel is 64 kbps, but it is available all during a complete session. A session is defined as the duration from the establishment of a connection between a pair of users to disconnect-time. Notice that all channels have equal bandwidth and occupy the same slot in the transmission channel. When the receiver synchronizes to the transmitter, it is able to de-multiplex the channels, but both transmitter and receiver know exactly which slot each user's data occupies. Since physical connection is set up between the two end stations prior to data transmission, the transition time delay is constant, which is essential for voice and video transmission. The nodes in the network using TDM are circuit switches. As we mentioned in Section 2.4.5, the end-to-end connection is physical. The video channel, which requires more bandwidth (the exact bandwidth depends on the compression of data and the quality of service required) occupies more channels.

Figure 2.27(b) shows the packet transmission mode. Note that the packets of different users are randomly multiplexed. While each user's data is traversing the medium, the full bandwidth of the medium is available to it. This is in contrast to TDM, where only a fraction of the medium's bandwidth is available to any user. Note also that the size of all the users' packets need not be the same. Another noticeable factor is that since the circuit connection is not pre-established, each packet contains the addresses of the originator and the destination. (We described packet switch in Section 2.3.10.) Obviously, packet switches are used with the packet transmission. The packet switch at each node looks at the address of the destination and routes it using the appropriate path. Each packet can take its own route, depending on the availability of links and bandwidth based on different algorithms used. The packets may arrive out of sequence at the receiver, and the end-to-end transmission time for each packet is different. This transmission mode is acceptable for data transmission, but not for voice and video. Data transmission can tolerate bursty traffic.

The cell transmission mode, shown in Figure 2.27(c), combines the best of the TDM and packet modes. The packets are all of the same size and small. Each packet has the full bandwidth of the medium and the packets are statistically multiplexed. The packets all take the same path as in the circuit-switched TDM mode, using the virtual path/virtual circuit concept. This mode of transmission is one of the fundamental concepts of ATM technology.

Most of the information now is transmitted in digital mode. It is a T-based hierarchy (T1, T3, ...) in the United States and an E-based hierarchy (E1, E2, ...) in the United

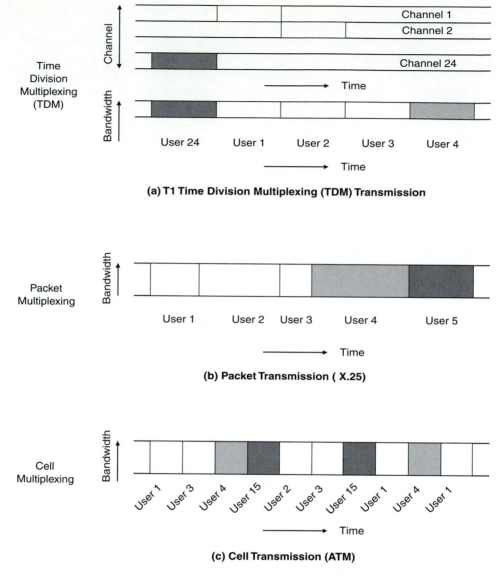

(a) T1 Time Division Multiplexing (TDM) Transmission

(b) Packet Transmission (X.25)

(c) Cell Transmission (ATM)

Figure 2.27   TDM, Packet, and Cell Transmission Modes

Kingdom and Europe and uses packet or frame technology. The latest digital mode of transmission is cell-based ATM traversing on **Synchronous Optical Network** (SONET)/ **Synchronous Digital Hierarchy** (SDH), which is addressed in the next section.

2.6   Integrated Services: ISDN, Frame Relay, and Broadband

Integrated Services Digital Network (ISDN) can be divided into narrow band and broadband, or broadband services. ISDN was introduced by Bell Systems to integrate voice and data over telephone loop facilities. The same principle is used to integrate voice, video, and data and provide them via broadband multimedia service.

The early form of integrated services network is the **Basic ISDN**, a full-duplex digital interface between the subscriber and the central office. It consists of two basic 56-kilobaud-rate channels, each combined with an 8-kilobaud signaling channel, and is referred to as 2B+D.

Basic ISDN was extended to T1 and E1 rates of 1.544 Mbps and 2.048 Mbps, called Primary ISDN interface. The T1 interface carries 24 channels and the E1 interface carries 32 channels.

With the improved quality of transmission media, the ISDN concept was extended from subscriber interfaces to wide-area networks. To achieve near real-time quality for voice, the performance of WANs must be improved. This was done by Frame Relay service, which eliminates hop-to-hop flow and error controls in traditional packet-switching networks, including X.25. The flow and error controls are relegated to higher layers at the ends of a link. Frame Relay access can go up to 2 Mbps.

However, on-line video requires a much larger bandwidth than could be achieved with Frame Relay. This has led to the early implementation of broadband ISDN, or, **broadband network**. Broadband network and service have contributed significantly to advances in three areas: ATM, SONET(terminology used in the United States)/SDH (terminology used in the United Kingdom), and broadband access technology. In Chapter 9, we discuss ATM, which is a cell-based transmission mode, and SONET/SDH, which is a digital hierarchy adopted universally.

The **broadband access technology**, which addresses the link from the central office to the customer's premises, is implemented using one of three technologies. **Hybrid fiber coax** (HFC) technology is a two-way interactive multimedia communication system that uses fiber and coaxial cable facilities and cable modems. The second technology uses **digital subscriber loop** (DSL), of which there are several variations, generically referred to as xDSL. For example, ADSL stands for asymmetric DSL. The third technology uses wireless transmission from the switching office or head end to the customer's premises via either satellite or terrestrial transmission. We will learn in detail about broadband service technologies in Chapter 10.

Figure 2.28 shows a broadband services network. The wide-area network is SONET/SDH. The wide-area network is linked to the customer premises using either optical links, OC-n (Optical Carrier-n)/STS (synchronous transport signal), or one of the three access technologies (HFC, xDSL, or wireless). The customer network consists of two classes, residential customers and corporate customers with campuslike networks. The residential customers are either residential homes or small corporations that use broadband services, but do not maintain the high-speed access network to a WAN. The service

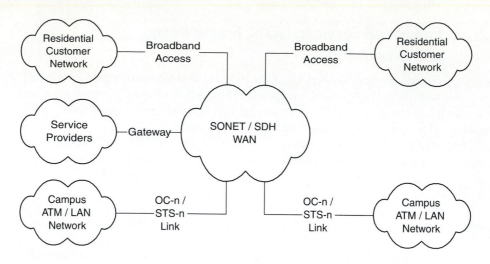

Figure 2.28   A Broadband Services Network

providers perform that function to bring radio, video, Internet, and other services to the customer. Multiple services are multiplexed by multiple system operators (MSO) and piped to customer premises via common facilities. The service providers interface via gateways, which could be either generalized routers or ATM switches.

Summary

In this chapter, we learned network concepts and technologies that would help us understand the network management in Parts II and III.

Network topologies can be classified as LAN and WAN topologies. There are three network topologies associated with wired LANs: bus, ring, and star topologies. The predominant commercial LANs use hub topology, a hybrid of star topology with either bus or ring topology.

A WAN is implemented using either a mesh or a tree topology. Mesh topology is the common implementation and is the topology of the Internet. Tree topology is used when a network is made up of bridges.

We discussed different types of common LAN implementation—Ethernet, Fast Ethernet, Gigabit Ethernet, switched hub, token ring, and FDDI. Of these, IEEE 802.3 10-Mbps Ethernet LAN is the predominant type. This uses CSMA/CD MAC protocol. We addressed the introduction of full-duplex types of Ethernet that double the bandwidth. Ethernet can be implemented using various types of transmission media: coaxial cable, unshielded twisted pair, and optical fiber. Fast Ethernet at 100 Mbps and Gigabit Ethernet at 1 Gbps can be implemented by employing hub technology. A switched hub multiplies the throughput by simultaneous conversations between pairs of nodes. Virtual LANs, implemented using switched hubs, enable logical association of workstations with VLANs.

Token ring and FDDI both use deterministic MAC and hence are more efficient over random access Ethernet. IEEE 802.5 defines the speed of the token ring as either 4 Mbps or 16 Mbps.

FDDI is based on IEEE 802.5 protocol and operates at 100 Mbps. It is typically used for backbone LANs. Because of the need for reliability of the backbone, FDDI can be configured as a dual ring with dual-attached stations (DAS), in contrast to a single ring with single-attached stations (SAS).

Network nodes comprise hubs, bridges, routers, gateways, and switches. Hubs play a significant role in forming LANs. Bridges function at the data link layer and can be connected to form a network. A network that consists of Ethernet bridges is called a transparent bridged network and should meet the criterion of having no loops. In contrast, a network made up of token-ring bridges, source routing bridges, can have loops in the network. This is because the source specifies the route in the data packet and the intermediate nodes do not make routing decisions.

Routers and gateways function at the network layer. Routers and gateways form the backbone of the Internet. The difference between routers and gateways is that the former just route, whereas the latter also do protocol conversion. If the protocol conversion is done at the application layer, the gateway is called a protocol converter.

Packet switches, in general, perform datagram service. That means the packets of one message can take different routes and arrive out of sequence. Therefore, they have to be reassembled in the correct sequence at the receiver.

We can also configure the packet switches to form a virtual circuit. In this case, all packets of a session between the source and the destination take the same path in the network and arrive in the same sequence that they were sent. A virtual circuit can be established on a per-session basis, in which case it is called a switched virtual circuit (SVC). The virtual circuit is set up and torn down each time. In contrast, for a permanent virtual circuit (PVC), call setup is done and left in place permanently.

A wide-area network (WAN) is established using either SVC or PVC. A WAN is distinguished from a LAN because it has a large geographical separation between source and destination. It is generally carried over the facilities of telecommunications network.

In discussing transmission technology, we covered wired and wireless LAN technologies. The roles of coaxial cable, twisted-pair cable, and optical fiber were reviewed. A LAN transmits data in digital format. WAN and broadband technology services transmit information in both digital and analog modes.

We ended our discussion of network technology by introducing ISDN and broadband multimedia services. They handle voice, video, and data transmission in an integrated manner. The WAN in broadband services is ATM-based SONET and the access to customer premises uses HFC, xDSL, or wireless technology.

Exercises

1. The maximum allowed segment for Ethernet is 500 meters and number of segments that can be connected by repeaters is limited to five. The minimum length of the frame that can be transmitted is the sum of the round-trip delay and the repeater delays. Assume the speed of transmission on the cable is 200

meters per microsecond and the total round-trip delay in traversing all the repeaters is 25 μs. Show that the minimum frame size (number of bits per frame) of an Ethernet frame is 64 bytes. *Note:* The maximum frame size is 1,518 bytes.

2. Gigabit Ethernet using CSMA/CD is specified to have a 100-meter drop cable. Show that this corresponds to a slot time of 512 bytes to detect collision. Assume a repeater delay of two microseconds.

3. The Engineering Department of twelve persons in a small corporation is on a regular 10Base-T Ethernet LAN hub with 16 ports. The busy group started complaining because of the slow network performance. The network was operating at 50% utilization, whereas 30% utilization is acceptable. If you are the corporation's Information Technology Engineer and have to resolve the problem technically,

   a. Describe four choices for resolving the problem, maintaining the LAN as an Ethernet LAN.
   b. State the advantages and disadvantages of each approach.

4. In Exercise 3, the IT Manager says the problem is to be solved by using bridges and the existing hub that could be configured for four subnets. A good rule of thumb is that LAN utilization of 20% yields good and satisfactory performance. Assume that twelve workstations are functioning at peer-to-peer level with distribution of traffic between any two stations being the same. What would be your new configuration?

5. Design an Ethernet LAN using a 10/100 Mbps switched Ethernet hub to handle the following specifications:

   Number of clients = 16 operating at 10 Mbps

   Number of server = 1

   50% of the traffic is directed to the server

   Draw the configuration and indicate the transmission modes (half-duplex or duplex) on the ports.

6. Repeat Exercise 5 if the traffic to the server increases to 80 percent.

7. Two virtual LANs, 145.50.50.1 belonging to NM lab, and 145.50.60.1 belonging to Networking lab, each have three workstations. The former has workstations 145.50.50.11-13, and the latter 145.50.60.21-23. They are connected to a switched hub (as shown in Figure 2.9) on ports 2 through 7. The NICs (network interface cards) associated with ports are made by Cabletron and their MAC addresses start with the vendor's global prefix 00-00-1D (hexadecimal notation) and end with 11, 12, 13, 21, 22, and 23 (same as the fourth decimal position of IP addresses).

   a. Create a conceptual matrix table, as shown below, that would be generated by the hub that relates the IP address, MAC address, and port number.

IP Address	MAC Address	Port Number

b. The workstation 23 is moved from Networking lab to NM lab. Show the appropriate parameter changes on the hub and the workstation.

8. In Exercise 7, port 1 of the hub is connected to a router (as shown in Figure 2.9). The IP and MAC addresses associated with the NIC on the hub interfacing to the router are 145.50.10.1 and 00-00-100-00-00-01, and that with the NIC on the router interfacing with the switched hub of 130.30.40.1 and 00-00-10-00.00-64. Extend the matrix of Exercise 7(a) to include port 1, using the same convention for MAC addresses.

9. In Exercise 8, the router is connected to the switched hub by a single physical cable. The router maintains two sets of tables, one to determine the subnets on its network and the other to determine the host on the subnet, as shown below. The third decimal of the IP address is allocated to subnet designation.

Network Table

Network	Subnet	Host
145.50	50	0
...	...	0
145.50	60	0

Subnet Address Tables

Network	Subnet	Host	Port
145.50	50	1	1
145.50	50	11	1
"	"	12	1
"	"	13	1
145.50	60	1	1
"	"	21	1
"	"	22	1
"	"	23	1

a. What is the mask used by the router to filter the subnet?
b. Show how two packets arriving in the router and addressed to 145.50.50.11 and 145.50.60.21 are directed to the switched hub by using the above table.

10. Design a client/server network with two servers operating at 100Base-T Fast Ethernet speed and the clients operating at regular 10Base-T Ethernet speed using a 10/100 Mbps NIC. The hub is located in a wiring closet, but the servers and clients are not. Assume that a satisfactory performance is achieved at 30% utilization of the LAN.

11. Which of the following is correct? The maximum throughput of an 8-port switched hub over an 8-port nonswitched hub is
   a. the same
   b. 2 times
   c. 4 times
   d. 8 times

12. It is assumed in Exercise 11 that the LAN operates at maximum utilization. How-ever, a regular LAN can degrade in performance to an intolerable level at 50% utilization. What is the approximate (ignore the contention of more than one sta-tion trying to reach the same destination at the same time) percentage utilization improvement of a 12-port switched-hub Ethernet LAN over a nonswitched-hub Ethernet LAN?

13. The minimum size of the frame is determined by the token size, which is 3 bytes long and should be contained in the ring under idle condition. Assume a 16-Mbps LAN and transmission of 200 meters per microsecond.

   a. What should be the minimum length of the ring in meters?
   b. Each station normally adds a bit delay in processing the data. What is the additional length gained by adding one station at a time?

14. Repeat Exercise 3 for an FDDI ring. Assume the speed of transmission is 300 meters per microsecond.

15. Explain why the performance of an Ethernet LAN decreases with an increase in the number of stations on the LAN, whereas it increases (at least initially) with the increase in the number of stations in a token-ring LAN.

16. Draw a network configuration and the protocol-layer interface architecture for a multiprotocol bridge that connects an Ethernet LAN and a token-ring LAN.

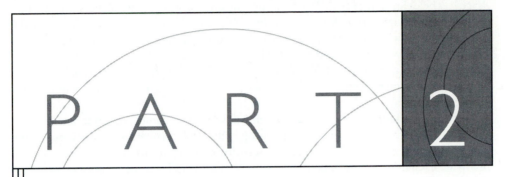

PART 2

SNMP, Broadband, and TMN Management

Part II, comprising Chapters 3 through 11, is devoted to understanding the principles of network and system management. Chapters 3 through 7 discuss the management of TCP/IP networks using SNMP versions 1, 2, and 3. Remote monitoring, which is also part of SNMP management, is discussed in Chapter 8. Broadband services that use multimedia technology are being deployed widely at present. Management of the high-speed ATM technology, which is the backbone of broadband services, and access technologies to connect homes form the contents of Chapters 9 and 10. Chapter 11 extends the management area to cover the broader aspects of network management to include service and business management as addressed in Telecommunications Management Network (TMN).

Chapter 3 introduces technical foundations of standards, models, and language that are needed to build network management systems based on various standards. The currently specified network management standards are SNMP (Internet), CMIP (OSI), TMN, IEEE, and Web-based management. SNMP (Simple Network Management Protocol) is the most widely deployed management system because of its truly simple architecture and implementation. An overview of the models and concepts of network management is also offered. The specifications of most of the protocols use Abstract Syntax Notation One, ASN.1, which is discussed in some detail.

Three versions of SNMP–based protocols manage TCP/IP networks. SNMPv1 is covered in Chapters 4 and 5. Chapter 4 is devoted to the organization and information models of SNMP in network management, and presents the system architecture and SNMP messages. The Structure of Management Information (SMI) is presented using ASN.1. The definition of SNMP objects and the organization of the objects in the structure of the Management Information Base (MIB) are described. Chapter 5 covers the SNMP communication protocol. Message data structures are presented along with the message protocol operations and SNMP MIB.

Studying Chapters 4 and 5 will help you understand the basic principles behind SNMP network management. Case histories and practical examples punctuate the presentation.

Chapter 6 addresses SNMPv2, which adds several significant enhancements to SNMPv1, including efficient transferring of bulk data between systems. One of the intended major enhancements, namely security considerations, was postponed from SNMPv2 to SNMPv3. In Chapter 7 we address security and privacy, as well as the generalized SNMP architecture and applications, which are part of SNMPv3 specifications.

SNMP is a management system based on polling. The goal of remote monitoring (RMON) of the network components using probes and sending only the relevant data to the network management system is discussed in Chapter 8.

The demarcation of telecommunications and computer communications is becoming increasingly fuzzy in broadband communication. The impact of ATM on broadband networks, as well as on ATM campus networks, is dealt with in Chapter 9. Broadband services to homes use cable modem, ADSL, and wireless technologies, which are all evolving technologies. Management considerations of these networks are explored in Chapter 10.

Management of a telecommunication network involves more than management of a network and its systems. It includes service and business management, which are addressed by TMN, which is discussed in Chapter 11.

CHAPTER 3

Basic Foundations: Standards, Models, and Language

In Part I we had an overview of networking and management of network and systems. We learned about network technology and components that need to be managed. To manage networks, systems, and services, there are several management standards and models in existence. We can understand and appreciate them better by first looking at the commonalities among them, and then the differences that distinguish them.

We will consider the foundations of various network management models and protocols, survey the network management standards, and present the general architecture of network management models in Section 3.1.

The International Standards Organization has defined a generalized model that addresses all aspects of network management. This is discussed in Section 3.2. In Sections 3.3 through 3.5 we cover the three models of the architecture that deal with organization, information, and communication. Then we will learn in Sections 3.6 through 3.8, the basics of the formal language, ASN.1, and the data structure that management systems use to store information and communicate with each other.

Section 3.9 presents the fourth model of network architecture, the functional model, which addresses the applications that fall into the categories of fault, configuration, performance, security, and accounting.

In a global perspective, three areas of network need managing: network, systems, and services; interlayer protocols; and intralayer protocols. In this book, our focus is on network and system management. We define *network management* as management of the network comprising nodes and links, and *system management* as management of a system's resources, such as central processor usage, disk usage, and application processes. *Service management* deals with services provided by organizations to customers. Service management is an extension of network and systems management.

The two leading models of network management are the Internet model and the OSI model. The Internet model is the most widely used for network management. It is a simple scalar model and, hence, easy to implement. The OSI model, which is object-oriented, is more complex and harder to implement. However, with the fast-paced progress of object-oriented technology and the melding of data and telecommunications technologies, the OSI model is gaining importance. Some of the commercial network management systems (Sun Enterprise, HP OpenView Network Node Manager) are based on the OSI model. A higher-level management network called Telecommunications Management Network (TMN) is also based on the OSI model. It addresses all levels of management including service and business aspects. We will study TMN in Chapter 11.

In this book, we are concerned primarily with the study of the Internet-based SNMP model. The OSI model is discussed in Appendix A.

3.1   Network Management Standards

Several network management standards are in use today. Table 3.1 lists four standards and their salient points, and a fifth standard based on emerging technology. They are the OSI model, the Internet model, TMN, IEEE LAN/MAN, and Web-based management. A detailed treatment of the various standards can be found in [Black U1].

The Open System Interconnection (OSI) management standard is the standard adopted by the International Standards Organization (ISO). The OSI management protocol standard is Common Management Information Protocol (CMIP), and has built-in services, Common Management Information Service (CMIS), that specify the basic services needed to perform the various functions. It is the most comprehensive set of specifications, and addresses all seven layers of the OSI Reference Model. The specifications are object-oriented and hence managed objects are based on object classes and inheritance rules. Besides specifying the management protocols, CMIP/CMIS also address the network management applications. Both LANs and WANs can be managed using CMIP/CMIS. Two of the major drawbacks of the OSI management standard are that it is complex and that the CMIP stack is large. Until recently, memory of an ordinary desktop workstation was not sufficient to load a complete CMIP stack.

In contrast to CMIP, Simple Network Management Protocol (SNMP) is truly simple, as its name indicates. It started as an industry standard and has since become very much like the standard specifications of a standards-setting organization. The Internet Engineering Task Force (IETF) is responsible for all Internet specifications including network management. The managed objects are defined as scalar objects in SNMP, which was primarily intended to manage Internet components, but is now used to manage WAN and telecommunications systems. Probably because it is easy to implement, SNMP is the most widely implemented network management system today.

The Telecommunications Management Network (TMN) is designed to manage the telecommunications network and is oriented toward the needs of telecommunications service providers. TMN is the standard of the International Telecommunication Union (ITU) and is based on OSI CMIP/CMIS specifications. TMN extends the concept of management beyond managing networks and network components; its specifications address service and business considerations.

The IEEE standards for LAN and MAN (metropolitan area network) specifications are concerned only with OSI layers 1 (physical) and 2 (data link), and they are structured similarly to OSI specifications. Both OSI/CMIP and Internet/SNMP protocols use IEEE standards for the lower layers. The IEEE 802.x series of specifications defines the standards for the various physical media and data link protocols. IEEE 802.1 specifications present overview, architecture, and management. The IEEE 802.2 standard specifies the logical link control (LLC) layer. As we saw in Chapter 1 (Figure 1.15), the LLC layer provides transparency of the various physical media and protocols to the network layer. The other specifications in the IEEE series are for specific media and protocols. For example, 802.3 specifications are for Ethernet LANs.

The last category in Table 3.1 is Web-based management, which is based on using Web technology, a Web server for the management system, and Web browsers for network management stations. Because this is an evolving technology, no standards exist at present. Two technologies are in vogue, Web-Based Enterprise Management (WBEM) and Java Management Extensions (JMX). A recently formed task force, Desktop Management Task Force (DMTF), is developing specifications for WBEM.

Table 3.1   Network Management Standards

Standard	Salient Points
OSI/CMIP	• International standard (ISO/OSI) • Management of data communications networks—LAN and WAN • Deals with all seven layers • Most complete • Object oriented • Well structured and layered • Consumes large resource in implementation
SNMP/Internet	• Industry standard (IETF) • Originally intended for management of Internet components, currently adopted for WAN and telecommunication systems • Easy to implement • Most widely implemented
TMN	• International standard (ITU-T) • Management of telecommunications network • Based on OSI network management framework • Addresses both network and administrative aspects of management
IEEE	• IEEE standards adopted internationally • Addresses management of LANs and MANs • Adopts OSI standards significantly • Deals with first two layers of the OSI Reference Model
Web-Based Management	• Web-Based Enterprise Management (WBEM) • Java Management Extensions (JMX)

The DMTF has chosen the Microsoft object-oriented management model, Common Information Model. JMX is based on a special subset of Java applets developed by Sun Microsystems that runs in the network components. (These technologies are covered in Chapter 14.)

Part I addressed the challenges that fast-moving technology presents to information technology managers. Network management is further complicated when the management system uses the new technology. The SNMP, based on scalar technology and simple definition of managed objects, was widely favored over CMIP. With the need for a total management of network, service, and business for telecommunications service providers, TMN, which uses CMIP, is being revived. CMIP, which was hard to implement because it required large memory and a better understanding of object-oriented technology, is now easier to implement. However, because of the numerous existing SNMP–based agents, SNMP is also being explored for implementing TMN. Both SNMP and CMIP use polling methodology, which puts an additional load on the network. Besides, both require dedicated workstations for the network management system. With the new Web-based management system, not only can object-oriented technology be implemented, but also the dedicated workstation constraint is removed by the use of a Web browser.

3.2   Network Management Model

The OSI network model is an ISO standard and is the most superior of all the models; it is structured and it addresses all aspects of management. Figure 3.1 shows an OSI network management architecture model that comprise four models: organization model, information model, communication model, and functional model. Although, the above classification of models is based on OSI architecture, and only some of the models are applicable to other architectures, it helps us understand the holistic picture of different aspects of network management.

The organization model describes the components of a network management system, their functions, and their infrastructure. The organization model is defined in ISO 10040 OSI Systems Management Overview. It defines the terms *object*, *agent*, and *manager*.

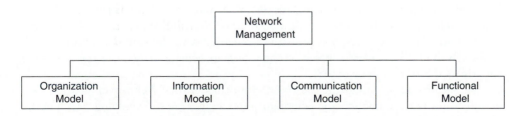

Figure 3.1   OSI Network Management Model

The OSI information model deals with the structure and organization of management information. ISO 10165 specifies the structure of management information (SMI) and the information database, Management Information Base (MIB). SMI describes how the management information is structured and MIB deals with the relationship and storage of management information.

The third model in OSI management is the communication model, which has three components: management application processes that function in the application layer, layer management between layers, and layer operation within the layers. We focus on the application processes in this book.

The functional model is the fourth component of OSI management, and it deals with the user-oriented requirements of network management. As mentioned in Chapter 1, OSI defines five functional application areas, namely, configuration, fault, performance, security, and accounting. These are defined as system management functions in OSI.

As mentioned earlier, only OSI presents the complete model for network management; others deal with only a subset or are still in the process of developing standards. OSI deals with all seven networking layers. Further, as we will see in Chapter 11, it lends itself to addressing service and business management, which is more than just networking.

The second standard listed in Table 3.1 is the SNMP/Internet standard. The IETF does not define architecture for the SNMP management model explicitly. However, it does exist implicitly. The organization, information, and communication models are similar to OSI models. The SNMP network management model addresses the functional model in terms of operations, administration, and security. SNMP–based management is widely used for campuswide networks, although enterprise-wide networks are also managed by using distributed configurations of SNMP–based network management systems. (SNMP-based management systems, tools, and applications are addressed in Chapters 12 and 13.)

The third standard in Table 3.1 is Telecommunications Management Network (TMN), which is based on the OSI model. The focus of the TMN standard is toward managing telecommunications networks. As mentioned earlier, it extends the application functions of OSI into service and business considerations. Operations systems support service and business management.

The fourth standard in Table 3.1 is the IEEE standard on management and is dedicated to the management of layers 1 and 2 of the OSI Reference Model. It is applicable to LANs and MANs and addresses standards on broadband network management, which is of great relevance to the current technology. Since the IEEE standard deals with only physical and data link layers, it is primarily concerned with the communication model. Although the IEEE standard is based on the OSI management model, the operations are slightly modified from those of OSI.

In Web-based management, the organization model uses Web server-Web browser architecture. The information and communication models are still evolving. Much of the object-oriented technology, such as hypermedia server, CORBA-oriented transportation, and client/server push technology are influencing Web-based management.

3.3   Organization Model

The organization model describes the components of network management and their relationships. Figure 3.2 shows a two-tier model. Network objects consist of **network elements** such as hosts, hubs, bridges, routers, and so on. They can be classified into managed and unmanaged objects or elements. The managed elements have a management process running in them, called an **agent**. The unmanaged elements do not have a management process running in them. For example, one can buy a managed or an unmanaged hub. Obviously, the managed hub has management capability built into it and hence is more expensive than the unmanaged hub, which does not have an agent running in it. The manager communicates with the agent in the managed element.

The **manager** manages the managed element. As shown in Figure 3.2, there is a database in the manager, but not in the agent. The manager queries the agent and receives management data, processes it, and stores it in its database. The agent can also send a minimal set of alarm information to the manager unsolicited.

Figure 3.3 presents a three-tier configuration, in which the intermediate layer acts as both agent and manager. As manager, it collects data from the network elements, processes it, and stores the results in its database. As agent, it transmits information to the top-level manager. For example, an intermediate system is used for making statistical measurements on a network and passing the information as needed to the top-level manager. Alternatively, an intermediate network management system could be at a local site of a network and pass the information to a remote site.

Network domains can be managed locally; and a global view of the networks can be monitored by a manager of managers (MoM), as shown in Figure 3.4. This configuration uses

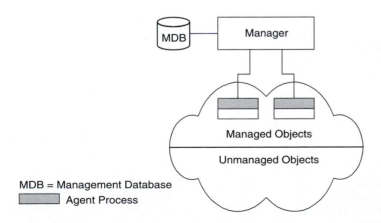

MDB = Management Database

▨ Agent Process

Figure 3.2   Two-Tier Network Management Organization Model

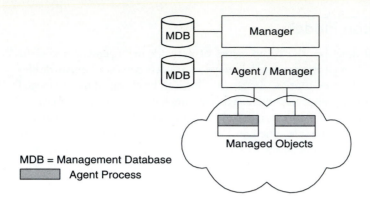

MDB = Management Database
▨ Agent Process

Figure 3.3   Three-Tier Network Management Organization Model

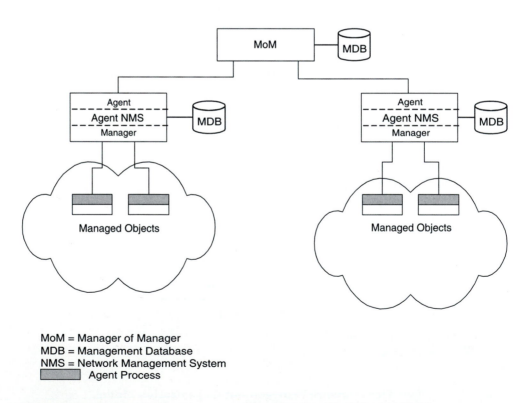

MoM = Manager of Manager
MDB = Management Database
NMS = Network Management System
▨ Agent Process

Figure 3.4   Network Management Organization Model with MoM

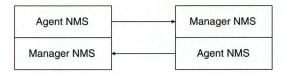

Figure 3.5   Dual Role of Management Process

an enterprise network management system and is applicable to organizations with sites distributed across cities. It is also applicable to a configuration in which vendor management systems manage the domains of their components, and MoM manages the entire network.

Network management systems can also be configured as peer-to-peer relationships, as shown in Figure 3.5. (This is the dumbbell architecture shown in Figure 1.23.) We can recognize the similarity between this and the client/server architecture where a host serves as both client and server. An example of such a situation would be two network service providers that need to exchange management information. From the user's point of view, the information traverses both networks and must be monitored end-to-end.

In the above discussion, we have used the term *network management system* (NMS) to mean a system that runs a management process. Thus, the agent and the manager devices are called agent NMS and manager NMS, as shown in Figures 3.4 and 3.5.

3.4   Information Model

An information model is concerned with the structure and the storage of information. Let us consider, for example, how information is structured and stored in a library and is accessed by all. A book is identified by an International Standard Book Number (ISBN). It is a ten-digit number that identifies a specific edition of a specific book. For example, ISBN 0-13-437708-7 refers to the book *Understanding SNMP MIBs* by David Perkins and Evan McGinnis. We can refer to a specific figure in the book by identifying chapter number and figure number; for example, Figure 3-1 refers to Figure 1 in Chapter 3. Thus, a hierarchy of designation (e.g., ISBN, chapter, figure) uniquely identifies the object, which is a figure in the book. "ISBN," "Chapter," and "Figure" define the *syntax* (format) of the three pieces of information associated with the figure; and their meanings in a dictionary would be the *semantics* (meaning) associated with them.

The representation of objects and information relevant to their management form the management information model. As discussed in Section 3.3, information on network components is passed between the agent and management processes. The information model specifies the information base to describe managed objects and their relationships. The **Structure of Management Information** (SMI) defines the syntax and semantics of management information stored in the **Management Information Base** (MIB). The MIB is used by both agent and management processes to store and exchange management information. The MIB associated with an agent is called the agent MIB and the MIB associated with a manager is designated the manager MIB. A manager MIB consists of information on all the network components that it manages, whereas an agent MIB needs to know only its local information, its MIB view. For example, a county may have many libraries. Each library has an index of all the books in that location—its MIB view. However, the central index at the county's main library, which manages all other libraries, has the index of all books in all the county's libraries—the global MIB view.

Figure 3.6 expands the network configuration shown in Figure 3.2 to include the MIB associated with the manager. Thus, the manager has both the management database (MDB) and the Management Information Base (MIB). It is important to distinguish between the two. The MDB is a real database and contains the measured or administratively configured value of the elements of the network. On the other hand, the MIB is a virtual database and contains the information necessary for processes to exchange information.

Let us illustrate the distinction between MIB and MDB by considering the scenario of adding a component to the network. Assume all the hubs in the network are made by a single vendor, say Cabletron. In Figure 3.6 the manager's knowledge about Cabletron hubs and their associated parameters is in its MIB, and its knowledge about the values associated with the parameters with the hubs are in its MDB. For example, number of ports in the hub is a parameter associated with the hub (MIB information) and if they are 12-port hubs, the values associated with the number of ports are 12 (MDB information). Suppose we add another Cabletron hub to the network. The manager would discover the new hub during its next discovery process, which could be just a broadcast ping from the manager. The new hub is another instance of the hub with a new IP address, and its MIB information is already in the manager's MIB. Its address and the number of ports associated with it are added to the MDB by the manager querying the agent.

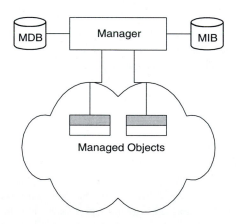

MDB = Management Database
MIB = Management Information Base
▨▨▨▨   Agent Process

Figure 3.6   Network Configuration with Data and Information Base

Now, let us add a 3Com hub to the network. Let this be the first time that a 3Com hub is added to the network. The manager would recognize the addition of a new component to the network by the periodic broadcast ping of the network. However, it would not know what component has been added until the MIB information on the 3Com hub is added to the manager's MIB. This information is actually compiled into the manager's MIB schema. After the information on the 3Com hub has been added to its MIB, the manager can send queries to the agent residing in the 3Com hub. It then retrieves the values for the type of hub, the number of ports, and so on, and adds them to its MDB.

The MIB that contains data on managed objects need not be limited to physical elements. For example, in network management, management information extends beyond that associated with the description of network elements or objects. Here are some examples of information that can be stored in the MIB:

Network Elements: hubs, bridges, routers, transmission facilities

Software Processes: programs, algorithms, protocol functions, databases

Administrative Information: contact person, account number

In fact, any type of information could be included in the MIB.

3.4.1   Management Information Trees

Managed objects are uniquely defined by a tree structure specified by the OSI model and are used in the Internet model. Figure 3.7 shows the generic representation of the management information tree (MIT). There is a root node and well-defined nodes underneath each node at different levels. Each managed object occupies a node in the tree. In the OSI model, the managed objects are defined by a containment tree that represents the MIT.

Figure 3.8 shows the internationally adopted OSI MIT. The root node does not have an explicit designation. There are three nodes in the layer beneath the root: **iso**, **ccitt** (**itu**), and **iso-ccitt**, (**iso-itu**). The **iso** defines the International Standards Organization and **itu** defines the International Telecommunications Union (the old name is **ccitt**). The two standards organizations are on the first layer and define management of objects under them. The joint **iso-itu** node is for management objects jointly defined by the two organizations. The number in each circle identifies the designation of the object in each layer.

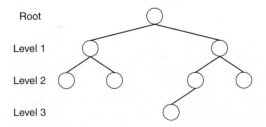

Figure 3.7   Generic Representation of Management Information Tree

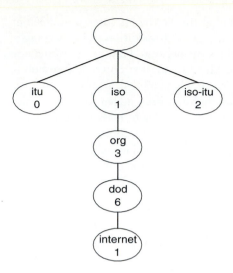

Figure 3.8   OSI Management Information Tree

Thus, **iso** is designated as 1 and **org** as 1.3, **dod** (Department of Defense) as 1.3.6 and the Internet as 1.3.6.1. All Internet-managed objects will be that number followed by more dots and numbers. Note that the names of the nodes are all in lowercase letters according to convention, which we formally define in Section 3.6.

3.4.2   Managed Object Perspectives

Although a managed object need not be a physical object that can be seen, touched, and felt, it is convenient to use a physical representation to understand the characteristics and operations associated with a managed object. Let us consider an object that is circular. We can define the object in English **syntax** as *circle*. To associate a meaning with the object's name, *circle*, we can use Webster's dictionary definition "a plane figure bounded by a single curved line every point of which is equally distant from the point at the center of the figure." In other words, the **definition** is a textual description of the object. The object can be viewed and its parameters changed by people who have **access** to it. The *access* privilege could be limited to just accessing it or performing some action on it, for example resetting a counter value to two. These are all defined as access attributes. If we envision a scenario in which the object is used by a nursery school to explain shapes to children, the school should have at least some basic shapes such as circle, square, and tri-angle. We can define each basic object that is required of a group (of objects) according to its **status**, such as whether it is mandatory or optional to have (implement) that object. There could be many types of circular objects in the nursery school. Each type has a unique *identification* and *name* (**object identifier** and **descriptor**) associated with it such as ring and donut. There could be many rings and donuts; but here we are addressing only the types of object, not instances of them. We have thus defined the five basic attributes of a managed object type from the Internet perspective. They are **object type** (**object identifier** and **descriptor**), **definition, syntax, access,** and **status.**

Figure 3.9(a) shows a pictorial view of a circular object in Internet perspective.

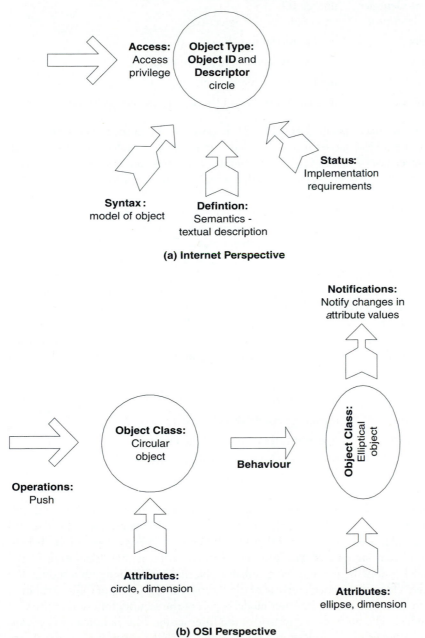

(a) Internet Perspective

(b) OSI Perspective

Figure 3.9   Conceptual Views of Managed Object

Specifications for the Internet are defined in Request for Comments (RFC) documents. A managed object in the Internet model is defined by five parameters [RFC 1155]:

- object identifier   unique ID
  and descriptor   and name for the object type
- syntax   used to model the object
- access   access privilege to a managed object
- status   implementation requirements
- definition   textual description of the semantics of object type

A modification of this is specified in [RFC 1212], as we will see in the next chapter.

The Internet object model is a scalar model and is easy to understand. In contrast, the OSI perspective of a managed object is complex and has a different set of characteristics. To illustrate an OSI perspective, we will extend the analogy of the circular object in a nursery school.

Figure 3.9(b) presents the conceptual OSI representation of the various characteristics of a managed object. As we mentioned earlier, OSI specifications are object-oriented, and hence a managed object belongs to an **object class.** The left side of Figure 3.9(b) presents the same circular object in the OSI model as is represented in Figure 3.9(a). The definition of an object in object-oriented perception includes both the shape and values. Thus, the attribute of the object is a circle with given dimensions. The **attribute** of an object defines the external perspective of the object. It undergoes an **operation** "push." Push is not really an OSI operational entity, but is used here to illustrate the concept. The **behaviour** of the object is to change its shape or attribute from circle to ellipse. It then sends **notifications** to the relevant community informing of its change. Thus an OSI managed object has the following characteristics:

- object class   managed object
- attributes   attributes visible at its boundary
- operations   operations that can be applied to it
- behaviour   behavior exhibited by it in response to an operation
- notifications   notifications emitted by the object

It is hard to compare the characteristics of a managed object in Internet and OSI models on a one-to-one basis because they are very different. However, it can be observed in the conceptual models in Figure 3.9 that the OSI characteristics of operations, behavior, and notification are part of the Internet communication model. Operation in the Internet model is done by get and set commands. Notification is done by response and alarm messages. The syntax characteristic of the Internet model is part of OSI's attributes. The access characteristic of the Internet model is part of the security function in the OSI functional model. The status characteristic of the Internet model is handled by conformance as part of application services in OSI. Further, in OSI we can create and delete objects; these concepts do not exist in the Internet. Objects in SNMP management are assumed to exist for management purposes.

Figure 3.10 shows the comparison of Internet and OSI specifications for the object, packet counter. An example of a packet counter as a managed object in the Internet model is given in Figure 3.10(a). The object type (we will define *object type* later) is Pkt-Counter. The syntax is Counter. The access mode is read-only. The status implementation is mandatory, which mandates that this object must be implemented if the group it belongs to is implemented. The description provides the semantics that the packet counter counts the packets.

The example of the same counter as a managed object in the OSI model is given in Figure 3.10(b). The counter is defined as an object class, Packet Counter. It could be related to either a subclass or superclass. The attribute value is single-valued. We can perform get and set operations on its attribute. Its behavior to a set operation would be to reset the counter, or just to retrieve data if the operation is get. The new value is sent out as notification.

Characteristics	Example
Object type	PktCounter
Syntax	Counter
Access	Read-only
Status	Mandatory
Description	Counts number of packets

(a) Internet Perspective

Characteristics	Example
Object class	Packet Counter
Attributes	Single-valued
Operations	get, set
Behavior	Retrieves or resets values
Notifications	Generates notifications on new value

(b) OSI Perspective

Figure 3.10   Packet Counter as an Example of a Managed Object

3.5   Communication Model

We discussed in the previous section how information content is defined (SMI) and stored (MIB). We will now address the model associated with the way information is exchanged between systems. Management data is communicated between agent and manager processes, as well as between manager processes. Three aspects need to be addressed in the communication of information between two entities: transport medium of message exchange (transport protocol), message format of communication (application protocol), and the actual message (commands and responses). Let us illustrate this by the example of Azita buying a car from an automobile salesperson, Roberto.

Azita could go to the automobile dealer and communicate in person with Roberto. Alternatively, she could communicate with Roberto via the Internet. In the former, visual and audio media are the transport mechanisms; electronic exchange is used in the latter. The communication at the application level could be exchanged in English, Spanish, or any other language that both people understand. This would be the application-level protocol that is decided between Azita and Roberto. Finally, there are messages exchanged between Azita and Roberto. For example, Azita could request what cars are available and Roberto would respond with the cars that are in stock. Azita then could set a price range and Roberto could respond with cars that match the price range. These exchanged messages are the commands/requests/operations and responses/notifications. They can be considered services requested by Azita and provided by Roberto.

Figure 3.11 presents the communication model. The applications in the manager module initiate **requests** to the agent in the Internet model. It is part of the **operations** in the OSI model. The agent executes the request on the network element, that is, the managed object, and returns **responses** to the manager. The notifications/traps are the unsolicited messages, such as alarms, generated by the agent.

Figure 3.12 presents the communication protocol used to transfer information between managed object and managing processes, as well as between management processes. The OSI model uses Common Management Information Protocol (CMIP) along with Common Management Information Services (CMIS). Internet uses Simple Net-

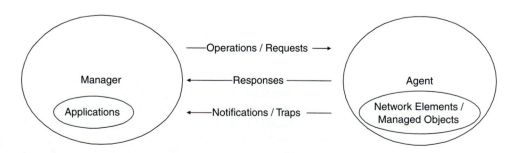

Figure 3.11   Management Communication Model

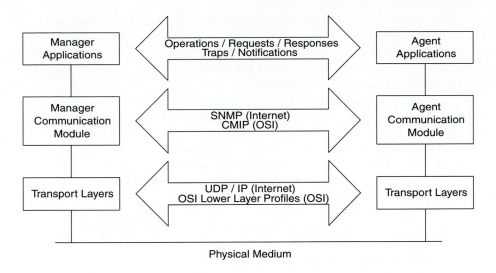

Figure 3.12   Management Communication Transfer Protocols

work Management Protocol (SNMP) for communication. The services are part of operations using requests, responses, and alarm notifications.

OSI uses both connection-oriented and connectionless protocols for transportation. For example, the TP4 transport-layer protocol riding on top of the x25 protocol could be used for connection-oriented transporting and application messages. TP4 over Connectionless Network Protocol is used for connectionless transportation. Internet uses connectionless UDP/IP protocol to transport messages.

CMIP and SNMP specify the management communication protocols for OSI and Internet management, respectively. CMIP is addressed in Appendix A. SNMP is covered extensively throughout this book.

The application processes invoke the management-communication layer protocols. OSI deals with messages in the specification of managed objects. Managed objects and their attributes could be manipulated by operations. Basic application service modules are defined by CMIS. In the Internet, operations are executed by SNMP messages.

3.6   Abstract Syntax Notation One: ASN.1

In both the information and communication models discussed in the previous sections, we addressed the functions. In these models, structure of management information needs to be specified syntactically and semantically, which is the focus of this section.

It is important for communication among systems that a formalized set of rules be agreed upon regarding the structure and meaning of the language of communication, namely, the syntax and semantics of the language. Because there are numerous sets of application and transport protocols, it is beneficial to choose a syntactical format for the language that specifies the management protocol in the application layer, which is transparent to the rest of the protocol layers. One old and well-proven format is Abstract Syntax Notation One, ASN.1. We introduce ASN.1 here to the extent needed to understand its use in network management. For greater depth on the subject, see [Cassel LN & Austing RAH, Chalks BS, Larmouth J, Stallings W2].

ASN.1 is more than just syntax. It is a formal language developed jointly by CCITT (now ITU-T) and ISO for use with application layers for data transfer between systems. It is also applicable within the system for clearly separating the abstract syntax and the transfer syntax at the presentation layer. We define **abstract syntax** as the set of rules used to specify data types and structures for storage of information. **Transfer syntax** represents the set of rules for communicating information between systems. Thus, abstract syntax would be applicable to the information model discussed in Section 3.4 and transfer syntax to the communication model discussed in Section 3.5. The abstract syntax can be used with any presentation syntax, depending on the medium of presentation. The abstract syntax in ASN.1 makes it independent of the lower-layer protocols. ISO 8824/X.208 standards specify ASN.1. The algorithm to convert the textual ASN.1 syntax to machine-readable code is called *basic encoding rules* (BER) and is defined in ISO 8825/X. 209 standards.

3.6.1   Terminology, Symbols, and Conventions

ASN.1 is based on the Backus system and uses the formal syntax language and grammar of the Backus-Nauer Form (BNF), which looks like:

```
<name> ::= <definition>
```

where the notation "<entity>" denotes an "entity" and the symbol "::=" represents "defined as".

Let us illustrate the Backus system by developing a simple arithmetic expression <SAE> [Maurer HA]:

We can define an entity <digit> in the following way:

```
<digit> ::= 0 | 1 | 2 | 3 | 4 | 5 | 6 | 7 | 8 | 9
```

where the symbol "|" represents "or". We can also define an operation entity <op> in the following way:

```
<op> ::= + | - | x | /
```

The definitions on the right side are called **primitives.** Using these primitives, we can construct more entities. Thus, an entity **number** can be constructed from the primitive, <digit>

```
<number> ::= <digit> | <digit><number>
```

For example, the number 9 is the digit 9; the number 19 is the concatenation of the digit 1 and the number 9; and the number 219 is the concatenation of the digit 2 with the number 19. We can now construct a simple arithmetic expression <SAE> from the primitives and the construct <number>. Thus,

<SAE> ::= <number> | <SAE> | <SAE><op><SAE>

The format of each line is defined as a **production** or **assignment.**

Let us consider an example with the following two assignments:

```
<BooleanType> ::= BOOLEAN
<BooleanValue> ::= TRUE | FALSE
```

The expression on the left side specifies the name of the type and the right side is the definition or value of the type. Thus, BooleanType is defined as BOOLEAN and Boolean-Value is defined as either TRUE or FALSE. This example illustrates the two basic parameters associated with an entity, namely, **data type** and **value.** The first line is called data type assignment and it defines the name of the entity; the second line, value assignment, specifies the assigned value to the data type. Thus, in the above example the entity BOOLEAN can have assigned values of TRUE or FALSE. Entities that are all in capital letters, such as TRUE and FALSE are called **keywords.**

A group of assignments makes up an ASN.1 module. For example, a name consists of first, middle, and last names, and they can be specified as:

```
person-name Person-Name ::=
{
first "John",
middle "T",
last "Smith"
}
```

Here **person-name**, beginning with lowercase letters, is the name of the module, which is a data type. **Person-Name** is a module and begins with capital letters. The module comprises three assignments, whose names are first, middle, and last with values "John", "T", and "Smith".

Figures 3.13 and 3.14 show examples of ASN.1 data type definition [Larmouth J]. The two ASN.1 modules define data types PersonnelRecord and Trade-Message. Because they are modules, they start with capital letters. PersonnelRecord describes the personnel record of an employee in a global corporation. The Trade-Message is a module that specifies a list of invoices that define customer name, part numbers, quantity, charge, and security authentication.

Note that in the examples of Figures 3.13 and 3.14 the data types are built up from primitive data types: INTEGER, REAL, NULL, and GraphicString. GraphicString is one of several CharacterString type primitives. These examples present three kinds of data types, which are built using three construction mechanisms:

alternatives:	CHOICE
list:	SET and SEQUENCE
repetition:	SET OF and SEQUENCE OF

```
PersonnelRecord ::= SET
     {           Name,
     title       GraphicString,
     division  CHOICE {
        marketing      [0]      SEQUENCE
           {Sector,
            Country},
        research       [1]      CHOICE
           {product-based  [0] NULL,
            basic          [1] NULL},
        production     [2]      SEQUENCE
           {Product-line,
            Country     }               } }
```

Figure 3.13   ASN.1 Data Type Definition Example 1

These constructs are used to build structured data types. Just as we saw in the <SAE> example, all data types are built from the ground up using primitive (also called atomic) entities. ASN.1 definition allows both backward and forward references, as well as in-line definition. For instance, in Figure 3.13 the data types **Name, Sector, Country,** and **Product-line** are defined externally either before or after the module that defines **Personnel-Record.** The data type whose name is **title** is defined in-line as the data type **GraphicString.** It could have been defined as data type **Title** as follows:

```
title    Title ::= GraphicString
```

Let us analyze the three construct types. In **PersonnelRecord,** the person works in one of the three divisions—*marketing, research,* or *production.* This is built using the

```
Trade-Message ::= SEQUENCE
     {invoice-no      INTEGER
      name            GraphicString,
      details         SEQUENCE OF
                          SEQUENCE
              {part-no     INTEGER
               quantity    INTEGER},
      charge              REAL,
      authenticator       Security-Type}
Security-Type ::= SET
     {      ...
            ...
            ...     }
```

Figure 3.14   ASN.1 Data Type Definition Example 2

CHOICE construction. Notice that in each of those divisions, research could be either *product-based* or *basic*.

The constructs SET and SEQUENCE are list builders. The PersonnelRecord module is a set of data types (Name, GraphicString, Sector, Country, etc.) that are all different data types. Because they are different and each is uniquely associated with a name, they can be encoded and transmitted in any order. For example, they could be arranged in any of the following orders:

```
"Smith", "Manager", {"North", "Chile"}
"Manager", "Smith", {"North", "Chile"}
{"North", "Chile"}, "Manager", "Smith"
```

Notice that "North" and "Chile" are always in the same order. This is because it is a list built with the SEQUENCE construction so the order in the list will be maintained.

The third type of construction is the repetitive types SET OF and SEQUENCE OF. In the example of TradeMessage in Figure 3.14, the SEQUENCE OF construction is shown. The *details* in the invoice are a repetition of data consisting of the ordered list (SEQUENCE construct) of *part-no* and *quantity* in each invoice. The repetitive records themselves are ordered in a SEQUENCE OF construction. This means that the data will be transmitted in the order in which it is entered. The encoding scheme will preserve that order while the data is transmitted from one process to another. For example, if data is entered for details in Figure 3.14 as a sequence {part-no, quantity} in the order {1, 5}, {60, 3}, {120, 40}, it will be transmitted in that order by the sending process. If the construct had been SET OF instead of SEQUENCE OF for details in Figure 3.14, order would be irrelevant. The order in this case for the example could be encoded and transmitted by the sending process as any of the combinations, {1, 5}, {60, 3}, {120, 40}; or {60, 3}, {1, 5}, {120, 40}; or {120, 40}, {1, 5}, {60, 3}; and so on, without relevance to the order.

In Figure 3.13 the NULL data type in PersonnelRecord is a placeholder. No value needs to be associated with it; it indicates that such a data type exists.

We observe in the PersonnelRecord example in Figure 3.13 that some assignments have integers in square brackets. For instance,

```
{product-based [0] NULL,
 basic         [1] NULL}
```

These are called tags. The definition of **tag** is introduced in ASN.1 to uniquely identify a data type; it will be discussed in more detail later.

We have used several symbols and primitive data types, including keywords, in the preceding examples. A complete list of ASN.1 symbols appears in Table 3.2.

Table 3.3 lists some of the frequently used ASN.1 keywords. For a more comprehensive list, see [Perkins D & McGinnis E].

As we said earlier, we can group assignments that are related; this group is called a module. A formal definition of a **module** is as follows:

```
<module name> DEFINITIONS ::= BEGIN
<name> ::= <definition>
<name> ::= <definition>
END
```

Table 3.2   ASN.1 Symbols

Symbol	Meaning
::=	defined as, or assignment
|	or, alternatives, options of a list
-	signed number
--	following the symbol are comments
{ }	start and end of a list
[ ]	start and end of a tag
( )	start and end of a subtype
..	range

For example, a MIB definition module will look like:

```
RFC1213-MIB DEFINITIONS ::= BEGIN
...
...
...
END
```

The terms DEFINITIONS, BEGIN, and END are primitives and are called keywords in ASN.1. They are built-in expressions that have special meanings. DEFINITIONS indicates that the named module, RFC 1213-MIB, is being defined. The body of a module always

Table 3.3   ANS.1 Keywords

Keyword	Brief Description
BEGIN	Start of an ASN.1 module
CHOICE	List of alternatives
DEFINITIONS	Definition of a data type or managed object
END	End of an ASN.1 module
EXPORTS	Data types that can be exported to other modules
IDENTIFIER	A sequence of non-negative numbers
IMPORTS	Data types defined in external modules
INTEGER	Any negative or non-negative number
NULL	A placeholder
OBJECT	Used with IDENTIFIER to uniquely identify an object
OCTET	Unbounded 8-bit bytes (octets) of binary data
OF	Used with SET and SEQUENCE
SEQUENCE	Ordered list maker
SEQUENCE OF	Ordered array of repetitive data
SET	Unordered list maker
SET OF	Unordered list of repetitive data
STRING	Used with OCTET for denoting string of octets

Table 3.4   ASN.1 Data Type Conventions

Data Types	Convention	Example
Object name	Initial lowercase letter	sysDescr, etherStatsPkts
Application data type	Initial uppercase letter	Counter, IpAddress
Module	Initial uppercase letter	PersonnelRecord
Macro, MIB module	All uppercase letters	RMON-MIB
Keywords	All uppercase letters	INTEGER, BEGIN

starts with BEGIN and always ends with END. Grouping assignments into modules has the great advantage that modules can be imported into and exported from other modules. Thus, they are reusable.

Notice that in the examples described so far in this section we have used both lowercase and uppercase letters. The ASN.1 conventions to designate the data are shown in Table 3.4.

3.6.2   Objects and Data Types

We will now use ASN.1 notation to define the various data types and apply them to describe objects in the context of SMI and MIB.

We observed in Section 3.6.1 that the data type could be either simple type (also called primitive, atomic, or basic), or structured. In addition, we talked about tag designation, which uniquely identifies the data type irrespective of the syntax version. In general, data types are defined based on structure and tag. The structure is divided into four categories. The tag is divided into two: class and tag number. This is shown in Figure 3.15. An object can be defined by its tag, that is, its class and tag number. For exchange of information between systems, the structure information is also included.

The four categories of data type structure, shown in Figure 3.15, are simple type, structured type, tagged type, and other type.

A **simple type** is one for which the values are specified directly. For example, we can define a page of a book as PageNumber of simple type, which can take on any integer value. INTEGER is a simple type. Thus,

```
PageNumber ::= INTEGER
```

Similarly, we can define the chapter number of the book as

```
ChapterNumber ::= INTEGER
```

Values for PageNumber can be specified as 1, 2, 3, ... and for ChapterNumber as 1, 2, 3, ...

A data type is a **structured type** when it contains other types. Types that are within a structured type are called component types. In the preceding example, a page number of

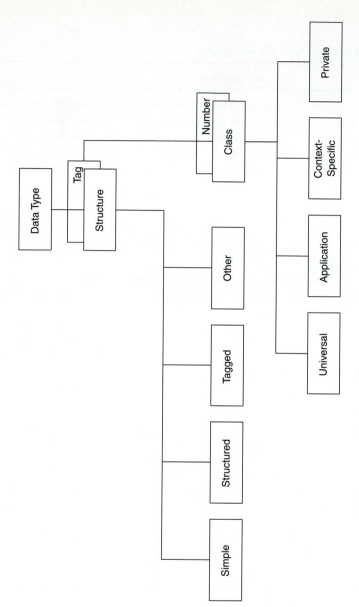

Figure 3.15   ASN.1 Data Type Structure and Tag

a book could be defined as a structured type by a SEQUENCE construction of Chapter-Number and PageNumber component data types. Let's call it BookPageNumber.

        BookPageNumber ::= SEQUENCE
                          {ChapterNumber, Separator, PageNumber}

where Separator is a VisibleString data type with value "-". BookPageNumber is a structured type. Values for BookPageNumber would then be like 1-1, 2-3, or 6-25.

We can define all the pages of the book as a collection of individual pages. If we want to define them in a sequential order from the first page of the first chapter to the last page of the last chapter we would use a SEQUENCE OF construction. Let us call it BookPages.

        BookPages ::= SEQUENCE OF {BookPageNumber}

We could define the same in an alternative manner as

        BookPages ::= SEQUENCE OF
                        {
                        SEQUENCE
                            {ChapterNumber, Separator, PageNumber}
                        }

These two definitions have the same meaning. Values for BookPages would then be 1-1, 1-2, 1-3, ..., 2-1, 2-2, 2-3, ... The ordering of the values is according to the order in which the data is specified and not according to any sorting of the component data types in the structured construct.

The pages of a book could also be specified as a collection of individual pages in random order. The structured type for BookPages would then be constructed with the SET OF data type construct as:

        BookPages ::= SET OF
        {
        SEQUENCE
            {ChapterNumber, Separator, PageNumber}
        }

Note that we could not have used the SET construct for BookPageNumber because the order of the chapter number, separator, and page number are important to keep. However, we could have used the SET construct to define BookPages as

        BookPages ::= SET {ChapterNumber, Separator, PageNumber}

and assigned values 1-2, 2-3, 1-1, ... in a random order. The order of the values in the transmission of data between sender and receiver is unimportant. Thus, SET is distinguished from SEQUENCE in two respects. First, the data types should all be distinct; and second, the order of values in SET is of no consequence, whereas it is critical in the SEQUENCE construct. It is also worth noting that the component data types in the SEQUENCE construct need not be distinct because the order is preserved.

Tagged type is a type derived from another type that is given a new tag id. Although a data type has a unique tag associated with it, a tagged data type is defined to distinguish types within an application. For instance, in Figure 3.14 although *invoice-no* is an

INTEGER type, which we will soon learn as a universal class with a tag number [2], it could have been assigned a local tag id. This is done sometimes to improve the efficiency of encoding.

The fourth and last category of structure is **other type,** which is a data type that is not predefined. It is chosen from CHOICE and ANY types, which are contained in other types. Type CHOICE defines the selection of one value from a specified list of distinct types. Thus, in Figure 3.13, "research" uses a CHOICE construct to select one of the two alternatives, *product-based* and *basic*. We can represent them with specific values, instead of NULL, as follows:

```
research Research ::= CHOICE
              {
               product-based   ProductType,
               basic           VisibleString
              }
              ProductType ::= VisibleString
```

The type ANY is always supplemented with any valid ASN.1 type defined in another module. We have given two representations for Research, the one above and the other in Figure 3.13, which is as follows:

```
research Research ::= CHOICE
              {
              product-based [0] NULL
              basic [1] NULL
              }
```

We could give a definition of these two options by defining **Research** as follows:

```
Research ::= CHOICE
        {
        product-based ANY,
        basic ANY
        }
```

This definition using ANY specifies that the *product-based* entity could be either NULL or ProductType data type, and similarly *basic* could be either VisibleString or NULL.

Figure 3.13 shows two perspectives of data type: structure and tag. The **structure** that we have so far described addresses how the data type is constructed. On the other hand, **tag** uniquely identifies the data type. It is required for encoding the data types for communication. Every data type except CHOICE and ANY has a tag associated with it. A tag has two components: class and tag number. There are four classes of tag: **universal, application, context-specific,** and **private.** Each data type that belongs to each class is assigned a unique number.

The **universal class** is the most common; and the ASN.1 list of universal class assignments is given in Table 3.5. A core set of assignments is used in all applications. Data types in the universal class are application-independent. It is similar to the use of a global variable in a software program, and is applicable anywhere in a program. It need not be defined repeatedly in the subroutines of the program. BOOLEAN and INTEGER are examples of the universal class, whose tag numbers are [1] and [2], respectively.

Table 3.5   Universal Class Tag Assignments

Tag	Type Name	Set of Values
Universal 1	BOOLEAN	TRUE or FALSE
Universal 2	INTEGER	0, Positive and negative numbers
Universal 3	BIT STRING	A string of binary digits or null set
Universal 4	OCTET STRING	A string of octets or null set
Universal 5	NULL	Null, single valued
Universal 6	OBJECT IDENTIFIER	Set of values associated with the object
Universal 7	Object description	Human readable text describing the object
Universal 8	EXTERNAL	The type is external to the standard
Universal 9	REAL	Real numbers, expressed in scientific notation Mantissa $\times$ base^{exponent}
Universal 10	ENUMERATED	Specified list of integers
Universal 11	ENCRYPTED	Encrypted information
Universal 12–15	Reserved for future use	
Universal 16	SEQUENCE and SEQUENCE OF	Ordered list of types
Universal 17	SET and SET OF	Unordered list of types
Universal 18	NumericString	Digits 0–9, space
Universal 19	PrintableString	Printable characters
Universal 20	TeletexString	Character set specified by CCITT Recommendation T.61
Universal 21	VideotexString	Character set specified by CCITT Recommendations T.100 and T.101
Universal 22	IA5String	International Alphabet 5, which is equivalent to ASCII
Universal 23	UTCTime	Time format YYMMDDHHMM[SS][local time differential from universal standard time]
Universal 24	GeneralizedTime	Time format YYYYMMDDH-HMM[SS][local time differential from universal standard time]
Universal 25	GraphicString	Graphic character set specified by ISO 8824
Universal 26	VisibleString	Character set specified by ISO 646, equivalent to ASCII
Universal 27	GeneralString	General character string
Universal 28	CharacterString	Character set
Universal 29–	Reserved for future use	

Tags in the **application class** are specific to applications. Examples of application-specific tag numbers are used in examples in Figure 3.13. A universal class tag number can be overridden with an application-specific tag number. Types in two different applications can have the same application-specific tag, but each tag could carry a different meaning in each application.

Application-specific assignments are classified as such. For instance, in the example of BookPageNumber, if we assign BookPageNumber, ChapterNumber, PageNumber and the tags APPLICATION 1, 2, and 3, respectively, the assignment will read

```
BookPageNumber ::= [APPLICATION 1] SEQUENCE {
                   [APPLICATION 2] ChapterNumber,
                                   Separator
                   [APPLICATION 3] PageNumber}
```

When defining large modules, the structure can become large. We can introduce descriptive names and comments on the structure for easy reading. Let's expand the BookPage-Number example as follows:

```
BookPageNumber ::= [APPLICATION 1] SEQUENCE {
    chapter-number [APPLICATION 2] ChapterNumber,
    separator                      Separator
    page-number    [APPLICATION 3] PageNumber}
-- page numbers are grouped by chapter numbers
```

The descriptive words *chapter-number*, *separator*, and *page-number* do not affect the result when encoding this structure, neither do the comments following the "--".

In the previous example, PageNumber is an INTEGER data type. INTEGER can be classified as either UNIVERSAL 2 or APPLICATION 3. This could be encoded either way. This is also the case for ChapterNumber. The efficiency of encoding can be improved if we add the data designation IMPLICIT as below:

```
PageNumber ::= [APPLICATION 3] IMPLICIT INTEGER
```

Such an expression forces the encoding to follow the local tag assignment.

The **context-specific type,** a subset of an application, is limited to that application. Thus, in Example 1 of Figure 3.13, research has a tag [1] associated with the application of PersonnelRecord and under that application, research has two context-specific tags [0] for product-based and [1] basic.

The **private type** is used extensively by vendors of network products. A vendor is assigned a node on the management information tree, and all branches and leaves under that node will be assigned private data types by the vendor.

Before leaving the subject of tags, it is worth noting a special case of the data type INTEGER. It is an ENUMERATED type and is similar to INTEGER. For example, we can define the colors of a rainbow as ENUMERATED type integers:

```
RainbowColors ::= ENUMERATED
    {
          violet(0)
          indigo(1)
          blue(2)
          green(3)
          yellow(4)
          orange(5)
          red(6)
    }
```

In this case, when a value of 5 is designated for the object type **RainbowColors**, it is implied that it is orange. **RainbowColors** could take on only the seven integer values defined.

An example for the **ENUMERATED** type for **INTEGER** from SNMP MIB, which we will cover in Chapter 5, error status in a get-response message is

```
ErrorStatus ::=
        INTEGER {
            noError(0)
            tooBig(1)
            noSuchName(2)
            badValues(3)
            readOnly(4)
            genErr(5)
            }
```

A subtype data type is derived from a parent type. For example, in the **PageNumber** example, if we limit the maximum page number to 255 (based on 2^8), then the assignment would read

```
PageNumber ::= INTEGER (0..255)
```

The parenthesis indicates that it is a subtype expression (see Table 3.2), where the range of integers is from 0 to 255.

Let us conclude this section with a real-life example in network management of a data type—an address translation table in SNMP IP MIB. An entry in the table is of data type **IpNetMediaEntry**, which is a sequence of four managed objects with associated date types. Each of the four objects starts with a lowercase letter, and the associated data type starts with either a capital letter or is all capital letters.

```
IpNetMediaEntry ::= SEQUENCE {
        ipNetToMediaIfIndex     INTEGER
        ipNetToMediaPhysAddress PhysAddress
        ipNetToMediaNetAddress  IpAddress
        ipNetToMediaType        INTEGER}
```

3.6.3   Object Names

In a MIB there is an identifier for each occurrence of an object. In ASN.1, it is the **OBJECT IDENTIFIER**. The object identifier for the Internet model shown in Figure 3.8 is

```
internet OBJECT IDENTIFIER ::= {iso(1) org(3) dod(6) internet(1)}
```

Thus, the object identifier for Internet has the value 1.3.6.1 that we discussed in Section 3.4.1. The MIT shown in Figure 3.8 has been extended to include in the MIB the class private type and is shown in Figure 3.16. Thus, the object identifier for private enterprise IBM is 1.3.6.1.4.1.2.

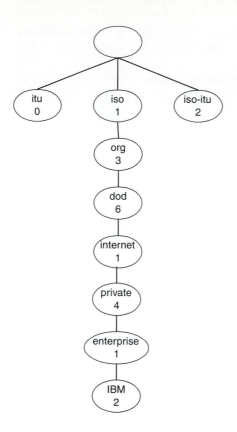

Figure 3.16   IBM as Example of Private Class in MIT

3.6.4   An Example of ASN.1 from ISO 8824

Figure 3.17 shows the ASN.1 structure for a personnel record. Part (a) shows the informal description, part (b) shows the ASN.1 description of the record's structure, and part (c) shows the description of the record value. There are several salient points to note in this example. First, there are no simple types like the page number defined in Section 3.6.2. The data type, Name, does not have an associated object name, although we could define one, for example personnel-name. In such a case, the second line in Figure 3.17(b) would read

```
personnel-name Name
```

PersonnelRecord is a structured data type, SET with the basic component types Name, Title, EmployeeNumber, Date, Name (nameOfSpouse), and ChildInformation. Child-Information itself is a structured data type, a SET consisting of Name and Date as component types. A third structured data type that we notice is SEQUENCE for the data type Name with VisibleString as the component types.

```
Name:                John P Smith
Title:               Director
Employee Number      51
Date of Hire:        17 September 1971
Name of Spouse:      Mary T Smith
Number of Children   2
Child Information
      Name           Ralph T Smith
      Date of Birth  11 November 1957
Child Information
      Name           Susan B Jones
      Date of Birth  17 July 1959
```

(a) Informal Description of a Personnel Record

```
PersonnelRecord ::= [APPLICATION 0] IMPLICIT SET {
    Name,
    title [0] VisibleString,
    number EmployeeNumber,
    dateOfHire [1] Date,
    nameOfSpouse [2] Name,
    children [3] IMPLICIT SEQUENCE OF ChildInformation DEFAULT { } }
ChildInformation ::= SET {
    Name,
    dateOfBirth [0] Date }
Name ::= [APPLICATION 1] IMPLICIT SEQUENCE {
    givenName VisibleString,
    initial VisibleString,
    familyName VisibleString }

EmployeeNumber ::= [APPLICATION 2] IMPLICIT INTEGER

Date ::= [APPLICATION 3] IMPLICIT VisibleString -- YYYYMMDD
```

(b) ASN.1 Description of the Record Structure

```
{ {givenName "John", initial "T", familyName "Smith"},
    title        "Director"
    number       51
    dateOfHire   "19710917"
    nameOfSpouse {givenName "Mary", initial "T", familyName "Smith"},
    children
    {{           {givenName "Ralph", initial "T", familyName "Smith"},
     dateOfBirth "19571111"},
    {            {givenName "Susan", initial "B", familyName "Jones"}
     dateOfBirth      "19590717"}}}
```

(c) ASN.1 Description of the Record Value

Figure 3.17   ISO 8824 Example of Use of ASN.1

The SEQUENCE type is used for Name and the SEQUENCE OF type is used for children, which contains the component type SEQUENCE. Thus, the first occurrence of Name in PersonnelRecord is a SEQUENCE construct and the same construct is embedded in children which is a SEQUENCE OF construct. Thus, we see a nested structure in this example.

The structure for PersonnelRecord is a structured type and it could have been defined without the data designation IMPLICIT, or the local tag [APPLICATION 0]. However, as mentioned in Section 3.6.2, the local tag type has been used to improve the efficiency of coding. Further use of the IMPLICIT designation makes the coding more efficient because INTEGER, for example, will be encoded with the [APPLICATION 2] tag and not the UNIVERSAL tag, which is also applicable. In this situation, it would not be encoded as UNIVERSAL type 2.

3.7   Encoding Structure

The ASN.1 syntax that contains the management information is encoded using the **basic encoding rules** (BER) defined for the transfer syntax. The ASCII text data is converted to bit-oriented data. We will describe one specific encoding structure, called TLV, which denotes type, length, and value components of the structure. This is shown in Figure 3.18. The full record consists of type, length, and value.

The type has three subcomponents: class, P/C, and tag number. P/C specifies whether the structure is a primitive, or simple, type or a construct, which is anything other than a simple type. It is encoded as a one-byte (an octet) field. The two most significant bits (7th and 8th bit) that specify the class are coded according to values defined in Table 3.6. The value of P/C is 0 for primitive and 1 for construct and is designated as the 6th bit. The lowest 5 bits (1–5) designate tag value in binary. For example, INTEGER, from Table 3.5 belongs to the universal class with a tag value of 2 and is a primitive data type. Hence, the type is 00000010.

The length specifies the length of the value field in number of octets. The length is defined as a series of octets. It is either one octet (short) or more than one octet (long). The most significant bit (8th bit) is set to 0 for short length with the low 7 bits indicating the length of the value. If the value field is longer than 127 (maximum specified by 7 bits), then the long form is used for length. The 8th bit of the first octet is marked as 1 and

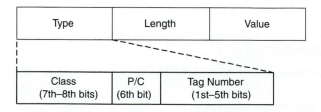

Figure 3.18   TLV Encoding Structure

Table 3.6   Value of Class in Type

Class	8th bit	7th bit
Universal	0	0
Application	0	1
Context-specific	1	0
Private	1	1

the rest of the seven bits of the first octet indicate how many octets follow to specify the length. For example, a value length of 128 would look like

    10000001 10000000

The value field is encoded based on the data type. It is a multiple number of octets. The simplest data type value to encode is an **OCTET STRING**. An octet string of '0C1B'H (the string is designated with apostrophes on both sides and an H to denote hexadecimal notation) would look like

    00001100 00011011

The complete TLV for the string of octets '0C1B'H is made up from universal (00) Primitive (0) data type of tag value of 4 with a one-octet long field to indicate that there are two octets of value field. It is

    00000100 00000010 00001100 00011011

The integer value is encoded using *twos-complement* form which is computed in the following manner. For positive value, the actual value is the binary representation, with the most significant always being 0 to indicate the positive sign. If the integer exceeds 127, an additional octet of 0s is prefixed. Thus a value of 255 is written as **00000000 11111111**, with the leading 0 indicating the positive sign bit. For a negative integer, the absolute value of the integer is written in binary form. The leading sign bit should be 0 to indicate the positive sign. Invert all the 1s to 0s and all the 0s to 1s. Then add 1 to the inverted binary digits. The leading sign bit will automatically become 1, indicating a negative integer. For example, a −5 will start as 00000101. Inverting the bits and adding 1, it becomes 11111011. Refer to [Perkins & McGinnis] for encoding of other values.

3.8   Macros

The data types and values that we have so far discussed use ASN.1 notation of syntax directly and explicitly. ASN.1 language permits extension of this capability to define new data types and values by defining ASN.1 macros. The ASN.1 macros also facilitate grouping of instances of an object and concisely defining various characteristics associated with an object.

```
<macroname> MACRO ::=
BEGIN
    TYPE NOTATION ::= <syntaxOfNewType>
    VALUE NOTATION ::= <syntaxOfNewValue>
    <auxiliaryAssignments>
END
```

Figure 3.19   Structure of an ASN.1 Macro

The structure of a macro takes the form shown in Figure 3.19.

As you can see from Table 3.4, the keyword for a macro is in capital letters. **TYPE NOTATION** defines the syntax of the new types and **VALUE NOTATION** defines the syntax of the new values. The auxiliary assignments define and describe any new types identified.

The **OBJECT-IDENTITY** macro is used to define information about an **OBJECT IDENTIFIER** assignment. Figure 3.20 shows an example from [RFC 1902] of creating an Internet object using the **OBJECT-IDENTITY** macro. The two syntactical expressions **STATUS** and **DESCRIPTION** are mandatory and the type **ReferPart** is optional. The value in **VALUE NOTATION** defines the object identifier.

As an example of the **OBJECT-IDENTITY** macro, let us consider a registration authority that registers all computer science courses offered in the College of Computing. Suppose we want to register the network management course *cs8113* under the object descriptor *csclasses* as the 50th subnode. We can specify an ASN.1 **OBJECT-IDENTITY** macro, as in Figure 3.21. The object identifier *cs8113* has a value {**csclasses 50**}. Its status is current and has a description that explains the course.

```
OBJECT-IDENTITY MACRO
BEGIN
TYPE NOTATION ::=
"STATUS" Status
"DESCRIPTION" Text
ReferPart
VALUE NOTATION ::=
value(VALUE OBJECT IDENTIFIER)
Status ::= "current" | "deprecated" | "obsolete"
ReferPart ::= "REFERENCE" Text I empty
Text ::= """"string""""
END
```

Figure 3.20   An OBJECT-IDENTITY Macro [RFC 1902]

```
cs8113    OBJECT-IDENTITY
     STATUS          current
     DESCRIPTION     "A graduate-level network management course
                     offered by College of Computing in
                     Georgia Institute of Technology."
          ::= {csclasses 50}
```

Figure 3.21   Example of an OBJECT-IDENTITY Macro

3.9   Functional Model

The functional model component of the OSI model addresses the user-oriented applications, which are formally specified in the OSI model and are shown in Figure 3.22. The functional model consists of five submodels: configuration management, fault management, performance management, security management, and accounting management. (Chapter 13 is devoted to the application aspects of network management.)

Configuration management addresses the setting and changing of configurations of networks and their components. Relevant management information is embedded in managed objects such as switches, hubs, bridges, and routers. Configuration management involves setting up these parameters. For example, alarm thresholds could be set to generate alarms when packet loss exceeds a defined value. Information on the object name and the person to be contacted when the component fails could be entered in the management agent. The configuration data is gathered automatically by and stored in the network management system (NMS) at the network operations center (NOC). NMS displays in real-time the configuration of the network and its status.

Fault management involves detection and isolation of the problem causing the failure in the network. An NMS constantly monitors and displays in real-time all major and minor alarms based on the severity of failures. Service is restored as soon as possible, and it could involve reconfiguration of the network, which is part of configuration management. In several failure situations, the network could do this automatically.

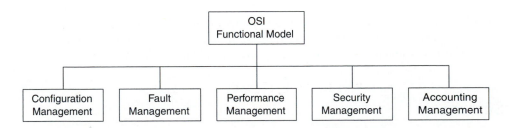

Figure 3.22   Network Management Functional Model

This network feature is called self-healing. In other situations, restoration of service does not include fixing the cause of the problem. Instead, a trouble ticket is generated and followed up for resolution of the problem.

The trouble ticket administration of fault management tracks all problems in the network, including nonproblems, until they are resolved. Periodic analysis of the data, which is maintained in a database, reveals patterns of the problems for follow-up action. There are automatic trouble-tracking systems that track problems from the NMS's generation of a trouble ticket until the resolution of the problem.

Performance management is concerned with the performance behavior of the network. The status of the network is displayed by a network-monitoring system that measures the traffic and performance of the network. The network statistics include data on traffic volume, network availability, and network delay. The traffic data can be captured based on traffic volume in the various segments of the network. In order to manage performance, data must be gathered by the NOC and kept up to date. If changes in the configuration are necessary to relieve traffic congestion temporarily, they are made by the NOC. Permanent relief is engineered by addition of equipment and facilities, as well as through policy changes. Performance-monitoring tools can gather statistics of all protocol layers. We can analyze the various application-oriented traffic such as Web traffic, Internet mail, file transfers, and so on. The statistics on applications could be used to make policy decisions that affect management of the applications. Performance data on availability and delay is useful for tuning the network to increase its reliability and to improve its response time.

Security management covers a broad range of security aspects. It involves physically securing the network, access to the network resources, and secured communication over the network. A security database is established and maintained by the NOC for access to the network and network information. Unauthorized access to the network generates an alarm on the NMS at the NOC. Firewalls protect corporate networks and network resources from being accessed by unauthorized personnel and programs, including virus programs. Secured communication prevents tampering of information as it traverses the network, so that it cannot be accessed or altered by unauthorized personnel. Cryptography plays a vital part in security management.

Accounting management administers costs of the network. Metrics are established to measure the use of resources and services. Traffic data gathered by performance management serves as input to this process.

Another dimension of application management concerns service and business management, which we discuss in Chapter 13. Service and business management is directed toward service providers, in order for them to provide customer satisfaction and to ensure the profitability of business. The traffic statistics, trouble ticket administration data, and accounting management results are inputs to service and business management.

Summary

This chapter addresses the foundations of standards, models, and language needed to delve into the study of network management. These are the tools of the four network management models—OSI, Internet, Telecommunications Network Management, and IEEE 802—and a fifth emerging model that uses Web technology.

The OSI management model categorizes the four functions of network management into four models: organization, information, communication, and application functions. Each of these has been addressed in detail. Some parts of the OSI model apply to the other three management models.

The organization model describes the management process in the network element, called the agent process, and the management process in the manager. We presented the two-tier and three-tier architectural models and the relationship between them.

The information model addresses the structure of management information that enables processes running in different components in the network to exchange management data. We defined the management object for both the OSI and Internet/SNMP management models.

The two primary communication protocols are CMIP in OSI and SNMP in the Internet.

We discussed the syntactical format Abstract Syntax Notation One and how it is applied to defining managed objects. We presented the terminology, symbols, and conventions of ASN.1 and then defined the various categories and structure of data types. We defined the managed objects in OSI and SNMP/Internet management models in adequate detail so that you will be prepared to study SNMP management in the next two chapters. We briefly covered how ASN.1 is applied to specifying the management information tree and MIB by giving some specific examples.

The text-oriented ASN.1 specifications need to be encoded for transmission of data between systems. We discussed the most widely adopted encoding scheme, basic encoding rules (BER).

We defined the extension to ASN.1 in defining an ASN.1 macro and presented an example from the SNMP management model used to create a new object.

The application functions are divided into five categories of management: configuration, fault, performance, security, and accounting. We have addressed each function briefly in this chapter.

Exercises

1. What are the standards used for the various layers in an Ethernet-based network that is managed by the Internet management protocol? Assume that the Ethernet runs on 10 Mbps on an unshielded twisted-pair cable.

2. Consider a network of multivendor components. Hubs are made by Cabletron and are managed by Cabletron's Spectrum NMS. Routers are made by Cisco and are managed by CiscoWorks NMS. The entire network is managed by a general-purpose NMS such as HP OpenView Network Node Manager. Draw a two-tier management network that performs configuration and fault management. Explain the rationale for your configuration.

3. Redraw the management network configuration of Exercise 2 as a three-tier configuration. What are the requirements on the three-tier network management system?

4. Explain succinctly the difference between the database of a network management system and its MIB. How do you implement each in a network management system?

5. You have been assigned the responsibility of adding a new vendor's components with its own NMS to an existing network managed by a different NMS. Identify the three sets of functions that you need to do to fulfill your task.

6. Write an ASN.1 module that specifies DaysOfWeek as a SEQUENCE type with each day of the week (day1, day2, ...) as the type VisibleString. Write the ASN.1 description (a) for the structure and (b) for the value.

7. Write an ASN.1 module that defines daysOfWeek as an ENUMERATED data type, with values from 0 to 6.

8. The following is the informal record structure of my home address:

Name	Mani M. Subramanian
Address	1652 Harts Mill Road
City	Atlanta
State	GA
Zip Code	30319

   Write for your record:

   a. the informal record structure
   b. an ASN.1 description of the record structure
   c. the record value for your home address

9. Given the definition

   ```
   class ::= SET {
   name     VisibleString
   size     INTEGER
   graduate BOOLEAN
   }
   ```

   which of the following set(s) of values is (are) compatible with the ASN.1 record structure in Exercise 8?

   a. "CS4803B", FALSE, 28
   b. CS8113B, TRUE, 28
   c. "CS4803B", 28, TRUE
   d. CS4803B, 28, TRUE

10. a. Describe a list and an ordered list in ASN.1 syntax.
    b. Identify the differences between them.
    c. Using examples, differentiate between list construction and repetitive construction.

11. In a ballroom dance class, the instructor asks the guests to form couples made up of a male and a female (order does not matter) for a dance. Write an ASN.1 module for *danceGroup* with data type *DanceGroup* that is composed of data type *Couple*; *couple is* constructed using *male* and *female*.

12. A high school class consists of four boys and four girls. The names of the boys with their heights are Adam (65"), Chang (63"), Eduardo (72"), and Gopal (62").

The names of the girls are Beth (68"), Dipa (59"), Faye (61"), and Keisha (64"). For each of the following cases, write an ASN.1 description for the structure and record values by selecting appropriate data types. Start with data type **StudentInfo**, listing information on each student.

a. a random list of the students

b. an alphabetized list of students

c. a sorted line up of students with increasing height

d. any one student to be a class representative to the faculty meeting

e. two groups, one of boys and one of girls

13. In Section 3.6.2, we defined the tag for Chapter-number type as APPLICATION [2] Encode this chapter (3) in TLV format.

14. You are establishing a small company. Give an example of each of the five functional applications that you would implement in your network management system.

CHAPTER 4

SNMPv1 Network Management: Organization and Information Models

SNMP management is also referred to as Internet management. We call it SNMP management because it has matured to the level that it manages more than the Internet, for example, intranet and telecommunications networks. Any network that uses the TCP/IP protocol suite is an ideal candidate for SNMP management. SNMP network management systems can manage even non–TCP/IP network elements through proxy agents.

SNMP management is the most widely used network management system (NMS). Most of the network components used in enterprise network systems have built-in network agents that can respond to an SNMP network management system. Thus, if a new component (e.g., a host, a bridge, or a router) that has a built-in SNMP agent, is added to a managed network, the NMS can automatically start monitoring the added component. The ease of adding

141

components and configuring them for management has contributed to the acceptance and popularity of the SNMP management system. To quote Marshall Rose [Rose MT], one of the early architects of SNMP management, the fundamental axiom is, "The impact of adding network management to managed nodes must be minimal, reflecting a lowest common denominator."

SNMP management got started as an interim set of specifications, the ultimate standard being OSI management. Since that did not materialize, SNMP specifications were enhanced by the development of SNMPv2 and SNMPv3; and the first version of SNMP is informally referred to as SNMPv1, as it is titled in this chapter. SNMPv2 and SNMPv3 are covered in Chapters 6 and 7, respectively.

We start with a real-world example of a managed network in Section 4.1 and show the kind of detailed information one could gather from a network management system. We then learn what SNMP management is and how it enables us to obtain that kind of information. The history of SNMP management goes back to 1970 in managing the Internet. The Internet Engineering Task Force (IETF) has the responsibility to develop Internet standards including network management standards. The standards documents are available free in Request for Comments (RFCs), which are covered in Sections 4.2 and 4.3.

Section 4.4 introduces the SNMP management model and addresses primarily organization, information, and communication. A network management system comprises management process, agent process, and network elements. We discuss the various possible configurations in Section 4.5. Three messages are transmitted by the manager and two by the agent for a total of five messages. The management data is obtained by the manager by polling the agents. The agents respond with the requested data, and generate a few alarms when needed. This simple architecture of SNMP management is described in Section 4.6.

The SNMP information model, described in Section 4.7, comprises the Structure of Management Information (SMI) and the Management Information Base. SMI uses ASN.1 syntax to define managed objects. SMIv1, developed in 1990, documented the specifications distinct from the formal ASN.1 definition because it was expected that OSI management would be the future standard. However, that did not happen. Hence, SMIv2 merged the two parts into a concise document. Management Information Base (MIB) defines the relationship between managed objects and groups of related objects into MIB modules. MIB-II is a superset of MIB-I and is used in SNMPv1.

The SNMP architecture, administration, and access policies, which fall under the communication model, are discussed in Chapter 5.

4.1   Managed Network: Case Histories and Examples

Let us look at some real-world experiences that demonstrate the power of network management before learning how it is accomplished. As with any good technology, the power of technology can result in both positive and negative results. Atomic energy is a great resource, but an atomic bomb is not! A network management system is a powerful tool, but it could also bring your network down if it is not "managed" properly.

As part of establishing a network operations center (NOC) as well as teaching a network management course, we made several visits to see how various corporations and institutions manage their networks. One of the visits was to an AT&T network control center, which monitored the network status of their network in the entire eastern half of the United States. We could see on a very large screen the network of nodes and links, mostly in green, indicating that the network was functioning well. The display screen would refresh automatically every few minutes. We saw nodes or links change color to yellow or red, indicating a minor or major alarm. We would also then see them turn back to green without human interference. What we were seeing was monitoring of a national network from a central monitoring center. The monitoring was done by the network management systems and operations support systems without human intervention. Even the healing of the network after a failure was accomplished automatically; it was a self-healing network. Any persistent alarm was pursued by the control center, which tested the network remotely using management tools to isolate and localize the trouble. It was an impressive display of the network management capability.

In another visit to a major international news network's world headquarters, we were shown the monitoring of not only network failures, but also the performance of networks around the globe. The NOC personnel were able to look at the networks in the various continents separately, as well as at the global integrated network. The system was putting out not only alarms, but also the causes of the failures, which was accomplished using the artificial intelligence built into the system.

On a more intimate level, one of the directors of information technology (IT) was narrating his experience of resolving a network failure using the discovery tool that identified new components in the network. A recently added host interface card was the culprit! The problem was solved from a network operations center, without sending an engineer to the remote site.

The flip side to the power of this awesome discovery tool was the experience of another network manager. He was once asked by one of the departments in the campus to shut off the discovery tool because it was flooding the network and degrading the performance. Thus, the powerful network management tools also need to be managed to avoid the degradation of network performance. There are horror stories of networks coming down when turning on network management systems.

When asked what is the greatest benefit of a network management system, one manager answered that it is the consistency of administering, for example configuring, the network. This struck me as an extremely interesting comment because I was once involved in automating the installation and maintenance of a telephone network. One of the operating telephone company managers, who helped in specifications then, commented that we were trying to accomplish an impossible task. He said that there were no standard operations procedures for the company that could be automated, and even in one single operations center, no two groups were following the same procedures! Believe it or not, the project was a success. It standardized the overall process while permitting local deviations.

Let us now illustrate what an NMS can do by monitoring a subnetwork that is using a commercial network management system. The addresses of the network components have been modified for security reasons.

Figure 4.1 shows a managed LAN that was discovered by a network management system. We show here only a subnetwork of a larger network managed by the NMS. As we mentioned, an NMS can automatically discover any component in the network as long as the component has a management agent. The management agent could be as simple as a TCP/IP suite that responds to a ping by the NMS. However, the agents in modern network components are more sophisticated. We will study how NMS does an autodiscovery of the elements in the network in Chapter 12. Let's accept for now that it has been accomplished somehow.

The managed subnetwork that we are discussing here is an Ethernet LAN that is shown below the backbone cloud in Figure 4.1. It consists of a router and two hubs and is connected to the backbone network. The LAN IP address is 172.16.46.1, and the two hub addresses have been configured as 172.16.46.2 and 172.16.46.3. The LAN IP address, 172.16.46.1, is the address assigned to the interface card in the router. The interface cards in the router and the interface card in each of the hubs are connected by a cat-5 cable, forming the Ethernet LAN.

The network management system, whose IP address is 192.168.252.1, is physically and logically located remotely from the 172.16.46.1 LAN. It is configured on the LAN 192.168.252.1, and is connected to the backbone network. Information system managers establish conventions to designate a network and a subnetwork. A 0 in the fourth decimal

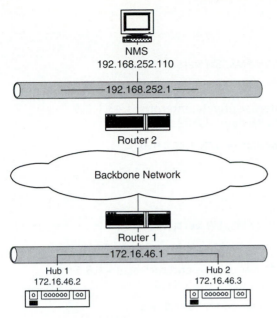

NMS = Network Management System

Figure 4.1   A Managed LAN Network

position of an IP address designates a network; and a subnetwork is designated with a 1 in the fourth position of the dotted decimal notation. Thus, 172.16.46.1 is a LAN subnetwork in the network 172.16.46.0.

Once the network components have been discovered and mapped by the network management system, we can query and acquire information on system parameters and statistics on the network elements. Figure 4.2 presents the system information on the three network elements in the managed LAN that the NMS gathered by sending specific queries about the system parameters.

Figure 4.2(a) shows that the network element is designated by 172.16.46.2. No specific title or name has been assigned to it. System description indicates that it is a hub made by 3Com vendor, with its model (LinkBuilder FMS) and software version (3.02). It also gives the system object ID and how long the system has been up without failure. The format of the system object ID follows the format shown in Figure 3.16 with the 3Com node under enterprises node being 43. The three node numbers, 1.8.5, that follow 43 describe the private management information base of 3Com. The System Up Time indicates that the system has been operating without failure for 286 days. The number in parentheses is in units of hundredths of a second. Thus, the hub designated by the IP address 172.16.46.2 has been up for 2,475,380,437 hundredths of seconds, or 286 days, 12 hours, 3 minutes, 24.37 seconds. System Description and System Object ID are set at the factory and the rest can be set by the user.

Title: System Information: 172.16.46.2
Name or IP Address: 172.16.46.2

System Name   :
System Description : 3Com LinkBuilder FMS, SW version:3.02
System Contact   :
System Location   :
System Object ID   : .iso.org.dod.internet.private.enterprises.43.1.8.5
System Up Time   : (2475380437) 286 days, 12:03:24.37

(a) System Information on 172.16.46.2 Hub

Title: System Information: 172.16.46.3
Name or IP Address: 172.16.46.3

System Name   :
System Description : 3Com LinkBuilder FMS, SW version:3.12
System Contact   :
System Location   :
System Object ID   : .iso.org.dod.internet.private.enterprises.43.1.8.5
System Up Time   : (3146735182) 364 days, 4:55:51.82

(b) System Information on 172.16.46.3 Hub

Title: System Information: router1.gatech.edu
Name or IP Address: 172.16.252.1

System Name   : router1.gatech.edu
System Description : Cisco Internetwork Operating System Software
                    : IOS (tm) 7000 Software (C7000-JS-M), Version
                    : 11.2(6),RELEASE SOFTWARE (ge1)
                    : Copyright (c) 1986-1997 by Cisco Systems, Inc.
                    : Compiled Tue 06-May-97 19:11 by kuong
System Contact   :
System Location   :
System Object ID   : iso.org.dod.internet.private.enterprises.cisco.ciscoProducts.
                      cisco 7000
System Up Time   : (315131795) 36 days, 11:21:57.95

(c) System Information on Router

Figure 4.2   System Information Acquired by an NMS

Figure 4.2(b) shows similar parameters for the second hub, 172.16.46.3, on the LAN. Figure 4.2(c) presents the system information sent by the router on the network in response to the network management system's queries. The system name for the router has been configured and hence the query received the response of the name, router1.gatech.edu.

Figure 4.3(a), (b), and (c) present the data acquired by the NMS from the interface cards on the two hubs and the router, which are on LAN 172.16.46.1. They are addresses associated with each interface. At the top of each figure are the titles and the

Title: Addresses: 172.16.46.2

Name or IP Address: 172.16.46.2

Index	Interface	IP Address	Network Mask	Network Address	Link Address
1	3Com	172.16.46.2	255.255.255.0	172.16 46.0	0x08004E07C25C
2	3Com	192.168.101.1	255.255.255.0	192.168.101.0	<none>

(a) Addresses on 172.16.46.2 Hub Ports

Title: Addresses: 172.16.46.3

Name or IP Address: 172.16.46.3

Index	Interface	IP Address	Network Mask	Network Address	Link Address
1	3Com	172.16.46.3	255.255.255.0	172.16 46.0	0x08004E0919D4
2	3Com	192.168.101.1	255.255.255.0	192.168.101.0	<none>

(b) Addresses on 172.16.46.3 Hub Ports

Title: System Information: router1.gatech.edu

Name or IP Address: 172.162.252.1

Index	Interface	IP Address	Network Mask	Network Address	Link Address
23	LEC.1.0	192.168.3.1	255.255.255.0	192.168.3.0	0x00000C3920B4
25	LEC.3.9	192.168.252.1	255.255.255.0	192.168.252.0	0x00000C3920B4
13	Ethernet2/0	172.16.46.1	255.255.255.0	172.16.46.0	0x00000C3920AC
16	Ethernet2/3	172.16.49.1	255.255.255.0	172.16.49.0	0x00000C3920AF
17	Ethernet2/4	172.16.52.1	255.255.255.0	172.16.52.0	0x00000C3920B0
9	Ethernet1/2	172.16.55.1	255.255.255.0	172.16.55.0	0x00000C3920A6
2	Ethernet0/1	172.16.56.1	255.255.255.0	172.16.56.0	0x00000C39209D
15	Ethernet2/2	172.16.57.1	255.255.255.0	172.16.57.0	0x00000C3920AE
8	Ethernet1/1	172.16.58.1	255.255.255.0	172.16.58.0	0x00000C3920A5
14	Ethernet2/1	172.16.60.1	255.255.255.0	172.16.60.0	0x00000C3920AD

(c) Addresses on Router Ports (Partial List)

Figure 4.3   Addresses Information Acquired by an SNMP NMS

IP address or name of the network interface card used by the NMS to access the network component. Thus, in Figure 4.3(a), the title and the name or IP address are 172.16.46.2. Note that the IP address 172.16.46.3 is the address as seen by the NMS traversing the router. In Figure 4.3(b), IP address 172.16.46.3 is the access address of the second hub on the 172.16.46.1 LAN. Figure 4.3(c) shows the title and name or IP address as router1.gatch.edu and 172.16.252.1, respectively. By using a network lookup command, the IP address of router1.gatech.edu can be recognized as 172.16.252.1. This is the backbone interface address of the router, and it is the interface on the router that is seen by the NMS as it traverses the backbone network.

In Figure 4.3(a), (b), and (c), note that there are six columns of data. The first column is index, which identifies the row in the matrix. Each row is a collection of various addresses associated with an interface. The second column describes the port id. For example, hubs 1 and 2 have 3Com cards in them. Column 2 of Figure 4.3(c) identifies the card and port of the interface. For example, the row with index 2 identifies Ethernet 0 card/port 1. The IP address of the interface card is presented in the third column of the matrix. The IP address in the third column and the network mask address in the fourth column are "and-ed" in modula-2 arithmetic to obtain the network address presented in the fifth column. This implies that all packets destined for network address 172.16.46.0 will be accepted by hub1. The sixth and last column in Figure 4.3, the link address, contains the MAC address. In the first row of Figure 4.3(a), 08004E07C25C is the MAC address of hub1 interface card. The link addresses in the second rows of Figure 4.3(a) and (b) are presented as "none," because they are non–LAN interfaces.

The Figure 4.3(c) matrix has many rows because it is a router with many interface cards, each with multiple ports. For example, each Ethernet card has four physical ports. LEC 1.0 and LEC 3.9 are ATM LAN emulation card (LEC) interfaces.

4.2   The History of SNMP Management

SNMP management began in the 1970s. Internet Control Message Protocol (ICMP) was developed to manage ARPANET (the U.S. government's Advanced Research Project Agency Network). ICMP is a mechanism to transfer control messages between nodes. A popular example of this is Packet Internet Groper (PING), which is part of the TCP/IP suite now. We learned to use PING in Chapter 1 Exercises. PING is a very simple tool that is used to investigate the health of a node and the robustness of communication with it from the source node. It started as an early form of a network-monitoring tool.

The ARPANET, which started in 1969, developed into the Internet in the 1980s with the advent of UNIX and the popularization of client/server architecture. Data was transmitted in packet form using routers and gateways. TCP/IP–based networks grew rapidly, mostly in the defense and academic communities and in small entrepreneurial companies that took advantage of the electronic medium for information exchange. The National Science Foundation officially dropped the name ARPANET in 1984 and adopted the name Internet. Note that Internet is spelled with capital I and is limited to TCP/IP–based networks. An Internet Advisory Board (IAB) was formed to administer Internet activities, which are discussed in the next section.

With the growth of the Internet, it became essential to have the capability to monitor and configure gateways remotely. The Simple Gateway Monitoring Protocol (SGMP) was developed for this purpose as an interim solution. The Internet Advisory Board recommended the development of SNMP, which is an enhancement of SGMP. Even SNMP was intended to be another interim solution, with the long-term solution being migration to the OSI standard CMIP/CMIS. However, due to the enormous simplicity of SNMP and its extensive implementation, it has become the de facto standard. SNMPv2 was developed to make it independent of the OSI standard, as well as to add features. SNMPv2 has only partially overcome some of the limitations of SNMP. The final version of SNMPv2 was released without one of the major enhancements on its security feature because there are strong differences of opinion among Working Group members on the specifications. SNMPv3 addresses the security feature.

4.3 Internet Organizations and Standards

In this section, we will review the organizations responsible for developing Internet standards. We will also trace the evolution of the Internet management documents relating to SNMPv1 and SNMPv2.

4.3.1 Organizations

We mentioned in the previous section that the Internet Advisory Board (IAB) recommended the development of SNMP. The IAB was founded informally in 1983 by researchers working on TCP/IP networks. Its name was changed from the Internet Advisory Board to the Internet Architecture Board in 1989 and it was charged with the responsibility to manage two task forces—the Internet Engineering Task Force (IETF) and the Internet Research Task Force (IRTF).

The IRTF is tasked to consider long-term research problems in the Internet. It creates focused, long-term, and small research groups to work on topics related to Internet protocols, applications, architecture, and technology. With the growth of the Internet, the IETF has grown to be the protocol engineering, development, and standardization arm of the IAB.

The InterNIC (Internet Network Information Center) is an organization that maintains several archives of documents related to the Internet and the IETF's activities. The archives include, among other documents, Request for Comments (RFC), Standard RFC (STD), and For Your Information RFC (FYI). The latter two are subseries of RFCs (more about these in the next section).

The Internet Assigned Numbers Authority (IANA) is the central coordinator for the assignment of unique parameter values for Internet protocols. It is the clearinghouse that assigns and coordinates the use of numerous Internet protocol parameters such as Internet addresses, domain names, autonomous system numbers (used in some routing protocols), protocol numbers, port numbers, management information base object identifiers (including private enterprise numbers), and many others. The common use of the Internet protocols by the Internet community requires that these values be assigned uniquely. It is the IANA's task to make those assignments as requested and to maintain a registry of the assigned values.

4.3.2 Internet Documents

Originally, RFC was just what the name implies, a Request for Comments. The early RFCs were messages between the ARPANET architects about how to resolve certain problems. Over the years, RFC has become more formal. It had reached the point that they were being cited as standards, even when they weren't. To help clear up some confusion, there are now two special subseries within the RFCs: FYIs and STDs. The "For Your Information" RFC subseries was created to document overviews and topics that are introductory. Frequently, FYIs are created by groups within the IETF user services area. The STD RFC subseries was created to identify those RFCs that do in fact specify Internet standards. Every RFC, including FYIs and STDs, have an RFC number by which they are indexed and can be retrieved. FYIs and STDs have FYI numbers and STD numbers, respectively, in addition to RFC numbers. This makes it easier for a new Internet user, for example, to find all of the helpful, informational documents by looking for the FYIs among all the RFCs. If an FYI or STD is revised, its RFC number will change, but its FYI or STD number will remain constant for ease of reference.

RFC documents are available in public libraries and can be accessed via the Internet. Some of the sources that are in the public domain to access RFC and other Internet documents are

ftp://ftp.internic.net/rfc

ftp://nic.mil/rfc

ftp.nic.it

http://nic.internic.net/

A novice to SNMP management could easily be confused as to which RFC document refers to what, namely, SMI, MIB, and SNMP, and so on. It is confusing because the management field and associated documents are continuously evolving. Figure 4.4 portrays a high-level view of the various document paths and documents that are relevant to SNMPv1 and SNMPv2. The documents associated with SNMPv3 are described in Chapter 7. It is not intended to be a complete list, but to identify the major core documents. There are three series of RFC and STD documents: SMI, MIB, and SNMP. As of autumn 1999 three standard documents, STD 15, 16, and 17 have been approved by IETF. STD 15/RFC 1157 defines the SNMP protocol. RFCs 1905, on protocol operations, and 1906, on transport mappings, are expanded updates of RFC 1157, but they are still in draft form. They both have gone through interim drafts, RFC 1448 and RFC 1449, respectively. In Figure 4.4 the RFCs in the back of the cascades are earlier versions of drafts that have become obsolete. For example, RFC 1448 has been replaced by RFC 1905.

Structure of Management Information (SMI) forms the contents of RFC 1155, shown in Figure 4.4. A more concise version of SMI is given in RFC 1212 and is a supplement to RFC 1155. They both comprise STD 16 document. RFC 1155 did not address trap events, which is covered in RFC 1215.

MIB has gone through a few iterations. RFC 1213/STD 17 is the version that is currently in use. It is backward compatible with MIB-I specified in RFC 1156, which is obsolete. Legacy systems that have implemented MIB-I can continue to be used with MIB-II implementation.

SNMP is currently under modification and is part of SNMPv2. RFC 1907 is a draft version of MIB-II for SNMPv2.

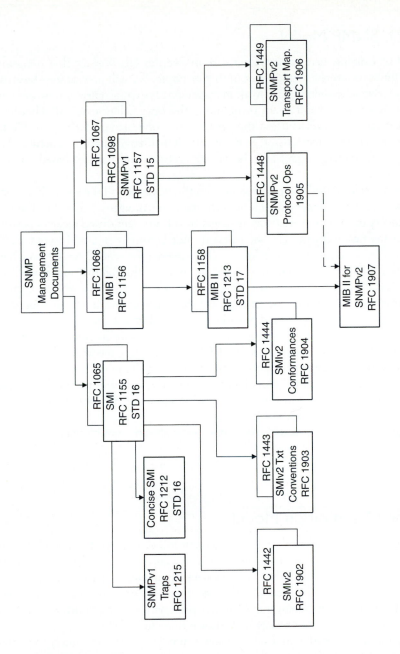

Figure 4.4   The Evolution of SNMP Documents (Versions 1 and 2)

4.4   The SNMP Model

We described an example of a managed network in Section 4.1. We saw that numerous management functions were accomplished in that example. We will now address how this is done in SNMP management. A network management system acquires a new network element through a management agent or monitors the ones it has acquired. There is a relationship between the manager and the agent. Since one manager is responsible for managing the designated functions of many agents, it is hierarchical in structure. The infrastructure of the manager-agent and the SNMP architecture that it is based on form the organization model.

Information is transmitted and received by both the manager and the agent. For example, when a new network element with a built-in management agent is added to the network, the discovery process in the network manager broadcasts queries and receives positive responses from the new element. The information must be interpreted both syntactically and semantically by the agent and the manager. (We covered the syntax, ASN.1, in Chapter 3.) Definition of syntax and semantics form the basis of the information model. We present a detailed definition of a managed object, rules for the Structure of Management Information (SMI), and a virtual information database, Management Information Base (MIB), that groups managed objects and provides a relational framework.

Communication between the manager and agents has to happen before information can be exchanged. The TCP/IP suite is used for the transport mechanism. SNMP is defined for the application layer protocol and is presented in Chapter 5.

The functions and services are not addressed explicitly in SNMP management. The security management is covered in the administration model as part of communication. The services are covered as part of SNMP operations.

The organization model, which has gone through an evolutionary process, is described in the next section.

4.5   The Organization Model

The initial organization model of SNMP management is a simple two-tier model. It consists of a network agent process, which resides in the managed object, and a network manager process, which resides in the NMS and manages the managed object. This is shown in Figure 4.5(a). Both the manager and the agent are software modules. The agent responds to any management system that communicates with it using SNMP. Thus, multiple managers can interact with one agent, as shown in Figure 4.5(b).

We can question the need of multiple managers in a system when it is easy to configure and monitor all objects in a network with standard messages. However, to configure a system in detail, more intimate knowledge of the object is needed, and hence an NMS provided by the same vendor would have more capabilities than other vendors' NMSs. Thus, it is common practice to use an NMS to monitor a network of multiple vendor products, and several vendors' NMSs to configure the respective network elements. Further, during fault tracking, a vendor's NMS can probe in more depth the source of failure, even to the level of identification of a component on a printed circuit board.

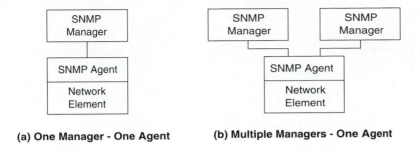

(a) One Manager - One Agent   (b) Multiple Managers - One Agent

Figure 4.5   Two-Tier Organization Models

In the two-tier models, the network manager receives raw data from agents and processes them. It is beneficial sometimes for the network manager to obtain preprocessed data. For example, we may want to look at the traffic statistics, such as input and output packets per second, at an interface on a node as a function of time. Alternatively, we may want to get the temporal data of data traffic in a LAN. Instead of the network manager continuously monitoring the events and calculating the information (e.g., data rate) an intermediate agent called RMON (Remote Monitoring) is inserted between the managed object and the network manager. This introduces a three-tier architecture as shown in Figure 4.6. The network manager receives data from the managed objects as well as data from the RMON agent about the managed objects. The RMON function, implemented in a distributed fashion on the network, has greatly increased the centralized management of networks.

The pure SNMP management system consists of SNMP agents and SNMP managers. However, an SNMP manager can manage a network element that does not have an SNMP agent. Figure 4.7 shows the organizational model for this case. This application occurs in many situations, such as legacy systems management, telecommunications management network, managing wireless networks, and so on. All of these systems are part of overall networks that have to be managed on an integrated basis. As an example in a

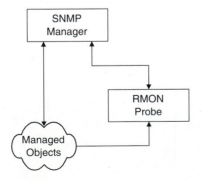

Figure 4.6   Three-Tier Organization Model

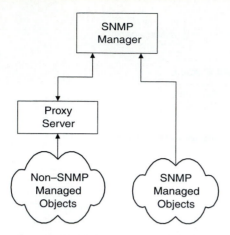

Figure 4.7   Proxy Server Organization Model

legacy case, we may want to manage equipment outside the plant and on the customer's premises for an HFC (hybrid fiber coax) access system in broadband services to home. There are amplifiers on the outside cable plant, which do not have built-in SNMP agents. The outside cable plant uses some of the existing cable technology and has monitoring tools built into it, as for example transponders that measure the various amplifier parameters. The information from the amplifiers could be transmitted to a central (head end) location using telemetry facilities. We can have a proxy server at the central location that converts the data into a set that is compatible with SNMP and communicates with the SNMP manager.

An SNMP management system can behave as an agent as well as a manager. This is similar to client/server architecture, where a host can function as both server and client (see Figure 1.8). In Figure 4.6, RMON, while collecting data from network objects, performs some of the functions (network monitoring) of a network manager. However, the preprocessed data by RMON may be requested by the network manager or sent unsolicited by RMON to the network manager to integrate with the rest of the network data and display it

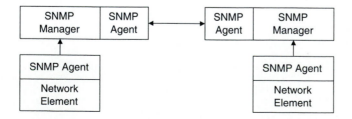

Figure 4.8   An NMS Behaving as Manager and Agent

to the user. In the latter situation, RMON acts as a network agent. Another example of a system acting as both agent and manager is an exchange of information between two NMSs that are managing two autonomous networks that are connected via a gateway. This model is presented in Figure 4.8 and is applicable to two telecommunication service providers managing their respective wide area networks. To provide end-to-end service to customers, the service providers may need to exchange management information.

4.6   System Overview

Now that we have learned the relationship between the network (management) agent and manager and the different ways they can be configured, let us consider SNMP management from a system point of view. We have opted to do this prior to discussing the details of the other three models—information, communication, and functional— because it will help to understand them better if you have the big picture first.

Figure 4.9 shows SNMP network management architecture. It portrays the data path between the manager application process and the agent application process via the

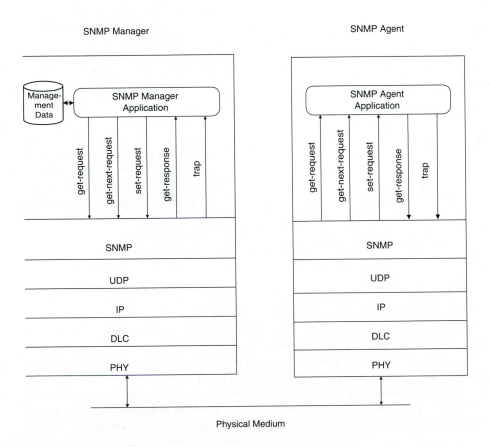

Figure 4.9   SNMP Network Management Architecture

four transport function protocols: UDP, IP, DLC (data link control), and PHY (physical). The three application layers above the transport layer are integrated in the SNMP process.

As we stated in Chapter 1, the Internet model is concerned only with the TCP/IP suite of protocols and does not address the layers above or below it. Thus, layers 1 (physical) and 2 (data link control) in the transport layers can be anything of the users' choice. In practice, SNMP interfaces to the TCP/IP with UDP as the transport layer protocol.

RFC 1157 describes SNMP system architecture. It defines SNMP "by which management information for a network element may be inspected or altered by logically remote users." The two companion RFCs are RFC 1155, which describes the structure and identification of management information, and RFC 1156, which addresses the information base that is required for management.

As the name implies, the SNMP protocol has been intentionally designed to be simple and versatile; this surely has been accomplished, as indicated by its success. The communication of management information among management entities is realized through exchange of just five **protocol messages.** Three of these (get-request, get-next-request, and set-request) are initiated by the manager application process. The other two messages (get-response and trap) are generated by the agent process. The message generation is called an event. In SNMP management scheme, the manager monitors the network by polling the agents as to their status and characteristics. However, efficiency is increased when agents generate unsolicited alarm messages, that is, traps. We'll summarize the messages here and describe structures associated with their PDUs in Chapter 5. RFC 1157 defines the original specifications.

The **get-request** message is generated by the management process requesting the value of an object. The value of an object is a scalar variable. The system group parameters in Figure 4.2 are single-instance values and are obtained using the get-request message.

The **get-next-request**, or simply get-next, is very similar to get-request. In many situations, an object may have multiple values because of multiple instances of the object. For example, we saw in Figure 4.3 that an interface can have multiple addresses associated with a given row. Another example is the routing table of a router, which has multiple values (instances) for each object. In such situations, get-next-request obtains the value of the next instance of the object.

The **set-request** is generated by the management process to initialize or reset the value of an object variable. The settable configuration parameters in Figure 4.2 can be set using the set-request message.

The **get-response** message is generated by an agent process. It is generated only on receipt of a **get-request, get-next-request,** or **set-request** message from a management process. The get-response process involves filling the value of the requested object with any success or error message associated with the response.

The other message that the agent generates is trap. A **trap** is an unsolicited message generated by an agent process without a message or event arriving from the manager process. A trap occurs when the agent observes the occurrence of a preset parameter in the agent module. For example, a node can send traps when an interface link goes up and down. Or, if a network object has a threshold value set for a parameter, such as maximum number of packets queued up, a trap could be generated and transmitted by the agent application whenever the threshold is crossed in either direction.

The SNMP manager, which resides in the NMS, has a database that polls the managed objects for management data. It contains two sets of data: one on the information about the objects, MIB, and a second on the values of the objects. These two are often confused with each other. A MIB is a virtual data (information) base and is static. In fact, a MIB needs to be there when an NMS discovers a new object in the network. It is compiled in the manager during the implementation. If the manager doesn't contain the information about the managed object, it could still detect the object but would mark it as unidentifiable. This is because the discovery process involves a broadcast Ping command by NMS and responses to it from the network components. Thus, a new network component will respond if it has a TCP/IP stack that normally has built-in ICMP (Internet Control Message Protocol). However, the response contains only the IP address. A MIB needs to be implemented in both the manager and the agent to acquire the rest of the information, such as system group information shown in Figure 4.2.

The second database is dynamic and contains the measured values associated with the object. This is a true database. It can be implemented using any database architecture chosen by the implementers.

It is worth noting in Figure 4.9 that the SNMP manager has a database, which is the physical database and the SNMP agent does not have a physical database. However, both have MIBs, which are compiled into the software module and not shown in the figure.

4.7   The Information Model

The information model deals with Structure of Management Information (SMI) and Management Information Base (MIB) and they are discussed in the following subsections.

4.7.1   Introduction

Figure 4.9 shows the information exchange between an agent and a manager. In a managed network, there are many managers and agents. For information to be exchanged intelligently between manager and agent processes, there has to be common understanding of both the syntax and semantics. The syntax used to describe management information is ASN.1 and a general introduction to it is given in Chapter 3. In this section, we will address SNMP–specific syntax and semantics of management information. We will address the specification and organizational aspects of managed objects. This is called the Structure of Management Information, SMI, and is defined in RFC 1155. The specifications of managed objects and the grouping of, and relationship between, managed objects are addressed in Management Information Base [RFC 1213].

There are generic objects that are defined by IETF and can be managed by any SNMP–compatible network management system. Objects that are defined by private vendors, if they conform to SMI defined by RFC 1155, and have MIBs specified by RFC

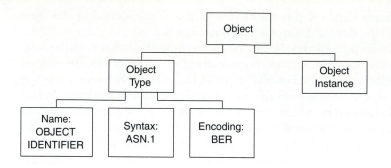

Figure 4.10   Managed Object: Type and Instance

1213, can be managed by SNMP–compatible network management systems. There are other RFCs that address specialized network objects, such as FDDI [RFC 1285], OSPF [RFC 1253], and ATM [RFC 1695]. Private vendor objects are specified in the private MIBs provided by the vendors for their specific products.

4.7.2   The Structure of Management Information

A managed object can be considered to be composed of an object type and an object instance, as shown in Figure 4.10. SMI is concerned only with the object type and not object instance. That is, the object instance is not defined by SMI. For example, Figure 4.2(a) and (b) present data on two 3Com hubs. They are identical hubs, except for a minor software release difference. The object types associated with both hubs are represented by the identical object ID, iso.org.dod.internet.private.enterprises.43.1.8.5. The hub 1 with an IP address 172.16.46.2 is an instance of the object.

Figure 4.11 shows the situation where there are multiple instances of an object type. In Figure 4.2(a) and (b), the hub 1 with an IP address 172.16.46.2 and hub 2 with an IP address 172.16.46.3 are two instances of the object.

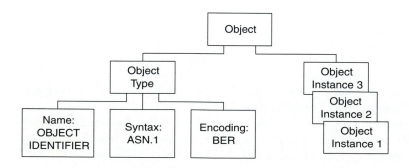

Figure 4.11   Managed Object: Type with Multiple Instances

A managed object need not be just a network element. It could be any object. For example, the Internet as an organization has an object name, "internet", with OBJECT IDENTIFIER 1.3.6.1. Of course, there can be only one instance of it! Thus, a managed object is only a means of identifying an object, whether it is physical or abstract.

Object type, which is a data type, has a name, syntax, and an encoding scheme as discussed in Chapter 3. The name is represented uniquely by a descriptor and object identifier. The syntax of an object type is defined using the abstract Syntax Notation ASN.1. basic encoding rules (BER) have been adopted as the encoding scheme for transfer of data types between agent and manager processes, as well as between manager processes. We will next discuss each of these for SNMP–managed objects in detail.

Names.   Every object type (i.e., every name) is uniquely identified by a DESCRIPTOR and an associated OBJECT IDENTIFIER. DESCRIPTOR and OBJECT IDENTIFIER are in uppercase letters because they are ASN.1 keywords. The **DESCRIPTOR** defining the name is mnemonic and is all in lowercase letters; at least it begins with lowercase letters, as we just described the Internet object as "internet". Since it is mnemonic and should be easily readable, uppercase letters can be used as long as they are not the first letter of the name. For example, the object IP address table is defined as *ipAddrTable*. **OBJECT IDENTIFIER** is a unique name and number in the management information tree, MIT, as we discussed in Chapter 3. We will henceforth use the term Management Information Base (MIB) for the Internet MIT. Thus, Internet MIB has its OBJECT IDENTIFIER 1.3.6.1, as shown in Figure 3.8. It can also be defined in a hybrid mode, as for example,

```
internet OBJECT IDENTIFIER ::= {iso org(3) dod(6) 1}.
```

The information inside the curly brackets can be represented in various ways. This is shown in Figure 4.12. We can use any combination of the unique name and the unique node number on the management tree.

```
internet OBJECT IDENTIFIER ::= { iso(1) standard(3) dod(6)
                                  internet(1) }
internet OBJECT IDENTIFIER ::= { 1 3 6 1 }
internet OBJECT IDENTIFIER ::= { iso standard dod internet }
internet OBJECT IDENTIFIER ::= { iso standard dod(6) internet(1) }
internet OBJECT IDENTIFIER ::= { iso(1) standard(3) 6 1 }
```

Figure 4.12   Different Formats of Declaration of OBJECT IDENTIFIER

Any object in the Internet MIB will start with the prefix 1.3.6.1 or *internet*. For example, there are four objects under the *internet* object. These four objects are defined as

```
directory       OBJECT IDENTIFIER ::= {internet 1}
mgmt            OBJECT IDENTIFIER ::= {internet 2}
experimental    OBJECT IDENTIFIER ::= {internet 3}
private         OBJECT IDENTIFIER ::= {internet 4}
```

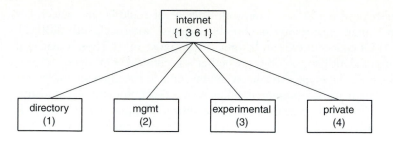

Figure 4.13   Subnodes under Internet Node in SNMPv1

The first line in this example states that the object, directory, is defined as the first node under the object internet. The four subnodes under the "internet" node are shown in Figure 4.13. We will discuss objects in a MIB tree in the next section.

The *directory*(1) node is reserved for future use of OSI Directory in the Internet. The *mgmt*(2) node is used to identify all IETF–recommended and IAB–approved subnodes and objects. As of now the only node connected directly to {internet 2} is *mib-2*. As we said earlier, MIB-II is a superset of MIB-I and hence *mib-2* is the only node under {mgmt} as shown below:

```
mib-2 OBJECT IDENTIFIER ::= {mgmt 1}
```

The *experimental*(3) node was created to define objects under IETF experiments. For example, if IANA has approved a number 5 for an experimenter, we would use the OBJECT IDENTIFIER {experimental 5}.

The last node is *private*(4). This is a heavily used node. Commercial vendors can acquire a number under enterprises(1), which is under the private(4) node. Thus, we have

```
enterprises OBJECT IDENTIFIER ::= {private 1}
```

or

```
enterprises OBJECT IDENTIFIER ::= {1 3 6 1 4 1}
```

Figure 4.14 shows an example of four commercial vendors—Cisco, HP, 3Com, and Cabletron—who are registered as nodes 9, 11, 43, and 52, respectively, under enterprises(1). Nodes under any of these nodes are entirely left to the discretion of the vendors.

Syntax.   The ASN.1 syntax that was introduced in Chapter 3 is used to define the structure of object types. Not all the constructs of ASN.1 are used in TCP/IP–based SNMP management. Figure 4.15 shows the TCP/IP–based ASN.1 data type. It is very similar to Figure 3.16, but has only three categories under structure: simple, defined, and constructor types, as defined in RFC 1155. The other common terms for these are primitive (or

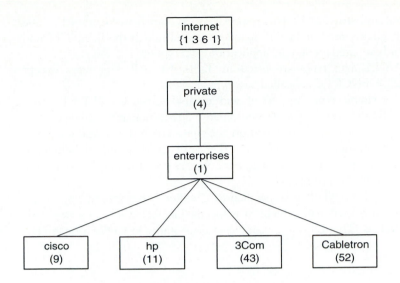

Figure 4.14   A Private Subtree for Commercial Vendors

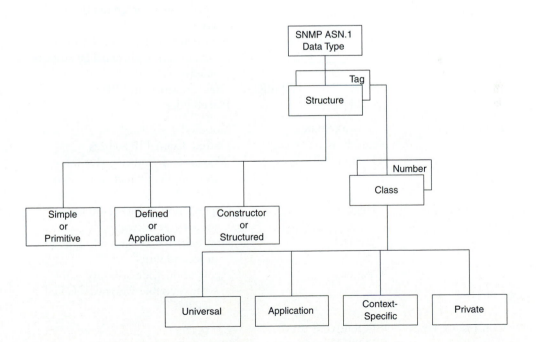

Figure 4.15   SNMP ASN.1 Data Type

atomic), application, and structured types, respectively, as shown in Figure 4.15. The tagged type is not explicitly used in TCP/IP management, although the IMPLICIT and EXTERNAL keywords are used for derived application data types.

The SNMP ASN.1 data types are listed in Table 4.1. All data types except SEQUENCE and SEQUENCE OF are called base types.

The primitive, or **simple types** are atomic and are INTEGER, OCTET STRING, OBJECT IDENTIFIER, and NULL. These are also referred to as nonaggregate types.

INTEGER has numerous variations based on the sign, length, range and enumeration. For a detailed presentation on the subject, see [Perkins D & McGinnis E]. When the integer value is restricted by a range, it is called a subtype, as presented in the comments column of Table 4.1, as INTEGER(n1..nN).

The data type ENUMERATED was specified in Chapter 3 as a special case of the INTEGER data type. In SNMP management, it is specified as INTEGER data type with labeled INTEGER values. The following example of error-status in **GetResponse-PDU**

Table 4.1   SNMP–Based ASN.1 Data Type Structure

Structure	Data Type	Comments
Primitive types	INTEGER	Subtype INTEGER (n1..nN)
		Special case: enumerated INTEGER type
	OCTET STRING	8-bit bytes binary and textual data
		Subtypes can be specified by range or fixed
	OBJECT IDENTIFIER	Object position in MIB
	NULL	Placeholder
Defined types	NetworkAddress	Not used
	IpAddress	Dotted decimal IP address
	Counter	Wraparound, non-negative integer, monotonically increasing, max 2^{32} -1
	Gauge	Capped, non-negative integer, increase or decrease
	TimeTicks	Non-negative integer in hundredths of second units
	Opaque	Application-wide arbitrary ASN.1 syntax, double-wrapped OCTET STRING
Constructor types	SEQUENCE	List maker
	SEQUENCE OF	Table maker

associated with GetRequest-PDU illustrates the use of it. Each enumerated INTEGER has a name associated with it.

```
error-status INTEGER {
     noError(0)
     tooBig(1)
     genErr(5)
     authorizationError(16)
}
```

Any nonzero value indicates the type of error encountered by the agent in responding to a manager's message. As a convention, the value 0 is not permitted in the response message. Thus, a noError message is filled with NULL.

The OCTET STRING data type is used to specify either binary or textual information that is 8 bits long. Just as in INTEGER data type, a subtype in OCTET STRING can be specified. In fact, the subtype value can be either ranged, fixed, or a choice between them. Some examples of the subtype are

```
OCTET STRING (SIZE 0..255)
OCTET STRING (SIZE 8)
OCTET STRING (SIZE 4 | 8)
OCTET STRING (SIZE 0..255 | 8)
```

The combination keyword OBJECT IDENTIFIER, as we discussed earlier, is the object position in the MIB. The fourth primitive type listed in Table 4.1 is NULL. SNMPv1 keywords are listed in Table 4.2

The second category of data types, shown in Figure 4.15 and Table 4.1, consists of **defined types**. These are application-specific data types, and are also SNMP–based types. They are defined using primitive types. The primitive types used are NetworkAddress (not used in SNMP management), IpAddress, Counter, Gauge, and TimeTicks. The base type Opaque is used to specify octets of binary information. It is intended for adding new base types to extend SNMP SMI. Other application-wide data types can be constructed as long as they are IMPLICITly defined using these application data types.

NetworkAddress is a choice of the address of the protocol family. For us, it is the TCP/IP–based Internet family, which uses the base type IpAddress.

IpAddress is the conventional four groups of dotted decimal notation of IPv4, for example 190.146.252.255. The 32-bit string is designated as OCTET STRING of length 4, in network byte order.

Counter is an application-wide data type and is a non-negative integer. It can only increase in value up to a maximum of $2^{32}-1$ (4,294,967,295) and then wraps around starting from 0. Counter type is useful for defining values of data types that continually increase, such as input packets received on an interface or output packet errors on an interface.

The data type **Gauge** is also a non-negative integer, but its value can move either up or down. It pegs at its maximum value of $2^{32}-1$ (4,294,967,295). Gauge is used for data types whose value increases or decreases, such as the number of interfaces that are active in a router or hub.

Table 4.2   SNMPv1 Keywords

ACCESS
BEGIN
CHOICE
Counter
DEFINITIONS
DEFVAL
DESCRIPTION
END
ENTERPRISE
FROM
Gauge
IDENTIFIER
IMPORTS
INDEX
INTEGER
IpAddress
NetworkAddress
OBJECT
OBJECT-TYPE
OCTET
OF
Opaque
REFERENCE
SEQUENCE
SIZE
STATUS
STRING
SYNTAX
TRAP-TYPE
TimeTicks
VARIABLES

TimeTicks is a non-negative integer and measures time in units of hundredths of a second. Its value indicates in hundredths of a second the number of units of time between the current instant and the time it was initialized to 0. The maximum value is $2^{32}-1$ (4,294,967,295). The System Up Time in Figure 4.2 is an example of this.

Opaque is an application-wide data type that supports the capability to pass arbitrary ASN.1 syntax. It is used to create data types based on previously defined data types. When it is encoded, it is double wrapped, meaning the TLV (tag, length, and version) for the new definition is wrapped around the TLV of the previously defined type. Its size is undefined in SNMPv1, which causes some problem in its implementation. It is limited in SNMPv2.

The Opaque data type can be defined both IMPLICITly and EXPLICITly. By use of EXTERNAL type, encoding other than ASN.1 may be used in opaquely encoded data.

The third and last type of structure shown in Figure 4.15 is **constructor**, or **structured, type**. SEQUENCE and SEQUENCE OF are the only two constructor data types in Table 4.1 that are not base types. They are used to build lists and tables. Note that the constructs SET and SET OF, which are in ASN.1, are not included in SNMP–based management syntax. SEQUENCE is used to build a list and SEQUENCE OF is used to build a table. We can conceptualize the list as values in a row of a table.

The syntax for list is

```
SEQUENCE { <type1>, <type2>,..., <typeN> }
```

where each type is one of ASN.1 primitive types.

The syntax for table is

```
SEQUENCE OF <entry>
```

where <entry> is a list constructor.

An illustration of building a list and a table are shown in Figure 4.16(a) and (b). Figure 4.16(a) shows the object *ipAddrEntry* as an entity that is created from a list of objects. The list of objects in Figure 4.16(a) is 1 through 5 in the table. They are all basic types and each row of an object has the object name, OBJECT IDENTIFIER and *ObjectSyntax*. For example, object 1 on row 1 is the IP address defined as *ipAdEntAddr*. It has an OBJECT IDENTIFIER {ipAddrEntry 1} and syntax IpAddress. Note that there are two data types (ObjectSyntax) in the table, namely IpAddress and INTEGER. Thus, the data types can be mixed in building a list. However, they are all basic data types and not constructor types.

The sixth object in the table is the object *ipAddrEntry*, and is made up of the list of the first five objects. The construction for that is a SEQUENCE data type structure as shown. In Figure 4.16(a), the object *ipAdEntReasmMaxSize* has the syntax INTEGER (0..65535), which denotes that it is a subtype and the integer can take on values in the range from 0 to 65535.

Figure 4.16(b) shows the seventh object, *ipAddrTable*. It is node 20 under *ip* node and has SEQUENCE OF construct. The *ipAddrTable* table is made up of instances of *ipAddrEntry* object.

Encoding.   SNMPv1 has adopted the basic encoding rules, BER, with its tag, length, and value (TLV) for encoding the information to be transmitted between agent and manager processes. We discussed this in Chapter 3 and illustrated a few ASN.1 data types. The SNMP data types and tags are listed in Table 4.3. Encoding rules for the various types follow.

OBJECT IDENTIFIER is encoded with each subidentifier value encoded as an octet and concatenated in the same order as in the object identifier. Since a subidentifier could be longer than an octet, the most significant bit (8th bit) is set to 0, if the subidentifier is only one octet long. The 8th bit is set to 1 for the value that requires more than one octet and indicates more octet(s) to follow. An exception to the rule of one or more octets for each subidentifier is the specification of the first two subidentifiers. For example, *iso(1)* and *standard(3)* {1 3}, are coded as 43 in the first octet of the value. As an illustration, let

	Object Name	OBJECT IDENTIFIER	ObjectSyntax
1	ipAdEntAddr	{ipAddrEntry 1}	IpAddress
2	ipAdEntIfIndex	{ipAddrEntry 2}	INTEGER
3	ipAdEntNetMask	{ipAddrEntry 3}	IpAddress
4	ipAdEntBcastAddr	{ipAddrEntry 4}	INTEGER
5	ipAdEntReasmMaxSize	{ipAddrEntry 5}	INTEGER
6	ipAddrEntry	{ipAddrTable 1}	SEQUENCE

```
List:    IpAddrEntry::=
                SEQUENCE{
                    ipAdEntAddr             IpAddress
                    ipAdEntIfIndex          INTEGER
                    ipAdEntNetMask          IpAddress
                    ipAdEntBcastAddr        INTEGER
                    ipAdEntReasmMaxSize     INTEGER (0..65535)
         }
```

(a) Managed Object IpAddrEntry as a List

	Object Name	OBJECT IDENTIFIER	Object Syntax
7	ipAddrTable	{ip 20}	SEQUENCE OF

```
Table:IpAddrTable ::=
             SEQUENCE OF     IpAddrEntry
```

(b) Managed Object ipAddrTable as a Table

Figure 4.16   Example of Building a List and a Table for a Managed Object

us consider the object identifier *internet* {1 3 6 1}. The first octet of the TLV is the UNI-VERSAL 6 tag, and the second octet defines the length of the value, which consists of three octets (43, 6, and 1). Thus the encoded format is

```
00000110 00000011 00101011 00000110 00000001
```

IP Address is encoded as straight octet strings. Counter, gauge, and TimeTicks are coded as integers. Opaque is OCTET STRING type.

Table 4.3 SNMP Data Types and Tags

Type	Tag
OBJECT IDENTIFIER	UNIVERSAL 6
SEQUENCE	UNIVERSAL 16
IpAddress	APPLICATION 0
Counter	APPLICATION 1
Gauge	APPLICATION 2
TimeTicks	APPLICATION 3
Opaque	APPLICATION 4

4.7.3 Managed Objects

In Chapter 3, we briefly looked at the perspective of a managed object in the SNMP model. We will now specify in detail the SNMP data type format that would serve the basis for defining managed objects. We will address the managed objects in the MIB in Section 4.7.4.

Structure of Managed Objects. A managed object, as we saw in Chapter 3, has five parameters: textual name, syntax, definition, access, and status as defined in RFC 1155. For example, *sysDescr* is a data type in the MIB that describes a system. The specifications for the object that describes a system are given in Figure 4.17.

As we notice in Figure 4.17, the **textual name** for an object type is mnemonic and is defined as OBJECT DESCRIPTOR. It is unique and made up of printable strings beginning with a lowercase letter, *sysDescr* in our example. OBJECT DESCRIPTOR defines only the object type, which is a data type. We will henceforth use the term *object type* and

```
OBJECT:
    sysDescr:   { system 1 }
    Syntax:     OCTET STRING
    Definition: "A textual description of the entity. This value
                should include the full name and version
                identification of the system's hardware type,
                software operating system, and networking
                software. It is mandatory that this contain only
                printable ASCII characters."
    Access:     read-only
    Status:     mandatory
```

Figure 4.17 Specifications for System Description

not *data type* when referring to a managed object. OBJECT DESCRIPTOR does not specify instances of a managed object. Thus, it describes the type of object and not the occurrence or instantiation of it, as we pointed out in Section 4.7.2. In Figure 4.2(a) and (b), the system description of the two hubs is 3Com LinkBuilder FMS and the appropriate software version. They both could use the same software version and, hence, could be identical. Identification of each instance is left to the specific protocol that is used, and is not part of the specifications of either SMI or MIB. Thus, the instances of the two hubs in Figure 4.2(a) and (b) are identified with their respective IP addresses, 172.16.46.2 and 172.16.46.3.

Associated with each OBJECT DESCRIPTOR is an OBJECT IDENTIFIER, which is the unique position it occupies in the MIB. In Figure 4.17, *sysDescr* is defined by OBJECT IDENTIFIER {system 1}.

Syntax is the ASN.1 definition of the object type. The syntax of *sysDescr* is OCTET STRING.

A **definition** is an accepted textual description of the object type. It is a basis for the common language, or semantics, to be used by all vendors. It is intended to avoid confusion in the exchange of information between the managed object and the management system, as well as between the various network management systems.

Access is the specification for the type of privilege associated with accessing the information: read-only, read-write, or not-accessible. The first two choices are obvious and the third choice, not-accessible, is applicable, for example, in specifying a table. We access the values of the entries in the table and not the table itself; the table is declared not-accessible. The access for sysDescr is read-only. Its value is defined by the system vendor during the manufacturing process.

Status specifies whether the managed object is current or obsolete. A managed object, once defined, can only be made obsolete and not removed or deleted. If it is current, the implementation of it is specified as either mandatory or optional. Thus, the three choices for status are mandatory, optional, and obsolete. The status for sysDescr is mandatory.

Related objects can be grouped to form an **aggregate object type**. In this case, the objects that make up the aggregate object type are called **subordinate object types**. The subordinate object type could either be simple (primitive type) or an aggregate type. However, it should eventually be made up of simple object types.

Macros for Managed Objects.   In order to encode the above information on a managed object to be processed by machines, it has to be defined in a formalized manner. This is done using macros. Figure 4.18(a) shows a macro where an object type is represented in a formal way [RFC 1155]. A macro always starts with the name of the type—in this case, OBJECT-TYPE—followed by the keyword MACRO, and then the definition symbol. The right side of the macro definition always starts with BEGIN and ends with END.

The body of the macro module consists of three parts: type notation, value notation, and supporting productions. TYPE NOTATION defines the object types in the module and VALUE NOTATION defines the name of the object. In Figure 4.18, the notations SYNTAX, ACCESS, and STATUS define the data types ObjectSyntax, Access, and Status. The notation for value specifies the ObjectName. Supporting

```
OBJECT-TYPE MACRO ::=
BEGIN
     TYPE NOTATION ::= "SYNTAX" type (TYPE ObjectSyntax)
          "ACCESS" Access
          "STATUS" Status
     VALUE NOTATION ::= value (VALUE ObjectName)
     Access ::= "read-only" | "write-only" | "not-accessible"
     Status ::= "mandatory" | "optional" | "obsolete"
END
```

(a) An OBJECT-TYPE Macro [RFC 1155]

```
sysDescr OBJECT-TYPE
     SYNTAX DisplayString (SIZE (0..255))
     ACCESS read-only
     STATUS mandatory
     DESCRIPTION
          "A textual description of the entity. This value should
          include the full name and version identification of the
          system's hardware type, software operating system, and
          networking software. It is mandatory that this contain
          only printable ASCII characters."
::= {system 1 }
```

(b) A Scalar or Single-Instance Macro: sysDescr [RFC 1213]

Figure 4.18   Scalar OBJECT-TYPE Macro and Example

productions in Figure 4.18 define the allowed values for access and status. Access can be only one of four options: read-only, read-write, write-only, or not-accessible. Allowed values for Status are mandatory, optional, or obsolete.

Figure 4.18(b) shows the application of the macro to the scalar, single-instance managed object, *sysDescr,* which is one of the components of the system group in the MIB, as we shall see in the next section. Its OBJECT IDENTIFICATION is {system 1}. DESCRIPTION gives the textual description of the object.

Aggregate Object.   An aggregate object is a group of related objects. Figure 4.19 shows specifications for an aggregate managed object, *ipAddrTable,* which we briefly considered as an example of structured object type in Figure 4.16. This is the IP address table that defines the IP address for each interface of the managed object. Objects 1 through 5 represent simple object types that make up an entry in a table. The textual name of the entry is *ipAddrEntry.* Thus object 1 with the OBJECT DESCRIPTOR, *ipAdEntAddr,* is the first element of the entity, *ipAddrEntry,* and is given the unique OBJECT IDENTIFICATION {ipAddrEntry 1}. This represents the IP address and has the syntax IpAddress, a keyword listed in Table 4.2. The access privilege is read-only and the status dictates that every managed object and management system is required to implement *ipAdEntAddr.*

OBJECT 1
        ipAdEntAddr   { ipAddrEntry 1 }
    Syntax   IpAddress
    Definition   "The IP address to which this entry's information pertains"
    Access   read-only
    Status   mandatory

OBJECT 2
        ipAdEntIfIndex   { ipAddrEntry 2 }
    Syntax   INTEGER
    Definition   "The index value that uniquely identifies the interface to which this
               entry is applicable. The interface identified by a particular value
               of this index is the same interface as identified by the same value of
               ifIndex."
    Access   read-only
    Status   mandatory

OBJECT 3
        ipAdEntNetMask   { ipAddrEntry 3 }
    Syntax   IpAddress
    Definition   "The subnet mask associated with the IP address of this entry. The value
               of the mask is an IP address with all the network bits set to 1 and the
               host bits set to 0."
    Access   read-only
    Status   mandatory

OBJECT 4
        ipAdEntBcastAddr   { ipAddrEntry 4 }
    Syntax   INTEGER
    Definition   "The value of the least significant bit in the IP broadcast address used
               for sending datagrams on the (logical) interface associated with the IP
               address of this entry. For example, when the Internet standard all-ones
               broadcast address is used, the value will be 1. This value applies to
               both the subnet and network broadcast addresses used by the entity on
               this (logical) interface."
    Access   read-only
    Status   mandatory

OBJECT 5
        ipAdEntReasmMaxSize { ipAddrEntry 5 }
    Syntax   INTEGER (0..65535)
    Definition   "The size of the largest IP datagram that this entity can reassemble
               from incoming IP fragmented datagrams received on this interface."
    Access   read-only
    Status   mandatory

OBJECT 6
        ipAddrEntry   { ipAddrTable 1 }
    Syntax   ipAddrEntry ::= SEQUENCE {
    ipAdEntAddr   IpAddress,
    ipAdEntIfIndex   INTEGER,
    IpAdEntNetMask   IpAddress,
    IpAdEntBcastAddr   INTEGER,
    ipAdEntReasmMaxSize INTEGER (0..65535) }
    Definition   "The addressing information for one of this entity's IP addresses."
    Access   not-accessible
    Status   mandatory

Figure 4.19   Specifications for an Aggregate Managed Object: ipAddrTable

```
OBJECT 7
        ipAddrTable           { ip 20 }
    Syntax         SEQUENCE OF IpAddrEntry
    Definition     "The table of addressing information relevant to this entity's IP
                   addresses."
    Access         not-accessible
    Status         mandatory
```

Figure 4.19   *(continued)*

Object 2 is *ipAdEntIfIndex* and is the second subordinate object type of *ipAddrEntry*. It identifies the interface to which this entry is applicable. The syntax of *ipAdEntIfIndex* is INTEGER, a primitive data type. Access is read-only and status is mandatory.

Objects 3, 4, and 5, *ipAdEntNetMask*, *ipAdEntBcastAddr*, and *ipAdEntReasmMaxSize*, respectively, specify the subnet mask, broadcast address information, and the size of the largest datagram. The definition for each describes the object.

Object 6 is the managed object *ipAddrEntry*, which consists of the subordinate object types of 1 through 5. It describes the complete set of information consisting of the five fields needed for an entry in the IP interface address table. The syntax for *ipAddrEntry* is a SEQUENCE data type consisting of the five data types. Each data type is identified with its OBJECT DESCRIPTOR and syntax. Note that the access for *ipAddrEntry* is not accessible. *IfAddrEntry* is itself a subordinate object type of the managed object *ipAddrTable*. It is the first (and only) element of *ipAddrTable* and has the OBJECT IDENTIFICATION {ipAddrTable 1}.

ipAddrTable is the OBJECT DESCRIPTOR for the IP address table, which has a unique place in the MIB tree with the OBJECT IDENTIFIER {ip 20}. We will see how the managed object *ip* group fits in the MIB tree in the next section. The syntax of *ipAddrTable* is the structure SEQUENCE OF the data type *ipAddrEntry*. Again, the access is not accessible.

As an example of the specifications in Figure 4.19 as they would be used in a table, let us consider the following entry in an IP address table:

```
OBJECT 1 {ipAdEntAddr } = { internet "123.45.2.1".}
OBJECT 2 {ipAdEntIfIndex} = { "1" }
OBJECT 3 {ipAdEntNetMask} = { internet "255.255.255.0" }
OBJECT 4 {ipAdEntBcastAddr} = { "0" }
OBJECT 5 {ipAdEntReasmMaxSize} = { "12000" }
```

The value of *ipAdEntIfIndex* for this entry in the IP address table is equal to 1, and the IP address defining this interface is 123.45.2.1 using the Internet-specific protocol. The value associated with network mask is 255.255.255.0, with *ipAdEntBcastAddr* 0, and with the maximum size of the packet 12,000.

Figure 4.20 presents the macro for the IP address table, a multiple-instance of aggregate managed object presented in Figure 4.19. The text following "--" are comments and

```
-- the IP address table
-- The IP address table contains this entity's IP addressing information.
     ipAddrTable OBJECT-TYPE
         SYNTAX SEQUENCE OF IpAddrEntry
         ACCESS not-accessible
         STATUS mandatory
         DESCRIPTION
             "The table of addressing information
relevant to this entity's IP addresses."
         ::= { ip 20 }

     ipAddrEntry OBJECT-TYPE
         SYNTAX IpAddrEntry
         ACCESS not-accessible
         STATUS mandatory
         DESCRIPTION
             "The addressing information for one of this entity's IP addresses."

         INDEX { ipAdEntAddr }
         ::= { ipAddrTable 1 }

     IpAddrEntry ::=
         SEQUENCE {
           ipAdEntAddr
              IpAddress,
           ipAdEntIfIndex
              INTEGER,
           ipAdEntNetMask
              IpAddress,
           ipAdEntBcastAddr
              INTEGER,
           ipAdEntReasmMaxSize
              INTEGER (0..65535)

     ipAdEntAddr OBJECT-TYPE
         SYNTAX IpAddress
         ACCESS read-only
         STATUS mandatory
         DESCRIPTION
             "The IP address to which this entry's addressing information
pertains."
```

Figure 4.20   Aggregate Managed Object Macro: ipAddrTable [RFC 1155]

```
        ::= { ipAddrEntry 1 }
ipAdEntIfIndex OBJECT-TYPE
    SYNTAX INTEGER
    ACCESS read-only
    STATUS mandatory
    DESCRIPTION
        "The index value that uniquely identifies the interface to which this
entry is applicable. The interface identified by a particular value of this
index is the same interface as identified by the same value of ifIndex."
        ::= { ipAddrEntry 2 }

ipAdEntNetMask OBJECT-TYPE
    SYNTAX IpAddress
    ACCESS read-only
    STATUS mandatory
    DESCRIPTION
        "The subnet mask associated with the IP address of this entry. The
value of the mask is an IP address with all the network bits set to 1 and all the
host bits set to 0."
        ::= { ipAddrEntry 3 }

ipAdEntBcastAddr OBJECT-TYPE
    SYNTAX INTEGER
    ACCESS read-only
    STATUS mandatory
    DESCRIPTION
        "The value of the least significant bit in the IP broadcast address
used for sending datagrams on the (logical) interface associated with the IP
address of this entry. For example, when the Internet standard all-ones broad-
cast address is used, the value will be 1. This value applies to both the subnet
and network broadcast addresses used by the entity on this (logical) interface."
        ::= { ipAddrEntry 4 }

ipAdEntReasmMaxSize OBJECT-TYPE
    SYNTAX INTEGER (0..65535)
    ACCESS read-only
    STATUS mandatory
    DESCRIPTION
        "The size of the largest IP datagram that this entity can reassemble
from incoming IP fragmented datagrams received on this interface."
        ::= { ipAddrEntry 5 }
```

Figure 4.20   *(continued)*

are not encoded. The module starts at the highest level; it defines the *ipAddrTable*, follows with *ipAddrEntry*, and then defines the subordinate object types of *ipAddrEntry*. Note that there is an additional clause, INDEX, in the *ipAddrEntry* macro in Figure 4.20. This uniquely identifies the instantiation of the entry object type in the table. Thus, the *ipAdEntAddr* object uniquely identifies the instantiation. We will discuss this more in the next section on columnar objects.

We have so far presented the structure of management information as it was originally developed in RFC 1155. This helped us understand the two aspects of an object module: specifications and formal structure. Obviously, there is duplication in this. Originally it was developed this way to migrate to OSI specifications. However, with the reality that the OSI standards were not implemented and SNMP standards had been deployed extensively, the specifications and the formal structure were combined into a concise definition of object macro, described in RFC 1212. It is presented in Figure 4.21.

Note that there is the definition of imports from other modules. Also, there are additional clauses—ReferPart, IndexPart, and DefVal—and their associated value definitions. The REFERENCE clause is the textual reference to the document from which the object is being mapped. The INDEX clause is the columnar object identifier, which will be discussed in the next section under columnar objects. DEFVAL is the default value to the object, if applicable.

Aggregate Object as Columnar Object.   The aggregate object that was discussed in the preceding section has been defined formally as columnar objects in RFC 1212. SNMP operations apply exclusively to scalar operations. This means that a single scalar value is retrieved or edited on a managed object with any one operation. However, managed objects do have multiple instances within a system and need to be represented formally. An aggregate object type comprises one or more subtypes; each subtype could have multiple instances, with a value associated with each instance.

It is convenient to conceptually define a tabular structure for objects that have multiple values, such as the IP address table. Such tables can have any number of rows including none, with each row containing one or more scalar objects. This is shown in Figure 4.22(a). Table T contains subordinate object Entry E that is a row in the table. Since the table is a SEQUENCE OF construction with entry E as components, there are multiple entries in the table; that is, there are multiple rows in the table. The entry E is a SEQUENCE construct consisting of subordinate objects, columnar objects 1 through 5.

Figure 4.22(b) shows a five-columnar object with four instances, that is, four rows. Note the convention used in denoting each object in the rows. The columnar objects in each row are denoted by the concatenation of the object identifier of the table, the entry, and then the object, and by the row number. Note that the last two numbers are not like what we would normally think of as row and column sequence in a matrix representation. It is more like column and row designation. Thus, the third occurrence (third row) of the fourth columnar object (fourth column) is T.E.4.3. The value for the row number is the value of the index of the table. For example, *ipAdEntAddr*, which is the IP address, is the index for the IP address table example in Figure 4.20. Hence, the value of the *ipAdEntAddr* will determine the row of the table.

```
IMPORTS
     ObjectName FROM RFC1155-SMI
     DisplayString FROM RFC1158-MIB

OBJECT-TYPE MACRO ::=
BEGIN
     TYPE NOTATION ::=
                     -- must conform to RFC 1155's ObjectSyntax
          "SYNTAX" type (TYPE ObjectSyntax)
          "ACCESS" Access
          "STATUS" Status
          DescrPart
          ReferPart
          IndexPart
          DefValPart
     VALUE NOTATION ::= value (VALUE ObjectName)

     Access ::= "read-only" | "write-only" | "not-accessible"
     Status ::= "mandatory" | "optional" | "obsolete"
     DescrPart ::= "DESCRIPTION" value (description DisplayString) | empty
     ReferPart ::= "REFERENCE" value (reference DisplayString) | empty
     IndexPart ::= "INDEX" "{" IndexTypes "}" | empty
     IndexTypes ::= IndexType | IndexTypes "," IndexType
     IndexType ::=
                  --if indexobject, use SYNTAX
                  --value of the correspondent
                  --OBJECT-TYPE invocation
          value (indexobject ObjectName)
                  --otherwise use named SMI type
                  -- must conform to IndexSyntax below
                   | (type IndexType)
     DefValPart ::=
          "DEFVAL" "{" value (defvalue ObjectSyntax) "}" | empty
END

IndexSyntax ::=
     CHOICE {
          number        INTEGER (0..MAX),
          string        OCTET STRING,
          object        OBJECT IDENTIFIER,
          address       NetworkAddress,
          ipAddress     IpAddress
}
```

Figure 4.21   OBJECT-TYPE Macro: Concise Definition [RFC 1212]

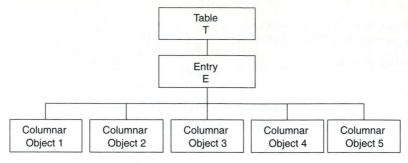

(a) A Multiple-Instance Managed Object

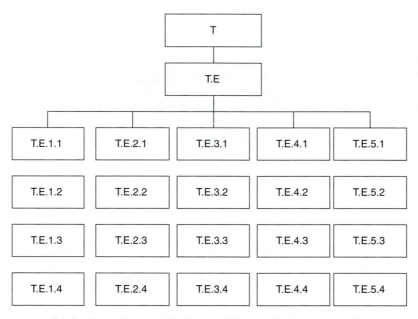

(b) An Example of a 5-Columnar Object with 4 Instances (Rows)

Figure 4.22   Numbering Convention of Managed Object Table

Let us apply this conceptual table to the IP address table we have been following. This is shown in Figure 4.23. Figure 4.23(a) presents the detail of the columnar object, *ipAdEntBcastAddr*, which is the fourth columnar object under *ipAddrEntry*, which is a subordinate object of *ipAddrTable*. The OBJECT IDENTIFIER of the *ipAddrTable* in the MIB is 1.3.6.1.2.1.4.20. The *ipAddrEntry* is node 1 under it and *ipAdEntBcastAddr* is the fourth node under ipAddrEntry. Thus, the columnar object identifier of *ipAdEntBcast-Addr* is {1.3.6.1.2.1.4.20.1.4}.

```
ipAddrTable {1.3.6.1.2.1.4.20}
      ipAddrEntry (1)
            ipAdEntAddr (1)
            ipAdEntIfIndex (2)
            ipAdEntNetMask (3)
            ipAdEntBcastAddr (4)
            ipAdEntReasmMaxSize (5)
```

Columnar object ID of ipAdEntBcastAddr is (1.3.6.1.2.1.4.20.1.4):

iso org dod internet mgmt mib-2 ip ipAddrTable ipAddrEntry ipAdEntBcastAddr
  1   3   6   1   2   1   4   20   1   4

(a) Columnar Objects under ipAddrEntry

Row	ipAdEntAddr	ipAdEntIfIndex	IpAdEntNetMask	IpAdEntBcastAddr	IpAdEntReasmMaxSize
1	**123.45.2.1**	1	255.255.255.0	0	12000
2	**123.45.3.4**	3	255.255.0.0	1	12000
3	**165.8.9.25**	2	255.255.255.0	0	10000
4	**9.96.8.138**	4	255.255.255.0	0	15000

(b) Object instances of ipAddrTable (1.3.6.1.2.1.4.20)

Columnar Object	Row no. in part (b)	Object Identifier
ipAdEntAddr 1.3.6.1.2.1.4.20.1.1	2	{1.3.6.1.2.1.4.20.1.1.123.45.3.4}
ipAdEntIfIndex 1.3.6.1.2.1.4.20.1.2	3	{1.3.6.1.2.1.4.20.1.2.165.8.9.25}
ipAdEntBcastAddr 1.3.6.1.2.1.4.20.1.4	1	{1.3.6.1.2.1.4.20.1.4.123.45.2.1}
IpAdEntReasmMaxSize 1.3.6.1.2.1.4.20.1.5	4	{1.3.6.1.2.1.4.20.1.5.9.96.8.138}

(c) Object ID for Specific Instances

Figure 4.23   A Multiple-Instance Managed Object: ipAddrTable

Figure 4.23(b) shows the tabular presentation of the IP address table. The table shows four rows and six columns. Each of the four rows in the IP address table indicates a set of values associated with each instance of *ipAddrEntry* in the table.

The first column in Figure 4.23(b) is the row number, which we have added to facilitate this explanation; it is not part of the managed objects. The first columnar object *ipAdEntAddr* is in bold letters to indicate that it is the index for the table. Just like each row in an aggregate object table is uniquely identified by the INDEX clause of the OBJECT-TYPE macro, each row in our example is uniquely identified by indexing the value of *ipAdEntAddr*. The second row is the columnar object *ipAdEntIfIndex*. Note that *ipAdEntIfIndex*, which is the same as the *ifNumber* of the Interfaces group, is not an index, but just an object associated with each row of the table. The last three columns in Figure 4.23(b) represent the columnar objects *ipAdEntNetMask*, *ipAdEntBcastAddr*, and *ipAdEntReasmMaxSize*.

Figure 4.23(c) shows the representation of the object identifier associated with each instance. There are four instances illustrated in the figure. The first column is the columnar object identifier, the second column is the row number shown in Figure 4.23(b), and the last column is the object identifier for the instance of the columnar object. Let us first look at the first row of Figure 4.23(c). We want to represent the object identifier associated with the columnar object *ipAdEntAddr* for the specific occurrence presented in the second row of Figure 4.23(b). The object identifier *ipAdEntAddr* in the first of row of Figure 4.23(c) is its columnar object identifier 1.3.6.1.2.1.4.20.1.1. It is suffixed with the value of the table index field *ipAdEntAddr* 123.45.3.4. The resultant object identifier 1.3.6.1.2.1..4.20.1.1.123.45.3.4, is shown in the first row of the last column in Figure 4.23(c). This is the instance of *ipAdEntAddr* in the second row of Figure 4.23(b).

The second entry in Figure 4.23(c) illustrates the object identifier 1.3.6.1.2.1.4.20.1.2.165.8.9.25 for the columnar object *ipAdEntIfIndex* for the instance indicated in the third row of Figure 4.23(b). The third and fourth entries in Figure 4.23(c) illustrate the object identifier values of *ipAdEntBcastAddr* and *ipAdEntReasmMaxSize* for rows 1 and 4 of Figure 4.23(b), respectively.

The formalized definitions of SMI as presented in STD 16/RFC 1155 are shown in Figure 4.24. In addition to the definition of the object type macro, it also specifies the

```
RFC1155-SMI DEFINITIONS ::= BEGIN

    EXPORTS - EVERYTHING
        internet, directory, mgmt, experimental, private, enterprises,
        OBJECT-TYPE, ObjectName, ObjectSyntax, SimpleSyntax,
        ApplicationSyntax, NetworkAddress, IpAddress, Counter, Gauge,
        TimeTicks, Opaque;

    - the path to the root

    internet        OBJECT IDENTIFIER ::= {iso org(3) dod(6) 1}

    directory       OBJECT IDENTIFIER ::= {internet 1}
    mgmt            OBJECT IDENTIFIER ::= {internet 2}
    experimental    OBJECT IDENTIFIER ::= {internet 3}
    private         OBJECT IDENTIFIER ::= {internet 4}
```

Figure 4.24   SMI Definitions [RFC 1155]

```
enterprises    OBJECT IDENTIFIER ::= {private 1}
```

— definition of object types

```
OBJECT-TYPE MACRO ::=
BEGIN
    TYPE NOTATION ::= "SYNTAX" type (TYPE ObjectSyntax)
            "ACCESS" Access
            "STATUS" Status
    VALUE NOTATION ::= value (VALUE ObjectName)

    Access ::= "read-only" | "read-write" | "write-only" | "not-accessible"
    Status ::= "mandatory" | "optional" | "obsolete"
END
```

— names of objects in the MIB

```
ObjectName ::=
  OBJECT IDENTIFIER
```

— syntax of objects in the MIB

```
ObjectSyntax ::=
  CHOICE {
    simple
      SimpleSyntax,
```

— Note that simple SEQUENCEs are not directly mentioned here to keep things simple (i.e., to prevent misuse). However, application-wide types, which are IMPLICITly encoded simple SEQUENCEs, may appear in the following CHOICE.

```
    application-wide
      ApplicationSyntax
}
SimpleSyntax ::=
  CHOICE {
    number
      INTEGER,
    string
      OCTET STRING,
    object
      OBJECT IDENTIFIER,
    empty
      NULL
  }
```

Figure 4.24   *(continued)*

```
ApplicationSyntax ::=
  CHOICE {
    address
      NetworkAddress,
    counter
      Counter,
    gauge
      Gauge,
    ticks
      TimeTicks,
    arbitrary
      Opaque

- Other application-wide types will be added here as they are defined.
  }

- application-wide types

NetworkAddress ::=
  CHOICE {
    internet
      IpAddress
  }
IpAddress ::=
  [APPLICATION 0]      - in network-byte order
    IMPLICIT OCTET STRING (SIZE (4))
Counter ::=
  [APPLICATION 1]
    IMPLICIT INTEGER (0..4294967295)
Gauge ::=
  [APPLICATION 2]
    IMPLICIT INTEGER (0..4294967295)
TimeTicks ::=
  [APPLICATION 3]
    IMPLICIT INTEGER (0..4294967295)
Opaque ::=
  [APPLICATION 4]      - arbitrary ASN.1 value,
    IMPLICIT OCTET STRING - "double-wrapped"
END
```

Figure 4.24   *(continued)*

exports of names and object types, as well as the Internet MIB, which is addressed in the next section.

4.7.4   Management Information Base

As stated in Section 4.7.1, MIB-II specified in RFC 1213 is the current standard, STD 17. It is a superset of MIB-I or simply MIB, as it was then addressed in RFC 1156. We present here MIB-II information. Both MIB-I and MIB-II can be implemented in SNMPv1. MIB is organized such that implementation can be done as needed. The entire MIB does not have to be implemented in either the manager or the agent process.

Let us remember that MIB is a virtual information store (base). Managed objects are accessed via this virtual information base. Objects in the MIB are defined using ASN.1. In the previous section, we discussed the Structure of Management Information (SMI), which defines the mechanism for describing these objects. The definition consists of three components:- **name** (OBJECT DESCRIPTOR), **syntax** (ASN.1), and **encoding** (BER).

The objects defined in MIB-II have the OBJECT IDENTIFIER prefix:

```
mib-2      OBJECT IDENTIFIER ::= {mgmt 1}
```

MIB-II has an additional attribute to the status of a managed object. The new term is "deprecated." This term mandates the implementation of the object in the current version of MIB-II, but it is most likely to be removed in future versions. For example, *atTable* is deprecated in MIB-II.

Object Groups.   Objects that are related are grouped into object groups. Notice that this grouping is different from grouping of object types to construct an aggregate object type. Object groups facilitate logical assignment of object identifiers. One of the criteria for choosing objects to be included in standards is that the object is essential for either fault or configuration management. Thus, if a group is implemented in a system by a vendor, all the components are implemented; that is, status is mandatory for all its components. For example, if external gateway protocol (EGP) is implemented in a system, then all EGP group objects are mandatory to be present.

The MIB module structure consists of the module name, imports from other modules, and definitions of the current module. The basic ASN.1 structure is shown in Figure 4.25.

Eleven groups are defined in MIB-II. The tree structure is shown in Figure 4.26, and Table 4.4 presents the name, object identification (OID), and a brief description of each group. Note that these groups are nodes under the MIB object *mib-2* whose OBJECT IDENTIFIER is 1.3.6.1.2.1.

The System group contains the objects that describe system administration. The Interfaces group defines the interfaces of the network component and the network parameters associated with each interface. The Address Translation group is a cross-reference table between the IP address and the physical address. IP, ICMP, TCP, UDP, and EGP groups are the groups of objects associated with the respective protocol of the system. The group, CMOT, is a placeholder for future use of the OSI protocol, CMIP over TCP/IP. The Transmission group was created as a placeholder for network transmission-related parameters and was a placeholder in RFC 1213. Numerous transmission systems and

```
<module name > DEFINITIONS ::= BEGIN
    <imports>
    <definitions>
END
```

Figure 4.25   A MIB Module Structure

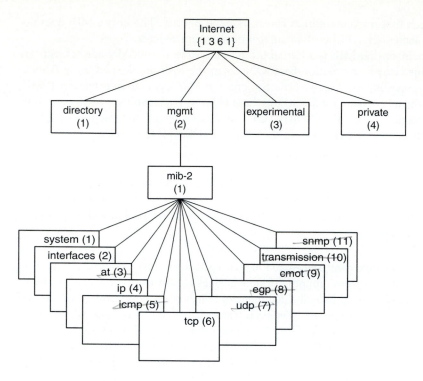

Figure 4.26   Internet MIB-II Group

Table 4.4   MIB-II Groups

Group	OID	Description (brief)
system	mib-2 1	System description and administrative information
interfaces	mib-2 2	Interfaces of the entity and associated information
at	mib-2 3	Address translation between IP and physical address
ip	mib-2 4	Information on IP
icmp	mib-2 5	Information on ICMP
tcp	mib-2 6	Information on TCP
udp	mib-2 7	Information on UDP
egp	mib-2 8	Information on EGP
cmot	mib-2 9	Placeholder for OSI
transmission	mib-2 10	Placeholder for transmission information
snmp	mib-2 11	Information on SNMP

objects have been developed under this group since then. The SNMP group is the communication protocol group associated with SNMP management. We will now learn more about some of these groups. It should be noted that there are more groups defined under the Internet node, which we will address in Chapter 5.

The following sections describe the details of each group except for CMOT, transmission, and SNMP. The CMOT group is a placeholder and is not yet defined. The Transmission group is based on the transmission media that underlie each interface of the system; the corresponding portion of the Transmission group is mandatory for that system. The SNMP group will be addressed in Chapter 5 as part of the communication model.

Although there are many more groups in MIB-II, we present here the details on only the generic groups directly related to physical properties of basic network elements (System and Interfaces) and the managed objects associated with Internet protocols (IP, TCP, and UDP). They are intended to familiarize you quickly with how to read and interpret RFCs that specify the MIBs. It is strongly recommended that you refer to the RFC for detailed specifications on each group and to understand the structure of each MIB group.

We will consider some examples associated with the managed objects in the groups along with a description of the groups so that you can appreciate the significance of each MIB. In Part III, we will learn to use the SNMP command using SNMP tools and retrieve the values associated with managed objects.

The System Group.   The System group is the basic group in the Internet standard MIB. Its elements are probably the most accessed managed objects. After an NMS discovers all the components in a network or the new components in the network, it has to obtain information on the system it discovered, such as system name, object ID, and so on. The NMS will initiate the get-request message on the objects in this group for this purpose. The data on the systems shown in Figure 4.2 were obtained by the NMS using the System group. The group also has administrative information, such as contact person and physical location, that helps a network manager.

Implementation of the System group is mandatory for all systems in both agent and manager. It consists of seven entities, which are presented in Figure 4.27 and Table 4.5. The vendor of the equipment programs the system description (*sysDescr*) and OBJECT IDENTIFIER (*sysObjectId*) during manufacturing. System uptime (*sysUpTime*), in hundredths of a second, is filled in dynamically during operation. Network management systems usually convert this into a more readable format of days, hours, and minutes in their presentation, as shown in Figure 4.2. Although the system services (*sysServices*) object is mandatory to be implemented, most NMSs do not show the information automatically.

The Interfaces Group.   The Interfaces group contains managed objects associated with the interfaces of a system. If there is more than one interface in the system, the group describes the parameters associated with each interface. For example, if an Ethernet

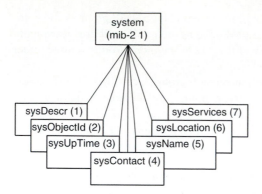

Figure 4.27   System Group

bridge has several network interface cards, the group would cover the information associated with each interface. However, the Interfaces MIB contains only generic parameters. In the Ethernet example, there is more information associated with the Ethernet LAN and these are addressed in the specific MIB associated with the particular medium, as in Definitions of Managed Objects for the Ethernet-like Interface types [RFC 2358]. A network management system would combine information obtained from the various groups to present the comprehensive data to the user.

The Interfaces group specifies the number of interfaces in a network component and the managed objects associated with each interface. Implementation of the Interfaces group is mandatory for all systems. It consists of two nodes, as shown in Figure 4.28 and Table 4.6. The number of interfaces of the entity is defined by *ifNumber*; and the information related to each interface is defined in the Interfaces table, *ifTable*.

Each interface in the Interfaces table can be visualized as attached to either a subnetwork or a system. The term **subnetwork** is not to be confused with the term **subnet,**

Table 4.5   The System Group

Entity	OID	Description (brief)
sysDescr	system 1	Textual description
sysObjectID	system 2	OBJECT IDENTIFIER of the entity
sysUpTime	system 3	Time (in hundredths of a second since last reset)
sysContact	system 4	Contact person for the node
sysName	system 5	Name of the system
sysLocation	system 6	Physical location of the node
sysServices	system 7	Value designating the layer services provided by the entity

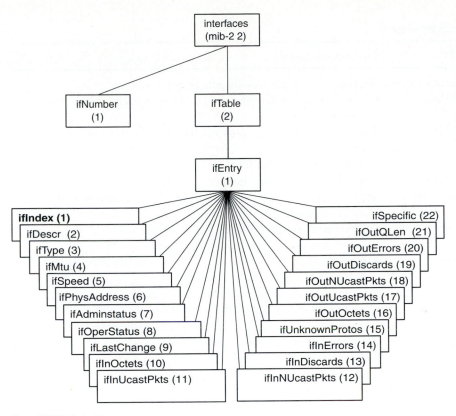

Note: INDEX in bold

Figure 4.28   The Interfaces Group

which refers to an addressing partitioning scheme in the Internet suite of protocols. The index for the table is just one entity, specified by *ifIndex*, as shown below in the definition of the *ifEntry* module under *ifTable*.

```
IfEntry OBJECT-TYPE
     SYNTAX     IfEntry
     ACCESS     not-accessible
     STATUS     mandatory
     DESCRIPTION
          "An interface entry containing objects at the subnet
          work layer and below for a particular interface."
     INDEX     {ifIndex}
     ::= {ifTable 1}
```

Table 4.6   The Interfaces Group

Entity	OID	Description (brief)
ifNumber	interfaces 1	Total number of network interfaces in the system
ifTable	interfaces 2	List of entries that describes information on each interface of the system
ifEntry	ifTable 1	An interface entry that contains objects at the subnetwork layer for a particular interface
ifIndex	ifEntry 1	A unique integer value for each interface
ifDescr	ifEntry 2	Textual data on product name and version
ifType	ifEntry 3	Type of interface layer below the network layer defined as an enumerated integer
ifMtu	ifEntry 4	Largest size of the datagram for the interface
ifSpeed	ifEntry 5	Current or nominal data rate for the interface in bps
ifPhysAddress	ifEntry 6	Interface's address at the protocol layer immediately below the network layer
ifAdminStatus	ifEntry 7	Desired status of the interface: up, down, or testing
ifOperStatus	ifEntry 8	Current operational status of the interface
ifLastChange	ifEntry 9	Value of sysUpTime at the current operational status
ifInOctets	ifEntry 10	Total number of input octets received
ifInUcastPkts	ifEntry 11	Number of subnetwork unicast packets delivered to a higher-layer protocol
ifInNUcastPkts	ifEntry 12	Number of non-unicast packets delivered to a higher-layer protocol
ifInDiscards	ifEntry 13	Number of inbound packets discarded, irrespective of error status
ifInErrors	ifEntry 14	Number of inbound packets with errors
ifInUnknownProtos	ifEntry 15	Number of unsupported protocol packets discarded
ifOutOctets	ifEntry 16	Number of octets transmitted out of the interface
ifOutUcastPkts	ifEntry 17	Total number of unicast packets that higher-level layer requested to be transmitted
ifOutNUcastPkts	ifEntry 18	Total number of non-unicast packets that higher-level layer requested to be transmitted
ifOutDiscrds	ifEntry 19	Number of outbound packets discarded, irrespective of error status
ifOutErrors	ifEntry 20	Number of outbound packets that could not be transmitted because of errors
ifOutQLen	ifEntry 21	Length of the output queue in packets
ifSpecific	ifEntry 22	Reference to MIB definitions specific to the particular media used to realize the interface

The index is also shown in boldface in Figure 4.28 and Table 4.6.

The entity *ifType* describes the type of data link layer directly below the network layer. It is defined as an Enumerated INTEGER. Examples of these are ethernetcsmacd(7), iso88025-tokenRing(9). See RFC 1213 for the specified type of standard interfaces. The administrative status and the operational status, indicated by object identifiers 7 and 8, should agree with each other when the system interface is functioning as administered. Object identifiers 11 through 15 refer to the measurements (with counter syntax) on inbound traffic and object identifiers 16 through 21 to measurements on outbound traffic.

An example of use of the interfaces MIB would be to measure the incoming and outgoing traffic rate on a given interface of an Ethernet hub. We can specify a port on an Ethernet network interface card by the value of *ifIndex* and query (**get-request**) the number of input unicast packets (*ifInUcastPkts*) and the number of output unicast packets (*ifOutUcastPkts*) every second. Remember that we get the reading of two counters, which are incremented with every packet coming in or going out of the port, from the management agent associated with the port. We would then take the difference in the consecutive counter readings to derive the packet rate of traffic.

The Address Translation Group.   The Address Translation group consists of a table that converts NetworkAddress to a physical or subnetwork address for all the interfaces of the system. For example, in Ethernet the translation table is ARP cache. Since in MIB-II each protocol group contains its own translation table, this is not needed and hence its status is deprecated. It is mandatory to be implemented to be backward compatible with MIB-I.

The IP Group.   The Internet uses IP as the networking protocol. The IP group has the information on the various parameters of the protocol. It also has a table that replaces the Address Translation table. The routers in the network periodically execute the routing algorithm and update its routing table, which are defined as managed objects in this group.

The IP group defines all the parameters needed for the node to handle network-layer IP protocol, as either a host or a router. The implementation is mandatory. Figure 4.29 and Table 4.7 present the MIB structure and details of the entities, respectively. The group contains three tables: IP address table, IP routing table, and IP Address Translation table.

We can use the IP MIB to acquire any information associated with the IP layer. For example, to learn the value of the managed object, *ipForwarding* will indicate whether the node is acting as just a route or gateway between two autonomous networks. We can measure the IP datagrams received that are in error, such as those with wrong addresses (*ipInAddrErrors*).

The three tables that belong to the IP group are shown in Figures 4.30, 4.31, and 4.32. Table 4.8 shows the entity table for an IP address table. The index for the table, *ipAdEntAddr,* is shown in boldface.

Figure 4.23(b) gives an example of four instantiations (rows) associated with an IP address table. The IP address table MIB shown in Figure 4.30 and Table 4.8 is used to retrieve the data from the router. It could be retrieved using **get-request** or **get-next-request** messages.

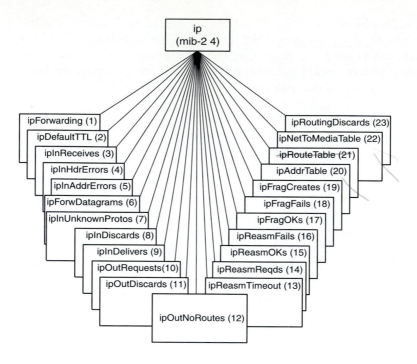

Figure 4.29   IP Group

Table 4.7   The IP Group

Entity	OID	Description (brief)
ipForwarding	ip 1	Node acting as a gateway or not
ipDefaultTTL	ip 2	Time-to-Live field of the IP header
ipInReceives	ip 3	Total number of input datagrams received from interfaces, including those in error
ipInHdrErrors	ip 4	Number of datagrams discarded due to header errors
ipInAddrErrors	ip 5	Number of datagrams discarded due to address errors
ipForwDatagrams	ip 6	Number of input datagrams attempted to forward to the destination; successfully forwarded datagrams for source routing
ipInUnknownProtos	ip 7	Number of locally addressed datagrams received successfully but discarded due to unsupported protocol
ipInDiscards	ip 8	Number of input datagrams discarded due to unsupported protocol
ipInDelivers	ip 9	Total number of input datagrams successfully delivered to IP user protocols
ipOutRequests	ip 10	Total number of IP datagrams which local IP user protocols supplied to IP
ipOutDiscards	ip 11	Number of no-error IP datagrams discarded due to lack of buffer space

Table 4.7   *(continued)*

Entity	OID	Description (brief)
ipOutNoRoutes	ip 12	Number of IP datagrams discarded because no route could be found to transmit them to their destinations
ipReasmTimeOut	ip 13	Maximum number of seconds that received fragments are held while they are awaiting reassembly
ipReasmReqds	ip 14	Number of IP datagrams received that need reassembly
ipReasmOKs	ip 15	Number of successfully reassembled datagrams
ipReasmFails	ip 16	Number of failures detected by the IP reassembly algorithm (not discarded fragments)
ipFragOKs	ip 17	Number of successfully fragmented datagrams
ipFragFails	ip 18	Number of IP datagrams not fragmented due to "Don't Fragment Flag" set
ipFragCreates	ip 19	Number of datagram fragments generated as a result of fragmentation
ipAddrTable	ip 20	Table of IP addresses
ipRouteTable	ip 21	IP routing table containing an entry for each route
ipNetToMediaTable	ip 22	IP Address Translation table that maps IP addresses to physical addresses
ipRoutingDiscards	ip 23	Number of routing entries discarded even though they were valid

The IP routing table is shown in Figure 4.31 and Table 4.9. It contains an entry for each route presently known to the entity. Multiple routes, up to five, to a single destination can appear in the table, but access to such multiple entries depends on the table-access mechanism defined by the network management protocol. The routes are indicated by the entities, *ipRouteMetricN*, where N is any integer from 1 to 5. An entry 0.0.0.0 in *ipRouteDest* is considered a default route. The index for the table is *ipRouteDest*.

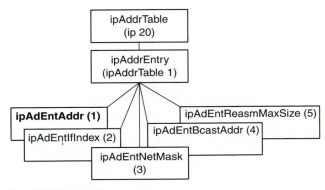

Note: INDEX in bold

Figure 4.30   The IP Address Table

Table 4.8   The IP Address Table

Entity	OID	Description (brief)
ipAddrTable	ip 20	Table of IP addresses
ipAddrEntry	ipAddrTable 1	One of the entries in the IP address table
ipAdEntAddr	ipAddrEntry 1	The IP address to which this entry's addressing information pertains
ipAdEntIfIndex	ipAddrEntry 2	Index value of the entry, same as ifIndex
ipAdEntNetMask	ipAddrEntry 3	Subnet mask for the IP address of the entry
ipAdEntBcastAddr	ipAddrEntry 4	Broadcast address indicator bit
ipAdEntReasmMaxSize	ipAddrEntry 5	Largest IP datagram that can be reassembled on this interface

As in IP address table, the *ipRouteIfIndex* has the same value as the *ifIndex* of the Interfaces table.

Figure 4.32 and Table 4.10 show the IP Address Translation table. It contains cross-references between the IP addresses and physical addresses, such as MAC address of Ethernet interface cards. In some situations, such as DDN-X.25 where this relationship is algorithmic, this table is not needed and hence has zero entries. The indices for this table

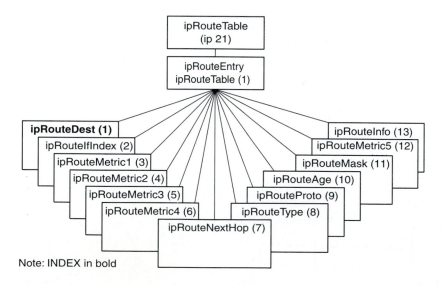

Note: INDEX in bold

Figure 4.31   IP Routing Table

Table 4.9   The IP Routing Table

Entity	OID	Description (brief)
ipRouteTable	ip 21	IP routing table
ipRouteEntry	ipRouteTable 1	Route to a particular destination
ipRouteDest	ipRouteEntry 1	Destination IP address of this route
ipRouteIfIndex	ipRouteEntry 2	Index of interface, same as ifIndex
ipRouteMetric1	ipRouteEntry 3	Primary routing metric for this route
ipRouteMetric2	ipRouteEntry 4	An alternative routing metric for this route
ipRouteMetric3	ipRouteEntry 5	An alternative routing metric for this route
ipRouteMetric4	ipRouteEntry 6	An alternative routing metric for this route
ipRouteNextHop	ipRouteEntry 7	IP address of the next hop
ipRouteType	ipRouteEntry 8	Type of route
ipRouteProto	ipRouteEntry 9	Routing mechanism by which this route was learned
ipRouteAge	ipRouteEntry 10	Number of seconds since routing was last updated
ipRouteMask	ipRouteEntry 11	Mask to be logically ANDed with the destination address before comparing with the ipRouteDest field
ipRouteMetric5	ipRouteEntry 12	An alternative metric for this route
ipRouteInfo	ipRouteEntry 13	Reference to MIB definition specific to the routing protocol

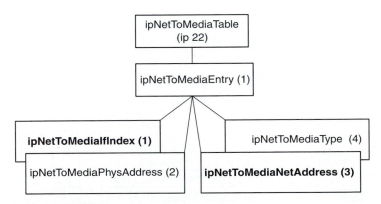

Note: INDEX in bold

Figure 4.32   IP Address Translation Table

Table 4.10   The IP Address Translation Table

Entity	OID	Description (brief)
ipNetToMediaTable	ip 22	Table mapping IP addresses to physical addresses
ipNetToMediaEntry	ipNetToMediaTable 1	IP address to physical address for the particular interface
ipNetToMediaIfIndex	ipNetToMediaEntry 1	Interfaces on which this entry's equivalence is effective; same as ifIndex
ipNetToMediaPhysAddress	ipNetToMediaEntry 2	Media-dependent physical address
ipNetToMediaNetAddress	ipNetToMediaEntry 3	IP address
ipNetToMediaType	ipNetToMediaEntry 4	Type of mapping

consist of two entities, *ipNetToMediaIfIndex* and *ipNetToMediaNetAddress*. Again, the *ipNetToMediaIfIndex* has the same value as *ifIndex* in the Interfaces group.

Baker [RFC 1354] has proposed an improved implementation of the IP routing table, called IP Forwarding Table, which is shown as a MIB tree in Figure 4.33 and the associated table in Table 4.11. The routing table that was originally proposed in RFC 1213 is inconsis-

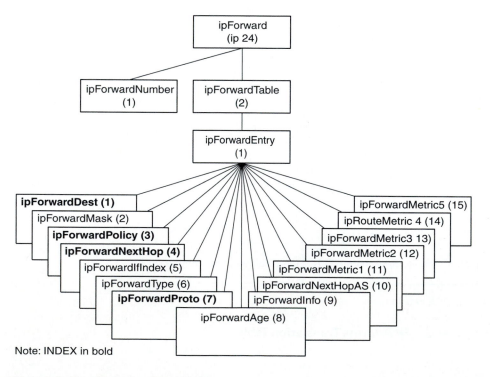

Figure 4.33   IP Forwarding Table

Table 4.11   The IP Forwarding Table

Entity	OID	Description (brief)
ipForward	ip 24	Contains information on IP forwarding table; deprecates IP routing table
ipForwardNumber	ipForward 1	Number of entries in the IP forward table
ipForwardTable	ipForward 2	Routing table of this entity
ipForwardEntry	ipForwardTable 1	A particular route to a particular destination under a particular policy
ipForwardDest	ipForwardEntry 1	Destination IP route of this address
ipForwardMask	ipForwardEntry 2	Mask to be logically ANDed with the destination address before comparing with the ipRouteDest field
ipForwardPolicy	ipForwardEntry 3	Set of conditions that selects one multipath route
ipForwardNextHop	ipForwardEntry 4	Address of the next system
ipForwardIfIndex	ipForwardEntry 5	ifIndex value of the interface
ipForwardType	ipForwardEntry 6	Type of route: remote, local, invalid, or otherwise; enumerated integer syntax
ipForwardProto	ipForwardEntry 7	Routing mechanism by which this route was learned
ipForwardAge	ipForwardEntry 8	Number of seconds since routing was last updated
ipForwardInfo	ipForwardEntry 9	Reference to MIB definition specific to the routing protocol
ipForwardNextHopAS	ipForwardEntry 10	Autonomous system number of next hop
ipForwardMetric1	ipForwardEntry 11	Primary routing metric for this route
ipForwardMetric2	ipForwardEntry 12	An alternative routing metric for this route
ipForwardMetric3	ipForwardEntry 13	An alternative routing metric for this route
ipForwardMetric4	ipForwardEntry 14	An alternative routing metric for this route
ipForwardMetric5	ipForwardEntry 15	An alternative routing metric for this route

tent with SNMP in that no specific policy was defined to choose the path among multiple choices in the IP route table. RFC 1354 has fixed this deficiency. Besides, it has added Next Hop Autonomous System Number, useful to the administrators of regional networks.

The entity *ipForwardPolicy* defines the general set of conditions that would cause the selection of one multipath route over others. Selections of path can be done by the protocol. If it is not done by the protocol, it is then specified by the IP TOS (type-of-service) Field. See Baker [RFC 1354] for more details.

The ICMP Group.   We used ICMP (Internet Control Message Protocol) to do some of the networking exercises in Chapter 1. It is part of the TCP/IP suite of protocols. All parameters associated with ICMP are covered in this group.

As mentioned in Section 4.3, ICMP is a precursor of SNMP and is part of the TCP/IP suite. It is included in MIB-I and MIB-II and implementation is mandatory. The ICMP

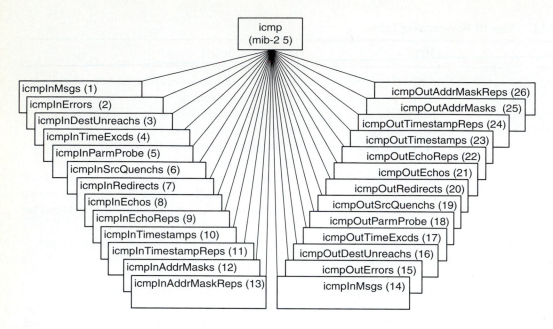

Figure 4.34   ICMP Group

group contains the statistics on ICMP control messages and is presented in Figure 4.34 and Table 4.12. The syntax of all entities is read-only counter. For example, statistics on the number of *ping* requests (icmp echo request) sent might be obtained from the counter reading of *icmpOutEchos*.

Table 4.12   The ICMP Group

Entity	OID	Description (brief)
icmpInMsgs	icmp 1	Total number of ICMP messages received by the entity including icmpInErrors
icmpInErrors	icmp 2	Number of messages received by the entity with ICMP-specific errors
icmpInDestUnreachs	icmp 3	Number of ICMP Destination Unreachable messages received
icmpInTimeExcds	icmp 4	Number of ICMP Time Exceeded messages received
icmpInParmProbs	icmp 5	Number of ICMP Parameter Problem messages received
icmpInSrcQuenches	icmp 6	Number of ICMP Source Quench messages received
icmpInRedirects	icmp 7	Number of ICMP Redirect messages received
icmpInEchos	icmp 8	Number of ICMP Echo (request) messages received
icmpInEchoReps	icmp 9	Number of ICMP Echo Reply messages received

Table 4.12   (continued)

Entity	OID	Description (brief)
icmpInTimestamps	icmp 10	Number of ICMP Timestamp (request) messages received
icmpInTimestampReps	icmp 11	Number of ICMP Timestamp Reply messages received
icmpInAddrMasks	icmp 12	Number of ICMP Address Mask Request messages received
icmpInAddrMaskReps	icmp 13	Number of ICMP Address Mask Reply messages received
icmpOutMsgs	icmp 14	Total number of ICMP messages attempted to be sent by this entity
icmpOutErrors	icmp 15	Number of good ICMP messages not sent, does not include the ones with errors
icmpOutDestUnreachs	icmp 16	Number of ICMP Destination Unreachable messages sent
icmpOutTimeExcds	icmp 17	Number of ICMP Time Exceeded messages sent
icmpOutParmProbs	icmp 18	Number of ICMP Parameter Problem messages sent
icmpOutSrcQuenchs	icmp 19	Number of ICMP Source Quench messages sent
icmpOutRedirects	icmp 20	Number of ICMP Redirect messages sent
icmpOutEchos	icmp 21	Number of ICMP Echo (request) messages sent
icmpOutEchoReps	icmp 22	Number of ICMP Echo Reply messages sent
icmpOutTimestamps	icmp 23	Number of ICMP Timestamp (request) messages sent
icmpOutTimestampReps	icmp 24	Number of ICMP Timestamp Reply messages sent
icmpOutAddrMasks	icmp 25	Number of ICMP Address Mask Request messages sent
icmpOutAddrMaskReps	icmp 26	Number of ICMP Address Mask Reply messages sent

The TCP Group.   The transport layer of the Internet defines TCP (Transmission Control Protocol) for connection-oriented circuits and UDP (User Datagram Protocol) for connectionless circuits.

The TCP group contains entities that are associated with the connection-oriented Transmission Control Protocol, TCP. They are present only as long as the particular connection persists. It is mandatory to implement this group. The entities are shown in Figure 4.35 and Table 4.13. It contains one table, the TCP connection table, which is presented in Figure 4.36 and Table 4.14. The table entry has four indices to uniquely define it in the table. They are *tcpConnLocalAddress*, *tcpConnLocalPort*, *tcpConnRemAddress*, and *tcpConnRemPort* and are identified in boldface. One can obtain all the TCP active sessions from this table with addresses and ports of local and remote entities.

The UDP Group.   The UDP group contains information associated with the connectionless transport protocol. Its implementation is mandatory. Figure 4.37 and Table 4.15 present the UDP group tree structure and entities, respectively. The group contains the

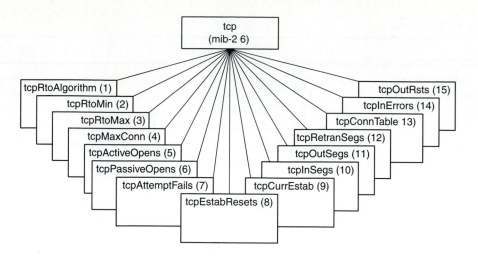

Figure 4.35   TCP Group

Table 4.13   The TCP Group

Entity	OID	Description (brief)
tcpRtoAlgorithm	tcp 1	Timeout algorithm for retransmission of octets
tcpRtoMin	tcp 2	Minimum value for timeout in milliseconds for retransmission
tcpRtoMax	tcp 3	Maximum value for timeout in milliseconds retransmission
tcpMaxConn	tcp 4	Maximum number of TCP connections
tcpActiveOpens	tcp 5	Number of active connections made CLOSED TO SYN-SENT state
tcpPassiveOpens	tcp 6	Number of passive connections made LISTEN to SYN-RCVD state
tcpAttemptFails	tcp 7	Number of failed attempts to make connection
tcpEstabResets	tcp 8	Number of resets done to either CLOSED or LISTEN state
tcpCurrEstab	tcp 9	Number of connections for which the current state is either ESTABLISHED or CLOSED-WAIT
tcpInSegs	tcp 10	Total number of segments received including with errors
tcpOutSegs	tcp 11	Total number of segments sent excluding retransmission
tcpRetransSegs	tcp 12	Total number of segments retransmitted
tcpConnTable	tcp 13	TCO connection table
tcpInErrs	tcp 14	Total number of segments received in error
tcpOutRsts	tcp 15	Number of segment sent containing RST flag

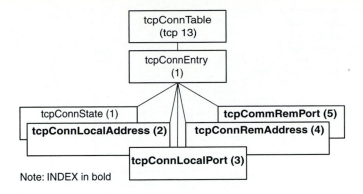

Note: INDEX in bold

Figure 4.36 TCP Connection Table

UDP Listener table, shown as part of Figure 4.37 and Table 4.15. The table contains information about the entity's UDP end-points on which a local application is currently accepting datagrams. The indices for the table entry are *udpLocalAddress* and *udpLocalPort*, and are indicated in boldface.

Table 4.14 The TCP Connection Table

Entity	OID	Description (brief)
tcpConnTable	tcp 13	TCO connection table
tcpconnEntry	tcpConnTable 1	Information about a particular TCP connection
tcpConnState	tcpConnEntry 1	State of the TCP connection
tcpConnLocalAddress	tcpConnEntry 2	Local IP address
tcpConnLocalPort	tcpConnEntry 3	Local port number
tcpConnRemAddress	tcpConnEntry 4	Remote IP address
tcpConnRemPort	tcpConnEntry 5	Remote port number

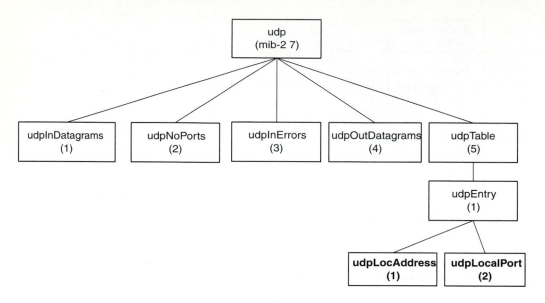

Figure 4.37   UDP Group

Table 4.15   The UDP Group

Entity	OID	Description (brief)
udpInDatagrams	udp 1	Total number of datagrams delivered to the users
udpNoPorts	udp 2	Total number of received datagrams for which there is no application
udpInErrors	udp 3	Number of received datagrams with errors
udpOutDatagrams	udp 4	Total number of datagrams sent
udpTable	udp 5	UDP Listener table
udpEntry	udpTable 1	Information about a particular connection or UDP listener
udpLocalAddress	udpEntry 1	Local IP address
udpLocalPort	udpEntry 2	Local UDP port

Summary

We have learned in this chapter the organization and information aspects of SNMP management. Communication and applications are covered in the next chapter. The subject matter included in this chapter has been approved as a standard by the IETF and implemented by most vendors.

We briefly reviewed the historical development of SNMP standards and documents. They grew more out of practical necessity than the need for setting standards.

The Internet Engineering Task Force is the standards organization and RFC, STD, and FYI are IETF documents on standards development.

SNMP management is organized as a two-tier management, in which a manager process and agent process communicate with each other. The agent process resides in the network element. The manager process is built into network management stations. The agent process does not perform analysis, which is done in the manager. The two-tier structure can be extended to three tiers by sandwiching a proxy agent, or RMON, between the manager and the agent.

All management operations are done using five messages in SNMPv1, which is the current standard. They are get-request, get-next, set-request, get-response, and trap. The first three are sent from the manager to the agent and the last two are sent by the agent to the manager.

The messages are exchanged according to the specifications defined in the Structure of Management Information (SMI). It is composed of a name, syntax, and encoding rules. The name is a unique name for the managed object and an associated unique object identifier. The syntax uses Abstract Syntax Notation 1 (ASN.1) language. The encoding is done using basic encoding rules (BER).

Objects or entities can be composed of other scalar objects. Multiple instances of a managed object, such as an IP address table, are handled by defining tables and columnar objects in the table. Managed objects are organized in a virtual database, called the Management Information Base (MIB). It is distinct from the management database that contains the values for the managed objects. Managed objects are grouped in MIBs according to their functions. MIB-II, which is a superset of MIB-I, consists of eleven groups. Several groups have since been added to the MIB.

Exercises

1. Refer to Figure 4.3 to answer the following questions:
   a. What are the classes of the networks shown in Figure 4.3(a)?
   b. Explain the function of a network mask.
   c. In Figure 4.3(c), network addresses 172.16.x.0 are subnets derived from the network address 172.16.0.0. Explain how the IP address bits are split between subnet and host addresses.

2. Access the Simple Gateway Monitoring Protocol (SGMP) RFC 1028 on the Internet. Describe the four message types defined in the document. (You do not have to present the structure of the message.)

3. Present the OBJECT IDENTIFIER for the object sun.products in two formats, one mnemonic and the other numeric.

4. Represent the objects as OBJECT IDENTIFIERs starting from the root for the three network components in Figure 4.2.
   a. hub in Figure 4.2(a) in hybrid format
   b. hub in Figure 4.2(b) in numeric format
   c. router in Figure 4.2(c) in hybrid format

5. Encode IP Address 10.20.30.40 in TLV format.

6. Refer to RFC 1213 for the following exercise:

   a. Write the ASN.1 specifications for sysServices.

   b. Illustrate the specifications with values for a bridge.

   c. Illustrate the specifications with values for a router.

7. Write the object DESCRIPTOR and syntax of the following SNMP managed entities:

   a. IP address

   b. A row in the Interfaces table (the row specifications only, not the objects in the row)

   c. The MAC address of an interface card

8. In Exercise 4 of Chapter 1, you measured the percentage of packet loss using *ping* tool, which depends on the ICMP group. Name the MIB objects that are used in the procedure and present the macros for the OBJECT TYPE.

9. Explain how you would determine whether a device is acting as a host or as a router using an SNMP command.

10. Refer to the IP Address Translation table shown in Figure 4.32 and Table 4.10 as well as the numbering convention shown in Figure 4.22 to answer the following questions:

   a. List the columnar objects under *ipNetToMediaEntry*.

   b. Draw the object instance table for *ipNetToMediaTable* as in Figure 4.23(b) without the <u>row</u> column. Fill three rows of data using MIB specifications.

   c. Redraw the table in (b), now filling each cell in the table with object instance identifiers. Use N = 1.3.6.1.2.1.4.22.1 for *ipNetToMediaEntry* in the table.

11. You own a specialty company, ABC (Atlanta Braves Company) that sells hats and jackets. You obtained an OBJECT IDENTIFIER 5000 under *enterprises* node from IANA. You have two branch locations. Each has an inventory system that can be accessed by the IP address; they have the following OBJECT DESCRIPTORS:

   branch1 - 100.100.100.15

   branch2 - 100.100.100.16

Each branch has two types of products whose inventory are

   hats

   jackets

Hats are all of the same size and the inventory is a scalar value, hatQuantity.

Jackets come in different sizes and the inventory is maintained in a table, jacketTable, whose columnar objects are

   jacketSize (index)

   jacketQuantity

Create a MIB module for your company. The objective is to find the inventory of any specific product while sitting in your office as president of the company.

   a. Draw a MIB subtree.

   b. Write a MIB module.

12. A network manager discovers that a network component is performing poorly and issues an order to the technician to replace it. Which MIB group contains this information for the technician to find out the physical location of the component?

13. How would you use one of the standard MIB objects to determine which of the stations in a LAN is functioning as a bridge to the external network?

14. TCP is a connection-oriented protocol and UDP is a connectionless protocol. Identify the differences in the two MIBs that exemplify this difference.

15. What OBJECT TYPE would you use to identify the address of the neighboring gateway from your local gateway?

16. An IT manager gets complaints from the users that there is excessive delay in response over the Ethernet LAN. The manager suspects the cause of the problem is excessive collisions on the LAN. She gathers statistics on the collisions using the dot3StatsTable and localizes the problem to a single faulty network interface card. Explain how she localized the problem. You may use RFC 2358 to answer this exercise.

17. FDDI is heavily used as a backbone network in a corporate complex.

   a. Draw a MIB tree for FDDI MIB. Limit your tree to the top five groups.

   b. Develop a three-column table presenting entity, OID, and brief descriptions of the groups and the tables under each group.

CHAPTER 5

*SNMPv1 Network Management:
Communication and Functional Models*

We have covered the organization and information models of SNMPv1 in the previous chapter. In this chapter, we will address the SNMPv1 communication and functional models. Although SNMPv1 does not formally define functional model, the applications are built in the community-based access policy of the SNMP administrative model.

5.1   The SNMP Communication Model

The SNMPv1 communication model defines the specifications of four aspects of SNMP communication: the architecture, the administrative model that defines data access policy, SNMP protocol, and the SNMP MIB. The architecture specifies the management messages between the management system and the management agents. Security in SNMP is managed by defining community, and only members of the same community can communicate with each other. A manager can belong to multiple communities and thus can manage multiple domains. This is the administrative model. We will discuss the protocol entities associated with SNMP protocol specifications. SNMP entities are grouped into an SNMP MIB module.

5.1.1   The SNMP Architecture

The SNMP architecture consists of communication between network management stations and managed network elements, or objects. Network elements have built-in management agents if they are managed elements. The SNMP communications protocol is used to communicate information between the network management stations and the management agents in the elements.

There are three goals of the architecture in the original specifications of SNMP [RFC 1157]. First, it should minimize the number and complexity of the management functions realized by the management agent. Second, it should be flexible enough to allow expansion (addition of new aspects of operation and management). Last, the SNMP architecture should be independent of the architecture and mechanisms of particular hosts and gateways.

Only nonaggregate objects are communicated using SNMP. The aggregate objects are communicated as instances of the object. This has been enhanced in SNMPv2, as we will see in the next chapter. Consistent with the rest of the SNMP standards, ASN.1 and BER are used for data transfer in SNMP.

The SNMP manages the network with the five messages shown in Figure 4.9 and discussed in Chapter 4. They comprise three basic messages: set, get, and trap. The information about the network is obtained primarily by the management stations polling the agents. The **get-request** and **get-next-request** messages are generated by the manager to retrieve data from network elements using the associated management agents. The **set-request** is used to initialize and edit the parameters of the network element. The **get-response-request** is the response from the agent to get (**get-request** and **get-next-request**) and set (**set-request**) messages from the manager. The number of unsolicited messages, in the form of **traps**, is limited to make the architecture simple and to minimize the traffic.

There are three types of traps: generic-trap, specific-trap, and time-stamp. The traps are application specific. The generic-trap type consists of *coldStart, warmStart, linkDown, linkUp, authenticationFailure, egpNeighborLoss,* and *enterpriseSpecific*. The specific-trap is a specific code and is generated even when an enterpriseSpecific trap is not present. For example, a specific-trap that occurs whenever a particular event occurs, such as use by a particular group, would help gather statistics. The time-stamp trap is the time elapsed between the last initialization or reinitialization of the element and the generation of the trap.

The SNMP messages are exchanged using the connectionless UDP transport protocol in order to be consistent with simplicity of the model, as well as to reduce the traffic. However, the mechanisms of the SNMP are suitable for a variety of protocols.

5.1.2   The Administrative Model

Although the administrative model usually would be discussed as part of security and privacy under the functional model, at this point it helps to understand the administrative relationship among entities that participate in the communication protocol in SNMP. Hence, we'll discuss it now.

In RFC 1157 the entities that reside in the management stations and network elements are called SNMP application entities. The peer processes, which implement the SNMP, and thus support the SNMP application entities, are termed protocol entities. We will soon discuss the protocol entities in detail. First, let's look at the application entities.

We'll refer to the **application entity** residing in the management station as the SNMP manager, and the application entity in the element as the SNMP agent. The pairing of the two entities is called an SNMP community. The SNMP community name, called the **community**, is specified by a string of octets. Multiple pairs can belong to the same community. Figure 5.1 shows multiple SNMP managers communicating with a single SNMP agent. While an SNMP manager is monitoring traffic on an element, another manager can be configuring some administrative information on it. A third manager can be monitoring it to perform some statistical study. We also have the analogous situation of a manager communicating with multiple agents.

With the one-to-many, many-to-one, and many-to-many communication links between managers and agents, the basic authentication scheme and the access policy have been specified in SNMP. Figure 5.1 shows the **authentication scheme**, which is a filter module in the manager and in the agent. The simplest form of authentication is the common community name between the two application entities. Encryption would be a higher level of authentication, in which case both the source and the receiver know the common encryption and decryption algorithms.

The SNMP authorization is implemented as part of managed-object MIB specifications. We discussed MIB specifications for managed objects in Chapter 4, and we will discuss MIB specifications for SNMP protocol in Section 5.1.5. A network element comprises many managed objects, both standard and private. However, a management agent may be permitted to view only a subset of the network element's managed objects. This is called the community **MIB view**. In Figure 5.2, the SNMP agent has a MIB view of objects 1, 2, and 3, although there may be other objects associated with a network element. In addition to the MIB view, each community name is also assigned an *SNMP* **access mode**, either READ-ONLY or READ-WRITE, as shown in Figure 5.2. A pairing of the SNMP MIB view with the SNMP access mode is called the **community profile**.

A community profile in combination with the access mode of a managed object determines the operation that can be performed on the object by an agent. For example,

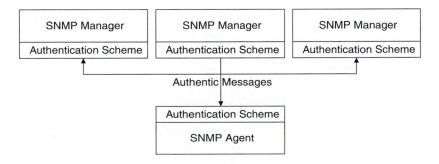

Figure 5.1   An SNMP Community

in Figure 5.2, the SNMP agent with READ-WRITE SNMP access mode can perform all operations—get, set, and trap—on objects 2, 3, and 4. On the other hand, if the SNMP agent has READ-ONLY access privilege, it can perform only get and trap operations on objects 2, 3, and 4. Object 1 has a not-accessible access mode and hence no operation can be performed on it.

There are four access privileges shown in Figure 5.2. They are none, read only, write only, and read-write. The tables are examples of no-access mode. One can only access the scalar objects associated with the entities under the table. Most of the objects available for the public community are read-only, such as the interface statistics and the IP table in a router. These are the get and trap operations. If the access mode is defined as read-write, that operand is available for all three operations (get, set, and trap). An example of read-write access is *sysContact* in the system group. The write-only access mode is used to set the value of MIB object by the network manager, for example *sysDescr* in the system group. This is done in network management systems as implementation-specific.

We can now define SNMP access policy in SNMP management. A pairing of an SNMP community with an SNMP community profile is defined as SNMP **access policy**. This defines the administrative model of SNMP management. Figure 5.3 shows an example of three network management systems in three network operation centers (NOCs), each having access to different community domains. Agents 1 and 2 belong to Community 1. However, they have different community profiles, community profiles 1 and 2. Manager 1, which is part of Community 1, can communicate with both Agents 1 and 2. However, it cannot communicate with Agents 3 and 4, which belong to Community 2. Manager 2 has access to them because it also belongs to Community 2. Agent 3 has community profile 3 and Agent 4 has community profile 4. Manager 3 has access to both Community 1 and 2 and hence can communicate with all the agents. We can picture an enterprise network management fitting this scenario. If a corporation has two operations in two cities, Manager 1 in NOC 1 and Manager 2 in NOC 2 are responsible for managing their respective domains. All of the operations can be viewed and managed by NOC 3 in the headquarters operation.

A practical application of the SNMP access policy can be envisioned in an enterprise management system of a corporation with headquarters in New York and domains

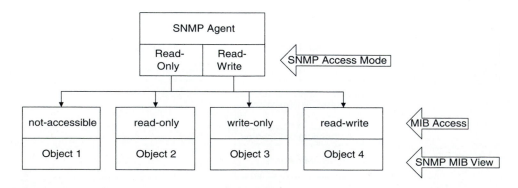

Figure 5.2   An SNMP Community Profile

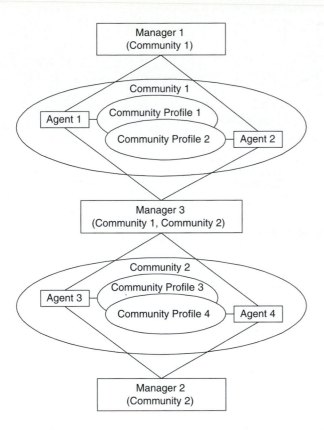

Figure 5.3   SNMP Access Policy

or network sites in New York and San Francisco. Let Manager 1 and Community 1 be associated with San Francisco, and Manager 2 and Community 2 with New York. Let Manager 3 be the overall network management system, MoM. Manager 1 manages Agents 1 and 2 associated with network elements in San Francisco. Manager 2 manages the New York network domain. Manager 1 does not have the view of New York and Manager 2 cannot perform operations on network elements in the San Francisco domain. Manager 3 has both community names defined in its profile and hence has the view of the total enterprise network that comprises New York and San Francisco.

The SNMP access policy has far-reaching consequences, beyond that of servicing a TCP/IP–based Internet SNMP community. It can be extended to managing a non–SNMP community that uses the SNMP proxy access policy. The SNMP agent associated with the proxy policy is called a proxy agent, or commercially a **proxy server**. The **proxy agent** monitors a non–SNMP community with non–SNMP agents and then converts the objects and data to SNMP–compatible objects and data to feed to an SNMP manager.

Figure 5.4 shows an illustration of SNMP and non–SNMP communities being managed by an SNMP manager. A practical example of this would be a network of a LAN and a WAN. The LAN could be a TCP/IP network with SNMP agents. The WAN could be

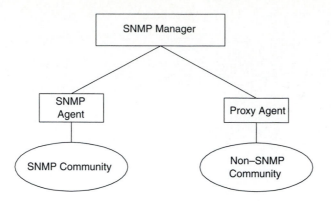

Figure 5.4   SNMP Proxy Access Policy

an X.25 network, which is not an Internet model, but can be managed by a proxy agent and integrated into the overall management system.

5.1.3   SNMP Protocol Specifications

The peer processes, which implement the SNMP, and thus support the SNMP application entities, are called **protocol entities**. Communication among protocol entities is accomplished using messages encapsulated in UDP datagrams. An SNMP message consists of a version identifier, an SNMP community name, and a protocol data unit (PDU). Figure 5.5 shows the encapsulated SNMP message. The version and community name are added to the data PDU and along with the application header the entire message is passed on to the transport layer as SNMP PDU. The UDP header is added at the transport layer, which then forms the transport PDU for the network layer. Addition of an IP header to the transport PDU forms the network PDU for the data link layer. The network or data link layer (DLC) header is added before the frame is transmitted on to the physical medium.

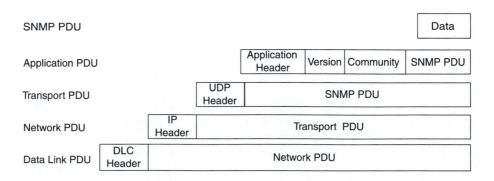

Figure 5.5   Encapsulated SNMP Message

An SNMP protocol entity is received on port 161 on the host except for trap, which is received on port 162. The maximum length of the protocol in SNMPv1 is 484 bytes (1472 bytes now in practice). It is mandatory that all five PDUs be supported in all implementations: GetRequest-PDU, GetNextRequest-PDU, GetResponse-PDU, SetRequest-PDU, and Trap-PDU. One of these five data PDUs is the data PDU that we start with at the top in Figure 5.5. RFC 1157-SNMP Macro definition is given in Figure 5.6.

Basic operations of the protocol entity involve the following steps as a guide to implementation [RFC 1157]. The protocol entity that generates the message constructs the appropriate data PDU as an ASN.1 object. It then passes the ASN.1 object, along

```
RFC1157-SNMP DEFINITIONS ::= BEGIN

IMPORTS
    ObjectName, ObjectSyntax, NetworkAddress, IpAddress, TimeTicks
        FROM RFC1155-SMI

--top-level message

    Message ::=
        SEQUENCE {
            version      -- version-1 for this RFC
             INTEGER {
                 version-1(0)
            },

            community  -- community name
             OCTET STRING,
            data       -- e.g., PDUs if trivial
             ANY       -- authentication is being used
            }

-- protocol data units

    PDUs ::=
        CHOICE {
            get-request          GetRequest-PDU,
            get-next-request     GetNextRequest-PDU,
            get-response         GetResponse-PDU,
            set-request          SetRequest-PDU,
            trap                 Trap-PDU
            }

-- the individual PDUs and commonly used data types will be defined
   later
END
```

Figure 5.6   RFC 1157-SNMP Macro

with a community name and the transport addresses of itself and the destination (e.g., 123.234.245.156:161), to the authentication scheme. The authentication scheme returns another ASN.1 object. The protocol entity now constructs the message to be transmitted with the version number, community name, and the new ASN.1 object, then serializes it using the basic encoding rules (BER), and transmits it.

The reverse process goes on at the receiver. The message is discarded if error is encountered in any of the steps. A trap may be generated in case of authentication failure. On successful receipt of the message, a return message is generated, if the original message is a get or set message.

A managed object is a scalar variable and is simply called a variable. Associated with the variable is its value. The pairing of the variable and value is called **variable binding** or **VarBind**. The data PDU in the message contains a VarBind pair. For efficiency sake, a list of VarBind pairs can be sent in a message. The ASN.1 construct for get and set type of messages is shown in Figure 5.7 and a conceptual presentation in Figure 5.8. The **VarBindList** contains n instances of VarBind (pairs).

```
-- request/response information

RequestId ::=
    INTEGER

ErrorStatus ::=
    INTEGER {
        noError(0)
        tooBig(1)
        noSuchName(2)
        badValue(3)
        readOnly(4)
        genErr(5)
    }

ErrorIndex ::=
    INTEGER

-- variable bindings

VarBind ::=
    SEQUENCE {
        name        ObjectName
        value       ObjectSyntax
    }

VarBindList ::=
    SEQUENCE OF
        VarBind
```

Figure 5.7   Get and Set Type PDU ASN.1 Construct [RFC 1157]

PDU Type	RequestID	Error Status	Error Index	VarBind 1 Name	VarBind 1 Value	...	VarBind n Name	VarBind n Value

Figure 5.8   Get and Set Type PDUs

The PDU type for the five messages is application data type, which is defined in RFC 1157 as:

```
get-request          [0]
get-next-request     [1]
set-request          [2]
get-response         [3]
trap                 [4]
```

In Figure 5.8 RequestID is used to track a message with the expected response or indicate loss of the message (remember UDP is unreliable). Loss-of-message detection is implementation specific, such as time out if no response is received for a request within a given time. A nonzero **ErrorStatus** is used to indicate that an error occurred. The convention is not to use 0 if no error is detected. **ErrorIndex** is used to provide additional information on the error status. The value is filled with NULL in cases where it is not applicable, such as in get-request data PDU. Otherwise, it is filled with the varBind number where the error occurred; for example, 1 if the error occurred in the first *varBind*, 5 if the fifth varBind had the error, and so on.

Figure 5.9 shows the structure for a trap PDU that contains n VarBinds, that is, n managed objects. The enterprise [RFC 1155] and agent-address pertain to the system generating the trap. The generic-trap consists of seven types as listed in Table 5.1. The integer in parenthesis associated with each name indicates the enumerated INTEGER. The specific-trap is a trap that is not covered by the enterpriseSpecific trap. Time-stamp indicates the elapsed time since last re-initialization.

5.1.4   SNMP Operations

SNMP operations comprise get and set messages from manager to agent, and get and trap messages from agent to manager. We will now look at these operations in detail.

The GetRequest-PDU Operation.   Figure 5.10 shows a sequence of operations in retrieving the values of objects in a System group. It starts with the get-request operation,

PDU Type	Enterprise	Agent Address	Generic Trap Type	Specific Trap Type	Timestamp	VarBind 1 name	VarBind 1 value	...	VarBind n name	VarBind n value

Figure 5.9   Trap PDU

Table 5.1   Generic Traps

Generic Trap Type	Description (brief)
coldStart(0)	Sending protocol entity is reinitializing itself; agent's configuration or protocol entity implementation may be altered
warmStart(1)	Sending protocol entity is reinitializing itself; agent configuration or protocol entity implementation not altered
linkDown(2)	Failure of one of the communication links
linkUp(3)	One of the links has come up
authenticationFailure(4)	Authentication failure
egpNeighborLoss(5)	Loss of EGP neighbor
enterpriseSpecific(6)	Enterprise-specific trap

using a **GetRequest**-PDU from a manager process to an agent process and the get-response from the agent with a **GetResponse**-PDU. The message from the manager starts from the left side and ends at the agent process on the right side of the figure. The message from the agent process starts on the right side of the figure and ends at the manager process on

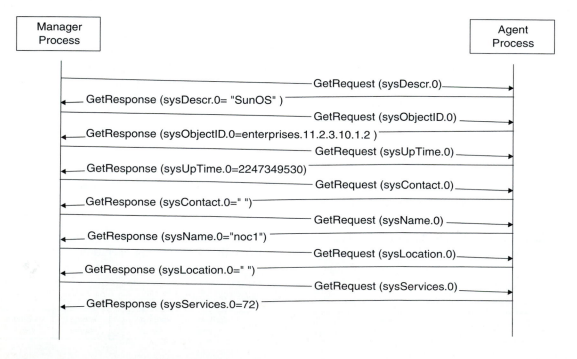

Figure 5.10   The Get-Request Operation for a System Group

the left side of the figure. The sequence of directed messages moves with time as we move down the figure. The messages depicted represent the values of the seven objects in the System group.

The manager process starts the sequence in Figure 5.10 with a **GetRequest**-PDU for the object *sysDescr*. Note that the .0 added to the managed object *sysDescr* indicates that the scalar value of the specified object should be retrieved. The agent process returns a **GetResponse**-PDU with a value "SunOS". The manager then sends a request for *sys-ObjectID* and receives the value "enterprises.11.2.3.10.1.2". The exchange of messages goes on until the value of 72 for the last object in the group *sysServices* is received. Although the figure shows messages as a sequence in time, they could also be obtained in one message using varBind shown in Figure 5.8.

GetNextRequest-PDU Operation.   A get-next-request operation is very similar to a get-request, except the requested record is the one next to the OBJECT IDENTIFIER specified in the request. Figure 5.11 shows the operations associated with retrieving data for the System group by the manager process using the get-next-request. The first message is a **GetRequest**-PDU for *sysDescr* and the response returns the value "SunOS". The

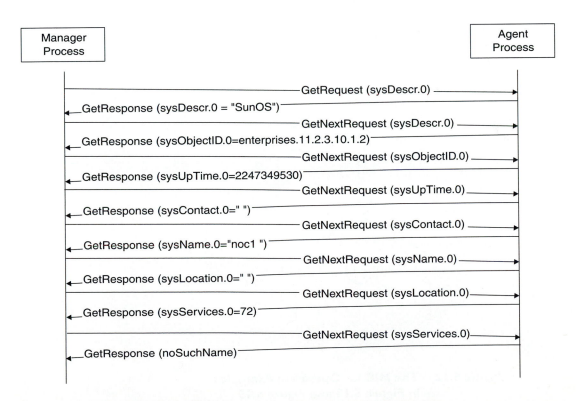

Figure 5.11   The Get-Next-Request Operation for a System Group

manager process then issues a **GetNextRequest-PDU** with the OBJECT IDENTIFIER *sysDescr*. The agent processes the name of the next OBJECT IDENTIFIER *sysObjectID* and its value "enterprises.11.2.3.10.1.2". The sequence terminates when the manager issues get-next-request for the object identifier next to *sysServices* and the agent process returns the error message "noSuchName".

The System group example we just looked at is a simple case where all the objects are single-valued scalar objects. Let us now consider a more complex scenario of a MIB that contains both scalar and aggregate objects. A generalized case of a conceptual MIB comprising three scalar objects and a table is shown in Figure 5.12. The first two objects, A and B, are single-valued scalar objects. They are followed by an aggregate object represented by the table T with an entry E and two rows of three columnar objects, T.E.1.1. through T.E.3.2. The MIB group ends with a scalar object Z.

Figure 5.13 shows the use of nine get-request messages to retrieve the nine objects. The left side of the figure shows the sequential operation for getting the MIB shown on the right side of the figure. The MIB shown is the same as in Figure 5.12, now drawn to follow the sequence of operations. We observe a few hidden assumptions in retrieving the data using the get-request operations. First, we need to know all the elements in the MIB including the number of columns and rows in the table. Second, we traversed the MIB from top to bottom, which is really from right to left in the MIB tree structure. Third, we retrieved

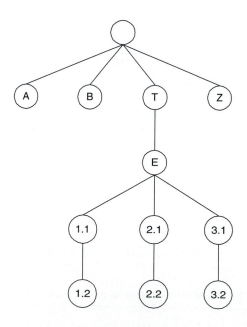

**Figure 5.12   The MIB for Operation Examples
in Figure 5.13 and Figure 5.15**

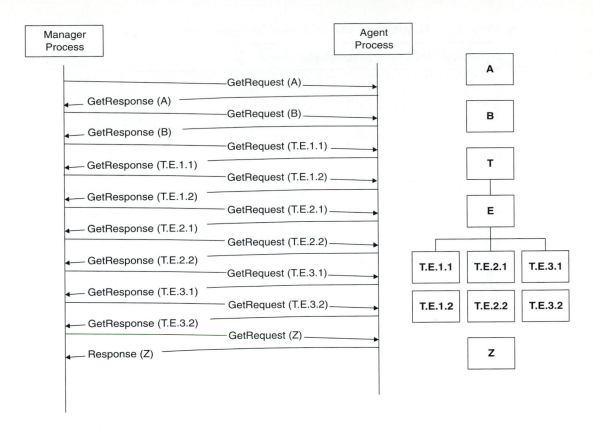

Figure 5.13   A Get-Request Operation for the MIB in Figure 5.12

the data in the table by traversing all the instances of a columnar object. The number of instances or rows in a table could be dynamic and is not always known to the management process. Thus, if the manager had issued a request for the object T.E.1.3 after acquiring T.E.1.2, it would have received an error message from the agent process. This is when get-next-request is very useful. However, we need to have a convention on the definition of the next object in a MIB tree, especially on the table representing an aggregate object. In SNMP, objects are retrieved using lexicographic convention. We will explain this convention before using the get-next-request operation to retrieve the same MIB group data.

The increasing order of entity used in SNMP operations is in lexicographic order. Let us understand lexicographic order by considering a simple set of integers shown in Table 5.2. The left side is a sequence of numbers in numeric order and the right side is the same group of numbers in lexicographic order. Notice that in the lexicographic order, we start with the lowest integer in the leftmost character, which in this case is 1. Before increasing the order in the first position, we select the lowest integer in the second position from the

Table 5.2   Numbers in Numeric and Lexicographic Orders

Numerical Order	Lexicographic Order
1	1
2	1118
3	115
9	126
15	15
22	2
34	22
115	250
126	2509
250	3
321	321
1118	34
2509	9

left, which is 11. There are two numbers (1118 and 115) that start with 11. We anchor at 11 for the first two positions, and then move on to select the lowest digit in the third position. This yields 111. We then move to the fourth position and obtain 1118 as the second number. Now, return to the third position and retrieve 115 as the third number. Having exhausted 1s (ones) in positions two to four, select 2 for the second position, and retrieve 126 as the next number. We continue this process until we reach 9.

We will now apply the lexicographic sequence to ordering the object identifiers in a MIB. Instead of each character being treated as a literal, we treat each node position as a literal and follow the same rules. Table 5.3 gives an example. The MIB associated with this example is shown in Figure 5.14. Notice that the lexicographically increasing order of nodes traces the traversal of the tree starting from the leftmost node 1. We traverse the path all the way to the leftmost leaf 1.1.5, keeping to the left whenever a fork is encountered. We then move up the tree and take a right on the first fork. This leads us to the leaf node 1.1.18. Thus, the rule at a forked node is to keep to the left while traversing down and keep to the right while going up. It actually turns out that we are always keeping to the right if you imagine ourselves walking along the tree path and looking in the forward direction. We turn around when we reach a leaf.

Returning to the get-next-request operation, the get-response message contains in each VarBind the value of the next lexicographic object value. If the request VarBind contains a scalar, nontabular object, the response contains the next scalar, nontabular value, or the first columnar object value of a table, if it is the next lexicographic entity. Figure 5.15 shows the principle of operation of get-next-request and response. We use the same MIB view that we had in Figure 5.12, which shows the get-request operation. The manager process starts the operation with a get-request message for the object A and receives the response with the value of A filled in. The subsequent requests from the manager are get-next-request type with the object ID of the response just received. The responses received are the next object ID with its value. The operations continue until Z

Table 5.3   A MIB Example of Lexicographic Ordering

```
1
1.1
1.1.5
1.1.18
1.2
1.2.6
2
2.2
2.10
2.10.9
3
3.4
3.21
9
```

is received. The subsequent request receives a response of an error message "noSuch-Name".

Get-next-request has several advantages. First, we don't need to know the object identifier of the next entity. Knowing the current OBJECT IDENTIFIER, we can retrieve the next one. Next, in the case of an aggregate object, the number of rows is changing dynamically. Thus, we do not know how many rows exist in the table. The get-next-request solves this problem. Another advantage of the get-next-request is that we can use

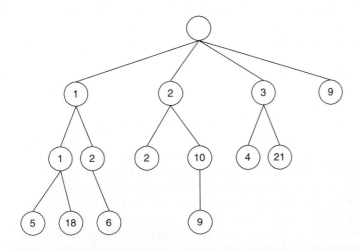

Figure 5.14   A MIB Example of Lexicographic Ordering

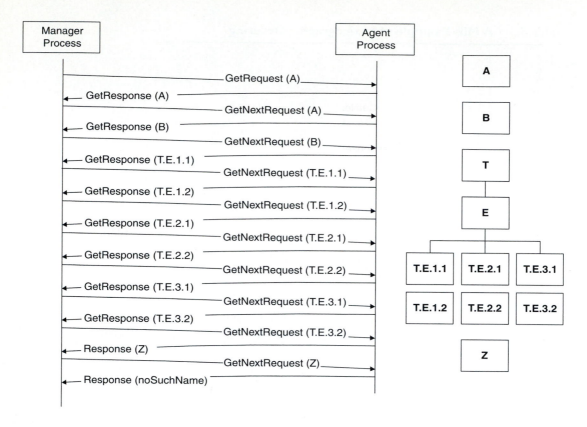

Figure 5.15   A Get-Next-Request Operation for the MIB in Figure 5.12

it to build a MIB tree by repeating the request from any node to any node. This is called MIB walk, and is used by a MIB browser in an NMS implementation.

Figure 5.16 shows a faster method to retrieve an aggregate object. It shows an address translation table with a matrix of three columnar objects, *atIfIndex*, *atPhysAddress*, and *atNetAddress*. The objects *atIfIndex* and *atNetAddress* are the indices that uniquely identify a row. There are three rows in the table. If we use the get-next-request operation shown in Figure 5.15, it would take us ten message exchanges. The VarBindList comprises the two VarBind name-value pairs, *sysUpTime* and *atPhysAddress*, suffixed with the values of *atIfIndex* and *atNetAddress*. Instead of issuing ten get-next-requests with a single VarBind in the message, the manager generates four GetNextRequest PDUs with a list of two VarBind fields. Although the address translation table is relatively stable, in general, a table is dynamic, and hence the time-stamp is requested by including *sysUpTime*.

In this method, the manager has to know the columnar objects of the table. The first query message retrieves the indices automatically. For the address translation table, the *atIfIndex* and *atNetAddress* are indices. This is shown in the request and response message OIDs. The first get-next-request message does not contain an operand value. The next

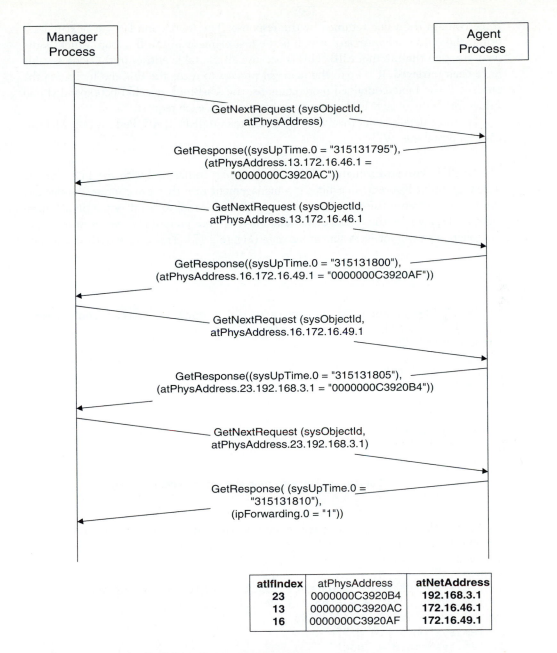

Figure 5.16   A GetNextRequest with Indices

three contain the value returned by the response. The fourth and last get-next-request brings the object, *ipForwarding,* which is the first element in the IP group, which is the next group in the Internet MIB. This is because all the table entries in the address table have been retrieved. It is up to the manager process to recognize this and terminate the process. If the table contained more columns, the VarBindList could be expanded and values for all the objects in the next row obtained with each request.

For more details about this PDU operation, refer to [RFC 1905, Perkins D & McGinnis E, and Stallings W2].

SNMP PDU Format Examples.   We will now use a sniffer tool with the PDU for the system group in Figure 5.10. Sniffer is a management tool that can capture the packets going across a transmission medium. We have used this tool to "sniff" some SNMP messages to display how the messages actually look. We are presenting a series of messages that query a system for its system group data (Figure 5.17). This corresponds to the data

```
13:55:47.445936 noc3.btc.gatech.edu.164 > noc1.btc.gatech.edu.snmp:
Community = public
GetRequest(111)
Request ID = 1
system.sysDescr.0
system.sysObjectID.0
system.sysUpTime.0
system.sysContact.0
system.sysName.0
system.sysLocation.0
system.sysServices.0
```

(a) Get-Request Message from Manager to Agent (before)

```
13:55:47.455936 noc1.btc.gatech.edu.snmp > noc3.btc.gatech.edu.164:
Community = public
GetResponse(172)
Request ID = 1
system.sysDescr.0 = "SunOS noc1 5.5.1 Generic_103640-08 sun4u"
system.sysObjectID.0 = E:hp.2.3.10.1.2
system.sysUpTime.0 = 247349530
system.sysContact.0 = ""
system.sysName.0 = "noc1"
system.sysLocation.0 = ""
system.sysServices.0 = 72
```

(b) Get-Response Message from Agent-to-Manager (before)

Figure 5.17   Sniffer Data of Get Messages (incomplete data in agent)

```
13:56:24.894369 noc3.btc.gatech.edu.164 > noc1.btc.gatech.edu.snmp:
Community = netman
SetRequest(41)
Request ID = 2
system.sysContact.0 = "Brandon Rhodes"

13:56:24.894369 noc1.btc.gatech.edu.snmp > noc3.btc.gatech.edu.164:
Community = netman
GetResponse(41)
Request ID = 2
system.sysContact.0 = "Brandon Rhodes"
```

Figure 5.18   Sniffer Data of Set-Request and Response for System Contact

shown in Figure 5.10. We, then, set the missing values for a couple of entities in the group (Figures 5.18 and 5.19) and reexamine them (Figure 5.20).

Figure 5.17(a) shows a GetRequest (-PDU in GetRequest-PDU is suppressed by the program) message for the system group values going from the manager, noc3.btc.gatech.edu (noc3, for short), to the agent, noc1.btc.gatech.edu (noc1, for short). The first line shows that it was sent at 13:55:47 from port 164 of noc3 to snmp port of noc1. The tool that was used has actually translated the conventional port number 161 to snmp. The community name is public and the GetRequest message is 111 bytes in length. The SNMP version number is not given. The seven object IDs from *system.sysDescr*.0 to *system.sysServices*.0 all end with zero to indicate that they are single-valued scalar objects. The agent, noc1, sends a GetResponse message of 172 bytes with values filled in for all the seven objects. The GetResponse message is shown in Figure 5.17(b). Notice that the values for *sysContact* and *sysLocation* in GetResponse are blank because they have not been entered in the agent. In addition, request number identified in the GetResponse-PDU is the same as the one in the GetRequest-PDU.

```
13:56:27.874245 noc3.btc.gatech.edu.164 > noc1.btc.gatech.edu.snmp:
Community = netman
SetRequest(37)
Request ID = 3
system.sysLocation.0 = "BTC NM Lab"

13:56:27.884244 noc1.btc.gatech.edu.snmp > noc3.btc.gatech.edu.164:
Community = netman
GetResponse(37)
Request ID = 3
system.sysLocation.0 = "BTC NM Lab"
```

Figure 5.19   Sniffer Data of Set-Request and Response for System Location

```
14:03:36.788270 noc3.btc.gatech.edu.164 > noc1.btc.gatech.edu.snmp:
Community = public
GetRequest(111)
Request ID = 4
system.sysDescr.0
system.sysObjectID.0
system.sysUpTime.0
system.sysContact.0
system.sysName.0
system.sysLocation.0
system.sysServices.0
```

(a) Get-Request Message from Manager to Agent (after)

```
14:03:36.798269 noc1.btc.gatech.edu.snmp > noc3.btc.gatech.edu.164:
Community = public
GetResponse(196)
Request ID = 4
system.sysDescr.0 = "SunOS noc1 5.5.1 Generic_103640-08 sun4u"
system.sysObjectID.0 = E:hp.2.3.10.1.2
system.sysUpTime.0 = 247396453
system.sysContact.0 = "Brandon Rhodes"
system.sysName.0 = "noc1"
system.sysLocation.0 = "BTC NM Lab"
system.sysServices.0 = 72
```

(b) Get-Response Message from Agent to Manager (after)

Figure 5.20   Sniffer Data of Get Messages (complete data in agent)

Figure 5.18 shows the use of **SetRequest** message to write the *sysContact* name in noc1 whose value is "Brandon Rhodes". Notice that the community name is changed to netman. The community of netman has the access privilege to write in noc1 and the object, *system.sysContact*, has read-write access for the netman community. The agent, noc1, makes the change and sends a GetResponse message to noc3. Figure 5.19 shows a similar set of messages for setting the entity *sysLocation* with the value "BTC NM Lab."

Figure 5.20(a) and (b) are repetitions of Figure 5.14 of the **GetRequest** and **Get-Response** messages. We now see the completed version of the system group data.

5.1.5   The SNMP MIB Group

Figure 5.21 shows the MIB tree for the SNMP group and Table 5.4 gives the description of the entities. Note that OID 7 and OID 23 are not used. The number of transactions in the description column in the table indicates the ins and outs of the SNMP protocol entity. All entities except *snmpEnableAuthenTraps* have the syntax, Counter. Implementation of the SNMP group is mandatory—obviously!

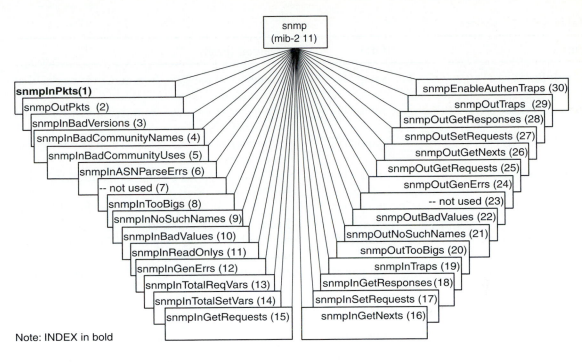

Figure 5.21 An SNMP Group

Table 5.4 An SNMP Group

Entity	OID	Description (brief)
snmpInPkts	snmp (1)	Total number of messages delivered from transport service
snmpOutPkts	snmp (2)	Total number of messages delivered to transport service
snmpInBadVersions	snmp (3)	Total number of messages from transport service that are of unsupported version
snmpInBadCommunityNames	snmp (4)	Total number of messages from transport service that are of unknown community name
snmpInBadCommunityUses	snmp (5)	Total number of messages from transport service, not allowed operation by the sending community
snmpInASNParseErrs	snmp (6)	Total number of ASN.1 and BER errors
	snmp (7)	Not used
snmpInTooBigs	snmp (8)	Total number of messages from transport service that have 'tooBig' errors
snmpInNoSuchNames	snmp (9)	Total number of messages from transport service that have 'noSuchName' errors

Table 5.5   *(continued)*

Entity	OID	Description (brief)
snmpInBadValues	snmp (10)	Total number of messages from transport service that have 'badValue' errors
snmpInReadOnlys	snmp (11)	Total number of messages from transport service that have 'readOnly' errors
snmpInGenErrs	snmp (12)	Total number of messages from transport service that have 'genErr' errors
snmpInTotalReqVars	snmp (13)	Total number of successful Get-Request and Get-Next messages received
snmpInTotalSetVars	snmp (14)	Total number of objects successfully altered by Set-Request messages received
snmpInGetRequests	snmp (15)	Total number of Get-Request PDUs accepted and processed
snmpInGetNexts	snmp (16)	Total number of Get-Next PDUs accepted and processed
snmpInSetRequests	snmp (17)	Total number of Set-Request PDUs accepted and processed
snmpInGetResponses	snmp (18)	Total number of Get-Response PDUs accepted and processed
snmpInTraps	snmp (19)	Total number of trap PDUs accepted and processed
snmpOutTooBigs	snmp (20)	Total number of SNMP PDUs generated for which error status is 'tooBig'
snmpOutNoSuchNames	snmp (21)	Total number of SNMP PDUs generated for which error status is 'noSuchName'
snmpOutBadValues	snmp (22)	Total number of SNMP PDUs generated for which error-status is 'badValue'
	snmp (23)	— not used
snmpOutGenErrs	snmp (24)	Total number of SNMP PDUs generated for which error status is 'genErr'
snmpOutGetRequests	snmp (25)	Total number of SNMP Get-Request PDUs generated
snmpOutGetNexts	snmp (26)	Total number of SNMP Get-Next PDUs generated
snmpOutSetRequests	snmp (27)	Total number of SNMP Set-Request PDUs generated
snmpOutGetResponses	snmp (28)	Total number of SNMP Get-Response PDUs generated
snmpOutTraps	snmp (29)	Total number of SNMP trap PDUs generated
snmpEnableAuthenTraps	snmp (30)	Override option to generate authentication failure traps

5.2   Functional Model

There are no formal specifications of functions in SNMPv1 management. Application functions are limited, in general, to network management in SNMP and not to the services provided by the network.

The OSI mode addresses five areas of functions: configuration, fault, performance, security, and accounting. Some of the configuration functions, as well as security and privacy-related issues, were addressed as part of the SNMP protocol entity specifications in the previous section. For example, the override function of traps is one of the objects in the SNMP group, which has the access privilege of read and write and hence can be set remotely. The security functions are built in as part of the implementation of the protocol entity. The community specifications and authentication scheme partially address these requirements.

The write access to managed objects is limited to implementation in most cases. Thus, configuration management in general is addressed by the specific network management system or by the use of console or telnet to set configurable parameters. We saw the configuration management function in the examples shown in Figures 5.18 and 5.19.

Fault management is addressed by the error counters built into the agents. They can be read by the SNMP manager and processed. Traps are useful to monitor network elements and interfaces going up and down.

Performance counters are part of the SNMP agent MIB. It is the function of the SNMP manager to do the performance analysis. For example, the counter readings can be taken at two instances of time and the data rate can be calculated. An intermediate manager/agent, such as RMON, can perform such statistical functions, as we will see in Chapter 8.

The administrative model in protocol entity specifications addresses security function in basic SNMP.

The accounting function is not addressed by the SNMP model.

Summary

All management operations are done using five messages in SNMPv1. They are get-request, get-next-request, set-request, get-response, and trap. The first three messages are sent from the manager to the agent and the last two are sent by the agent to the manager.

The SNMP communication model deals with the administrative structure and the five SNMP message protocol data units (PDU). The administrative model defines the community within which messages can be exchanged. It also defines the access policy—who has access to what data. The five protocol entities are defined in ASN.1 format and macros. We learned SNMP operations by tracing messages exchanged between manager and agent processes. We then looked inside the PDU formats for the various messages to learn the data formats.

There is no formal specification for the functional model in SNMP management. However, management functions are accomplished by built-in schemes and managed objects. The administrative model in SNMP and the operations using managed objects are employed to accomplish the various functions.

Exercises

1. Three managed hubs with interface id 11-13 (fourth decimal position value) in subnetwork 200.100.100.1 are being monitored by a network management system for mean time between failures using the *SysUpTime* in *system {internet.mgmt.mib-2.system}* group. The NMS periodically issues the command

   ```
   get-request object-instance community OBJECT IDENTIFIER
   ```

   Fill the operands in the three set of requests that the NMS sends out. Use "public" for the *community* variable.

2. You are assigned the task of writing specifications for configuring SNMP managers and agents for a corporate network to implement the access policy. The policy defines a community profile for all managed network components where a public group (community name *public*) can only look at the system group, a privileged group (community name *privileged*) that can look at all the MIB objects, and an exclusive group (community name *exclusive*) that can do a read-write on all allowed components. Present a figure (similar, but not identical, to the flowchart in Figure 5.2) showing the paths from the SNMP managers to managed objects of a network component.

3. Fill in the data in the trap PDU format shown in Figure 5.9 for a message sent by the hub shown in Figure 4.2(a) one second after it is reset following a failure. Treat the trap as generic and leave the specific trap field blank. The only *varBind* that the trap sends is the *sysUpTime*. (Refer to RFC 1157 and RFC 1215.)

4. An SNMP manager sends a request message to an SNMP agent requesting *sysUpTime* at 8:00 A.M. Fill in the data for the fields of an SNMP PDU shown in Figure 5.5. Please use "SNMP" for the application header, enumerated INTEGER 0 for version-1 and "public" for community name.

5. In Exercise 4, if the SNMP manager sent the request at 8:00 A.M. and the SNMP agent was reset at midnight after a failure, fill in the fields for the SNMP PDU on the response received.

6. An SNMP manager sends a request for the values of the *sysUpTime* in the System group and *ifType* in the interfaces group for *ifNumber* value of 3. Write the PDUs with the fields filled in for

   a. the get-request PDU, and

   b. the get-response PDU with noSuchName error message for *ifType*.

7. The following data response information is received by the manager for a get-request with a *varBindList*. Compose

   a. the get-request PDU, and

   b. the get-response PDU.

Object	Value
Error Status	Too big
Error Index	udpInErrors
udpInDatagrams	500,000
udpNoPorts	1,000
udpInErrors	5000
udpOutDatagrams	300,000

8. Draw the message sequence diagram similar to the one in Figure 5.10 for the hub example given in Figure 4.2(a). Assume that a separate get-request message is sent for each data value.

9. Repeat Exercise 7 with a VarBindList. Use the format of Figure 5.16.

10. For the UDP Group MIB in Figure 4.38, assume that there are three rows for the columnar objects in the *udpTable*. Write the OBJECT IDENTIFIER for all the objects in the lexicographic order.

11. Draw the message sequence diagram for the following *ipNetToMediaTable*, retrieving all the values objects in each row with single get-next-request commands, similar to the one shown in Figure 5.16. The indices are *ipNetToMediaIfIndex* and *ipNetToMediaNetAddress*. Ignore obtaining *sysUpTime*.

ipNetToMedia IfIndex	IpNetToMediaPhys Address	ipNetToMediaNet Address	ipNetTo MediaType
25	00000C3920B4	192.68.252.15	4
16	00000C3920AF	172.16.49.1	4
9	00000C3920A6	172.16.55.1	4
2	00000C39209D	172.16.56.1	4

12. Compose the data frames for SNMP PDUs for the example in Figure 5.16 for the following two cases:
    a. the first GetNextRequest (*sysUpTime*, *atPhysAddress*) and the GetResponse
    b. the second GetNextRequest and GetResponse with values obtained in part (a).

13. A data analyzer tool is used to look at a frame of data traversing a LAN. It is from the station noc3 in response to a request from noc1. Use the following system status to answer this question:

```
Version = 0
Community = netMan
```

Object	Value	Units
Request ID	100	
Error Status	Too big	udpInErrors too high
Error Index	udpInErrors	
sysUpTime	1,000,000	hundredths of a second
udpInDatagrams	500,000	datagrams
udpNoPorts	1,000	datagrams
udpInErrors	5000	datagrams
udpOutDatagrams	300,000	datagrams

Compose the expected data frames for SNMP PDU types. Your frames should look like the frames in Figure 5.17.

a. **GetRequest** from manager to managed object

b. **GetResponse** from managed object to manager

CHAPTER 6

SNMP Management: SNMPv2

SNMPv1, which was originally called SNMP, was developed as an interim management protocol; OSI was expected to be the ultimate network management protocol. A placeholder, CMOT (CMIP over TCP/IP), was created in Internet MIB for migrating from SNMP to CMIP. But the "best-laid plans..." never came about. SNMP caught on in the industry. Major vendors had incorporated SNMP modules in their network systems and components. SNMP now needed enhancements.

Version 2 of Simple Network Management Protocol, SNMPv2, was developed when it became obvious that OSI network management standards were not going to be implemented in the foreseeable future. The working group that was commissioned by the IETF to define SNMPv2 released it in 1996. It is a community-based administrative framework similar to SNMPv1 defined in STD 15 [RFC 1157], STD 16 [RFCs 1155 and 1212], and STD 17 [RFC 1213]. Although the original version was known as SNMP, it is now referred to as SNMPv1 to distinguish it from SNMPv2.

6.1   Major Changes in SNMPv2

Several significant changes were introduced in SNMPv2. One of the most significant changes was to provide the security functions that SNMPv1 lacked. Unfortunately, after significant effort there was a lack of consensus, so the security feature was dropped from the final specifications. The security function continued to be implemented on an administrative framework based on community name, and the same administrative framework as in SNMPv1 was adopted for SNMPv2. The SNMPv2 Working Group has presented a summary of the community-based Administrative Framework for the SNMPv2 framework, and referred to it as SNMPv2C, in RFC 1901. RFC 1902 through RFC 1907 present the details of the framework. There are significant differences between the two versions of SNMP, and unfortunately version 2 is not backward-compatible with version 1. RFC 1908 presents implementation schemes for the coexistence of the two versions.

The basic components of network management in SNMPv2 are the same as in version 1. They are agent and manager, both performing the same functions. The manager-to-manager communication, shown in Figure 4.8, is formalized in version 2 by adding an additional message. Thus, the organizational model in version 2 remains essentially the same. In spite of the lack of security enhancements, major improvements to the architecture have been made in SNMPv2.

Bulk Data Transfer Message: Two significant messages were added. The first is the ability to request and receive bulk data using the get-bulk message. This speeds up the get-next-request process and is especially useful to retrieve data from tables.

Manager-to-Manager Message: The second additional message deals with interoperability of two network management systems. This message extends the communication of management messages between management systems and thus makes network management systems interoperable.

Structure of Management Information (SMI): In SNMPv1, SMI is defined as STD 16, which is described in RFCs 1155 and 1212, along with RFC 1215, which describes traps. They have been consolidated and rewritten in RFCs 1902 through 1904 for SMI in SNMPv2. RFC 1902 deals with SMIv2, RFC 1903 with textual conventions, and RFC 1904 with conformances.

SMIv2 is divided into three parts: module definitions, object definitions, and trap definitions. An ASN.1 macro, MODULE-IDENTITY, is used to define an information module. It concisely conveys the semantics of the information module. OBJECT-TYPE macro defines the syntax and semantics of a managed object. Trap is also termed notification and defined by NOTIFICATION-TYPE macro.

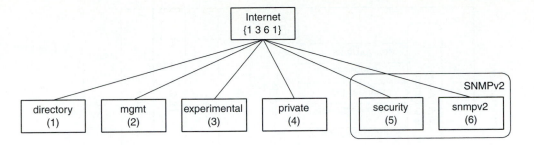

Figure 6.1   SNMPv2 Internet Group

Textual Conventions are designed to help define new data types. They are also intended to make the semantics consistent and clear to the human reader. Although new data types could have been created using new ASN.1 classes and tags, the decision was made to use the existing defined class types and apply restrictions to them.

Conformance Statements help the customer objectively compare the features of the various products. It also keeps the vendors honest in claiming their products are compatible with a given SNMP version. Compliance defines a minimum set of capabilities. Vendors can offer additional capabilities as options.

Table Enhancements: Using a newly defined columnar object with a Syntax clause, *RowStatus*, conceptual rows can be added to or deleted from an aggregate object table. Further, a table can be expanded by augmenting another table to it, which is helpful in adding columnar objects to an existing aggregate object.

MIB Enhancements: In SNMPv2, the Internet node in the MIB has two new subgroups: security and snmpV2, as shown in Figure 6.1. There are significant changes to the system and SNMP groups of version 1. Changes to the system group are under the mib-2 node in the MIB. The SNMP entities in version 2 are a hybrid, with some of the entities from the SNMP group, and the rest from the groups under the newly created snmpV2 node.

Transport Mappings: There are several changes to the communication model in SNMPv2. Although UDP is the preferred transport protocol mechanism for SNMP management, other transport protocols can be used with SNMPv2. The mappings needed to define other protocols on to UDP are the subject of RFC 1906.

6.2   SNMPv2 System Architecture

The SNMPv2 system architecture looks essentially the same as that of version 1, shown in Figure 4.9. However, there are two significant enhancements in the SNMPv2 architecture, which are shown in Figure 6.2. First, there are seven messages instead of five (compare Figure 4.9). Second, two manager applications can communicate with each other at peer level. Another message, report message, is missing from Figure 6.2 because, even

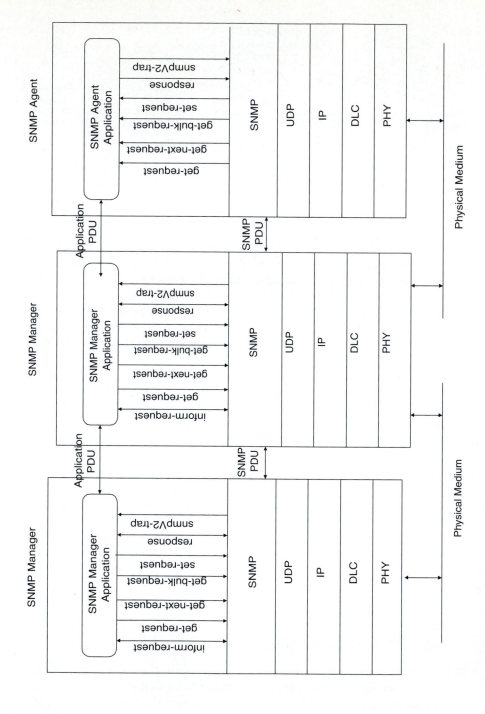

Figure 6.2   SNMPv2 Network Management Architecture

though it has been defined as a message, the SNMPv2 Working Group did not specify its details. It is left for the implementers to generate the specifications. It is not currently being used.

The messages **get-request**, **get-next request**, and **set-request** are the same as in version 1 and are generated by the manager application. The message **response** is also the same as get-response in version 1, and is now generated by both the agent and the manager applications. It is generated by the agent application in response to a get or set message from the manager application. It is also generated by the manager application in response to an **inform-request** message from another manager application.

An **inform-request** message is generated by a manager application and transmitted to another manager application. The receiving manager application responds with a response message. This set of communication messages is a powerful enhancement in SNMPv2, because it makes two network management systems interoperable.

The message **get-bulk-request** is generated by a manager application. It is used to transfer large amounts of data from the agent to the manager, especially if it includes retrieval of table data. The retrieval is fast and efficient. The receiving entity generates and fills data for each entry in the request and transmits all the data as a response message to the originator of the request.

An **SNMPv2-trap** event, known as trap in version 1, is generated and transmitted by an agent process when an exceptional situation occurs. The destination to which it is sent is implementation-dependent. The PDU structure has been modified to be consistent with other PDUs.

Another enhancement in SNMPv2 over version 1 is the mapping of SNMP layer over multiple transport domains. An example of this is shown in Figure 6.3, in which an SNMPv2 agent riding over a connectionless OSI transport layer protocol, CLNS (Connectionless-Mode Network Service), communicates with an SNMPv2 manager over UDP transport layer. RFC 1906, which describes the transport mappings, addresses a few well-known transport-layer mappings; others can be added using similar structure.

The details on the MIB relating to SNMPv2 are covered in Section 6.4 and the communication protocol aspects of the messages are covered in Section 6.5. Although not a standard, RFC 1283 specifies SNMP over COTS (Connection-Oriented Transport Service), a connection-oriented OSI transport protocol. However, SNMP is not specified over the connection-oriented Internet protocol, TCP.

6.3   SNMPv2 Structure of Management Information

There are several changes to SMI in version 2, as well as enhancements to SMIv2 over that of SMIv1. As stated earlier, the SMIv2 [RFC 1902], is divided into three parts: module definitions, object definitions, and notification definitions.

We introduced the concept of a module in Chapter 3, which is a group of assignments that are related to each other. The **module definitions** describe the semantics of an information module and are formally defined by an ASN.1 macro, MODULE-IDENTITY.

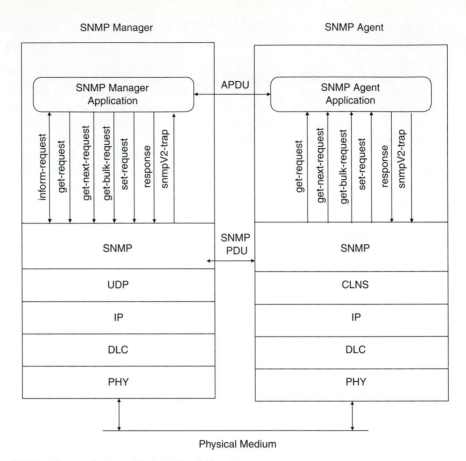

Figure 6.3   SNMPv2 Network Management Architecture on Multiple Transport Domains

CLNS = Connectionless-Mode Network Service
UDP = User Datagram Protocol
DLC = Data Link Control

Object definitions are used to describe managed objects. The OBJECT-TYPE macro that we discussed in Chapter 4 is used to define managed objects. OBJECT-TYPE conveys both syntax and semantics of a managed object.

Notification in SMIv2 is equivalent to trap in SMIv1. In SMIv1, trap is formally specified by an ASN.1 macro, TRAP-TYPE. In SMIv2, notification is specified by an ASN.1 macro, NOTIFICATION-TYPE, and conveys both its syntax and semantics.

SMIv2 defines an additional part that formalizes the assignment of OBJECT IDEN-TIFIER. Even though we have two assignments in SMIv1, namely, object name and trap, they are not formally structured. In SMIv2, an ASN.1 macro, OBJECT-IDENTITY, is introduced for the assignment of object name and notification to OBJECT IDENTIFIER, as shown in Figure 6.4.

```
SNMPv2-SMI DEFINITIONS ::=
BEGIN

-- the path to the root
    org             OBJECT IDENTIFIER ::= {iso 3}
                    ...
    private         OBJECT IDENTIFIER ::= {internet 4}
    enterprises     OBJECT IDENTIFIER ::= {private 1}
    security        OBJECT IDENTIFIER ::= {internet 5}
    snmpV2          OBJECT IDENTIFIER ::= {internet 6}
    -- transport domains
    snmpDomains     OBJECT IDENTIFIER ::= {snmpV2 1}
-- transport proxies
    snmpProxys      OBJECT IDENTIFIER ::= {snmpV2 2}
    --module identities
    snmpModules     OBJECT IDENTIFIER ::= {snmpV2 3}
    -- definitions for information modules
    MODULE-IDENTITY MACRO
    BEGIN
        <clauses> ::= <values>
    END
    -- definitions for OBJECT IDENTIFIER assignments*
    OBJECT-IDENTITY MACRO ::=
    BEGIN
            <clauses> ::= <values>
    END
    --names of objects
            objectName ::=      OBJECT IDENTIFIER
            NotificationName ::= OBJECT IDENTIFIER
    -- syntax of objects
            <objectSyntax Productions>
            <dataType Productions>
    -- definition of objects
    OBJECT-TYPE MACRO ::=
    BEGIN
        <clauses> ::= <values>
    END
    -- definition for notification
    NOTIFICATION-TYPE MACRO ::=
    BEGIN
        <clauses> ::= <values>
    END
    -- definition of administration identifiers
    zeroDotZero ::= {0 0}      -- a value for null identifiers
END
```

Figure 6.4   Definitions (skeletal) of SMI for SNMPv2

6.3.1   SMI Definitions for SNMPv2

Figure 6.4 shows a skeleton of the SMIv2; see RFC 1902 for complete definitions. We have taken the liberty of presenting the definitions with some additional comments (marked by *) and structural indentations to bring out clearly the BEGIN and END of macros. The definitions begin with the high-level nodes under the Internet MIB. Two additional nodes, security and SNMPv2, are introduced. Security node is just a place-holder and is reserved for the future. The *snmpV2* node has three subnodes: *snmpDomains*, *snmpProxys*, and *snmpModules*. The MIB tree showing all these nodes defined in SMIv2 is presented in Figure 6.5.

6.3.2   Information Modules

RFC 1902 defines *information module* as an ASN.1 module that defines information relating to network management. The SMI describes how to use a subset of ASN.1 to define an information module. Three kinds of information modules that are defined in SNMPv2: MIB modules, compliance statements for MIB modules, and capability statements for agent implementations. This classification scheme does not impose rigid taxonomy in the definition of managed objects. Figure 6.6 shows an example where *conformance information* and *compliance statements* are part of the SNMP group of SNMPv2 MIB. As we will see later, the SNMP group in SNMPv2 contains some of the objects of version 1 and some new objects and object groups (to be defined later). It also has information on conformance requirements. In the example shown, the mandatory groups in implementing SNMPv2 are *snmpGroup*, *snmpSetGroup*, *systemGroup*, and *snmpBasicNotificationsGroup*. Thus, if a network component vendor claims that its

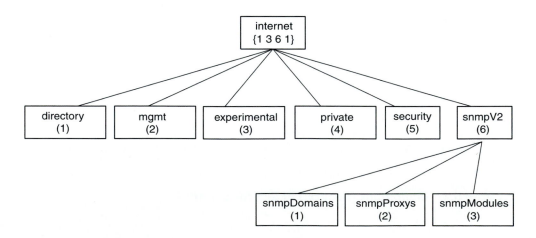

Figure 6.5   SNMPv2 Internet Nodes Defined in SMIv2

```
SNMPv2-MIB DEFINITIONS ::=
BEGIN
     ...         ...          ...            ...
snmpMIB      MODULE IDENTITY ::= {snmpModules 1}
     ...         ...          ...            ...
snmpMIBObjects     OBJECT IDENTIFIER ::= {snmpMIB 1}
-- the SNMP group
snmp               OBJECT IDENTIFIER ::= {mib-2 11}
snmpInPkts            OBJECT-TYPE ::= {snmp 1}
snmpOutPkts           OBJECT-TYPE ::= { snmp 2}
     ...         ...          ...
snmpSet            OBJECT IDENTIFIER ::= {snmpmibObjects 6}
snmpSetSerialNo      OBJECT-TYPE ::= { snmpSet 1}
-- conformance information
snmpMIBConformance
OBJECT IDENTIFIER ::= {snmpMIB 2}
snmpMIBCompliances
                   OBJECT IDENTIFIER ::= {snmpMIBConformance 1}
snmpMIBGroups      OBJECT IDENTIFIER ::= {snmpMIBConformance 2}
-- compliance statements
snmpBasicCompliance MODULE-COMPLIANCE
     STATUS        current
     DESCRIPTION
                   "The compliance statement for SNMPv2 entities
                   which implement the SNMPv2 MIB"
     MODULE        -- this module
          MANDATORY-GROUPS {snmpGroup, snmpSetGroup,
                            systemGroup,
                            snmpBasicNotificationsGroup}
          GROUP    snmpCommunityGroup
          DESCRIPTION
                   "This group is mandatory for SNMPv2 entities
                    which support community-based authentication."
     ::= {snmpMIBCompliances 2 }
-- units of conformance
snmpGroup      OBJECT-GROUP    ::= {snmpMIBGroups 8}
snmpCommunityGroup     OBJECT-GROUP ::= {snmpMIBGroups 9}
snmpObsoleteGroup OBJECT-GROUP ::= {snmpMIBGroups 10}
     ...         ...          ...            ...
END
```

Figure 6.6   Example of SNMP Group including Conformance and Compliance in SNMPv2 MIB

management agent is SNMPv2 compliant, these groups as they are defined in SNMPv2 should be implemented.

The MIB specifications contain only compliance statements. The *agent-capability statements* are part of implementation in the agent by the vendor. It might be included as part of an "enterprise-specific" module.

The information on SMIv2 has been split into three parts in the documentation. MIB modules for SMIv2 are covered in RFC 1902. The textual conventions to be used to describe MIB modules have been formalized in RFC 1903. The conformance information, which encompasses both compliance and agent capabilities, is covered in RFC 1904.

6.3.3   SNMP Keywords

The keywords used in the specifications of SMIv2 are a subset of ASN.1. But it is a different subset from that of SMIv1. Table 6.1 shows the comparison of keywords used in the two versions. We'll address the new keywords for specific applications as we discuss them.

Table 6.1   SNMP Keywords

KEYWORD	SNMPv1	SNMPv2
ACCESS	Y	Y
AGENT-CAPABILITIES	N	Y
AUGMENTS	N	Y
BEGIN	Y	Y
BITS	N	Y
CONTACT-INFO	N	Y
CREATION-REQUIRES	N	Y
Counter	Y	N
Counter32	N	Y
Counter64	N	Y
DEFINITIONS	Y	Y
DEFVAL	Y	Y
DESCRIPTION	Y	Y
DISPLAY-HINT	N	Y
END	Y	Y
ENTERPRISE	Y	N
FROM	Y	Y
GROUP	N	Y
Gauge	Y	N
Gauge32	N	Y
IDENTIFIER	Y	Y
IMPLIED	N	Y
IMPORTS	Y	Y
INCLUDES	N	Y

Table 6.1   *(continued)*

KEYWORD	SNMPv1	SNMPv2
INDEX	Y	Y
INTEGER	Y	Y
Integer32	N	Y
IpAddress	Y	Y
LAST-UPDATED	N	Y
MANDATORY-GROUPS	N	Y
MAX-ACCESS	N	Y
MIN-ACCESS	N	Y
MODULE	N	Y
MODULE-COMPLIANCE	N	Y
MODULE-IDENTITY	N	Y
NOTIFICATION-GROUP	N	Y
NOTIFICATION-TYPE	N	Y
NetworkAddress	Y	N
OBJECT	Y	Y
OBJECT-GROUP	N	Y
OBJECT-IDENTITY	N	Y
OBJECT-TYPE	Y	Y
OBJECTS	N	Y
OCTET	Y	Y
OF	Y	Y
ORGANIZATION	N	Y
Opaque	Y	Y
PRODUCT-RELEASE	N	Y
REFERENCE	Y	Y
REVISION	N	Y
SEQUENCE	Y	Y
SIZE	Y	Y
STATUS	Y	Y
STRING	Y	Y
SUPPORTS	N	Y
SYNTAX	Y	Y
TEXTUAL-CONVENTION	N	Y
TRAP-TYPE	Y	N
TimeTicks	Y	Y
UNITS	N	Y
Unsigned32	N	Y
VARIABLES	Y	N
VARIATION	N	Y
WRITE-SYNTAX	N	Y

It's worth noting here that some general keywords have been replaced with limited keywords. Thus, Counter is replaced by Counter32, Gauge by Gauge32, and INTEGER by Integer32. The NetworkAddress is deleted from use and only the IpAddress is used.

Note that reference in IMPORTS clause or in clauses of SNMPv2 macros to an informational module is not through "descriptor" as it was in version 1. It is referenced through specifying its module name, an enhancement in SNMPv2.

Note also that the expansion of the ASN.1 module macro occurs during the implementation phase of a product, and not at run-time.

6.3.4   Module Definitions

The MODULE-IDENTITY macro is added to SMIv2 to specify an informational module. It provides administrative information regarding the informational module as well as revision history. The SMIv2 MODULE-IDENTITY macro is presented in Figure 6.7.

Figure 6.8 shows an example of a MODULE-IDENTITY macro (a hypothetical example of a nonexistent module) for a network component vendor, InfoTech Services, Inc. (isi), that is updating its private-enterprises-isi MIB module {private.enterprises.isi}.

The last-updated clause is mandatory and contains the date and time in UTC (universal time) format [RFC 1902]. "Z" refers to Greenwich mean time (GMT). The Text clause uses the NVT ASCII character set [RFC 854], which is a printable set. All clauses, except the revision clause, must be present in the macro.

```
MODULE-IDENTITY MACRO ::=
BEGIN
    TYPE NOTATION ::=
                      "LAST-UPDATED" value (Update UTCTime)
                      "ORGANIZATION" Text
                      "CONTACT-INFO" Text
                      "DESCRIPTION" Text
                      RevisionPart
    VALUE NOTATION ::=
                      value (VALUE OBJECT IDENTIFIER)
    RevisionPart ::= Revisions | empty
    Revisions ::= Revision | Revisions Revision
    Revision ::=
        "REVISION" value (UTCTime)
        "DESCRIPTION" Text
    -- uses the NVT ASCII character set
    Text ::= """" string """"
END
```

Figure 6.7   MODULE-IDENTITY Macro

```
isiMIBModule      MODULE-IDENTITY
     LAST-UPDATED      "9802101100Z"
     ORGANIZATION      "InfoTech Services, Inc."
     CONTACT-INFO      "Mani Subramanian
                       Tele: 770-111-1111
                       Fax: 770-111-2222
                       email: manis@bellsouth.net"
     DESCRIPTION       "Version 1.1 of the InfoTech Services MIB
                        module"
     Revision          "9709021500Z"
     DESCRIPTION       "Revision 1.0 on 2 September 1997 was a draft
                        version."
```

Figure 6.8   Example of MODULE-IDENTITY Macro

6.3.5   Object Definitions

The OBJECT-IDENTITY macro, new in SMIv2, is used to define information about an OBJECT-IDENTIFIER. It is presented in Figure 6.9. The STATUS clause has one of three values: current, deprecated, or **obsolete**. The value *mandatory* in SMIv1 is replaced with the value **current** in SMIv2. The value **optional** is not used in SMIv2. The new value, **deprecated**, has been added to define objects that are required to be implemented in the current version, but which may not exist in future versions of SNMP. This allows for backward compatibility during the transition between versions.

Whereas the REFERENCE clause was used only in the OBJECT-TYPE construct in SMIv1, it is used in many constructs in version 2.

```
OBJECT-IDENTITY MACRO ::=
BEGIN
     TYPE NOTATION ::=
                        "STATUS"          Status
                        "DESCRIPTION"     Text
                        ReferPart
     VALUE NOTATION ::=
                        value (VALUE OBJECT IDENTIFIER)
     Status ::=         "current" | "deprecated" | "obsolete"
     ReferPart ::=      "REFERENCE" Text | empty
     Text ::=           """" string """"
END
```

Figure 6.9   OBJECT-IDENTITY Macro

Let us extend our hypothetical example of InfoTech Services, Inc. (ISI) and suppose ISI makes a class of router products. It is given an OBJECT IDENTIFIER as isiRouter OBJECT IDENTIFIER ::= {private.enterprises.isi 1}. The class of router products can be specified at a high level using the OBJECT-IDENTITY macro as shown in Figure 6.10(a). The status of the *isiRouter* is current and is described as an 8-slot IP router. A reference is given for obtaining the details.

A specific implementation of the router in the *isiRouter* class of products is routerIsi123. This is a managed object specified by the OBJECT-TYPE macro shown in Figure 6.10(b).

Let us make sure that we understand the terminology used with OBJECT. OBJECT IDENTIFIER defines the **administrative identification** of a node in the MIB. The OBJECT IDENTITY macro is used to **assign** an object identifier value to the object node in the MIB. The OBJECT-TYPE is a macro that defines the **type** of a managed object. It is also used to describe a new type of object. As we learned in previous chapters, an **object instance** is a specific instance of the *object (type)*. Thus a specific instance of the *routerIsi123* could be identified by its IP address 10.1.2.3.

Comparing Figure 6.10(a) and Figure 6.10(b), we observe the difference between OBJECT-IDENTITY and OBJECT-TYPE. The status clause appears in both. The description clause that also appears in both describes different aspects of the object. The OBJECT-IDENTITY describes the high-level description; whereas the OBJECT-TYPE description focuses on the details needed for implementation.

Let us now visualize the router in Figure 6.10 with several slots for interface cards. We want to define the parameters associated with each interface. The parameters that are

```
isiRouter     OBJECT-IDENTITY
    STATUS        current
    DESCRIPTION   "An 8-slot IP router in the IP router family"
    REFERENCE     "ISI Memorandum No. ISI-R123 dated 20 January
                  1997"
    ::= {private.enterprises.isi 1}
```

(a) An OBJECT-IDENTITY Macro

```
routerIsi123  OBJECT-TYPE
    SYNTAX        DisplayString
    MAX-ACCESS    read-only
    STATUS        current
    DESCRIPTION   "An 8-slot IP router that can switch up to
                  100 million packets per second"
    ::= {isiRouter 1}
```

(b) An OBJECT-TYPE Macro

Figure 6.10   OBJECT-IDENTITY and OBJECT-TYPE Macros

managed objects (or entities) are defined by an aggregate object, *IfTable*. For example, the *ifNumber* for our router example could be 32 if the router has eight slots and each card has four ports.

SMIv2 extends the concept table for an aggregate object from a single table to multiple tables. This allows for the expansion of managed objects when the number of columnar objects needs to be increased, or when the objects are best organized by grouping them hierarchically. Let us first consider the case of adding columnar objects to an existing table with the following restrictions: (a) the number of conceptual rows is not affected by the addition; (b) there is one-to-one correspondence between the rows of the two tables; and (c) the INDEX of the second table is the same as that of the first table. This is shown in Figure 6.11.

Table 1 is called the aggregate object *table1* and has three columns and four rows; and Table 2 is called aggregate object *table2* and has two columns and four rows. There is a

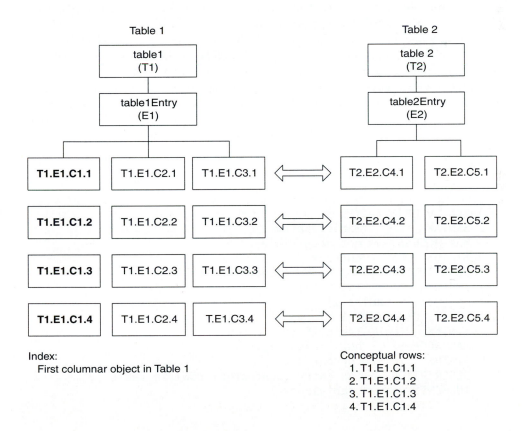

Index:
   First columnar object in Table 1

Conceptual rows:
   1. T1.E1.C1.1
   2. T1.E1.C1.2
   3. T1.E1.C1.3
   4. T1.E1.C1.4

Figure 6.11   Augmentation of Tables

one-to-one correspondence in rows between the two tables. The row object of table1 is *table1Entry* and for table 2 is *table2Entry*. The INDEX is defined in Table1 for both tables and it is the columnar object T1.E1.C1. We are using the notations T1, E1, C1, and so on, for easier visual conceptualization of the instance of an object in a table using the prefixes of table ID (e.g., T1) and entry (e.g., E1). The columnar object notation starts with C (e.g., C1). The value or values suffixed with the columnar object identifier uniquely identifies the row. Objects in a row in a table are identified by the index. For example, the objects in the second row of Table 1 and Table 2 are identified by index T1.E1.C1.2. The value of the columnar object T2.E2.C4 in Table T2 corresponding to index T1.E1.C1.2 is T2.E2.C4.2. Table 1 is called the **base table** and Table 2 is the **augmented table**. The indexing scheme comprises two clauses, INDEX clause and AUGMENTS clause. The constructs for the rows of the two tables in Figure 6.11 are shown in Figure 6.12. The object *table1Entry* has the INDEX clause and *table2Entry* has the AUGMENTS clause that refers to *table1Entry*. The combination of the two tables still provides four conceptual rows, T1.E1.C1.1 through T1.E1.C1.4 (identified by the index), the same number of rows as in the base table.

Figure 6.13 shows an example of augmentation of tables. We have augmented *ipAddrTable* in the standard MIB with a proprietary table, *IpAugAddrTable*, that could add information to the rows of the table. *IpAddrTable* is the base table and *ipAugAddrTable* is the augmented table. In a practical case, the *ipAugAddrTable* could add two more columnar objects to define the board and port number associated with the *ipAdEntIfIndex*.

A table with a larger number of rows (**dense table**) than the base table can be appended to the base table with combined indices of both, as shown in Figure 6.14. The INDEX clause for combining tables of differed sizes is the combined indices; that is, combined columnar objects as the INDEX clause for the added aggregate object. In

```
table1Entry OBJECT-TYPE
     SYNTAX          TableT1Entry
     MAX-ACCESS      not-accessible
     STATUS          current
     DESCRIPTION     "An entry (conceptual row) in table T1"
     INDEX           {T1.E.C1}
        ::= { table1 1}
table2Entry OBJECT-TYPE
     SYNTAX          TableT2Entry
     MAX-ACCESS      not-accessible
     STATUS          current
     DESCRIPTION     "An entry (conceptual row) in table T2"
     AUGMENTS        {table1Entry}
        ::= {table2 1}
```

Figure 6.12   ASN.1 Constructs for Augmentation of Tables

```
ipAddrTable OBJECT-TYPE
    SYNTAX          SEQUENCE OF IpAddrEntry
    MAX-ACCESS      not-accessible
    STATUS          current
    DESCRIPTION     "The table ..."
    ::= {ip 20}
ipAddrEntry  OBJECT-TYPE
    SYNTAX          IpAddrEntry
    MAX-ACCESS      not-accessible
    STATUS          current
    DESCRIPTION     "The addressing information"
    INDEX           {ipAdEntAddr}
    ::= {ipAddrTable 1}
ipAugAddrTable   OBJECT-TYPE
    SYNTAX          SEQUENCE OF IpAugAddrEntry
    MAX-ACCESS      not-accessible
    STATUS          current
    DESCRIPTION     "The augmented table to IP address table
                    defining board and port numbers"
    ::= {ipAug 1}
ipAugAddrEntry OBJECT-TYPE
    SYNTAX          IpAugAddrEntry
    MAX-ACCESS      not-accessible
    STATUS          current
    DESCRIPTION     "The addressing information ..."
    AUGMENTS        {ipAddrEntry}
    ::= {ipAugAddrTable 1}
```

Figure 6.13   Example of Augmentation of Tables

Figure 6.14, Table 1 consists of two rows and three columnar objects, T1.E1.C1, T1.E1.C2, and T1.E1.C3, with the first columnar object T1.E1.C1 being the index. Table 2 has four rows and two columnar objects, T2.E2.C4 and T2.E2.C5 with its first columnar object, T2.E2.C4 being the index. The combined index for specifying the aggregate object of Table 2 appended to Table 1 is the set of both first-columnar objects, T1.E1.C1 and T2.E2.C4. Table 1 is called the **base table** and Table 2 is called the **dependent table**. As we see in Figure 6.14, the combined base table and dependent table could have a maximum of eight conceptual rows (multiplication of the number of rows of the two tables).

Figure 6.15 shows the constructs for appending a dense table to a base table. The two table objects, *table1* and *table2*, are nodes under the node table. The *table1Entry* defines a

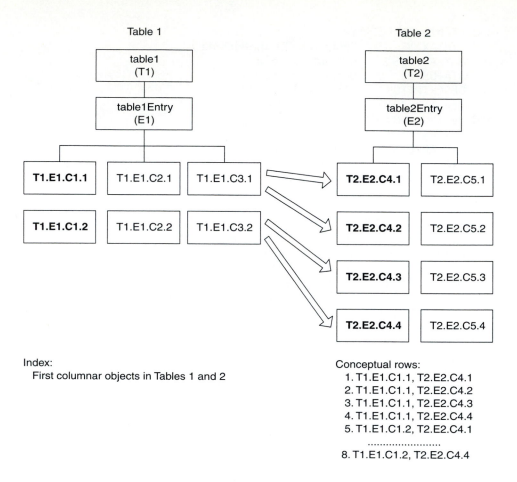

Figure 6.14   Combined Indexing of Tables

row in *table1* with the columnar object T1.E1.C1 as the index. The *table2Entry* is a row in *table2*. Its index is defined by the indices of both tables, namely, T1.E1.C1 and T2.E2.C3.

We can visualize application of combining a base table with a dense table with an example of a router with multiple slots, each slot containing a particular type of board. For example, see the LEC and Ethernet shown in Figure 4.3(c). The slot and the board type will be defined in Table 1. The boards can have different numbers of physical ports. The port configuration is defined by Table 2. By using the combination of the two tables, we can specify the details of a given port in a given slot.

The third possible scenario in appending an aggregate object to an existing aggregate object is the case where the appended table has fewer rows than that of the base table.

```
table1 OBJECT-TYPE
    SYNTAX          SEQUENCE OF table1Entry
    MAX-ACCESS      not-accessible
    STATUS          current
    DESCRIPTION     "Table 1 under T"
        ::= { table 1}
table1Entry OBJECT-TYPE
    SYNTAX          Table1Entry
    MAX-ACCESS      not-accessible
    STATUS          current
    DESCRIPTION     "An entry (conceptual row) in Table 1"
    INDEX           {T1.E1.C1}
        ::= {table1 1}
table2 OBJECT-TYPE
    SYNTAX          SEQUENCE OF table2Entry
    MAX-ACCESS      not-accessible
    STATUS          current
    DESCRIPTION     "Table 2 under T"
        ::= {table 2}
table2Entry OBJECT-TYPE
    SYNTAX          Table2Entry
    MAX-ACCESS      not-accessible
    STATUS          current
    DESCRIPTION     "An entry (conceptual row) in Table 2"
    INDEX           {T1.E1.C1, T2.E2.C4}
        ::= {table2 1}
```

Figure 6.15   ASN.1 Constructs for Appending a Dense Table

This is called a **sparse dependent table** case and is shown in Figure 6.16. In this example, the index for the second table is the same as that for the base table and the constructs are similar to the ones shown in Figure 6.12 except the AUGMENTS clause is substituted with INDEX clause for *table2Entry*. This is shown in Figure 6.17.

In SNMPv2, operational procedures were introduced for the creation and deletion of a row in a table. However, prior to discussing these procedures, let us first look at the textual convention that was specified to create a new object type in designing MIB modules. We will return to row creation and deletion in Section 6.3.7.

6.3.6   Textual Conventions

Textual conventions are designed to help definition of new data types following the structure defined in SMIv2. They are also intended to make the semantics consistent and clear to the human reader. Although new data types could have been created using new ASN.1

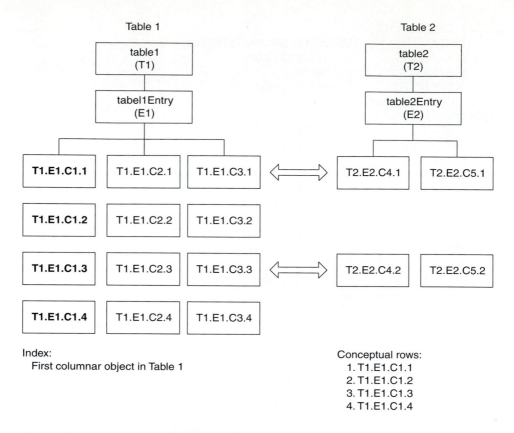

Figure 6.16   Addition of a Sparse Table to Base Table

classes and tags, the decision was made to use the existing defined class types and apply restrictions to them. This is accomplished by defining an ASN.1 macro, TEXTUAL-CONVENTION, in SMIv2.

The TEXTUAL-CONVENTION macro concisely conveys the syntax and semantics associated with a textual convention. SNMP–based management objects defined using a textual convention are encoded by the same basic encoding rules that define their primitive types; however, they have the special semantics as defined in the macro. For all textual conventions defined in an information module, the name is unique and mnemonic, similar to data type and cannot exceed 64 characters. However, it is usually limited to 32 characters.

Let us now compare the definition of a type in SMIv1 with SMIv2. The textual convention was defined in SNMPv1 as an ASN.1 type assignment. For example, textual

```
table1 OBJECT-TYPE
    SYNTAX          SEQUENCE OF table1Entry
    MAX-ACCESS      not-accessible
    STATUS          current
    DESCRIPTION     "Table 1 under T"
        ::= { table 1}
table1Entry OBJECT-TYPE
    SYNTAX          Table1Entry
    MAX-ACCESS      not-accessible
    STATUS          current
    DESCRIPTION     "An entry (conceptual row) in Table 1"
    INDEX           {T1.E.1}
        ::= {table1 1}
table2 OBJECT-TYPE
    SYNTAX          SEQUENCE OF table2Entry
    MAX-ACCESS      not-accessible
    STATUS          current
    DESCRIPTION     "Table 2 under T"
        ::= {table 2}
table2Entry OBJECT-TYPE
    SYNTAX          Table2Entry
    MAX-ACCESS      not-accessible
    STATUS          current
    DESCRIPTION     "An entry (conceptual row) in Table 2"
    INDEX           {table1Entry}
        ::= {table2 1}
```

Figure 6.17   ASN.1 Constructs for Appending Sparse Table

convention for data type *DisplayString* in SNMPv1, from RFC 1213 is

```
DisplayString ::= OCTET STRING
- This data type is used to model textual information taken from
- the NVT ASCII character set. By convention, objects with this
- syntax are declared as having
- SIZE (0..255).
```

The same example of *DisplayString* in SNMPv2 is defined as

```
DisplayString ::= TEXTUAL-CONVENTION
DISPLAY-HINT    "255a"
STATUS          current
DESCRIPTION     "Represents textual information taken from the
                NVT ASCII character set, as defined in pages 4,
                10-11 of RFC 854. ..."
SYNTAX          OCTET STRING (SIZE (0..255))
```

As we can see, the TEXTUAL-CONVENTION in SNMPv2 is defined as data type, and is used to convey the syntax and semantics of a textual convention. The macro for textual conventions is defined in RFC 1903 and a skeleton of it is presented in Figure 6.18. It has the definition of type and value notations with the formalized definition of data types.

All clauses except *DisplayPart* in the TEXTUAL-CONVENTION macro are self-explanatory and represent similar clauses in SMIv1. The *DISPLAY-HINT* clause, which is optional, gives a hint as to how the value of an instance of an object, with the syntax defined using this textual convention, might be displayed. It is applicable to the situations where the underlying primitive type is either INTEGER or OCTET STRING.

For INTEGER type, the display consists of two parts. The first part is a single character denoting the display format: "b" for binary, "d" for decimal, "o" for octal, and "x" for hexadecimal. It is followed by a hyphen and an integer in the case of decimal display to indicate the number of decimal points. For example, a hundredths value of 1234 with DISPLAY-HINT "d-2" is displayed as 12.34.

For the OCTET-STRING type, the display hint consists of one or more octet-format specifications. A brief description of each part is shown in Table 6.2. For example, the DISPLAY-HINT "255a" indicates that the *DisplayString* is an ASCII string of up to a maximum of 255 characters.

Table 6.3 shows the types for which textual conventions were specified in SMIv2, and a brief description of each type. They are applicable to all MIB modules. Only those textual conventions whose status is current are given in the table. One of the important textual conventions is *RowStatus*, which is used for creation and deletion of conceptual rows, which we will discuss next.

```
TEXTUAL-CONVENTION MACRO ::=
BEGIN
    TYPE NOTATION ::=
                    DisplayPart
                    "STATUS" Status
                    "DESCRIPTION" Text
                    ReferPart
                    "SYNTAX" Syntax
    VALUE NOTATION ::=
                    value (VALUE Syntax)
    DisplayPart ::= "DISPLAY-HINT" Text | empty
    Status ::=      "current" | "deprecated" | "obsolete"
        .........
END
```

Figure 6.18   TEXTUAL-CONVENTION Macro [RFC 1903]

Table 6.2   DISPLAY-HINT for Octet Format

1	(Optional) repeat indicator "*"	An integer, indicated by *, that specifies how many times the remainder of this octet-format should be repeated
2	Octet length	One or more decimal digits specifying the number of octets
3	Display format	"x" for hexadecimal, "d" for decimal, "o" for octal, and "a" for ASCII for display
4	(Optional) display separator character	A single character other than a decimal digit or "*", produced after each application of the octet-specification.
5	(Optional) repeat terminator character	A single character other than a decimal digit or "*" present if display character is present. Produced after the second and third part.

Table 6.3   SMIv2 Textual Conventions for Initial Data Types

DisplayString	Textual information from NVT ASCII character set [RFC 854]
PhysAddress	Media- or physical-level address
MacAddress	IEEE 802 MAC address
TruthValue	Boolean value; INTEGER {true (1), false (2)}
TestAndIncr	Integer-valued information used for atomic operations
AutonomousType	An independently extensible type identification value
VariablePointer	Pointer to a specific object instance; e.g., sysContact.0, ifInOctets.3
RowPointer	Pointer to a conceptual row
RowStatus	Used to manage the creation and deletion of conceptual rows and used as the value of the SYNTAX clause for the status column of a conceptual row
TimeStamp	Value of sysUpTime at which a specific occurrence happened
TimeInterval	Period of time, measured in units of 0.01 seconds
DateandTime	Date-time specifications
StorageType	Implementation information on the memory realization of a conceptual row as to the volatility and permanency
Tdomain	Kind of transport service
Taddress	Transport service address

6.3.7   Creation and Deletion of Rows in Tables

The creation of a row and deletion of a row are significant new features in SMIv2. This is patterned after a similar procedure that was developed for RMON, which we discuss in Chapter 8. There are two methods of creating a row in a table. The first is to create a row and make it active, which makes it available immediately. The second method is to create the row and make it available at a later time. This means that we need to know the status of the row as to its availability.

The information on the status of the row is accomplished by introducing a new column, called the *status* column. In Table 6.3 we observed that for the textual convention, RowStatus is used as the value of the SYNTAX clause for the *status* column of a conceptual row. Table 6.4 shows the status with enumerated integer syntax for the six states associated with the row status. The manager uses the last three states, along with the first one, (1, 4, 5, and 6) to create or delete rows on the agent. The agent uses the first three states (1, 2, and 3) to send responses to the manager.

The MAX-ACCESS clause is extended to include "read-create" for the *status* object, which includes read, write, and create privileges. It is a superset of read-write. If a *status* columnar object is present, then no other columnar object of the same conceptual row can have a maximal access of read-write. But it can have objects with maximum access of read-only and not-accessible. If an index object of a conceptual row is also a columnar object (it does not always have to be), it is called an *auxiliary object* and its maximum access is made not-accessible. Remember that there could be more than one index object to define a conceptual row in a table.

Let us now analyze the create and delete operations using the conceptual table shown in Figure 6.19. The table, *table1*, originally has two rows and three columns. The first column, *status*, has the value of the status of the row as indicated by the enumerated integer syntax of the RowStatus textual convention. The second columnar object, *index*, is the index for the conceptual row of *entry1*, and the third columnar object contains nonindexed data. We will illustrate the two types of row-creation and row-deletion operations by adding a third row and then deleting it.

As we notice from Table 6.4, there are two states for RowStatus, *createAndGo* and *createAndWait*, which are action operations. In *createAndGo* the manager sends a message to

Table 6.4   RowStatus Textual Conventions

State	Enumeration	Description
active	1	Row exists and is operational.
notInService	2	Operation on the row is suspended.
notReady	3	Row does not have all the columnar objects needed.
createAndGo	4	This is a one-step process of creation of a row, immediately goes into active state
createAndWait	5	Row is under creation and should not be commissioned into service.
destroy	6	Same as Invalid in EntryStatus. Row should be deleted.

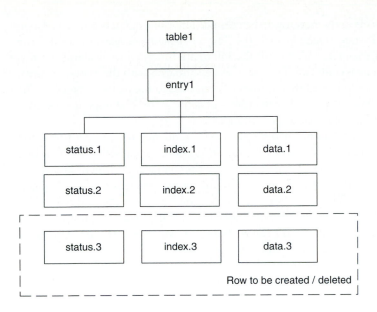

Figure 6.19   Conceptual Table for Creation and Deletion of a Row

the agent to create a row and make its *status* active immediately. In the *createAndWait* operation, the manager sends a message to create a row, but not make it active immediately. Figure 6.20 shows the create-and-go operation. The manager process initiates a **Set-Request-PDU** to create a conceptual row with the values given for the three columnar instances of the row. The value for the index column is specified by the VarBind *index* = 3. This is suffixed to the

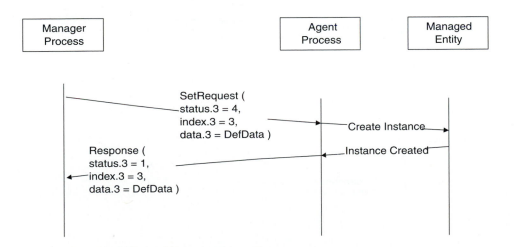

Figure 6.20   Create-and-Go Row Creation

other two columnar objects in the new row to be created. The value of *status* is specified as 4, which is the *createAndGo* state as seen in Table 6.4. The set-request message also specifies the default value *DefData* for *data.3*, and thus all the information needed to establish the row and put it in an active state is complete. The agent process interacts with the managed entity, creates the instance successfully, and then transmits a response to the manager process. The value of the *status* is 1, which denotes that the row is in active state. The response also contains the values of the other columnar object instances.

Figure 6.21 presents a scenario for the operational sequence to create a row using the create-and-wait method. Again, this illustration takes the same scenario of adding the third row to the table shown in Figure 6.19. Only the manager and agent are shown and not the managed entity in this figure. The manager process sends a Set-Request-PDU to the agent process. The value for *status* is 5, which is to create and wait. The third columnar object expects a default value, which is not in the set-request message. Hence, the agent process responds with a *status* value of 3, which is *notReady*. The manager sends a get-request to get the data for the row. The agent responds with a *noSuchInstance* message, indicating that the data value is missing. The manager subsequently sends the value for *data* and receives a response of *notInService (2)* from the

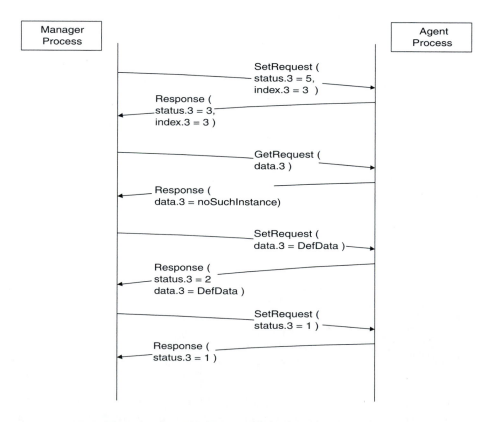

Figure 6.21   Create-and-Wait Row Creation

agent. The fourth and final exchange of messages in the figure is to activate the row with a *status* value of 1. With each message received from the manager, the agent either validates or sets the instance value on the managed entity.

Table 6.5 gives a summary of possible state transitions. The first column lists the action; and the next four columns list the transitions based on the present state.

The operation of deletion of a row is simple. A set-request with a value of 6, which denotes destroy for status is sent by the manager process to the agent process.

Table 6.5   Table of States for Row Creation and Deletion

Action	A Status column does not exist	B Status column notReady	C Status column notInService	D Status column active
Set status column to create-AndGo	noError -> D	inconsistent-Value	inconsistent-Value	inconsistent-Value
Set status column to createAnd-Wait	noError, see 1 or wrongValue	inconsistent-Value	inconsistent-Value	inconsistent-Value
Set status column to active	inconsistent-Value	inconsistent-Value or see 2 ->D	noError ->D	noError ->D
Set status column to notInService	inconsistent-Value	inconsistent-Value or see 3 -> C	noError ->C	noError ->C or wrongValue
Set status column to destroy	noError ->A	noError ->A	noError ->A	noError ->A
Set any other column to some value	see 4	noError see 1	noError ->C	see 5 ->D

1. goto B or C, depending on information available to the agent.

2. If other variable bindings included in the same PDU, provide values for all columns that are missing but required, then return noError and goto D.

3. If other variable bindings included in the same PDU, provide values for all columns that are missing but required, then return *noError* and goto C.

4. At the discretion of the agent, the return value may be

inconsistentName: because the agent does not choose to create such an instance when the corresponding RowStatus instance does not exist, or

inconsistentValue: if the supplied value is inconsistent with the state of some other MIB object's value, or

noError; because the agent chooses to create the instance.

If *noError* is returned, then the instance of the status column must also be created, and the new state is B or C, depending on the information available to the agent. If *inconsistentName* or *inconsistentValue* is returned, the row remains in state A.

5. Depending on the MIB definition for the column/table, either *noError* or *inconsistentValue* may be returned.

Note: Other processing of the set request may result in a response other than *noError* (e.g., wrongValue, noCreation, etc.).

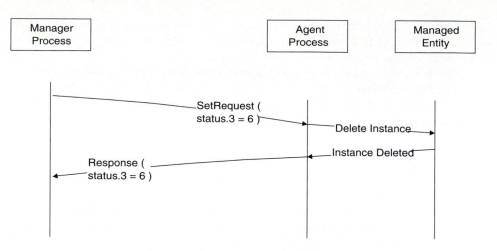

Figure 6.22   Row Deletion

Independent of the current state of the row, the row is deleted and a response sent by the agent. The instance in the managed entity is deleted in the process. This is shown in Figure 6.22.

6.3.8   Notification Definitions

The trap information in SMIv1 has been redefined using the NOTIFICATION-TYPE macro in SMIv2. As we will see in Section 6.5, the PDU associated with the trap information is made consistent with other PDUs. The NOTIFICATION-TYPE macro contains unsolicited information that is generated on an exception basis, for example, when set thresholds are crossed. It can be transmitted within either an SNMP-Trap-PDU from an agent or an InformRequest-PDU from a manager. Two examples of a NOTIFICATION-TYPE macro, drawn from RFC 1902 and RFC 1907 are shown in Figure 6.23. The first example, linkUp, is generated by an agent when a link that has been down comes up.

The OBJECTS clause defines the ordered sequence of MIB objects, which are included in the notification. It may or may not be present. The second example in Figure 6.23, coldStart, has the OBJECTS clause missing and is not needed. The other two clauses, STATUS and DESCRIPTION, have the usual mappings.

We have not presented here discussions on refined syntax in some of the macros, or extension to the informational modules. For information on them, refer to RFC 1902, which also discusses the conversion of a managed object from the OSI to the SNMP version.

6.3.9   Conformance Statements

RFC 1904 defines the SNMPv2 conformance statements for the implementation of network management standards. A product is considered to be in compliance with a particular standard when it meets the minimum set of features in its implementation. The

```
linkUp NOTIFICATION-TYPE
    OBJECTS     {ifIndex}
    STATUS      current
    DESCRIPTION
        "A linkUp trap signifies that the SNMPv2 entity, acting
        in an agent role, recognizes that one of the communication
        links represented in its configuration has come up."
    ::= {snmpTraps 4}

coldStart NOTIFICATION-TYPE
    STATUS      current
    DESCRIPTION
        "A coldStart trap signifies that the SNMPv2 entity, acting
        in an agent role, is reinitializing itself such that its
        configuration is unaltered."
::= {snmpTraps 1}
```

Figure 6.23   Examples of NOTIFICATION-TYPE Macro

minimum requirements for SNMPv2 compliance are called module compliance and are defined by an ASN.1 macro, MODULE-COMPLIANCE. It specifies the minimum MIB modules or subset of modules that should be implemented. The actual MIB modules that are implemented in an agent are specified by another ASN.1 module, AGENT-CAPA-BILITIES. For the convenience of defining module-compliance and agent-capabilities, the objects and traps have been combined into groups, which are subsets of MIB modules. The object grouping is defined by an ASN.1 macro, OBJECT-GROUP, and the group of traps is defined by the NOTIFICATION-GROUP macro.

The Object Group.   The OBJECT-GROUP macro defines a group of related objects in a MIB module. Used for defining conformance specifications, the OBJECT-GROUP macro is compiled during implementation, not at run-time. The macro is shown in Figure 6.24. Implementation of an object in an agent implies that it executes the get and set operations from a manager. If an agent in SNMPv2 has not implemented an object, it returns a noSuchObject error message.

The OBJECTS clause names each object contained in the conformance group. Each of the named objects is defined in the same informational module as the OBJECT-GROUP macro and has a MAX-ACCESS clause of "accessible-for-notify", "read-only", "read-write", or "read-create". Every object that is defined in an informational module with a MAX-ACCESS clause other than "not-accessible" is present in at least one object group. This prevents the mistake of adding an object to an information module, but forgetting to add it to a group.

The STATUS, DESCRIPTION, and REFERENCE clauses have the usual interpretations.

An example of an OBJECT-GROUP, systemGroup in SNMPv2, is shown in Figure 6.25. The system group defines the objects that pertain to the overall information about

```
OBJECT-GROUP MACRO
    BEGIN
        TYPE NOTATION ::=
                            ObjectsPart
                            "STATUS" Status
                            "DESCRIPTION" Text
                            ReferPart

        VALUE NOTATION ::=
                            value (VALUE OBJECT IDENTIFIER)
        ObjectsPart ::=     "OBJECTS" "{"objects"}"
        Objects ::=         Object | Objects "," Object
        Object ::=          value (Name Object Name)
        Status ::=          "current" | "deprecated" | "Obsolete"
        ReferPart ::=       "REFERENCE" Text | empty

        -- uses the NVT ASCII character set
        Text ::=            """" string """"
END
```

Figure 6.24   The OBJECT-GROUP Macro

the system. Because it is so basic, it is implemented in all agent and management systems. All eight entities defined as values for OBJECTS should be implemented. The group has some entities that were not in SNMPv1, such as *sysORLastChange*. These will be addressed when we discuss SMPv2 MIB in Section 6.4.1.

The Notification Group.   The notification group contains notification entities, or what was defined as traps in SMIv1. The NOTIFICATION-GROUP macro, shown in Figure 6.26, is compiled during implementation, not during run-time. The value of an invocation of the NOTIFICATION-GROUP macro is the name of the group, which is an OBJECT IDENTIFIER.

```
systemGroup    OBJECT-GROUP
    OBJECTS    {sysDescr, sysObjectID, sysUpTime, sysContact,
               sysName, sysLocation, sysServices, sysORLastChange,
               sysORID, sysORUptime, sysORDesc}
    STATUS     current
    DESCRIPTION    "The system group defines objects that are
                    common to all managed systems."
    ::= {snmpMIBGroups 6}
```

Figure 6.25   Example of an OBJECT-GROUP Macro

```
NOTIFICATION-GROUP MACRO
BEGIN
    TYPE NOTATION ::=
                       NotificationsPart
                       "STATUS" Status
                       "DESCRIPTION" Text
                       ReferPart
    VALUE NOTATION ::=
                       value (VALUE OBJECT IDENTIFIER)


NotificationsPart ::=  "NOTIFICATIONS" "{"Notifications"}"
Notifications ::=      Notification | Notifications "," Notification
Notification ::=       value (Name NotificationName)


    Status ::=         "current" | "deprecated" | "obsolete"
    ReferPart ::=      "REFERENCE" Text | empty


    -- uses the NVT ASCII character set
    Text ::= """" string """"


END
```

Figure 6.26   The NOTIFICATION-GROUP Macro

An example of NOTIFICATION-GROUP, *snmpBasicNotificationsGroup*, is shown in Figure 6.27. According to this invocation, the conformance group, *snmpBasicNotifications-Group*, has two notifications: *coldStart* and *authenticationFailure*.

Module Compliance.   The MODULE-COMPLIANCE macro, shown in Figure 6.28, defines the minimum set of requirements for implementation of one or more MIB modules. The expansion of the MODULE-COMPLIANCE macro is done during the implementation and not during run-time. The MODULE-COMPLIANCE macro can be defined as a component of the information module or as a companion module.

The STATUS, DESCRIPTION, and REFERENCE clauses are self-explanatory.

```
snmpBasicNotificationsGroup NOTIFICATION-GROUP
    NOTIFICATIONS    {coldStart, authenticationFailure}
    STATUS           current
    DESCRIPTION      "The two notifications that an SNMP-2 entity is
                     required to implement."
    ::= {snmpMIBGroups 7}
```

Figure 6.27   Example of a NOTIFICATION-GROUP Macro

```
MODULE-COMPLIANCE MACRO
BEGIN
    TYPE NOTATION ::=
                        "STATUS" Status
                        "DESCRIPTION" text
                        ReferPart
                        ModulePart

    VALUE NOTATION ::=
                        value (VALUE OBJECT IDENTIFIER)

    Status ::=                "current" | "deprecated" | "obsolete"
    ReferPart ::=             "REFERENCE" Text | empty
    ModulePart ::=            Modules | empty
    Modules ::=               Module | Modules Module
    Module ::=                -- name of module --
                              "MODULE" ModuleName
                              Mandatory Part
                              CompliancePart
    ModuleName ::=            moduleReference ModuleIdentifier | empty
-- must not be empty unless contained in MIB module
ModuleIdentifier ::=          value (ModuleID OBJECT IDENTIFIER) |
empty
    MandatoryPart ::=         "MANDATORY-GROUPS" "{" Groups "}"
                              | empty
    Groups ::=                Group | Groups "," Group
    Group ::=                 value (Group OBJECT IDENTIFIER)
    CompliancePart ::=        Compliances | empty
    Compliances ::=           Compliance | Compliances compliance
    Compliance ::=            ComplianceGroup | Object
    ComplianceGroup ::=       "GROUP" value (Name OBJECT IDENTIFIER)
                              "DESCRIPTION" Text
    Object ::=                "OBJECT" value (Name ObjectName)
                              SyntaxPart
                              WriteSyntaxPart
                              AccessPart
                              "DESCRIPTION" Text
    --must be a refinement for object's SYNTAX clause
    SyntaxPart ::=            "SYNTAX" type (SYNTAX) | empty
    --must be a refinement for object's SYNTAX clause
    WriteSyntaxPart ::=       "WRITE-SYNTAX" type (WriteSYNTAX) | empty
    AccessPart ::=            "MIN-ACCESS" Access | empty
    Access ::=                "not-accessible" | "accessible-for-
                              notify" | read-only" | "read-write" |
                              "read-create"
-- uses the NVT ASCII character set
    Text ::=                  """ string """
END
```

Figure 6.28   The MODULE-COMPLIANCE Macro

The MODULE clause is used to name each module for which compliance requirements are specified. The modules are identified by the module name and by its OBJECT IDENTIFIER. The latter can be dropped if the MODULE-COMPLIANCE is invoked in a MIB module and refers to the encompassing MIB module.

Two CLAUSES of groups are specified by the MODULE-COMPLIANCE macro: MANDATORY-GROUPS and GROUP. As the name implies, the MANDATORY-CLAUSE modules have to be implemented for the system to be SNMPv2 compliant. The group specified by the GROUP clause is not mandatory for the MIB module, but helps vendors define specifications of the features that have been implemented.

When both the WRITE-SYNTAX and the SYNTAX clauses are present, restrictions are placed on the syntax for the object mentioned in the OBJECT clause. These restrictions are tabulated in Section 9 of RFC 1902.

The *snmpBasicCompliance* macro is an example of a MODULE-COMPLIANCE macro and is part of the SNMPv2 MIB presented in Figure 6.6. A system is defined as SNMPv2 compliant if and only *if snmpGroup, snmpSetGroup, systemGroup,* and *snmpBasicNotificationsGroup* are implemented. The GROUP, *snmpCommunityGroup,* is optional.

Agent Capabilities.   The AGENT-CAPABILITIES macro is lengthy; refer to RFC 1904 for exact specifications. A skeleton of the macro and significant points of the macro is shown in Figure 6.29.

```
AGENT-CAPABILITIES
BEGIN
    TYPE NOTATION ::=
                        "PRODUCT-RELEASE" Text
                        "STATUS" Status
                        "DESCRIPTION" Test
                        ReferPart
                        ModulePart
    VALUE NOTATION ::=
                        value (VALUE OBJECT IDENTIFIER)
    Status ::=          "current" | "obsolete"
    ReferPart ::=       "REFERENCE" | empty
    ModulePart ::=      Modules | empty
    Modules ::=         Module | Modules Module
    Module ::=          – name of module –
                        "SUPPORT" ModuleName
                        "INCLUDES" "{"Groups"}"
                        VariationsPart
    ...         ...             ...             ...
END
```

Figure 6.29   The AGENT-CAPABILITIES Macro (Skeleton)

```
routerIsi123 AGENT-CAPABILITIES
     PRODUCT-RELEASE       "InfoTech Router isiRouter123 release 1.0"
     STATUS                current
     DESCRIPTION           "InfoTech High Speed Router"
     SUPPORTS              snmpMIB
        INCLUDES           {systemGroup, snmpGroup, snmpSetGroup,
                           snmpBasicNotificationsGroup }
        VARIATION          coldStart
        DESCRIPTION            "A coldStart trap is generated on all
                              reboots."
     SUPPORTS              IF-MIB
        INCLUDES           {ifGeneralGroup, ifPacketGroup}
     SUPPORTS              IP MIB
        INCLUDES           {ipGroup, icmpGroup}
     SUPPORTS              TCP-MIB
        INCLUDES           {tcpGroup}
     SUPPORTS              UDP-MIB
        INCLUDES           {udpGroup}
     SUPPORTS              EGP-MIB
        INCLUDES           {egpGroup}
::= { isiRouter 1 }
```

Figure 6.30   Example of an AGENT-CAPABILITIES Macro

The AGENT-CAPABILITIES macro for the router example given in Figure 6.10 is
shown in Figure 6.30. Note that the *snmpMIB* module, which is SNMPv2-MIB, includes
system and *snmp* MIBs. Those MIBs and the associated groups are supported by the router.
Other standard MIBs and groups supported by the router are indicated in Figure 6.30.

6.4   The SNMPv2 Management Information Base

As mentioned in Section 6.3 and shown in Figure 6.5, two new MIB modules, security and
SNMPv2, have been added to the Internet MIB. The SNMPv2 module has three submodules: SNMPDomains, SNMPProxys, and SNMPModules. SNMPDomains extends
the SNMP standards to send management messages over transmission protocols other than
UDP, which is the predominant and preferred way of transportation [RFC 1906]. Since
UDP is the preferred protocol, systems that use another protocol need a proxy service to
map onto UDP. Not much work has been done on SNMPProxys, as of now.

There are changes made to the core MIB-II defined in SNMPv1. Figure 6.31 presents
an overview of the changes to the Internet MIB and their relationships. The system module and *snmp* module under *mib-2* have significant changes as defined in RFC 1907. A
new module *snmpMIB* has been defined, which is {snmpModules 1}. There are two modules under *snmpMIB: snmpMIBObjects* and *snmpMIBConformance*.

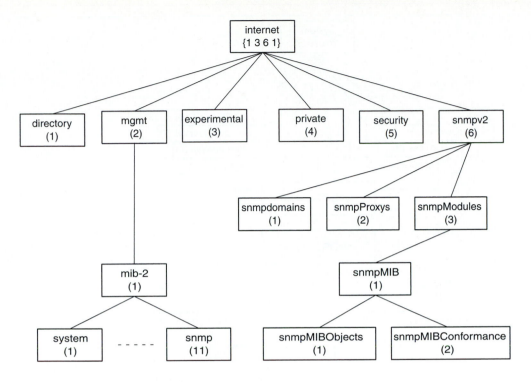

Figure 6.31   The SNMPv2 Internet Group

The MIB module *snmpMIBObjects* addresses the new objects introduced in SNMPv2, as well as those that are obsolete. This module is concerned primarily with trap, which has been brought into the same format as other PDUs. Also, many of the unnecessary objects in the SNMP group have been made obsolete.

We discussed the conformance specifications and object groups in the previous section. They are specified under the *snmpMIBconformance* module. As SNMPv2 is currently defined, there is a strong coupling between *system*, *snmp*, *snmpMIBObjects*, and *snmpMIBconformance* modules. With this picture in mind, it will be a lot easier to follow RFC 1907, which discusses all these modules.

6.4.1   Changes to the System Group in SNMPv2

There are seven entities, or objects, in SNMPv2 system group that are the same as in SNMPv1. Two additional objects are added to the System group in SNMPv2; both are collection of objects, called object resources that support various MIB modules. Object resources are configurable both statically and dynamically. Figure 6.32 shows the MIB tree

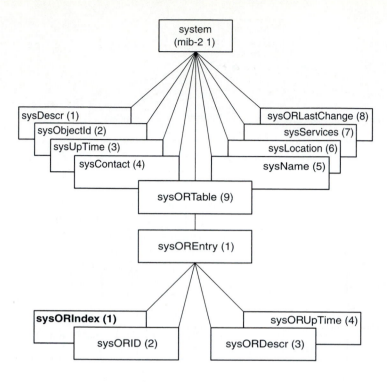

Figure 6.32   The SNMPv2 System Group

for the System group in SNMPv2. The *sysORLastChange* entity and *sysORTable* have been added to the set of objects in the System group. Table 6.6 presents the entity, OID, and a brief description of each entity for the System group.

6.4.2   Changes to the SNMP Group in SNMPv2

The SNMP group in SNMPv2 has been simplified considerably from SNMPv1 by eliminating a large number of entities that were considered unnecessary. The simplified SNMP group is shown in Figure 6.33 (compare with Figure 5.21!). It has only eight entities—six old ones (1,3,4,5,6,30) and two new ones (31,32). Figure 6.33 also presents the four groups of all SNMP entities: *snmpGroup, snmpCommunityGroup, snmpObsoleteGroup,* and the group of two objects, 7 and 23, not used even in version 1. We will soon see that the *snmpGroup* is mandatory to implement for compliance of SNMPv2 and the *snmpCommunityGroup* is optional. The *snmpObsoleteGroup* is self-explanatory.

The SNMPv2 SNMP group is shown in Table 6.7. All the unused and obsolete entities have been omitted for clarity.

Table 6.6   The SNMPv2 System Group

Entity	OID	Description (brief)
sysDescr	system 1	Textual description
sysObjectID	system 2	OBJECT IDENTIFIER of the entity
sysUpTime	system 3	Time (in hundredths of a second) since last reset
sysContact	system 4	Contact person for the node
sysName	system 5	Administrative name of the system
sysLocation	system 6	Physical location of the node
sysServices	system 7	Value designating the layer services provided by the entity
sysORLastChange	system 8	SysUpTime since last change in state or sysORID change
sysORTable	system 9	Table listing system resources that the agent controls; manager can configure these resources through the agent
sysOREntry	sysORTable 1	An entry in the sysORTable
sysORIndex	sysOREntry 1	Row index, also index for the table
sysORID	sysOREntry 2	ID of the resource module
sysORDescr	sysOREntry 3	Textual description of the resource module
sysORUpTime	sysOREntry 4	system up-time since the object in this row was last instantiated

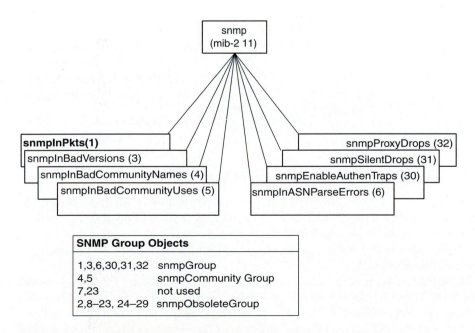

Figure 6.33   The SNMPv2 SNMP Group

Table 6.7   The SNMPv2 SNMP Group

Entity	OID	Description (brief)
snmpInPkts	snmp (1)	Total number of messages delivered from transport service
snmpInBadVersions	snmp (3)	Total number of messages from transport service that are of unsupported version
snmpInBadCommunityNames	snmp (4)	Total number of messages from transport service that are of unknown community name
snmpInBadCommunityUses	snmp (5)	Total number of messages from transport service, of not allowed operation by the sending community
snmpInASNParseErrs	snmp (6)	Total number of ASN.1 and BER errors
snmpEnableAuthenTraps	snmp (30)	Override option to generate authentication failure traps
snmpSilentDrops	snmp (31)	Total number of the five types of received PDUs that were silently dropped due to exceptions in varbinds or max. message size
snmpProxyDrops	snmp (32)	Total number of the five types of received PDUs that were silently dropped due to inability to respond to a target proxy

6.4.3   Information for Notification in SNMPv2

The information on traps in SNMPv1 has been restructured in version 2 to conform to the rest of the PDUs. The macro TRAP-TYPE, used in version 1 and described in RFC 1215, has been made obsolete in SNMPv2. At the same time, enhancement to the specifications has been made, and the terminology has been generalized to "notification", as the subheading indicates.

The information on notifications is defined under *snmpMIBObjects* and is shown in Figure 6.34. There are three modules under the *snmpMIBObjects* node: *snmpTrap* (4), *snmpTraps* (5), and *snmpSet* (6). The subnode designations 1, 2, and 3 under *snmpMIBObjects* have been made obsolete. Table 6.8 gives a brief description of the subnodes and leaf objects under *snmpMIBObjects*.

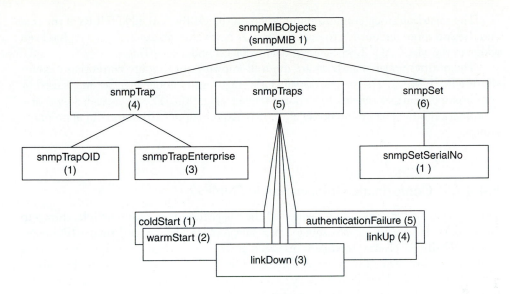

Figure 6.34 MIB Modules under snmpMIBObjects

Table 6.8 snmpMIBObjects MIB

Entity	OID	Description (brief)
snmpTrap	snmpMIBObjects 4	Information group that contains trap ID and enterprise ID
snmpTrapOID	snmpTrap 1	OBJECT IDENTIFIER of the notification
snmpTrapEnterprise	snmpTrap 2	OBJECT IDENTIFIER of the enterprise sending the notification
snmpTraps	snmpMIBObjects 5	Collection of well-known traps used in SNMPv1
coldStart	snmpTraps 1	Trap informing of a cold start of the object
warmStart	snmpTraps 2	Trap informing a warm start of the object
linkDown	snmpTraps 3	Agent detecting a failure of a communication link
linkUp	snmpTraps 4	Agent detecting coming up of a communication link
authentificationFailure	snmpTraps 5	Agent reporting receipt of an unauthenticated protocol message
snmpSet	snmpMIBObjects 6	Manager-to-manager notification messages
snmpSetSerialNo	snmpSet 1	Advisory lock between managers to coordinate set operation

The *snmpTrap* group contains information on the OBJECT IDENTIFIERs of the trap and the enterprise responsible to send the trap. A new value, *accessible-for-notify*, has been added to the MAX-ACCESS clause to define objects under *snmpTrap*.

The entities under *snmpTraps* are the well-known traps that are currently in extensive use in SNMPv1. The *snmpSetSerialNo* is a single entity under *snmpSet* and is used by coordinating manager objects to perform the set operation. This is intended as coarse coordination only; fine-grain coordination may require more MIB objects in appropriate groups.

6.4.4   Conformance Information in SNMPv2

The conformance information is defined by the *snmpMIBConformance* module, shown in Figure 6.35. It consists of two submodules: *snmpMIBcompliances* and *snmpMIBGroups*. The *snmpMIBCompliances* module is discussed extensively in Section 6.3.9. The units of conformance are defined in terms of OBJECT-GROUPs. Table 6.9 presents the various OBJECT-GROUPs defined in SNMPv2 and associated OBJECTS for all but *snmpObsoleteGroup*, which is shown in Figure 6.33.

6.4.5   Expanded Internet MIB-II

As SNMP network management expands to cover legacy as well as new technology, MIB modules are continuously increasing. Figure 6.36 shows an expanded MIB-II [Miller MA] that has more modules than those covered in RFC 1213. It is not intended to be an exhaustive list. Table 6.10 gives a description of each group in the MIB.

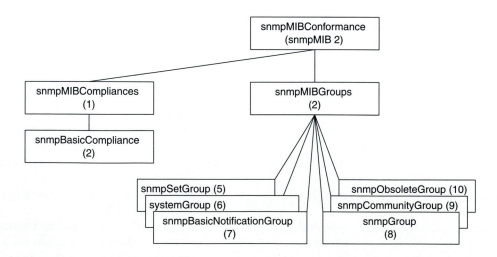

Figure 6.35   MIB Modules under snmpMIBConformance

Table 6.9 SNMPv2 OBJECT-GROUPs

OBJECT-GROUPs	OID	OBJECTS
snmpSetGroup	snmpMIBGroups 5	snmpSetSerialNo
systemGroup	snmpMIBGroups 6	sysDescr
		sysObjectID
		sysUpTime
		sysContact
		sysName
		sysLocation
		sysServices
		sysORLastChange
		sysORID
		sysORUpTime
		sysORDescr
snmpBasicNotification Group	snmpMIBGroups 7	coldStart
		authenticationFailure
snmpGroup	snmpMIBGroups 8	snmpInPkts
		snmpInBadVersions
		snmpInASNParseErrs
		snmpSilentDrops
		snmpProxyDrops
		snmpEnableAuthenTraps
snmpCommunityGroup	snmpMIBGroups 9	snmpInBadCommunityNames
		snmpInBadCommunityUses
snmpObsoleteGroup	snmpMIBGroups 10	Please see Figure 6.33

6.5 SNMPv2 Protocol

SNMPv2 protocol operations are based on a community administrative framework, which is the same as in SNMPv1; this was discussed in Chapter 5. We presented the SNMPv2 protocol operations from a system architecture viewpoint in Section 6.2. In this section we'll discuss the details of the PDU data structures and protocol operations.

6.5.1 The Data Structure of SNMPv2 PDUs

The PDU data structure in SNMPv2 has been standardized to a common format for all messages. This improves the efficiency and performance of message exchange between systems. The significant improvement is that the trap data structure is in the same format as the rest. The generic PDU message structure is shown in Figure 6.37 and is the same as Figure 5.8 of SNMPv1. The PDU type is indicated by an application-wide data type. The error-status, defined as Enumerated INTEGER, and error-index fields are

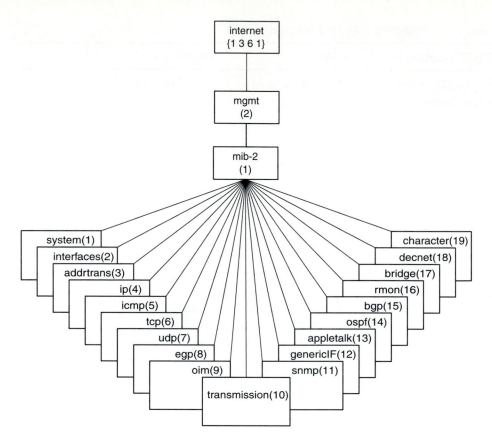

Figure 6.36   An Expanded Internet MIB-II Group

Table 6.10   Expanded MIB-II Group

Group	OID	Description (brief)
genericIF	mib-2 12	Extension to generic interfaces in interfaces group
appletalk	mib-2 13	MIB for appletalk networks
ospf	mib-2 14	Open Shortest Path First routing protocol MIB
bgp	mib-2 15	MIB for Border Gateway Protocol for inter-autonomous network routing
rmon	mib-2 16	MIB for remote monitoring using RMON probe; there are MIBs under this for Ethernet and token-ring networks
bridge	mib-2 17	MIB for bridges
decnet	mib-2 18	Digital Equipment Corporation DECnet MIB
character	mib-2 19	MIB for ports with character stream output for computer peripheral

PDU Type	RequestID	Error Status	Error Index	VarBind 1 name	VarBind 1 value	...	VarBind n name	VarBind n value

Figure 6.37   SNMPv2 PDU (all but bulk)

either set to zero or ignored in the get-request, get-next-request, and set messages. Error-status is set to zero in the get-response message if there is no error; otherwise, the type of error is indicated. Table 6.11 lists the types of PDU and error-status. The error-index is set to zero if there is no error. If there is error, it identifies the first variable binding in the variable-binding list that caused the error message. The first variable binding in a request's variable-binding list is index one, the second is index two, and so forth.

Table 6.11   Values for Types of PDU and Error-Status Fields in SNMPv2 PDU

Field	Type/Enumeration	Value
PDU	0	Get-Request-PDU
	1	GetNextRequest-PDU
	2	Response-PDU
	3	Set-Request-PDU
	4	obsolete
	5	GetBulkRequest-PDU
	6	InformRequest-PDU
	7	SNMPv2-Trap-PDU
Error Status	0	noError
	1	tooBig
	2	noSuchName
	3	badValue
	4	readOnly
	5	genErr
	6	noAccess
	7	wrongType
	8	wrongLength
	9	wrongEncoding
	10	wrongValue
	11	noCreation
	12	inconsistentValue
	13	resourceUnavailable
	14	commitFailed
	15	undoFailed
	16	authorizationError
	17	notWritable
	18	inconsistentName

PDU Type	RequestID	Non-Repeaters	Max Repetitions	VarBind 1 name	VarBind 1 value	...	VarBind n name	VarBind n value

Figure 6.38   SNMPv2 GetBulkRequest PDU

The error-status and error-index fields function differently in SNMPv1 and SNMPv2. In version 1, any error encountered by the agent in responding to the requests from the manager generates a nonzero value either in the error-status field or in both the error-status and error-index fields. Values in the variable bindings are returned only under nonerror conditions.

In SNMPv2, however, if only the error-status field of the Response-PDU is nonzero, the value fields of the variable binding in the variable-binding list are ignored. If both the error-status and the error-index fields of the Response-PDU are nonzero, then the value of the error-index field is the index of the variable binding (in the variable-binding list of the corresponding request) for which the request failed. The values in the other variable bindings in the variable-binding list are returned with valid values and processed by the manager.

The generic PDU format is applicable to all SNMPv2 messages except the Get-Bulk-Request PDU, the format for which is shown in Figure 6.38. You can see that the format of the structure is the same in both cases, except that in the get-bulk-request message the third and fourth fields are different. The third field, the error-status field, is replaced by non-repeaters; and the fourth field, the error-index field, is replaced by max-repetitions. As we mentioned in Section 6.2, the get-bulk-request enables us to retrieve data in bulk. We can retrieve with a single message a number of both nonrepetitive scalar values and repetitive tabular values. The non-repeaters indicate the number of nonrepetitive field values requested; and the max-repetitions field designates the maximum number of table rows requested. Next we will look at the SNMPv2 operations using the PDUs.

6.5.2   SNMPv2 Protocol Operations

There are seven protocol operations in SNMPv2, as discussed in Section 6.3. We will ignore the report operation, which is not used. The messages *get-request*, *get-next-request*, *set-request*, and *get-response* are in both SNMPv1 and SNMPv2 and operate in a similar fashion. The two messages in SNMPv2 that are not in version 1 are the *get-bulk-request* and the *inform-request*. The command get-bulk-request is an enhancement of get-next request and retrieves data in bulk efficiently.

The GetBulkRequest-PDU Operation.   The **get-bulk-request** operation is added in SNMPv2 to retrieve bulk data from a remote entity. Its greatest benefit is in retrieving multiple rows of data from a table. The basic operation of get-bulk-request is the same as get-next-request. The third and fourth field positions are used in the get-bulk-request message PDU as non-repeaters and max-repetitions, as shown in Figure 6.38. The non-repeaters field indicates the number of nonrepetitive (scalar) objects to be retrieved. The max-repetitions field defines the maximum number of instances to be returned in the response message. This would correspond to the number of rows in an aggregate object. The value for the max-repetitions field is operation-dependent and is determined by such factors as the maximum size of the SNMP message, the buffer size in implementation, and the expected size of the aggregate object table.

The data structure of the response for the get-bulk-request operation differs from other get and set operations. Successful processing of the get-bulk-request produces variable bindings (larger array of VarBindList) in the response PDU, which is larger than that contained in the corresponding request. Thus, there is no one-to-one relationship between the VarBindList of the request and response messages.

Figure 6.39 shows a conceptual MIB to illustrate the operation of get-next-request and get-bulk-request shown in Figures 6.40 and 6.41. It is similar to Figure 5.12, but has

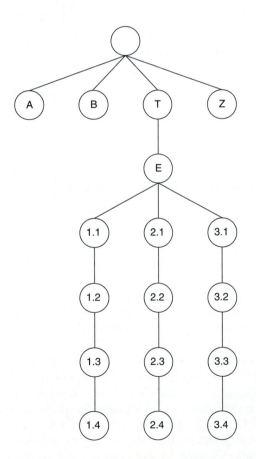

Figure 6.39   The MIB for Operation Sequences in Figures 6.40 and 6.41

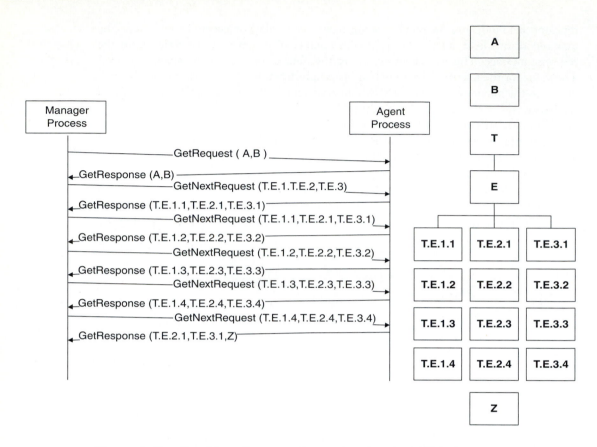

Figure 6.40   Get-Next-Request Operation for the MIB in Figure 6.39

two more rows added to the table. To show the difference in improvement of get-bulk-request over get-next-request, Figure 6.40 shows the sequence of operations for get-next-request for the MIB in Figure 6.39. The sequence starts with a get-request message from the manager process with a VarBindList array of two scalar variables, A and B. It is subsequently followed by the get-next-request message with three columnar OBJECT IDENTIFIERs T.E.1, T.E.2, and T.E.3. The get-response returns the first instance values T.E.1.1, T.E.2.1, and T.E.3.1. The sequence of operation continues until the fourth instance is retrieved. The last get-next-request message with the OBJECT IDENTIFIERs T.E.1.4, T.E.2.4, and T.E.3.4 generates the values T.E.2.1, T.E.3.1, and Z. This is because there are no more instances of the table. It retrieves the three objects, which are logically the next lexicographically higher objects—namely, T.E.2.1 (next to T.E.1.4), T.E.3.1 (next to T.E.2.4), and Z (next to T.E.3.4). The manager would stop the sequence at this message. However, if it continues the operation, it would receive a *noSuchName* error message.

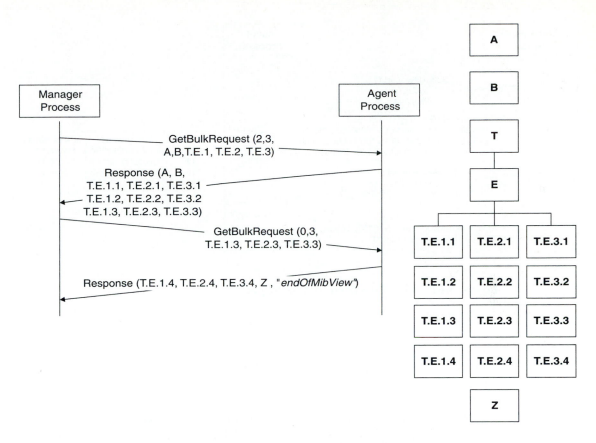

Figure 6.41   Get-Bulk-Request Operation for the MIB in Figure 6.39

Figure 6.41 shows the sequence of operations to retrieve the MIB shown in Figure 6.39 using the get-bulk message. The entire MIB data is retrieved in two requests. The first message GetBulkRequest-PDU (2, 3, A, B, T.E.1, T.E.2, T.E.3) is a request for two nonrepetitive objects (the first operand (2) in the request command) and three repetitive instances (the second operand (3) in the command) of the columnar objects (T.E.1, T.E.2, and T.E.3). The Response-PDU returns values of A and B for the nonrepetitive objects, and the first three rows of the aggregate object table. The second request is for three more rows of the table. Because there is only one row left to send, the response message contains the information in the last row, the next lexicographic entity, Z, and the error message endOfMibView. The manager interprets this as the end of the table. (Note that "-PDU" is not shown in the figure for clarity.)

Figure 6.42 shows the retrieval of the address translation table shown in Figure 5.16 using the get-bulk-request operation. Instead of four sets of get-next-request and

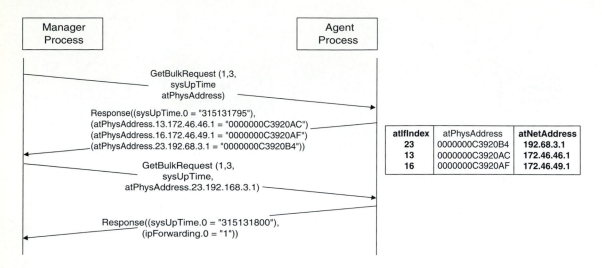

Figure 6.42   Get-Bulk-Request Example

get-response messages, only two get-bulk-request and response messages are needed in the get-bulk-request operation. Instead of endOfMibView as shown in Figure 6.41, the agent returns the first scalar in the IP group, which the manager interprets as the end of the table.

The SNMPv2-Trap-PDU and InformRequest-PDU Operations. The SNMPv2-Trap-PDU performs the same function as in version 1. The name and the data structure have been changed from the generic format shown in Figure 6.37. The variable bindings in position 1 and 2 are specified as *sysUpTime* and *snmpTrapOID,* as shown in Figure 6.43. The destination(s) to which a trap is sent is implementation dependent.

A trap is defined by using the NOTIFICATION-TYPE macro. If the macro contains an OBJECTS clause, then the objects defined by the clause are in the variable bindings in the order defined in the clause. For example, we may want to know what interface is associated with a *linkUp* trap. In this case the linkUp NOTIFICATION-TYPE would have *ifIndex* as an object in its OBJECTS clause, as shown in Figure 6.44.

An InformRequest-PDU is generated by a manager (in contrast to a trap generated by an agent) to inform another manager of information in its MIB view. Although a trap is received passively by a manager, an InformRequest-PDU generates a response in the receiving manager to send to the sending manager.

PDU Type	RequestID	Error Status	Error Index	VarBind 1 sysUpTime	VarBind 1 value	VarBind 2 snmpTrapOID	VarBind 2 value	...

Figure 6.43   SNMPv2 Trap PDU

```
linkUp NOTIFICATION-TYPE
    OBJECTS          { ifIndex }
    STATUS           current
    DESCRIPTION      "A linkUp trap signifies that the SNMPv2 entity,
                     acting in an agent role, recognizes that one of
                     the communication links represented in its
                     configuration has come up."
```

Figure 6.44   An OBJECTS Clause in the NOTIFICATION-TYPE Macro

6.6   Compatibility with SNMPvI

An SNMP proxy server, in general, converts a set of non–SNMP entities into a set of SNMP–defined MIB entities. Unfortunately, SNMPv2 MIB is not backward compatible with SNMPv1 and hence requires conversion of messages. The SNMPv2 IETF Working Group has proposed [RFC 1908] two schemes for migration from SNMPv1 to SNMPv2: bilingual manager and SNMP proxy server.

6.6.1   The Bilingual Manager

One of the migration paths to transition to SNMPv2 from version 1 is to implement both SNMPv1 and SNMPv2 interpreter modules in the manager with a database that has profiles of the agents' version. The interpreter modules do all the conversions of MIB variables and SNMP protocol operations in both directions. The **bilingual manager** does the common functions needed for a management system. The SNMP PDU contains the version number field to identify the version (see Figure 5.5). This arrangement, which is expensive to implement and maintain, is shown in Figure 6.45. The alternative scheme is to use a proxy server.

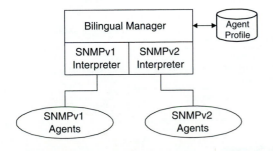

Figure 6.45   The SNMP Bilingual Manager

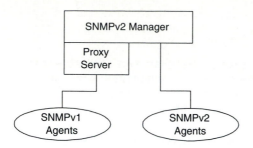

Figure 6.46   The SNMPv2 Proxy Server Configuration

6.6.2   The SNMP Proxy Server

The **SNMPv2 proxy server** configuration is shown in Figure 6.46. The requests to and responses from, as well as traps, from SNMPv2 agents are processed by the SNMPv2 manager in a straightforward manner. A proxy server is implemented as a front-end module to the SNMPv2 manager to allow communication with SNMPv1 agents.

Figure 6.47 details the conversions done by an SNMP v2-v1 proxy server. The get-Request, GetNextRequest-PDU, and Set-Request-PDU from the SNMPv2 manager are passed through unaltered by the proxy server. There are two modifications done to the GetBulkRequest-PDU. The values for the two fields, non-repeaters and max-repetitions, are set to zero and transmitted as GetNextRequest-PDU. The GetResponse-PDU from

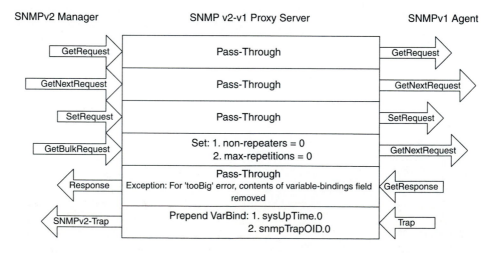

Figure 6.47   The SNMP v2-v1 Proxy Server

SNMPv1 is passed through unaltered by the proxy server to the SNMPv2 manager, unless a response has a *tooBigError* value. In the exception, the contents of the variable binding field are removed before propagating the response. The trap from the SNMPv1 agent is prepended with two VarBind fields, *sysUpTime*.0 and *snmpTrapOID*.0, with their associated values and then passed on to the SNMPv2 manager as an SNMPv2-Trap-PDU.

Summary

A significant number of network management systems and agents that are on the market today use SNMP version 1, referred to as SNMPv1. However, some features have been added to SNMPv1 and formally defined in SNMPv2. In this chapter, we have discussed the enhancements of SNMPv1 that exist in SNMPv2.

The enhancements to SNMP architecture are the formalization of manager-to-manager communication and the inclusion of traps as part of the SMI and messages, instead of as an appendix to SMI as in SNMPv1. Three messages have been added: get-bulk-request, inform-request, and report. Only get-bulk-request and inform-request details have been defined and the report is left to the implementers of a system. The report is not used in practice at present.

There are several changes to SMI in SMIv2. Modules are formally introduced using the MODULE-IDENTITY macro. An OBJECT-IDENTITY macro defines the MIB objects, and a NOTIFICATION-TYPE macro defines the traps and notifications. SMIv2 has been split into three parts, each defined in a separate RFC: module definitions, textual conventions, and conformance specifications. The module definitions specify the rules for defining new modules. The textual conventions help define precise descriptions of modules for human understanding. The conformance specifications are intended to interpret what the vendor is specifying in the network component with regard to compliance with SNMP management. Object groups are introduced to group a number of related entities. The conformance specifications detail the mandatory groups that should be implemented to be SNMP conformant. The object groups also help vendors define the capabilities of the system when they implement additional groups beyond the mandatory ones.

Two new modules have been added to the Internet module: security and snmpV2. The security module is, as of now, a placeholder in the MIB tree because consensus could not be reached within the working group to define it. It is specified in SNMPv3, which is covered in Chapter 7. The system and SNMP groups have been modified in the Internet MIB. Additional objects have been added to the system group to support various MIB modules. Many entities have been made obsolete in the SNMP module. The obsolete entities are defined as an obsolete group in the SNMPv2 module. The SNMPv2 module also defines the MIB definition for compliance groups. Object groups defining collection of related entities are defined to specify vendor compliance and capabilities.

All protocol PDUs, including trap, have been unified into a common data format. The new get-bulk-request is intended to improve the efficiency of the get-next request in SNMPv1 by retrieving data in large quantities. The get-next-request is maintained in version 2. The interoperability of management systems has been facilitated by a new message, inform-request. We have given a conceptual presentation of the table management, because this has become important when multiple management systems try to set configurations on one agent at the same time.

The unfortunate part of SNMPv2 is that it is not backward compatible with SNMPv1. Two schemes have been recommended for migrating from version 1 to version 2. Proxy server is the preferred approach over that of bilingual manager. Proxy server can also be developed for managing non–SNMP agents with an SNMP manager.

Exercises

1. Define the OBJECT-IDENTITY module for the following objects mentioned in Exercise 4.10:

   a. hats
   b. jacketQuantity

2. Write the OBJECT TYPE modules for ipAddrTable, ipAddrEntry, and ipAdEnt-IfIndex in the IP address translation table shown in Figure 4.20 in SMIv2.

3. Add two columnar objects, cardNumber (of interface card) and portNumber (port in the interface card) to an IP address table in a router. The index values for the IP address table rows are 150.50.51.1, 150.50.52.1, 150.50.53.1, and 150.50.54.1. The packets to the first two addresses are directed to ports 1 and 2 of interface card 1. The last two addresses refer to ports 1 and 2 of interface card 2.

   a. Draw the conceptual base table and augmented table (ipAug 1).
   b. Present the ASN.1 constructs for both, down to the leaf level of the MIB tree. Limit your leaf for *ipTable* to *ipAdEntAddr* object.

4. Table 6.12 shows the output of a network management system that details the addresses of a router in a network. Three columnar objects (Index, IP Address, and Physical Address) belong to the address translation table, atTable. Treat the other three columns as belonging to an augmented table, atAugTable (atAug 1). Repeat Exercise 3(a) and 3(b)for this case. Use SMIv2 textual conventions.

Table 6.12   Table for Exercise 4

atIfIndex	intType	intNumber	PortNumber	IP Address atNetAddress	Physical Address atPhysAddress
3	6	0	2	172.46.41.1	00:00:0c:35:C1:D2
4	6	0	3	172.46.42.1	00:00:0c:35:C1:D3
5	6	0	4	172.46.43.1	00:00:0c:35:C1:D4
6	6	0	5	172.46.44.1	00:00:0c:35:C1:D5
2	6	0	1	172.46.63.1	00:00:0c:35:C1:D1
7	15	1	0	172.46.165.1	00:00:0c:35:C1:D8
1	6	0	0	172.46.252.1	00:00:0c:35:C1:D0

5. In Exercise 3, the router interfaces with subnets are reconfigured as virtual LANs. There is only one interface card with two ports, each handling two subnets. The packets to the two subnets, 150.50.51.1 and 150.50.52.1, are directed to port 1 of the interface card and the packets to 150.50.53.1 and 150.50.54.1 are connected to port 2. The second table is the dependent table ipDepTable (ipDep 1).

   a. Draw the conceptual base table and the dependent table.
   b. Present the ASN.1 constructs for both, down to the leaf level of the MIB tree. Limit your leaf for *ipTable* to *ipAdEntAddr* object.

6. A table is used in a corporation for each branch to maintain an inventory of its equipment in the agent system located at the branch. The inventory table is maintained remotely from the central location. Items can be added, deleted, or changed. The objects that make up the table are

Table name	invTable	{corp 100}
Row name	invEntry	
Columnar object 1	invStatus	
Columnar object 2	invNumber (index)	
Columnar object 3	make	
Columnar object 4	model	
Columnar object 5	serNumber	

   a. Draw the inventory conceptual table.
   b. Write the detailed ASN.1 constructs for the table.

7. In Exercise 6, the following equipment is to be added as the 100th inventory number:

make	Sun
model	Ultra5
serNumber	S12345

   a. Add the conceptual row to the table in Exercise 6(a).
   b. Draw the operational sequence diagram for a create-and-go operation to create the new row.

8. In Exercise 6, the equipment with the inventory number 50 is no longer in use. Draw the operational sequence to delete the conceptual row.

9. Generate an ASN.1 OBJECT-GROUP macro for the address translation group in SNMPv2 implementation.

10. Draw request-response messages, as shown in Figures 6.40 and 6.41, for Table 6.13. Assume that you know the number of rows in the table in making requests.

   a. Draw the get-next-request and response messages.
   b. Draw the get-bulk-request and response messages.
   c. Compare the results of parts (a) and (b).

Table 6.13   Table for Exercises 10

Index	IP Address	Physical Address
3	172.46.41.1	00:00:0c:35:C1:D2
4	172.46.42.1	00:00:0c:35:C1:D3
5	172.46.43.1	00:00:0c:35:C1:D4
6	172.46.44.1	00:00:0c:35:C1:D5
2	172.46.63.1	00:00:0c:35:C1:D1
7	172.46.165.1	00:00:0c:35:C1:D8
1	172.46.252.1	00:00:0c:35:C1:D0

11. Fill in the values for the SNMPv2 Trap PDU shown in Figure 6.43 for a message sent by the hub shown in Figure 4.2(a) one second after it is reset following a failure. (You may want to compare the result with that of Exercise 3 in Chapter 5 for SNMPv1.)

CHAPTER 7

SNMP Management: SNMPv3

After much controversy, SNMPv2 was released as a community-based SNMP framework, SNMPv2C, without any security enhancements. Subsequently, SNMPv3 was developed to meet the need for better security in SNMP management. Fortunately, SNMPv3 addressed more than just security: It now provides a framework for all three versions of SNMP and future development in SNMP management with minimum impact on existing operations.

One of the key features of SNMPv3 is the modularization of documentation and architecture. The design of the architecture integrated the SNMPv1 and SNMPv2 specifications with those of the newly developed SNMPv3. This integration enables the continued use of legacy SNMP entities by SNMPv3 agents and managers. That's good news, as there are tens of thousands of SNMPv1 and SNMPv2 agents in use.

283

An SNMP engine is defined with explicit subsystems that include dispatch and message processing functions. It allows all three versions of SNMP to coexist in a single management entity. Application services and primitives are explicitly defined in SNMPv3, which formalizes the various types of messages used in the earlier versions.

Another key feature is improved security. The SNMP configuration can be set remotely with secure communication links that protect against modification of information and masquerade with encryption schemes. The security feature also is intended to ensure against malicious modification of messages by reordering and delaying message streams and protect against eavesdropping.

The access policy used in SNMPv1 and SNMPv2 is enhanced and formalized in the View-based Access Control Model (VACM) in SNMPv3. The SNMP engine defined in the architecture checks whether a specific type of access (read, write, create, or notify) to a particular object (instance) is allowed.

7.1   SNMPv3 Documentation

The documentation of SNMPv3 is described in five Requests for Comments (RFCs) published in January 1998 and listed in Table 7.1.

RFC 2271 presents an overview of SNMPv3. It defines a vocabulary for SNMP management frameworks and an architecture for the major portions of those frameworks.

Table 7.1   SNMPv3 RFCs

RFC 2271	An Architecture for Describing SNMP Management Frameworks
RFC 2272	Message Processing and Dispatching for SNMP
RFC 2273	SNMPv3 Applications
RFC 2274	User-based Security Model (USM) for SNMPV3
RFC 2275	View-based Access Control Model for SNMP

RFC 2272 describes message processing and dispatching for SNMP messages. Procedures are specified for dispatching multiple versions of SNMP messages to the proper SNMP message processing models, and for dispatching PDUs to SNMP applications.

RFC 2273 defines five types of SNMP applications: command generators, command responders, notification originators, notification receivers, and proxy forwarders. It also defines the MIB modules for specifying targets of management operations, for notification filtering, and for proxy forwarding.

RFC 2274 addresses the User-based Security Model (USM) for SNMPv3 and specifies procedures for providing SNMP message security. A MIB for remotely monitoring and managing configuration parameters is also specified.

RFC 2275 describes the User-based Access Control Model which deals with procedures for controlling access to management information. A MIB is specified for remotely managing the configuration parameters for the View-based Access Control Model (VACM).

7.2   SNMPv3 Documentation Architecture

The numerous SNMP documents have been organized into a document architecture. It addresses how existing documents and new documents can be designed to be autonomous and, at the same time, be integrated to provide documentation for the various SNMP frameworks. The representation shown in Figure 7.1 reflects the contents of the specifications, but is a different perspective than that given in [RFC 2271]. It can be correlated with what we presented in Figure 4.4. Two sets of documents are general in nature. One is the set of documents covering the roadmap, the applicability statement, and coexistence and transition. It provides placeholders for documents yet to be written.

The other set of documents, SNMP frameworks, comprise the three versions of SNMP. An SNMP framework represents the integration of a set of subsystems and models. Models describe specific subsystem designs. The implementation of an SNMP entity is based on a specific model for a specific framework. For example, a message in an SNMP manager is processed by using a specific message processing model (we will discuss these models later) in a specific SNMP framework. The SNMP frameworks document set is not explicitly shown in the pictorial presentation in RFC 2271, as we have done here. RFC 1901 in SNMPv2 and RFC 2271 in SNMPv3 are SNMP framework documents.

The information model and MIBs cover the Structure of Management Information (SMI), textual conventions, and conformance statements, as well as various MIBs. These topics are covered in the STD 16, STD 17, and SMIv2 documents [RFCs 1902–1904].

The message handling and PDU handling sets of documents address transport mappings, message processing and dispatching, protocol operations, applications, and access control. They correspond to the SNMP STD 15 documents and the draft documents for SNMPv2 [RFCs 1905–1907] shown in Figure 4.4. RFCs 2273–2275 address these topics in SNMPv3.

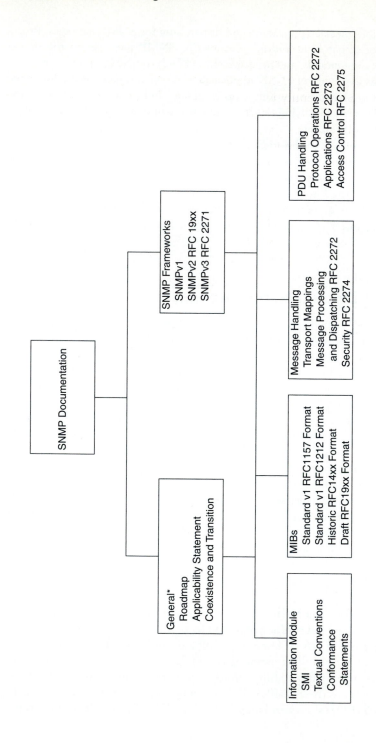

Figure 7.1   SNMP Documentation (recommended in SNMPv3)

7.3   Architecture

An SNMP management network consists of several nodes, each with an SNMP entity. They interact with each other in monitoring and managing the network and its resources. The architecture of an SNMP entity is defined as the elements of that entity and the names associated with them. There are three kinds of naming: naming of entities, naming of identities, and naming of management information. Let us first look at the elements of an entity, including naming of the entity.

7.3.1   Elements of an Entity

The elements of the architecture associated with an SNMP entity, shown in Figure 7.2, comprise an SNMP engine and a set of applications. The SNMP engine, named snmpEngineID, consists of a dispatcher, a message processing subsystem, a security subsystem, and an access control subsystem.

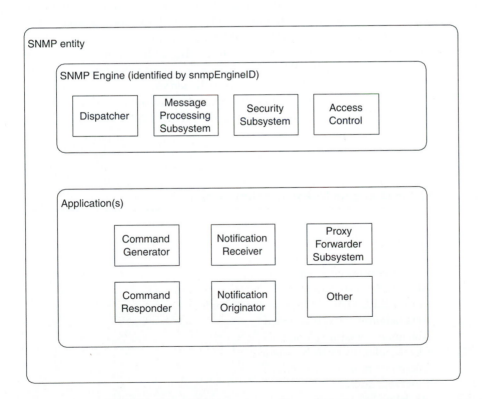

Figure 7.2   SNMPv3 Architecture

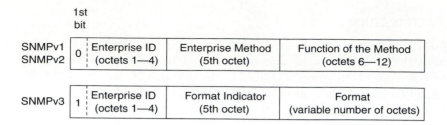

Figure 7.3   SNMP Engine ID

The SNMP Engine.   As shown in Figure 7.2, an SNMP entity has one **SNMP engine**, which is identified by a unique *snmpEngineID*. The SNMP engine ID is made up of octet strings. The length of the ID is twelve octets for SNMPv1 and SNMPv2, and is variable for SNMPv3, as shown in Figure 7.3. The first four octets in both formats are set to the binary equivalent of the agent's SNMP management private enterprise number. The first bit of the four octets is set to 1 for SNMPv3 and 0 for earlier versions. For example, if Acme Networks has been assigned {enterprises 696}, the first four octets would read '800002b8'H in SNMPv3 and '000002b8'H in SNMPv1 and SNMPv2.

The fifth octets for SNMPv1 and SNMPv2 indicate the method that the enterprise used for deriving the SNMP engine ID, and octets 6–12 indicate the function of the method. For a simple entity, it could be just the entity's IP address.

The fifth octet for SNMPv3 ID indicates the format used in the rest of the variable number of octets. Table 7.2 shows the values of the fifth octet for SNMPv3.

Table 7.2   SNMPv3 Engine ID Format (fifth octet)

0	Reserved, unused
1	IPv4 address (4 octets)
2	IPv6 (16 octets)
	Lowest nonspecial IP address
3	MAC address (6 octets)
	Lowest IEEE MAC address, canonical order
4	Text, administratively assigned
	Maximum remaining length 27
5	Octets, administratively assigned
	Maximum remaining length 27
6–127	Reserved, unused
128–255	As defined by the enterprises
	Maximum remaining length 27

The Dispatcher Subsystem.   There is only one **dispatcher** in an SNMP engine, but it can handle multiple versions of SNMP messages. It performs three sets of functions. First, it sends messages to and receives messages from the network. Second, it determines the version of the message and interacts with the corresponding message processing model. Third, it provides an abstract interface (described in Section 7.3.3) to SNMP applications to deliver an incoming PDU to the local application and to send a PDU from the local application to a remote entity.

The three separate functions in the dispatcher subsystem are accomplished with (1) a transport mapper, (2) a message dispatcher, and (3) a PDU dispatcher.

The transport mapper delivers the message over the appropriate transport protocol of the network. The message dispatcher routes the outgoing and incoming messages to the appropriate module of the message processor. If a message is received and cannot be handled by the message processing subsystem of a particular SNMP version, it would be rejected by the message dispatcher. The PDU dispatcher handles the traffic routing of PDUs between applications and the message processor.

The Message Processing Subsystem.   The SNMP **message processing subsystem** of an SNMP engine interacts with the dispatcher to handle version-specific SNMP messages. It contains one or more **message processing models**. The version is identified by the version field in the header.

The Security and Access Control Subsystems.   The **security subsystem** provides authentication and privacy protection at the message level. The access control subsystem provides access authorization security.

The Applications Module.   The **application(s) module** is made up of one or more applications, which comprise command generator, notification receiver, proxy forwarder, command responder, and notification originator. The first three applications are normally associated with an SNMP manager and the last two with an SNMP agent. The application(s) module may also include other applications, as indicated by the Other box in Figure 7.2.

7.3.2   Names

Naming of entities, identities, and management information is part of SNMPv3 specifications. We have already mentioned the naming of an entity by its SNMP engine ID, *snmpEngineID*. Two names are associated with identities, *principal* and *securityName*. The *principal* is the "who" requesting services. It could be a person or an application. The *securityName* is a human-readable string representing a principal. The principal could be a single user—for example, the name of a network manager—or a group of users—for example the names of operators in the network operating center. The principal is made nonaccessible; it is hidden and is protected by the security method being used. However, it is administratively given a security name—for example, User 1 or Admin—which is made readable by all.

A management entity can be responsible for more than one managed object. For example, a management agent associated with a managed object at a given node could also be managing a neighboring node. Each object is called a **context** and has a *context-EngineID* and a *contextName*. When there is a one-to-one relationship between the management entity and the managed object, *contextEngineID* is the same as *snmpEngineID*. A **scopedPDU** is a block of data containing a *contextEngineID*, a *contextName*, and a PDU. An example would be a switched hub by which a common SNMP agent in the hub is accessed to manage the interfaces of the hub. The agent would have an SNMP engine ID and each interface would have a context engine ID. In contrast, in a nonswitched hub with each interface being managed individually, the SNMP engine ID and context ID are the same.

7.3.3   Abstract Service Interfaces

The subsystems in an SNMP entity communicate with each other across an interface, one subsystem providing a service and the other using the service. If the interface is defined so that it is generic and independent of specific implementation, it becomes a conceptual interface, called **an abstract service interface**. A set of primitives define these abstract services. Figure 7.4(a) shows subsystem A sending a request for service via *primitiveAB* to subsystem B. The *primitiveAB* is associated with the receiving subsystem B, which is the one providing the service in this illustration. A primitive has IN and OUT as operands or parameters, which are data values, and are indicated by a1 and a2, and b1 and b2, respectively. The IN parameters are input values to the called subsystem from the subsystem calling for service. The OUT parameters are the responses expected from the called subsystem to the calling subsystem. The OUT parameters are sent unfilled in the message format by the calling subsystem (recall the Get-Request-PDU) and returned filled (Get-Response-PDU) by the called subsystem. When the calling subsystem expects a response from the called subsystem, directed messages flow in both directions, with a two-directional arrow coupling the two. In this case *primitiveAB* is indicated only in the forward direction. In addition to returning the OUT parameters, the called subsystem could also return a value associated with the result of the request in terms of *statusInformation* or result (for example, success or failure or tracking ID). Because of the execution of *primitiveAB*, subsystem B may initiate a request for service from another subsystem, subsystem C, using *primitiveBC* over the abstract service interface between subsystems B and C.

In general, except for the dispatcher, primitives are associated with the receiving subsystem. Dispatcher primitives are used in receiving messages from and sending messages to application modules, as well as registering and unregistering them, and in transmitting messages to and receiving messages from the network.

Figure 7.4(b) illustrates the use of a command generator, which is sending a request, *sendPdu* (destined for a remote entity), to the dispatcher. After successful execution of the service requested and sending it on the network, the dispatcher returns *sendPduHandle* to the application. The command generator will use it to correlate the response from the remote entity. The only OUT parameter to be filled in this primitive is the status information. The command generator expects the status information, hence the coupling

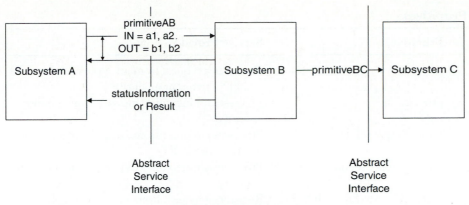

(a) Abstract Service Interface

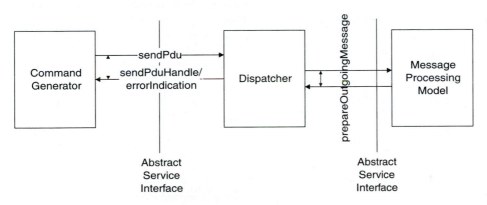

(b) Abstract Service Interface for sendPdu

Figure 7.4   Abstract Service Interfaces

arrow indicator. The dispatcher sends an error indicator instead of *sendPduHandle* for the status information if the *sendPdu* transaction is a failure. The dispatcher also generates a request to the message processing model: *prepareOutgoingMessage*. The *prepareOutgoing-Message* has both IN and OUT parameters and hence information flows in both directions. The numerous IN and OUT parameters associated with primitives are not identified in Figure 7.4(b) for the sake of simplicity.

Table 7.3 lists the primitives served by the dispatcher, message processing, security, and access control subsystems. A brief description of each primitive and the service provided, including the user of service is presented.

Table 7.3   List of Primitives

Module	Primitive	Service Provided
Dispatcher	sendPdu	Processes a request from an application to send a PDU to a remote entity
Dispatcher	processPdu	Processes an incoming message from a remote entity
Dispatcher	returnResponsePdu	Processes a request from an application to send a response PDU
Dispatcher	processResponsePdu	Processes an incoming response from a remote entity
Dispatcher	registerContextEngineID	Registers a request from a context engine
Dispatcher	unregisterContextEngineID	Unregisters a request from a context engine
Message Processing Model	prepareOutgoingMessage	Processes a request from the dispatcher to prepare an outgoing message to a remote entity
Message Processing Model	prepareResponseMessage	Processes a request from the dispatcher to prepare an outgoing response to a remote entity
Message Processing Model	prepareDataElements	Processes a request from the dispatcher to extract data elements from an incoming message from a remote entity
Security Model	generateRequestMsg	Processes a request from a message processing model to generate a request message
Security Model	processIncomingMsg	Processes a request from a message processing model to process security data in an incoming message
Security Model	generateResponseMsg	Processes a request from a message processing model to generate a response message
Intra-Security Model	authenticateOutgoingMsg	Processes a request to the authentication service to authenticate an outgoing message
Intra-Security Model	authenticateIncomingMsg	Processes a request for the authentication service to authenticate an incoming message
Intra-Security Model	encryptData	Processes a request from the security Model to the privacy service to encrypt data
Intra-Security Model	decryptData	Processes a request for the privacy service to decrypt an incoming message
Access Control Model	isAccessAllowed	Processes a request from an application to access and authorize the service requested

7.4   SNMPv3 Applications

SNMPv3 formally defines five types of applications, but they are not the same as those of the functional model that the OSI model addresses. They may be considered as the application service elements used to build applications. They are the command generator,

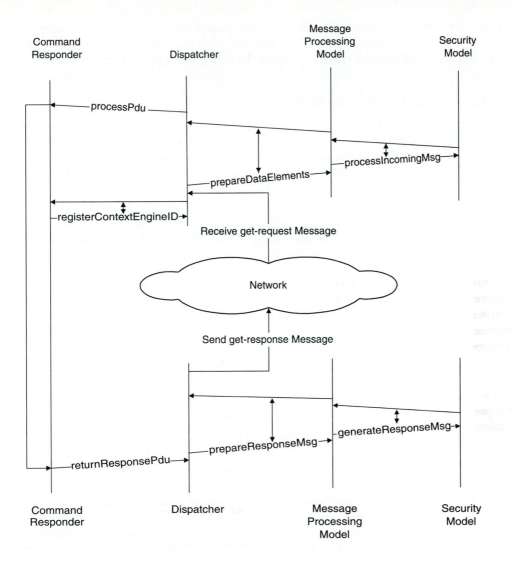

Figure 7.6   The Command Responder Application

performs the security functions, and the dispatcher eventually transmits the get-response message on the network.

Continuing the example discussed in Section 7.4.1 for the command generator, the Dispatcher in the SNMP agent receives the message. The message is processed by the MPM and SM and is returned to the dispatcher. The message is delivered to the command responder via *processPdu*. When the command responder acquires the system group information, it fills the PDU received with system group object values, as previously shown in

Figure 5.17(b). The *returnResponsePdu* primitive is used by the command generator to deliver the message to the dispatcher. The dispatcher, after processing the get-response message through MPM and SM, transmits it across the network using UDP protocol.

7.4.3   The Notification Originator

The notification originator application generates either a trap or an inform message. Its function is somewhat similar to that of the command responder, except that it needs to find out where to send the message and what SNMP version and security parameters to use. Further, the notification generator must determine the *contextEngineID* and the name of the context that has the information to be sent. It obtains these data using newly created MIBs for the notification and target groups, as well as using other modules in the system. In Section 7.5 we will describe the MIBs that define the new groups. The notification group contains information on whether a notification should be sent to a target and, if so, what filtering should be used on the information. The target that the notification should be sent to is obtained from the target group.

7.4.4   The Notification Receiver

The notification receiver application receives SNMP notification messages. It registers with the SNMP engine to receive these messages, just as the command responder application does to receive get and set messages.

7.4.5   The Proxy Forwarder

The proxy forwarder application performs a function similar to that discussed in Chapter 6 for the proxy server. However, *proxy* has been clearly defined and restricted in SNMPv3 specifications. The word is used to refer to a proxy forwarder application, which forwards SNMP requests, notifications, and responses without regard for the managed objects contained in those messages. Non-SNMP object translation does not fall under this category. The proxy forwarder handles four types of messages: those generated by the command generator, command responder, and notification generator, and those that contain a report indicator. The proxy forwarder uses the translation table in the proxy group MIB created for this purpose.

7.5   SNMPv3 Management Information Base

The new objects defined in SNMPv3 follow the textual convention specified in SNMPv2 and described in Chapter 6. Refer to the RFCs listed in Table 7.1 for complete details on managed objects and MIBs in SNMPv3. We will cover a subset of the MIBs here. Figure 7.7 shows the MIBs of the new object groups. They are nodes under the *snmpModules* {1.3.6.1.6.3}, previously shown in Figure 6.31. There are seven new MIB groups. The *snmpFrameworkMIB* (node 10 under *snmpModules*) describes the SNMP management architecture. The MIB group *snmpMPDMIB* (node 11) identifies objects in the message processing and dispatching subsystems.

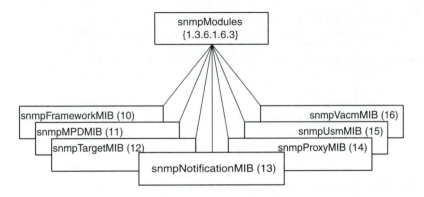

Figure 7.7   SNMPv3 MIB Groups

Three groups are defined under *snmpModules* for applications: *snmpTargetMIB* (node 12), *snmpNotificationMIB* (node 13), and *snmpProxyMIB* (node 14). The first two are used for the notification generator. The *snmpTargetMIB* contains two tables that are of specific interest in generating notification and are shown in Figure 7.8. The first table, *snmpTargetAddrTable*, in the snmpTargetObjects group contains the addresses to be used in the generation of SNMP messages. These are grouped in the SNMP Notification Table and identified by tags under SNMP Notification MIB (to be discussed soon). The nine columnar objects in the table are listed in Table 7.4.

The second table of interest in the snmpTargetObjects group is the *snmpTargetParamsTable*. The lead into this table is via the columnar object *snmpTargetAddrParams* in the

Table 7.4   The SNMP Target Address Table

Entity	OID	Description (brief)
snmpTargetAddrTable	snmpTargetObjects 2	Table of transport addresses
snmpTargetAddrEntry	snmpTargetAddrTable 1	Row in the target address table
snmpTargetAddrName	snmpTargetAddrEntry 1	Locally administered name associated with this entry
snmpTargetAddrTDomain	snmpTargetAddrEntry 2	Transport type of the addresses
snmpTargetAddrTAddress	snmpTargetAddrEntry 3	Transport address
snmpTargetAddrTimeOut	snmpTargetAddrEntry 4	Expected maximum round-trip time
snmpTargetAddrRetryCount	snmpTargetAddrEntry 5	Number of retries
snmpTargetAddrTagList	snmpTargetAddrEntry 6	List of tag values used to select the target addresses for a particular operation
snmpTargetAddrParams	snmpTargetAddrEntry 7	Value that identifies an entry in the snmpTargetParams Table
snmpTargetAddrStorageType	snmpTargetAddrEntry 8	Storage type for this row
snmpTargetAddrRowStatus	snmpTargetAddrEntry 9	Status of the row

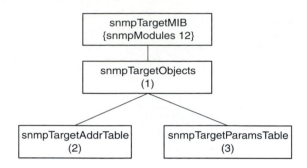

Figure 7.8   Target Address and Target Parameter Tables

snmpTargetAddrTable. It contains the security parameters for authentication and privacy. The columnar objects in the *snmpTargetParamsTable* are listed in Table 7.5.

The *snmpNotificationMIB* shown in Figure 7.9 deals with MIB objects for generation of notifications. The three tables in this group are the notification table, notification filter profile table, and notification filter table. They fall under the node *snmpNotifyObjects*. The SNMP notification table, *snmpNotifyTable* contains groups of management targets that should receive notifications, as well as the type of notification to be sent. The addresses in the SNMP Target Address Parameters to be selected are tagged in this table. Table 7.6 shows the columnar objects in the group. The Notification Profile Table group, *snmpNotifyProfileTable*, is used to associate a notification filter profile with a particular set

Table 7.5   The SNMP Target Parameters Table

Entity	OID	Description (brief)
snmpTargetParamsTable	snmpTargetObjects 3	Table of SNMP target information to be used
snmpTargetParamsEntry	snmpTargetParamsTable 1	A set of SNMP target information
snmpTargetParamsName	snmpTargetParamsEntry 1	Locally administered name associated with this entry
snmpTargetParamsMPModel	snmpTargetParamsEntry 2	Message processing model to be used
snmpTargetParamsSecurity Model	snmpTargetParamsEntry 3	Security model to be used
snmpTargetParamsSecurityName	snmpTargetParamsEntry 4	Security name of the principal
snmpTargetParamsSecurityLevel	snmpTargetParamsEntry 5	Level of security
snmpTargetParamsStorageType	snmpTargetParamsEntry 6	Storage type for the row
snmpTargetParamsRowStatus	snmpTargetParamsEntry 7	Status of the row

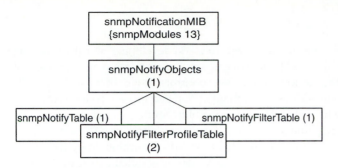

Figure 7.9   SNMP Notification Tables

of target parameters. The Notification Filter Table group, *snmpNotifyFilterTable*, contains table profiles of the targets. The profile specifies whether a particular target should receive particular information.

The *snmpProxyMIB* in Figure 7.7 is concerned with objects in a proxy forwarding application, such as the SNMPv2 proxy server previously shown in Figure 6.46. It contains a table of translation parameters used by the proxy forwarder application for forwarding SNMP messages.

The SNMP user-based security model objects are defined in *snmpUsmMIB* module (node 15). Last, the objects for the SNMP view-based access control model are defined in the *snmpVacmMIB* module (node 16). We will discuss the details of these MIBs shortly.

Table 7.6   The SNMP Notification Table

Entity	OID	Description (brief)
snmpNotifyTable	snmpNotifyObjects 1	List of targets and notification types
snmpNotifyEntry	snmpNotifyTable 1	Set of management targets and the type of notification
snmpNotifyName	snmpNotifyEntry 1	Locally administered name associated with this entry
snmpNotifyTag	snmpNotifyEntry 2	A single value used to select entries in the snmpTargetAddrTable
snmpNotifyType	snmpNotifyEntry 3	Selection of trap or inform to send
snmpNotifyStorageType	snmpNotifyEntry 4	Storage type for the row
snmpNotifyRowStatus	snmpNotifyEntry 5	Status of the row

7.6   Security

One of the main objectives—if not the main objective—in developing SNMPv3 was the addition of security features for SNMP management. Authentication and privacy of information, as well as authorization and access controls, have been addressed in SNMPv3 specifications. We will address the authentication and privacy issues in this section and in Section 7.7. We will deal with access control in Section 7.8.

The SNMPv3 architecture permits flexibility to use any protocol for the authentication and privacy of information. However, the IETF SNMPv3 working group has specified for its security subsystem a User-based Security Model. It is called *user-based* because it follows the traditional concept of a user, identified by a user name with which to associate security information. The working group has specified HMAC-MD5-96 and HMAC-SHA-96 (see Section 7.7.1 for an explanation) as the authentication protocols. CBC-DES has been adopted for privacy protocol.

We will discuss the general aspects of security associated with the types of threats, the security models, the message data format to accommodate security parameters, and the use and management of keys in this section. We will address specifically the User-based Security Model in the next section.

7.6.1   Security Threats

Four types of threats to network management information while it is being transported from one management entity to another must be addressed: (1) modification of information, (2) masquerade, (3) message stream modification, and (4) disclosure. These threats are depicted in Figure 7.10, where information is being transported from management entity A to management entity B. With regard to the first three threats, an intruder must intercept the signal in order to tamper with it, whereas the disclosure threat involves tapping into but not intercepting the signal.

Modification of information is the threat that some unauthorized user may modify the contents of the message while it is in transit. The data contents are modified, including falsifying the value of an object. Modification does not include changing the originating or destination address. The modified message is received by entity B, which is unaware that it has been modified. For example, the response by an SNMP agent to a request by an SNMP manager could be altered by this threat.

Masquerade is the threat that some unauthorized user may send information to another user, assuming the identity of an authorized user. This can be done by changing the originating address. Using both masquerade and modification of information, an unauthorized user can perform operation on a management entity, which he or she is not otherwise permitted to do. The SNMP set operation should be protected against such an attack.

Because SNMP communication uses connectionless transport service, such as UDP, a message could be fragmented into packets, with each packet taking a different path. The packets could arrive at the destination out of sequence and have to be reordered. The threat

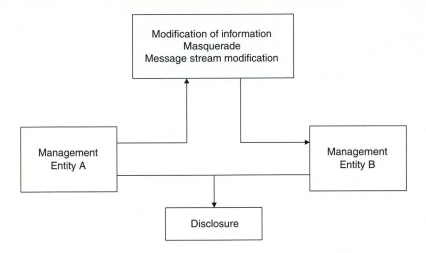

Figure 7.10   Security Threats to Management Information

here is that an intruder may **modify the message stream** and maliciously reorder the data packets to change the meaning of the message. For example, the sequence of data of a table could be reordered to change the values in the table. The intruder could also delay messages so that they arrive out of sequence. Moreover, the message could be interrupted, stored, and replayed at a later time by an unauthorized user.

The threat of **disclosure** of management information does not require modification, just interception and eavesdropping. For example, accounting department message stream could be monitored by an employee with a TCP/IP dump procedure and the information be used against the organization.

At least two more threats are normally considered in traditional data communication, but in the SNMP User-based Security Model they are classified as nonthreats. The first is denial of service, when an authorized user is denied service by a management entity. This is not considered to be a threat, as a network failure could cause such a denial, and the protocol should address this issue. The second is traffic analysis by an unauthorized user. The IETF SNMPv3 working group determined that no significant advantage is achieved by protecting against this attack.

7.6.2   Security Model

Under normal operational conditions, the message processing model interacts with the security subsystem model. For example, in Figure 7.5, we showed that an outgoing message is generated by an application and handled first by the dispatcher, then by the message processing model, and finally by the security model. If the message is to be authenticated, the security model authenticates it and forwards it to the message

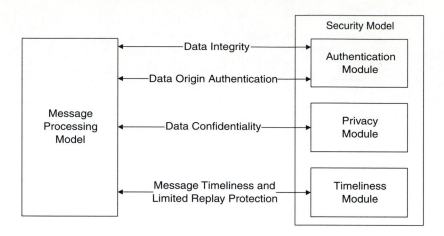

Figure 7.11   Security Services

processing model. Similarly for an incoming message, the message processing model requests the service of the security model to authenticate the user ID. Figure 7.11 shows the services provided by the three modules—the authentication module, privacy module, and timeliness module—in the security model to the message processing model.

The Authoritative SNMP Engine.   When two management entities communicate, the services provided by each entity are determined by the role it plays (i.e., whether the entity is authorized to perform the service). This condition led to the concept of authoritative and nonauthoritative SNMP engines. In the SNMPv3 architecture, when two SNMP engines communicate, one acts as an **authoritative engine** and the other as a **non-authoritative engine**. The set of rules as to which is the authoritative SNMP engine for each message communicated is well defined. For get-request, get-next-request, get-bulk-request, set-request, or inform messages, the receiver of the message is the authoritative SNMP engine. As these messages are originated by a manager process in a network management system, the receiver is the SNMP agent. Thus the agent is the authoritative SNMP engine. For trap, get-response, and report messages, the sender is the authoritative SNMP engine. Thus an SNMP engine that acts in the role of an agent is the designated authoritative SNMP engine. In general, an SNMP agent is the authoritative SNMP engine in SNMP communication.

An authoritative SNMP engine is responsible for the accuracy of the time stamp and a unique SNMP engine ID in each message. Thus every nonauthoritative SNMP engine must keep a table of the time and authoritative engine ID of every SNMP engine with which it communicates.

Security Authentication.   Communication between two entities could satisfy the condition of an authoritative and a nonauthoritative pair, but it has to be the right set of pairs. Thus the source from which the message is received should be authenticated by the receiver. Authentication is also needed for the security reasons discussed in Section 7.6.1 and is performed by the authentication module in the security model.

The **authentication module** provides two services: **data integrity**, and **data origin authentication**. The data integrity service authenticates a message at the originating end and validates it at the receiving end, ensuring that the message has not been modified during the communication process by an unauthorized intruder. Validation also catches any nonmalicious modification of data in the communication channel. The authentication process involves the use of protocols such as HMAC-MD5-96 or HMAC-SHA-96 in SNMPv3, or any other authentication protocol.

The data origin authentication service ensures that the claimed identity of the user on whose behalf the message was sent is truly the originator of the message. The authentication module appends to each message a unique identifier associated with an authoritative SNMP engine.

Privacy of Information.   The **privacy module** provides a **data confidentiality service**. Data confidentiality ensures that the information is not made available or disclosed to unauthorized users, entities, or processes. The privacy of the message is accomplished by encrypting the message at the sending end and decrypting it at the receiving end.

Timeliness of Message.   The **timeliness module** provides a **message timeliness check** preventing message redirection, delay, and replay. Based on the concept of authoritative SNMP engine, a window of time is set in the receiver for accepting a message. A message's travel time between sender and receiver should fall within this time interval. The time clock in both the sender and receiver are synchronized to the authoritative SNMP engine. The recommended value for the window of time in SNMPv3 is 150 seconds.

For implementation of the timeliness module, the SNMP engine maintains three objects: *snmpEngineID*, *snmpEngineBoots*, and *snmpEngineTime*. The *snmpEngineID* uniquely identifies the authoritative SNMP engine. The *snmpEngineBoots* is a count of the number of times the SNMP engine has rebooted or reinitialized since *snmpEngineID* was last configured. The *snmpEngineTime* is the number of seconds since the *snmpEngine-Boots* counter was last initialized or reset.

The timeliness module also checks the message ID of a response with that of the request message and drops the message if they do not match.

7.6.3   Message Format

The SNMPv3 message format consists of four groups of data and is shown in Figure 7.12. Details of the fields in each group except security parameters are given in Table 7.7. The first group is a single field, which is the version number and is in the same position as in SNMPv1 and SNMPv2.

Global/header data defined by the data type comprise the second group of data in the message format. It contains administrative parameters of the message: message ID, message maximum size, message flag, and message security model. (An SNMP engine can handle many models concurrently in the message processing subsystem.) The dispatcher

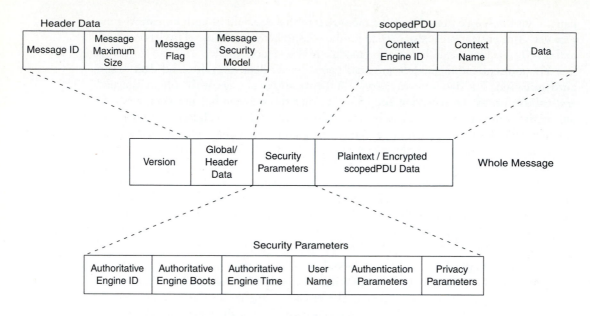

Figure 7.12   The SNMPv3 Message Format

Table 7.7   SNMPv3 Message Format

Field	Object name	Description
Version	msgVersion	SNMP version number of the message format
Message ID	msgID	Administrative ID associated with the message
Message maximum size	msgMaxSize	Maximum size supported by the sender
Message flags	msgFlags	Bit fields identifying report, authentication and privacy of the message
Message security model	msgSecurityModel	Security model used for the message; concurrent multiple models allowed
Security parameters (see Table 7.8)	msgSecurityParameters	Security parameters used for communication between sending and receiving security models
Plaintext/encrypted scopedPDU data	scopedPduData	Choice of plaintext or encrypted scopedPDU; scopedPDU uniquely identifies context and PDU
Context engine ID	contextEngineID	Unique ID of a context (managed entity) with a context name realized by an SNMP entity
Context name	contextName	Name of the context (managed entity)
PDU	data	Contains unencrypted PDU

subsystem examines the version number in the message and sends it to the appropriate message processing model in the message subsystem. For example, if *msgVersion* is set to snmpv2, SNMPv2 message processing model would be invoked.

The third group of data, the security parameter fields, are used by the security model in communications between sending and receiving entities. The values of the parameters depend on the message security model set in the header data. The parameters shown will be discussed in Section 7.7.

The fourth group of data in the message record comprises the plaintext/encrypted *scopedPDU* fields. The *scopedPduData* field contains either unencrypted or encrypted *scopedPDU*. If the privacy flag is set to zero (no privacy) in the message flag (see header data), then this field contains plaintext *scopedPDU*, or unencrypted *scopedPDU*. The plaintext *scopedPDU* consists of the context engine ID, context name, and the PDU. A management entity can be responsible for multiple instances of managed objects. For example, in an ATM switch, a single managed entity acts as agent for all the network interface cards in all its ports. We could treat each interface card as a context with a context engine ID and a context name. Thus a particular context name, in conjunction with a particular context engine ID, identifies the particular context associated with the management information contained in the PDU portion of the message. The object name for the PDU is *data*.

7.7 SNMPv3 User-Based Security Model

The security model for SNMPv3 is a User-based Security Model (USM) that reflects the traditional user name concept. Just as we have defined abstract service interfaces between the various subsystems in an SNMP entity, we can define abstract service interfaces in USM. These definitions cover conceptual interfaces between generic USM services and self-contained authentication and privacy services. Two primitives are associated with an authentication service, one to generate an outgoing authenticated message (*authenticate-OutgoingMsg*) and another one to validate the authenticated incoming message (*authenticateIncomingMsg*). Similarly, two primitives are associated with privacy services: *encryptData* for encryption of outgoing messages and *decryptData* for decryption of incoming messages. They were included in the list of primitives in Table 7.3.

The services provided by the authentication and privacy modules in the security subsystem for outgoing and incoming messages are shown in Figures 7.13 and 7.14, respectively. The message processing model invokes the User-based Security Model (USM) in the security subsystem. Based on the security level set in the message, the USM in turn invokes the authentication and privacy modules. The results are returned to the message processing model by the USM.

Figure 7.13 shows the process of an outgoing message. We will assume that both privacy and authentication flags are set in the message flag in the header data. The message processing model inputs to the security model the message processing model (MPM) information, header data, security data, and *scopedPDU*. The USM invokes the privacy module first, providing as input the encryption key and *scopedPDU*. The privacy module outputs privacy parameters (such as *salt* value in the CBC-DES encryption) that are sent as part of the message and the encrypted *scopedPDU*. The USM

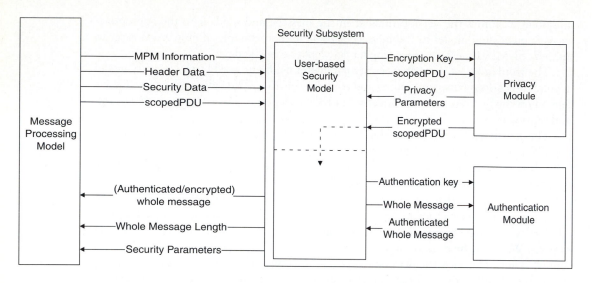

Figure 7.13   Privacy and Authentication Services for Outgoing Message

passes the unauthenticated whole message with encrypted *scopedPDU* to the authentication module along with the authentication key. The authentication module returns the authenticated whole message to the USM. The USM returns to the message processing model the authenticated and encrypted whole message along with the message length and the security parameters. Figure 7.14 shows the reverse process of an incom-

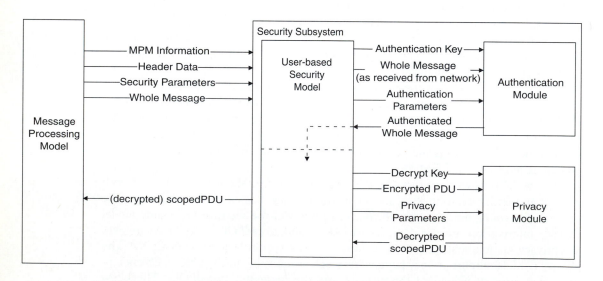

Figure 7.14   Privacy and Authentication Services for Incoming Message

ing message going through the authentication validation first and then decryption of the message by the privacy module.

The security parameters used in the security model were shown in Figure 7.12. Table 7.8 lists the parameters and the corresponding SNMPv3 MIB objects. The position of the relevant MIB objects associated with the security parameters belongs to the two modules *snmpFrameworkMIB* and *snmpUsmMIB*, under *snmpModulesMIB* (see Figure 7.7). The details of the positions of the objects in the MIB are presented in Figure 7.15.

We have already discussed the first three parameters in Table 7.8, which are associated with the engine ID, the number of boots, and the time since the last boot. They are in the *snmpEngine* group shown in Figure 7.15. The last three parameters in the table (*msgUserName, msgAuthentication Parameters,* and *msgPrivacyParameters*) are in the usmUserTable in the *usmUser* group shown in Figure 7.15.

The fourth parameter is the user (principal) on whose behalf the message is being exchanged. The authentication parameters are defined by the authentication protocol columnar object in the *usmUserTable*. The *usmUserTable* describes the users configured in the SNMP engine and the authentication parameters the type of authentication protocol used. Likewise, the privacy parameters describe the type of privacy protocol used.

The *usmUserSpinLock* is an advisory lock that is used by SNMP command generator applications to coordinate their use of the set operation in creating or modifying secrets in the *usmUserTable*.

Now let us return to Figure 7.13 and follow the detailed processes and data flow involved in the User-based Security Model (USM). Figure 7.13 shows the operation for

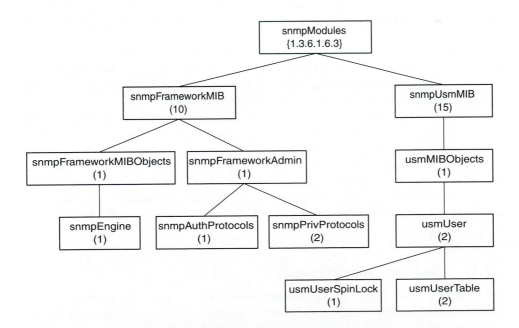

Figure 7.15   SNMPv3 MIB Objects for Security Parameters

Table 7.8   Security Parameters and Corresponding MIB Objects

Security Parameters	USM User Group Objects
msgAuthoritativeEngineID	snmpEngineID (under snmpEngine group)
msgAuthoritativeEngineBoots	snmpEngineBoots (under snmpEngine group)
msgAuthoritativeEngineTime	snmpEngineTime (under snmpEngine group)
msgUserName	usmUserName (in usmUserTable)
msgAuthenticationParameters	usmUserAuthProtocol (in usmUserTable)
msgPrivacyParameters	usmUserPrivProtocol (in usmUserTable)

an outgoing message, which could be either a request message or response message. The message processing model (MPM) inputs to the USM information on the model to be used (normally the SNMP version number), header data, security data (security model, SNMP engine ID, security name, and security level) and *scopedPDU*. This information is received by the USM in the security subsystem.

In the USM, the security-level settings for privacy and authentication determine the modules invoked. The encryption key and *scopedPDU* (context engine ID, context name, and PDU) are fed into the privacy module. The privacy module encrypts the PDU and returns the encrypted PDU along with privacy parameters to the calling module, USM.

The USM then communicates with the authentication module and inputs the encrypted whole message along with the authentication key. The authentication module returns the authenticated whole message to the USM. The USM passes back to the MPM the authenticated and encrypted whole message, whole message length, and securities parameters.

The detailed processes and data flow for an incoming message are shown in Figure 7.14. The inputs to the security model are the message processing model information, header data, security parameters for the received message, and the whole message. The output of the security model is *scopedPDU* in plaintext format.

The operational sequence of authentication and privacy for an incoming message is the reverse of that for outgoing message. The message is first sent to the authentication module along with the authentication key, a whole message received from the network, and authentication parameters received from the network as inputs. It outputs an authenticated whole message to the calling module in USM. The USM then feeds in the decrypt key, privacy parameters, and the encrypted *scopedPDU* and receives in return the decrypted *scopedPDU*. The decrypted *scopedPDU* is then passed on to the message processing model.

7.7.1   Authentication Protocols

The basis for security in the use of authentication and privacy schemes are the secret keys shared by sender and user—one for authentication and another for encryption and decryption. The secret keys for the USM are developed from the user password. Two algorithms are recommended in SNMPv3 for developing keys from the password: HMAC-MD5-96 and HMAC-SHA-96. The first letter in the designation stands for the cryptographic hash function (H) used for generating message access code (MAC). The second part of the designation is the hashing algorithm used, the first being the MD5 hashing algorithm, and the second being the SHA-1 hashing algorithm used to generate MAC. The MAC is derived by truncating the hashing code generated to 96 bits, as indicated by the last set of characters in the designation.

Authentication Key.   The secret key for authentication is derived from a password chosen by the user. The user in our case is the nonauthoritative SNMP engine, which is generally a network management system. In both MD5 and SHA-1 algorithms, the password is repeated until it forms a string of 2^{20} octets (1,048,576 octets), truncating the last repetition, if necessary. This result is called *digest0* [Stallings W]. In the second step, the *digest0* is hashed by using either MD5 or SHA-1 algorithm to derive *digest1*. The MD5 algorithm yields a 16-octet *digest1*, and SHA-1 results in a 20-octet *digest1*. A second string is formed by concatenating the authoritative SNMP engine ID and *digest1*. This string is fed into the respective hashing algorithm to derive *digest2*. The derived *digest2* is the user's authentication key, *authKey*, that is input to the authentication modules shown in Figures 7.13 and 7.14. Details on the MD5 and SHA-1 algorithms are covered in Chapter 13.

The choice between the 16-octet MD5-based *authKey* and the 20-octet SHA-1-based *authKey* depends on the implementation. Breaking the code in the 20-octet key is more difficult than for the 16-octet key. However, processing is faster with the 16-octet key. Furthermore, the same 16-octet key derived from the same password could be used for the privacy key, although the same key should not be used for both.

The HMAC Procedure.   The 96-bit long code MAC is derived by using the HMAC procedure [RFC 2104, RFC 2274]. First, two functions K1 and K2 are derived, using the *authKey* previously obtained, and two fixed but different strings, *ipad* and *opad*, as defined in the following manner. A 64-byte *extendedAuthKey* is derived by supplementing *authKey* with zeros:

ipad = the hexadecimal byte 0x36 (00110110) repeated 64 times

opad = the hexadecimal byte 0x5c (01011100) repeated 64 times

K1 = *extendedAuthKey* XOR *ipad*

K2 = *extendedAuthKey* XOR *opad*

The HMAC is computed by performing the following nested hashing functions on K1, K2, and *wholeMsg*, which is the unauthenticated whole message shown in Figure 7.13:

H (K2, H (K1, *wholeMsg*))

The first twelve octets of this final digest are the MAC. These are the authentication parameters, *msgAuthenticationParameters*, shown in Figure 7.12 and are included as part of the authenticated whole message, *authenticatedWholeMsg* shown in Figure 7.13.

Key Management. A user (network management system) has only one password and hence one *secret* key, *digest1* (mentioned in the authentication key discussion). However, it communicates with all the authoritative SNMP engines (all the agents in the network). The shared information is again a secret between the two communicating engines. The concept of a localized key is introduced to avoid having to store a separate password for each authoratative engine with which the user communicates. A hash function, which is the same as that used to generate the secret key, is used to generate the localized key:

$$\text{Localized key} = H\,(secret,\,authoritativeSnmpEngineID,\,secret)$$

where *secret* is the secret key (*digest1*) and the *authoritativeSnmpEngineID* is the SNMP engine ID of the authoritative SNMP engine with which the local user is communicating. This localized key is different for each authoritative engine and is localized for the user (NMS) at the authoritative SNMP engine (agent). It is stored in each authoritative engine with which the user communicates.

SNMPv3 permits the operation of changes and modification in keys, but not the creation of keys, to ensure that the secret key does not become stale. Note that the localized key is the same as authKey.

Discovery. One of the important functions of a network management system as a user is the discovery of agents in the network. Discovery is accomplished by generating a request message with a security level of no authentication and no privacy, a user name of "initial", an authoritative SNMP engine ID of zero length, and a varBind list that is empty. The authoritative engines respond with response messages containing the engine ID and the security parameters filled in. Additional information is then obtained via pair-wise communication messages.

7.7.2 Encryption Protocol

The encryption generates nonreadable **ciphertext** from readable **plaintext**. The SNMPv3 recommendation for data confidentiality is to use the Cipher Block Chaining mode of the Data Encryption Standard (CBC-DES) Symmetric Encryption Protocol. The USM specifications require the *scopedPDU* portion of the message to be encrypted. A secret value in combination with a timeliness value is used to create the encryption/decryption key and initialization vector (IV). Again, the secret value is user-based, and hence is associated typically with a network management system. The 16-octet privacy key, *privKey*, is generated from the password as described in the generation of authentication code with the MD-5 hashing algorithm.

The first 8 octets of the 16-octet privacy key are used in creating the DES key. It is only 56 bits long, so the least significant bit of each octet in the privacy key is discarded. The 16-octet IV is made up of two parts: an 8-octet pre-IV concatenated with an 8-octet **salt**. The pre-IV comprises the last eight octets of the privacy key. The *salt* is added to ensure that two identical instances of ciphertext are not generated from two different plaintexts that are using the same key. The *salt* is generated by an SNMP engine by concatenating a 4-octet *snmpEngineBoots* with a locally generated integer. The *salt* constitutes the privacy parameters shown in Figures 7.12–7.14.

The encryption process first divides the plaintext of scopedPDU into 64-bit blocks. The plaintext of each block is XOR-ed with the ciphertext of the previous block, and the result is encrypted to produce a ciphertext for the current block. For the first block, the IV is used instead of the ciphertext of the previous block.

7.8   Access Control

In the previous two sections we covered security considerations in network management with regard to data integrity, message authentication, data confidentiality, and the timeliness of message. We will now address access control, which deals with who can access network management components and what they can access. In SNMPv1 and SNMPv2, this topic was covered by the community-based access policy. In SNMPv3, access control has been made more secure and more flexible by introduction of the **View-based Access Control Model** (VACM).

VACM defines a set of services that an application in an agent can use to validate command requests and notification receivers. It validates sending sources and their access privilege for command requests. One of the assumptions made is that the authentication of the source has been done by the authentication module. In order to perform the services, a local database containing access rights and policies, called the local configuration datastore (LCD), has been created in the SNMP entity. The LCD is typically in an agent or in a manager functioning in an agent's role when it communicates with another manager.

The LCD needs to be configured remotely and security considerations need to be addressed, so a MIB module for VACM has been introduced.

7.8.1   Elements of the Model

Five elements comprise VACM: (1) groups, (2) security level, (3) contexts, (4) MIB views and view families, and (5) access policy.

Groups.   A group, identified as *groupName*, is a set of zero or more security model (*vacmSecurityModel*)–security name (*vacmSecurityName*) pairs on whose behalf SNMP management objects can be accessed. A security name is a principal, as defined in Section 7.3.2, and is independent of the security model used. All elements belonging to a group have identical access rights. Community name is equivalent to a group in SNMPv1. Thus all network management systems (security names) in SNMPv1 (security model) with a community name public (group) would have equal access privilege to an agent.

Security Level.   Security level (*vacmAccessSecurityLevel*) is the level of security of the user—namely, no authentication–no privacy, authentication–no privacy, and authentication–privacy. This level is set by the message flag shown in Figure 7.12. A member using a specific security model and with a given security name in a group could have different access rights by using different security levels for various tasks.

Contexts.   As mentioned in Section 7.3, an SNMP context is a collection of management information accessible by an SNMP entity (agent). An SNMP entity has access to potentially more than one context. Each SNMP engine has a context table that lists the locally available contexts by *contextName*.

MIB Views and View Families.   As in SNMPv1 and SNMPv2, access rights to contexts are controlled by a MIB view (see Figure 5.2). A MIB view is defined for each group and it details the set of managed object types (and optionally, the specific instances of object types). Following the approach of the treelike naming structure for MIB, a MIB view is defined as a set of *view subtrees* with each view subtree being in the managed object naming tree. A simple MIB view could be all nodes defined under an object identifier—for example, *system*. A view subtree is identified by the OBJECT IDENTIFIER value that is the longest OBJECT IDENTIFIER prefix common to all (potential) MIB object instances in that subtree. For the system example, it is {1.3.6.1.2.1.1}.

An example of a complex MIB view could be all information relevant to a particular network interface. This information can be represented by the union of multiple view subtrees, such as a set of *system* and *interfaces* for viewing all managed objects in the System and Interfaces groups.

A more complex MIB view occurs when all the columnar objects in a conceptual row of a table appear in separate subtrees, one per column, each with a similar format. Because the formats are similar, the required set of subtrees can be aggregated into one structure, called a *family of view subtrees*. A family of view subtrees is a pairing of an OBJECT IDENTIFIER value (called the family name) together with a bit string value (called the family mask). The family mask indicates which subidentifiers of the associated family name are significant to the family's definition. A family of view subtrees can be either included or excluded from a MIB view.

Access Policy.   The access policy determines the access rights to objects such as *read-view*, *write-view*, and *notify-view*. For a given *groupName*, *contextName*, *securityModel*, and *securityLevel*, that group's access rights are defined by the combination of the three views or by *not-accessible*. The read-view is used for get-request, get-next-request, and get-bulk-request operations. The write-view is used with the set-request operation. The notify-view represents the set of object instances authorized for the group when objects are being sent in a notification.

7.8.2   The VACM Process

The VACM process is presented as a flowchart in Figure 7.16. We will explain the process in terms of an SNMP agent with an SNMP engine having responsibility for many contexts. In the next section we will describe the tables shown. The VACM process answers the six questions related to access of management information [RFC 2275]:

1. Who are you (group comprising security model and security name)?
2. Where do you want to go (context to be accessed)?
3. How secure are you in accessing the information (security model and security level)?
4. Why do you want to access the information (to read, write, or send notification)?
5. What object (object type) do you want to access?
6. Which object (object instance) do you want to access?

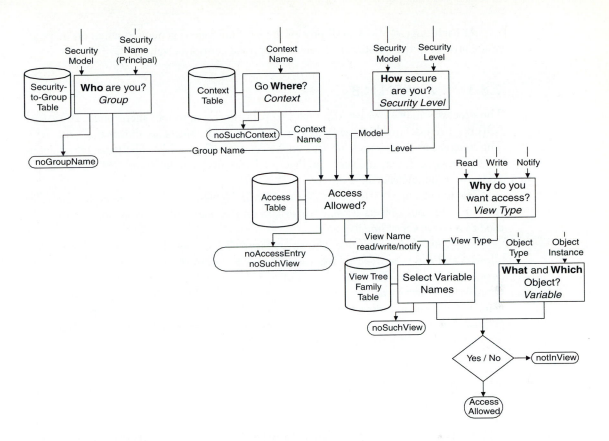

Figure 7.16   The VACM Process

The first question is answered by the introduction of the group concept. The group that the requester belongs to is determined by the VACM from the security model and security name. It uses the security-to-group table for validating the principal and deriving the group name.

The second question is answered by checking whether the context that needs to be accessed is within the responsibility of the agent. If the first two questions are answered in the affirmative, then the results, *group name* and *context name*, along with the *security model* and *security level* (answers to the question "how"), are fed into the "access allowed?" process. With these four inputs as indices, the access table provides the views permitted, *view name*, as one or more of the read-view, write-view, and notify-view.

The answer to the fourth question regarding why access is needed is used to select the family of view subtrees eligible to be accessed. In the view tree family table a match is made between the result of the selection process and the answers to the fifth and sixth questions regarding what (object type) and which (object instance), to make a decision on whether access is to be allowed.

At each stage of the overall process an error message is generated when an inappropriate answer to the question is given and approval cannot be validated.

7.8.3   A VACM MIB

The processes in VACM use the tables to perform the functions mentioned. A VACM MIB has been defined by specifying the newly created objects, as shown in Figure 7.17. The *snmpVacmMIB* is a node under *snmpModules* (see Figure 7.7). The three tables defining the group, context, and access in Figure 7.16 are nodes under *vacmMIBObjects*, itself a node under *snmpVacmMIB*.

The *vacmContextTable* is a list of *vacmContextNames*. The *vacmSecurityToGroupTable* has the columnar objects *vacmSecurityModel* and *vacmSecurityName* as indices that are used to retrieve *vacmGroupName*.

The VACM Access Table, shown in Figure 7.18, is used to determine the access allowed and the *viewName*. It has *vacmGroupName* from the *vacmSecurityToGroupTable* as one of the indices. The other three indices from this table are *vacmAccessContextPrefix*, *vacmAccessSecurityModel*, and *vacmAccessSecurityLevel*. The *viewName* representing the three views *vacmAccessReadViewName*, *vacmAccessWriteViewName*, and *vacmAccessNotifyViewName* are retrieved from the table. The *vacmAccessStorageType* and *vacmAccessStatus* are the administrative information objects relating to storage volatility and row status.

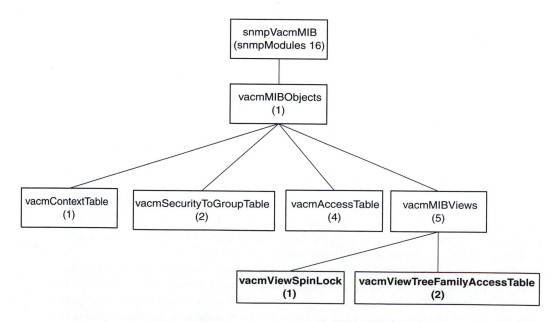

Figure 7.17   A VACM MIB

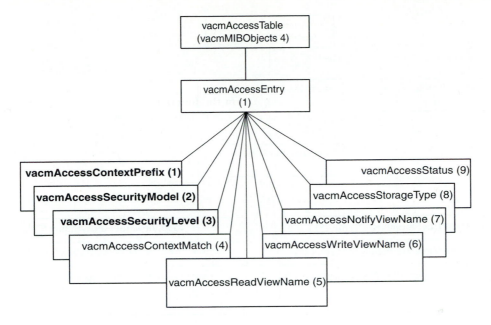

Figure 7.18   The VACM Access Table

The *vacmMIBViews*—the fourth node under *vacmMIBObjects*, shown in Figure 7.19—has the subordinate nodes *vacmViewSpinLock* and *vacmViewTreeFamilyAccessTable*. The *vacmViewSpinLock* is an advisory lock used by SNMP command generator applications to coordinate their use of the set operation in creating or modifying views in agents. It is an optional implementation object.

The *vacmViewTreeFamilyTable* describes families of subtrees that are available within MIB views in the local SNMP agent for each context. Each row in this table describes a subtree for a viewName and an OBJECT IDENTIFIER. For example, if the "access allowed?" process in Figure 7.16 yields three values for *viewName*, that would result in three conceptual rows in this table. The *vacmViewTreeFamilyViewName* representing *viewName* is one of the columnar objects and an index in the table; two indices define a conceptual row in this table. The second is the *vacmViewTreeFamilySubtree*, which is a node representing the top of the tree. For example, if the object identifier were 1.3.6.1.2.1.1, it would represent the *system* subtree. The object identifier for the local agent is determined by the highest object identifier that would address all object instances in the local view.

In some situations, we may want to view different subsets of a subtree. In such cases, we can form a family of view subtrees by using a combination of two parameters. The first is selection of the view, which is done by a family mask defined by *vacmViewTreeFamily-Mask*, and the second is a family type defined by *vacmViewTreeFamilyType*. The family mask is a bit string that is used with the *vacmViewTreeFamilySubtree*. When this feature is

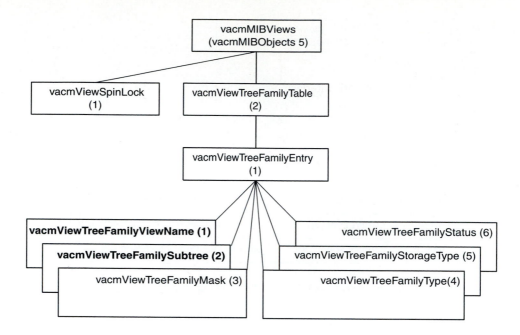

Figure 7.19   VACM MIB Views

used, specific objects in a subtree are selected if the corresponding object identifier matches. If the corresponding bit value is 0 in the family mask, it is considered to be a wild card and any value of the object identifier would be selected. After the selection has been made, if the family type value is included(1), the view is included; if it is excluded(2), the view is excluded. Flexibility in the views can be obtained by introducing a columnar object *vacmViewTreeFamilyType* that indicates whether a particular subtree in the family of subtrees derived from *vacmViewTreeFamilySubtree* and *vacmViewTreeFamily-Mask* is to be included or excluded in a context's MIB view.

As an example of the system group to be included, the values of the various parameters of the family entry in Figure 7.19 are:

Family view name = "system"

Family subtree = 1.3.6.1.2.1.1

Family mask = ""

Family type = 1

The zero length string, "", for mask value designates all 1s by convention.

We could extend the view by adding a second row to the table. For example, we could add a SNMP group by adding another row to the table containing the family subtree 1.3.6.1.2.1.11.

We could also extend the view by adding a columnar object to the table. We could extend the view to all the columnar objects of a conceptual row in a table. A useful convention for doing this is to use the definition of columnar object 0, which designates all columnar objects in a table. For example, {1.3.6.1.2.1.2.2.1.0.5} identifies all columnar objects associated with the 5th interface (corresponding to an *ifIndex* value of 5) in the *ifTable*.

If more than one family name is present with the same number of subidentifiers, the lexicographic convention is followed for predominance. This technique helps in the following way. Suppose that we wanted to choose all columnar objects in the *ifTable* example, except the *ifMtu*, which is the 4th columnar object. We would then choose {1.3.6.1.2.1.2.2.1.4.5} and the Type = 2 to exclude it. This set is lexicographically higher than {1.3.6.1.2.1.2.2.1.0.5}, so the latter takes precedence. Thus the combination of the two will select all 5th row objects except *ifMtu*.

Summary

In this chapter we reviewed the latest version of SNMP, SNMPv3. Its two main features are the specifications for a formalized SNMP architecture and security. The first addresses the three SNMP frameworks for the three versions. Two new members, Dispatcher and Message Processing Model, are defined. These additions enable a network management system to handle messages from and to agents that belong to all three current versions. It also will accommodate future versions as necessary.

The second of these features is the inclusion of security. A security model is defined that addresses data integrity, data origin authentication, data confidentiality, message timeliness, and limited message replay protection. The authentication module in the security model addresses the first two issues, the privacy module protects data confidentiality, and the timeliness module deals with message timeliness and limited replay protection. The security model is the User-based Security Model (USM), which was derived from the traditional concept of user ID and password.

The access policy of SNMPv1 and SNMPv2 has been extended and made more flexible by the View-based Access Control Model (VACM). An SNMP agent handling multiple objects (contexts) can be configured to present a set of MIB views and a family of subtrees in its MIB views. These views can be matched with seven input parameters to determine the access allowed to the principal. They are the security model (version of SNMP), security name (principal), security level (dependent on the authentication and privacy parameters), context name, type of access needed, object type, and object instance.

Exercises

1. The first four octets of an SNMP engine ID in a system are set to the binary equivalent of the system's SNMP management private enterprise number as assigned by the IANA. Write the first four octets of the SNMP engine ID in hexadecimal

notation for the four enterprises, cisco, hp, 3com, and cabletron, shown in Figure 4.14 for the following two versions.

a. SNMPv1
b. SNMPv3

2. Write the full SNMP engine ID for:

a. SNMPv1 for a 3Com hub with the IPv4 address 128.64.46.2 in the 5th to 8th octets followed by 0s in the rest.
b. SNMPv3 for the Cisco router interface with the IPv6 address ::128.64.32.16

3. Describe the SNMPv3 *scopedPdu* that the SNMP agent (router) uses to respond to NMS with the data shown in Figure 4.2(c).

4. Figure 7.20 Exercise 4 shows a generalized time-sequenced operation for get-request message going from a manager to an agent. Complete the primitives in Figure 7.20 and explicitly identify the application modules you used.

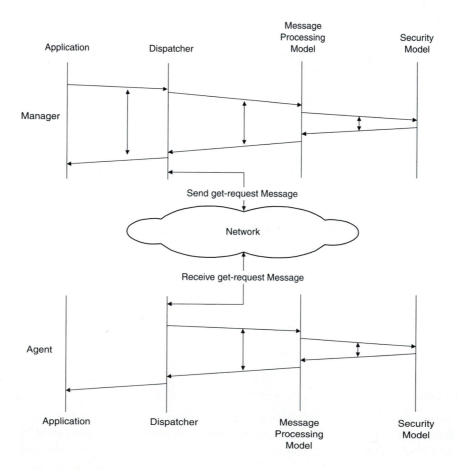

Figure 7.20   Exercise 4

5. Draw the time-sequence operation similar to that shown in Figure 7.20 detailing the elements of procedure for get-response message from the agent to the manager.

6. Detail the IN and OUT parameters of the *sendPdu* and *prepareOutgoingMsg* primitives shown in Figure 7.4 by referring to RFC 2271.

7. Identify the authoritative and nonauthoritative entities in Figure 7.20.

8. Define the configuration parameters for a notification generator to send traps to two network management systems, *noc1* and *noc2*, by filling in the objects in the *snmpTargetAddressTable*, *snmpTargetTable*, and *snmpNotifyTable*. The specifications for the two targets are as follows. You may use the Appendix of RFC 2273 as a guide to complete this exercise.

	noc1	noc2
messageProcessingModel	SNMPv3	SNMPv3
securityModel	3 (USM)	3 (USM)
securityName	"noc1"	"noc2"
snmpTargetParamsName	"NOAuthNoPriv-noc1"	"NOAuthNoPriv-noc1"
securityLevel	noAuthNoProv(1)	authPriv(3)
transportDomain	snmpUDPDomain	snmpUDPDomain
transportAddress	128.64.32.16:162	128.64.32.8:162
tagList	"group1"	"group2"

9. Access RFC 2274 and list and define the primitives provided by the authentication module at the sending and receiving security models. Describe the services provided by the primitives.

10. Access RFC 2274 and list and define primitives provided by the privacy module at the sending and receiving security models. Describe the services provided by the primitives.

11. Specify family name, family subtree, family mask, and family type, in the *vacmViewTreeFamilyTable* for an agent to present a view of

    a. the complete IP group.
    b. the IP Address Table (*ipAddrTable*).
    c. the row in the IP address table corresponding to the IP address 172.46.62.1.

12. Write the *vacmViewTreeFamilyTable* for the three rows that present the system group in the IP address table for the row with IP address 172.46.62.1 without using the *ipAdEntReasmMaxSize*.

CHAPTER 8

SNMP Management: RMON

The success of SNMP management resulted in the rapid growth of managed network components in computer networks. SNMPv1 provided the foundation for monitoring a network remotely from a centralized network operations center (NOC) and performing fault and configuration management. However, the extent to which network performance could be managed was limited. The characterization of computer network performance is statistical in nature. That led to the logical step of measuring the statistics of important parameters in the network from the NOC and development of remote network monitoring specifications.

8.1   What Is Remote Monitoring?

In Chapter 5 we gave some examples of SNMP messages going across a network between a manager and an agent. We did so with a tool that "sniffs" every packet going across a LAN, opens it, and analyzes it. It is a passive operation and does nothing to the packets, which continue on to their destinations. This approach is called *monitoring* (or probing) *the network*, and the device that performs that function is called a *network monitor* (or probe). We need to make a distinction between the two components of a probe: (1) the physical object that is connected to the transmission medium, and (2) the processor that analyzes the data. If both are at the same place geographically, the probe is local, which is how sniffers used to function. We will discuss this topic further in Chapter 9, when we consider management systems and tools.

The monitored information, gathered and analyzed locally, can be transmitted to a remote network management station. In such a case, remotely monitoring the network with a probe is referred to as Remote Network Monitoring (RMON). Figure 8.1 shows an FDDI backbone network with a local Ethernet LAN. Two remote LANs, one a token ring LAN and another, an FDDI LAN, are connected to the backbone network. The network manage-

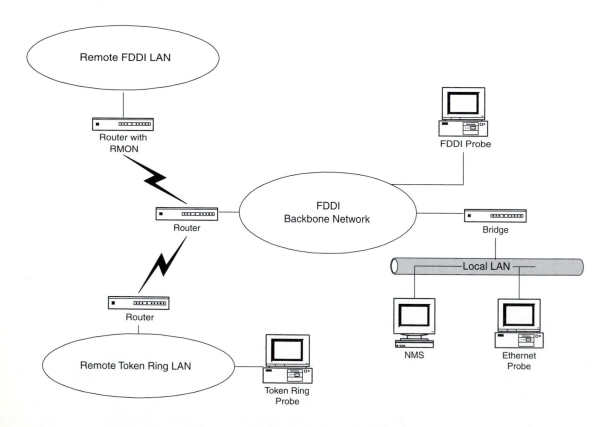

Figure 8.1   Network Configuration with RMONs

ment system (NMS) is on the local Ethernet LAN. Either an Ethernet probe or an RMON is on the Ethernet LAN monitoring the local LAN. The FDDI backbone is monitored by an FDDI probe via the bridge and Ethernet LAN. A token ring probe monitors the token ring LAN. It communicates with the network management system via the routers, the WAN (shown by the lightning bolt symbol of the telecommunications link), and the backbone network. The remote FDDI is monitored by the built-in probe on the router. The FDDI probe communicates with the network management system. All four probes that monitor the four LANs and communicate with the network management system are RMON devices.

The use of RMON devices has several advantages. One advantage is that each RMON device monitors the local network segment and does the necessary analyses. It relays information in both solicited and unsolicited fashion to the network management system. For example, RMON could be locally polling the network elements in a segment. If it detects an abnormal condition, such as heavy packet losses or excessive collisions, it sends an alarm. Because the polling is local, the information is fairly reliable. This example of local monitoring and reporting to a remote network management system significantly reduces SNMP traffic in the network. This reduction is especially true for the segment in which the network management system resides, as all the monitoring traffic would otherwise converge there.

The following case history illustrates another advantage: that RMON reduces the need for agents in the network to be visible at all times to the network management system. A network management system frequently indicated that one of the hubs showed failure, but the hub recovered without any intervention. The performance study of the hub that the LAN was part of, indicated that the LAN would frequently become overloaded with heavy traffic and would experience significant packet loss. The lost packets included the ICMP packets that the NMS was using to poll the hub. The NMS had been set to indicate a node failure if three successive ICMP packets did not receive responses. Increasing the number of packets needed to indicate a failure stopped the failure indication.

Monitoring packets, such as ICMP pings, may get lost in long-distance communication, especially under heavy traffic conditions. Such losses may wrongly be interpreted by the network management system that the managed object is down. RMON pings locally and hence has less chance of losing packets, thus increasing monitoring reliability.

Yet another advantage of local monitoring with RMON is that the individual segments can be monitored almost continuously. This capability provides better statistics and control. Thus a fault can be diagnosed more quickly by the RMON and reported to the network management system. In some situations, a failure may even be prevented by proactive management.

The overall benefits of implementing RMON technology in a network are higher network availability for users and greater productivity for administrators. A study report [CISCO/RMON] indicates significantly increased productivity for network administrators who use RMON in their networks.

8.2   RMON SMI and MIB

For a network configuration system like the one shown in Figure 8.1 to work successfully, several conditions must be met. The network components are made by different vendors, and even the RMON devices may be from different vendors. Thus, as in the communication of network management information, standards need to be established for common syntax and semantics for the use of RMON devices. The syntax used is ASN.1, and the RMON structure of management information is similar to that of SMIv2 in defining the object types. The Remote Network Monitoring Management Information Base (RMON MIB), which defines RMON groups, has been developed in three stages. The original RMON MIB, now referred to as RMON1, was developed for the Ethernet LAN in November 1991 [RFC 1271], but it was made obsolete in 1995 [RFC 1757]. Token ring extensions to RMON1 were developed in September 1993 [RFC 1513]. The use of RMON1 for remote monitoring was extremely beneficial, but RMON1 addressed parameters at the OSI layer 2 only. Hence RMON2 [RFC 2021] was developed and released in January 1997; it addressed the parameters associated with OSI layers 3–7.

The RMON group is node 16 under MIB-II (mib-2 16), as previously shown in Figure 6.36. All the groups in the overall RMON group are shown in Figure 8.2. The overall group

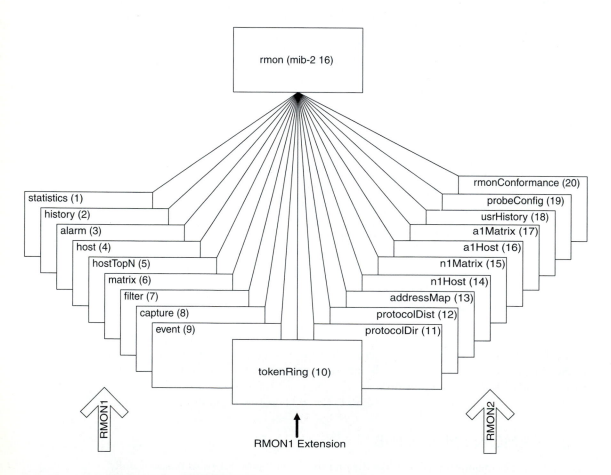

Figure 8.2   **RMON Group**

consists of nine Ethernet RMON1 groups (rmon 1–rmon 9), one token ring extension group to RMON1 (rmon 10), and ten RMON2 groups (rmon 11-rmon 20) for the higher layers.

We will cover RMON1 in Section 8.3 and RMON2 in Section 8.4. We will discuss the applications of RMON in Part III.

8.3   RMON I

RMON1 is covered by RFC 1757 for Ethernet LAN and by RFC 1513 for extensions to token ring LAN. Two data types were introduced, as textual conventions, along with ten MIB groups (rmon 1–rmon 10).

8.3.1   RMON I Textual Conventions

Two new data types defined in the RMON1 textual conventions were *OwnerString* and *EntryStatus*. Both are extremely useful in the operation of RMON devices, which are used by management systems to measure and produce statistics on network elements. We will soon demonstrate that this function involves setting up tables that control parameters to be monitored. Typically, a network has more than one management system, which could be permitted to create, use, and delete the control parameters in a table. Or, a human network manager in charge of network operations could perform such functions. For this purpose, the owner identification is made part of the control table defined by the *OwnerString* data type. The *EntryStatus* is used to resolve conflicts that might arise between management systems in the manipulation of control tables.

The **OwnerString** is specified in the NVT ASCII character set as *DisplayString*. The information content of *OwnerString* contains information about the owner, such as IP address, management station name, network manager's name, location, or telephone number. If the agent itself is the owner, as, for example, in the addition of an interface card, the *OwnerString* is set to "monitor."

In order to understand the data type **EntryStatus**, we need to understand the concept of creation and deletion of rows in tables (see Chapter 6). For a table to be shared by multiple users, a columnar object using *EntryStatus* (for example, *etherStatsStatus*), similar to *RowStatus* in SNMPv2, is added to the table that contains the information on the row's status. The *EntryStatus* data type can exist in one of four states: (1) *valid*, (2) *createRequest*, (3) *underCreation*, and (4) *invalid*; these four states are shown in Table 8.1. Under the *valid*

Table 8.1   EntryStatus Textual Convention

State	Enumeration	Description
valid	1	Row exists and is active. It is fully configured and operational.
createRequest	2	Create a new row by creating this object.
underCreation	3	Row is not fully active.
invalid	4	Delete the row by disassociating the mapping of this entry.

state condition, the instantiation or row of the table is operational and is probably measuring the number of input octets in the IF group on an interface. Any management system authenticated to use the RMON device may use this row of data. Of course, if the owner of the row decides to make it invalid, other systems lose the data. The *invalid* state is used to delete a row. Based on the implementation used, the row may be deleted immediately and the resource claimed, or it may be deleted in batch mode later. If the desired row of information does not already exist, the management system can create a row. The *EntryStatus* is then set to *createRequest*. The process of creation may involve more than one exchange of PDUs between the manager and the agent. In such a situation, the state of the *EntryStatus* is set to *underCreation* so that others won't use it. After the creation process has been completed, it is set to the *valid* state.

8.3.2   RMON1 Groups and Functions

RMON1 performs numerous functions at the data link layer. Figure 8.3 depicts the RMON1 groups and functions. The data gathering modules, which are LAN probes, gather data from the remotely monitored network comprising Ethernet and

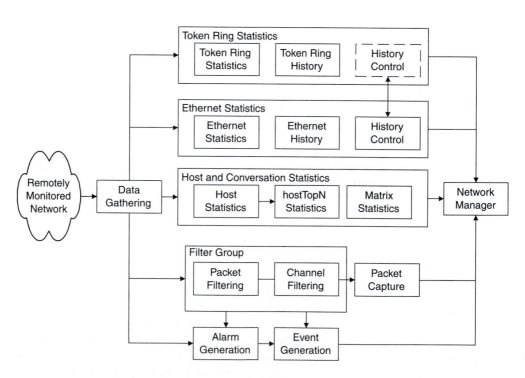

Figure 8.3   RMON1 Groups and Functions

token ring LANs. The data can serve as inputs to five sets of functions, three of which monitor traffic statistics. The host and conversation statistics group deals with traffic data associated with the hosts, ranking the traffic for the top N hosts, and conversation between hosts. The group of statistical data associated with Ethernet LAN—namely, Ethernet statistics and Ethernet history statistics—is addressed by the groups and functions in the Ethernet statistics box. The history control table controls the data to be gathered from various networks. It is also used by the token ring statistics modules in the token ring statistics box. The outputs of the various modules are analyzed and presented in tabular and graphical forms to the user by the network manager in the network management system.

The filter group is a cascade of two filters. The packet filter filters incoming packets by performing a Boolean and/or XOR with a mask specified, which can be quite complex. The filtered packet stream is considered a channel, and we can make further selections based on the channel mask. The filtered outputs may generate either alarms or events, which are reported to the network manager. The output of the data gatherer could also generate an alarm directly.

The output of the filter group can be stored in the packet capture module for further analysis by the network manager. Examples of analyses include special studies of traffic patterns or troubleshooting of abnormalities in the network.

The functions associated with the various groups are performed by ten groups associated with the RMON1 MIB, as is shown in Table 8.2. The first nine groups are applicable to common data and to the Ethernet LAN, and the tenth group extends it to the token ring LAN: most of the groups have one or more tables. The groups fall into three categories, the largest of which is the category of statistics gathering groups. These are the statistics groups, history groups, host group, host Top N group, and matrix group. The second category deals with the network event reporting functions. These are the alarm group and the event group. The third category deals with filtering the input packets according to selected criteria and capturing the data if desired for further analysis. These are the filter group and the packet capture group. We will consider RMON1 groups and the token ring extension to RMON1 in Sections 8.3.4 and 8.3.5, respectively.

In the tables column in Table 8.2 some of the groups have tables with "2" as part of the name—for example, the *etherStats2Table* in the statistics group. These are additional tables created during RMON2 specifications development and are enhancements of RMON1. Hence they are included here as part of RMON1. The enhancements of RMON1 include the standard *LastCreateTime* textual convention for all control tables and the *TimeFilter* textual convention that provides capability for the filter to handle rows to be used for the index to a table. The *LastCreateTime* enhancement helps keep track of data with the changes in control. The *TimeFilter* enables an application to download only those rows that changed after a particular time. The agent returns a value only if the time mark is less than the last update time.

For example, let's consider a *fooTable* with two rows and three columnar objects, *fooTimeMark* (with *TimeFilter* as the data type), *fooIndex*, and *foocounts*. The indices defining a row are *fooTimeMark* and *fooIndex*. Let the *TimeFilter* index start at 0, the last update of *fooCounter* in row #1 occur at time 3, and its value be 5. Assume that the update

Table 8.2   RMON1 MIB Groups and Tables

Group	OID	Function	Tables
Statistics	rmon 1	Provides link level statistics	-etherStatsTable
			-etherStats2Table
History	rmon 2	Collects periodic statistical data and stores them for later retrieval	-historyControlTable
			-etherHistoryTable
			-historyControl2Table
			-etherHistory2Table
Alarm	rmon 3	Generates events when the data sample gathered crosses pre-established thresholds	-alarmTable
Host	rmon 4	Gathers statistical data on hosts	-hostControlTable
			-hostTable
			-hostTimeTable
			-hostControl2Table
Host Top N	rmon 5	Computes the top N hosts on the respective categories of statistics gathered	-hostTopNControlTable
Matrix	rmon 6	Gathers statistics on traffic between pairs of hosts	-matrixControlTable
			-matrixSDTable
			-matrixDSTable
			-matrixControl2Table
Filter	rmon 7	Performs filter function that enables capture of desired parameters	-filterTable
			-channelTable
			-filter2Table
			-channel2Table
Packet capture	rmon 8	Provides packet capture capability for gathering packets after they flow through a channel	-bufferControlTable
			-captureBufferTable
Event	rmon 9	Controls the generation of events and notifications	-eventTable
Token ring	rmon 10	See Table 8.3	See Table 8.3

of row #2 occurred at time 5 and that the value was updated to 9. This scenario would yield the following instance of *fooCounts* in the fooTable at time 7. Each row has the value of its latest update at any given time.

```
fooCounts.0.1  5
fooCounts.0.2  9
fooCounts.1.1  5
fooCounts.1.2  9
fooCounts.2.1  5
fooCounts.1.2  9
fooCounts.3.1  5
fooCounts.3.2  9
fooCounts.4.2  9    (Note that row #1 does not exist for times 4
                    and 5 since the last update occured at time-
                    mark 3.)
fooCounts.5.2  9
(Both rows #1 and #2 do not exist for timemark greater than 5.)
```

8.3.3   Relationship Between Control and Data Tables

In the tables column in Table 8.2, notice that several of the groups have both a data table and a control table. The data table contains rows (instances) of data. The control table defines the instances of the data rows in the data table and can be set to gather and store different instances of data. The generic relationship between control and data tables is illustrated in Figure 8.4. The value of the *dataIndex* in the data table is the same as the value of *controlIndex* in the control table.

We can illustrate how data and control tables work together by using the matrix group in Table 8.2. We can base the data collection on source and destination addresses appearing in the packets for a given interface using the *matrixSDTable* (matrix source–destination table). The control index is an integer uniquely identifying the row in the control table. It can have a value of 1 for the first interface of a managed entity. The value of the columnar object, *controldataSource*, identifies the source of the data being collected. In our example, if interface #1 belongs to the interfaces group, then *controlDataSource* is *ifIndex.1*.

The *controlTableSize* identifies the entries associated with this data source. In our matrix source–destination table example, it is the source–destination pair in each row of the table.

The *controlOwner* columnar object is the entity or person that created the entry. The entity could be the agent or NMS, or a management person. The *controlStatus* is one of the entries listed in Table 8.1. The *controlOther* could be any other object.

To identify a unique conceptual row in the data table, we may need to specify more indices than the *dataIndex*, as indicated by *dataAddlIndex* in Figure 8.4. In our matrix source–destination example, the additional indices are source and destination address objects. The dataOther in the data table indicates data being collected, such as the number of packets.

8.3.4   RMON1 Common and Ethernet Groups

So far we have covered the global picture of the RMON1 Ethernet MIB and how data and control tables are related to each other. Let us now address the nine common RMON1 and Ethernet groups.

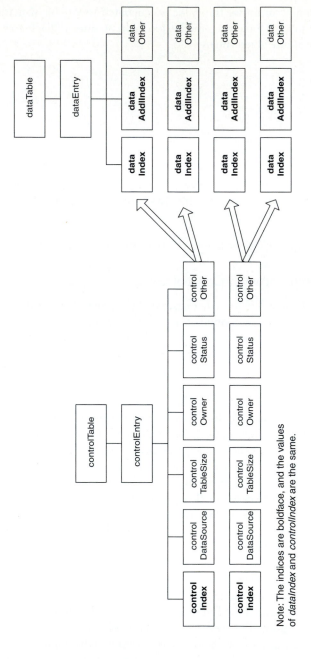

Note: The indices are boldface, and the values
of *dataIndex* and *controlIndex* are the same.

Figure 8.4   Relationship Between Control and Data Tables

The Statistics Group.   The statistics group contains statistics measured by the probe for each monitored Ethernet interface on a device. The *etherStatsTable* in this group has an entry for each interface. The data include statistics on packet types, sizes, and errors. Also provided is the capability to gather statistics on collisions of the Ethernet segment. The number of collisions is a best estimate, as the number detected depends on where the probe is placed on the segment.

The statistics group is used to measure live statistics on nodes and segments. Commercial network management systems include features such as dynamic presentation of various traffic patterns. The number of MIB collisions can also be used to generate an alarm when the number exceeds a set high threshold value.

The History Group.   The history group consists of two subgroups: the history control group and the history (data) group. The history control group controls the periodic statistical sampling of data from various types of networks. The control table stores configuration entries comprising interface, polling period, and other parameters. The information is stored in a media-specific table, the history table, which contains one entry for each specific sample. Short-term and long-term intervals, such as 30-second and 30-minute intervals, may be specified to obtain two different statistics. The data objects defined are dropped events, number of octets and packets, different types of errors, fragments, collisions, and utilization.

The history group is extremely helpful in tracking the overall trend in the volume of traffic. Because historical data are accumulated at the data link layer, they include traffic emanating from all higher layer protocols. The short-term history statistics can also be used to troubleshoot network performance problems. For example, in one study of traffic patterns short-term history statistics revealed that a significant volume of "transparent" data was contributed by servers in the network, which were functioning as "mirrors" for a public news service on the Internet. Although the service was considered to be desirable because it was generated and consumed externally, it behaved somewhat transparently with regard to the local network traffic.

The Alarm Group.   The alarm group periodically takes statistical samples on specified variables in the probe and compares them with the preconfigured threshold stored in the probe. Whenever the monitored variable crosses the threshold, an event is generated. To avoid excessive event generation on the threshold border, rising and falling thresholds are specified. This technique works in the following manner. Suppose that an alarm event is generated when the variable crosses the falling threshold while dropping in value. Another event would be generated only after the value crosses the rising threshold at least once.

The group contains an *alarm table* with a list of entries that define the alarm parameters. The columnar objects *alarmVariable* and *alarmInterval* are used to select the variable and the sampling interval. The sampling type is either the absolute or delta value. In the former, the absolute value of the variable at the end of the previous period is stored as an alarm value. In the latter, the absolute value at the end of a period is subtracted from the beginning of the period, and the computed value is stored. These values are compared to the rising and falling thresholds to generate alarms as appropriate.

An example of an absolute value is a new interface card on a test for infant mortality. The threshold of the sum of outgoing and incoming packets could be set to 1 gigaoctects, and the RMON would generate an alarm/event when the threshold is reached. An example of a delta value is a threshold set to 10,000 packets in a 10-second interval for excessive packet loss.

The Host Group.   The host group contains information about the hosts on the network. It compiles a list of hosts by looking at the good packets traversing the network and extracting source and destination MAC addresses; it also maintains statistics on these hosts. The group comprises three tables: *hostControlTable, hostTable,* and *hostTimeTable.* The *hostControlTable* controls the interfaces on which the data gathering is done. The other two tables depend on this information. The *hostTable* contains statistics about the host. The *hostTimeTable* contains the same data as the host table, but it is stored in the time order in which the host entry was discovered. This ordering helps in the fast discovery of new hosts in the system. The entries in the two data tables are synchronized with respect to the host in the *hostControlTable.* We can obtain statistics on a host by using this MIB.

The Host Top N Group.   The host top N group generates reports ranking the top *N* hosts in selected statistics categories. For example, we can rank-order the top ten hosts with maximum outgoing traffic. The *hostTopNControlTable* is used to initiate generation of such a report.

An example of the type of data that can be acquired with a RMON probe is the chart shown in Figure 8.5, which was derived with an RMON probe for the output octets of the top ten hosts in a network. The names of the hosts have been changed to generic host numbers for security reasons.

The Matrix Group.   The matrix group stores statistics on conversations between pairs of hosts. An entry is created for each conversation that the probe detects. There are three tables in the group: The *matrixControlTable* controls the information to be gathered; the *matrixSDTable* keeps track of the source to destination conversations; and the *matrixDSTable* keeps the data by destination to source traffic. We can obtain a graph similar to that shown in Figure 8.5 for the conversation pairs in both directions by using this group.

The Filter Group.   The filter group is used to base the capture of filter packets on logical expressions. The stream of data based on a logical expression is called a *channel.* The group contains a filter table and a channel table. The filter table allows packets to be filtered with an arbitrary filter expression, a set of filters is associated with each channel, and each filter is defined by a row in the filter table. A channel may be associated with several rows. For each channel, the input packet is validated against each filter associated with that channel and is accepted if it passes any of the tests. A row in the channel table of the filter group includes the ID for the interface (same as *ifIndex*) with which the channel is associated, along with acceptance criteria. The combination of the filter and channel filtering provides enormous flexibility in selecting packets to be captured.

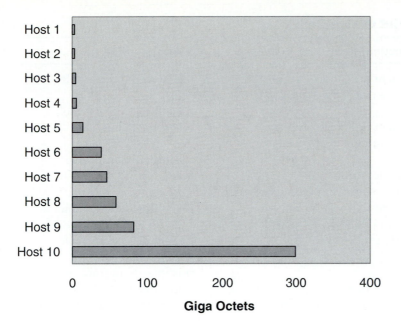

Figure 8.5 Host Top-10 Output Octets

The Packet Capture Group. The packet capture group is a post-filter group. It captures packets from each channel, based on the filter criteria of packet and channel filters in the filter group. The channel filter criteria for acceptance of filter group output is controlled by the *bufferControlTable* and the captured channel data in the *captureBufferTable*. Each packet captured is stored in the buffer as an instance.

The Event Group. The event group controls the generation and notification of events. Both rising and falling alarms can be specified in the *eventTable* associated with the group. In addition to transmitting events, the system maintains a log.

8.3.5   RMON Token Ring Extension Groups

As we mentioned earlier, the token ring RMON MIB is an extension to RMON1 MIB and is specified in RFC 1513. Table 8.3 presents the token ring MIB groups and tables. Each of the eight groups has a data table and two have control tables.

   There are two token ring statistics groups, one at the MAC layer (the token ring statistics group) and the other on packets collected promiscuously (the token ring promiscuous statistics group). Both contain statistics on ring utilization and ring error statistics. The MAC layer statistics group collects data on token ring parameters (e.g., token packets, errors in packets, bursts, polling, etc.). The promiscuous statistics group collects statistics on

Table 8.3   RMON Token Ring MIB Groups and Tables

Token Ring Group	Function	Tables
Statistics	Current utilization and error statistics of the MAC Layer	tokenRingMLStatsTable
		tokenRingMLStats2Table
Promiscuous statistics	Current utilization and error statistics of promiscuous data	tokenRingPStatsTable
		tokenRingPStats2Table
MAC-layer history	Historical utilization and error statistics of the MAC Layer	tokenRingMLHistoryTable
Promiscuous history	Historical utilization and error statistics of promiscuous data	tokenRingPHistoryTable
Ring station	Station statistics	ringStationControlTable
		ringStationTable
		ringStationControl2Table
Ring station order	station order	ringStationOrderTable
Ring station configuration	Active configuration of ring stations	ringStationConfigControlTable
		ringStationConfigTable
Source routing	Utilization statistics of source routing information	sourceRoutingStatsTable
		sourceRoutingStats2Table

the number of packets of various sizes and the type of packets—multicast or broadcast data. There are two corresponding history statistics groups: current and promiscuous. One data table is associated with each of the four statistics groups. The history control table is common to both Ethernet and Token ring.

Three groups are associated with the stations on the ring. The ring station group provides statistics on each station being monitored on the ring, along with its status. The data are stored in the *ringStationTable*. The rings and parameters to be monitored are controlled by the *ringStationControlTable*. The ring station order group provides the order of the station on the monitored rings and has only a data table. The ring station configuration group manages the stations on the ring.

The last of the ring groups is the source routing group. It is used to gather statistics on routing information in a pure source routing environment.

8.4   RMON2

RMON1 dealt primarily with data associated with the OSI data link layer. The success and popularity of RMON1 led to the development of RMON2 [RFC 2021]. It extends monitoring capability to the upper layers, from the network layer to the application layer. The term *application level* is used in the SNMP RMON concept to describe a class of protools, and not strictly in the OSI layer 7 protocol. The error statistics in any layer include all the errors below that layer, down to the network layer. For example, the network layer errors do not include data link layer errors, but transport layer errors include network layer errors.

Several of the groups and functions in RMON2 at higher layers are similar to those of the data link layer in RMON1. We will discuss the groups and their similarity here. We will cover in detail how protocol analyzer systems incorporate the higher layer data gathered with the use of RMON2 in Chapter 12 when we discuss network management systems and tools.

8.4.1   The RMON2 Management Information Base

The architecture of RMON2 is the same as that of RMON1. The RMON2 Management Information Base (MIB) is arranged in ten groups. Table 8.4 shows the RMON2 MIB groups and tables. We have already discussed the enhancements of RMON1 MIB in the preceding section.

The protocol directory group identifies the protocols that the probe can monitor. Probe capability can be altered by reconfiguring the *protocolDirTable*. The protocols range from the data link control layer to the application layer and are identified by the columnar object on the unique protocol ID. Each protocol is further subdivided by parameters, such as fragments. The protocol identifier and the protocol parameters are used as indices for the table's rows. The table contains one entry for each protocol. The protocols that can be used with the Protocol Directory have been defined in RFC 2074.

The protocol distribution group provides information on the relative traffic of different protocols, either in octets or packets. It collects basic statistics that help a network management system manage bandwidth allocation utilized by different protocols. The *protocolDistControlTable* is configured according to the data to be collected, and *protocolDistStatsTable* stores the data collected. Each row in the *protocolDistStatsTable* is indexed by the *protocolDistControlIndex* in the *protocolDistControlTable* and the *protocolDirLocalIndex* in the *protocolDirTable*. The data table stores the packet and octet counts.

The address map group is similar to the address translation table binding the MAC address to network address on each interface. It has two tables for control and data.

The network layer host group measures the traffic sent from and to each network address representing each host discovered by the probe, as the host group in RMON1 does.

The network layer matrix group provides information on the conversation between pairs of hosts in both directions. It is very similar to the matrix tables in RMON1. The group also ranks the top *N* conversations. It has two control tables and three data tables.

The application layer functions are divided into the application layer host group and the application layer matrix group. Both calculate traffic by protocol units and use their respective control tables in the network layer host group and the network layer matrix group. The application layer matrix group can also generate a report of the top *N* protocol conversations.

Alarm and history information have been combined into the user history collection group in RMON2. This function, normally done by network management systems, can be off-loaded to RMON. It has multiple control tables and data tables. Data

Table 8.4   RMON2 MIB Groups and Tables

Group	OID	Function	Tables
Protocol directory	rmon 11	Inventory of protocols	protocolDirTable
Protocol distribution	rmon 12	Relative statistics on octets and packets	protocolDistControlTable
			protocolDistStatsTable
Address map	rmon 13	MAC address to network address on the interfaces	addressMapControlTable
			addressMapTable
Network layer host	rmon 14	Traffic data from and to each host	n1HostControlTable
			n1HostTable
Network layer matrix	rmon 15	Traffic data from each pair of hosts	n1MatrixControlTable
			n1MatrixSDTable
			n1MatrixDSTable
			n1MatrixTopNControlTable
			n1MatrixTopNTable
Application layer host	rmon 16	Traffic data by protocol from and to each host	a1HostTable
Application layer matrix	rmon 17	Traffic data by protocol between pairs of hosts	a1MatrixSDTable
			a1MatrixDSTable
			a1MatrixTopNControlTable
			a1MatrixTopNTable
User history collection	rmon 18	User-specified historical data on alarms and statistics	usrHistoryControlTable
			usrHistoryObjectTable
			usrHistoryTable
Probe configuration	rmon 19	Configuration of probe parameters	serialConfigTable
			netConfigTable
			trapDestTable
			serialConnectionTable
RMON conformance	rmon 20	RMON2 MIB compliances and compliance groups	See Section 8.4.2

objects are collected in bucket groups. Each bucket group pertains to a MIB object, and the elements in the group are the instances of the MIB object. Users can specify the data to be collected by entering data in the *usrHistoryControlTable*, which will then be assembled with rows of instances in the *usrHistoryObjectTable*. Each row in the former specifies the number of buckets to be allocated for each object, and the latter contains rows of instances of the MIB object. There could be multiple instances of *usrHistoryObjectTable* under *usrHistoryControlTable*. The data are stored in the *userHistoryTable*. There could be one or more instances of *userHistoryTable* associated with each *userHistoryObjectTable*.

The probe configuration group provides the facility for configuring the probe. The data can be accessed via a modem connection. The pertinent data are stored in the *serialConfigTable* and *serialConnectionTable*. The *netConfigTable* contains the network configuration parameters, and the *trapDestTable* defines the destination addresses for the traps.

8.4.2   RMON2 Conformance Specifications

Conformance specifications were not specified in RMON1, but they have been added in RMON2. As shown in Figure 8.6, the RMON2 conformance group consists of two subgroups: rmon2MIBCompliances and rmon2MIBGroups. The compliance requirements are separated into basic RMON2 MIB compliance and application layer RMON2 MIB compliance. Each compliance module defines mandatory and optional groups. Vendors are required to implement the mandatory groups; optional groups may be used by the vendors to specify additional capabilities.

The thirteen groups in rmon2MIBGroups are listed in Table 8.5, along with the mandatory (M) and optional (O) requirements for basic and application level conformance to RMON2. The *rmon1EnhancementGroup* is mandatory for systems that implement RMON1 with RMON2. Notice that *probeConfigurationGroup* is a basic group and hence is marked as mandatory, even though it is not specified as such in the RFC 2021 definitions. The *rmon1EthernetEnhancementGroup* and *rmon1TokenRingEnhancementGroup* are enhancements of RMON1 that help management stations. The enhancements include filter entry which provides variable-length offsets into packets and the addition of more statistical parameters.

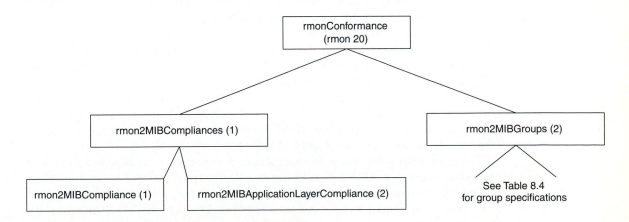

Figure 8.6   The RMON2 Conformance Group

Table 8.5 RMON2 Groups and Compliances

Object Group	RMON2 MIB Compliance	RMON2 MIB Application Layer Compliance
protocolDirectoryGroup	M	M
protocolDistributionGroup	M	M
addressMapGroup	M	M
n1HostGroup	M	M
n1MatrixGroup	M	M
a1HostGroup	N/A	M
a1MatrixGroup	N/A	M
usrHistoryGroup	M	M
probeInformationGroup	M	M
probeConfigurationGroup	M*	M*
rmon1EnhancementGroup	O†	O†
rmon1EthernetEnhancementGroup	O	O
rmon1TokenRingEnhancementGroup	O	O

*One of the basic groups in RMON2 and hence mandatory.
†Mandatory for systems implementing RMON1.

8.5   ATM Remote Monitoring

We will be discussing the management of ATM in Chapter 9. However, there is a similarity in the use of remote probes for remote monitoring of an ATM network. We will address their commonalities and differences here. You may skip this section now, if you so choose, and return to it after you have studied ATM management.

So far we have described remote monitoring and its advantages for gathering statistics on Ethernet and token ring LANs. RMON1 dealt with data link layer and RMON2 with higher level layers. IETF RMON MIBs have been extended to perform traffic monitoring and analysis for ATM networks (see af-nm-test-0080.000 in Table 9.3). Figure 8.7 shows the RMON MIB framework for the extensions, as portrayed by the ATM Forum. Switch extensions for RMON and ATM RMON define RMON objects at the "base" layer, which is the ATM sublayer. ATM protocol IDs for RMON2 define additional objects needed at the higher levels [RFC 2074].

There are several differences between remote monitoring of the Ethernet and token ring and monitoring of ATM devices. Extending RMON to ATM devices requires design changes and new functionality. Particular attention must be paid to high-speed requirements, cells versus frames, and the connection-oriented nature of ATM. At the data link

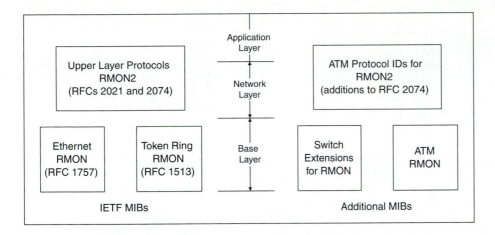

Figure 8.7   The RMON MIB Framework (© 1995 The ATM Forum)

sublayer, ATM RMON measures cells instead of packets or frames, and provides cell-based per-host and per-conversation traffic statistics. The high-speed nature of ATM imposes a severe set of requirements in ATM RMON implementation. At the application layer, RMON provides basic statistics for each monitored cell stream, for each ATM host, and for conversations between pair-wise hosts. It also provides the capability for flexible configuration mechanisms suited to the connection-oriented nature of ATM.

Four different collection perspectives are possible for ATM RMON, as shown in Figure 8.8. Figure 8.8(a) shows a stand-alone probe attached to a single port of a switch, and ATM traffic is copied somehow to the RMON probe. Figure 8.8(b) shows an embedded probe within a switch but with no access to the switch fabric; again, ATM traffic is somehow copied to the RMON probe. Figure 8.8(c) shows an embedded probe with access to the switch fabric. However, this type of probe measures traffic at cell header level only. Figure 8.8(d) shows a stand-alone probe, tapping a network-to-network interface between two switches. ATM traffic in both directions is monitored directly without switch intervention. When RMON instrumentation is embedded in the switch fabric, as in part (c) or placed between two switches, as in part (d), no modification of the circuit is needed. In parts (a) and (b), circuit steering is needed to copy the cells onto the probe. The two-way arrows indicate two half-duplex circuits that carry the steered traffic.

The ATM RMON MIB is under the experimental node of the IETF Internet MIB, as shown in Figure 8.9. The functions of the groups and the tables in each group are given in Table 8.6. The MIB contains four groups: *portSelect*, *atmStats*, *atmHost*, and *atmMatrix*.

The *portSelect* group is used to define the ports to be monitored in a particular statistics, host, or matrix collection. It contains two tables. The *portSelGrpTable* controls the setting up of ports and the ATM connection selection criteria used on behalf of any collection associated with the entries in this table, such as *atmHostTable*. The *portSelTable* is then used to control the setting up of selection criteria for a single ATM port.

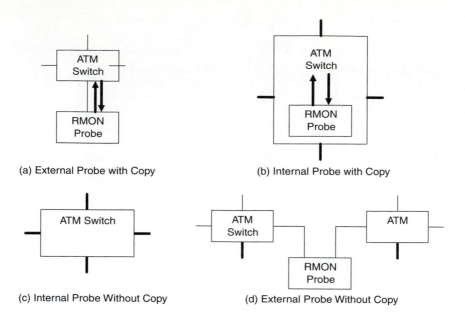

(a) External Probe with Copy   (b) Internal Probe with Copy

(c) Internal Probe Without Copy   (d) External Probe Without Copy

Figure 8.8   ATM Probe Location (© 1995 The ATM Forum)

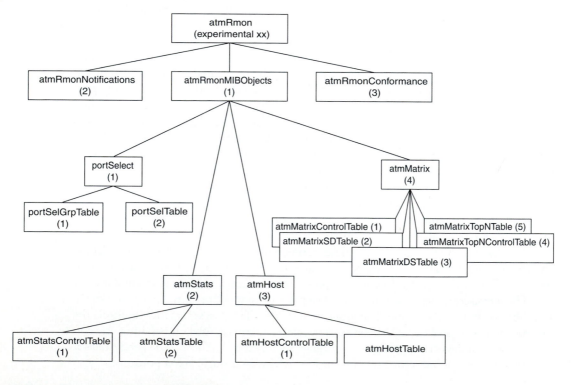

Figure 8.9   The ATM RMON MIB

Table 8.6 ATM RMON MIB Groups and Tables

Group	OID	Function	Tables
portSelect	atmRmonMIBObjects 1	Port selection	portSelGrpTable portSelTable
atmStats	atmRmonMIBObjects 2	Basic statistics	atmStatsControlTable atmStatsTable
atmHost	atmRmonMIBObjects 3	ATM per-host statistics	atmHostControlTable atmHostTable
atmMatrix	atmRmonMIBObjects 4	ATM per-circuit statistics	atmMatrixControlTable atmMatrixSDTable atmMatrixDSTable atmMatrixTopNControlTable atmMatrixTopNTable

The *atmStats* group collects basic statistics. It counts the total amount of traffic on behalf of one or more *portSelectGroups*. The two tables in this group are *atmStatsControlTable* and *atmStatsTable*.

The *atmHost* group collects per-host statistics. It counts the amount of traffic sent on behalf of each ATM address discovered by the probe, according to associated *portSelect* Group criteria. It contains a data table and a control table.

The *atmMatrix* group collects per-circuit statistics and reports the top *N* circuit traffic. It gathers traffic data by pair-wise source–destination address, according to *portSelect* Group criteria, in both directions. It contains three data tables and two control tables. The *atmMatrixControlTable* is used to define the source to destination (*atmMatrixSDTable*) and destination to source (*atmMatrixDSTable*) traffic. The *atmMatrixTopNControlTable* and *atmMatrixTopNTable* are used to analyze and present the top *N* traffic carriers.

8.6   A Case Study of Internet Traffic Using RMON

At the Georgia Institute of Technology a study was undertaken, for planning purposes, to gather statistics on Internet growth. Technical objectives of the study were to analyze (1) the traffic growth and trend and (2) traffic patterns. The latter analysis was to cover (a) weekly and monthly patterns, (b) diurnal patterns, (c) distribution of traffic by users, packet size, and protocol, and (d) source of traffic based on source–destination data.

The network comprised multiple domains of the Ethernet and FDDI LANs. The network complex was connected to the Internet via a high-speed gateway. The data were gathered by measurements made on the various domains individually and on the gateway.

Various tools were used to gather the data, including RMON statistics. Hewlett-Packard's Netmetrix® Protocol Analyzer was used for the Ethernet LANs. The statistics were gathered by using the *hostTopN* and history groups to select the top generators of traffic over the period. The matrix group was used to measure incoming and outgoing traffic. The filter and packet capture groups were helpful in analyzing the type of traffic, based on application-level protocols such as HTTP and NNTP.

In addition to the commercial tools, special tools were developed for the study. For example, the commercial probes were not fast enough to measure the packets traversing an FDDI ring. Hence a promiscuous mode of counting the packets (the function of a probe) was developed to measure traffic on the gateway. We will discuss management tools and their use in management applications further in Part III. However, the case study described here is intended to illustrate the importance of gathering statistics and the use of RMON for that purpose.

A partial summary of the results follows. The names in the results have been changed to protect the privacy and security of the institution.

Results

1. **Growth Rate:** Internet traffic grew at a significant rate from February to April at a monthly rate of 9% to 18%.

February	12%
March	9%
April	18%

   Note: A sudden drop in May–June reflected the ending of the spring quarter and the beginning of the summer quarter.

2. Traffic Pattern:

   - **Monthly/Weekly:** The only discernible variation was lower traffic over weekends.
   - **Daily:** 2/3 of the top 5% peaks occurred in the afternoon.
   - Users:

     The top six domains of users (96%) were:

Domain 1	20%
Domain 2	30%
Subdomain 1	(25%)
Subdomain 2	(3%)
Domain 3	34%
Domain 4	7%
Domain 5	3%
Domain 6	2%

     The top three hosts sending or receiving data were:

     Newsgroups

     Mbone

     Linux host

What was learned:

1. The three top groups of users contributing to 84% of the Internet traffic were students (surprise!), newsgroup services, and domain 1.
2. The growth rate of Internet use during the study period (spring quarter) was 50%.

Summary

In this chapter we discussed enhancement of SNMP management by the introduction of Remote Network Monitoring (RMON). Remote monitoring of the network involves the use of remotely positioned probes in various segments of the network. RMON1 was initially defined for data link level parameters of the Ethernet LAN. It was then extended to the token ring LAN. The RMON2 development that followed allowed monitoring of the upper layers and production of statistics concerning the parameters associated with them—from the network to the application level. A case study of the use of RMON involving Internet traffic was presented to illustrate the use of RMON MIR. We will pursue the use of RMON in managing networks in practice in Part III.

Exercises

1. An NMS connected to an Ethernet LAN is monitoring a network of 10,000 nodes comprising routers, hubs, and workstations. It sends an SNMP query to each station once a minute and receives a response when the stations are up. Assume that an average frame size is 1000 bytes long for get-request and response messages.
   a. What is the traffic load on the LAN that has the NMS?
   b. If the Ethernet LAN operates at a maximum efficiency of 40% throughput, what is the overhead due to network monitoring?

2. In Exercise 1, assume the network comprises ten subnetworks, with an RMON monitoring each subnet.
   a. Design a heartbeat monitoring system, using RMONs, that indicates failures to the NMS within a minute of a failure.
   b. What is the monitoring load on each subnet?
   c. If the NMS is still expected to detect any failure within one minute of occurrence, what is the overhead on the LAN to which the NMS is connected due to this traffic?

3. a. Describe qualitatively how the utilization (number of frames offered/number of frames transmitted) depends on frame size.
   b. How would you measure the distribution of the frame size on the LAN?

4. a. Describe the two methods of measuring collisions on an Ethernet LAN.
   b. Compare the two methods in terms of what you can measure.

5. Two identical token rings with the same number of stations operate at different efficiencies (the ratio of time spent in data transmission to total time). One

operates at a higher efficiency than the other. You suspect that this difference is due to the different frame sizes of the data frames in the two rings.

a. Why would you suspect the frame size?

b. How would you use RMON to prove your suspicion?

6. How would you measure the types and distribution of frames in a token ring LAN?

7. An RMON probe in a network measures Ethernet packets on hub interfaces (*ifIndex*) 1 and 2. The counters were set to zero as the measurements started, and interface 1 has counted 1000 1500-byte packets and interface 2 has measured 100 64-byte packets. These counts are stored in rows 1 and 2 of the *protocolDistStatsTable*. They are indexed by the *protocolDistControlIndex* of 1 and 2 and the *protocolDirLocalIndex* of 11 and 12.

a. Draw the conceptual rows of the tables involved with the relevant columnar objects and values.

b. Write each instance of the columnar object of the data with its associated index and value.

CHAPTER 9

Broadband Network Management: ATM Networks

Broadband networks can be classified into two distinct categories, the wide area network (WAN) and the access network. The WAN is predominantly based on ATM technology. The access network is based on cable modem, digital subscriber loop, and wireless technologies. In this chapter, we cover the ATM technology and the management of ATM networks. We will address the access technologies and their management in Chapter 10.

9.1   Broadband Networks and Services

As new technologies emerge, service providers use them to offer new and expanded services to commercial and residential communities. In turn, the offering of such services propels information technology to new heights. This cycle is especially true of broadband technology, which we briefly introduced in Chapter 2. Let us first define what broadband networks and services are.

Broadband networks and narrowband ISDNs provide multimedia integrated analog and digital services over the same network. A narrowband ISDN—also known as Basic ISDN—is a low-bandwidth network that can carry two 56-kilobaud rate channels. A broadband network can transport very high data rate signals.

There are three types of information technology services: voice, video, and data. In traditional terminology, voice and video information and services are transported over telecommunication networks in either analog or digital mode. The telecommunication network can be topologically separated into a wide-area network (WAN) and local loops. The former transports signals over long distances between switching offices, and the latter covers the "last mile" from a switching office to the customer's premises.

As we showed in Chapter 1, data are transported over computer networks made up of LANs and WANs. The switches and multiplexers of the telecommunication network are replaced with bridges, routers, and gateways. Computer networks use the facilities of tele-communication networks for WAN services.

The term **broadband network** has several interpretations. One of the chief charac-teristics of broadband services is the integration of voice, video, and data and their trans-portation over the same medium; in other words, it is multimedia networking. Sometimes, broadband networks are confused with the high-speed networks, especially in terms of data traffic. However, we limit our definition of broadband networks to those that can handle multimedia services. Broadband networks are also called broadband inte-grated services digital networks (B-ISDNs). Those who provide multimedia services to customers are broadband service providers and are referred to as **multiple system opera-tors** (MSOs).

The early form of an integrated services network was the **Basic Integrated Services Digital Network** (ISDN). It consisted of two basic channels: B-channels, each with a 56-kilobaud rate, combined with an 8-kilobaud signaling D-channel. Together, they are referred to as 2B+D. As we stated earlier, this system is also called narrowband ISDN. However, on-line video requires a much larger bandwidth. Moreover, voice and video require low latency and latency fluctuations, which are achieved by ATM technology. These requirements led to the early development and implementation of the broadband ISDN, or more simply the broadband network.

Broadband networks and services have contributed significantly to advances in three areas: the Asynchronous Transfer Mode (ATM), Synchronous Optical Network (SONET)/Synchronous Digital Hierarchy (SDH), and broadband access technology. The ATM technology can be viewed as a hybrid of circuit- and packet-switched trans-mission modes. As a switch, ATM makes a physical connection of a virtual circuit. However, data are transmitted as cells (or packets) unlike in a circuit-switched connec-tion (see Chapter 2). The data rate of SONET/SDH WAN is an integral multiple of the basic Optical Carrier (OC-1)/synchronous transport signal (STS), which is 51.84 Mbps. Broadband access technology is implemented in one of four ways. The first, hybrid fiber coaxial (HFC) technology, is a two-way interactive multimedia communi-cation system that uses fiber and coaxial cable facilities and cable modems. The second, digital subscriber loop (DSL) technology, has several variations, generically referred to as xDSL; for example, ADSL stands for asymmetric DSL. The third and fourth technol-ogies involve the use of wireless transmission from the switching office or head end to

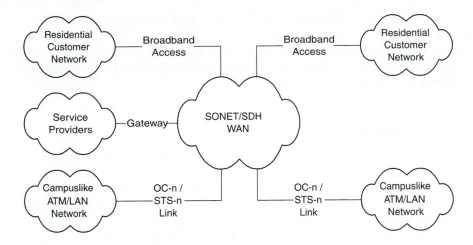

Figure 9.1   Broadband Services Networks

the customer's premises. In both cases the transmission is either terrestrial or via satellite. We will also discuss these access technologies in Chapter 10.

Although ATM has become an integral part of broadband services, this technology can be used for any high-speed, high-bandwidth environment. Thus, for example, a campus network with conventional LANs can use ATM switches to speed up data traffic, even without having broadband services.

Figure 9.1 shows a broadband services network. The wide-area network is SONET/SDH and is linked to the customer premises by means of either OC-n/STS optical technology or a broadband access network utilizing the emerging HFC, xDSL, or wireless technology. The customer network consists of two classes: residential customers and corporate customers having campuslike networks. The residential customers are either homes or small businesses that use broadband services but do not require as high-speed access to WAN as corporate customers.

Radio, video (television), ISP (Internet service provider), and others comprise the service providers. Multiple services are multiplexed at the central office or MSO head end and piped to customer premises through common transmission facilities. The service providers interface with WAN via gateways.

Management of a broadband network is more complex than that of either the conventional computer network or telecommunication network. It is based on ATM technology and broadband access technology, both of which are relatively new. An ATM network is based on switches with point-to-point connections (in contrast to one-to-many connections as in broadcast protocols). It is also a connection-oriented protocol and needs to be integrated in the connectionless Internet environment. These conditions provide challenges to the management of an ATM network, which is being implemented in a traditional computer network environment, with IP over an ATM protocol.

We will discuss ATM technology in Section 9.2 and ATM network management in Section 9.3. We have already discussed ATM remote monitoring in Chapter 8. We will cover access technologies involving the use of cable modems and hybrid fiber coaxial cable (HFC), digital subscriber loop (DSL) through existing local telephone loop facilities, and wireless in Chapter 10.

9.2   ATM Technology

The Asynchronous Transfer Mode (ATM) has helped bring about the merger of computer and telecommunication networks. Five important concepts comprise ATM technology [Keshav S]: (1) virtual path–virtual circuit, (2) fixed packet sizes or cells, (3) small packet sizes, (4) statistical multiplexing, and (5) integrated services. Implementation of these concepts in a network made up of ATM switches achieves a high-speed network that can transport all three multimedia services (voice, video, and data). The desired quality of service is provided to individual streams (unlike the current Internet) at the same time. The network is also easily scalable. The ATM Forum, an organization that specifies standards for ATM implementation, has also provided a framework for network management, which we will address in Section 9.3.

ATM terminology is filled with acronyms. Hence we have included a special acronym table, Table 9.1, containing those that we use here. However, many more acronyms are associated with ATM, and you undoubtedly will encounter them in your studies and work.

Table 9.1   ATM Acronyms

AAL	ATM adaptation layer
ABR	Adjustable bit rate
AIS	Alarm indication signal
ATM	Asynchronous Transfer Mode
BICI	Broadband Inter Carrier Interface
BISDN	Broadband Integrated Services Digital Network
BISSI	Broadband Inter Switching System Interface
BUS	Broadcast and unknown server
CBR	Constant bit rate
DS3	Digital signal 3
DXI	Digital Exchange Interface
EL	Element layer
ELAN	Emulated local-area network
EML	Element management layer
ILMI	Interim/Integrated Local Management Interface
LANE	LAN emulation
LATA	Local access and transport area
LCD	Loss of cell delineation
LE	LAN emulation

Table 9.1   (continued)

LE_ARP	LAN Emulation Address Resolution Protocol
LEC	LAN emulation client
LECS	LAN emulation configuration server
LES	LAN emulation server
LOF	Loss of frame
LOP	Loss of pointer
LOS	Loss of signal
LUNI	LAN Emulation User-Network Interface
NE	Network element
NEL	Network element layer
NEML	Network element management layer
NML	Network management layer
NPC	Network parameter control
OAM	Operations, administration, and maintenance
PMD	Physical media dependent
QoS	Quality of service
RD	Route descriptor
RDI	Remote defect indication
SDH	Synchronous Digital Hierarchy
SONET	Synchronous Optical Network
TMN	Telecommunications Management Network
UBR	Unspecified bit rate
UNI	User Network Interface
UPC	User parameter control
VBR-rt	Variable bit rate—real time
VBR-nrt	Variable bit rate—nonreal time
VC	Virtual channel
VCC	Virtual channel connection
VCI	Virtual channel identifier
VCL	Virtual channel link
VP	Virtual path
VPC	Virtual path connection
VPI	Virtual path identifier
VPL	Virtual path link

9.2.1   Virtual Path–Virtual Circuit

You learned about the cell transmission mode in Chapter 2. As we showed in Figure 2.27(c), it combines the best of the circuit- and packet-switched modes of transmission. The packets are all of the same small size. Each cell has the full bandwidth of the medium, and the cells are statistically multiplexed. The packets all take the same path in accordance with the virtual path–virtual circuit concept. This mode of transmission is called

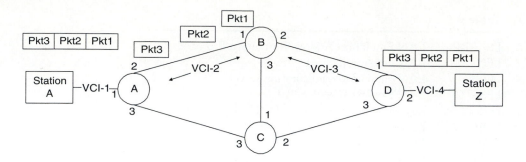

Figure 9.2   A Virtual Circuit Configuration

Asynchronous Transfer Mode (ATM) and is one of the fundamental concepts of ATM technology. Let us now look at other aspects of that technology.

In Chapter 2 we discussed how the virtual path–virtual circuit (VP–VC) concept is used in packet switches. Figures 2.26(a) and (b) showed the distinction between the datagram and the virtual circuit configuration, which is used in ATM technology. A virtual circuit between two stations, A and Z, is shown in Figure 9.2. The routing tables in the ATM switches, A, B, and D, associated with this virtual circuit are shown in Table 9.2. The virtual circuit is established before data are sent. Here, the virtual circuit is the combination of virtual circuit links VCI-1, VCI-2, VCI-3, and VCI-4. Once the virtual circuit has been established, all packets are transported in the sequence in which they were transmitted by the source along the same path during a given session. Thus packets 1, 2, and 3 transmitted by station A traverse the same links and arrive at station Z in the correct sequence. Because the path is fixed for the entire session, the transmission rate is considerably faster than a non-virtual circuit packet-switched network.

Although the speed of packet transmission has been enhanced, a delay is associated with preestablishing the links for the virtual circuit. This delay can be reduced by preassigning links to a virtual circuit by grouping a number of virtual circuits between two switches into a virtual path. A virtual path identifier (VPI) comprises virtual circuit identifiers

Table 9.2   A–Z Virtual Circuit Routing Tables

Switch	Input VCI/Port	Output VCI/Port
A	VCI-1/Port-1	VCI-2/Port-2
	VCI-2/Port-2	VCI-1/Port-1
B	VCI-2/Port-1	VCI-3/Port-2
	VCI-3/Port-2	VCI-2/Port-1
D	VCI-3/Port-1	VCI-4/Port-2
	VCI-4/Port-2	VCI-3/Port-1

(VCIs). Thus establishing the route from station A to station Z requires consulting the VPI–VCI tables. The price that we pay for using this approach is that some VCIs may remain idle during nonbusy traffic periods, and thus waste bandwidth. However, this amount of wasted bandwidth is a lot less than that for dedicated physical links in the circuit-switched transmission mode.

A virtual path–virtual circuit can be established for each session as needed and removed after the session; this method is called switched virtual circuit (SVC). Or a connection can be established for long periods of time and not switched between sessions, creating a permanent virtual circuit (PVC) between a pair of end stations that carry large traffic volumes. PVCs are established between locations of large corporations.

9.2.2   ATM Packet Size

ATM packets are of fixed size, each being 53 bytes long. A fixed-size packet was chosen so that fast and efficient switches could be built. Many switches can be operated in parallel because all are performing switching on packets of the same size.

The ATM packet size of 53 bytes comprises a header of 5 bytes and a payload of 48 bytes. This size was arrived at by optimizing two factors. The packet size should be as small as possible to reduce the delay in switching and packetization. However, it should also be large enough to reduce the overhead of the header relative to the payload.

9.2.3   Integrated Service

The main challenge in integrating the three multimedia services is to meet the different requirements of each. Voice and video traffic require low tolerance on variations in delay and low end-to-end (roundtrip) delays for good interactive communication. Once voice data has been lost or delayed, real-time communication is garbled and it cannot be reproduced. Thus avoiding delays has to be given the highest priority in transmission. The same is true with the voice portion of video transmission, and, in addition, the voice and video have to be synchronized. Otherwise, the transmission would be like watching a movie with the conversation lagging behind the mouth motion owing to incorrect threading of the film. Pure video without sound can have less priority in terms of delay than a combination of audio and video can.

Data traffic can have a much higher tolerance on latency because it is primarily a store and forward technology and the traffic itself inherently occurs in bursts. However, data speed is important for large data transmission applications, although it has the lowest priority in transmission.

Latency priorities can be set in ATM switches by assigning priorities to the different services being provided. We do so by guaranteeing a quality of service (QoS) for each accepted call setup. A traffic descriptor is specified by the user, and the system ensures that acceptable quality of the service requested can be met by the virtual circuit that was set up.

Four main classes of traffic have been defined to implement quality of service: constant bit rate (CBR), real-time variable bit rate (VBR-rt), non-real–time variable bit rate

(VBR-nrt) and available bit error rate (ABR). Transmission of voice is assigned CBR. Streaming video such as real-time video on the Internet is assigned VBR-rt. The VBR-nrt is assigned to transmission of still images. IP data traffic gets the lowest bandwidth priority, ABR.

There are two markets for ATM switches using ATM technology: public and private. A public network is established by service providers. A private network is primarily a campuslike network. Network management clearly distinguishes between these two markets, as we will show in Section 9.3.

9.2.4   WAN/SONET

Although analog high-frequency multiplexing is still in vogue for wide-area network transportation in legacy systems, digital transmission is the predominant mode of transportation. The basic voice band, 0–4 kHz, is converted to a 64-Kbps digital signal universally. However, multiplexing hierarchy of the basic signal has evolved differently in North America, Europe, and Japan. For example, the T1 transmission carrier previously shown in Figure 2.25(a) has a data rate of 1.544 Mbps and carries 24 voice channels. Equivalent to this carrier is the European E1 transmission that has a data rate of 2.048 Mbps and carries 30 channels. Thus, whenever digital transmission occurs across the "pond" between Europe and North America, an expensive conversion is involved between the two types of systems.

The digital hierarchy has been synchronized throughout the world, using 155.52 Mbps as the basic data rate in carrier technology and using fiber optics. However, the names are different in Europe and North America: in Europe, **synchronous digital hierarchy** (SDH); in North America, **synchronous optical network** (SONET). The SDH units are synchronous transport signal (STS-n), where n is the hierarchical level. The **optical carrier** starts with the unit of OC-1 (optical carrier–level 1), which is 51.84 Mbps, and thus the basic SONET is level OC-3.

9.2.5   ATM LAN Emulation

In the future ATM may well be available at all desktop workstations. However, for the foreseeable future the IP LAN network will continue to dominate. Even in that arena, IP over Ethernet LAN is dominant. There is competition from high-speed 802.3 LAN functioning at 100 Mbps and even at 1 Gbps speed. However, ATM LAN has many advantages and hence is being deployed in many campuses. One advantage is that it interfaces nicely with an ATM SONET network. It is also adaptable for a high-speed backbone for a campus network that can function at a higher speed than FDDI, which is what is mostly deployed at present.

The services provided by ATM differ from conventional LAN in three ways. First, ATM is connection-oriented. Second, ATM makes a one-to-one connection between pairs of workstations in contrast to the broadcast and multicast mode in the conventional LAN. Third, a LAN MAC address is dedicated to the physical network interface card and this is independent of network topology; the 20-byte ATM address is not.

In order to use ATM with a LAN, it has to fit into the current TCP/IP LAN environment. Because of the basic differences between the systems, the ATM Forum has developed ATM specifications for **LAN emulation** (LE or LANE) that emulates the services of a current LAN network across an ATM network by using layered architecture, as shown

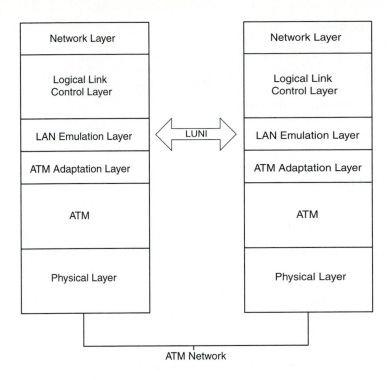

Figure 9.3   Layered Architecture of a LAN Emulation

in Figure 9.3. The ATM layer is adjacent to the physical layer as are other MAC layers. Two layers—the ATM adaptation layer and the LAN emulation layer—are inserted between the ATM layer and the LLC layer. The ATM adaptation layer interfaces with the ATM layer underneath it, and the LAN emulation layer is sandwiched between the ATM adaptation layer and the LLC layer. Thus, looking upward from the LLC layer, the ATM LAN Emulation environment sees the usual TCP/IP environment.

The ATM Forum also specified a LAN Emulation User-Network Interface (LUNI), which provides the interface between the user and the LAN emulation layer. The user, which is an ATM end station, is called the LE client and the LE layer provides LE services.

Two LECs communicate with each other over an ATM network, using LE services, as shown in Figure 9.4. The three LE services are the **LE configuration server** (LECS), **LE server** (LES), and **broadcast and unknown server** (BUS).

The LECS implements assignment of individual LECs to different emulated LANs. The LES performs a control coordination function for ELAN, registering and resolving MAC addresses and/or route descriptors to ATM addresses. An LEC may also register additional MAC addresses besides its primary one if it represents other destinations. The BUS handles data sent by the LEC to a broadcast MAC address, a multicast address, and the initial unicast frames before the address resolution is performed by the LEC.

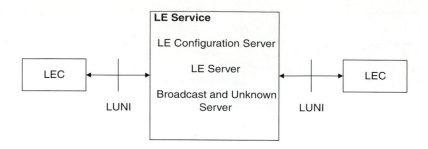

Figure 9.4   The LUNI Interface

Four functions are performed across LUNI: (1) initialization, (2) registration, (3) address resolution, and (4) data transfer. Initialization involves (a) obtaining ATM address(es) of LES(s) that are available on a particular ATM network; (b) joining or leaving a particular emulated LAN specified by the ATM address of the LES; and (c) declaring whether the LEC across this LUNI is to receive address resolution requests for all unregistered destinations.

The second function, registration, informs the LES of the individual MAC address that the LEC represents and route descriptors for source–route bridging. The third function, address resolution, involves obtaining the ATM address representing the LEC with a particular MAC address. The fourth function involves transporting the data from source to destination. The data are encapsulated in an ATM frame AAL-5, forwarded in the frame by the LE source, and decapsulated from the frame at the destination.

Let us now look at how an ATM workstation and a traditional LAN workstation coexist in an ATM LAN emulation environment. An ATM workstation behaves as a LAN emulation client (LEC) and interfaces to the outside via a LAN user-to-network interface (LUNI), as shown in Figure 9.5. The Ethernet LAN interfaces, through a bridge, which acts as an LEC. The LEC may be considered as an entity in the end system, which performs data forwarding, address resolution, and other control functions across LUNI. It provides a MAC level emulated Ethernet (or token ring) interface to higher level software—the logical link control (LLC) layer.

The LEC requires various services to function in a LAN Emulation environment. Shown in Figure 9.5 are three servers: LES, BUS, and LECS. All could be part of an ATM switch or distributed over the network, including being embedded in the LEC. Two types of connections are also established: a data connection (indicated by the solid lines) and a control connection (indicated by the dashed lines). Let us examine further what these services and connections do and why we need them.

ATM is a switch that establishes a connection-oriented circuit between input and output ports. An ATM LAN establishes a virtual circuit connection between pairs of LECs going through the switch. However, to establish this connection over a conventional LAN, it needs to know the MAC address of the non-ATM station. The LES provides the translation between 20-byte ATM address and the 6-byte MAC address. Clients

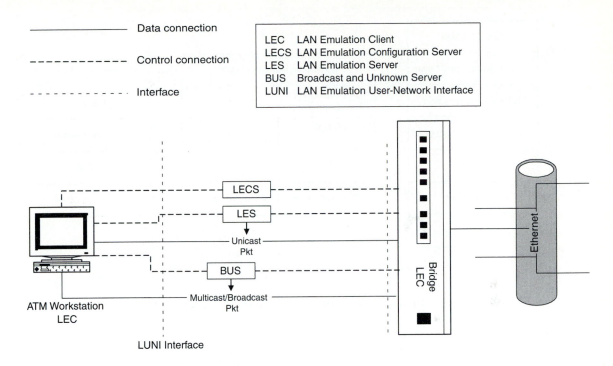

Figure 9.5   LAN Emulation Client Connections Across LUNI

register their addresses with the LES, so, when a station wants to send data to another station, associating the LEC with the source establishes a control connection to the LES and retrieves the ATM address. It then establishes a virtual-circuit connection to the destination through ATM switch(es). The data, which may be an Ethernet or token ring packet, is encapsulated in an ATM packet by the source client and transmitted via an ATM LAN to the destination client over the virtual-circuit connection.

We have used the LAN emulation server to address the connection-oriented issue and the address resolution issue. However, we still need to resolve the issue of one-to-many connections needed for broadcast and multicast protocols. The BUS shown in Figure 9.5 helps accomplish this function. The LEC sends the broadcast or multicast PDU to the broadcast and unknown server via a controlled connection. The BUS converts it to a series of unicast packets and sends them to a group of attached LECs, who in turn transmit them to the destination stations. The LECs know the address of the BUS because of the address resolution protocol that it performs. The unknown server function of the BUS is used when the LEC cannot obtain the address translation from the LES.

Every LAN emulation client belongs to a BUS. The LECS implements the assignment of the individual LEC to various LAN segments. Thus switching a station from one LAN segment to another without requiring any physical change is easy. This capability is

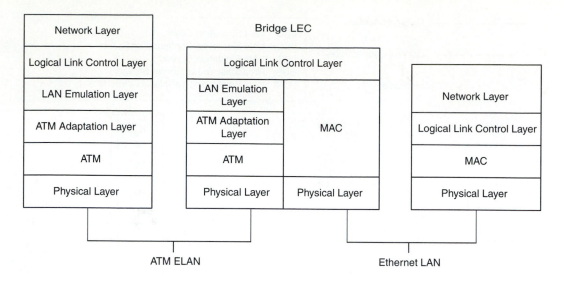

Figure 9.6   Protocol Architecture of an ATM ELAN with an Ethernet LAN

an advantage in that an ATM LAN or an emulation of an ATM LAN can be used for a virtual LAN, which we will address in the next section.

Figure 9.6 shows the protocol architecture in the communication between ATM and Ethernet end stations that reside in an ATM LAN and an Ethernet LAN, respectively. The protocol layers logically come together at the LLC level in the intermediate LAN emulation bridge client.

The most popular implementation of LAN emulation currently is to use ATM switches in the backbone network of a campus environment, called the **collapsed backbone design**. The backbone is built inside a router and consists of a router with an ATM switch acting as a bridge between the router port and the Ethernet LAN going to a hub or router at buildings housing terminals. Another design, which is more adaptable for handling larger traffic, is to have distributed routers connected in an FDDI-ring. The interfaces in the routers are connected to hubs and routers through ATM switches, as shown in Figure 9.7. A router port is connected to an ATM switch, which is geographically located in the main information services building. A multitude of LANs connect to routers and hubs in other campus buildings. Communication between the end stations attached across the routers or hubs in the end buildings shown in Figure 9.7 go through the ATM switch, using the services just described.

9.2.6   Virtual LAN

A virtual LAN (VLAN) is a topology and location-independent group of stations that are communicating as though they were on the same physical LAN. Although sometimes confused with ATM emulated LANs (ELANs), VLANs can be implemented on any switched LAN, as we pointed out in Chapter 2. The stations could be on different ports of

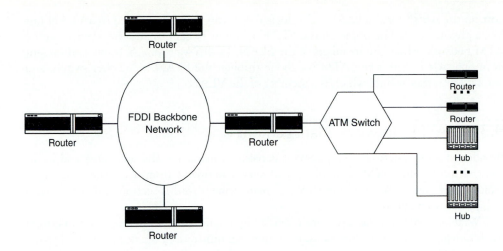

Figure 9.7   An ATM Switch as a Bridge in a Campus Network

the same switch or on different switches, but to the stations they appear to be on the same physical network as all the other stations in the VLAN.

Recall that ATM emulation LANs can be used to extend virtual LANs across an ATM backbone, as shown in Figure 9.8. The LAN emulation configuration server (and there is normally only one in a geographic location) can be configured to form VLAN groups. Each ATM switch has an interface to the ATM ELAN, which creates a logical

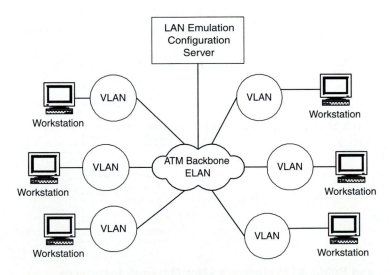

Figure 9.8   ATM VLAN Configuration

port on the switch for the ELAN. This logical port can then be assigned to a VLAN just like a physical port. The traffic on the VLAN will now be sent to all other devices in the ATM network, which are members of the ELAN. In this way, VLAN traffic can be sent from one switch, across the ATM backbone through the ELAN to another switch, and out a port on that switch, which is a member of the VLAN.

9.3   ATM Network Management

Broadband service network management consists of managing the wide-area and local-area networks with ATM technology and access networks from a central office to a remote workstation. We will discuss WAN management in this section and access technology management in Chapter 10.

Wide-area network facilities are provided by public service providers, who perform the following management functions: operation, administration, maintenance, and provisioning (OAM&P). Typically, large institutions and corporations service their private networks. However, they too use the public service providers' facilities to transport information long distance, or over a public network. ATM networks are classified as both private and public networks, as shown in Figure 9.9. The standards for management of each and the interactions between them have been addressed by the ATM Forum (the international organization accelerating cooperation on ATM technology). The user interface to the private network is the private User Network Interface (UNI), and the interface to the public network is the public UNI. The ATM Forum documents and related RFCs that are referenced are listed in Table 9.3.

9.3.1   The ATM Network Reference Model

The ATM Forum has defined a management interface architecture—the ATM network reference model—as shown in Figure 9.10 [af-nm-0020.000]. Private network managers or private network management systems manage private networks. Public network man-

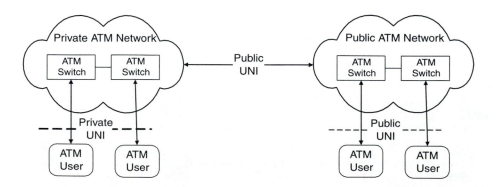

Figure 9.9   Private and Public ATM Network User Network Interfaces (© 1995 The ATM Forum)

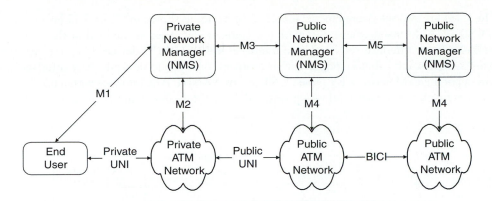

Figure 9.10   The ATM Forum Management Interface Reference Architecture (© 1995 The ATM Forum)

agers or public network management systems manage public networks. To distinguish between a human manager and a management system, we will refer to a network manager in the context of a network management system (NMS), unless explicitly stated otherwise. Of the five interfaces (M1–M5) between systems and networks, M1 and M2 are the interfaces between a private NMS and either an end user or a private network, respectively. The end user can be a workstation, ATM switch, or any ATM device. A private ATM network is an enterprise network.

A private network management system can access its own network-related information in a public network via an M3 interface to the public network management system. The public NMS responds to the private NMS via the M3 interface with the relevant information or takes the action requested.

The M4 interface is between the public NMS and the public network. The final interface, M5, is between the NMSs of two service providers. The ATM Forum has not yet specified this interface.

9.3.2   The Integrated Local Management Interface

In addition to the five M interfaces, Figure 9.10 also shows interfaces between an ATM end user or device and an ATM network, as well as interfaces between ATM networks. These interfaces are distinct from the M interfaces between NMSs and networks or end users. Although the M interfaces provide a top–down management view of a network or device, the ATM Forum defines an ATM link-specific view of configuration and fault parameters across a User-Network Interface (UNI). These are the UNI interfaces presented in Figures 9.9 and 9.10. The specifications for them are contained in the Integrated Local Management Interface (ILMI), which we will discuss further in Section 9.3.4.

The first "I" in ILMI originally stood for "Interim," not "Integrated." The af.ilmi.0065.000 specifications were supposed to have been replaced by IETF specifications, some were and others were not. Hence the "I" in ILMI now designates "Integrated."

The ILMI fits into the overall model for an ATM device as shown in Figure 9.11 [af-ilmi-0065.000]. ATM management information is communicated across the UNI or the Network–Network Interface (NNI). These interfaces are with ATM devices (e.g., end systems, switches, etc.) that belong to either a private or a public network. Any interface with a public ATM network is a public UNI or a public NNI. Any interface with a private ATM network is a private UNI or a private NNI. The devices communicate across UNI

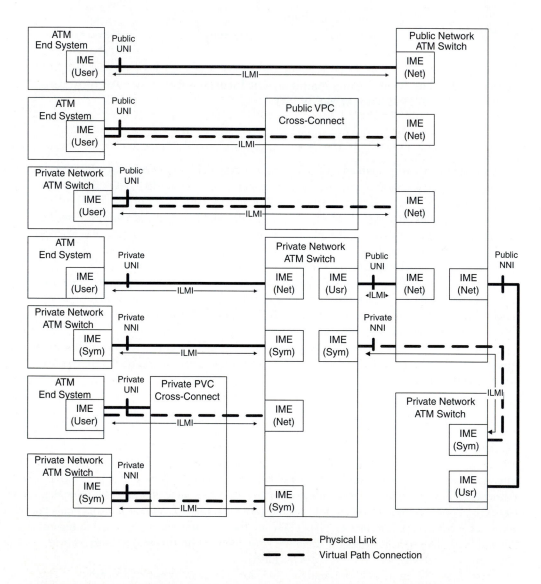

Figure 9.11   Definitions and Context of ILMI (© 1995 The ATM Forum)

and NNI via an ATM interface management entity (IME) module in the entity. The three versions of IME—user, network, and system—are based on where the IME is used.

Figure 9.11 shows the various physical connections, virtual connections, and ILMI communication links between the devices and networks. ILMI communication takes place over both physical and virtual links by means of SNMP or AAL-5 protocols. We will discuss the MIB related to management in the following sections.

Two public carrier networks interface via a Broadband Inter Carrier Interface (BICI), as shown in Figure 9.10. The BICI is also known as an NNI.

9.3.3 The ATM Management Information Base

The management information base and the structure of management information required for an ATM network are specified in two sets of documents, one by IETF and the other by the ATM Forum. The global view of the Internet MIB tree associated with ATM is presented in Figure 9.12. The two major branches are *mib-2* and *atmForum* (under *enterprises*). The structure of management information is defined in ASN.1 syntax. The MIB associated with ATM is primarily concerned with ATM sublayer parameters. The parameters associated with higher layers are handled by the standard MIB discussed in Chapter 4. The documents that cover the various groups are listed in Table 9.3.

Five nodes are shown under mib-2 in Figure 9.12. We described the system and interfaces groups in Chapter 4, but the interfaces group has evolved to handle the sublayers, such as ATM; the details are described in RFC 1573. As all the needed parameters could not be defined within the confines of the interfaces group, additional tables were added in the *ifMIBObjects* group under *ifMIB* [RFC 1573]. The transmission group contains subgroups for each medium of transmission. ATM objects, as defined in the *atmMIBObjects* group under *atmMIB*, are specified in RFC 1695.

The *atmForum* group is subnode 353 under the *enterprises* node. The *atmForum* group contains the five subgroups shown in Figure 9.12: *atmForumAdmin*, *atmForumUni*, *atmUniDxi*, *atmfLanEmulation*, and *atmForumNetworkManagement*. The ATM Administrative group (*atmForumAdmin*) and the ATM User–Network Interface (*atmForumUni*) group are defined in the Integrated Local Management Interface (ILMI) specification, af-ilmi-0065.000. The ATM DXI (*atmUniDxi*) group is the Data Exchange Interface and will be discussed in Section 9.3.10. It is the ATM interface between DTE and DCE and is described in af-dxi-0014.000. The ATM emulated LAN MIB (*atmfLanEmulation*) defines entities for ATM LAN emulation servers and is specified in af-lane-0057.000. The MIB for M4 interface (*atmForumNetworkManagement*) is covered in af-nm-0095.001.

9.3.4 The Role of SNMP and ILMI in ATM Management

Although ILMI was conceived as a set of interim specifications, it has become permanent. ATM network management uses both the SNMP MIB and the ATM Forum MIB. Figures 9.13 and 9.14 [af-ilmi-0065.000 and Section 4 of af-uni-0010.002] present conceptually the role of the two network management protocols. Figure 9.13 presents the M1 interface. An SNMP agent is shown embedded in an ATM device, and the NMS communicates with it through SNMP protocols and IETF MIB modules. Interface

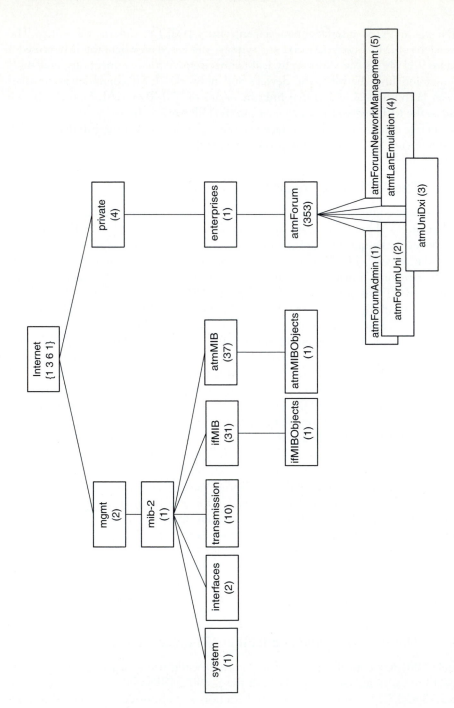

Figure 9.12   The Internet ATM MIB

Table 9.3   Internet ATM MIB Groups and Documents

Entity	OID	Description	Document
system	mib-2 1	System	RFC 1213
interfaces	mib-2 2	Interfaces (modified)	RFC 1213
			RFC 1573
ifMIB	mib-2 31	Interface types	RFC 1573
transmission	mib-2 10	Transmission	RFC 1213
ds1	transmission 18	DS1 carrier objects	RFC 1406
ds3	transmission 30	DS3/E# interface objects	RFC 1407
sonetMIB	transmission 39	SONET MIB	RFC 1595
atmMIB	mib-2 37	ATM objects	RFC 1695
atmForum	enterprises 353	ATM Forum MIB/M3 specification	af-nm-0019.000
		M4 interface	af-nm-0020.000
			af-nm-0020.001
		CMIP specification for M4 interface	af-nm-0027.000
		M4 Network–View Interface	af-nm-0058.000
		AAL management for the M4 NE view	af-nm-0071.000
		Circuit emulation service internetworking requirements—logical and CMIP MIB.	af-nm-0072.000
		M4 network–view CMIP MIB spec v1.0	af-nm-0073.000
		M4 network–view requirements and logical MIB addendum	af-nm-0074.000
atmRmon	experimental xx	Remote monitoring MIB extensions for ATM networks	af-nm-test-0080.000
		Network management M4 security requirements and logical MIB	af-nm-0103.000
atmForumAdmin	atmForum 1	ATM administrative	af-ilmi-0065.000
atmForumUni	atmForum 2	ATM User–Network Interface	af-ilmi-0065.000
atmUniDxi	atmForum 3	Data Exchange Interface (DXI) specification	af-dxi-0014.000
atmfLanEmulation	atmForum 4	ATM emulated LAN MIB	af-lane-0057.000
atmForumNetwork-Management	atmForum 5	SNMP M4 network Element view MIB	af-nm-0095.001
		LAN emulation over ATM	af-lane-0021.000
		LAN emulation client management specification	af-lane-0038.000
		LANE 1.0 addendum	af-lane-0050.000
		LANE servers management Specv1.0	af-lane-0057.000

Documents with af- prefix are © 1995 The ATM Forum.

Table 9.3   *(continued)*

Entity	OID	Description	Document
		LANE v2.0 LUNI Interface	af-lane-0084.000
		LAN emulation client	af-lane-0093.000
		Multi-protocol over ATM	af-mpoa-0087.000
		Multi-protocol over ATM version 1.0 MIB	af-mpoa-0092.000
		D53/SONET STS3-C Physical Layer	af-uni-0010.002

Documents with af- prefix are © 1995 The ATM Forum.

parameters and types, including the additional tables required to manage the ATM sub-layer, are specified in RFC 1213 and RFC 1573, and ATM objects are specified in RFC 1695. The transport MIB module is dependent on the transmission medium.

Figure 9.14, which shows the M2 interface, comprises the network of two ATM devices. The NMS is managing the network with an interface to device A. The ILMI protocol is used for communication between the agent management entity (AME) in device A and the AME in device B. A proxy agent that resides in device A does the translation between the ILMI MIB and the SNMP MIB.

9.3.5   M1 Interface: Management of ATM Network Element

As mentioned earlier, the M1 interface is between an SNMP management system and an SNMP agent in an ATM device, as shown in Figure 9.13. The *interfaces* and *ifMIB* groups under the *mib-2* node are shown in Figure 9.15. Four tables have been added to handle sublayers and are shown in Figure 9.15 under *ifMIBObjects*. Table 9.4 gives a brief description of the functions that each table performs.

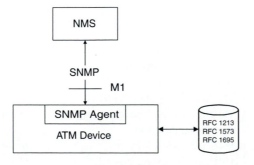

Figure 9.13   SNMP ATM Management (M1 Interface) (© 1995 The ATM Forum)

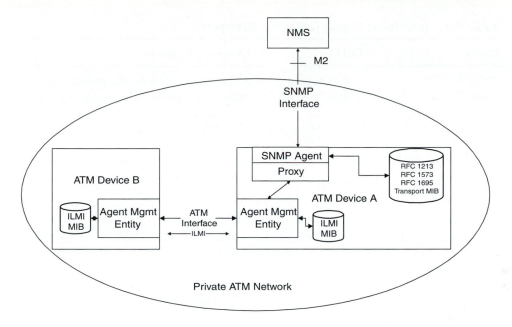

Figure 9.14   Role of SNMP and ILMI in ATM Management (M2 Interface) (© 1995 The ATM Forum)

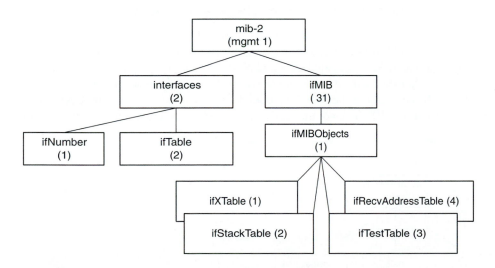

Figure 9.15   Interfaces Group Tables for Sublayers

Table 9.4   Interfaces Group Tables for Sublayers

Entity	OID	Description (brief)
ifXTable	ifMIBObjects 1	Additional objects for the interface table
ifStackTable	ifMIBObjects 2	Information on the relationship between sublayers
ifTestTable	ifMIBObjects 3	Tests that NMS instructs the agent to perform
ifRecvAddressTable	ifMIBObjects 4	Information on the type of packets/frames accepted on an interface

Figure 9.16 shows the three transmission modes used for ATM: DS1 (1.544 Mbps twisted-pair cable), DS3 (44.736 Mbps coaxial cable), and SONET (n×155.52 Mbps optical fiber). DS1 and DS3 are transmitted over T1 and T3 carriers, respectively. Only one of these MIBs needs to be implemented in the agent, depending on which transmission medium is used. RFCs dealing with transmission group MIB modules are listed in Table 9.3.

Figure 9.17 and Table 9.5 show the ATM MIB objects group. This group contains information needed to manage the ATM sublayer entities: traffic descriptors, DS3 physical layer convergence parameters (PLCPs), transmission convergence (TC) sublayer parameters, virtual path link/virtual channel link and their associated cross-connect tables, and performance parameters for AAL-5 (ATM adaptation layer).

9.3.6   M2 Interface: Management of Private Networks

The M2 interface for ATM management was shown in Figure 9.14. The management information on ATM links between devices is gathered from ILMI MIB. The roles of each were shown in Figure 9.14. Detailed UNI and NNI for both private and public interfaces, specified in af-ilmi-0065.000, were shown in Figure 9.11 and discussed in Section 9.3.2.

The ILMI specifications [af-ilmi-0065.000] define the administrative and UNI groups of the ATM Forum MIB. The administrative group defines a general-purpose registry for

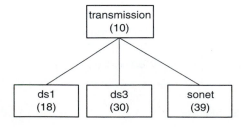

Figure 9.16   Transmission Groups for ATM

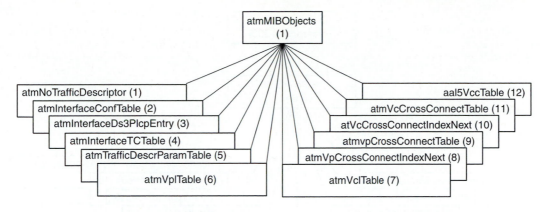

Figure 9.17   The ATM Managed Objects Group

Table 9.5   The ATM Managed Objects Group

Entity	OID	Description (brief)
atmNoTrafficDescriptor	atmMIBObjects 1	ATM traffic descriptor type
atmInterfaceConfTable	atmMIBObjects 2	ATM local interface configuration parameter table
atmInterfaceDs3PlcpEntry	atmMIBObjects 3	ATM interface DS3 PLCP parameters and state variables table
atmInterfaceTCTable	atmMIBObjects 4	ATM TC sublayer configuration and state parameters table
atmTrafficDescrParamTable	atmMIBObjects 5	ATM traffic descriptor type and associated parameters
atmVplTable	atmMIBObjects 6	Virtual path link table
atmVclTable	atmMIBObjects 7	Virtual channel link table
atmVpCrossConnectIndexNext	atmMIBObjects 8	Index for virtual path cross-connect table
atmVpCrossConnectTable	atmMIBObjects 9	Virtual path cross-connect table
atmVcCrossConnectIndexNext	atmMIBObjects 10	Index for virtual channel cross-connect table
atmVcCrossConnectTable	atmMIBObjects 11	Virtual cross-connect table
aal5VccTable	atmMIBObjects 12	AAL VCC performance parameters table

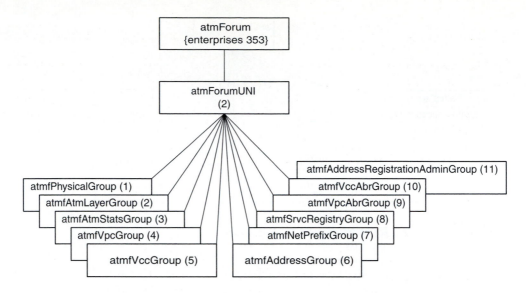

Figure 9.18   The ATM Interface MIB Object Group (© 1995 The ATM Forum)

locating ATM network services, such as the LAN emulation server (LECS) and the ATM name answer server (ANS). Other subgroups under the administrative group have been deprecated and handled by IETF specifications.

Figure 9.18 and Table 9.6 show the ATM interface MIB object group. They define the management objects associated with the ATM layer and the physical layer. The statistics group is deprecated. The parameters associated with virtual path/virtual connections, as well as the adjustable bandwidth rate (ABR) and QoS, are covered.

9.3.7   M3 Interface: Customer Network Management of Public Networks

The M3 management interface is between the private NMS and the public NMS. It allows customers to monitor and configure their portions of the public ATM network. The M3 interface specifications are defined in the ATM Forum document af-nm-0019.000. Figure 9.19 shows how a customer would typically interact with the public NMS via the carrier management system [af-nm-0019.000]. Two classes of M3 requirements are shown: status and configuration monitoring (class I), and virtual configuration control (class II).

Class I requirements are those that a public NMS offers to the customer, monitoring and management of configuration, fault, and performance of a specific customer's portion of a public ATM network. This service is offered only for a permanent virtual circuit

Table 9.6   ATM Interface MIB Object Group

Entity	OID	Description (brief)
atmfPhysicalGroup	atmForumUni 1	Defines a table of physical layer status and parameter information
atmfAtmLayerGroup	atmForumUni 2	Defines a table of ATM layer status and parameter information
atmfAtmStatsGroup	atmForumUni 3	Deprecated
atmfVpcGroup	atmForumUni 4	Defines a table of status and parameter information on the virtual path connections
atmfVccGroup	atmForumUni 5	Defines a table of status and parameter information on the virtual channel connections
atmfAddressGroup	atmForumUni 6	Defines the network-side IME table containing the user-side ATM-layer addresses
atmfNetPrefixGroup	atmForumUni 7	Defines a user-side IME table of network prefixes
atmfSrvcRegistryGroup	atmForumUni 8	Defines the network-side IME table containing all services available to the user-side IME
atmfVpcAbrGroup	atmForumUni 9	Defines a table of operational parameters related to ABR virtual path connections
atmfVccAbrGroup	atmForumUni 10	Defines a table of operational parameters related to ABR virtual channel connections
atmfAddressRegistration AdminGroup	atmForumUni 11	

(PVC) configuration. Examples of this service are (1) retrieving performance and configuration information for a UNI link and (2) public NMS reporting of a UNI link failure via an alarm or trap message to the user NMS.

Class II service provides greater capability to the user, who can request the public NMS to add, delete, or change virtual connections between pairs of the customer's UNIs. An example would be a customer wanting to establish a new virtual path or increase the number of virtual circuits in a given virtual path.

A customer network management (CNM) manages both private and public ATM networks. A CNM agent residing in the public ATM network provides the M3 service. As previously mentioned, the service is limited to the portion of the public service provider's network that the user's circuit traverses. If the user's circuit traverses multiple service providers, a separate interface with each provider is needed. The CNM sends requests to the carrier management system (see Figure 9.19), which acts as an agent to the CNM. The carrier management system then invokes the request on the network elements or other NMS and returns the responses to CNM. CNM manages its own ATM networks at sites 1, 3, and 4.

The requirements for M3 and M4 are specified as mandatory or required, conditionally required, and optional. Class I requirements are mandatory, and Class II requirements are optional.

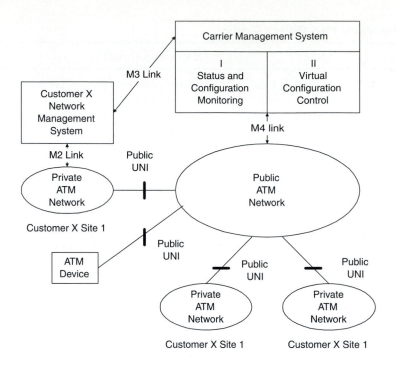

Figure 9.19   Customer Management of Private and Public Networks

Class I Interface Management Functions.   Table 9.7 presents M3 Class I requirements and the MIB groups used to obtain the information. The request has SNMP "read-only" capability. The public network service provider should give the CNM customer the ability to retrieve all the information listed in Table 9.7.

Class II Interface Management Functions.   M3 Class II functionality is divided into three subgroups: (1) ATM-level subgroup, (2) VPC/VCC-level subgroup, and (3) traffic subgroup. The provider can implement one or more of these subgroups.

The ATM-level subgroup provides the CNM the ability to modify ATM-level information configuration information. The VPC/VCC-level subgroup provides the CNM the ability to modify:

1. virtual path link configuration and status configuration information
2. virtual channel link configuration and status information
3. virtual path connection configuration and status information
4. virtual channel connection configuration and status information

Table 9.7   M3 Class I Interface Requirements and MIB

General UNI protocol stack information	System group [RFC 1213], interfaces group, including ifTable and ifStackTable [RFC 1213, RFC 1573], and SNMP group [RFC 1213]
ATM performance information on customer's UNI	ifTable [RFC 1573]
Physical layer performance and status information	All tables except dsx3ConfigTable [RFC 1407], all tables except dsx1ConfigTable [RFC 1406], all tables except the configuration tables and VT tables of SONET MIB [RFC 1595], and atmInterfaceDs3PlcpTable/atmInterfaceTCTable of ATM MIB [RFC 1695]
ATM-level information configuration information	atmInterfaceConfTable of ATM MIB [RFC 1695]
Physical layer configuration information	dsx3ConfigTable [RFC 1407], dsx1ConfigTable [RFC 1406], and all configuration tables except the sonetVtConfigTable of SONET MIB [RFC 1595]
ATM layer virtual path link configuration and status information	atmVplTable of ATM MIB [RFC 1695]
ATM layer virtual channel link configuration and status information	atmVclTable of ATM MIB [RFC 1695]
ATM layer virtual path connection configuration and status information	atmVpCrossConnectTable and atmVpCrossConnectIndexNext of ATM MIB [RFC 1695]
ATM layer virtual channel connection configuration and status information	atmVcCrossConnectTable and atmVcCrossConnectIndexNext of ATM MIB [RFC 1695]
ATM layer traffic characterization (traffic descriptors for customer's UNIs) information	atmTrafficDescrParamTable of ATM MIB [RFC 1695]
Event notifications on ATM link going up or down	warmStart, coldStart, linkUp, linkDown of SNMP group [RFC 1695]

The traffic subgroup provides the CNM the ability to modify:

1. traffic descriptors and information objects for virtual channel connections
2. traffic descriptors and information objects for virtual path connections

Table 9.8   M3 Class II Interface Requirements and MIB

ATM level information configuration information	atmInterfaceConfTable in ATM MIB [RFC 1695]
Virtual path link configuration and status configuration information	atmVplTable in ATM MIB [RFC 1695]
Virtual channel link configuration and status information	atmVclTable in ATM MIB [RFC 1695]
Virtual path connection configuration and status information	atmVpCrossConnectTable and atm-VpCrossConnectIndexNext of ATM MIB [RFC 1695]
Virtual channel connection configuration and status information	atmVcCrossConnectTable and atmVcCross-ConnectIndexNext of ATM MIB [RFC 1695]
Traffic descriptors and information objects for virtual path and channel connections	atmTrafficDescrParamTable in ATM MIB [RFC 1695]

Table 9.8 presents the M3 Class II requirements and the MIB objects in the ATM MIB group.

9.3.8   M4 Interface: Public Network Management

The management of public ATM networks is primarily the responsibility of network service providers—carriers, PTTs, and RBOCs. They are challenged not only to manage public networks, but also to keep up with the rapidly changing technology. To help this process, ITU-T has defined [M.3010] a five-layer model of operations—the Telecommunications Management Network (TMN), which we will discuss in detail in Chapter 11. The relationship of ATM to TMN is shown in Figure 9.20. The top two layers, business management and service management, deal with the business and service aspects of TMN and have not been addressed by the ATM Forum.

The element layer (EL) contains network elements (NEs). The NEs specific to ATM technology are components, such as workstations, switches, transport devices (cross-connect systems and concentrators), and the like. The element management layer (EML) manages network elements. The network management layer (NML) manages the network either directly or via EML.

Figure 9.21 shows the dual view of the M4 interface [af-nm-0058.000]. Both views are present in the architecture across the M4 interface plane. These views are conceptual and the physical connections can be the same for both.

In the NE-level management architecture, shown in Figure 9.22, the NMS environment, consisting of one or more NMSs, directly interfaces with the ATM network ele-

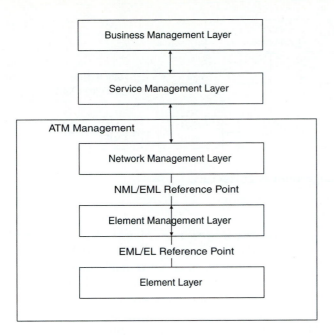

Figure 9.20   ATM Relationship to TMN Layered Architecture

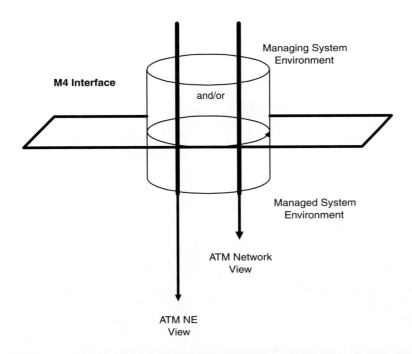

Figure 9.21   Dual Views of the M4 Interface (© 1995 The ATM Forum)

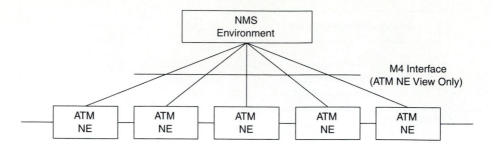

Figure 9.22   NE-Level Management Architecture

ments and manages them. A single M4 interface is between ATM network elements and the NMS environment. Although links exist between network elements, the NMS communicates directly with each ATM network element. In an actual implementation, the NMS likely interfaces with another NMS, and while managing the network elements it can still present a network view to the higher level management system.

Figure 9.23 presents an example of a network view of management's physical configuration. It consists of two ATM networks, one a single supplier subnetwork and the other a multiple supplier subnetwork. A subNMS manages the network elements for each subnetwork. In the single supplier subnetwork (shown on the right) the subNMS has only an ATM NE view. In the multiple supplier subnetwork environment (shown

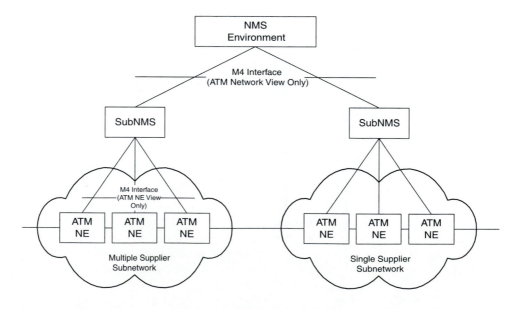

**Figure 9.23   Example of a Network View of Management's Physical
Configuration (© 1995 The ATM Forum)**

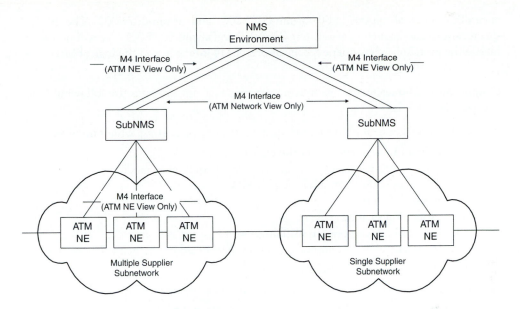

Figure 9.24   Example of the NE + Network View of Management's Physical Configuration (© 1995 The ATM Forum)

on the left) the subNMS is presented only in ATM NE view, although it may actually be communicating with lower level NMSs of each supplier. This situation is explicitly shown and is similar to the manager-of-manager architecture discussed in Chapter 4. Both subNMSs shown in Figure 9.23 present an ATM network view only to the NMS environment shown at the top. Thus, the top-level NMS sees the network view of the subnetworks but not the NE view.

The NMS environment can manage both network elements and networks, as shown in Figure 9.24. Such a hybrid situation can exist in some remote ATM devices that don't need to be under a group's NMS and are managed by an enterprise NMS.

M4 Network Element View Requirements and Logical MIB.   The ATM Forum M4 network element view specifications currently support only permanent virtual circuits (PVCs). Based on the OSI application model, the specifications are confined to configuration management, fault management, and performance management. Basic security features are also included to ensure user authorization and authentication and data protection and privacy, and the M3 interface responds to queries. The ATM security framework is similar to that discussed for management in Chapter 7. It is covered in af-sec-0096-000. Network management considerations are presented in af-nm-0103.000, which includes security requirements and logical MIB.

The MIB specifications are presented in a logical format in af-nm-0020.000 and were updated in af-nm-0020.001. They can be implemented by using either CMIP or SNMP protocols. The CMIP specifications are presented in af-nm-0027.000, af-nm-0058.000, af-nm-0071.000, af-nm-0072.000, af-nm-0073.000, and af-nm-0074.000. The SNMP specifications are detailed in af-nm-test-0080.000 and af-nm-0095.001. We will now summarize the protocol-independent specifications of M4 interface and the logical MIB.

Configuration Management.   Configuration management provides the following functions to manage NEs:

1. ATM NE configuration identification and change reporting, which involves
    a. operations performed over the craft interface
    b. human intervention (removal/insertion of equipment modules)
    c. customer control channels (e.g., ILMI)
    d. network failures
    e. protection switching events
    f. subATM NE component initialization
    g. secondary effects of atomic operations performed by the management system
2. configuration of UNIs, BICIs, and BISSIs
3. configuration of VPL/VCL termination points and cross-connections
4. configuration of VPC and VCC OAM segment end points
5. event flow control, the event forwarding discriminator function

Fault Management.   The following set of functions is specified for detecting, isolating, and correcting abnormal operations:

1. notifying the NMS of a detected failure
2. logging failure reports
3. isolating faults via demand testing

The specific functions are:

1. failure reporting of the various alarms listed in Table 9.9; the generic troubles that cause the alarm are also listed in the table
2. OAM (operations, administration and maintenance) cell loopback testing

Performance Management.   The functions of performance monitoring for an ATM network are:

1. performance monitoring
2. traffic management
3. UPC (user parameter control)/NPC (network parameter control) disagreement monitoring
4. performance management control
5. network data collection

Table 9.9   Generic Troubles in ATM NEs

Alarm Category	Generic Trouble
Communication	Alarm indication signal (AIS)
	Loss of cell delineation (LCD)
	Loss of frame (LOF)
	Loss of pointer (LOP)
	Loss of signal (LOS)
	Payload type mismatch
	Transmission error
	Path trace mismatch
	Remote defect indication (RDI)
	Signal label mismatch
Equipment	Back-plane failure
	Cell establishment error
	Congestion
	External interface device problem
	Line card problem
	Multiplexer problem
	Power problem
	Processor problem
	Protection path failure
	Receiver failure
	Replaceable unit missing
	Replaceable unit problem
	Replaceable unit type mismatch
	Timing problem
	Transmitter failure
	Trunk card problem
Processing error	Storage capacity problem
	Memory mismatch
	Corrupt data
	Software environment problem
	Software download failure
	Version mismatch
Environmental	Cooling fan failure
	Enclosure door open
	Fuse failure
	High temperature
General	Vendor specific

The following specific functions carry out these general functions:

1. physical layer performance monitoring
2. ATM cell–level protocol monitoring
3. UPC/NPC disagreement monitoring

Network View Requirements and Logical MIB.   The M4 network view for the management of an ATM public network is concerned with network management layer information. It addresses the different perspectives of service providers, each of whom need both network management and service management capabilities.

ATM Forum document af-nm-0058.000 details the requirements for ATM network management across the M4 network view interface. The associated MIB is specified in logical form and is not management protocol–specific. The functional areas addressed in the specifications are:

1. transport network configuration provisioning (including subnetwork provisioning and link provisioning)
2. transport network connection management (including set up, reservation, and modification for subnetwork connections, link connections, trails, and segments)
3. network fault management (including congestion, and connection, and segment monitoring)
4. network security management

Managed entities that meet all these requirements have not yet been defined in the MIB.

Transport Network Provisioning and Layered Network Provisioning.   Transport network provisioning includes subnetwork provisioning of network nodes and links:

1. subnetwork provisioning for the addition and monitoring information on addition, deletions, and changes in NEs and their configurations
2. link provisioning for the set up, modification, and release of subnetwork links

Subnetwork Connection Management.   The M4 network view managed entities support the subnetwork management of reservation and modification of subnetwork connections, link connections, trails, and segments, which involves:

1. point-to-point VP/VC subnetwork connections between pairs of end points
2. multipoint subnetwork VP/VC connections between pair-wise end points
3. link VP/VC connections between subnetworks
4. segment set up and support of VP/VC segment termination end points
5. trail set up and support of trails containing information on subnetwork connections and links; when part of the ATM trail spans multiple administrative

domains, each NMS is responsible for setting up and maintaining the trails for its domain

Connection Release.   The connections release across the M4 interface involves the management of resources to be made available after use, and should support:

1. release of subnetwork connections and release of resources of both point-to-point and multipoint connections

2. release of link connections between subnetworks

Subnet State Management.   The NMS needs to be aware of the operational status of the subnetworks with regard to network readiness to perform its intended functions, including link connections, trail operational changes, and network components.

Transport Network Fault Management.   M4 interface management is required to report network view alarms and provide testing to isolate the problems reported, including:

1. provision of log network alarms within a subnetwork to be retrieved by the NMS

2. autonomous notification of failures, such as termination point failures

3. provision of loopback-testing capability that supports OAM cell loopback along a subnetwork connection or a segment of it.

Network Security Management.   The security framework for ATM networks is described in ATM Forum document af-sec-0096.000. It addresses the security concerns from the perspectives of customers, public communities, and network operators. The main security objectives are (1) confidentiality of stored and transferred information, (2) data integrity of stored and transferred information, (3) accountability for all ATM network service invocations and for ATM network management activities, and (4) availability of correct access to ATM facilities.

Seven generic threats are considered in the threat analysis of an ATM network: (1) masquerade or spoofing, or pretence by an entity to be a different entity; (2) eavesdropping, or breach of confidentiality by monitoring of communications; (3) unauthorized access; (4) loss or corruption of information; (5) repudiation, or subsequent denial by an entity that it was involved in a communication exchange; (6) forgery; and (7) denial of service, or failure of an entity to fulfill its functions or prevent others from fulfilling theirs.

Table 9.10 relates the threats to the objectives. Not all threats affect all security objectives. For example, masquerade and unauthorized access threaten all security objectives, whereas eavesdropping affects only the confidentiality of information.

A set of functional security requirements addresses the generic threats, and security services should be provided to deal with these threats. Table 9.11 relates the security requirements to the services needed to meet them. Refer to af-sec-0096.000 for specifications of each service. Security recovery and security management security do not have associated services; they are part of the requirements.

Table 9.10   Relation of Threats to Objectives

| Threat | Objective | | | |
	Confidentiality	Data Integrity	Accountability	Availability
Masquerade	x	x	x	x
Eavesdropping	x	—	—	—
Unauthorized access	x	x	x	x
Loss or corruption of information	—	x	x	—
Repudiation	—	—	x	—
Forgery	x	—	x	—
Denial of service	—	—	—	x

The security framework is applied across the M4 interface. The network management M4 security requirements and logical MIB are documented in af-nm-0103.000. The MIB is defined independently of protocol implementation and is used to transfer information across ATM management interfaces. Both resources and services are defined in the MIB as *managed entities* in the ATM network element.

Table 9.11   Relation of Security Requirements to Services

Functional Security Requirement	Security Services
Verification of identities	User authentication
	Peer entity authentication
	Data origin authentication
Controlled access and authorization	Access control
Protection of confidentiality	
Stored data	Access control
Transferred data	Confidentiality
Protection of data integrity	
Stored data	Access control
Transferred data	Integrity
Strong accountability	Nonrepudiation
Activity logging	Security alarm, audit trail, and recovery
Alarm reporting	Security alarm, audit trail, and recovery
Audit	Security alarm, audit trail, and recovery
Security recovery and security management	—

9.3.9   Management of LAN Emulation

The management of an ATM network in a LAN emulation environment involves the management of ATM LAN as in any other switched LAN. A good reference on the practical aspects of switched LAN management is [Black, D]. Switched LAN management, in general, and ATM LANE, in particular, is handled with traditional SNMP management and IETF MIBs specified in RFC 1213, RFC 1573, and RFC 1695.

In addition to traditional LAN management, LANE requires management of LANE servers and clients. This requirement is addressed by the ATM Forum specifications on LANEmulation servers, af-lane-0057.000. The three servers that we are concerned with are the LANE server (LES), the broadcast and unknown server (BUS), and the LANE configuration server (LECS). The fourth component is the LANE client (LEC). Specifications are given for configuration, performance, and fault management.

In Figure 9.12 we showed the ATM LAN emulation group MIB under the ATM Forum node. Figure 9.25 shows three MIB modules under the overall ATM LANE module: *elanMIB*, *lesMIB*, and *busMIB*. The *elanMIB* enables a network manager to change the configuration of ELANs. The *lesMIB* and the *busMIB* allow reading back the current

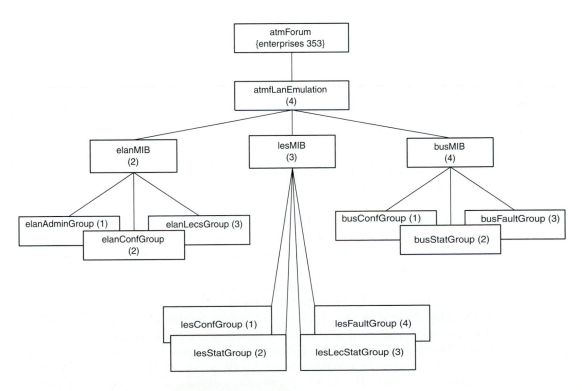

Figure 9.25   The ATM LAN Emulation MIB

Table 9.12   LAN Emulation Module

Entity	OID	Description (brief)
elanMIB	atmfLanEmulation 2	Information required for LEC to join ELAN
elanAdminGroup	elanMIB 1	Registry for LEC assignment policy types
elanConfGroup	elanMIB 2	Construction and destruction of ELAN configuration
elanLecsGroup	elanMIB 3	Configuration and monitoring of LECs
lesMIB	atmfLanEmulation 3	Information for creating and configuring LES
lesConfGroup	lesMIB 1	LES configuration and topology information
lesStatGroup	lesMIB 2	Measurement of performance and fault statistics
lesLecStatGroup	lesMIB 3	Information on LE-ARP and error statistics on LEC-LES pairs
lesFaultGroup	lesMIB 4	Information on faults
busMIB	atmfLanEmulation 4	Information on BUS
busConfGroup	busMIB 1	Information on the BUS configuration
busStatGroup	busMIB 2	Information on BUS and BUS-LEC statistics
busFaultGroup	busMIB 3	Maintenance of BUS error statistics

status of the ELANs. Table 9.12 describes the functions of the various entities in the ATM LAN emulation module.

Emulated LAN MIB.   The Emulated LAN (ELAN) MIB deals with information required for a LEC to join an ELAN. It is a repository of static information about the emulated LAN. As we demonstrated in Sections 9.2.5 and 9.2.6, in an ATM emulated LAN environment we can easily create and reconfigure components of LANs. As the *elanMIB* specifies only static information, the following manual steps are necessary in creating an ELAN: (1) create a new ELAN in the *elanMIB*; (2) create a LES entry for that ELAN, using the *lesMIB*; and (3) create a BUS entry for that ELAN, using the *busMIB*. These operations must be performed in the three separate MIBs because the components may not be collocated. Although a LES and a BUS may reside on the same platform and hence can be managed by a single agent, a LAN client is normally on a different platform at a different location. The LANE specification currently does not provide a standard method for centralized creation of LAN emulation servers.

The *elanMIB* consists of three groups: ELAN administration, ELAN configuration, and ELAN LECS. The ELAN administration group is a registry for the LEC assignment policy types. The ELAN configuration group provides the configuration for emulated LANs, which can be either created or destroyed. The operation in this group should be accompanied by concurrent operations in the LES and BUS groups as previously mentioned. The LECS configuration group allows the configuration and monitoring of LECS. It also provides configuration information on type, length, and value (TLV) for the managed entity.

LAN Emulation Server MIB.   The LAN emulation sever MIB is used to manage LESs. We can create, configure, and monitor LESs using this MIB. It also serves to assign LECs to various LESs. It contains four groups: the LES configuration group, LES statistics group, LES-LEC statistics group, and LES fault management group. The LES configuration group provides information on LES configuration and topology. The LES statistics group measures performance and fault data. It defines a table that augments the LES configuration table in the LES configuration group. The LES-LEC statistics group has the entire LAN emulation Address Resolution Protocol (ARP) request-related counter and error counts on a per LEC-LES pair basis. The fourth group in *lesMIB* is the LES fault management group, which is responsible for maintaining a log of errors in LES.

Broadcast and Unknown Server MIB.   The *busMIB* is used to create, destroy, configure, and determine the current status of BUSs and topology portions of ELANs being served by BUSs. It consists of three groups: the BUS configuration group, BUS statistics group, and BUS fault management group. The BUS configuration group provides information on BUS topology. The BUS statistics group provides information on BUS statistics and BUS-LEC statistics. The BUS fault management group addresses BUS errors and maintains a log of the errors.

9.3.10   ATM Digital Exchange Interface Management

The Digital Exchange Interface (DXI) is between digital terminal equipment (DTE) and digital circuit equipment (DCE) and connects to a public data network. In an ATM network, the public data network is a network of ATM switches. Figure 9.26 shows high-level view of the DXI interface. Typically, a DTE is a hub or router, and a DCE is a digital service unit (DSU), which interfaces with an ATM switch. More details on this interface and its management are presented in the ATM Forum document covering the data exchange interface specification, af-dxi-0014.000.

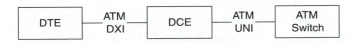

Figure 9.26   The ATM DXI Interface (© 1995 The ATM Forum)

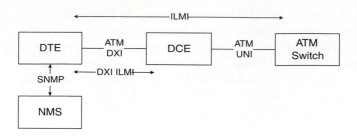

Figure 9.27   The ATM DXI Local Management Interface (© The ATM Forum)

Figure 9.27 shows the ATM DXI Local Management Interface (LMI). The ATM LMI defines the protocol for exchanging information across the DXI and supports DXI-, AAL-, and UNI-specific management information. The LMI protocol supports the SNMP management system and the ILMI management entity (IME) running on an ATM switch. The ATM DXI LMI MIB [af-dxi-0014.000] supports the IETF ATM MIB and the ATM Forum UNI MIB.

Summary

In this chapter we described the emerging broadband network technology and the management of broadband networks. There are two distinct aspects of broadband networks. One is concerned with wide-area and local-area networks, based on ATM technology. The other is concerned with the access technology that carries multimedia information from central offices or cable distribution centers to residences and enterprises.

The ATM is based on cell transmission, which is a hybrid of circuit and packet mode transmissions. Virtual paths and virtual circuits are created and deleted in this mode. Priorities are assigned to ensure quality of service for voice and video transmissions, which have tight requirements on latency and delay. These requirements have allowed integrated services to be extended from narrowband ISDN to broadband (ISDN) networks.

Because of its speed, ATM technology has been adopted for corporate LAN implementation, especially for the backbone network. With the proliferation of Ethernet LAN, ATM technology has been adapted to emulate the existing LAN, creating a LAN emulation (LANE) mode. Virtual LAN, which is an outgrowth of switched hub development, is well suited for the ATM environment.

ATM technology has brought the private and public switched network services closer together. In fact, they now overlap and thus their network management functions overlap. Several user interfaces in OSI standards have been specified by the International Standards Organization (ISO) to manage broadband wide-area networks. The ATM Forum has developed an ATM MIB that supplements the SNMP MIB developed by IETF.

The OSI standards have identified five M interfaces for managing ATM networks. M1 manages ATM network elements. M2 manages private ATM networks. M3 allows private enterprises to access their domains on the public ATM network, and based on the privilege granted—Class I or Class II—can perform limited management of the public network.

M4 defines the management interface of the ATM network for public service providers. They can manage the network at the network element level, using the network element view, or at the network management level, using the network view. These two views are part of the five-level Total Management Network (TMN) defined by OSI standards, which we will address in detail in Chapter 10. Fault, performance, and security management specifications are addressed in the M4 interface specifications. Circuit provisioning is covered as part of configuration management. M5 is between the NMSs of two service providers.

We have presented the emulated LAN environment in terms of both technological and management considerations. The RMON MIB developed by IETF has been extended to ATM by the ATM Forum to monitor remotely ATM networks. We covered this development in Section 8.6, along with other RMONs in Chapter 8.

Exercises

1. Switched virtual circuit transmission overhead could be high for sending small amounts of information. Calculate the minimum time required to transmit one ATM cell from Miami to San Francisco on a basic SONET network (OC-3) for the following cases. Assume that the distance is 4500 km and that the propagation speed is 300 meters per microsecond.

   a. datagram service
   b. switched virtual circuit service
   c. permanent virtual circuit service

2. Packet-switched transmission of voice affects real-time information because of packetization delay, which is defined as the delay caused by the need to buffer all the bits of a packet before it can be processed. Voice signal is normally digitized at a rate of 64 kbps. Calculate the packetization delay for the packet of the following sizes (use only the information bits).

   a. 1 byte
   b. an Ethernet packet of 1500 bytes of information
   c. an ATM cell

3. Although cell transmission of multimedia services offers numerous benefits, there is an inefficiency penalty. Calculate the maximum efficiency (data bytes/(data bytes + overhead bytes) for ATM transmission.

4. Calculate the efficiency of transmission to transmit:

   a. an Ethernet packet of 1500 bytes (including the overhead with 6-byte addresses)
   b. equivalent data using ATM cells

5. Figure 9.6 shows the protocol architecture of a bridge connecting an Ethernet LAN to an ATM LAN with an ATM LANE station. In actual implementation, an ATM ELAN workstation goes through an ATM switch with a LUNI interface.

Insert an ATM switch between the bridge and ATM workstation and redraw Figure 9.6.

6. A new LEC is added to an ATM LAN containing other LECs, LES, LECS, a BUS, and an ATM switch. Starting from the initial conditions, six steps (or phases) are required to make the new LEC part of the ELAN network: (1) LEC connection, (2) configuration, (3) join, (4) initial registration, (5) BUS connection, and (6) operation. Describe these steps.

7. Communication between two ATM switches is broken in a private ATM network. You are troubleshooting the problem from a network management station. What M interfaces would you use?

8. In Exercise 7:

   a. What IETF MIB would you use from your NMS station to isolate the problem? What MIB objects would you use?

   b. Can you perform the task by using ATM MIB? If so, what MIB object group would you use and why?

9. The ATM ILMI MIB covers both the physical and virtual configuration of ATM links. How would you use the ILMI MIB to isolate a break in link and distinguish a physical link failure from a virtual link failure?

10. Customer network management is used to look at the QoS classes associated with VCIs across an ATM link interface. What three MIB groups and objects are used to collect the information? Describe the relationships among them.

11. In Figure 9.19, identify the M interfaces and SNMP and ILMI management systems and agents involved in measuring the QoS information if the observed interface of the link is:

   a. in Customer X Site 1

   b. in Customer X Site 3

   c. in a public ATM network and connected to Customer X Site 2

CHAPTER 10

Broadband Network Management

In Chapter 9 we presented the general concepts of broadband network and services, comprising WAN and access networks. We then focused on the role of ATM technology and management in broadband networks. In this chapter we will address the management of access networks.

As we showed in Figure 9.1, three different types of customers have access to broadband networks: (1) corporate or enterprise users who have campuswide networks; (2) service providers; and (3) residential and small business customers who have multimedia requirements. However, the last type of customers typically has neither a sophisticated LAN environment nor large bandwidth requirements in both directions.

Access to broadband WANs for corporate or enterprise customers is accomplished by an optical fiber link from the WAN ATM switch to a campus ATM device, which can be either an ATM switch or a router with an ATM interface.

Service providers are one of the following: cable operators, local exchange carriers or telephone companies, or multiple systems operators (MSOs) that multiplex several services, such as telephony, video, and data services. Interfaces to WANs in these cases are via gateways. The physical link between a gateway and a WAN depends on the choice of the service provider.

Residential users and small business offices are the focus of broadband access network and technology. We will address services for these customers in this chapter.

An overview of broadband access networks and technologies will be presented in Section 10.1. Cable modem technology using hybrid fiber coaxial (HFC) cable will be covered in Sections 10.2 and 10.3. HFC management will be discussed in Section 10.4. We will present digital subscriber loop technology in Section 10.5 and ADSL in Section 10.6. In Section 10.7 we will cover ADSL management, which is the only DSL technology field for which management issues have been addressed.

10.1   Broadband Access Networks and Technologies

In this section, we will first look at the high level view of bradband access technologies based on customer type. Then, we will review the access technologies available specifically for the residential customer base.

10.1.1   Broadband Access Networks

The access networks serving the customer premises from the backbone SDH/SONET WAN are shown in Figure 10.1. One of the access networks comprises the OC-n/STS-n links, which we discussed in Chapter 9. It has a router or an ATM switch at either end of the access network and is used primarily for enterprise connections. The link to service providers is via gateways (not shown in figure 10.1).

Two types of access technology are currently available to residential and small business customers. They are based on the hybrid fiber coaxial (HFC)/cable modem and the

Digital Subscriber Line (DSL). Network access based on either of these two technologies can potentially support the transmission of voice, video, and data. In the case of the HFC network, information is transmitted to the cable modem at the customer site from an MSO facility. The access network based on DSL uses the existing twisted-pair loop facility from a central office to the customer premises. Based on which of the various DSL technologies is being offered, a particular type of xDSL modem is used at the customer premises. Corresponding equipment is used at the central office.

Figure 10.1 also shows the wireless customer network, which is in the early stage of development and thus trails the availability of HFC and ADSL. Consequently, we have not shown an actual implementation scheme for this type of network. It is currently envisioned as one-way wireless transmission to the customer premises, with a telephone return path. However, two-way wireless systems may also become available.

The alternative method of getting broadband services to the home is via a satellite communication network. As with wireless, this network is envisioned as being one-way to the customer's location and telephony return. Again, the potential of two-way satellite communication exists.

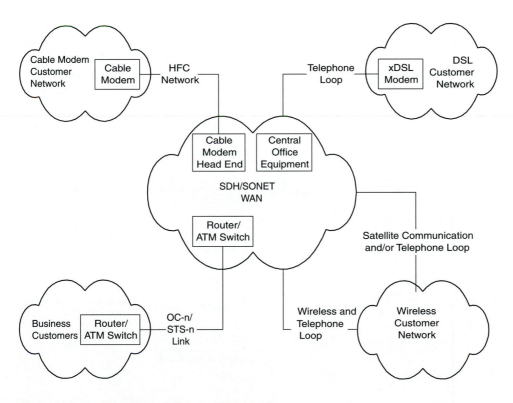

Figure 10.1   Broadband Access Networks

To summarize, broadband access technologies currently consist of four mutually independent methods—other than ATM technology—of transporting multimedia data to a customer premises. They are based on cable modem, digital subscriber line, and two wireless media methods. Not only are such networks in an embryonic stage, but so also is their management.

10.1.2   Broadband Access Technology

Broadband access technology is an emerging field. Several books [Abe G; Azzam A; Black U2; Black U3; Maxwell K & Maxwell K; Wu CH & Irwin JD] on this subject have been published recently.

Four modes of access rely on four different technologies. As shown in Figure 10.2, they are hybrid fiber coaxial (HFC) cable, Digital Subscriber Line (DSL), wireless, and satellite communication. The HFC uses television transmission facilities and cable modems, and is the most widely deployed means of access of the four. HFC can be implemented as either a one-way network with telephony return or a two-way network. In the one-way telephony return configuration, the downstream signal to the customer traverses cable. The return upstream signal from the customer premises is carried over telephone facilities via regular modem. Typically, the types and amounts of data transmitted by a residential customer are significantly less than those transmitted to the customer; hence this approach—one-way or two-way communication—is acceptable. For example, a residential customer may request a movie or a file download from the Internet; these requests require only a small bandwidth. However, the actual transmission of a movie and digital video or the downloading of a file, requires a large bandwidth. In

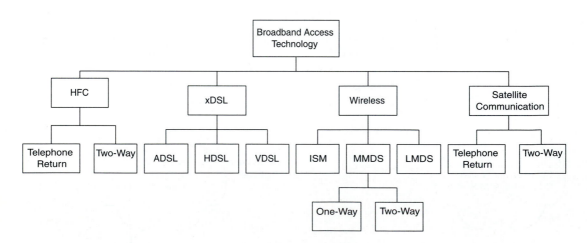

Figure 10.2   Broadband Access Technologies

two-way HFC mode, both upstream and downstream are handled by the HFC medium, using a cable modem.

Digital Subscriber Line (DSL) technology has three different implementations and is generally referred to as xDSL, where the x represents asymmetric (A), high-speed (H), or very high-speed (V) transmission. We'll discuss the differences among the three implementations in Section 10.5. All are based on the use of existing local loop telephone facilities and are currently being introduced in the market.

Wireless access technology uses wireless transmission for the downstream link to the customer site and either wireless or telephony return for the upstream link from the customer site. Various frequency spectrums and technologies are used in wireless transmission, but this industry and market for its products and services are just emerging. As mentioned earlier, the management of wireless access technology remains to be addressed.

Three broad categories of services—MMDS/WCS, LMDS, and ISM—are being offered in wireless access technology. The multichannel multipoint distribution service (MMDS)/wireless communication services (WCS) operates over the 2,500–2,686-MHz band and includes both one-way wireless with telephony return and two-way wireless implementations; it has a range of up to 35 miles. Local multipoint distribution service (LMDS) operates over two frequency bands (27,500–28,350 MHz and 31,000–31,300 MHz); it has a range of about 3 miles. The instructional scientific and medical (ISM) service also operates over two frequency bands (902–928 MHz and 2,400–2,483.5 MHz); the lower band has a range of only 0.5 mile, but the higher band has a range of up to 15 miles. Figure 10.2 also shows how wireless satellite communication has been extended to broadband access service, again either as one way with telephony return or two way.

10.2   HFC Technology

HFC technology is based on existing cable television (cable TV, or CATV) technology. Originally, cable TV systems were based on coaxial cable facilities from an MSO to a customer premises and used a tree topology. Most of these systems have been upgraded to HFC, by which the signal is brought to a fiber node via a pair of optical fibers and then distributed via coaxial cable to customers, as illustrated in Figure 10.3. At the head end, signals from various sources, such as traditional satellite services, analog and digital services using WAN, and Internet service provider (ISP) services using private backbone network, are multiplexed and converted up from an electrical (radio frequency) signal to an optical signal. Communication is one way on the optical fiber; each of a pair of optical fibers from the head end to the fiber node carry one-way traffic in opposite directions. The optical signal is converted down to RF at the fiber node and travels over the coaxial cable in a duplex mode. The signal going from the head end to the customer premises is called a **downstream signal** or a **forward path signal**. The signal going from the customer premises to the *head end* is called an **upstream signal** or a **reverse path signal**.

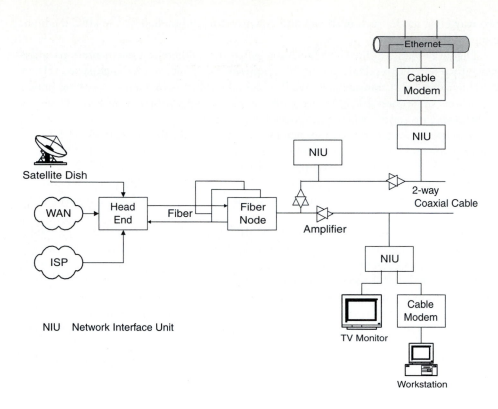

Figure 10.3   An HFC Network

The broadband signal transmitted over coaxial cable differs from the base band signal transmitted over a pair of wires (e.g., a telephone signal of up to 4 kHz). The base band signal is transmitted over only a few kilometers. The coaxial cable is a shared access medium designed to carry a signal for tens of kilometers. However, it is amplified on the way in both directions, as shown in Figure 10.3. The duplex mode of communication is achieved in the United States by transmitting downstream signal in the high-frequency band (50 MHz–860 MHz) and the upstream signal in the low-frequency band (5 MHz–42 MHz). The downstream signal includes the analog cable television spectrum.

At the customer premises, a **network interface unit** (NIU)—also referred to as network interface device (NID)—is the demarcation point between the customer network and service provider network. The analog signal is split at the NIU: The TV signal is directed to the TV and the data to the cable modem. The **cable modem** converts the analog signal to an Ethernet output, feeding either a PC or LAN. The telephone signal is also transmitted along with video and data at some cable sites.

Table 10.1   Comparative Data Transmission Speeds

Telephone modem, 28.8 kbps	6–8 minutes
ISDN, 64 kbps	1–1.5 minutes
Cable modem, 10 Mbps	Approximately 1 second

The HFC broadband system with a cable modem can process data much faster than can a conventional telephone modem or ISDN. A comparative data transmission rate to transmit a single 50-kilobyte message is shown in Table 10.1 [CableLabs-1]. A companion reference presents a more elaborate treatment of cable modem performance [CableLabs-2].

Several components must be managed in an HFC network. Let us first review the basics of HFC technology that underlie the functions of the various components to be managed. HFC technology is based on (1) broadband LAN; (2) asymmetric bandwidth allocation to achieve two-way communication; (3) a radio frequency spread spectrum technique for carrying multiple signals over the HFC; and (4) radio frequency spectrum allocation to carry multimedia telephony (voice), television (video), and computer communication (data) services.

10.2.1   The Broadband LAN

Figure 10.4 shows the architecture of several cable modems communicating with each other on a broadband LAN, as well as outside the LAN. Although the modems share a common coaxial cable that allows communication in both directions, we show the downstream (forward) and upstream (reverse) paths separately in order to represent the concept clearly. The downstream and upstream paths are separated in the frequency spectrum: The downstream signals are in the 50–860-MHz band and the upstream signals are in the 5–42-MHz band. The downstream bandwidth of a channel is 6 MHz, and the

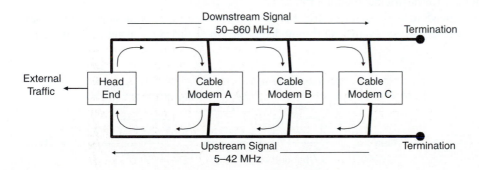

Figure 10.4   Broadband LAN Architecture

upstream bandwidth varies, based on the implementation. It ranges from 200 kHz to 3.2 MHz. The cable modems receive signals in the downstream signal band and transmit in the upstream signal band. Let us trace the path of a message from cable modem B to cable modem A. The message first goes past cable modem A (because A cannot pick up the signal from the bottom path) to the head end, where it is converted to the downstream frequency band and retransmitted. Cable modem A then gets the message addressed to it from cable modem B coming downstream (from the top path) and picks it from the LAN. The terminations prevent signals from reflecting at the end of the cable. If the message is to be transmitted outside the LAN, the head end-acting as either a bridge or router—redirects it appropriately.

10.2.2   The Cable Modem

The cable modem modulates and demodulates the digital signal from the customer equipment to the radio frequency signal carried on the cable. Similar operations are performed at the head end equipment. A single 6-MHz channel in the downstream bandwidth can support multiple data streams. Three different modulation techniques support different capabilities: amplitude shift keying (ASK), frequency shift keying (FSK), and phase shift keying (PSK). Variations and combinations of these techniques are used in cable modem technology. Of these, the modulation techniques most commonly used are **quadrature phase shift keying** (QPSK) and **quadrature amplitude modulation** (QAM). In order to understand how the different modulation techniques accomplish their objectives, we need to review digital-to-analog encoding schemes.

Figure 10.5 shows the basic concept. For example, a digital signal from a computer is converted to an analog signal by the modem, in our case a cable modem. The converted analog signal modulates a radio frequency (RF) carrier. The modulated signal occupies a band of frequencies around the carrier frequency, shown as the channel bandwidth. For example, if the digital signal in Figure 10.5 varies at a rate of 1 Mbps, alternating between 0 and 1, its base band is 1 MHz. Its frequency is modulated with a carrier frequency of 100 MHz. Thus the modulated RF signal will have a carrier frequency of 100 MHz and a channel bandwidth of 1 MHz. At the receiving end the receiving modem converts the signal back to the original digital format.

You need to understand clearly the telecommunication transmission terminology used in managing and evaluating the modems: bit rate, baud rate, carrier frequency, and

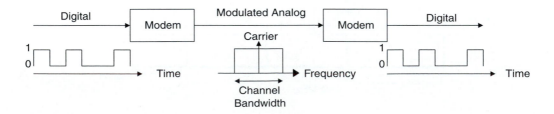

Figure 10.5   Digital-to-Analog Encoding

bandwidth. *Bit rate* is the number of bits per second traversing the medium. The *baud rate* is the number of signal units (symbols) per second. The bit rate equals the baud rate times the number of bits per symbol. In Figure 10.5, the digital signal is shown as binary 0 and 1 (i.e., two levels, 2^1). Hence the number of bits per symbol is 1. The bit rate and baud rate (symbol rate) are the same in this case.

The input signal can also be quantized into multiple levels—for example, into four levels, or 2^2. We would then need two bits to represent each signal unit (00, 01, 10, and 11). In this situation, the bit rate would be twice the baud rate. The information is carried as a digital RF signal by modulating the base band signal by the RF carrier band. For example, in the ASK method, the carrier frequency is turned on and off for each bit, representing 1 and 0.

The channel bandwidth and the data rate depend on the rate at which the signal unit changes and on the type of modulation. Thus, for the simple binary case shown in Figure 10.5, the bit rate, the baud rate, and the bandwidth (in Hz) are all the same. For the four-level technique mentioned earlier, the bandwidth needed for amplitude and phase modulation (which are the techniques of interest to us here) can be visualized as the frequency corresponding to the rate at which the signal unit changes (i.e., the baud rate of 10^6). The data rate, as we noted, is twice the baud rate (i.e., 2 Mbps).

In QPSK modulation, the four levels (00, 01, 10, and 11) are represented by the four phase states (0°, 90°, 270°, and 180°). Because PSK is relatively insensitive to external noise amplitude, it is preferred over AM for data transmission at low frequencies, where the noise is more predominant. Thus QPSK is the preferred method of modulation for the upstream signal shown in Figure 10.4. A 6-MHz channel transmitting a signal with QPSK modulation would support a 6×10^6 baud rate and 12 Mbps (2^2 levels, or 2 bits, and hence $2 \times 6 \times 10^6$ bps) bit rate capacity.

Phase shift keying is limited by the difficulty of detecting small phase shifts, but it can be combined with amplitude modulation to increase the number of levels of a signal. In the name of this technique, quadrature amplitude modulation (QAM), *quadrature* indicates the ability to distinguish clearly between the levels and does not imply four levels. The number of possible levels is the number of PSK levels times the AM levels. Thus we can create 16 QAM by combining eight levels of PSK and two levels of AM, or four levels each of PSK and AM. The downstream signal is at a higher frequency band and carries much more information than the upstream signal. As the downstream signal uses more bandwidth and a spectrally more efficient modulation technique could be used, it has higher information capacity. QAM is the preferred method of modulation for the downstream signal shown in Figure 10.4. The same 6-MHz signal channel using 16 QAM would require a channel capacity of 24 Mbps (2^4 levels or 4 bits per symbol). A detailed treatment of analog-to-digital encoding can be found in [Forouzan B, Coombs CA, & Fegan SG].

When we observe Figures 10.4 and 10.5 together, we notice that the signals in the upstream and downstream bands are at different carrier frequencies and hence can be carried on the same medium. The cable modems transmit and listen at their respective frequencies for duplex operation.

Table 10.2 shows a sample of commercially available cable modem speeds. All but Toshiba specify the data rates in terms of bits per second, whereas Toshiba specifies it in

Table 10.2   Sample Cable Modem Speeds

	Upstream	Downstream
Toshiba	2.56 Msym/sec	5.36 Msym/sec
RCA DCM105	10 Mbps	38 Mbps
Cisco	10 Mbps	38 Mbps
LANcity	10 Mbps	10 Mbps
Motorola	10 Mbps	40 Mbps

terms of symbols per second or baud rate. Cable modems with a downstream speed of 40 Mbps and an upstream speed of 10 Mbps are commonly available now.

HFC uses pseudotree topology, and the upstream and downstream transmissions are handled differently. The downstream signal on each RF channel is transmitted in broadcast mode, as a TV broadcast is. The upstream signal from each customer's equipment has to be coordinated by the head end equipment. Different vendors have adopted various schemes for implementing upstream transmission in currently deployed cable modems. They generally involve the use of a combination of time division multiplexing and Ethernet LAN. With a physical configuration of a tree and shared (Ethernet) media access, the upstream tree configuration is not a pure tree topology—hence our use of the term pseudotree topology. Unfortunately, until recently, all the schemes were proprietary, which presented interoperability problems.

Interoperability could be achieved by standardizing cable modem system specifications. Several groups have been working on standard specifications for broadband service over cable networks. These standards are being developed by the Multimedia Cable Network System (MCNS), the Digital Audio/Video Interoperability Council (DAVIC), the IETF, the IEEE 802.14 Working Group, and the ATM Forum. The **Digital Over Cable Service Interface Specifications** (DOCSIS) standard being developed by the MCNS is the industry standard. Several vendors' modems are undergoing interoperability tests and they will soon be interoperable. Thus we will soon be able to buy any vendor's cable modems and use them for broadband service, just as we buy dial-up modems for dial-up data transmission.

A cable modem, along with the head end, can handle two-way data traffic over the HFC link. Some cable modems are designed as one way, and the return path is via telephone link, called *telco return*. A cable modem is connected to the subscriber's PC on an Ethernet LAN interface. Depending on the modem, the LAN interface can be either for a single PC connection or for a LAN with multiple PCs. Many cable modem vendors offer both options.

Thanks to SNMP standards in network management, most of the cable modems have an SNMP management agent embedded in them, which makes remote management of cable modems feasible. Outsourcing companies manage cable modem sites for some of the MSOs from remote locations.

10.2.3   The Cable Modem Termination System

All cable modems terminate at a server, called the **cable modem termination system** (CMTS), at the head end. The HFC link connects the cable modems to the CMTS at the head end. The CMTS provides various services to the access networks. It is the gateway to the external network from the access network. It also multiplexes and demultiplexes the signals from the cable modems to interface with the external network.

As we would expect with the topology of a broadband LAN, the upstream and downstream propagation frequencies are different. The CMTS performs the frequency conversion. For example, when a cable modem wants to communicate with another cable modem, the signal goes upstream to the CMTS at the head end. It is converted to the downstream carrier frequency by the CMTS and propagated downstream as a broadcast message. The receiving cable modem picks up the message by reading the destination address in the message.

Thus the CMTS performs the function of routing (to the external network) or bridging (intra-access network). Some vendors build these functions into the CMTS. The routing function can also be accomplished by the use of an external router.

The CMTS interfaces with operations support systems that manage the access network. It also supports security and access controller systems that handle the integrity and security of the access network. We will discuss the architecture and components of the CMTS in Section 10.3.

10.2.4   The HFC Plant

The HFC plant consists of multiple pairs of optical fibers connecting fiber nodes. Each fiber carries traffic to a fiber node. The head end equipment converts the telephony, digital data, digital video, and analog TV signals to optical signals and transmits them to the fiber nodes. Each node serves 200 to 2,000 households [Davis AW]. Fiber nodes are connected to the home via multipoint coaxial cable. As the signals are attenuated and dispersed (with frequency), amplifiers are inserted in the coaxial cables. Because the coaxial cable supports traffic in both directions (in contrast to the fiber, which supports it only in one direction), the amplifiers have to be two-way amplifiers (see Figure 10.3). They enable coaxial cable systems to be extended tens of miles. The last section of the HFC plant is the coaxial cable that connects to the NIU in the home, referred to as *tap-to-TV* in CATV terminology.

10.2.5   The RF Spectrum for Cable Modem

Some of the key components in the broadband services to the home are the various aspects of (frequency) spectral decomposition and the consequent necessity for spectrum management. An asymmetric configuration is required to achieve two-way communication, and the allocation of bandwidth in the two directions is different, based on the type of service. Although the spectrum use in HFC extends to 860 MHz, the typical spectrum allocation extends only to 750 MHz. Figure 10.6 shows an example of a

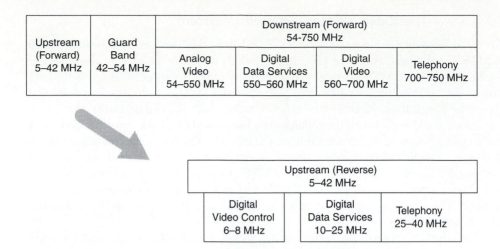

Figure 10.6   An Example of Radio Frequency Assignment

spectrum allocation for the different services in the upstream and downstream directions [Ahmed A & Vecchi MP, Davis AW]. The upstream, or reverse, signal is allocated the low end of the spectrum from 5 MHz to 42 MHz. The downstream, or forward, signal is allocated from 54 to 750 MHz. A guard band from 42 to 50 MHz (or 54 MHz depending on the cable modem) separates the forward and reverse spectral bands. Currently, spectrum allocations vary from vendor to vendor.

The downstream band contains the analog video from 54 to 550 MHz and is compatible with current TV requirements. The digital data services providing data service to the home are offered at a data rate of up to 30 Mbps. Distinguishing between the bandwidth allocation and the data rate is important. For example, 64 QAM can produce 6 bits per symbol ($2^6 = 64$), and thus a 6-MHz bandwidth used for conventional cable channel can produce 36 Mbps (6 bits/symbol $\times$ 6 MHz) of data. Digital data, digital video, and telephony services have bandwidths allocated in both the forward and reverse directions.

The downstream channel bandwidth is 6 MHz, and the upstream channel bandwidth varies, depending on the symbol rate. The Toshiba cable modem, which is DOCSIS compliant, offers upstream channel bandwidths from 200 kHz to 3.2 MHz, using QPSK/16-QAM schemes.

Cable modems are designed to tune themselves automatically to the upstream and downstream channel frequencies upon initial installation. They listen to the downstream data channels from the head end and initiate communication with them. The head end assigns specific downstream and upstream channels for the cable modem.

Under noisy conditions, the cable modem could dynamically switch to different downstream and upstream channels to improve the quality of service. Such a feature is called the *frequency-agile capability* and the corresponding cable modem the **frequency-agile cable modem**.

10.3   Data Over Cable Reference Architecture

The top part of Figure 10.7 shows the system reference architecture of HFC data over cable services and interfaces. It is a higher level representation of the HFC network that links the subscriber workstation to the WAN connection (see Figure 10.3). It is made up of head end, HFC link, cable modem, and subscriber PC [CableLabs-1]. The head end is connected to WAN, and multiple head ends can be connected via the WAN to a regional center head end. In such a case, the local head end is referred to as a **distribution hub**. The HFC link consists of fiber links and coaxial cable, connecting the head end to cable modem at the subscriber's location.

The bottom part of Figure 10.7 shows an expanded view of the head end. It comprises the cable modem termination system (CMTS), switch/router, combiner, transmitter, receiver, splitter and filter, servers, operations support system/element manager, and security and access controller. The CMTS consists of a modulator, *mod*, and a demodulator, *demod*,

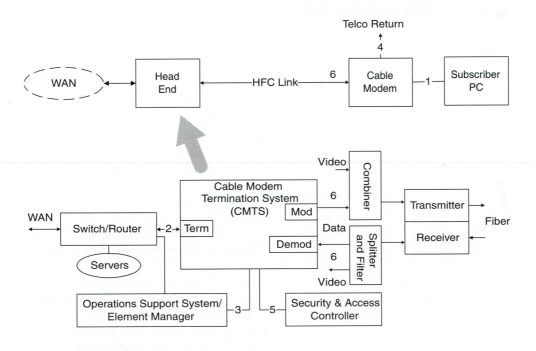

INTERFACES:
1 CMCI   Cable Modem to CPE Interface
2 CMTS-NSI CMTS Network Side Interface
3 DOCS-OSSI   Data Over Cable Services Operations Support System Interface
4 CMTRI   Cable Modem to Telco Return Interface
5 DOCSS   Data Over Cable Security System
6 RFI   Cable Modem to RF Interface

Figure 10.7   Data Over Cable System Reference Architecture

on the HFC link side and a network terminator, *term*, to the switch/router connecting to the WAN. The modulator is connected to the combiner, which multiplexes the data and video signals and feeds them to the transmitter. The RF signal is converted to an optical signal in the transmitter. The receiver converts the optical signal down to the RF level and feeds it to the splitter, where the various channels are split. The demod in the CMTS demodulates the analog signal back to digital data.

Servers at the head end handle the applications and databases. The security function (to be described shortly) is managed by the security and access controller. The operations support system and element manager perform the functions of management at various management levels—elements, network, and service.

Six interfaces are indicated in Figure 10.7. Data over Cable Service Interface Specifications (DOCSIS) places them in three interface categories: (1) data interfaces; (2) operations support system interfaces and telephony return interface; and (3) RF and security interfaces. The references to MCNS documents pertaining to these categories are listed in SP-BPI-I01-970922, which we summarize in Table 10.3. These documents can be downloaded from *http://www.cablemodem.com*.

Table 10.3   HFC/Data Over Cable System Documentation

tr-docs-ossiw08-961016	OSSI framework
sp-ossi-i02-990113	OSSI specification overview
sp-ossi-rfi-i03-990113	OSSI RF Interface specification
draft-ietf-ipcdn-interface-mib-03.txt, January 1998	MCNS Interface MIB
sp-ossi-bpi-i01-980331.pdf	OSSI Baseline Privacy Interface MIB
draft-ietf-ipcdn-cable-device-mib-07.txt, February 20, 1999	DOCSIS Cable Device MIB
draft-ietf-ipcdn-mcns-bpi-mib-00.txt, January 17, 1999	Baseline Privacy MIB
draft-ietf-ipcdn-rf-interface-mib-07.txt, February 17, 1999	DOCSIS RF Interface MIB
draft-ietf-ipcdn-tri-mib-00.txt, July 30, 1998	Telephony Return Interface MIB for cable modems and CMTS
draft-ietf-ipcdn-qos-mib-00.txt, August 7, 1998	DOCSIS quality of service MIB
SP-CMCI-I02-980317, 03/17/98	Cable Modem to Customer Premises Equipment Interface (CMCI) specification
SP-NSI-I01, 07/22/96	Cable Modem Termination System—Network-Side Interface specification
SP-OSSI-BPI-I01-980331	Operations Support System Interface specification Baseline Privacy Interface MIB
SP-CMTRI-I01-970804	Cable Modem Telephony Return Interface specification
SP-RSMI-I01-980204	Removable Security Module Interface specification—interim
SP-BPI-I02-990319	Baseline Privacy Interface specification
SP-SSI-I01-970506	Security System specification
SP-RFIv1-I01-990311	RF Interface specification

Two interfaces in the data interfaces category are shown in Figure 10.7. They are the Cable Modem to Customer Premises Equipment (CPE) interface, CMCI (1), and the CMTS-NSI interface (2), which is the network side of the interface of CMTS with the switch/router.

The second category of interfaces includes the operations support system interfaces, Data Over Cable Services Operations Support System Interface (DOCS-OSSI) (3), and the Telephony Return Interface Cable Modem to Telco Return Interface (CMTRI) (4). The element management system is considered to be an operations support system. Other operations support systems can include administrative systems that manage the service, business layer management, and test systems.

The third category of interfaces includes the Security System Interface, Data Over Cable Security System (DOCSS) (5), and the RF Interfaces (RFI) (6). There are three security requirements: the security system, cable modem removable security module, and data over cable baseline privacy interface. Many of the security and privacy issues associated with a shared medium become especially important in cable modem systems. We addressed some of these security and privacy issues in Chapter 7. Privacy issues become even more complex when privacy within a customer premises also needs to be considered. However, DOCSS does not deal with that. The RF interfaces are between the cable modem and the HFC network, and between the CMTS and the HFC network in the upstream and downstream directions, respectively. Since the HFC carries information about multiple customers over the same medium, privacy of information is a serious issue.

10.4   HFC Management

Management of an HFC system with cable modems is more complex than management of either a computer network or a telecommunication network. Management of a computer communication network is involved with data layers—the data link layer and above. Management of a telecommunication network is involved with physical layer management. HFC management encompasses both data layer and physical layer management. Part of the HFC link is fiber optics and the other part is coaxial cable, so frequency spectrum management is complex. Because HFC access technology is under the administration of a multiple systems operator (MSO), who has to deal with other service providers in close business relationships, the service and business management functions previously shown in Figure 9.20 also need to be addressed.

Figure 10.8 presents the protocol layer architecture for HFC, showing both applications and network management components. The head end is connected to the SONET wide-area network via an ATM link and to the HFC via an HFC link. The head end contains both the applications and SNMP manager in the application layer. The network manager in the head end can also be configured as RMON if the NMS at a regional center is configured to manage multiple head ends. An SNMP agent resides in the cable modem that monitors both the RF and Ethernet interfaces. Communication between the head end and the cable modem is via the HFC link, which contains both fiber optics and coaxial cable. The interface between the cable modem and the subscriber PC is an Ethernet interface.

Three functional areas are identified in the management of broadband interactive data services (BIDS): network maintenance, subscriber (customer) support, and planning

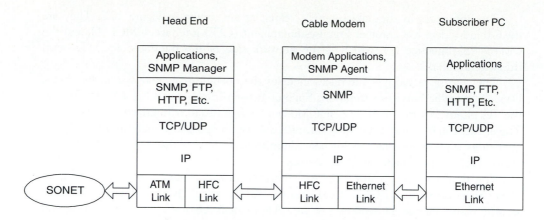

Figure 10.8   Protocol Layer Architecture in an HFC System

[Perry E & Ramanathan S]. In the following sections, we will focus only on network maintenance associated with the element management layer, although higher layers of management—network, service, and business—are important. They are yet to be developed for access networks. At the physical layer, HFC access network management functions include detection of errors and correction of ingress noise interference, amplifier gains, signal levels at the cable modems, and power supply voltages. At the data layer, HFC access network management functions include the traditional configuration, fault, and performance of the various components and the network.

We can broadly divide the HFC element management into four components: cable modem management, CMTS management, HFC link management, and RF spectrum management.

10.4.1   Cable Modem and CMTS Management

Cable modems (CM) and the cable modem termination system (CMTS) can be managed with SNMP management. Different vendors implement network management functions in two different ways. For example, LANCity cable modems and CMTS (called *head end reference*), have agents built in them and are managed directly from a centralized NMS. However, Motorola has the network management agent interface built into its head end router, which acquires information on individual modems.

Figure 10.9 shows the MIBs associated with cable modems and the MIB associated with CMTS that are relevant to managing cable modems and the CMTS. These MIBs may be grouped as follows. The first category is the generic set of IETF MIBs: *system* {mib-2 1}, *interfaces* {mib-2 2} [RFC 1213], and *ifMIB* {mib-2 31}, which describes interface types [RFC 1573]. The second category comprises MIBs for the interfaces of cable modem and CMTS:

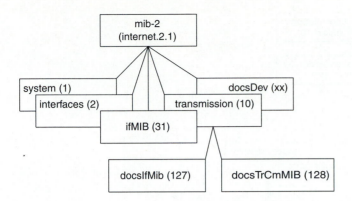

Figure 10.9   Cable Modem Management MIBs

docsIfMib. The *docsIfMib* {mib-2.transmission 127} is a subnode under transmission and includes objects for the Baseline Privacy Interface. The *docsTrCmMIB* {mib-2.transmission 128} specifies the telephony return (or telco return) interfaces for cable modems and CMTS. The third category deals with the set of objects for cable modems and CMTS. We will now discuss the second and third categories.

Figure 10.10 shows the data over cable system (DOCS) interface MIB that supplements the standard SNMP interface MIBs [RFC 1213, RFC 1573 (made obsolete by RFC 2233)]. The original specifications covered only the CM and CMTS objects, which are subnodes 1, 2, and 3 under *docsIfMIB* (Table 10.3, Draft-ietf-ipcdn-rf-interface-mib-07.txt). The baseline privacy MIB, *docsBpiMIB*, was added later as subnode 5 and contains the same subgroup structure as nodes 1, 2, and 3 under *docsIfMIB* [Table 10.3, draft-ietf-ipcdn-mcns-bpi-mib-00.txt]. It deals with the privacy issues mentioned in Section 10.3. The notification subgroups in the interface MIBs are currently placeholders. DOCSIS quality of service MIB, *docsQoSMIB*, is node 6 under *docsIfMIB* and describes the control of QoS features for cable modems and CMTS [Table 10.3, draft-ietf-ipcdn-qos-mib-00.txt].

The DOCS interface objects group, *docsIfMIBObjects*, has three subgroups. The base interface objects group specifies objects common to the CM and CMTS. The CM interface objects group, *docsIfCmObjects*, pertains to the CM. The CMTS interface objects group, *docsIfCmtsObjects*, pertains to the CMTS.

The RF spectrum has a layered interface similar to that of ATM sublayers. However, the multiple RF channels in the upstream and downstream bands also need to be specified in this case. Fortunately, the specifications of RFC 1573 permit this extension. The layered structure of the RF interface is shown in Figure 10.11, depicting one downstream and two upstream channels interfacing with the RF MAC channel on the user interface on top and with the RF physical layer on the service provider interface on the bottom.

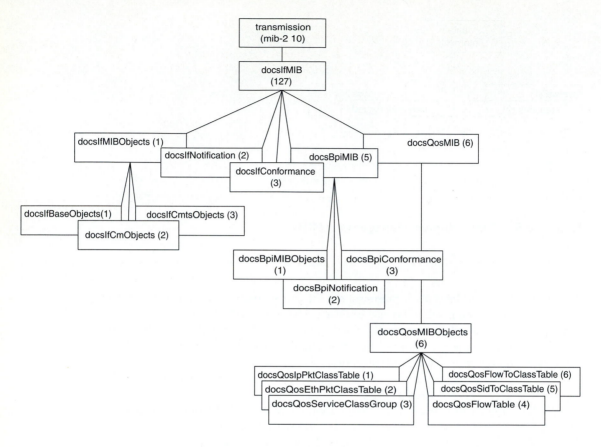

Figure 10.10   **The DOCS Interface MIB**

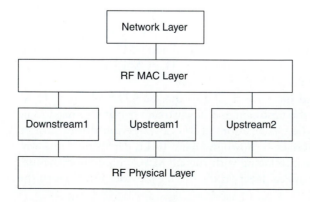

Figure 10.11   **The RF MAC Interface**

The baseline privacy objects group, *docsBpiMIBObjects*, has eight subgroups, as shown in Table 10.4. The subgroups define the baseline privacy requirements for the CM and CMTS. The specifications include definition of objects, authorization tables, encryption keys, and multicast control tables. The conformance specifications are defined in the *docsBpiConformance* group.

The DOCS quality of service MIB extends the QoS objects defined in *docsIfMIBObjects* and *docsDev*. The six tables under *docsQosMIBObjects* are shown in Figure 10.10. Table 10.5 presents the entities, OID, and a brief description of each. The *docsQosMIBObjects* is a node under *docsQosMIB* that contains the six tables. The IP packet classification table describes the IP packet classification. Each packet that is either received or routed through may be compared to an ordered list of rules pertaining to the IP (and UDP/IP) packet header. The Ethernet packet classification table serves a similar purpose at the data link layer.

A service class represents a level of service provided by the CMTS to a service identifier (SID) or to a packet flow. An SID and a flow are associated with only one service class. The *docsQosServiceClassTable* describes the set of DOCSIS QoS service classes defined in the managed device. The *docsQosFlowTable* describes the flows in the device. The mapping of service classes to SIDs is contained in the *docsQosSidToClassTable*. The mapping of flow to service class is described in the *docsQosFlowToClassTable*.

Figure 10.12 shows the DOCS cable device MIB. It provides a set of objects required for the management of MCNS-compliant cable modems and the CMTS. It consists of three groups: *docsDevMIBObjects*, *docsDevNotification*, and *docsDevConformance*.

Table 10.4   The DOCS Baseline Privacy MIB

Entity	OID	Description
docsBpiCmObjects	docsBpiMIBObjects 1	Baseline privacy objects for CM
docsBpiCmBaseTable	docsBpiMIBCmObjects 1	Baseline privacy CM base and authorization table
docsBpiCmTEKTable	docsBpiMIBCmObjects 2	Baseline privacy traffic encryption key table
docsBpiCmtsObjects	docsBpiMIBObjects 2	Baseline privacy CMTS objects
docsBpiCmtsBaseTable	docsBpiMIBCmtsObjects 1	Baseline privacy CMTS base table
docsBpiCmtsAuthTable	docsBpiMIBCmtsObjects 2	Baseline privacy CMTS authorization table
docsBpiCmtsTEKTable	docsBpiMIBCmtsObjects 3	Baseline privacy CMTS traffic encryption key table
docsBpiMulticastcontrol	docsBpiMIBObjects 4	Baseline privacy CMTS multicast control group

Table 10.5   The DOCS QoS MIB

Entity	OID	Description
docsQosMIBObjects	docsQoSMIB 1	DOCSIS QoS extensions of MIB objects
docsQosIpPktClass-Table	docsQosMIBObjects 1	IP packet classification table containing class information on direction, type, flow, source, and destination
docsQosEthPktClass-Table	docsQosMIBObjects 2	Ethernet packet classification containing information similar to the IP packet
docsQosServiceClassGroup	docsQosMIBObjects 3	Contains QoS table
docsQosServiceClassTable	docsQosServiceClass Group 1	Set of DOCSIS QoS service classes defined in the managed object
docsQosFlowTable	docsQosMIBObjects 4	Set of DOCSIS QoS flows active in the device; an extension of *intSrvFlowTable* [RFC 2213]
docsQosSidToClass-Table	docsQosMIBObjects 5	Mapping of service classes to SIDs
docsQosFlowToClassTable	docsQosMIBObjects 6	Mapping of flows to service classes

Table 10.6 summarizes the seven groups under DOCS device MIB objects. The base group extends the MIB-II system group to cable modem and CMTS devices. A minimum level of access security is defined in the access table. Software upgrades can be temporarily loaded by using the SNMP command defined in the software group for test purposes. The server group describes server access and parameters used for initial provisioning and bootstrapping. The event group specifies the control and login of events and traps. The trap/

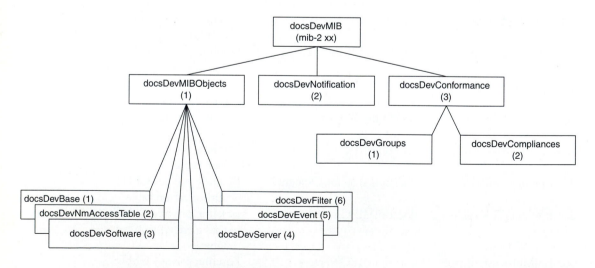

Figure 10.12   The DOCS Cable Device MIB

Table 10.6 The DOCS Cable Device MIB

Entity	OID	Description
docsDevMIBObjects	docsDevMIB 1	Objects of the cable modem and CMTS device
docsDevBase	docsDevMIBObjects 1	Extends MIB-II System Group with objects needed for cable device system management
docsDevNmAccessTable	docsDevMIBObjects 2	Defines the minimum level of SNMP access security
docsDevSoftware	docsDevMIBObjects 3	Provides information for network-downloadable software upgrades
docsDevServer	docsDevMIBObjects 4	Provides information about the progress of the interaction with various provisioning servers
docsDevEvent	docsDevMIBObjects 5	Provides control and logging for event reporting
docsDevFilter	docsDevMIBObjects 6	Configures filters at link layer and IP layer for bridged data traffic
docsDevCpe	docsDevMIBObjects 7	CPE IP management and anti-spoofing group on cable modems

notification is to be defined in the notification group, which is currently just a placeholder. The filter group provides objects for both LLC and IP protocol filters. The conformance group, consisting of groups and compliances groups, addresses conformance and compliance objects.

10.4.2 HFC Link Management

Management of plant facilities in HFC system is extremely important. As mentioned earlier, the functioning of cable modems depends on the strength of the signal, which can be neither too high nor too low. Signal strengths are determined by the gain of the amplifiers on the HFC link and source strength at the high end. Thus the controlling parameters of the HFC plant need to be monitored continually to ensure the reliability of the cable modem system. This function is currently performed by implementing transponders that monitor the amplifiers and distribution hubs and telemeter information to the head end [CheetahNet™]. A proxy server is used to convert this information to SNMP objects. MIB development in this area is minimal as of now.

10.4.3 RF Spectrum Management

The **spectrum management system** (SMS) deals with the management of RF spectrum allocations to different digital services, both in the downstream and upstream bands. A private proposal [Ahmad A & Vecchi MP] has been made regarding the subject, but no public specifications are currently available.

10.5   DSL Technology

The main motivating factor for employing Digital Subscriber Line (DSL) for access technology in multimedia services is the preexistence of local loop facilities to most residences. The information capacity of a 3,000-Hz analog voice channel with a 30-dB signal-to-noise ratio (based on the Shannon limit) is 30,000 bits per second [Tanenbaum AS, Hawley GT]. However, an unloaded twisted pair of copper wires from a central office to a residence can carry a digital T1/DS1 signal at 1.544 Mbps as far as 18,000 feet, a DS2 signal at 6.312 Mbps as far as 12,000 feet, and an STS-1 signal at 51.840 Mbps as far as 1,000 feet [ADSL Forum-1]. Thus Shannon's fundamental limitation of data rate prevalent in an analog modem can be overcome by direct digital transmission. This is the basic concept behind xDSL technology, which we will now discuss briefly. See [Chen WY, Gorlaski W, Maxwell K & Maxwell K, Abe G] for in-depth treatments of this topic.

These distances can be increased for analog telephony if loaded cables that compensate for loss and dispersion are used. However, they cannot support digital subscriber lines because the loaded coils attenuate high frequencies. Many communities have been wired with fiber-optic cable coming to the curb and a digital multiplexer at the end of the fiber-optic line. The length limitation of copper cable is practically eliminated by the use of this fiber-optic configuration. However, special digital subscriber line multiplexing needs to be done at the termination of the fiber-optic line. Other configurations are covered in [Hawley GT].

The basic DSL architecture consists of an unloaded pair or pairs of wires connected between a transceiver unit at a central office and a transceiver unit at a customer premises. This transceiver multiplexes and demultiplexes voice and data and converts the signal to the format suitable for transmission on the DSL link. Table 10.7 [ADSL Forum-1] shows the various forms of DSL, including the conventional analog modem and ISDN, and their characteristics.

Table 10.7   Copper Access Transmission Technologies

Meaning	Data rate	Mode	Cable	Applications
Voice band modems	1200 bps to 28,800 bps	Duplex	2-pair	Low data rate data communications
Integrated services digital network (ISDN)	160 kbps	Duplex		ISDN service, voice and data communications
High data rate digital subscriber line (HDSL)	1.544 Mbps 2.048 Mbps	Duplex Duplex	2-pair	T1/E1 service feeder plant, WAN, LAN, and server access
Single line digital subscriber line (SDSL)	1.544 Mbps 2.048 Mbps	Duplex Duplex	1-pair	Same as HDSL plus premises access for symmetric services
Asymmetric digital subscriber line (ADSL)	1.5 to 9 Mbps 16 to 640 kbps	Down Up	1-pair	Internet access, video demand, simplex video, LAN access, interactive multimedia
Very high data rate digital subscriber line (VDSL)	13 to 52 Mbps 1.5 to 2.3 Mbps	Down Up	2-pair	Same as ADSL plus HDTV

A **high data rate digital subscriber line** (HDSL) operates at a T1 or E1 data rate in a duplex mode with two pairs of wires. The duplex mode is defined as two-way communication with the same speed in both directions. The **single line digital subscriber line** (SDSL) is the same as the HDSL, except the 2-way duplex communication occurs over a single twisted pair.

The asymmetric digital subscriber line (ADSL) and the **very high data rate digital subscriber line** (VDSL) both operate asymmetrically. As in HFC, the downstream signal has a larger bandwidth and is at the high end of the spectrum, whereas the upstream signal is at the lower end of the spectrum and has a lower bandwidth. The difference between ADSL and VDSL is that VDSL operates at higher data rates over shorter lines than ADSL.

10.6   Asymmetric Digital Subscriber Line Technology

Of all the xDSLs available, the **asymmetric digital subscriber line** (ADSL) technology is being deployed most widely in the United States. A simplified access network using ADSL is shown in Figure 10.13; it consists of an ADSL transmission unit (ATU) and a splitter at each end of the ADSL line. The ATU acronym has also been expanded to ADSL transceiver unit and ADSL terminating unit, although ADSL TR-001 defines it as ADSL transmission unit. The ATU at a central office is ATU-C, and the ATU at the customer premises is ATU-R. The ATU is also called the ADSL modem. The data and video signal from the broadband network is converted to an analog signal by the ATU-C and multiplexed and demultiplexed. The splitter at the central office combines the plain old telephone service (POTS) voice signal and the broadband signal. The reverse process occurs at the splitter and ATU-R at the customer premises. Development is in progress to eliminate the splitter at the customer site. This configuration is referred to as ADSL-Lite.

As previously mentioned, the upstream and downstream signals are placed asymmetrically in the frequency spectrum, as shown in Figure 10.14(a) [ADSL Forum-2]. The POTS signal is always allocated the base band of 4 kHz and is separated from the broadband signal by a guard band. There are two schemes for separating the upstream and downstream frequency bands: frequency division multiplexing (FDM) and echo cancellation. In FDM, after the upstream and downstream bands have been separated, each band is divided into one or more high-speed channels and one or more low-speed channels. As shown in Figure 10.14(b), the upstream and downstream bands overlap, but are separated

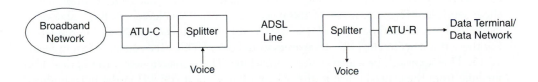

Figure 10.13   A Simplified ADSL Access Network

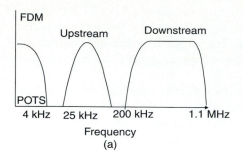

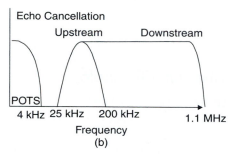

Figure 10.14   ADSL Spectrum Allocation

by echo cancellation. The low-frequency end of the spectrum is made available for downstream signals, thus increasing the overall downstream spectral band.

Within the upstream and downstream bands, individual channels are allocated a multiple of a 4-kHz band, using either the standard discrete multitone (DMT) or the carrierless amplitude phase (CAP) modulation. The former modulation scheme is more efficient, but it is more complex and costly; both schemes are currently in use. Further details on spectrum allocation schemes are presented in [Goralski W, Wu CH & Irwin JD, Greggains D].

The standards for DSL are addressed by the various standards organizations, including the American National Standards Institute (ANSI). T1-413 is the ANSI standard for DSL at the physical layer protocol level. To accelerate the interoperability and implementation of ADSL, the industry has established a consortium, the ADSL Forum. It is addressing issues associated with end-to-end system operation, management, and security.

Only residential customers who have a direct copper connection from a central office can receive ADSL services. The telephone loop facilities with loaded coils cannot handle these services. Moreover, many of the newer residential developments have fiber-optic cable to the neighborhood (FTTN) and twisted pairs from the FTTN to the residence. For these residences, telephone companies would offer VDSL services, as shown in Figure 10.15. This approach provides greater bandwidth. The signal traverses the optical fiber medium from the central office to the optical network unit (ONU) in the neighborhood and carries multiple channels. It is demultiplexed at the ONU and fed through VDSL

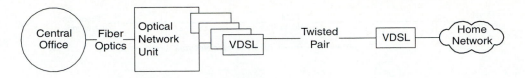

Figure 10.15   A VDSL Access Network

modems and twisted-pair cable to the residence. Bandwidths of 12.96 to 55.2 Mbps could be achieved for downstream signals and up to 2.3 Mbps for upstream signals with single-pair cable. Multiple configurations are being proposed for home networks, which we will not cover here.

Much of the latest documentation on ADSL is available on TRs published by the ADSL Forum and in ANSI standard T1-413. The ADSL Forum's approved documentation list is available on its Web page, *www.adsl.com*. Some of the TRs that we will be referring to are listed in Table 10.8.

10.6.1   Role of the ADSL Access Network in an Overall Network

The ADSL Forum's view [TR-001] of how the ADSL access network fits into an overall network for broadband services is presented in Figure 10.16. It shows the components of the overall network comprising private, public, and premises networks and the role that the ADSL access network plays in it. The service providers network consists of service systems, various types of networks that are behind the access node, operations systems (OS) that perform the operations, administration, and maintenance (OAM) of the networks and access nodes, and the ATU-Cs. The customer premises network consists of ATU-R, premises distribution network (PDN), various service modules (SM), and terminal equipment (TE).

The service systems are on a private network that provides on-line services, Internet access, LAN access, interactive video services, and videoconference services. The private

Table 10.8   ADSL Documents

TR-001	ADSL Forum System Reference Model
TR-005	ADSL Network Element Management System
TR-006	SNMP-Based ADSL Line MIB; see also draft-ietf-adslmib-adsllinemib-09.txt
TR-014	DMT Line Code Specific MIB
TR-015	CAP Line Code Specific MIB
TR-016	CMIP-Based Network Management Framework

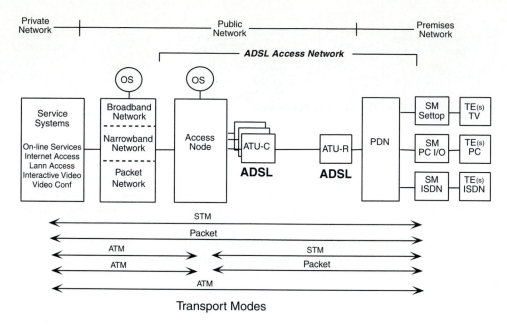

Transport Modes

ADSL = Asynchronous Digital Subscriber Line
ATM = Asynchronous Transfer Mode
STM = Synchronous Transfer Mode
TE = Terminal Equipment
OS = Operations System
PDN = Premises Distribution Network
SM = Service Module

Figure 10.16   Role of the ADSL in an Overall Network

network interfaces with the public network, which consists of the broadband (e.g., SONET/SDH), narrowband (e.g., T1/E1), or packet (e.g., IP) networks. The access node is the concentration point for the broadband signal, narrowband data, and packet data. It is located in a central office or at a remote location such as an Optical Network Unit (ONU). The access node may include the ATU-Cs, as in a Digital Subscriber Line Access Multiplexer (DSLAM). The access network commences at the access node and extends to the PDN in the customer premises.

The premises network starts from the network interface at the output of ATU-R. The PDN, which is part of the customer premises network may be a LAN, twisted-pair cable of a telephone network, consumer electronics bus (CEBus), which distributes signal over power lines, coaxial cable, fiber-optic cable (in future homes), or a combination of these transmission media. The service modules, such as set-top boxes and ISDN, perform the terminal adaptation functions for the terminal equipment.

Five transport modes are shown in Figure 10.16. The first is what the ADSL Forum called the synchronous transfer mode (STM), or the bit synchronous transmission mode.

An example of this mode is the bit pipe such as T1/E1, ISDN, or a simple modem. In this mode the PDN outputs bits out of the service modules, and the access node delivers bits to the narrowband network.

The second transport mode is end-to-end packets such as IP packets. In this mode, the service modules are expected to deliver packets to the ADSL access network through PDN. This mode is probably one of the most common uses of the small office home office (SOHO) network. The digital data terminals are interconnected via an Ethernet LAN PDN, and packets are delivered to the ADSL access network via a router. The reverse process occurs at the access node to the network interface.

The next two transport modes are hybrids. The output to the network from the access node is ATM. The services module at the premises network delivers either a bit synchronous output or a packet output. A conversion is involved in the access node. For example, the access node to a broadband network could be an emulated LAN, wherein the IP packets are transferred as ATM cells to the network.

The fifth transport mode is the end-to-end ATM, whereby the service modules put out cells instead of packets. We would expect the home network in this case to be wired with fiber-optic lines.

10.6.2   ADSL Architecture

Let us now look at the architecture of the ADSL access network presented in Figure 10.13. The ADSL Forum's system reference model [TR-001] is shown in Figure 10.17. We have already discussed some of its components in Section 10.6.1. The additional components are the splitters at the central office and the customer premises, which separate the low-frequency telephony signal from the video and digital data. The Public Switched Telephone Network (PSTN) is the switch connected at the central office, whereas the telephones operate off the splitter at the customer end. The digital broadcast and network management interface with the access node. The digital broadcast is the typical broadcast video. Network management may be treated as one of the operations system components. We will go into more detail on operations system interfaces and functions in Section 10.7.

Several interesting aspects of the ADSL system reference model are shown in Figure 10.17. They include the interfaces between components of the ADSL network and interfaces between the ADSL access network and the external networks. There are five basic interfaces: V, U, T, B, and POTS. The interface between the access node and the network, V_c, is usually a physical interface; V_A is the logical interface between ATU-C and access node. An interface can have multiple physical connections (as shown), or multiple logical interfaces can be connected through a physical interface. Network management is implemented through the V_c interface. All network monitoring of central office and home network components must go through this interface.

The U interfaces are all off the splitters. In fact, these U interfaces may disappear when ADSL-Lite is implemented. The POTS interfaces also are from the splitters. The B interface is for auxiliary data input—for example a satellite feed directly into a service module such as set-top box.

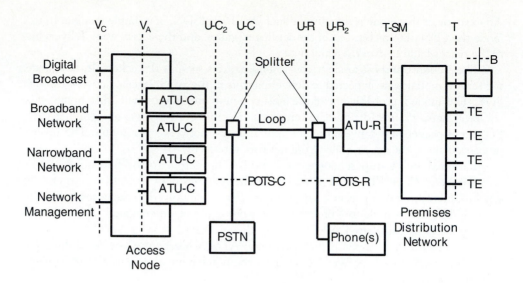

Interfaces:

B = Auxiliary Data Input (e.g., a satellite feed to a service module)
POTS-C = Interface Between PSTN and POTS Splitter at Network End
POTS-R = Interface Between Phones and POTS Splitter at Premises End
T = Interface Between Premises Distribution Network and Service Modules
T/SM = Interface Between ATU-R and Premises Distribution Network
U-C = Interface Between Loop and ATU-C (analog)
U-C$_2$ = Interface Between POTS Splitter and ATU-C
U-R = Interface Between Loop and ATU-R (analog)
U-R$_2$ = Interface Between POTS Splitter and ATU-R
V$_A$ = Logical Interface Between ATU-C and Access Node
V$_C$ = Interface Between Access Node and Network
TE = Terminal Equipment
POTS = Plain Old Telephone Service
PSTN = Public Switched Telephone Network

Figure 10.17   The ADSL System Reference Model

10.6.3   ADSL Channeling Schemes

There are two aspects of transport channels in ADSL access networks. The first is the traditional transport bearer channels as they are defined in ISDN. For ADSL transport frames, seven AS bearer channels are defined for the downstream signal operating in a simplex mode. The AS bearer channels are in multiples (1, 2, 3, or 4) of the T1 rate of 1.536 Mbps. In addition to the downstream AS channels, three additional LS duplex channels can carry signals in both the downstream and upstream directions. The LS bearer channels are 160, 384, or 576 Kbps. See [Goralski W] for a detailed discussion of these channels. Incidentally, AS and LS are not specific acronyms.

The second is how the signal is buffered while traversing the ADSL link. Real-time signals, such as audio and real-time video, use a fast buffering scheme and hence are referred to as a *fast channel*. Digital data that can tolerate delay make use of slow buffers and are interleaved between fast signals. The digital data channel is referred to as an *interleaved channel*. Thus a physical interface can carry both the fast channel and interleaved channel, which needs to be addressed in network interface management. We will discuss the interfaces of physical, fast, and interleaved channels more in Section 10.7.

10.6.4   ADSL Encoding Schemes

ADSL management is dependent on the line encoding scheme used. We will briefly discuss the two types of encoding schemes used in ADSL line encoding: **carrierless amplitude modulation** (CAP) and **discrete multitone** (DMT) technology. Both are based on the quadrature amplitude modulation (QAM) scheme that we discussed in Section 10.2.2. In both cases, the basic approach is to separate the POTS band (0–4 kHz) (see Figure 10.14) either by separating the upstream signal from the downstream signal with a guard band or by distinguishing overlapping upstream and downstream signals by echo cancellation.

The echoing phenomenon occurs in telephone systems because of crosstalk between neighboring pairs of wires in a bundle. Two signals transmitted from a central office can couple with each other, which is referred to as *near-end crosstalk*. Two signals traversing in opposite directions can also interfere with each other, which is referred to as *far-end crosstalk*. Both types of crosstalk can be mitigated by using the echo cancellation technique. The same technique can be used to separate the overlapping band between upstream and downstream signals.

Although ANSI has recommended the use of DMT for ADSL, a significant number of the currently deployed systems use the CAP system. Recall that CAP is carrierless. In other words, the signal is quadrature amplitude modulated at a specific carrier frequency, the carrier is suppressed at the transmitter and then sent, and the carrier is regenerated at the receiver to detect the signal bits. In CAP, the entire local loop bandwidth (25 to 200 kHz for upstream signals or 200 kHz to 1.1 MHz for downstream signals) is used in the encoding.

In DMT, the entire bandwidth of approximately 1.1 MHz is split into 256 subchannels, each of an approximately 4-kHz band. Subchannels 1 through 6 are used for voice signal, and the rest are used for broadband signal. The number of upstream subchannels is 32 (7 through 38). The number of downstream subchannels is either 250 if echo cancellation is used or 218 if echo cancellation is not used.

10.7   ADSL Management

The general framework for ADSL management is described in ADSL Forum document TR-005. TR-006 presents the SNMP-based ADSL line MIB, and TR-016 contains the CMIP specification for ADSL network element management. TR-014 and TR-015 document the DMT line code specific MIB and CAP line code specific MIB, respectively. The management documentation is specific to ADSL and is a supplement to standard management MIB documentation.

Figure 10.18 shows the ADSL system reference model that is used in the ADSL management framework. It is similar to the one shown in Figure 10.17, but it has additional

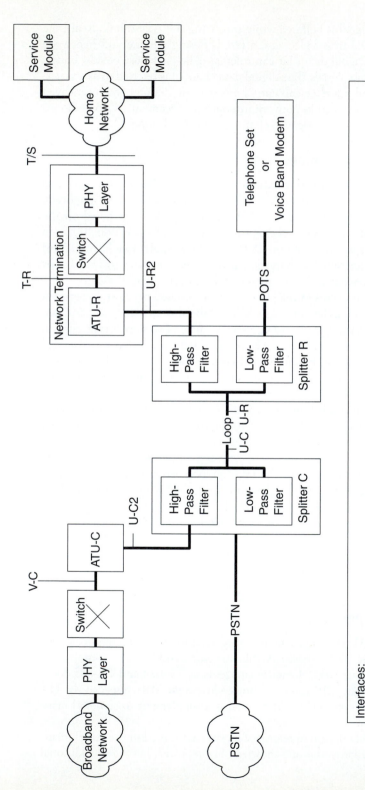

Figure 10.18   ADSL Forum Management System Reference Model

Interfaces:
T-R Interface Between ATU-R and Switching Layers
T/S Interface Between ADSL Network Termination and Customer Installation or Home Network
U-C Interface Between Loop and ATU-C (analog)
UC2 Interface Between POTS Splitter and ATU-C
U-R Interface Between Loop and ATU-R (analog)
U-R2 Interface Between POTS Splitter and ATU-R
V-C Logical Interface Between ATU-C and a Digital Network Element (e.g., one or more switching systems)

components that identify the switching and physical layer functions explicitly. The management functions addressed in the ADSL-specific documents address the physical layer functions. The management of data layers is addressed by the conventional NMS. The low- and high-pass filters are also explicitly shown.

10.7.1   ADSL Network Management Elements

ADSL network management addresses the parameters, operations, and protocols associated with configuration, fault, and performance management. Security and accounting management are not explicitly dealt with, although they are important management functions and are addressed by other models (e.g., SNMP security management, discussed in Chapters 7 and 13).

Management of the ADSL network involves five network elements: (1) management communications protocol across the network management subinterface of the V interface; (2) management communications protocol across the U interfaces between ATU-C and ATU-R; (3) parameters and operations with the ATU-C; (4) parameters and operations within the ATU-R; and (5) ATU-R side of the T interface. All management functions in the ADSL network are accomplished via the V interface. Thus the management of elements 2–5 is accomplished via the V interface, not the U interface.

As discussed in Section 10.6.3, the management function at the physical layer involves three entities: physical channel, fast channel, and interleaved channel. The fast and interleaved channels need to be managed separately. They use the physical transmission medium, which also needs to be managed. In addition to physical links and channel parameters, parameters associated with the type of line coding need to be monitored.

10.7.2   ADSL Configuration Management

The various parameters that need to be managed for configuration are listed in Table 10.9 [adapted from ADSL Forum TR-005]. It shows the component with which the parameter is associated, as well as whether it pertains to the physical line or fast or interleaved channel. A brief description of each parameter is also given. A link can be configured in one of five ways: no separation of channels, fast, interleaved, either, or both.

There are five levels of noise margin—the highest defined by the maximum noise margin and the lowest defined by the minimum noise margin. Decreases or increases in the transmission power of the modem are based on these thresholds. The transmission rate can be increased if the noise margin goes above a threshold level that is less than the maximum noise margin threshold. Similarly, the transmission rate can be decreased if the noise margin falls below a threshold that is greater than the minimum noise margin. At the middle of these thresholds lies steady state operation. These levels are shown in Figure 10.19.

Some modems support one of the three rate adaptation modes. In mode 1 the rate is changed manually. In mode 2, the rate is automatically selected at start-up, but remains at that level afterward. In mode 3, the rate is dynamic and is based on the noise margin.

Table 10.9   ADSL Configuration Management Parameters

Parameter	Component	Line	Description
ADSL line type	ADSL Line	N/A	Five types: no channel, fast, interleaved, either, or both
ADSL line coding	ADSL Line	N/A	ADSL coding type
Target noise margin	ATU-C/R	Physical	Noise margin under steady state (BER=$<10^{-7}$)
Maximum noise margin	ATU-C/R	Physical	Modem reduces power above this threshold
Minimum noise margin	ATU-C/R	Physical	Modem increases power below this margin
Rate adaptation mode	ATU-C/R	Physical	Mode 1: Manual Mode 2: Select at start-up Mode 3: Dynamic
Upshift noise margin	ATU-C/R	Physical	Threshold for modem increases data rate
Minimum time interval for upshift rate adaptation	ATU-C/R	Physical	Time interval to upshift
Downshift noise margin	ATU-C/R	Physical	Threshold for modem decreases data rate
Minimum time interval for downshift rate adaptation	ATU-C/R	Physical	Time interval to downshift
Desired maximum rate	ATU-C/R	Fast/Interleave	Maximum rates for ATU-C/R
Desired minimum rate	ATU-C/R	Fast/Interleave	Minimum rates for ATU-C/R
Rate adaptation ratio	ATU-C/R	Physical	Distribution ratio between fast and interleaved channels for available excess bit rate
Maximum interleave delay	ATU-C/R	Fast/Interleave	Maximum transmission delay allowed by interleaving process
Alarm thresholds	ATU-C/R	Physical	15-minute count threshold on loss of signal, frame, poser, and error-seconds
Rate up threshold	ATU-C/R	Fast/Interleave	Rate-up change alarm
Rate down threshold	ATU-C/R	Fast/Interleave	Rate-down change alarm
Vendor ID	ATU-C/R	Physical	Vendor ID assigned by T1E1.4
Version Number	ATU-C/R	Physical	Vendor specific version
Serial Number	ATU-C/R	Physical	Vendor specific Serial Number

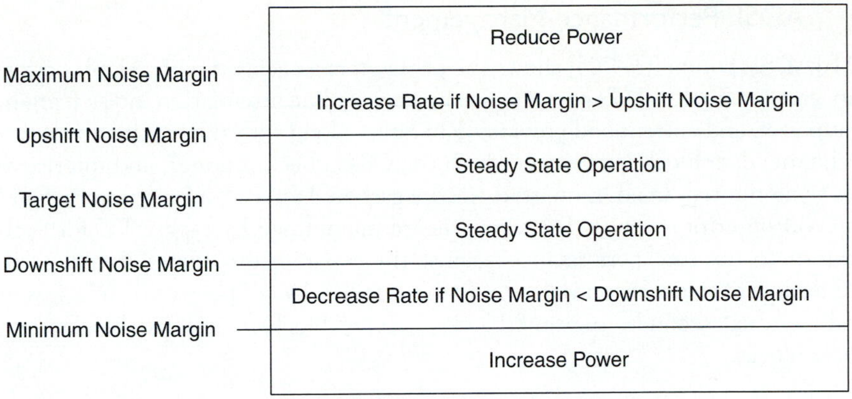

Figure 10.19   **Noise Margins**

10.7.3   ADSL Fault Management

Fault isolation parameters are shown in Table 10.10 [ADSL Forum TR-005], and should be displayed by the network management system. After the automatic indication of faults, ATU-C and ATU-R self-tests as specified in T1.413 could be used to assist in the diagnostics.

ADSL line status shows the current state of the line—whether it is operational or there is a loss of any of the frame, signal, power, or link parameters. It also indicates initialization errors. Alarms are generated when the preset counter reading exceeds 15 minutes on loss of signal, frame, power, link, and error-seconds.

Table 10.10   **ADSL Fault Management Parameters**

Parameter	Component	Line	Description
ADSL line status	ADSL line	Physical	Indicates operational status and various types of failures of the link
Alarms thresholds	ATU-C/R	Physical	Generates alarms on failures or crossing of thresholds
Unable to initialize ATU-R	ATU-C/R	Physical	Initialization failure of ATU-R from ATU-C
Rate change	ATU-C/R	Physical	Event generation upon rate changes when shift margins are crossed in both upstream and downstream

10.7.4   ADSL Performance Management

Table 10.11 [ADSL Forum TR-005] shows the parameters associated with ADSL performance management. Each ATU's performance in terms of line attenuation, noise margin, total output power, and current and previous data rate—along with the maximum attainable rate, channel data block length (on which the CRC check is done), and interleave delay—can be monitored. In addition, statistics are gathered for a 15-minute interval and a 1-day interval on error-seconds. Two counters are maintained by each ATU for each error condition to measure performance against these parameters. Error statistics are maintained for loss of signal seconds, loss of frame seconds, loss of power seconds, loss of link seconds, errored seconds, transmit blocks, receive blocks, corrected blocks, and uncorrectable blocks.

10.7.5   SNMP-Based ADSL Line MIB

Both SNMP-based [ADSL Forum TR-006] and CMIP-based [ADSL Forum TR-016] specifications have been developed for ADSL. We will discuss the updated SNMP-based MIB [Table 10.8, draft-ietf-adslmib-adsllinemib-09.txt] in this section. The ADSL SNMP MIB is presented in Figure 10.20. The *adslForum* is shown as a yet-to-be assigned node (xx) under *enterprises* (1.3.6.1.4.1). This MIB is still in draft form and is subject to change. However, we present it here to bring out some significant issues associated with defining SNMP MIB for ADSL.

Table 10.11   ADSL Performance Management Parameters

Parameter	Component	Line	Description
Line attenuation	ATU-C/R	Physical	Measured power loss in dB from transmitter to receiver ATU
Noise margin	ATU-C/R	Physical	Noise margin in dB of the ATU with respect to received signal
Total output power	ATU-C/R	Physical	Total output power from the modem
Maximum attainable rate	ATU-C/R	Physical	Maximum currently attainable data rate by the modem
Current rate	ATU-C/R	Fast/Interleave	Current transmit rate to which the modem is adapted
Previous rate	ATU-C/R	Fast/Interleave	Rate of the modem before the last change
Channel data block length	ATU-C/R	Fast/Interleave	Data block on which the CRC check is done
Interleave delay	ATU-C/R	Fast/Interleave	Transmit delay introduced by the interleaving process
Statistics	ATU-C/R	Physical Fast/ Interleave	15-minute/1-day failure statistics

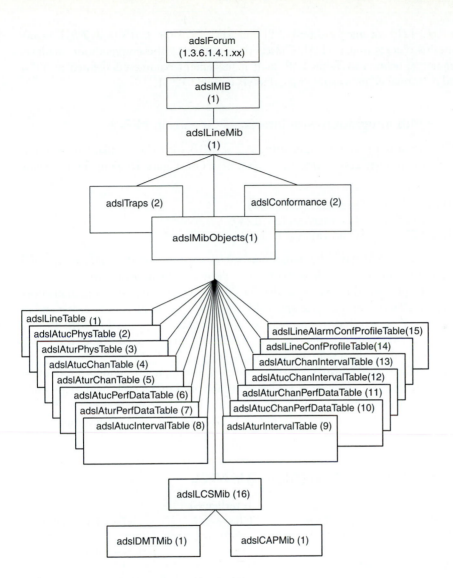

Figure 10.20   The ADSL SNMP MIB

Five nodes are defined under *adslLineMib* {adslForum.adslMIB 1}. Discussed in TR-006 are the details of *adslMibObjects* {adslLineMib 1}, which are shown in part in Figure 10.20. Two other nodes, *adslTestTypes* (4) and *adslTestCodes* (5) are not shown. Notice that there are complimentary physical and channel objects for the link. For example, there are the *adslAtucPhysTable* and the corresponding *adslAtucChanTable*. The former specifies a table in which each row contains the physical layer parameters associated with the link on an interface. The latter specifies a table in which each row contains parameters associated with a channel on that interface. The definitions of these interfaces are based on RFC 1213 for *interfaces* {mib-2 2} and RFC 1573 for *ifMIB* {mib-2 31}. Figure 10.20 contains objects under *adslMibObjects* that pertain to the configuration management parameters defined in Table 10.9, fault management parameters defined in Table 10.10, and performance management parameters in Table 10.11.

10.7.6   MIB Integration with Interfaces Groups in MIB-2

The ADSL Forum has proposed integrating ADSL MIB with the standard IETF Interfaces group MIB-II *interfaces*, ifMIB, and *transmission* (see Figure 10.9) in the following manner:

```
adslPhysIf ::= {transmission 94}
adslInterIf ::= {transmission 124}
adslFastIf ::= {transmission 125}
```

Each MIB branch would have the appropriate tables for that interface *ifType* type and would augment the interfaces table with *ifIndex* in *ifEntry* as the accessing index.

Table 10.12 presents the objects needed for ADSL, which are part of the mandatory *ifGeneralGroup* [RFC 1573]. They are applicable to the line generally, not to either end in particular. Normal means that the variable is used normally as specified in MIB-II. The designations i, j, and k indicate three arbitrary *ifIndex* values corresponding to the physical, interleaved, and fast entries for a single ADSL line.

The *ifStackTable* {ifMIB.ifMIBObjects 2}, which is the table containing information on the relationships between multiple sublayers of network interfaces, is used to associate the fast and interleaved channels with the physical line. Their relationship with each other and with higher layers is shown in Figure 10.21. The fast channel and interleaved

Table 10.12   Use of Interfaces [Objects] in ADSL

MIB Variable	Physical Line, i	Interleaved Channel, j	Fast Channel, k
ifDescr	Normal	Normal	Normal
ifType (IANA)	94	124	125
ifSpeed	ATU-C line Tx rate	ATU-C channel Tx rate	ATU-C channel Tx rate
ifPhyAddress	Null	Null	Null
ifAdminStatus	Normal	Normal	Normal
ifOperStatus	Normal	Normal	Normal
ifLastChange	Normal	Normal	Normal
ifLinkUpDownTrap-Enable	Normal (default: Enable)	Normal (default: Enable)	Normal (default: Enable)
ifConnectPresent	True	False	False
ifHighSpeed	Null	Null	Null

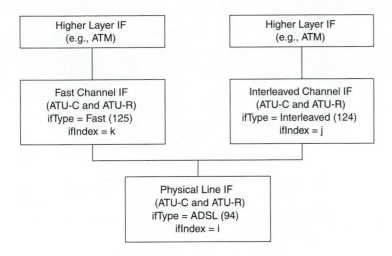

Figure 10.21 Relationship Among ADSL Entries

channel, which are at the same level, are stacked on the physical layer. They interface above with a higher layer—for example, the ATM if it is over the ADSL.

10.7.7 ADSL Configuration Profiles

In a typical configuration of the ADSL system, the access node shown in Figure 10.17 has hundreds of ATU-Cs. Provisioning all the parameters for each ATU-C individually would be impractical. Two MIB tables address this issue—one for the configuration profile and another for the performance profile. One of the tables is *adslLineConfProfile-Table {adslMibObjects.14}*, which contains the information on the ADSL line configuration shown in Table 10.9. One or more ADSL lines may be configured to share common profile information. Figure 10.22 shows the dynamic mode, MODE-I, configuration profile scheme. Profile tables are created and indexed 1–n. Each ADSL line interface, with the given value of *ifIndex*, shown in the range 1–x share the configuration profiles 1–n. Again, the three entries for the physical layer, the interleaved channel, and the fast channel for each ADSL line are represented by i, j, and k. Only the ADSL line entry contains the pointer to the configuration profile table. The *ifStack-Table* [RFC 1573] is used to link the channel entries and the corresponding physical layer to acquire the channel configuration parameters.

The second mode, denoted MODE-II, specifies the static mode for setting up the ADSL configuration profile. Each ADSL line interface has a static profile, as shown in Figure 10.23. Each ADSL line interface 1–x has its own configuration profile $i1$–ix, indicated by profile indices $i1$–$1x$.

The alarm profile can also be structured in a manner similar to the configuration profile. That is how the *adslLineAlarmConfProfileTable {adslMibObjects.15}* is designed.

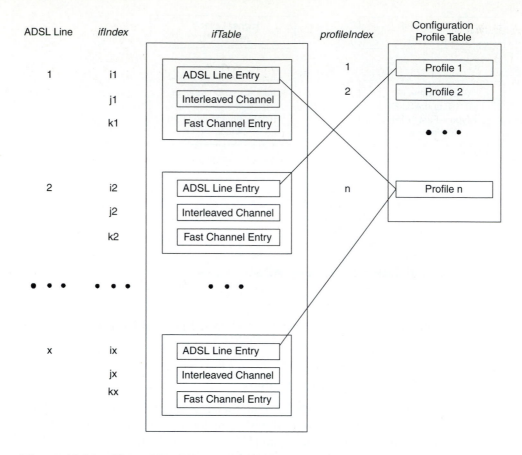

Figure 10.22   Use of Profiles in MODE-I (dynamic)

The line code specific (LCS) MIBs for the DMT and CAP ADSL lines are described in ASDL Forum documents TR-014 and TR-015. They are nodes under *adslLCSMib* {*adslMibObjects.16*}. The tables and other information follow a structure and organization similar to that of the ADSL line MIB shown in Figure 10.20 as {*adslMibObjects 1-15*}.

Figure 10.20 shows three nodes under *adslLineMib*. The first contains the ADSL MIB objects that we have discussed. The other two are traps and conformance groups. Of these two, only the traps group is specified in TR-006 [see Table 10.8, draft-ietf.adslmib-adsllinemib-05.txt] as of now. In addition to the generic traps, alarms are generated by the ATU-C and ATU-R for the loss of frame, loss of signal, loss of power, errored seconds threshold, data rate change, loss of link duration threshold, and ATU-C initialization failure. All are specified in the *adslTraps* MIB.

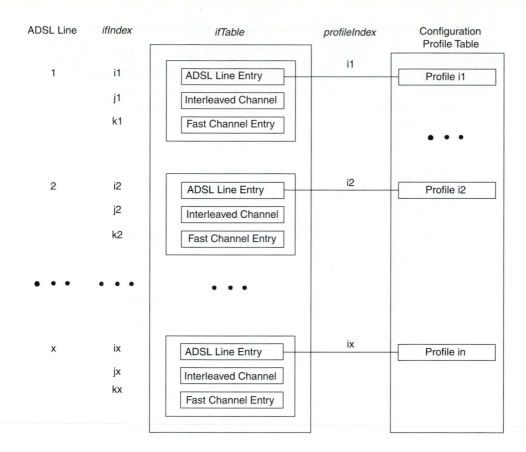

Figure 10.23   Use of Profiles in MODE-II (static)

Summary

In this chapter we described the emerging technology of broadband access networks and the management of some broadband access networks. Broadband access technology is primarily focused on bringing multimedia services to residences. We addressed three emerging technologies: hybrid fiber coaxial cable (HFC)/cable modem technology, Asymmetric Digital Subscriber Line (ADSL) technology, and wireless technology. Of the three, implementations of HFC and ADSL are the most advanced. Therefore we covered them in greater depth, both in terms of their technology and management.

HFC carries information from the head end to the customer premises via fiber-optic and coaxial cables. Cable modems are located at the customer site and a cable modem termination system at the head end. In most of the implementations transmission is two-way, although some one-way downstream and telephony-return upstream systems are still in use. Management of cable modems and facilities uses SNMP management, as has been developed by DOCSIS.

ADSL is the most widely implemented configuration of DSL in the United States. HDSL and VDSL configurations, which can handle greater bandwidths and quantities of information, are also being introduced. We covered ADSL technology and the early stages of ADSL management, as specified by the ADSL Forum.

Exercises

1. A half-duplex channel is carrying a 2-Mbps signal. Calculate the baud rate and bandwidth in Hz for the following modulated signals.

   a. ASK (binary)
   b. PSK (binary)
   c. QPSK
   d. 16 QAM

2. The downstream channel bandwidth for cable modem is 6 MHz. Calculate the bit rate if the signal is

   a. QPSK
   b. 64 QAM

3. The upstream bandwidth for a cable modem is user settable for the following bandwidths. Calculate the channel data rate that can be accommodated for each case for the QPSK modulation scheme.

   a. 200 kHz
   b. 800 kHz
   c. 1.6 MHz
   d. 3.2 MHz

4. Repeat Exercise 3 for 16-QAM modulation scheme.

5. Most of the cable modem manufacturers use quadrature amplitude modulation (QAM) for downstream and quadrature phase shift keying (QPSK) for upstream traffic on HFC. Explain why.

6. Cable modems on the coaxial part of the topology of the HFC configuration shown in Figure 10.3 are a tree structure. The cable modems with Ethernet stations resemble an Ethernet LAN. Contrast HFC coaxial broadband LAN with regular Ethernet LAN with regard to

   a. topology
   b. downstream protocol
   c. upstream protocol

7. Configure a cable modem for the following four upstream and one downstream channels using the *ifTable* and *ifStackTable*. Your answer should present two tables with only the relevant objects in the *ifTable* (index, *ifType*, and *ifSpeed*) and the *ifStackTable* (*ifStackHigherLayer* and *ifStackLowerLayer*). Refer to Table 10.3, draft-ietf-ipcdn-rf-interface-mib-07.txt, for additional information.

MAC Layer:	10 Mbps	Index 1
Downstream:	10 Mbps	Index 2
Upstream:	6 Mbps (video)	Index 3
	1.5 Mbps (data)	Index 4
	8.0 kbps (telephony)	Index 5
	8.0 kbps (telephony)	Index 6

The *ifType* for each subchannel is:

docsCableMacLayer	127
docsCableDownstream	128
docsCableUpstream	129

The upper layer above the MAC Layer and the lower layer below the upstream and downstream layers are designated 0 in the *ifStackTable*.

8. The *QoS* table for the cable modem in Exercise 7 is configured with the following priorities: video 4, data 1, and telephony 7. Complete Table 10.13 for the upstream channels. The "*" in the column heads stands for *docsIfQosProf*. Assume that the maximum bandwidth for all channels is 10 Mbps for both the up bandwidth and the down bandwidth and that the guaranteed bandwidth is the specified bandwidth for each subchannel.

Table 10.13   Exercise 8

*Index	*Priority	*MaxUpBandwidth	*GuarUpBandwidth	*MaxDownBandwidth

9. Telephone service providers are now offering ADSL service to homes, using the existing twisted-pair telephone wires. The signal can be carried up to a maximum of 1 MHz base band with a S/N (signal power/noise power in ratio) of 30 dB. S/N in decibels (dB) is defined as $10 \log_{10}$(signal power/noise power). Using MPEG-2 compression techniques, (a) a nonsports video channel can be broadcast at a 3-Mbps data rate and (b) a sports video channel can be broadcast at a 6-Mbps data rate. Shannon's limitation for information capacity for a channel is given by

$$\text{Maximum bit rate (bits/sec)} = B \log_2(1+S/N),$$

where S/N is a ratio (not in dB) and B is the bandwidth. How many video channels can simultaneously be transmitted over the line for the two cases?

10. For a capacity of 1.104 MHz, what is the maximum number of DMT subchannels (at 4.3125 kHz) that can be transmitted over an ADSL channel in both directions?

11. Each subchannel in a DMT is line coded with QAM.
    a. What is the baud rate in each subchannel?
    b. The bit rate in each channel can be dynamically varied according to the noise of the channel. The range of operation is 2 bits/baud to 15 bits/baud. What is the range of *n* in *n*-QAM modulation?

12. Estimate the number of voice subchannels available for the POTS shown in Figure 10.14 if DMT line coding is used.

13. A 50-Mbyte file is downloaded by using FTP from a host attached to a cable modem to a station on an ATU-R. Assume that full bandwidth for the channels is available and that the ADSL is a relatively noiseless channel.

14. Repeat Exercise 13 for a download in the opposite direction.

15. Four tables are involved in the configuration of ADSL line interface parameters: *ifTable* [RFC 1213], *ifStackTable* [RFC 1573], *adslLineTable*, and *adslLineConfProfileTable* [Table 10.8, draft-ietf-adslmib-adsllinemib-09.txt]. Identify the relationships among them and the links (index clause values) that relate them in a MODE-I configuration.

16. Repeat Exercise 14 for a MODE-II configuration profile.

17. Which tables are involved in the configuration of an alarm profile for an ADSL line? Refer to Table 10.8, draft-ietf-adslmib-adsllinemib-09.txt.

CHAPTER 11

Telecommunications Management Network

So far in this second part of the book, we have addressed the principles of network management associated with data communication networks and broadband communication networks. They carry information over long distances and are dependent to a large extent on a telecommunications network that has evolved from long-distance telephone networks. These networks are owned by public utility companies, which are either long-distance carriers, such as AT&T and British Telecom, or local exchange telephone companies, such as the Bell Operating Companies. In this chapter, we will discuss management of telecommunications networks and services provided by such public utility companies.

Management of telecommunications networks was developed by the International Standards Organization as part of ISO management. Hence it is strongly based on ISO network management, which in

429

turn is based on the Common Management Information Protocol (CMIP) and Common Management Information Services (CMIS). Although we address telecommunications network management without the requirement of CMIP/CMIS-based management, you may want to learn it. Toward that end, we cover OSI network and systems management in Appendix A.

In 1986, the International Telecommunications Union-Telecommunications (ITU-T) proposed the concept of a Telecommunications Management Network (TMN) to address the interoperability of multivendor equipment used by service providers and to define standard interfaces between service provider operations. In addition, it also extended the concept of management to include not only the management of networks and network elements, but also the service functions of the service providers. It was envisioned as a solution to the complex problems of operations, administration, maintenance, and provisioning (OAM&P) for telecommunications networks and services.

We will begin by describing TMN in Section 11.1 and then introduce operations systems, which form the building blocks of TMN, in Section 11.2. In Section 11.3 we address the concept of TMN. TMN is based on a large number of standards, which we delineate in Section 11.4. The TMN architecture is described in Section 11.5, TMN management service architecture is covered in Section 11.6, and an integrated view is presented in Section 11.7. We deal with implementation issues in Section 11.8, including the OMNIPoint program that was developed by the Network Management Forum.

11.1   Why TMN?

With the proliferation of SNMP management that has left OSI network management by the wayside, you may well ask why we are spending time discussing TMN. Historically, TMN was born of necessity to extend the private and proprietary—but well-developed network management systems—and make them interoperable. In the early days, the large telecommunications companies referred to the systems that maintained the network and network elements as operations systems. The ITU formed a working group in 1988 to develop a framework for telecommunications management networks. The ISO was also working on standardizing network management with the OSI management framework, using the Common Management Information Protocol (CMIP). With globalization and deregulation of the telecommunications industry, the need for interoperability of network management systems became urgent. Because of the slowness of the standards bodies, industry sponsored groups such as the Network Management Forum (NMF) began developing standards in parallel to speed up the process.

Unfortunately, the standards and frameworks developed were so complex and expensive to implement using the then available technology that TMN and OSI network management never got off the ground. However, TMN was the only framework that addressed not only the management of network elements, but also the management of networks, services, and business. The resolution of these issues is crucial in today's business environment with its numerous network and service providers (they are not one and the same as in the past). Customer service, quality, and cost form a three-legged stool [Adams EK & Willetts KJ]. Knock out one leg and the stool falls down.

Moreover, in today's corporate environment, buyouts and mergers demand interoperability and greater efficiency in business management. With work environments going into cyberspace and the Internet facilitating global communications that traverse multiple service providers' networks, the exchange of management information has become essential. For all these reasons, interest in the TMN architecture has been revived.

Although TMN was based on OSI management principles, it can be implemented—as is now being done—using other management technology, such as SNMP management. Organizations such as the NMF are promoting alternative approaches.

11.2   Operations Systems

The TMN is built on the foundation of the operations support system. This terminology, used in the telephone industry, has been changed to **operations system** (OS), as it is also used to control networks and network elements. For example, user configurable parameters in an ATM network can be controlled by the users via the M3 interface, as we showed in Chapter 10. The OS (don't confuse operations system with operating system) does not play a direct role in information transfer, but it does help in the **OAM&P** of network and information systems. Two examples of OSs used in the operation of telephone networks and services are the trunk test system and the traffic measurement system.

The trunk test system, illustrated in Figure 11.1, is used to monitor the loss and signal-to-noise ratio in the trunk transmission system. A trunk is a logical entity that links two switching offices. The transmission test system can seize any available cable facility between the switches while not carrying traffic. To ensure quality of service, losses and the signal-to-noise ratio on the trunks are measured at regular intervals by accessing from a centralized test center every trunk at each switching office. Any trunk that fails to meet minimum quality control criteria is removed from service. When a trunk is taken out of service as it is failing (but before it actually fails), the customer does not experience any degradation of service. The same test systems are used for on-demand tests to track troubles.

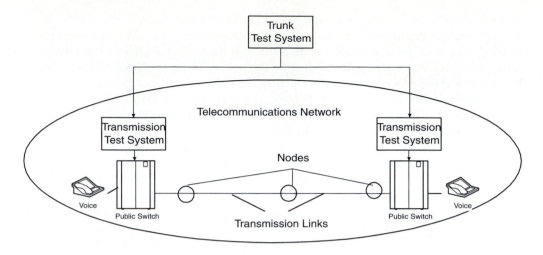

Figure 11.1   Operations System for Testing Transmission

Except during popular holidays such as Mother's Day, telephone service is almost always available for communication at any time of the day. Careful planning and implementation of facilities adequate to handle the traffic avoid delays and blockages. The traffic measurement operations system, illustrated in Figure 11.2, measures the busy status of switch appearance (access point) on each switch. As the number of busy paths increases, either owing to lack of access points or lack of adequate trunk facilities, additional equipment is added to avoid blockages.

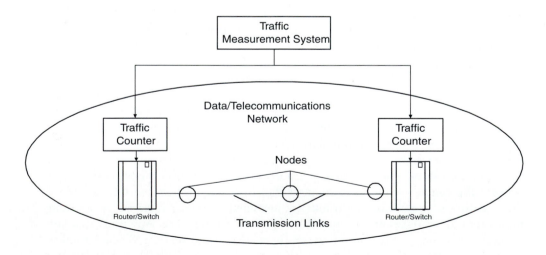

Figure 11.2   Operations System for Traffic Measurement

These two OS examples illustrate the essential role of operations systems in the OAM&P of telecommunications networks. They are part of telecommunications network management activities, and come under the performance management function of the OSI model defined in Chapter 3.

11.3   TMN Conceptual Model

From a TMN point of view, the network management system (NMS) is treated as an operations system, as shown in Figure 11.3. It manages the data communication and telecommunications network, although from a TMN perspective, we consider only the latter.

Recall that we differentiated the data, or computer, communication network from the telecommunications network in Chapter 1 (see Figure 1.4). Figure 11.3 extends Figure 1.4 to TMN, where operations systems, including the NMS, form a support network. It is logically a separate network, but it may or may not be physically separate, based on the implementation selected. The telecommunications network shown consists of switching exchange and transmission system network elements. It is primarily the WAN of communications. The switching systems contain both analog and digital switches. Hence the transmission systems are both analog and digital and include all transport facility modes, including twisted pair, coaxial, fiber optics, and wireless.

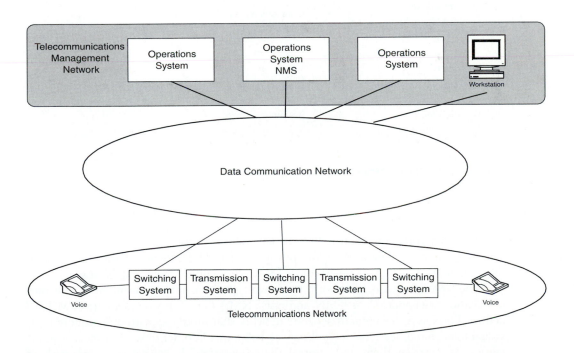

Figure 11.3   TMN Relationship to Data and Telecommunications Networks

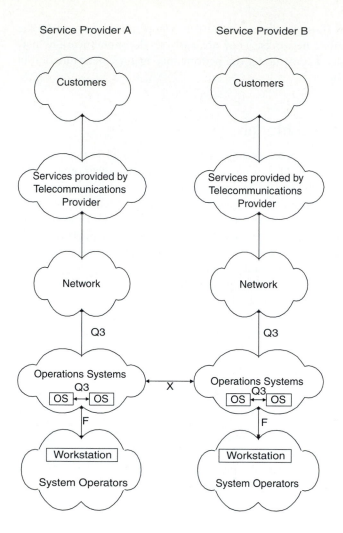

Figure 11.4   The TMN Conceptual Model

The data communication network components consist of LANs, bridges, routers, gateways, and hosts. The workstation shown in Figure 11.3 attached to the data communication network is a distinct element of TMN, whose interface we will discuss later.

The TMN shown is a network in its own right, not just management of telecommunications network. (It is TMN and not TNM.) ITU-T Recommendation M.3010 defines **TMN** as a conceptually separate network that interfaces with one or more individual telecommunications networks at several points in order to send or receive information to or from them and control their operation. It consists of a network of operations systems, including a network management system, which, as we stated earlier, is also considered an OS.

Figure 11.4 shows the TMN conceptual model. Notice that not only are networks and the OSs depicted, but also the services provided and the human resources required are included. The two columns in the figure show the identical components of two service providers, A and B. These components are workstations, OSs, networks, services, interfaces, operators of the systems, and customers who use the services.

Customers buy services from service providers, and providing quality customer services should be a key part of a service provider's business. Thus service management is an important consideration in the TMN model.

The service provider sells telecommunication services to customers, which means that the telecommunications network needs to be operated efficiently and economically. The OAM&P of a network needs to be automated as much as possible to decrease both response time and costs. Cost considerations lead to business management, which also is addressed by the TMN model.

Service management, business management, and network management can all be accomplished, partially or totally, by using the OSs shown in Figure 11.4. System operators interface with the OSs via workstations. The **interfaces associated with the various functions and services** have been standardized in the TMN model. Notice the three interfaces—**Q3**, **F**, and **X**. Q3 is the interface between an operations system and a network element. F is the interface between a workstation and an operations system. Information exchange between operations systems within a TMN is accomplished with the Q3 interface, whereas OSs belonging to different TMNs communicate via the X interface. We will discuss these interfaces in more detail in Section 11.5.

11.4   TMN Standards

The ITU-T is the standards body that developed TMN standards, based on the OSI framework. However, the scope of its work has been expanded recently and [Sidor DJ1] has published a good review of it. The scope of the TMN recommendations is summarized in Figure 11.5 [NMF]. The ITU-T document M.3000 presents a TMN tutorial. The other documents in the M series address TMN architecture, methodology, and terminology. The Q series addresses the Q interface (e.g., Q3) and G.733, the protocol profile for the Q interface. TMN documents are listed in Table 11.1, and some of the ITU-T study groups responsible for various TMN activities are listed in Table 11.2.

Supporting documents are also shown in Figure 11.5. Network traffic management, maintenance, and security are covered in the E and M series documents. The communication protocol, CMIP, and service elements, the Common Management Information Service Element (CMISE) are covered in the I and X series documents. The X series is discussed in Appendix A. Appendix A [NMF] contains a complete list of the series shown in Figure 11.5.

TMN standards define two types of telecommunications resources: managed and operations systems and the interfaces between them [Sidor DJ1, Sidor DJ2]. Architectural definitions of the communicating TMN entities, their roles in TMN, and their interrelationships are described in M.3010. The common services of OAM&P functions are defined in M.3200. The functions associated with individual TMN management services

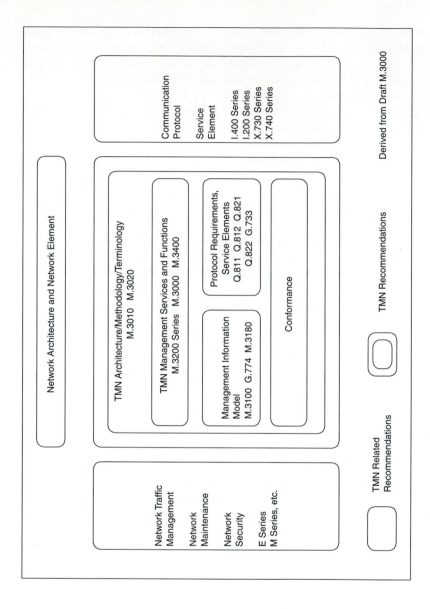

Figure 11.5   Scope of the TMN Recommendations [NMF]

Table 11.1   TMN Documents

M.3000	Tutorial Introduction to TMN (1992)
M.3010	Principles for TMN (1992)
M.3020	TMN Interface Specifications Methodology (1992)
M.3100	Generic Network Information Model for TMN (1995)
M.3180	Catalogue of TMN Managed Objects (1992)
M.3200	TMN Management Services Introduction (1996)
	TMN Management Services 1 (1996)
	TMN Management Services n (1996)
M.3300	F-interface Management Capabilities (1998)
M.3400	TMN Management Functions (1996)
Q.811	Protocols for the Q Interface—Lower Layer (1996)
Q.812	Protocols for the Q Interface—Upper Layer (1996)
G.773	Protocol Profiles for the Q Interface (1990)
G.774	SDH Network Information Model for TMN (1992–1996)

Table 11.2   ITU-T Study Groups

Study Group	Study Topic	Recommendation Series
SG 2	Traffic management	
SG 4	TMN architecture definition	M series
	Generic network model	
	F interface	
SG 7	OSI base management standards	X series
	Data network management and MHS	
	Customer network management	
SG 10	User interfaces	
	Specification languages	
SG 11	TMN protocols and profiles	Q series
	Switching and signaling system managed objects	
	ISDN management protocol and information models	
	Intelligent network management	
	UPT management	
SG 13	B-ISDN requirements (transport networks)	
	ISDN	
SG 14	Modem management	V series
SG 15	Transmission system management	G series
	Transmission system modeling	
	SDH, PDH, ATM management	
SG 18	Broadband management requirements	
JRM (JCG)	Overall coordination of TMN	

are described in the M.3200 series. A generic set of TMN management functions, based on OSI management functional areas, is specified in M.3400.

Management application messages and information models to support OAM&P requirements are specified in the M.3100 series and G.774. A generic network information model is defined in M.3100; it addresses common solutions for the management of network resources such as switching, transmission, and other technologies. OSI management services and Common Management Information Services (CMIS) are defined in X.710. TMN-related messages are contained in the information model defining application protocols and support objects, which are covered in Q-series documents.

Communication protocols are addressed in the respective protocol-specific standards documents. The G series addresses those not covered there but that are relevant to TMN, such as SDH network management in G.784.

11.5   TMN Architecture

TMN architecture is defined in M.3010, which describes the principles for a TMN. Three architectural perspectives are presented: functional, physical, and information, as shown in Figure 11.6. The **functional architecture** identifies functional modules, or blocks, in the TMN environment, including the reference points between them, and specifies interface requirements. The **physical architecture** defines the physical blocks and interfaces between them. The **information architecture** deals with the information exchange between managed objects and management systems, using a distributed object-oriented approach. We will look at each of these three perspectives in the next three subsections. You may also obtain more details from [ITU-T, M.3010, NMF, Cohen RS, Raman LG, Sidor DJ2].

11.5.1   Functional Architecture

TMN Recommendation M.3010 defines TMN architecture as five function blocks: operations systems, network element, mediation, workstation, and Q adapter, as shown in Figure 11.7. Each function block contains a set of functions, and there are multiple instances of each function. Thus, for example, many OSs may be performing various operational functions in the operations systems' function block. Communication between function

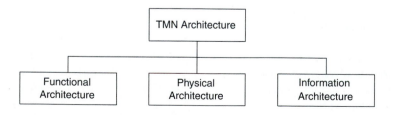

Figure 11.6   TMN Architecture

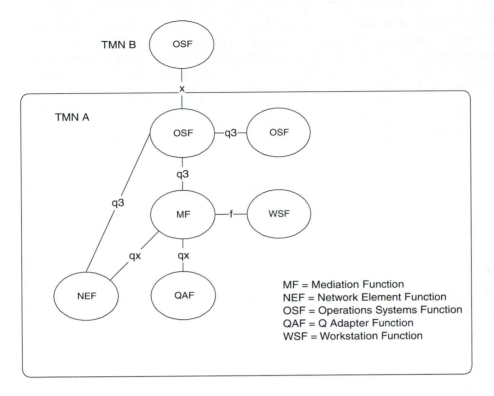

Figure 11.7   TMN Functional Architecture

blocks is itself a function, but not a function block, and is defined as the **TMN data communication function** (DCF), which supports the standard transport protocols.

The **TMN operations systems function** (OSF) is implemented in operations systems. As we demonstrated in Section 11.2, operations systems, such as the network trunk test system OS and traffic measurement OS, help monitor, manage, and control telecommunications networks and services. Network management, both as manager and agent, is also considered to be an OS. This system includes the MIB in Internet management and the naming tree in OSI management as a function of the OSF.

The **TMN network element function** (NEF) is concerned with managed network elements. The network elements themselves are not part of TMN, but are supported by TMN over the standard interfaces. Network elements include hardware, software, and systems such as hubs, routers, switches, processes, and the like. The network management agent and the associated MIB are part of the NEF. Network elements providing information for management (e.g., packets dropped, collision rate, etc.) are considered to be part of TMN (i.e., NEF).

The **TMN mediation function** (MF) block addresses the operations performed on the information content passing between the network elements and OSs. Such operations include filtering, store and forward, protocol conversion, and threshold detection. A physical entity in which the MF is implemented can be shared between multiple OSs and network elements. For example, a remote monitoring device (RMON) can monitor a remote LAN on various parameters, such as statistics on users, protocols, and packet loss, and report the raw or analyzed data to accounting and performance management operations systems. In this situation, the RMON device acts as a mediation device, performing mediation function between the network elements on the remote LAN and the OSs (or NMSs).

The **TMN workstation function** (WSF) provides an interface between human personnel and TMN activities. More specifically, it addresses the presentation aspect of the system. The function that converts machine readable information to human interpretable format in the presentation function belongs in one of the other three function blocks: the OSF, MF, or Q adapter function (explained later). Putting it there would cover presentation functions such as the Graphical User Interface (GUI) and the human–machine interface of workstations.

Communication among the four functional blocks—OSF, WSF, MF, and NEF—is assumed to be standardized. Of course, that is far from the reality of the situation. Therefore, in order to accommodate legacy functionality as part of TMN, a **TMN Q adapter function** (QAF) has been defined. It is somewhat similar to a proxy server in SNMP management, where non-SNMP network elements are managed by an SNMP manager via a proxy server. Thus TMN noncompliant devices are connected to a TMN compliant system/network with a Q-adapter interface.

Each function in the function block can be considered as providing a service and each function in the service block as providing a set of services. An example is a security management application function that is either part of an OS or a stand-alone OS. As shown in Figure A.13, Appendix A, several security system management functions (e.g., alarm reporting, audit trail, etc.) are associated with overall security. In fact, all five management functional areas—configuration, fault, performance, security, and accounting—residing in a network management system would belong to OSF.

Function blocks are designed to be nonoverlapping. However, that does not keep different function blocks from using some of the same functions. For example, the MIB is a function used by several function blocks that enables them to exchange management information. Another example is the scheduling function shown in Figure A.13. It can be used in a performance management application to gather traffic statistics, in a configuration system to discover and delete network elements, and in a fault management system to gather errored-seconds on unstable elements.

Notice that the function blocks in Figure 11.7 are connected with interfaces denoted by x, q3, qx, and f. They are called **TMN service interfaces**, or simply **TMN interfaces**. The TMN interface between function blocks, shown in Figure 11.8, is called a **TMN reference point**. A reference point can be considered to be a conceptual point of information exchange between function blocks. An interface between a management agent embedded in a network element and a network management system is a q3 reference point. When a network management system automatically creates a trouble ticket in a trouble tracking system in another domain (TMN B), it is communicating via an x reference point. When a Web browser interfaces with a Web-based management system, it is accessing an f reference point. When a TMN noncompliant switch is managed by a TMN compliant operations system using a Q adapter interface, it is interfacing via a qx interface.

Figure 11.8   TMN Reference Point

Summarizing, some examples of network devices implementing TMN functional components are operations systems, a network management system, applications, a network element, a management network agent, a management information base, an RMON, a proxy server, a GUI, and a Web browser. Recall that a data communication function (e.g., SNMP, CMIP, or CORBA) is not included here.

The information exchange across TMN reference points can be classified as q-class, f-class, and x-class. The **q-class reference point** interfaces with a management application function. In Figure 11.7, the q-class reference point includes both q3-class and qx-class TMN reference points. An **f-class TMN reference point** is an interface between the workstation function block and any other function block in TMN. An **x-class TMN reference point** is an interface between two OS function blocks belonging to two different TMNs. The interface information pertains to similar functionalities.

TMN reference points are designated by the lowercase letters q, f, and x. The associated physical interfaces are identified by the uppercase letters Q, F, and X.

11.5.2   Physical Architecture

ITU-T recommendation M.3010 presenting a model for the TMN physical architecture is illustrated in Figure 11.9. A TMN physical block could be an embodiment of one or more blocks, besides its equivalent function block. For example, an OS could have its operation function as well as a mediation device, which filters information. Five types of physical blocks represent the five functions discussed in Section 11.5.1, excluding the TMN data communication function.

Operations systems are embodiments of the TMN operations system function. This function is connected to the mediation device, placing the mediation function on a data communication network. The data communication network is the physical implementation of the data communication function, which, to repeat, is not a function block but a TMN function, DCF. The network elements, Q adapter, and workstations reflect their respective TMN functions.

The **Q**, **F**, and **X TMN interfaces** between the physical devices are also shown in Figure 11.9, representing the physical implementation of the respective TMN reference points. The Q3 interface is used between the OS and an NE or a QA. The Qx interface is used between an MD and a QA or an NE. An example is an MD being a proxy server communicating with legacy systems via a QA interface. The F interface is implemented to connect a workstation to TMN. The X interface is used between OSs belonging to two different TMNs.

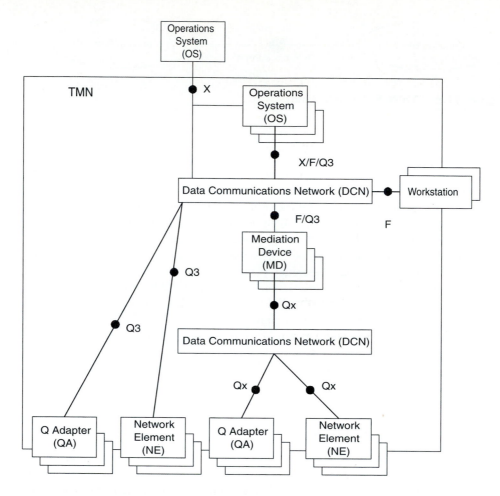

Figure 11.9   TMN Physical Architecture

11.5.3   Information Architecture

The TMN information architecture initially adopted the OSI management information architecture, CMIP/CMIS, defined in the ITU-T X.700 series and discussed in Appendix A. However, with the wide acceptance of the Internet SNMP, which we covered extensively in earlier chapters, deployment of both models in TMNs is underway. We have covered both management models in this book. To review briefly, the OSI information model is object oriented, and the SNMP model is scalar. Both models are based on the dual roles that entities play in information exchange: manager and agent. Figure 11.10 shows the information exchange between the two types of entities. The manager performs

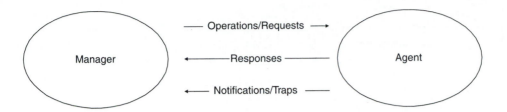

Figure 11.10   TMN Information Architecture

operations or makes requests from an agent. The agent executes the operations on the network elements that it is managing and sends responses to the manager. The agent also sends unsolicited messages to the manager indicating alarm events.

Information models specified by SNMP and OSI management deal with the management of network elements. The TMN information model has been used with specific technologies, such as ATM and SDH/SONET, which we covered in Chapter 9.

The information architecture should transport information reliably across functional boundaries. There are two types of **communication services** between interfaces: **interactive** and **file-oriented**. We will discuss the interactive service in Appendix A. It is supported in OSI by the Common Management Information Service Element (CMISE) over the Remote Operations Service Element (ROSE). In the Internet distributed computing environment, this function is handled by the remote procedure call (RPC). The file-oriented category is supported by File Transfer Access Management (FTAM) in OSI [Raman LG] and on the Internet by the File Transfer Protocol (FTP). In the OSI model, the Association Control Services Element (ACSE) is needed to establish, release, and abort application associations. In the Internet model, it is integrated into the RPC presentation service. More details on this subject are presented in [Piscitello DM & Chapin AL].

11.6   TMN Management Service Architecture

Another functional model of TMN is based on the services provided in a TMN environment. The TMN services are grouped and presented as TMN layered architecture, as shown in Figure 11.11 [ITU-T, M.3400]. This layered architecture is not in the strictest sense the same as protocol layered architecture because communication can occur between nonadjacent layers.

The lowest layer is the **network element layer**, comprising network elements, such as switches, routers, bridges, and transmission facilities. The second layer is the **element**

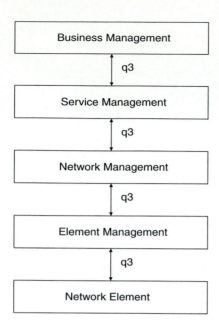

Figure 11.11   TMN Service Architecture

management layer, which manages the network elements. The third layer is the **network management layer**, which manages the network. The network management functions in this layer include bandwidth, performance, quality of service, end-to-end flow control, and network congestion control. (We presented these three layers in relationship to ATM management in Figure 9.20.) The network element layer and network element management layer are vendor dependent, whereas the network management layer is not.

The **service management layer** is concerned with managing the services provided by a network service provider to customers or to other network service providers. They include services such as billing, order processing, complaints, and trouble ticket handling. The top layer is the business management layer. It is concerned with managing the operations of a communications business, including fiscal considerations, human resource needs, project management, and customer needs and satisfaction.

The TMN reference point between the various service layers is q3. It is the standard interface between the operations system, network element, and mediation functions previously shown in Figure 11.7.

TMN management services are classified by **OSI system management functional area**. These areas are the five **OSI application functions** described in Chapter 3: configuration management, fault management, performance management, security management, and accounting management. The TMN management services and the system management functional areas are presented in Figure 11.12.

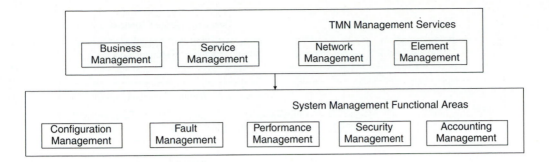

Figure 11.12   TMN Management Services and Management Functional Areas

11.7   An Integrated View of TMN

Let us now look at the overall picture of how the various aspects of the TMN architecture fit together. A representation of this view is shown in Figure 11.13.

The four TMN management services—business, service, network, and element—are at the top of the hierarchy. They invoke the system management functions defined as the five components comprising the system management functional areas: configuration, fault, performance, security, and accounting.

The management applications in the system functional areas perform either system management functions or TMN functions. The TMN function blocks OSF, WSF, NEF, MF, and QAF consist of TMN functional components such as the NMF and MIB. The data communication function (DCF), although not part of the TMN function blocks, is included for completeness.

The system management functions include object management and alarm management. We will discuss system management functions in Appendix A. In Figure 11.13, we could have embedded the system management functions in TMN function blocks and TMN functional components, but we show them separately in order to present a non-OSI environment. Again, in the past TMN was exclusively associated with the OSI environment and only recently has it been considered for use in the popular SNMP environment.

System management functions and TMN functions invoke the primitive services. Figure 11.13 also shows the OSI primitive services of M-GET, M-SET, and so on. Equivalent SNMP services are GET-REQUEST, SET-REQUEST, and so on.

The TMN environment is a distributed environment. The applications communicate remotely with the communication transport service by means of the RPC. In the OSI model, the RPC is accomplished with ROSE and ACSE. The former does the remote operation and the latter establishes and releases the application association. In the SNMP management model, the remote operation is accomplished by using the RPC and TCP/IP.

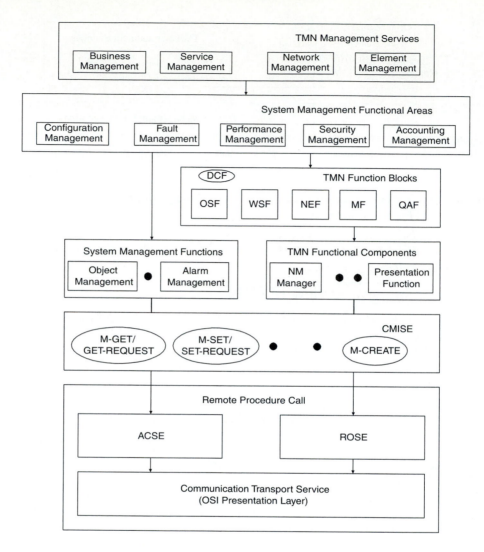

Figure 11.13   TMN Services and Functions

11.8   Implementation Issues

Although the TMN concept was proposed in the early 1980s, it has not been widely accepted for several reasons [Glitho & Hayes-1, Raman LG1]. These reasons include heavy dependence on exclusive OSI network management, high resource requirements, technical complexity, lack of complete standards, the popularity and simplicity of SNMP management, and implementation difficulties.

Computer technology and the computer industry were not quite ready in the 1980s to implement (even partially) object-oriented OSI network management because of its complexity. The object-oriented and layered OSI protocol stack demanded processor resources that were beyond the capability of the technology at that time. However, current hardware resources can handle such demands. OSI toolkits are currently available both commercially and as freeware. As a result of these advances, products have been developed recently for trouble ticket administration (TMN X interface) and the integrated digital loop carrier (TMN Q3 interface) [Raman LG1].

The object-oriented technology in the 1980s—for example, the distributed computing environment (DCE) and common object request broker architecture (CORBA)—was not at the same level as it is today. Recent advances in hardware and technology have revived work on the distributed management environment [Autrata M & Strutt C], using an object-oriented approach.

Even with the resources and toolkits now available, we cannot avoid the legacy systems interfacing with TMN [Glitho & Hayes-2]. Dealing with these systems necessitates using either the TMN Q adaptation (TMN QA) interface or adding a new Q (TMN Q3) interface. The choice between the two depends on the cost of each approach for achieving adequate and efficient OAM&P of a telecommunications network.

Two forums have actively promoted implementation of TMN: the ATM Forum and NMF (formerly known as the Network Management Forum). We covered the ATM Forum's application for ATM in Chapter 9. We will now briefly consider NMF's activities.

Implementation Using OMNIPoint.   An example of TMN architecture realization is presented in Figure 11.14 [NMF]. Figure 11.14(a) shows the TMN logical layered architecture and Figure 11.14(b) shows a physical realization of it. Each layer consists of several management systems that provide the various services. The layered architecture shows the TMN q3 reference points, and the physical realization shows the corresponding Q3 interfaces.

The NMF is an industry-sponsored forum. It has developed a program called the Open Management Interoperability Point (OMNIPoint). The objective is to help companies implement management standards for a broad range of suppliers' equipment. It has developed documents that specify mapping between the Internet and OSI standards to help TMN implementation in a hybrid management environment [NMF].

Summary

In this chapter we presented a brief introduction to the complex subject of the Telecommunications Management Network (TMN). Although it was proposed by ITU-T in the early 1980s, this approach is just now becoming a reality because of advances in technology and the availability of OSI standards and toolkits.

We defined and demonstrated the role of operations systems (OSs) in operation, administration, maintenance, and provisioning (OAM&P), as currently being implemented by

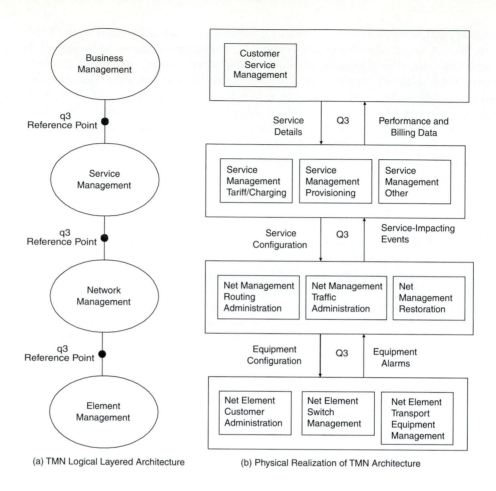

(a) TMN Logical Layered Architecture   (b) Physical Realization of TMN Architecture

Figure 11.14   An Example of TMN Realization [NMF]

telecommunications service providers. The network management system (NMS) is considered to be an OS in the TMN environment.

We defined the TMN concept as customers, services provided by telecommunications service providers, networks, operations systems, and system operators. Owing to the many services provided by a multitude of service providers using a variety of vendor equipment, TMN utilizes reference points between the components that define standard service interfaces. The original TMN proposal was based exclusively on OSI standards.

We presented three views of TMN architecture: functional, physical, and information. TMN functional architecture comprises five functions: operations system function (OSF), network element function (NEF), mediation function (MF), Q adapter function (QAF), and workstation function (WSF). The interface between them is defined by three TMN reference points: f, q3/qx, and x.

TMN physical architecture is the physical manifestation of the functional architecture. The functions are implemented by means of operations systems, mediation devices, network elements, Q adapter functions interfacing with non-TMN legacy systems, and workstations. The information architecture is the OSI management information architecture, CMIP/CMIS. The data communication function is a distributed function that carries the information between function blocks via network management operations, responses, and notifications.

TMN service architecture consists of four layers of management and a fifth layer of network elements. The four layers of management are element management, network management, service management, and business management. We presented an integrated view of the components, showing how they all fit together to form the TMN environment.

We discussed the issues and recent activities in implementing TMN, touching on recent advances in technology and tools that have helped implementation of TMN. The roles played by two forums—the ATM Forum and the NMF—were highlighted.

Exercises

1. Shannon's channel capacity theorem provides the following relationship for maximum channel capacity (bits per second), in terms of bandwidth B and signal-to-noise ratio S/N.

$$C = B \log_2(1+S/N).$$

   The S/N in decibels (dB) is related to S/N as a power ratio by

   $$S/N \text{ in dB} = 10(\log_{10}S/N).$$

   The transmission operations system described in Figure 11.1 monitors the S/N of a telephone channel with a 3-kHz bandwidth and a channel capacity of 30 kbps. When S/N decreases by 3 dB, the operations system issues a warning alarm and the telephone trunk facility is taken out of service if S/N drops by 6 dB. Calculate the channel capacity in bps at (a) the warning threshold and (b) the out-of-service limit, keeping the same 3-kHz bandwidth for the telephone channel.

2. Design a traffic measurement operations system that monitors the packet traffic at layer-2 on the nodes shown in Figure 11.2. Assume that all traffic is made up of unicast packets and that the links and nodes are such that the packets dropped at any node are due primarily to traffic overload on the node. The system measures the incoming and outgoing packets handled by the data link layer as it interfaces with the physical and network layers. Assume that the system permits the user to set the thresholds for action based on percent packet loss.

   a. What MIB objects would you monitor?
   b. Express the threshold parameters for congestion (percent packet loss) on the node as a function of the measured parameters.

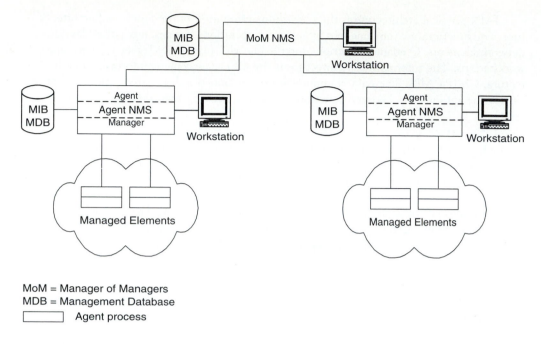

MoM = Manager of Managers
MDB = Management Database
☐ Agent process

Figure 11.15   Exercise 3

3. Figure 11.15 shows a network management environment consisting of an MoM NMS, several agent NMSs that manage individual network domains, and managed network elements. Identify the TMN functions performed by

   a. MoM NMS
   b. agent NMS
   c. managed elements

4. A proxy server configuration (see Figure 6.46) is used to manage SNMPv1 network elements by an SNMPv2 network management system.

   a. What TMN function does a proxy server play in an NMS environment?
   b. Identify the interfaces of the proxy server with the network manager and network elements.

5. In Figure 11.15, identify all

   a. TMN reference points
   b. TMN interfaces

6. Associate the M1–M5 interfaces in ATM management (Figures 11.9 and 11.10) with TMN reference points and TMN service interfaces.

7. CMISE services are listed in Table A.3. Map these services, wherever possible, to SNMPv1 services.

8. Repeat Exercise 7, comparing CMISE and SNMPv2 services.

9. TMN can be applied to ATM switch management by using either SNMP or CMIP specifications. Research the ATM Forum specifications referenced in Table 9.3 and identify the OBJECT IDENTIFIERS for the two modules, *atmfM4CmipNEView* and *atmfM4SnmpView*.

10. ATM objects are defined under the node *informationModule(0)*, which is a subclass of *atmfCmipNEView*. Five managed object classes are defined under the *informationModule*: the *atmfM4ObjectClass*, *atmfM4Package*, *atmfM4Attribute*, *atmfM4NameBinding*, and *atmfM4Action*. Draw a naming tree for these classes, explicitly identifying the *ObjectID*.

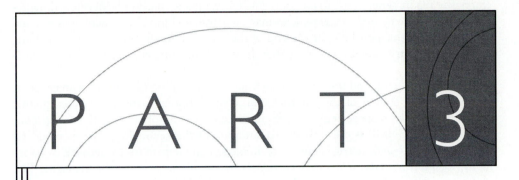

PART 3

Management Tools, Systems, and Applications

In Part I we dealt with background and in Part II laid the foundations for SNMP management, broadband management, and TMN. In Part III we will address management tools, systems, and applications.

Chapter 12 is devoted to networking tools, management tools, and management systems. You will learn about some basic networking tools that can be of immense help in the day-to-day operations of a network. SNMP command tools are convenient and are part of operating systems. They can be used for network management even without having a network management system. After describing these tools, we will cover a range of network management systems, ranging from low-end to high-end solutions. We will cover in more detail mid-range enterprise network management systems and present examples of commercial systems that are in widespread use.

Applications are the focus of Chapter 13. We will first describe how the tools and systems discussed in Chapter 12 are used for configuration, fault, and performance management. We will then go into more depth on correlation technology as a way of localizing and diagnosing problems that cause multiple alarms. Six correlation techniques applicable to correlation technology are discussed. Information security is a very important application in network and system management. Besides basic SNMP security management, you will learn about firewalls and the role of cryptography in authentication and authorization. We will then cover authentication systems and secure messaging systems, including e-mail. Accounting and reporting are important to the efficient operation of any enterprise, but especially to those providing information technology services. We will emphasize report generation. To use tools efficiently, policies need to be developed, established, and implemented. Some policies may be automated in management systems, and we will address this possibility at the end of the chapter. Finally, we cover the evolving service-level management technology that deals with meeting customer needs and quality of service.

We end this part, and the book, by looking into the future of network management. With the rapid growth of the Internet and Web technology, the industry is moving toward Web-based management. A Web interface to a traditional network management system, such as SNMP, is the early implementation of this technology. We then address embedded Web-based management. A technology complementary to network management, Desktop Management Interface (DMI), has come into vogue for managing PCs and servers. Web-Based Enterprise Management (WBEM) is currently under development by the Desktop Management Task Force (DMTF). It is attempting to integrate various network management protocols under the umbrella of an object-oriented Web-based system. Microsoft's Common Information Model (CIM) is being used as the integrating framework. An alternative to WBEM is the Java Management Extensions™ (JMX), which is a distributed embedded Web-based technology and is based on the Java Dynamic Management Kit™. It is an extension of the Java language classes for network management. We will introduce you to these two future Web-based technologies in Chapter 14. We will also address the Java-based solution that is under development for management of storage area networks.

CHAPTER 12

Network Management Tools and Systems

In this chapter we will describe the tools and systems used to monitor and manage a network. The available tools help people who work on and manage networks and those who are network users. With the proliferation of Internet and Web sites, a *user* is anyone who owns a personal computer or workstation and is connected to an external data communication network. You have already used some of these tools in the exercises in Chapter 1.

In the early part of Section 12.1 we cover the general-purpose tools used in daily network maintenance. Classification of the various tools that are available is presented in Section 12.1.1. Digital data in the physical layer are affected by noise in the transmission channel. We cover tools to measure the bit error rate in Section 12.1.2. Numerous software tools exist for obtaining information on

455

networks and for monitoring the status of nodes and hosts, traffic analysis, and route tracing. We present them in Section 12.1.3, using a practical approach to network management without having to rely on sophisticated management systems.

As you learned in Part II, network management strongly depends on standards, especially the SNMP with its MIB. There are Internet standard MIBs, as well as MIBs defined by other forums and private vendors. In Section 12.1.4 we describe the SNMP tools used to obtain the MIB view of a network component and to discover managed objects and their characteristics.

A protocol analyzer analyzes data packets in all layers of the OSI Reference Model. It is used as a diagnostic tool and to gather network statistics. In Section 12.1.5 we describe the protocol analyzer as a diagnostic tool.

In Section 12.2 we discuss the use of the protocol analyzer as a system tool for gathering statistics. Data can be collected on traffic load, performance, applications, protocols, and errors, using RMON and the protocol analyzer. These results are used to analyze trends in network traffic and usage. We also describe a public domain software toolkit to measure live traffic statistics.

The management of all the functions associated with an enterprise has been continuously evolving. Enterprise management covers a spectrum of functions, as identified in our discussion of TMN concepts in Chapter 11. The history of enterprise management systems is recounted in Section 12.3.

In Section 12.4 we describe the functional components of the network management system. We then discuss how multiple network management systems are configured for managing an enterprise network. Basic requirements are specified for a manager of managers network management system for enterprise use. In Section 12.5, we describe three commercially popular NMSs.

In addition to managing a network, resources on the network also need to be monitored and managed. For example, when a processor on a server is used excessively, we may want to add another server to distribute the load. In Section 12.6 we address system management.

How can all aspects of enterprise management be taken into consideration? No single product or vendor can provide a system that would answer this question. However, company and product line mergers are providing some integrated enterprise management solutions, which we explore in Section 12.7.

12.1   Network Management Tools

The catalog of network management tools is extensive, and we cannot do justice to the full range of these tools here. They are necessary for troubleshooting of problems in networks and supplement system tools that detect problems or failures and notify the various alarms. In this section, we will consider the tools used daily by network managers and operators to conduct their activities. Some of these tools can also be utilized by network users in their normal use of network services.

12.1.1   Tools Catalog

A tools catalog listing the tools available in 1993 was generated by the IETF Working Group on Network Operations Center tools (NOCtools) [RFC 1470]. Updates are available via the Web sources news:comp.networks.noctools and ftp://wuarchive.wustl.edu/doc/noctools. Figure 12.1 shows the categories of tools, with examples, listed in RFC 1470. In the examples given, the catalog's keywords tersely characterize the tools in each of the five classifications: (1) the tool's functional role in management, (2) the network resource or component managed, (3) the mechanism or method that a tool uses to perform its function, (4) the tool's operating system or hardware environment, and (5) how the product can be acquired. An entity is listed with multiple keywords in different categories.

Under the functional category, the keyword Alarm identifies a reporting/logging tool that can be triggered by specific events within a network, such as the NetMetrix™ Protocol analyzer. The keyword Manager represents a distributed network management system or system component, such as the MIB Manager™ from Empire Technologies. The keyword Security indicates a tool for analyzing or reducing threats to security, such as SNMP Libraries and Utilities™ from SNMP Research. Traffic is the keyword for the tool that monitors packet flow, such as *tcpdump*.

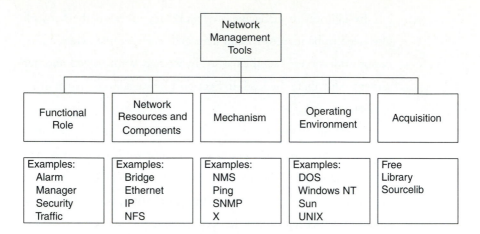

Figure 12.1   NOC Tool Categories [RFC 1470]

Under the Network Resources and Components category, the keyword Bridge identifies a tool for controlling or monitoring LAN bridges, such as XNETMON™ from SNMP Research. The keyword Ethernet indicates a tool for controlling or monitoring network components on Ethernet LANs—for example, manipulating the Address Resolution Protocol (ARP). The keyword IP represents a tool for controlling or monitoring implementations of the TCP/IP protocol suite or network components that use it, for example, *ARP*. The keyword NFS indicates a network file system debugging tool, such as *etherfind* or *tcpdump*.

Under the category of Mechanism, NMS is the keyword describing a tool that is a component of a Network Management System. Ping is the keyword for a tool that sends packet probes, such as ICMP echo messages. SNMP is the keyword that describes a network management system or component based on SNMP. The keyword X indicates a tool that uses X-Windows.

The Operating Environment classification covers both hardware and software platforms. Each keyword under this category identifies an operating system or a hardware platform tool. For example, UNIX™ and Microsoft Windows NT™ are two popular platforms for network management systems.

The Acquisition category defines the characteristics of product availability. The Free keyword indicates that a tool is available at no charge, such as freeware that can be downloaded from a public source. The keyword Library describes a tool packaged with either an Application Programming Interface (API) or object-level subroutines that may be loaded with programs. Sourcelib is the keyword for a collection of source code (subroutines) from which developers may construct other tools.

Tables 12.1–12.4 [RFC 1470] give the keywords for tools under the first four categories. The list is not current, but is a good start toward understanding the classification system. The Microsoft operating systems Windows 95™ and Windows NT have been added to the original RFC 1470 table. The Acquisition category has only the three entries already described.

Table 12.1   Functional Role of Management Tools

Function	Description
Alarm	A reporting/logging tool that can be triggered by specific events with a network
Analyzer	A traffic monitoring tool that reconstructs and interprets protocol messages that span several packets
Benchmark	A tool used to evaluate the performance of network components
Control	A tool that can change the state or status of a remote network resource
Debugger	A tool that, by generating arbitrary packets and monitoring traffic, can drive a remote network component to various states and record its responses
Generator	A traffic generation tool
Manager	A distributed network management system or system component
Map	A tool that can discover and report a system's topology or configuration
Reference	A tool for documenting MIB structure or system configuration
Routing	A packet route discovery tool
Security	A tool for analyzing or reducing threats to security
Status	A tool that remotely tracks the status of network components
Traffic	A tool that monitors packet flow

Table 12.2   Resources and Components Managed by Tools

Resource/ Component	Description
Bridge	A tool for controlling or monitoring LAN bridges
CHAOS	A tool for controlling or monitoring implementations of the CHAOS protocol suite or network components that use it
DECnet	A tool for controlling or monitoring implementations of the DECnet protocol suite or network components that use it
DNS	A domain name system debugging tool
Ethernet	A tool for controlling or monitoring network components on Ethernet LANs
FDDI	A tool for controlling or monitoring network components on FDDI LANs or WANs
IP	A tool for controlling or monitoring implementations of the TCP/IP protocol suite or network components that use it
OSI	A tool for controlling or monitoring implementations of the OSI protocol suite or network components that use it
NFS	A Network File System debugging tool
Ring	A tool for controlling or monitoring network components on token ring LANs
SMTP	An SMTP debugging tool
Star	A tool for controlling or monitoring network components on StarLANs

Table 12.3   Mechanism Used in Management Tool

Mechanism	Description
CMIS	A network management system or component based on the Common Management Information System and Protocol (CMIS/CMIP)
Curses	A tool that uses the "curses" tty interface package
Eavesdrop	A tool that silently monitors communications media (e.g., by putting an Ethernet interface into "promiscuous" mode)
NMS	The tool is a component of or queries a Network Management System
Ping	A tool that sends packet probes such as ICMP echo messages; to help distinguish tools, we do not consider NMS queries or protocol spoofing as probes
Proprietary	A distributed tool that uses proprietary communications techniques to link its components
RMON	A tool that employs the RMON extensions to SNMP
SNMP	A Network Management System or component based on the Simple Network Management Protocol (SNMP)
Spoof	A tool that tests operation of remote protocol modules by peer-level message exchange
X	A tool that uses X-Windows

Table 12.4   Keywords Used for Operating Environment (Modified)

Operating Environment	Description
DOS	A tool that runs under MS-DOS
HP	A tool that runs on Hewlett-Packard systems
Linux/FreeBSD	A tool that runs under Linux/FreeBSD operating systems
Macintosh	A tool that runs on Macintosh personal computers
OS/2	A tool that runs under the OS/2 operating system
Standalone	An integrated hardware/software tool that requires only a network interface for operation
Sun	A tool that runs on Sun Microsystems platforms (Solaris 1.x/SunOS 4.x, Solaris 2.x).
UNIX	A tool that runs under 4.x BSD UNIX or related OS
Windows 95	A tool that runs under Microsoft Windows 95
Windows NT	A tool that runs under Microsoft Windows 98
VMS	A tool that runs under DEC's VMS operating system

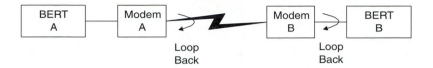

Figure 12.2   Bit Error Rate Testing of Modems with BERT

12.1.2   Bit Error Rate Tester

Modems play a significant role in remote access of hosts on a network. They have gained importance with the introduction of broadband access technology (see Chapter 10). The bit error rate tester (BERT) has been used for a long time as a network test tool that can test bit error rate and block error rate. It can also test digital circuit equipment (see Figures 9.26 and 9.27) on a loop back, sending the data back to BERT, which generated it.

Figure 12.2 shows the configuration for bit error rate (BER) testing of modems with BERT. Bit or block patterns are generated by BERT A. The error is measured by BERT B after the signal has passed through modem A, a WAN link, and modem B. It gives a one-way end-to-end error rate of the link. A two-way or round-trip error rate can be measured by using the loop back function built into most of the modems at the far end. The same BERT can also generate data as well as measure the error rate. The error rate introduced by a single modem at different signal levels can be measured by doing the loop back at the near end, as shown.

We can also make BER measurements in a LAN environment by setting MAC/IP addresses in BERT's software configuration for the transmitting and receiving ends. The advantage of such a setup is that the test can be performed in a shared LAN medium. Figure 12.3 shows a configuration for such a measurement on a cable modem, using Netcom Systems' SmartBits. Data are injected at the head end Ethernet port, and noise is introduced on the HFC link. The packet loss and cyclic redundancy check (CRC) errors, which are correlated to BER, are measured at the Ethernet port of the cable modem at the subscriber's end (see Chapter 10 for details on cable modems). Figure 12.4 shows the result of such a test [Chu LC & Subramanian M]. As the noise level increases, forward error correction keeps the error rate low. However, at higher noise levels, the error rate rises rapidly, and the modem loses synchronization.

Figure 12.3   HFC Testing Using BERT

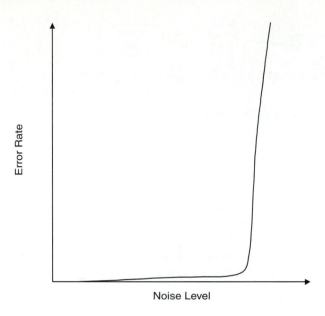

Figure 12.4   Results of an Error Rate Test on a Cable Modem

12.1.3   Basic Software Tools

Numerous basic tools are either part of an operating system or are available as add-on applications that aid in obtaining network parameters or diagnosing network problems. We will describe some of the more popular ones here, under the three categories of status monitoring, traffic monitoring, and route monitoring.

Network Status Tools.   Table 12.5 lists some of the network status monitoring tools that are available in the UNIX and Microsoft Windows (95 and NT) environments.

Table 12.5   Status Monitoring Tools

Name	Operating System	Description
Ifconfig	UNIX	Obtains and configures networking interface parameters and status
ping	UNIX Windows	Checks the status of node/host
nslookup	UNIX Windows NT	Looks up DNS for name-IP address translation
dig	UNIX	Queries DNS server
host	UNIX	Displays information on Internet hosts/domains

```
netman: ifconfig -a
lo0: flags=849<UP,LOOPBACK,RUNNING,MULTICAST> mtu 8232
        inet 127.0.0.1 netmask ff000000
hme0: flags=863<UP,BROADCAST,NOTRAILERS,RUNNING,MULTICAST>
        mtu 1500 inet 192.207.8.31 netmask ffffff00 broadcast 192.207.8.255
```

Figure 12.5   An Interface Configuration (ifconfig) Example

The command **ifconfig** on a UNIX system is used to assign an address to a network interface or to configure network interface parameters. Usually, someone needs to be a super-user (su) in UNIX to set interface parameters. However, the command can be used without options by any user to obtain the current configuration of the local system or of a remote system. With this and other commands, you may invoke **man commandname** to obtain the manual page of a command in a UNIX system. An example of **ifconfig** is shown in Figure 12.5.

The option -a is for displaying all interfaces. There are two interfaces: the loopback interface, lo0, and the Ethernet interface, hme0. Option -a provides information on whether the interface is up or down, what maximum transmission unit (mtu) it has, Ethernet interface address, and the like.

One of the most basic tools is the packet Internet groper (*ping*). It is frequently used when an execution of a command on a remote station fails. As one of the first diagnostics, we want to ensure that the connection exists, for which the *ping* utility is executed on the remote host. If it fails, there is problem with the link. If it passes, the trouble is with the application or is something else.

You used the *ping* tool in doing the Chapter 1 exercises. It is based on the ICMP echo_request message and is available in both UNIX and Microsoft Windows operating systems. Pinging a remote IP address verifies that the destination node and the intermediate nodes have live connectivity and provides the round-trip delay time. By pinging multiple times, we can obtain both the average time delay and the percentage loss of packets, which is a measure of throughput. This feature can be used to check the performance of the connection. Because of the numerous implementations of *ping,* you may want to read the manual page covering the details of the specific implementation on each host.

The UNIX commands **nslookup**, **host**, and **dig** are useful for obtaining names and addresses on hosts and domain name servers. A domain name server locates IP addresses. The *nslookup* tool is an interactive program for making queries to the domain name server for translating a hostname to an IP address and vice versa. The command, by default, sends the query to the local domain name server, but any other server can also be specified. For example, the command **nslookup 172.152.8.138** on the host noc2 (192.77.147.142) yields the result shown in Figure 12.6.

In this case the host, noc2, with the IP address 192.77.147.142 obtained the name of mani.bellsouth.net corresponding to IP address 172.152.8.138 from the domain name server 192.77.147.28. Instead of hostname, the IP address could also be used as an option parameter in the **nslookup** command.

```
noc2% nslookup 172.152.8.138
Server: ada.btc.gatech.edu
Address: 192.77.147.28

Name: mani.bellsouth.net
Address: 172.152.8.138
```

Figure 12.6   A Network Address Translation (nslookup) Example

We could use **nslookup** if we wanted to find all the names of the hosts on a LAN. We first execute a broadcast *ping* on the LAN and acquire all the IP addresses. Then, we obtain the host names using **nslookup**.

The domain information groper (**dig**) sends a query to a domain name server and gathers information from it. The interactive command **host** can also be used to get the host name with the domain name server. However, with the appropriate security privilege, it can be used to get all the host names maintained by a domain name server. The *dig* and *host* utilities also provide additional data on the hosts, besides the host names, which you may obtain from the manual page.

Network Traffic Monitoring Tools.   Table 12.6 lists seven traffic monitoring tools. One of the tools is *ping*, which we have just described as a status monitoring tool. As we stated earlier, by executing repeatedly a large number of **ping** commands (ICMP echo_request messages) and measuring how many were successfully received, we can calculate the percentage of packet loss. Recall that packet loss is a measure of throughput. The example presented in Figure 12.7 displays zero percent packet loss when five packets are transmitted and received. It also shows the round-trip packet transmission time, with minimum, average, and maximum of 40, 40, and 42 milliseconds respectively.

Table 12.6   Traffic Monitoring Tools

Name	Operating System	Description
ping	UNIX Windows	Used for measuring round-trip packet loss
bing	UNIX	Measures point-to-point bandwidth of a link
etherfind	UNIX	Inspects Ethernet packets
snoop	UNIX	Captures and inspects network packets
tcpdump	UNIX	Dumps traffic on a network
getethers	UNIX	Acquires all host addresses of an Ethernet LAN segment
iptrace	UNIX	Measures performance of gateways

```
netman: ping -s mit.edu
PING mit.edu: 56 data bytes
64 bytes from MIT.MIT.EDU (18.72.0.100): icmp_seq=0. time=42. ms
64 bytes from MIT.MIT.EDU (18.72.0.100): icmp_seq=1. time=41. ms
64 bytes from MIT.MIT.EDU (18.72.0.100): icmp_seq=2. time=41. ms
64 bytes from MIT.MIT.EDU (18.72.0.100): icmp_seq=3. time=40. ms
64 bytes from MIT.MIT.EDU (18.72.0.100): icmp_seq=4. time=40. ms

--mit.edu PING Statistics--
5 packets transmitted, 5 packets received, 0% packet loss
round-trip (ms) min/avg/max = 40/40/42
```

Figure 12.7   A Traffic Monitoring (ping) Example

Another useful tool, heavily based on *ping,* is the point-to-point bandwidth *ping* (*bing*). The *bing* utility determines the raw throughput of a link by calculating the difference in round-trip times for different packet sizes from each end of the link. For example, if we want to measure the throughput of a hop or point-to-point link between L1 and L2, we derive it from the results of the measurements of ICMP echo requests to L1 and L2 (L1 being in the path of L2). The difference between the two results yields the throughput of the link L1–L2. This method has the advantage of yielding accurate results, even though the path to the link L1–L2 from the measuring station could have a lower bandwidth than the link L1–L2 for which the measurement is made. However, there is a practical limit to this difference (about 30 times). In practice, this means that if you have a 64-kbps connection to the Internet, the maximum throughput of the link you can measure is 2 Mbps.

The other five commands examine the packets that traverse the network to provide different outputs. The commands **etherfind**, **snoop**, and **tcpdump** put a network interface in a promiscuous mode (a mode in which raw data are gathered from the network without any filtering) and log the data. All of them could generate an output text file, associating each line with a packet containing information on protocol type, length, source, and destination. Because of the security risk associated with looking at data in a promiscuous mode in these cases, the user ID is limited to a super-user. An example of the output of a *snoop* command execution is shown in Figure 12.8. The option -d instructs the command to use the device interface hme0 and count (-c) 5 packets. We can observe the result of the analysis on the transport protocol packets TCP and UDP and the Ethernet packets exchanged between the *noc2* and *noc4* hosts. We also notice the sequence and acknowledge the numbers of the packets, their lengths, source and port addresses, and so on. For an example of **tcpdump** command output, refer back to the SNMP get-request and get-response PDUs shown in Figure 4.50 that were obtained by using *tcpdump* tool.

The command **getethers** discovers all host and Ethernet address pairs on the LAN segment (a.b.c.1 to a.b.c.254). It generates an ICMP echo_request message much the same as *ping* does, using an IP socket. The replies are compared with the ARP table to determine the Ethernet address of each responding system.

```
root@noc2:~# snoop -d hme0 -c 5
Using device /dev/hme (promiscuous mode)
noc2.btc.gatech.edu -> noc4.btc.gatech.edu TCP D=22 S=1221 Ack=2845521735
Seq=24552727 Len=0 Win=7368
      ? -> (multicast) ETHER Type=809B (EtherTalk (AppleTalk over Ethernet)),
          size = 80 bytes
      ? -> (multicast) ETHER Type=809B (EtherTalk (AppleTalk over Ethernet)),
          size = 86 bytes
noc2.btc.gatech.edu -> 199.77.147.255 UDP D=137 S=137 LEN=108
noc2.btc.gatech.edu -> 199.77.147.255 UDP D=137 S=137 LEN=108
noc2.btc.gatech.edu -> 199.77.147.255 UDP D=137 S=137 LEN=108
noc2.btc.gatech.edu -> 199.77.147.255 UDP D=137 S=137 LEN=108
      ? -> (broadcast) ETHER Type=8137 (Novell (old) NetWare IPX), size = 88
noc4.btc.gatech.edu -> noc2.btc.gatech.edu TCP D=1221 S=22 Ack=24552727
Seq=2845521735 Len=64 Win=8760
noc2.btc.gatech.edu -> noc4.btc.gatech.edu TCP D=22 S=1221 Ack=2845521799
Seq=24552727 Len=0 Win=7304
noc4.btc.gatech.edu -> noc2.btc.gatech.edu TCP D=1221 S=22 Ack=24552727
Seq=2845521799 Len=56 Win=8760
snoop: 5 packets captured
```

Figure 12.8   An Example of the snoop Command Output

The *iptrace* tool uses the NETMON program in a UNIX kernel and produces three types of outputs: IP traffic, host traffic matrix output, and abbreviated sampling of a predefined number of packets.

Network Routing Tools.   Table 12.7 lists three sets of route monitoring tools. The *netstat* tool displays the contents of various network-related data structures in various formats, depending on the option selected. The network-related data structures that can be displayed by using *netstat* include routing table, interface statistics, network connections, masquerade connections, and multicast memberships. An example of the routing tables obtained with *netstat* is shown in Figure 12.9, which also shows the ports associated with

Table 12.7   Route Monitoring Tools

Name	Operating System	Description
netstat	UNIX	Displays the contents of various network-related data structures
arp/rarp	UNIX, Windows 95/NT	Displays and modifies the Internet-to-Ethernet address translation tables
traceroute/tracert	UNIX/Windows	Traces route to a destination with routing delays

```
netstat -r
Routing tables

Internet:
Destination           Gateway            Flags   Refs    Use        Netif   Expire
Default               gw.litech.net      UGC     44      541550     de0
172.16.15.1           gw.litech.net      UGH     0       0          de0
ah.litech.net         0:80:48:ee:74:b4   UHLW    9       2653683    de0     202
uucp.litech.net       uucp.litech.net    UH      0       0          lo0
sip-17.litech.net     big                UH      0       5551       ppp3
dip-244.litech.net    gw.litech.net      UGH     0       2472       de0
univers-litech-gw     gw.litech.net      UGH     0       47         de0
194.44.232            gw.isr.lviv.ua     Ugc     0       171831     ppp9
OSPF-ALL.MCAST.NET    localhost          UH      1       86491      lo0
OSPF-DSIG.MCAST.NE    localhost          UH      1       25127      lo0
```

Figure 12.9   A Network Status (netstat) Example, showing the Routing Table

various destinations. The netstat command is a useful diagnostic tool for troubleshooting. For example, the routing table information shown in Figure 12.9 informs the network operator of which nodes have been active since the last purge of the table, which is typically on the order of a minute. The most frequently used options of *netstat* are -r, which obtains the contents of the routing tables; -i, which prints the table of all networking interfaces; and -a, which prints the information about all active Internet connections and UNIX-domain sockets.

We could also obtain the routing table by using the *arp* utility. The *arp* tool displays and modifies the Internet-to-Ethernet address translation tables (ARP cache) used by the Address Resolution Protocol (ARP). Some UNIX systems provide an additional tool, the RARP cache, for manipulating the contents of Ethernet-to-Internet address translation tables. The name of the tool is *rarp* and its use is similar to that of *arp*.

The third type of routing tool shown in Table 12.7 is the *traceroute* (UNIX) or *tracert* (MS Windows), which is the tool used most extensively for diagnostics associated with routing problems. The tool discovers the route taken by packets from source to destination through each hop. It is very useful in localizing the source of route failure and in performance/packet delay evaluation, as the result gives the delay time to each node along the route. The *traceroute* is based on the ICMP time_exceeded error report mechanism. When an IP packet is received by a node with a time-to-live (TTL) value of 0, an ICMP packet is sent to the source. The source sends the first packet with a TTL of zero to its destination. The first node looks at the packet and sends an ICMP packet because its TTL value is greater than 0. The source then sends the second packet with a TTL value larger than that needed to get to the first node, and thus *traceroute* acquires the second node. This process continues until all the nodes between the source and the destination have been determined.

Figure 12.10 presents two sample traces taken close to each other in time between the same source *mani.bellsouth.net* and destination *mani.btc.gatech.edu*. Notice the significant differences in route taken, delay times, and number of hops. We would expect these differences because each packet in a packet-switched network takes a different route. Each line shows the routers that the packet traversed in sequence. The three time counts on each line indicate the round-trip delay for each router on three attempts from the source. A jump in round-trip delay from 2 to 5 milliseconds to more than 10 milliseconds occurred when the packet crossed over from the local BellSouth network. In some lines— for example, in lines 9 and 13 in Figure 12.10(a), one of the round-trip delay reads high, which could be attributed to a router being busy. In Figure 12.10(b), the second half of the route appears congested, indicating consistently large round-trip delays. Some of the routers respond with their IP address, but others don't. The lines marked with asterisks are responses from those routers, which have been administratively prevented from revealing their identities in their responses.

Web-based *traceroute* and *ping* utilities are also available on some systems. The use of these tools significantly decreases the time required to detect and isolate a routing problem.

```
Tracing route to mani.btc.gatech.edu [199.77.147.96]
over a maximum of 30 hops:

1  2 ms  3 ms  3 ms  bims008001.bims.bellsouth.net [205.152.8.1]
2  4 ms  2 ms  3 ms  172.16.11.2
3  5 ms  4 ms  3 ms  172.16.4.2
4  5 ms  3 ms  3 ms  bims011033.bims.bellsouth.net [205.152.11.33]
5  4 ms  4 ms  4 ms  205.152.13.98
6  *      *      *    Request timed out
7  5 ms  9 ms  12 ms  205.152.2.249
8  33 ms  31 ms  31 ms  Hssi0-0-0.GW2.ATL1.ALTER.NET [157.130.65.229]
9  68 ms  10 ms  11 ms  105.ATM3-0-0.XR1.ATL1.ALTER.NET [146.188.232.66]
10 11 ms  14 ms  12 ms  195.ATM12-0-0.BR1.ATL1.ALTER.NET [146.188.232.49]
11 16 ms  14 ms  14 ms  atlanta1-br1.bbnplanet.net [4.0.2.141]
12 19 ms  15 ms  17 ms  atlanta2-br2.bbnplanet.net [4.0.2.158]
13 21 ms  56 ms  328 ms  atlanta2-cr99.bbnplanet.net [4.0.2.91]
14 17 ms  18 ms  17 ms  192.221.26.3
15 32 ms  20 ms  18 ms  130.207.251.3
16 20 ms  17 ms  17 ms  mani.btc.gatech.edu [199.77.147.96]

Trace complete
```

(a) Sample 1

Figure 12.10   Route Tracing (traceroute) Examples

```
Tracing route to mani.btc.gatech.edu [199.77.147.96]
over a maximum of 30 hops:

1 3 ms 3 ms 4 ms bims008001.bims.bellsouth.net [205.152.8.1]
2 3 ms 3 ms 2 ms 172.16.11.2
3 5 ms 4 ms 4 ms 172.16.4.2
4 5 ms 3 ms 4 ms bims011033.bims.bellsouth.net [205.152.11.33]
5 7 ms 4 ms 4 ms 205.152.13.98
6 *    *    *  Request timed out
7 9 ms 8 ms 9 ms 205.152.2.249
8 228 ms 214 ms 191 ms 206.80.168.9
9 230 ms 246 ms 234 ms maeeast.bbnplanet.net [192.41.177.2]
10 243 ms 222 ms 212 ms vienna1-nbr2.bbnplanet.net [4.0.1.93]
11 230 ms 213 ms 202 ms vienna1-nbr3.bbnplanet.net [4.0.5.46]
12 247 ms 227 ms 236 ms vienna1-br2.bbnplanet.net [4.0.3.149]
13 228 ms 235 ms 238 ms atlanta1-br1.bbnplanet.net [4.0.2.58]
14  *    257 ms 238 ms atlanta2-br2.bbnplanet.net [4.0.2.158]
15 225 ms 234 ms 233 ms atlanta2-cr99.bbnplanet.net [4.0.2.91]
16 240 ms 229 ms 251 ms 192.221.26.3
17 235 ms 245 ms 225 ms 130.207.251.3
18  *    268 ms 243 ms mani.btc.gatech.edu [199.77.147.96]

Trace complete
```

(b) Sample 2

Figure 12.10   Route Tracing (traceroute) Examples *(continued)*

12.1.4   SNMP MIB Tools

Several tools are available for obtaining the MIB tree structure and its values from a net-work object. Each of these tools has several implementations. We will not go into the spe-cific implementations here, but will describe the functionality involved in the tools' use. You may obtain details on uses and options from the manual page describing each tool.

There are three types of SNMP MIB tools. First is the SNMP MIB browser that uses the browser interface and can be used on any platform supporting a Web browser. Second is a set of SNMP command line tools that are primarily UNIX-, and LINUX/FreeBSD-based tools. Third is a LINUX/FreeBSD-based tool, *snmpsniff*, which is useful for reading the SNMP PDUs.

SNMP MIB Browsers.   SNMP MIB browsers are user-friendly tools that can be accessed from public libraries or purchased commercially. All of them extract the MIB-II of SNMPv1, and some of them extract the SNMPv2 MIB. Some specific implementa-tions can also acquire private MIB objects. We specify the host name or IP address and request information on a specific MIB object, MIB group, or the entire MIB in the command. The response returns the object identifier(s) and value(s). Some of the sophisticated implementations even have graphical user interfaces.

Let us use the MIB browser http://mystery.inp.nsk.su/~pasha/sbrowser.cgi to request the variable *system.sysDescr* from host 199.77.147.182. The response is shown in Figure 12.11. Figure 12.12 shows the results obtained by using the browser to retrieve system group.

SNMP Command-Line Tools.   Several SNMP command-line tools are available for either the UNIX or the LINUX/FreeBSD operating system environment; a few DOS-based add-ons may also be available. The command-line tools are basically the SNMPv1 messages *get, get-next, set, get-response,* and *trap.* Public domain software packages that are capable of operating either as an SNMPv1 or SNMPv2 agent can be downloaded. The following commands are described in SNMPv1 format: "+" or "/" character added to the community string would be interpreted by the agent as SNMPv2c or SNMPv2u, respectively. The former is the community-based SNMPv2 (see Chapter 6) and the latter is the user-based security model, as in SNMPv3.

```
Object Type:
   sysDescr
Object Identifier:
   1.3.6.1.2.1.1.1
Access:
   read-only
Syntax:
   OCTET STRING
Textual Convention:
   DisplayString
Format:
   255a
Description:
   A textual description of the entity. This value should include the full name and
version identification of the system's hardware type, software operating system,
and networking software.
File:
   /usr/local/lib/tnm2.1.8/mibs/rfc1907.mib

199.77.147.182:

   sysDescr.0 : SunOS noc5 5.6 Generic_105181-03 sun4u
```

Figure 12.11   MIB Browser Example for a System Descriptor Object

```
199.77.147.182:

    sysDescr.0 : SunOS noc5 5.6 Generic_105181-03 sun4u
    sysObjectID.0 : 1.3.6.1.4.1.11.2.3.10.1.2
    sysUpTime.0 : 8d 22:21:53.74
    sysContact.0 :
    sysName.0 : noc5
    sysLocation.0 :
    sysServices.0 : 72
    sysORLastChange.0 : 0d 0:00:00.00
```

Figure 12.12   MIB Browser Example for System Group

The SNMP Get Command.   The command

```
snmpget [options] host community objectID [objectID]...
```

communicates with a network object by using the SNMP *get-request* message. The *host* may be either a host name or an IP address. If the SNMP agent resides on the host, with the matching *community* name, it responds with a *get-response* message returning the value of the *objectID*. If multiple *objectID*s are requested, the *varBind* clause is used to process the message containing multiple object names (see Figure 5.8).

For example,

```
snmpget 199.77.147.182 public system.sysdescr.0
```

retrieves the system variable system.sysDescr

```
system.sysdescr.0 = "SunOS noc5 5.6 Generic_105181-03 sun4u"
```

The 0 at the end of the *objectID* indicates that the request is for a single scalar variable. If the get-request message is invalid, the get-response message contains the appropriate error indication.

The SNMP Get-Next Command.   The command

```
snmpgetnext [options] host community [objectID]...
```

communicates with a network object via the SNMP *get-next-request* message. The object responds with the expected get-response message on the *objectID* that is lexicographically next to the one specified in the request. This command is especially useful for getting the values of variables in an aggregate object (i.e., a table).

For example,

```
snmpgetnext 199.77.147.182 public
                           interfaces.ifTable.ifEntry.ifIndex.1
```

retrieves

```
interfaces.ifTable.ifEntry.ifIndex.2 = "2"
```

The SNMP Walk Command.   The command

```
snmpwalk [options] host community [objectID]
```

uses *get-next-request* messages to get the MIB tree starting from the *objectID* specified in the request. It literally walks through the MIB. Without the *objectID*, the command displays the entire MIB-II tree. The command gets the *objectIDs* and their values.

The SNMP Set Command.   The snmpset command sends the SNMP set-request message and receives the *get-response* command.

The SNMP Trap Command.   The snmptrap command generates a trap message. Some implementations handle only SNMPv1 traps. Others handle both SNMPv1 and SNMPv2, which can be specified in the argument.

The SNMP Sniff Tool.   The SNMP Sniff tool, *snmpsniff,* is similar to the *tcpdump* tool and is implemented in a Linux/FreeBSD environment. It captures SNMP packets going across the segment and stores them for later analysis.

12.1.5   The Protocol Analyzer

The protocol analyzer is a powerful and versatile network management tool. We will consider it as a test tool in this section and later look at its use as a system management tool. It analyzes data packets on any transmission line. Although it could be used for the analysis of any line, its primary use is in a LAN environment, which is what we will focus on here. Protocol analyzer measurements can be made either locally or remotely. The basic configuration used for a protocol analyzer is shown in Figure 12.13. It consists of a data capture device that is attached to a LAN and can be a specialized tool; it can also be a personal computer or workstation with a network interface card. The captured data are

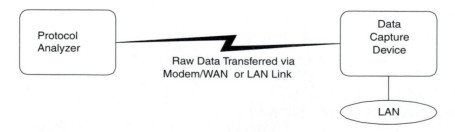

Figure 12.13   Basic Configuration of a Protocol Analyzer

transmitted to the protocol analyzer via a dial-up modem connection, a LAN or campus network, or WAN. The protocol analyzer analyzes the data and presents the results to the user on a user-friendly interface.

The protocol analyzers available commercially are capable of presenting a multitude of results derived from the data. Contents of the data packets can be viewed and analyzed at all layers of the OSI reference model. Distribution of the various protocols at each layer can be ascertained. At the data link layer, both statistical counts and collision rates can be measured for an Ethernet LAN. At the transport layer, port information for the different applications and sessions can be obtained. Distribution of the application-level protocols provides valuable information on the nature of traffic in the network, which can be used for network performance tuning.

Two popular commercial protocol analyzers are the Sniffer™ by Network Associates (previously Network General) and the NetMetrix™ protocol analyzer by Hewlett-Packard. Sniffer can be used as a stand-alone portable protocol analyzer and on a network. NetMetrix is a software package loaded on to a workstation. It uses LanProbe as a collector device, which can also be configured as an RMON. Communication between an RMON and the protocol analyzer is based on SNMP protocol, as shown in Figure 12.14.

A protocol analyzer functioning as a remote monitoring analyzer collects data using an RMON probe. The raw data gathered is preanalyzed by the RMON and transmitted as SNMP traffic instead of raw data in the basic configuration mentioned earlier. Statistics can be gathered over time for analysis or displayed in real time. In the promiscuous mode, the actual data collected by the probe can be looked at in detail or statistics at various protocol layers can be displayed. The results are used to perform diagnostics on network problems such as traffic congestion and to perform network management functions such as traffic reroute planning, capacity planning, and load monitoring.

Using an RMON probe for each segment of the network and one protocol analyzer for the entire network, as shown in Figure 12.15, allows monitoring of the complete network. The RMON probe for each type of LAN is physically different. Even for the same type of LAN, a separate probe is needed for each segment, which could be expensive to implement.

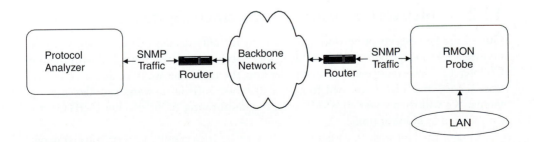

Figure 12.14   A Protocol Analyzer with an RMON Probe

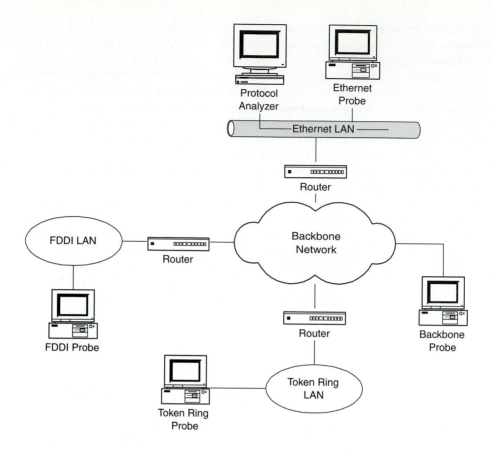

Figure 12.15   Monitoring of a Total Network with Individual RMON Probes

12.2   Network Statistics Measurement Systems

One of the key aspects of network management is traffic management. We will consider performance management as one of the application functions when we deal with them in Chapter 13. However, we will first consider how the tools that we have discussed in Sections 12.1.4 and 12.1.5 are used to gather network statistics at various nodes and segments. We will then cover an SNMP tool, the multi router traffic grapher (MRTG) that can be used to monitor traffic.

One of the best ways to gather network statistics is to capture packets traversing network segments or node interfaces in a promiscuous mode. We have shown that protocol analyzers do just that. Thus they are good tools to use for gathering network statistics.

Another way to gather network statistics is to develop a simple application having a function similar to *tcpdump*, using a high-performance network interface card and processor, and analyze the data for the required statistics. After all, that is the basis on which protocol analyzers are built.

The RMON MIB that we discussed in Chapter 8 along with the SNMP communication protocol, provides a convenient mechanism for building network monitoring systems. The configurations shown in Figures 12.14 and 12.15 can be the network monitoring system used to gather the various RMON objects. The RMON1 MIB groups and tables shown in Tables 8.2 and 8.3 are used to gather statistics at the data link layer in Ethernet and token ring LANs. The RMON2 MIB groups and tables presented in Table 8.4 define parameters for higher layer statistics.

12.2.1   Traffic Load Monitoring

Traffic load monitoring can be based on source, destination, and source–destination pairs. If we want to balance the traffic load among various LAN segments we may also want to measure the total traffic in each network segment or domain. The data for traffic monitoring can be sampled at the data link layer, using the RMON1 MIB History Group. Traffic relevant to a host—either as a source or as a destination—is available in the Host Group. The hosts can be ranked on the traffic load that they carry using the HostTopN Group. Unfortunately, there is no convenient way to measure the traffic in a segment directly, except to compute it externally if we know the hosts in the segment.

The load statistics in an IP network can also be obtained by measuring the IP packets at the network layer. The entities in the Network Layer Host and Network Layer Matrix Groups in RMON2 MIB can be used for this measurement. Figures 12.16–Figure 12.18 show the load statistics measured in an FDDI LAN segment, using the NetMetrix protocol analyzer as Load Monitor and FDDI probe.

Figure 12.16 shows that 1,609 sources generated data packets. The top ten have been identified, with the highest entry being *news-ext.gatech.edu*. The entry LOW-CONTRIB is a combination of sources other than those specifically identified. Traffic is measured as the number of octets. Figure 12.17 presents similar statistical data on traffic destined to the hosts in the network segment. Figure 12.18 presents top ten conversation pairs of hosts. Each line identifies the host pairs and traffic from NetHost1 to NetHost2. Oct1to2 and Oct2to1 denote the traffic in octets from NetHost1 to NetHost2 and NetHost2 to NetHost1, respectively. For example, news-ext.gatech.edu transmitted 3K octets/sec of outgoing traffic to and received 50K octets of incoming traffic from howland.erols.net.

12.2.2   Protocol Statistics

Packets can be captured by data capture devices, based on the filter setting for the desired criteria. From the captured data, we can derive the protocol statistics for the various protocols at each layer of the OSI Reference Model. This capability is very useful at the application layer. We can get the traffic load for different

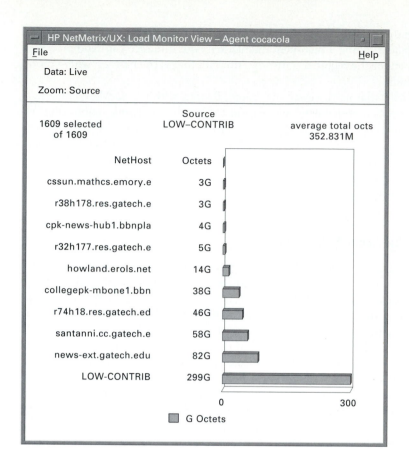

Figure 12.16   Load Statistics: Monitoring of Sources

applications such as file transfer (FTP), Web data (HTTP), and news groups (NNTP). This information can be used for bandwidth management of real-time and non–real time traffic.

Figure 12.19 shows the distribution of protocols at data link (top left), network (top right), transport (bottom left), and application (bottom right) layers, obtained using Net-Metrix LanProbe and a protocol analyzer. Data link and network layers show 100 percent LLC and IP protocols. The majority of the transport layer protocol packets belong to TCP, followed by UDP. The other category is undefined. At the application layer(s), the distribution contains http (Web protocol), nntp (news protocol), ftp-data, UDP-other, TCP-other, and undefined other. The Georgia Tech Internet backbone network in which the measurements were made carries a complex variety of protocol traffic including multi-media traffic and next generation Internet traffic.

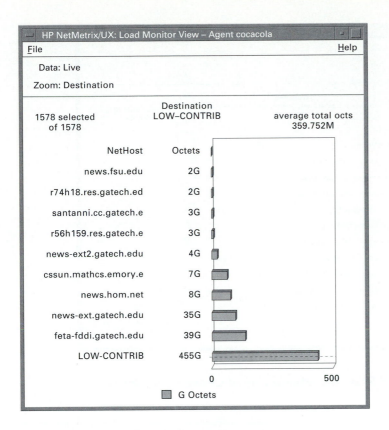

Figure 12.17   Load Statistics: Monitoring of Destinations

12.2.3   Data and Error Statistics

Data and error statistics can be gathered directly from managed objects by using the specifications defined in various MIB groups. The RMON Statistics Groups for Ethernet [RFC 1757] and Token Ring [RFC 1513] contain various types of packets and errors in the data link layer. Similar information is available on higher level layers from specifications detailed in RMON2 [RFC 2021]. Information on statistics can also be gathered for an individual medium from the respective MIB in the Transmission Group. For example, statistics on the Ethernet can be derived from the Ethernet-like Statistics Group in the Ethernet-like Interface Types MIB [RFC 1284], token ring statistics from the IEEE 802.5 MIB [RFC 1748], and FDDI data from the FDDI MIB [RFC 1285].

12.2.4   Using MRTG to Collect Traffic Statistics

The Multi Router Traffic Grapher (MRTG) is a tool that monitors the traffic load on network links [Oetiker T & Rand D]. It generates live visual representations of traffic data by

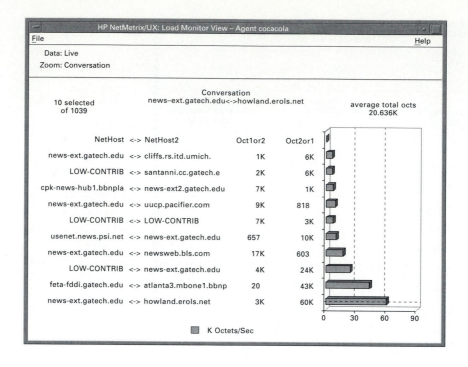

Figure 12.18   Load Statistics: Monitoring of Conversation Pairs

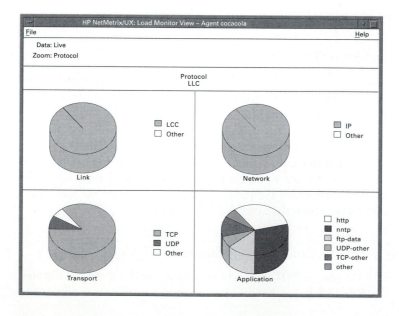

Figure 12.19   Protocol Distribution (NetMetrix)

reading the SNMP traffic counters on routers and creating graphs that are embedded in Web pages and can be viewed with any Web browser. Visual presentations of traffic data are presented daily, for the last 7 days, for the past 4 weeks, and for the last 12 months. The generic software can be implemented on either a UNIX or a Windows NT platform. An example of the presentations can be viewed on http://www.ee.ethz.ch/stats/mrtg/.

12.3   History of Enterprise Management

The origin of enterprise management depends on how we define the term. Some authors [Hegering HG & Abeck S, Lewis L1, Strutt C & Sylor MW] have attempted to define it as broadly as possible to allow for the evolution of telecommunications. We choose to define *enterprise management* as functions that support networks and systems that are directly involved with user data.

One view of enterprise management starts with network management, which had its origin in the late 1980s and early 1990s. Several commercial systems were introduced by vendors such as IBM (NetView™), Sun (Solstice), HP (OpenView™), and Cabletron (Spectrum™). These systems were primarily concerned with managing the transport of data. They addressed transport protocols at the data link, network, transport, and application layers.

Another view of enterprise management traces its origin to the introduction of commercial systems management products such as Tivoli's TME and Computer Associate's Unicenter in the early 1990s. These systems were primarily concerned with the management of system resources.

Network management and systems management products evolved independently. Information technology managers needed to manage both networks and systems and wanted the management systems industry to merge the two technologies. This desire gave rise to the term *enterprise management*. Enterprise management systems, having matured to an industry standard of monitoring networks of multivendor systems, started focusing on application management in the mid 1990s. Application-oriented issues such as fault correlation, performance management, and security management were included in enterprise management.

A third perspective of enterprise management dates back to the telephone companies' introduction of operations (support) systems. These systems were intended to support telephone networks. They helped maintain quality by monitoring performance and testing telephone networks and systems at the physical layer. In addition, operations systems were developed to administer customer service functions. The importance of all these functions led to the development of TMN standards, which we discussed in Chapter 11. The management of access technology involves management of the network at the physical and data layers. This produces new challenges for enterprise management.

With the data and telecommunications fields coming together, the management of services became increasingly important to all enterprises, not just the traditional telecommunications industry. The enterprise management systems of the late 1990s are introducing service and policy management functions, moving the industry into the service layer level of TMN. Some enterprise management solutions will be discussed in Section 12.7. The last, but certainly not the least aspect of enterprise management systems, business management, is on the horizon.

12.4   Network Management Systems

A network management system (NMS) is an automated system tool that helps networking personnel perform their functions efficiently. For an SNMP-based NMS, that involves the implementation of the management functions and messages that we have discussed in Part II of this book. The SNMP-based NMS manages the network components that have the SNMP agent process integrated in them. Non-SNMP components can be managed by an SNMP NMS by using a proxy server (see Chapter 5), which creates equivalent SNMP MIB objects for non-SNMP objects.

12.4.1   Functional Components

A network management system can be divided into five functional components, as shown in Figure 12.20: hardware, operating system, core application services, common SNMP services, and vendor-specific NMS services. Types of service (not intended to be an exhaustive list) and some examples of the more popular systems are presented in Table 12.8. The innermost component is the hardware platform. The two most popular sets of hardware platforms are those that can house either a UNIX (usually a workstation such as Sun Sparc™ or Hewlett-Packard HP 9000™) or Microsoft Windows NT operating sys-

Figure 12.20   Network Management System Components

Table 12.8   Network Management System Components

Component	Service	Example
Hardware	Processor Monitor Mouse and keyboard Communications	Sun Sparc HP 9000 PC
Operating system	OS services	UNIX LINUX/FreeBSD Solaris MS Windows 95/98/NT
Core application services	Display GUI Database Report generation Communication services	OpenView SunNet Manager Solstice Enterprise Manager MS Windows

Common SNMP
services
	SNMPv1 messages
	SNMPv2 messages
	MIB management
	Basic SNMP applications
	Third party NMS API
		SNMPc
		HP OpenView Network Node
		   Manager
		Cabletron Spectrum Enterprise
		   Manager
		IBM NetView
		SunNet Manager
		Sun Solstice Enterprise Manager

Vendor-specific
NMS services
	MIB management
	SNMP applications
	Configuration management
	Physical entity display
		CiscoWorks
		Transcend
		Spectrum Element Manager/
		   Spectrum Portable Manage-
		   ment Application

tem (normally an Intel x86-based processor). The next component layer is the operating system. Sun Sparc and HP 9000 are workstations that run one of the UNIX operating systems or a variation of it (Sun Solaris™). The personal computer (PC) is used with Microsoft Windows operating systems. Linux and FreeBSD are two similar UNIX-based operating systems that run on a PC platform. The *platform*, which refers to the combination of hardware and operating system, has built-in application service modules, such as presentation services that include a graphical user interface (GUI) and database management system. The current network management systems primarily use a relational database, such as Oracle or Sybase. Report generation is a basic utility in the next component layer, core application services. Some of the network management systems provide an application program interface (API) that third-party vendors can integrate with their NMSs. Core application services also include basic communication services that communicate data over networks.

The fourth layer of components comprises the common SNMP services. They include the manager process that can interpret and generate the SNMP MIB and messages. It has a broad MIB view; in addition to the standard MIB, private MIBs may be compiled into it to interpret multiple vendors' private MIBs. It is capable of performing the required network management application functions of fault, performance, configuration, and security management. The only security functional requirement is the SNMP security policy. The configuration function of a centralized network management system (manager of managers) is to execute *set-request* messages, although most of the configuration functions on network components are performed with vendor-specific network management systems. There are no specific account management requirements in SNMP. Most of the network management systems are based on SNMPv1. However, some vendors have implemented SNMPv2 agents in some of their network components. Thus a proxy server is needed for a manager of managers (MoM) to convert SNMPv2 messages to SNMPv1 messages. The same condition applies to the SNMPv2 network management system, which has to have a proxy server to convert SNMPv1 messages to SNMPv2 messages.

The outermost component layer is vendor-specific network management services. Each vendor of telecommunications equipment has specific hardware and software implementations and consequently is in the best position to configure them. Thus equipment vendors have their own network management systems that configure their equipment. The alternative is to have a telnet connection to the console interface to configure the system. In addition, manufacturers of telecommunications equipment present the physical configuration of the equipment on a GUI for ease of operation by personnel in the network operations center. This presentation requires detailed knowledge of the equipment, which is the responsibility of the particular vendor.

12.4.2   Multiple NMS Configuration

Figure 12.21 shows the functional configuration for the use of multiple network management systems in a network. The three vendor-specific network management systems shown are used in configuring a multivendor equipment network. For example, the network elements could be Cabletron hubs, 3Com Ethernet switches, and Cisco routers. In this case, the vendor-specific network management systems are Cabletron's Spectrum Element Manager, 3Com's Transcend™, and Cisco's CiscoWorks™. The MoM, which presents the global view of the network (see Chapter 3) does the overall monitoring and management of fault and performance. This system could be any of those shown in the example column of the common SNMP services row in Table 12.8—for example, HP's OpenView Network Node Manager™, Cabletron's Spectrum Enterprise Manager, or Sun's Solstice Enterprise Manager™.

The vendor-specific NMS can be either a stand-alone system or integrated with a MoM NMS. In the latter case, the vendor-specific system uses the platform and core application services of the MoM NMS, as well as some of the common SNMP services. An integrated network management system not only presents a more unified user interface, but it also conserves space by not having to use multiple monitors, keyboards, and

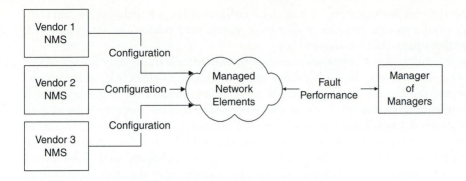

Figure 12.21   A Functional NMS Configuration

mice. An integrated system approach also has other economic benefits, such as shared use of platforms and peripherals.

The security function is required and built into all network management systems. For example, only the network engineers set up the configuration and make changes to it. Hence this aspect of vendor-specific network management systems normally is inaccessible to operators in the network operations center. However, the MIB view of the equipment's physical configuration in these systems may be available to the network operations center for the purpose of monitoring problems. Moreover, all the MIB views of the MoM may be made accessible to the network operations center, but access is restricted to the read-only mode.

12.4.3   Network Management System Requirements

The requirements for a network management system depend on the needs of the enterprise network and the price of the system. The choice of a network management system also depends on whether it is intended to be used as a vendor-specific network management system or as a manager of managers function. We will not define features and functions required in selecting a network management system to meet particular needs; rather, we will discuss some of the basic features of a network management system.

In general, establishing a management network system for an enterprise network is a complex task. Both network and system management need to be considered, and the network overhead caused by management traffic needs to be addressed. Because an enterprise network is dynamic, it could grow or diminish in size. Hence the management solution should be scalable and have a modular and distributed architecture. Further, networking technology is constantly evolving with its future directions not always being clear. Thus a human network manager needs to design the enterprise network to be flexible enough to adapt to emerging technologies, as we discussed in Chapter 10 regarding broadband technology. This reality also is an argument for designing all network and system solutions, including network management, in a modular fashion with open architecture and standards. A vendor-specific network management system may need to be integrated with MoM, so third-party API is a requirement.

The daily users of network management systems are people in the network operations center who do not have the same engineering background as those who designed and implemented the systems. Therefore ease of use is an important factor in the selection of network management systems. For example, an operator does not constantly sit in front of a monitor and watch for failures and alarms. Thus, when an alarm goes off, it should attract the attention of the operator visibly, audibly, or both. It should present a global picture of the network and give the operator the ability to "drill down" to the lowest level of component failure by successive point and click operation of the icon indicating an alarm.

Figures 12.22–12.24 show hierarchical views of a complex network at the Georgia Institute of Technology, which were captured with an HP OpenView Network Node Manager. (The IDs of the nodes have been removed for security reasons.) Figure 12.22 shows the global view with network segments and numerous domains behind routers and gateways. Figure 12.23 is obtained by clicking the mouse (also colloquially referred to as *drilling*) on the campus-rtr domain icon in Figure 12.22 and shows the networks connected to the campus-rtr. The interface cards on the campus-rtr are obtained by drilling on the campus-rtr icon in Figure 12.23. The result shown in Figure 12.24 contains nine network segments as seen by the nine interface cards in campus-rtr.

Next, we address the key high-level considerations associated with a network management system. First, the network management systems and agents have to be configured. Then, the network components need to be discovered, network maps presented, and components monitored. Finally, the management application functions need to be handled by the management system.

Configuration.   The configuration function involves configuring the agents and the management systems. The network components with built-in management agents are usually manufactured with default settings. For example, the community string is set to "public," in which case any SNMP message with "public" as a data value for community can communicate with the agent.

The network management system should have the capability to configure easily the network components. Because the network is geographically spread out, the NMS should have the capability to remotely set, reset, edit, and delete the components' parameters. The SNMP set-request is the main tool used for configuration changes, with the get-response message serving the acknowledgement function.

In addition to the configuration of network and system parameters, the management agent needs to be configured for security and trap notification. The community associations for security purposes need to be configured with regard to which management systems can access each component (community string and access mode) and what information they are authorized to view (MIB view). In addition, traps need to be configured in terms of what alarms need to be sent to which management systems.

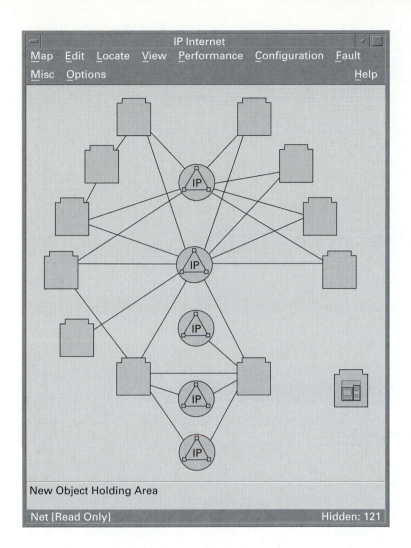

Figure 12.22 Global View of Network

Configuration management requires that an NMS perform autodiscovery during start up, as well as update and identify new components as they are added. Removed components are indicated by hard failure, but one should prevent valid actions—such as purposely turning workstations on and off—from being indicated as failures. Thus, to limit the scope of the NMS domain, appropriate filtering schemes should be made available for configuration.

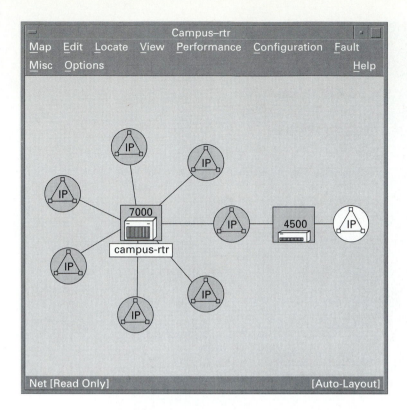

Figure 12.23   Domain View

Monitoring. Let us briefly review the two alternatives for network monitoring by a net-work management system: polling and traps. In polling, the managed objects are polled periodically and a lack of response or poor results, such as a high collision rate on an Ethernet LAN is reported by the network management system. In the second approach, traps are sent unsolicited to the network management system by a network component. Then, a hub could report the failure of an interface for a failed component or report a collision rate that exceeds a preset threshold value.

The first step in implementing an NMS is to do an autodiscovery of the network. That can be done in several ways. The system could detect the addresses in the local seg-ment and in other known segments, using broadcast *ping*. The routing tables and arp tables in the routers can then be accessed to discover the topology of the network and the network structured for presentation in layers. The top layer comprises the backbone net-work of routers and gateways. Pointing and clicking ("drilling") on the respective icons displays the network behind each router or gateway. Repeating this process successively allows us to reach the ultimate component (a leaf of the topology tree), behind each node on the top layer.

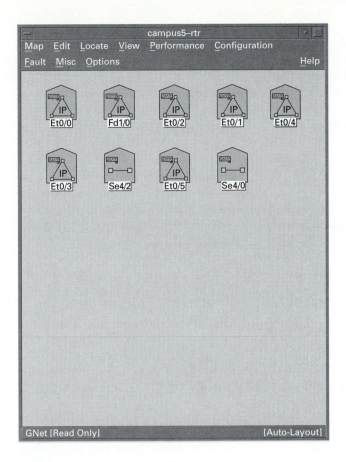

Figure 12.24 Interfaces View

Monitoring of network elements is accomplished by the NMS using the ICMP *ping* messages and *traps*. Normally, when the network is fully operational, the colors of all the icons are green, If a component fails to respond to a multiple succession of pings, the icon turns red, indicating that it is a failed component. A hard failure of a component at a lower level is reflected as a soft failure at higher levels with colors other than red. The frequency of pinging may be configured to optimize between the overhead caused by the ping messages on the network traffic and the rapidity with which a failure needs to be recognized. The more frequent the ping, the heavier the traffic load, but the faster will be the failure detection.

Component failures and restarts are also monitored with trap messages, such as *linkDown*, *linkUp*, *coldStart*, and *warmStart*. Either a restart trap from a failed component or a successful ping turns the NMS icons back to green.

Network performance can be monitored by error counts in the various MIB or RMON groups or as packet losses from pings. The RMON agent can transmit this information as a trap when the set threshold is crossed. In the absence of such traps a performance application module in NMS can calculate it from the periodic counter readings and display an alarm when performance falls below a certain level.

The SNMP messages *get-request, get-next-request,* and *get-bulk-request* are used as monitoring tools to troubleshoot problems identified by the processes just described.

Management Application Functions.   The network management system, along with the agents and RMON, should be capable of performing the five types of application functions that we defined in Chapter 3. They are management of configuration, fault, performance, security, and accounting. We have already addressed some of these functions, and we will discuss them in more detail in Chapter 13, when we deal with some sophisticated methods.

12.5   Commercial Network Management Systems

Numerous network management systems are commercially available today, and we do not intend to survey them all here. Rather, our purpose is to present a broad perspective by highlighting the use of and techniques involved in some of them. We can classify the commercially available network management systems broadly as low-end NMS, enterprise NMS, and enterprise management solutions.

The low-end systems are either PC-based or vendor-specific network management systems. An example of a PC-based system is SNMPc™. Examples of vendor-specific systems are CiscoWorks, which manages Cisco network products; Transcend, which manages 3Com products; and Spectrum Portable Management Applications, which manages Cabletron products.

An enterprise management solution deals with network and systems management and unifies various management systems and functions. Such solutions are built on open architecture so that systems can be integrated easily. However, they are still customized for the individual corporate environment. Two major contributors in this field are Computer Associates Unicenter/The Next Generation (TNG) and Tivoli TME/NetView. We will discuss these systems in Sections 12.6 and 12.7.

The broadest range of the network management system is the middle-range enterprise network management system. Three of the popular ones are Hewlett-Packard's OpenView, Cabletron's Spectrum, and Sun's family of Solaris network managers. These three vendor products share most of the enterprise network management market, so we will look at each of them in some detail.

Enterprise network management systems manage networks globally, using standard protocol-based managed objects, such as SNMP-based managed objects. Detailed object management is accomplished with vendor-specific management systems, which are integrated with enterprise management systems. There are two types of integrated enterprise network management systems. The first approach utilizes systems such as OpenView to launch vendor-specific management systems such as CiscoWorks. This approach is referred to as loose and open integration and is implemented by the vendor-specific system vendor, with API provided by the enterprise system vendor. The alternative approach of tight integration is utilized by an enterprise manager or a vendor management system, which contains management modules for multiple vendor-specific devices. Both approaches have advantages and disadvantages.

For most computer communication networks, a network management system that manages SNMP-based scalar objects is adequate. As we showed in Part II, an aggregate object is defined as a table with columnar objects. Each instance of a set of values is described as a row in the table, each being associated with a scalar value. All three systems—Hewlett-Packard's OpenView Network Node Manager, Cabletron's Spectrum, and Sun's family of network management systems—are capable of managing scalar objects. Recently, attention has been paid to managing telecommunications and computer communication networks with TMN. Recall that TMN is OSI based, with CMIP as the management protocol. Hewlett-Packard's Network Node Manager and Sun's Enterprise Manager have this capability built into them. As our focus in this book has been on SNMP-based management of scalar objects, we will restrict our discussion here to that aspect of network management systems.

12.5.1   Hewlett-Packard's OpenView Network Node Manager

HP's network management platform is OpenView, and Network Node Manager is the network management system built on that platform. The NetMetrix Protocol Analyzer that we discussed earlier in the chapter is also built on the OpenView platform. When implemented together, these two systems perform the fault and performance management functions of the enterprise network efficiently.

The HP OpenView platform provides the common management services that are accessed through standard application programming interfaces (APIs). Figure 12.25 shows the OpenView platform architecture. It is open, modular, and distributed and has an object-oriented design that can manage telecommunications networks. The management applications, including the agent and manager processes, interface with the display services via an API and with the common management services via another API. These interfaces allow easy development and integration of vendor-specific management systems with the OpenView platform by third-party vendors.

A communication infrastructure provides the foundation for integrating all the common services, as well as the capability to establish a distributed management platform, as shown in Figure 12.26 [Chadayammuri PG]. We simplified the representation of the distributed management platform by omitting the TMN components. The heart of the distributed platform is the postmaster, which integrates all the management services. It handles multiple protocol stacks—SNMP, CMIP, and TCP/IP. The routing services manage the distributed message routing. Event services control event and alarm messages. The managed services interface with different application processes via APIs.

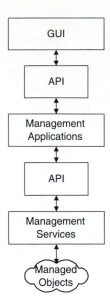

Figure 12.25   The HP OpenView Platform Architecture

Figure 12.27 shows how an enterprise network is managed by HP OpenView Network Node Managers (NNMs). The site collectors are also NNMs, or they could be Entry NNMs, which can manage as many as 100 nodes. Filtered information is sent to the centralized network management station for an aggregate view. Proximity of the collection station to the site enables a lot of data to be collected with great reliability. Filtered transmission of information to the management station also reduces the management traffic load on the network.

12.5.2   Cabletron's Spectrum Platform

Spectrum is an enterprise network management platform made by Cabletron. It has two components: SpectroSERVER and SpectroGRAPH. The platform is a distributed client/server architecture, with SpectroSERVER as the server and SpectroGRAPH as the client. The SpectroSERVER is a modeling engine containing a multiprotocol communications handler, database, and artificial intelligence (AI) technology for modeling and event correlation; it gathers information from the network. The SpectroGRAPH is the client that interfaces with the user via a GUI and accesses information from the SpectroSERVER.

The architecture of the Spectrum network management platform is shown in Figure 12.28 [Lewis L & Frey J]. Each domain of the enterprise network has a SpectroSERVER. The domain can be functional, geographic, or administrative. All domains are managed

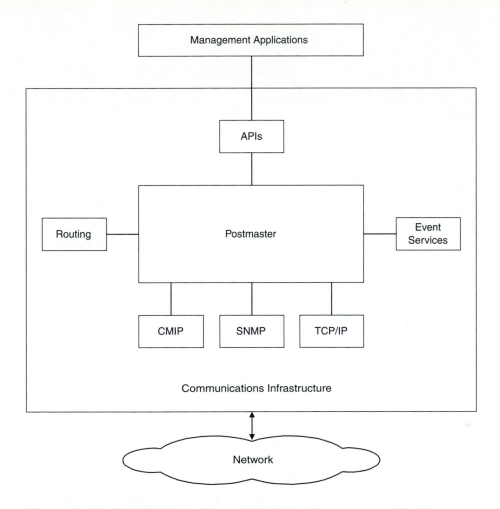

Figure 12.26   The HP OpenView Distributed Management Platform

from a single SpectroGRAPH. Thus, in Figure 12.28, the SpectroGRAPH is shown attached to SpectroSERVER 2 by a solid line, but it could be switched to other Spectro-SERVERs, as indicated by the dashed lines.

Spectrum's distributed architecture in the SpectroSERVER has the advantage of the server being close to the network domain that it is managing. Further, AI technology limits the management traffic on the network by sending the alarms and relevant events to the SpectroGRAPH and other SpectroSERVERs. Cabletron, other vendors, customers, or independent development companies build the third-party management modules for managing other vendor equipment.

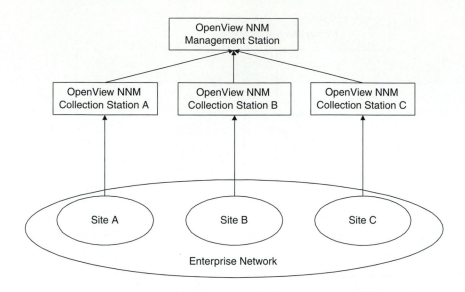

Figure 12.27   The HP OpenView Distributed Network Management System

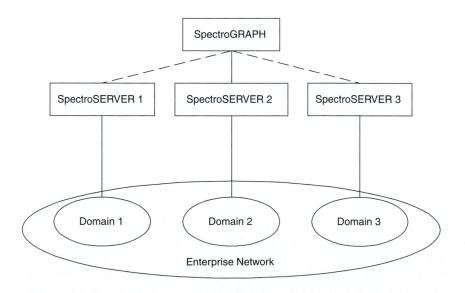

Figure 12.28   The Cabletron Spectrum Platform Architecture

12.5.3   Sun Network Management Systems Family

Sun has a family of three network management systems: the Solstice Site Manager, Solstice Domain Manager, and Solstice Enterprise Manager. Sun's earlier version, the Sun-Net Manager™, has been incorporated into the Solstice Domain Manager and Solstice Site Manager.

The Solstice Site Manager is a low-end platform designed to manage up to 100 nodes. The Solstice Domain Manager is designed for larger sites (1,000 to 10,000 nodes), and can be configured in three ways. The first configuration is a stand-alone for large site management. The second configuration is a MoM configuration, in which Solstice Site Managers feed data to the Solstice Domain Manager. In the third configuration, Solstice Domain Managers are connected peer-to-peer as cooperative management platforms, sending and receiving information between each other.

The earlier design architecture of a cooperative console is implemented in both the Solstice Site Manager and the Solstice Domain Manager, which enables the console function to be transferred to remote sites during off hours of a network operations center. The Solstice Site Manager also includes a proxy agent for remote management. With the proxy agent, the polling is localized at the remote site, thus reducing network overhead. It also manages alarms for the local network. Both the Solstice Site Manager and the Solstice Domain Manager have a statistics agent for managing Sun Solaris platforms. The remote procedure call (RPC)-based agent monitors CPU usage. A technical white paper by Sun [Sun Site and Domain] provides considerable detail on the design and features of Solstice Site Manager and Solstice Domain Manager.

The Solstice Enterprise Manager is the top-of-the-line platform. It is designed for very large enterprise networks and is capable of handling both computer and telecommunications networks. Its AI technology performs advanced event correlation. It uses an object-oriented server and supports multiple protocols such as SNMP, CMIP, and proprietary protocols.

The architecture of the Solstice Enterprise Manager is shown in Figure 12.29 [Sun Enterprise]. It has an event-driven, transaction-oriented, distributed, and multi-process architecture. The architecture has four components: management applications, a portable management interface, a management information server, and a management protocol adapter. Management applications interface with the management information server (MIS) through a portable management interface (PMI). The PMI is a high-level abstraction of the interface for manipulating objects, using the services available in the Enterprise Manager. The MIS contains services, functions, and management data. It communicates with managed objects via the appropriate protocol stack. For each protocol adapter housing the protocol stack, a separate PMI is defined in the Enterprise Manager.

The Solstice Enterprise Manager architecture is designed for TMN [Sun Enterprise]. Using CMIP protocol, it supports the TMN functions OSF, MF, and QAF (see Chapter 11). Recently, Sun has extended the Solstice Enterprise Manager to Java technology–based computing. The TMN/SNMP Q-adapter function enables implementation of TMN in an Internet management environment.

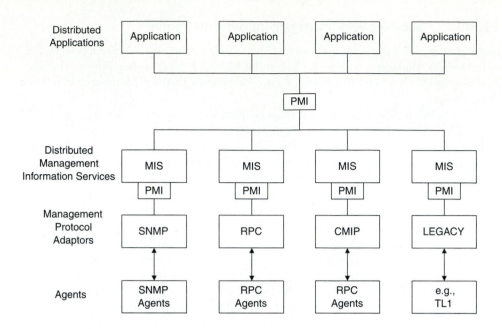

Figure 12.29   The Sun Solstice Enterprise Manager Architecture

12.6   System Management

Network management addresses only the managing of a network (i.e., managing the transportation of information). System management deals with managing system resources, which complements network management. For example, *ping* is used to test whether a host is alive. However, we want to know more about the use of system resources on the host, such as the amount of central processing unit (cpu) use on the host or whether a specific application is running on the host.

Historically, corporations had two separate and distinct organizations. The telecommunications department took care of communications, giving rise to network management. The management of information systems (MIS) department took care of the computers, a task that involves system management. However, in the current distributed environment of client/server architecture, the communication network depends heavily on computers (e.g., servers) and the distinction has disappeared. System and network management now form a single umbrella, headed by a chief information officer. System and network management are beginning to be considered together as a solution for information management issues and problems. System management tools, which used to be custom developed, are currently available as commercial systems, and are being integrated with network management.

System management tools monitor the performance of computer systems. Some of the parameters that can be monitored are (1) cpu use, which measures the number of processes that are running and the resource consumption of each; (2) status of critical background processes (called *daemons* in UNIX terminology); and (3) application servers such as the Simple Mail Transfer Protocol (SMTP), File Transport Protocol (FTP), and Domain Name Server (DNS). System management may also include backup of server databases, desktop workstations, and operations systems that support operations such as help desk and trouble ticket tracking.

Several UNIX-based tools can be used to monitor systems. Such tools are constantly evolving and are updated on Web sites that are used to track them. One of the long-established sites that provide this information is http://netman.cit.buffalo.edu/Archives.html; and a recently established Linux-based site is http://www.btc.gatech.edu/net/management/linux. More references may be obtained from these sources.

12.6.1   High-End System Management

The Computer Associates (CA) Unicenter TNG and Tivoli Enterprise Manager TME 10 are two integrated systems solutions available commercially (ZDNet 1998). Both solutions offer features that can be classified as high end and thus require the vendor's ongoing active participation. They meet the requirements of large enterprises, particularly as they are offered as integrated solutions, which we will discuss in Section 12.7.

12.6.2   Low-End System Management

System management of hosts can be accomplished by installing simple and free public domain software and configuring it to local system management. Two well-known low-end system management products are Big Brother [MacGuire S] and Spong [Hill E]. Although they have very serious limitations in terms of both platforms and functionality, they may be adequate for small and medium-sized company networks.

Big Brother and Spong are two examples of software that can be implemented with relative ease to manage system resources. The systems are quite similar, as Spong was derived from Big Brother, and both are Web-based. A central server on a management workstation runs on a UNIX platform, and clients are on managed objects. Big Brother is written in C and UNIX shell scripts, whereas Spong is written in Perl code and hence can be run on multiple platforms. The central management station presents the status of all the systems and applications being monitored in a matrix of colored cells, each color designating a particular status. Both systems can support pager and e-mail functions that report the occurrence of alarms. For both systems, the software can be downloaded and modified to meet local requirements for the operations, services, and applications to be monitored.

Big Brother performs the dual function of polling clients and listening to periodic status reports from clients that are UNIX based. Polling checks the network connectivity to any system. The client software periodically wakes up, monitors the system, transmits the information to the central server, and then goes back to sleep. Textual details can be obtained on the exact nature of a problem. The systems are grouped for ease of administration.

Spong is a simple system according to its author [Hill E]. Communication is via simple TCP messages, not SNMP messages. The client behaves the same way as in Big Brother. It generates data on the system periodically and reports it to the server. The server saves the information reported by the client and displays the status on the matrix display. Besides the ability to display a large amount of information about problems, the server can also present the history of problems.

12.7   Enterprise Management Solutions

We will next describe the two commercially available integrated solutions to system and network management. The two solutions are offered by two vendors, Computer Associates and IBM, which has acquired Tivoli. Both partner with several network management system vendors to provide integrated solutions.

12.7.1   Computer Associates Unicenter TNG

The CA Unicenter TNG framework provides infrastructure to support integrated distributed enterprise management. It is based on a client/server architecture having an agent in each host and a centralized workstation. CA provides Unicenter TNG agents that can run on a large number of platforms, and the list continues to increase as the customer base diversifies. Besides TCP/IP and SNMP, the TNG framework supports numerous other network protocols, accommodating a varied enterprise environment.

CA describes Unicenter TNG as a framework comprising three components: Real World Interface, object repository, and distributed services. The Real World Interface presents visual depiction of managed objects from different user perspectives. Both two-dimensional and three-dimensional presentations are available. The object repository is a management information database that includes multiplicity of data, such as managed objects, metadata class definitions, business process views, policies, topology, and status information. The distributed services link elements at the communications level.

Because of the TNG agents running in the hosts, during autodiscovery the system discovers not just the host identifications, but also details of the processor, disk, and other components of the system. The discovered components are presented in a Real World Interface that presents a unified GUI at the higher levels. An object repository stores all the autodiscovered information and any other management information needed to support the Real World Interface. System and network management views are extended to business process views, whereby objects related to an administrative group or functional group can be presented. This approach makes operations easier for human personnel because they don't have to know the technical details behind the operations they are performing.

Event management in the TNG framework includes a rule-based paradigm that correlates events across cross-platforms and presents the resultant alarms at the central console. These events include the standard SNMP traps. The standard drilling through layers to detect the lowest level component failure is built in as desktop support.

An additional feature of the TNG framework is calendar management, which provides a shared calendar so that all personnel can view each other's activities. The calendar handles both one-time and periodic activities. Operations such as triggering an alarm pager or e-mail can be programmed according to weekly and weekend shift schedules.

Some of the other notable features of the TNG framework are backup and disaster recovery, customized and canned report generation, and virus detection—all of which can be programmed as part of calendar management activities. In addition to these standard features, numerous optional modules, such as advanced help desk management, Web server management, and software delivery, are available.

12.7.2   Tivoli Enterprise Manager

Tivoli's management framework, originally named the Tivoli TME 10 framework, provides system and network management and is in the same class as the Unicenter TNG framework. Tivoli has changed the TME 10 from a two-tier, client/server architecture to a three-tier architecture and has renamed it Tivoli Enterprise Manager. Tivoli claims that the new architecture has increased the capability of handling from 300 to 10,000 managed nodes. The extended three-tier architecture also has a gateway as a middle layer that is designed to handle as many as 2,000 agents. The agent module has been redesigned to consume less resources.

Tivoli merged with IBM, allowing it to integrate the features of its systems with IBM's NetView network management system. NetView performs the network management function, and the complementary features of the Tivoli management applications perform the system management functions. The platform is object-oriented, and the system uses the standard CORBA-compliant object model for use with diverse and distributed platforms. This feature is somewhat similar to the Sun Enterprise Manager, which also uses the CORBA-compliant OSI object model and standard CMIP protocol. In the management framework, Tivoli management agents reside in the managed host applications. Although the TME Enterprise system does not use SNMP as the management protocol, NetView handles SNMP traps.

Tivoli Enterprise Manager monitors network, systems, and applications in a distributed architecture, as in most other systems. Event management has a built-in rule-based engine that correlates events and diagnoses problems. It further has an automated or operator-initiated response mechanism to correct problems wherever possible, using a decision support system. Service desk technology is integrated with network and system management technology in the service-level management framework.

Tivoli service management comprises problem management, asset management, and change management. The problem management module tracks customer requests, complaints, and problems. The asset management module handles inventory management. The change management module incorporates and manages business change processes.

The Tivoli Enterprise Manager framework contains an applications manager module (global enterprise manager), that coordinates business applications residing in diverse multiple platforms. An API is provided to permit third-party vendors to integrate their application software into the Tivoli Enterprise Manager framework. The applications manager also measures the response and throughput performance of applications.

The security management module provides encryption and decryption capabilities (optional). A software distribution module automates software distribution and updates. Operations can be scheduled by the workload scheduler module.

Summary

In this chapter we described various networking and network management tools and systems. The Network Operations Center Tools Working Group of IETF, which is no longer active, produced a document that classified tools—both commercial and public.

We surveyed networking tools and showed how they are used to monitor and test networks. The network's physical layer is tested by the bit error rate tester. Other tools test network status, network traffic, and network routing. Even more such tools are available in UNIX operating system environments.

SNMP queries can be made by using SNMP command tools, which are the commands that you learned in Part II of this book. These command tools are implemented in the network management systems that we discussed in the last several sections of this chapter.

Protocol analyzers play a significant role in network maintenance. They are useful for testing network performance and for gathering packet statistics on all OSI layers. We looked at examples of commercial protocol analyzers and network traffic statistics obtained using them.

Finally, we discussed network and system management solutions, differentiating between network and system management. We looked at the requirements for a network management system and gave examples of some commercially available systems for both low-end and enterprise levels. We identified some public software that can be used to implement system management solutions. We also described two commercially available solutions for integrated system and network management applicable to enterprise management.

Exercises

Note: *For some of the following exercises, the instructor needs to set up appropriate network configurations and host parameters.*

1. Execute the commands **nslookup** and **dig** on a host IP address and present your results.
   a. Compare the two results for the common information and present it.
   b. What kinds of additional information do you get from *dig?*
2. Use *dig* to determine the authoritative domain name servers for the zone associated with *altavista.com.*
3. Using *dig,* list all the hosts associated with the zone of *altavista.com.*

4. Using *dig*, determine the domain name that corresponds to the IP address 198.116.142.34.

5. a. As a network engineer, you are required to add and configure a nonmanaged network component that has multiple interfaces remotely. What network utility would you use?

   b. Discover the details on interfaces available on a host that has already been configured.

6. As a network manager, you are responsible for the operation of a network. You notice heavy traffic in a host that is on a TCP/IP network and want to find out the details.

   a. What basic network monitoring tool(s) would you use?

   b. What would you look for in your results?

7. Using *tcpdump* on an Ethernet interface on a host, capture ten IP packets.

8. a. What are the five major forms of display formats available in the *netstat* command? Give a one- or two-sentence description of each.

   b. Cite an application for each of the display formats mentioned in part (a) in the daily network operations.

9. Execute the three options (a) -N, (b) -r, and (c) -i of *netstat* on a host and explain your results.

10. Compare the results of routing tables obtained from using the *arp* and *netstat* utilities.

11. Ping an international site 100 times and determine the percentage packet loss.

12. Execute **traceroute** to a well-known host name and measure the effective throughput for one of the point-to-point links in the path using *bing*. (*Hint:* Vary the packet size in *bing* if your results do not look right.)

13. In diagnosing poor network performance—for example, delay—you need to know where the bottleneck is. Use *traceroute* to an international site on another continent and isolate the delay in the path.

14. Execute the **arp** command on a host or router in your network multiple times. Comment on the content and size of your results. (Your network may keep you from exercising this utility.)

15. From a workstation in a segment of your institute's network, discover all other workstations in your segment, using a network tool. Substantiate your result with the gathered data.

16. If your network segment is bridged to another subnet, you would have noticed it in Exercise 15. Using network tools, discover the workstations on the neighboring segment if there is one. Substantiate your result with the gathered data.

17. Monitor and capture SNMP network connectivity test packets from a network management system. Explain the contents of the packets.

18. Using an SNMP tool, determine which of the nodes given by your instructor has the longest and shortest up time. Substantiate your result with the gathered data.

19. Using an SNMP tool, for the host nodes provided by your instructor, determine which ones offer FTP service. Confirm your results by direct queries.

20. Using a MIB tool, for the network node given by your instructor, determine its private MIB.

CHAPTER 13

Network Management Applications

The management of networked information services involves both network and system resources. OSI defines network management as a five-layer architecture. We extended the model to include system management and present the integrated architecture in Figure 13.1. At the highest level is business management that deals with the functions associated with managing an enterprise. These functions apply to all enterprises, be they commercial businesses, educational institutions, telecommunications service providers, or any other organizations that use networked information systems to help manage their operations.

For our purposes an enterprise is an organization, public or private, that provides a product or service. In either case, the second level, service management must be addressed. For example, a business that makes a product also has to be concerned with customer

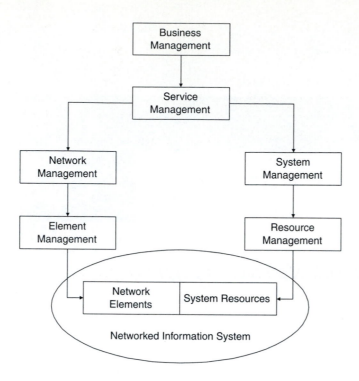

Figure 13.1   Network and System Management

service, as well as internal services. Service management for a service provider, including a telecommunications organization, is an
absolute necessity. (See Figure 11.14 for an illustration of some service applications.)

The third level deals with network management or system management. Network management aggregates and correlates data from
network element management activities at the fourth level. Likewise, system management aggregates and coordinates data from the
resource management activities. The complementary functions of
network and system management deal with the networked information system composed of network elements and system resources at
the fifth and lowest level.

Our focus in this chapter will be on network management
applications. As we discussed in Chapter 3, they are configuration

management, fault management, performance management, security management, and accounting management. Others [Leinwand A & Conroy KF] have treated the five categories of applications and presented both simple and complex tools to manage them.

Configuration management may be looked at not only from the operational viewpoint, but also from the engineering and planning viewpoints. In our treatment of configuration management in Section 13.1, we will discuss network provisioning and inventory management. These topics supplement the configuration of network topology, which is part of traditional network management.

Fault management involves detecting a fault as it occurs in the network and subsequently locating its source. We will cover isolating the root cause of the problem in Section 13.2.

Defining performance of a network in quantitative terms is harder than defining it in qualitative terms. For example, when we observe that network performance is slow, we need to define slowness and which segment of the network is slow. However, the application, which could be running on a server, may be what is behaving slowly. We will discuss performance management in Section 13.3, including performance metrics and how to monitor a network for performance. Performance statistics play an essential part in network management, so we will cover several system tools available for gathering statistics.

When a fault occurs in a network, either because of component failure or performance, it may manifest itself in many places. Thus, in a centralized management system, alarms can come from multiple locations. Correlating alarm events and finding the causes of the problems is a challenge. We will discuss various correlation technologies in Section 13.4.

Network security is concerned with preventing illegal access to information by unauthorized personnel. It involves not only technical issues, but also establishment of well-defined policies and procedures. We will discuss the various issues associated with authentication and authorization in Section 13.5. We will also deal with the establishment of secure (i.e., without illegal monitoring and manipulation) communication between source and receiver.

The business health of an enterprise depends on well-maintained accounting management and reporting. Reports for management have a different purpose from that of reports generated for day-to-day network operation. For example, reports are needed to measure the quality of service being provided as per the service level agreement. We will cover these topics in Sections 13.6 and 13.7.

Network management at the third level and service management at the fourth level of the hierarchy are based not just on technical considerations, but also on policy decisions. Once policies have been established, some of them can be implemented in the system. For example, solving network congestion owing to heavy traffic may mean automatically adjusting network parameters to increase the bandwidth or decreasing traffic into the network. A policy decision preselecting one of these options can be implemented as part of the management system. We will discuss this topic in Section 13.8.

Service level management is fast becoming an important aspect of network and system management. It goes beyond managing resources, being concerned with service level agreements between customers and service providers regarding the quality of network, system, and business application services to be provided and maintained. We will cover this topic in Section 13.9.

13.1   Configuration Management

Configuration management in network management is normally used in the context of discovering network topology, mapping the network, and setting up configuration parameters in management agents and management systems. However, as discussed in Chapter 1 and shown in Figure 1.21, network management in the broad sense also includes network provisioning, which includes network planning and design. Network provisioning is considered to be part of configuration management.

13.1.1   Network Provisioning

Network provisioning, also called circuit provisioning in the telephone industry, is an automated process. A trunk (circuit from the originating switching center to the destination switching center) and a special service circuit (customized to meet customer specifications) are designed by application programs written in operation systems. Planning and inventory systems are integrated with design systems to build an overall system (often referred to as a *system of systems*). Thus a circuit designed for the future automatically derives its turn-on date from the planning system and ensures that the components are available in the inventory system. Similarly, disconnecting a circuit is coordinated with the planning system, and the freed-up components are added to the inventory system, making the design system aware of the availability of components for future designs.

An example of a circuit provisioning system is the one developed by the Bell System (before it was broken up), called the Trunk Integrated Record Keeping System (TIRKS™). It is used in the automated circuit provisioning of trunks, which are logical circuits between switching offices and traverse many facilities. TIRKS is an operations system in the context of TMN, which we examined in Chapter 11. Given the requirements of a trunk, such as transmission loss and noise, type of circuit, availability date, and the like, as input to the system, the system automatically designs trunk components. The designed circuit identifies the transmission facilities between switching offices and equipment in intermediate and end offices. Equipment selection is based on the devices available when the circuit is to be installed.

Network provisioning in a computer communications network has different requirements. Instead of circuit-switched connections, packet-switched paths are used to transmit information from source to destination. In a connectionless packet-switched circuit, each packet takes an independent path and the switching of each packet by the routers at various nodes is based on the load in the links. Provisioning of the links is based on average and peak demands. In store-and-forward communication, excess packets can be stored in buffers in routers or retransmitted in the event that packets are lost or discarded. In connection-oriented circuit communication, permanent and switched-virtual circuit demands need to be accommodated for end-to-end demands on the various links. Network provisioning for packet-switched network is based on performance statistics and quality of service requirements.

Network provisioning in broadband WAN communication using ATM technology is more complex. The virtual-circuit concept is always used and has to be taken into account in the provisioning process. The switches are cell-based, in contrast to frame-based packet switching. Each ATM switch has knowledge of the virtual path–virtual circuit (VP–VC) of each session connection only to the neighboring nodes and not end-to-end. Each ATM switch vendor has built into the ATM switch their proprietary assignment of VP–VC for end-to-end design. The architecture of end-to-end provisioning of ATM circuits could be either centralized or distributed. It is based on whether the circuit is a permanent virtual circuit (PVC) or a switched virtual circuit (SVC). Commercial products, which provision PVCs for multiple vendor products, have recently been introduced.

13.1.2   Inventory Management

An efficient database system is an essential part of an inventory management system. We need to be aware of the specification details associated with various components. The data should be accessible by means of different indices. Some of the obvious indices or access keys are the component description or part number, components that match a set of characteristics, components in use and in spare, and components to be freed-up for future use.

In Section 13.1.1 we cited the example of TIRKS, which is a system of systems. Two of the systems that TIRKS uses are equipment inventory (E1) and facilities inventory (F1). The E1 system maintains an inventory of all equipment, identifying what is currently available and what will become available in the future with dates of availability. Similar information is maintained on facilities by the F1 system. With these detailed inventory systems, TIRKS can anticipate circuit provisioning for the future with components that would be available.

Legacy inventory management systems use hierarchical and scalar-based database systems. Such databases limit the addition of new components or extend the properties of existing components by adding new fields. These limitations can be removed by using relational database technology. Further, new network management systems, such as OSI CMIP and Web-based management, use object-oriented technology. These systems manage object-oriented managed objects. An object-oriented relational database is helpful in configuration and inventory management in such an environment.

13.1.3   Network Topology

Network management is based on knowledge of network topology. As a network grows, shrinks, or otherwise changes, network topology needs to be updated automatically. Such updating is done by the discovery application in the network management system. However, the scope of the discovery process needs to be constrained. For example, the *arp* command can discover any network component that responds with an IP address, which can then be mapped by the network management system. If the response includes workstations that are turned on only when they are in use, the network management system would indicate failure whenever they are off. Obviously, that is not desirable. In addition, some hosts should not be discovered for security reasons and should be filtered out during the discovery process. Hence the discovery application should have the capability to set filter parameters to impose constraints.

Autodiscovery can be done by using the broadcast ping on each segment and following up with further SNMP queries to gather more details on the system. A more efficient method is to look at the ARP cache in the local router. The ARP cache table is large and contains the addresses of all the hosts and nodes used in recent communications. Use of this table also allows subsequent ARP queries to be sent to other routers. This process is continued until the desired information is obtained on all IP addresses defined by the scope of the autodiscovery procedure. A map showing network topology is presented by the autodiscovery procedure after the addresses of the network entities have been discovered.

The autodiscovery procedure becomes more complex in the virtual LAN configuration. We briefly described virtual LAN in the context of ATM emulated LAN in Chapter 9. At that time, we pointed out that virtual LAN could be implemented in any switched LAN environment. Let us now look at it in more detail. Figure 13.2 shows the *physical* configuration of a conventional LAN. The router can be visualized as part of a backbone (not shown). Two LAN segments, segment A and segment B, are connected to the router. They are physically connected to two physical ports in the router (i.e., one port for each segment is used on the interface card). They are identified as port A and port B and correspond to segment A and segment B, respectively. Both LANs are Ethernet LANs and use hub configuration. Two hosts, A1 and A2, are connected to hub 1 on LAN segment A and two hosts, B1 and B2, are connected to hub 2 on LAN segment B.

Figure 13.3 shows the *logical* configuration for Figure 13.2, which is what the autodiscovery process detects. It is similar to the physical configuration: Segment A corresponds to LAN on hub 1 with the hosts A1 and A2. This configuration is easy to visualize conceptually and easy to configure.

Let us now contrast Figures 13.2 with 13.4, which shows the *physical* configuration of two virtual LANs (VLANs). Notice that only one physical port, port A, is used in the router—not two as in the case of a traditional LAN. Hosts A1 and A2 are configured to be on VLAN 1, and hosts B1 and B2 are configured to be on VLAN 2. Although VLAN grouping can be done according to different criteria, let us assume that it is done here on a port basis on the switch. Thus the two ports marked segment A on the switch are grouped as VLAN 1. The other two ports, marked segment B, are grouped as VLAN 2. Hence segment A corresponds to VLAN 1, and segment B corresponds to VLAN 2. Moreover, VLAN 1 and VLAN 2 are spread across the two physical hubs, hub 1 and hub 2. With a layer-2 bridged network, the VLAN network is efficient. As standards are established, this configuration will be deployed more and more, along with an ATM backbone.

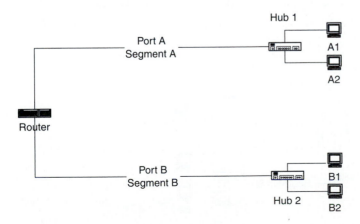

Figure 13.2   LAN Physical Configuration

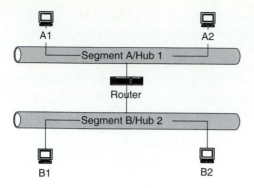

Figure 13.3   Logical Configuration of Two LAN Segments

The *logical* view of the physical VLAN configuration shown in Figure 13.4 is presented in Figure 13.5. Hosts A1 and A2 still belong to segment A, but they are on different hubs. Likewise, hosts B1 and B2 belong to segment 2. The autodiscovery process would not detect the physical hubs that are identified in Figure 13.5. In many situations, the switch also would be transparent, as no IP addresses are associated with switch ports. Consequently, associating the logical configuration with the physical configuration would be more difficult.

Inability to map the logical configuration with the physical configuration makes the network management task a complex one. First, two separate maps must be maintained continually as changes are made to the network. Second, when a new component is added and autodiscovered by the system, a manual procedure is needed to follow up on the physical configuration.

Figure 13.4 shows the establishment of VLAN using one switch. However, as was shown in Figure 9.8, VLANs can be established across multiple switches in an ATM

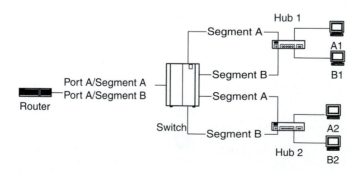

Figure 13.4   VLAN Physical Configuration

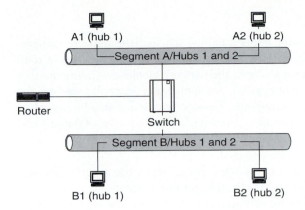

Figure 13.5   Logical Configuration of Two VLAN Segments

backbone. This approach makes keeping track of logical versus physical configurations even harder.

In the preceding example, we talked about basing the grouping of VLAN on ports on the switches. We could also base VLAN grouping on MAC address, IP address, or protocol type. Grouping by IP address has some benefits in the management of a VLAN network. Basing the logical grouping of components on IP network segments makes sense. In addition, as a policy the *sysLocation* entity in a system group should be filled in for easier management.

13.2   Fault Management

Fault in a network is normally associated with failure of a network component and subsequent loss of connectivity. Fault management involves a five-step process: (1) fault detection, (2) fault location, (3) service restoration, (4) identification of the problem's root cause, and (5) problem resolution. The fault should be detected as quickly as possible by the centralized management system, preferably before or at about the same time as users would notice it. Fault location involves identifying where the problem has occurred. We distinguish this step from problem isolation, although in practice they could be the same. The reason for doing so is that restoring service to users as quickly as possible, using alternative means, is important. Service restoration has a higher priority than diagnosing the problem and fixing it. However, that may not always be possible. Identification of the problem's root cause could be a complex process, which we will consider in greater depth shortly. After the source of the problem has been identified, a trouble ticket can be generated to resolve the problem. In an automated network operations center, the trouble ticket could be generated automatically by the network management system.

13.2.1   Fault Detection

Fault detection is accomplished by using either a polling scheme (the network management system polling management agents periodically for status) or by generation of traps (management agents based on information from the network elements sending unsolicited alarms to the network management system). An application program generates the **ping** command periodically and waits for response. Connectivity is declared broken when a preset number of consecutive responses are not received. The frequency of pinging and the preset number for failure detection may be optimized for balance between traffic overhead and the rapidity with which failure is detected.

The alternative detection scheme is to use traps. For example, the generic trap messages *linkDown* and *egpNeighborLoss* in SNMPv1 can be set in the agents, giving them the capability to report events to the network management system with the legitimate community name. One of the advantages of traps over polling is that failure detection is accomplished faster with less traffic overhead.

13.2.2   Fault Location and Isolation Techniques

Fault location using a simple approach (we'll look at the complex approach using correlation technology in Section 13.4) would be to detect all the network components that have failed. The origin of the problem could then be traced by walking down the topology tree to where the problem starts. Thus, if an interface card on a router has failed, all managed components connected to that interface would indicate failure.

After having located where the fault is, the next step is to isolate the fault (i.e., determine the source of the problem). First, we should determine whether the problem is failure of the component or failure of the physical link. Thus, in the preceding example, the interface card may be functioning well, but the link to the interface may be down. We need to use various diagnostic tools to isolate the cause.

Let us assume for the moment that the link is not the problem and that the interface card is. We then proceed to isolate the problem to the layer that is causing it. Excessive packet loss may be causing disconnection, and we can measure the packet loss by pinging, if pinging can be used. We can query the various MIB parameters on the node itself or on other related nodes to localize further the cause of the problem. For example, error rates calculated from the interface group parameters *ifInDiscards*, *ifInErrors*, *ifOutDiscards* and *ifOutErrors* with respect to the input and output packet rates could help us isolate the problem in the interface card.

The ideal solution to locating and isolating the fault is to have an artificial intelligence solution. By observing all the symptoms, we might be able to identify the source of the problem. Several techniques can be used to do so, which we will address in Section 13.4.

13.3   Performance Management

We have already addressed performance management applications both directly and indirectly under the various headings. In Chapter 12 we discussed two popular protocol analyzers, Sniffer and NetMetrix. Also in Chapter 12, we used the protocol analyzer as a system tool to measure traffic monitoring on Ethernet LANs, which is within the realm of performance management. We looked at load monitoring based on various parameters such as source and destination addresses and protocols at different layers. We addressed traffic statistics collected over periods of from hours to a year, using the MRTG tool. We detailed the use of statistics obtained using a protocol analyzer as an RMON in the case study in Chapter 8 to identify the overall trend in Internet-related traffic and the type of traffic.

Network performance is a nebulous term, which is hard to define or quantify in terms of global metrics. The purpose of the network is to carry information, and thus performance management actually is (data) traffic management. It involves following data monitoring, problem isolation, performance tuning, analysis of statistical data for recognizing trends, and resource planning.

13.3.1   Performance Metrics

The parameters that can be attributed to defining network performance on a global level are throughput, response time, network availability, and network reliability. The metrics of these parameters depend on what, when, and where the measurements are made.

These macro-level parameters can be defined in terms of micro-level parameters. Some of the parameters that affect network throughput are bandwidth or capacity of the transmission media, its utilization, channel error rate, peak load, and average traffic load. They can be measured at specific points in the network. For example, bandwidth or capacity will be different in different segments of the network. An Ethernet LAN with a capacity of 10 Mbps can function to full capacity with a single workstation on it, but it reaches full capacity with a utilization factor of only 30 to 40 percent when it is densely populated with workstations. This utilization factor can further be defined in terms of collision rate, which is measurable. In contrast, in a WAN, the bandwidth is fully utilized except for the packet overhead.

The response time of a network not only depends on the throughput of the network, but also on the application; in other words, it depends on both network and system performance. Thus, in a client/server environment, the response time as seen by the client could be slow, either owing to the server being heavily used, the network traffic being overloaded, or a combination of both. According to [Feldmeir J], "The application responsiveness on the network, more than any other measure, reflects whether the network is meeting the end users' expectations and requirements." He defines three types of metrics to measure application responsiveness: application availability, response time between user and server, and burst frame rate, which is the rate at which the requested data arrives at the user station.

The IETF Network Working Group developed several RFCs on traffic flow measurement. RFC 2063 defines the architecture for the measurement and reporting of network traffic flows. The network is characterized as traffic passing through four representative levels, as shown in Figure 13.6. Backbone networks are typically connected to other networks and do not have individual hosts connected to them. A regional network is similar to a backbone but is smaller. It may have individual hosts connected to it, and its hosts

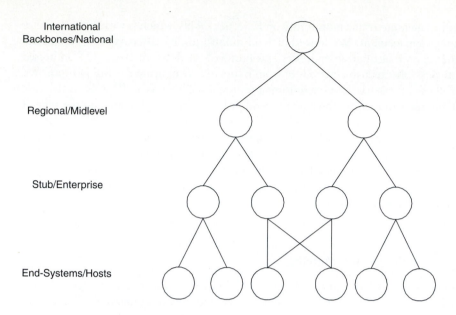

Figure 13.6   Traffic Flow Measurement Network Characterization

are subscribers to a backbone network. Stub/enterprise networks connect hosts and LANs and are subscribers to regional and backbone networks. End systems or hosts are subscribers to all these networks.

The architecture defines three entities for traffic flow measurements: meters, meter readers, and managers. Meters observe network traffic flows and build a table of flow data records for them. Meter readers collect traffic flow data from meters. Managers oversee the operation of meters and meter readers. RFC 2064 defines the MIB for the meter, and RFC 2123 describes NeTraMet, an implementation of a flow meter based on RFC 2063 and RFC 2064.

13.3.2   Data Monitoring

Data monitoring in the network for abnormal performance behavior, such as a high collision rate in an Ethernet LAN and excessive packet drop because of overload, are detected by traps generated by agents and RMON. Performance-related issues are detected primarily with trap messages generated by RMON probes. Thresholds are set for important SNMP parameters in the RMON, which then generate alarms when the preset thresholds are crossed. For example, the parameters in the alarm group and the event group in the RMON MIB [RFC 1757] may be set for the object identifier to be monitored. The time interval over which the data are to be collected for calculation and the rising and falling thresholds are specified. In addition, the community names are set for who would receive the alarm.

Network management systems generally report all events selected for display, including alarms. Alarms are set for criticality, and the alarm icon changes color according to the criticality. Depending on the implementation, the alarm is either automatically cleared when the alarm condition clears, or it is manually cleared by an operator. The latter case is useful for alerting operations personnel as to what happened.

13.3.3   Problem Isolation

Performance-related problem isolation depends on the type of problem. As we have indicated before, a high percentage of packet loss will cause loss of connectivity, which could be intermittent. In this situation, monitoring the packet loss over an extended period of time will isolate the problem. Another example is the performance problem associated with a long delay, which may be attributable to excessive drop of packets. We can identify the source of packet delay from a route-tracing procedure and then probe for the packet discards at that node. Refer to [Rose MT & McCloghrie K] for a detailed analysis of the performance degradation cases in various components and media.

As in fault management, problems can occur at multiple locations simultaneously. They can be reported to the central management system as multiple independent events, although they may be related. For example, an excessive drop in packets in one of the links may switch the traffic to an alternative route. That could cause an overload in that link, which would be reported as an alarm. A more sophisticated approach, using correlation technology is again required here (which we will discuss in Section 13.4).

13.3.4   Performance Statistics

Performance statistics are used in tuning a network, validating a service level agreement (SLA), which we will cover in Section 13.9, analyzing use trends, planning facilities, and functional accounting. Data are gathered by means of an RMON probe and an RMON MIB for statistics. To be accurate, statistics require large amounts of data sampling, which create overhead traffic on the network and thus have an impact on its performance. One of the enormous benefits of using an RMON probe for collecting statistical data is that it can be done locally without degrading overall network performance. An RMON MIB contains the history and statistics groups (see Chapter 8) for various media and can be used efficiently to collect the relevant data and store them for current and future analysis.

One application of the results obtained from performance statistics is to tune the network for better performance. For example, two segments of the network may be connected by a gateway and excessive intersegment traffic could produce excessive delay. Error statistics on dropped packets on the gateway interfaces would manifest this problem. The solution is to increase the bandwidth of the gateway by either increasing its capacity or by adding a second gateway between the segments. Of course, adding the extra gateway could cause configuration-related problems and hence reconfiguration of traffic might be needed.

Various error statistics at different layers are gathered to measure the quality of service and lead to performance improvements, if needed. Some of the other performance parameters that can be tuned by monitoring network statistics are bandwidth of links, utilization of links, and controlling the peak-to-average ratio of inherently bursty data traffic. In addition, traffic utilization can be improved by redistributing the load during the day, with essential traffic occupying the busy hours and nonessential traffic the slack hours.

An important statistic, especially in broadband services, is the variation in network delay, known as *jitter*. Variation affects the quality of service (QoS) guaranteed to the customer by the SLA. For example, in cable modem, a managed object *docsQoSServiceClass-MaxJitter* (see the DOCSIS Quality of Service MIB in Table 10.3) is proposed for monitoring jitter.

Another performance application is validation of the SLA between service user and service provider. The SLA may require limiting the input to the service provider network. If the packet rate is tending toward the SLA threshold, the bandwidth of the access to the service provider network may have to be controlled. Control can be achieved by implementing application interfaces that use algorithms such as the leaky bucket or the token bucket [Tanenbaum AS]. The leaky bucket algorithm limits the maximum output data rate, and the token bucket algorithm controls its average value. Combining the two, we can tune the peak-to-average ratio of the output. Some ATM switches have such interfaces built into them, and they are easily tunable. This approach would be desirable if a service provider's pricing is based on peak data rate use instead of average data rate use.

Performance statistics are also used to identify and project traffic use trends and to plan future resource requirements (see case study in Chapter 8). Statistical data on traffic are collected and periodic reports generated on use trends and to project needs.

As we pointed out in Chapter 12, statistics can be gathered on the network load created by various users and applications. They can be used as a basis for functional accounting so that network operating costs can be fairly apportioned to users and justified.

13.4   Event Correlation Techniques

We have illustrated some simple methods of diagnosing and isolating the source of a problem in fault and performance management. When a centralized network management system receives a trap or a notification, it is called *receiving an event*. A single problem source may cause multiple symptoms, and each symptom detected is reported as an independent event to the management system. Obviously, we do not want to treat each event independently and act to resolve it. Hence we want the management system to correlate all these events and isolate the root cause of the problem. The methods used to do so are called *event correlation techniques*.

Several correlation techniques are used to isolate and localize fault in networks. All are based on (1) detecting and filtering of events, (2) correlating observed events to isolate and localize the fault either topologically or functionally, and (3) identifying the cause of the problem. In all three cases, different reasoning methods distinguish one technique from another.

We will discuss six approaches to correlation techniques: (1) rule-based reasoning, (2) model-based reasoning, (3) case-based reasoning, (4) codebook, (5) state transition graph model, and (6) finite state machine model. See [Lewis L6] for a detailed comparison of the various methods.

13.4.1   Rule-Based Reasoning

Rule-based reasoning (RBR) is the earliest form of correlation technique. It is also known by many other names, including rule-based expert system, expert system, production system, and blackboard system. It has a working memory, an inference engine and a knowledge base as shown in Figure 13.7 [Cronk R, Callahan P & Berstein L; Lewis L2]. The three levels representing the three components are the data level, control level, and knowledge level, respectively. Cronk, Callahan, and Berstein's work also presents a good review of RBR network applications. The knowledge base contains expert knowledge as to (1) definition of a problem in the network and (2) action that needs to be taken if a particular condition occurs. The knowledge base information is rule-based in the form of *if-then* or *condition-action*, containing rules that indicate which operations are to be performed when. The working memory contains—as working memory elements—the topological and state information of the network being monitored. The working memory recognizes when the network goes into a faulty state. The inference engine, in cooperation with the knowledge base, compares the current state with the left side of the rulebase and finds the closest match to output the right side of the rule. The knowledge base then executes an action on the working memory element.

In Figure 13.7, the rule-based paradigm is interactive among the three components and is iterative. Several strategies are available for the rule-based paradigm. A specific strategy is implemented in the inference engine. When a specific rule has been chosen, an action is performed on the working memory element, which can then initiate

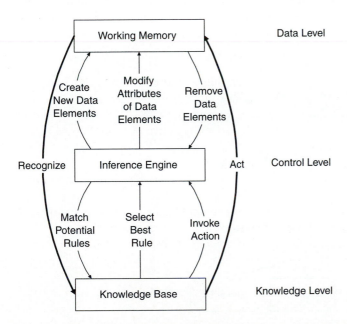

Figure 13.7   The Basic Rule-Based Reasoning Paradigm

another event. This process continues until the correct state is achieved in the working memory.

Rules are established in the knowledge base from the expertise of people in the field. The rule is an exact match and the action is very specific. If the antecedent and action in the rule do not match, the paradigm breaks and it is called *brittle*. However, it can be fixed by adding more rules, but doing so increases the database size and degrades performance, called a *knowledge acquisition bottleneck*. As the number of working memory elements grows, memory requirements grow exponentially. In addition, the action is specific, which can cause unwanted behavior. For example, we can define the alarm condition for packet loss as follows:

```
If packet loss < 10%          alarm green
If packet loss => 10% < 15%   alarm yellow
If packet loss => 15%         alarm red
```

The left side conditions are the working memory elements, which if detected would execute the appropriate rule defined in the rule-base. As you can see, this action could cause the alarm condition to flip back and forth in boundary cases. An application of fuzzy logic is used to remedy this problem [Lewis L2], but it is difficult to implement.

The RBR is used in Hewlett-Packard OpenView Element Management framework [Hajela S]. Figure 13.8 is an adaptation of Hajela's scenario, used here to illustrate an implementation of RBR. It shows a four-layer network. Backbone router A is linked to router B. Hub C is connected to router B and has four servers, D1–D4, in its LAN. Without a correlation engine, failure in the interface of router A will generate an alarm. This fault then propagates to router B, hub C, and finally to servers D1–D4. Recall that a time delay is involved in alarm generation. In general, propagation of faults and the time delay associated with them need to be fully recognized in fault management.

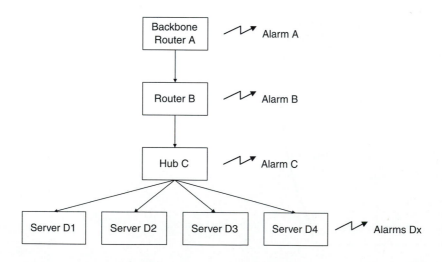

Figure 13.8   An RBR-Based Correlation Example Scenario

```
      Rule 0: Alarm A : Send rootcause alarm A
      Rule 1  Alarm B   If Alarm A present    Related to A and ignore
      Rule 2  Alarm C   If Alarm B present    Related to B and ignore
      Rule 3  Alarm Dx  If Alarm C present    Related to C and ignore
Correlation window: 20 seconds.
```

Figure 13.9   Rule Specifications for the RBR Scenario Presented in Figure 13.8

Four correlation rules are specified in Figure 13.9. Rule 0 has no associated condition with, but rules 1–3 are conditional. To allow for propagation time, a correlation window of 20 seconds is set.

The inference engine at the control level interprets these rules and takes the actions shown in Figure 13.10.

In the preceding example, only alarm A is sent, and the others are ignored so long as they arrive within the correlation window. The alarms could even be generated out of sequence. However, because of the specification of correlation window size, the inference engine waits before sending alarms B, C, and Dx.

Several commercial systems using RBR have been built. They include Computer Associates TNG and Tivoli TME.

13.4.2   Model-Based Reasoning

In model-based reasoning, an event correlator is built on an object-oriented model associated with each managed object. As a representation of the component it models, the traditional object-oriented model has attributes, relations to other models, and behaviors. The relationship between objects is reflected in a similar relationship between models.

```
         Correlation Window = 20 seconds
         ◄─────────────────────────────────►

Arrival of Alarm A      | Alarm A sent
Arrival of Alarm B              |
       (Correlated by Rule 1)
Arrival of Alarm C                  |
       (Correlated by Rule 2)
Arrival of Alarms Dx                    |
       (Correlated by Rule 3)
End of Correlation Window                   |
```

Figure 13.10   Control Actions for the RBR Scenario Presented in Figure 13.8

Let us picture a physical network of hubs connected to a router, as shown in Figure 13.11 (a). The corresponding event correlator model in the network management system (NMS) is shown in Figure 13.11(b). The NMS pings every hub and the router (really a router interface to the backbone network) periodically to check whether each component is working. We can associate communication between the NMS and a managed component with a model (software object) in the NMS/correlator and its counterpart of a managed object. Thus in our example, the model of each hub periodically pings its hub, and the model of the router pings the router. So long as all the components are working, no additional operation is needed.

If Hub1 fails, it is recognized by the Hub1 model. Let us assume that the Hub1 model is programmed to wait for a lack of response to three consecutive pings. After three pings with no response, the Hub1 model suspects a failure of Hub1. However, before it declares a failure and displays an alarm, it analyzes its relation to other models and recognizes that it should query the router model. If the router model responds that the router is working, the Hub1 alarm is triggered. If the router model responds that it is not receiving a response from the router, the Hub1 model deduces that the problem is with the router and not Hub1. At least, it cannot definitively determine a Hub1 failure so long as it cannot communicate with Hub1 because of the router failure.

This example is modeled on the one by [Lewis L6], who presented an interesting scenario of a classroom with teacher. Outside the classroom is a computer network with a router and workstations. Each student is a model (software mirror) of the workstation, and the teacher is a model of the router. Each student communicates with his or her real-world counterpart, which is the workstation outside the classroom. The teacher communicates

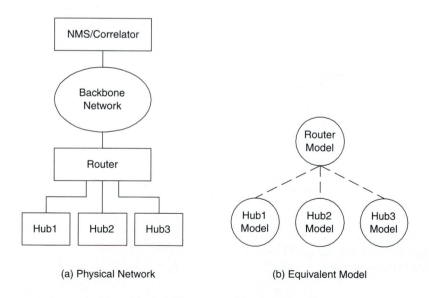

(a) Physical Network   (b) Equivalent Model

Figure 13.11   A Model-Based Reasoning Event Correlator

with the router. If a student is unable to communicate with the workstation, he or she queries the teacher as to whether the teacher could communicate with the teacher's router. Depending on the teacher's answer, the student declares a "fail" (yes) or "no-fail" (no) condition. Model-based reasoning is implemented in Cabletron Spectrum.

13.4.3   Case-Based Reasoning

Case-based reasoning (CBR) overcomes many of the deficiencies of RBR. In RBR, the unit of knowledge is a rule, whereas in CBR the unit of knowledge is a case [Lewis L4]. The intuition of case-based reasoning is that situations repeat themselves in the real world and that what was done in one situation is applicable to others in a similar, but not necessarily identical, situation. Thus, when we try to resolve a trouble, we start with the case that we have experienced before [Kolodner J, Lewis L4]. Kolodner treats CBR from an information management viewpoint, and Lewis applies CBR specifically to network management.

The general CBR architecture is shown in Figure 13.12 [Lewis L4]. It consists of four modules: input, retrieve, adapt, and process, along with a case library. The CBR approach uses knowledge gained previously and extends it to the current situation. The former episodes are stored in a case library. If the current situation, as received by the input module, matches one in the case library (as identified by the retrieve module), it is applied. If it does not, the closest situation is chosen by the adapt module and adapted to the current situation to resolve the problem. The process module takes the appropriate action(s). Once the problem has been resolved, the newly adapted case is added to the library.

Lewis also described the application of CBR in a trouble-tracking system, CRITTER™ [Lewis L5]. The CRITTER application has evolved into a CBR application for network management named SpectroRx™, produced by Cabletron. When a trouble ticket is created on a network problem, it is compared to similar cases in the case library containing previous trouble tickets with resolutions. The current trouble is resolved by adapting the previous case in one of three ways: (1) parameterized adaptation, (2) abstraction/respecialization adaptation, and (3) critic-based adaptation. The resolved trouble ticket is then added to the library. We will use the examples given by Lewis to illustrate the three adaptation methods.

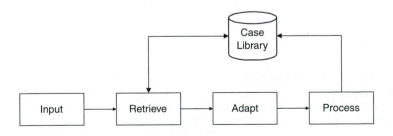

Figure 13.12   General CBR Architecture

```
Trouble: file_transfer_throughput=F
Additional data: none
Resolution: A=f(F), adjust_network_load=A
Resolution status: good
```

Figure 13.13   Matching Trouble Ticket for the CBR Example

Parameterized Adaptation.   Parameterized adaptation is used when a similar case exists in the case library, but the parameters may have to be scaled to resolve the current situation. Consider the current trouble with file_transfer_throughput, which matches the following trouble ticket in the case library, as shown in Figure 13.13.

In the parameterized adaptation of the trouble ticket shown in Figure 13.14, variable F has been modified to F′, and the relationship between network load adjustment variable A′ and F′ remain the same as between A and F. In the default situation, where the match is exact, F′ and A′ are F and A.

Abstraction/Respecialization Adaptation.   Figure 13.15 shows three trouble tickets. The first two are two cases from the case library matching the problem that we have been discussing. The first option adjusts the network load, and the second option adjusts the network bandwidth. The user or the system has the option of adapting either of the two, based on restrictions to be placed on adjusting the workload or adjusting the bandwidth. Let us choose the option of not restricting the network load, which means that we have to increase the bandwidth. We can add this adjustment as additional data to the trouble ticket that chooses the bandwidth option and create a new trouble ticket (the third trouble ticket in Figure 13.15). It is now added to the library.

This CBR adaptation is referred to as abstraction/respecialization. Choosing to adjust the bandwidth and not the load is a policy decision, which we will discuss in Section 13.8.

Critic-Based Adaptation.   In the third option, critic-based adaptation, a critic or craft person decides to add, remove, reorder, or replace an existing solution. Figure 13.16 shows an example where the network_load has been added as an additional parameter in adjusting the network load and resolution A is a function of two variables, F and N. It is added as a new case to the library.

```
Trouble: file_transfer_throughput=F′
Additional data: none
Resolution: A′=f(F′), adjust_network_load=A′
Resolution status: good
```

Figure 13.14   Parameterized Adaptation for the CBR Example

```
Trouble: file_transfer_throughput=F
Additional data: none
Resolution: A=f(F), adjust_network_load=A
Resolution status: good

Trouble: file_transfer_throughput=F
Additional data: none
Resolution: B=g(F), adjust_network_bandwidth=B
Resolution staus: good

Trouble: file_transfer_throughput=F
Additional data: adjust_network_load=no
Resolution: B=g(F), adjust_network_bandwidth=B
Resolution status: good
```

Figure 13.15   Abstraction/Respecialization Adaptation for the CBR Example

CBR-Based CRITTER.   The architecture of CRITTER is shown in Figure 13.17 [Lewis L5]. It is integrated with the network management system, Spectrum, which we described in Chapter 12. The core modules of CRITTER are the four basic modules of the CBR system shown in Figure 13.12: input, retrieve, adapt, and process. A fifth additional module, propose, displays potential solutions found by the reasoning module and allows the user to inspect and manually adapt these solutions.

The input module receives its input from the fault detection module of Spectrum. The process module updates the ticket library with the new experience. The retrieve module uses determinators to retrieve a group of tickets from the library that are similar to an outstanding ticket. The initial set of determination rules is based on expert knowledge and is built into the determinators module. The application technique is the strategy used by the adapt module. User-based adaptation is the interface module, allowing the user to propose critic-based adaptation.

Kolodner has compared and identified the differences between RBR and CBR [Kolodner J]. In RBR, the retrieval is based on an exact match, whereas in CBR the retrieval is based on a partial match. RBR is applied to an iterative cycle of microevents, but CBR is applied as a total solution to the trouble and then adapted to the current situation.

```
Trouble: file_transfer_throughput=F
Additional data: network_load=N
Resolution: A=f(F,N), adjust_network_load=A
Resolution status: good
```

Figure 13.16   Critic-Based Adaptation for the CBR Example

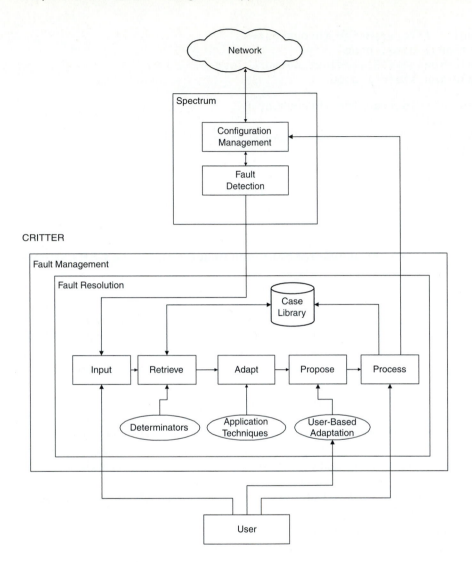

Figure 13.17   CRITTER Architecture

13.4.4   Codebook Correlation Model

Algorithms have been developed to correlate events generated in networks, based on network modeling and network component behavior. Because correlators are based on algorithms, a claim is made that they do not require expert knowledge to associate events with problems. Although this claim is true, expert knowledge is still needed in selecting the right kinds of input that are to be fed to the correlator to develop an efficient system.

Figure 13.18 [Kliger S, Yemini S, Yemini Y, Ohsie D, & Stolfo S] shows the architecture of a model-based event correlation system. The term "model-based event correlation" should not be confused with the term "model-based reasoning approach" that we discussed in Section 13.4.2. As this section's heading states, we will refer to this method as *codebook correlation*.

Monitors capture alarm events and input them to the correlator. The configuration model contains the network's configuration. The event model represents the various events and their causal relationships (we will define the causality relationship shortly). The correlator correlates the alarm events with the event model and determines the common problems that caused the alarm event.

One of the correlation algorithms based on generic modeling is a coding approach to event correlation [Kliger S, Yemini S, Yemini Y, Ohsie D, & Stolfo S]. In this approach, problem events are viewed as messages generated by a system and "encoded" in sets of alarms that they cause. The function of the correlator is to "decode" those messages to identify the problems. Thus the coding technique comprises two phases. In the first phase, called the *codebook selection phase*, problems to be monitored are identified and the symptoms or alarms that each of them generates are associated with the problem. (As we stated previously, this phase is where expert knowledge is needed.) This phase produces a problem–symptom matrix. In the second phase, the correlator compares the stream of alarm events with the codebook and identifies the problem.

To generate the problem–symptom matrix codebook, we first need to consider a causality graph, which represents symptom events caused by other events. An example of such a causality graph is shown in Figure 13.19. Each node in the graph represents an event. Nodes are connected by directed edges, which begin at a causing event and end at a resulting event. For example, event E1 causes events E4 and E5. Notice that events E1, E2, and E3 have directed edges only leaving them and none coming into them. We can identify these nodes as problem nodes and the rest as symptom nodes, as they all have at least one directed edge pointing inward. With problems labeled as Ps and symptoms as Ss, the newly labeled causality graph is shown in Figure 13.20. There are three problem nodes, P1, P2, and P3, and four symptom nodes, S1, S2, S3, and S4. We have eliminated directed arrows where one symptom causes another symptom, as they do not add any information to the overall graph.

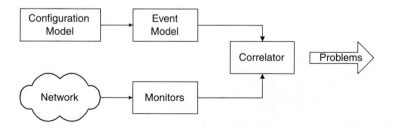

Figure 13.18   Generic Architecture of an Event Correlation System

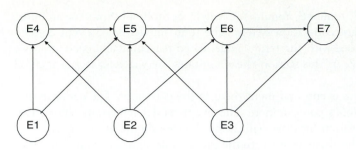

Figure 13.19   A Causality Graph

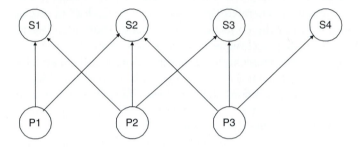

Figure 13.20   A Labeled Causality Graph for Figure 13.19

We can now generate a problem–symptom matrix codebook for the labeled causality graph (we will drop the qualifier "labeled" from now on), as shown in Figure 13.21, with three columns as problems and four rows as symptoms.

In general, the number of symptoms will exceed the number of problems, and hence the codebook can be reduced to a minimal set of symptoms needed to uniquely identify the problems. Showing that two rows are adequate to identify uniquely the three problems in the codebook shown in Figure 13.21 is easy. We will keep row S1 and

	P1	P2	P3
S1	1	1	0
S2	1	1	1
S3	0	1	1
S4	0	0	1

Figure 13.21   The Codebook for Figure 13.20

	P1	P2	P3
S1	1	1	0
S3	0	1	1

Figure 13.22   The Correlation Matrix for Figure 13.20

try eliminating subsequent rows, one at a time. At each step, we want to be sure that the remaining codebook distinguishes between the problems. You can prove to yourself that eliminating rows S2 and S3 does not preserve the uniqueness, whereas eliminating S2 and S4 does. The reduced codebook, called the *correlation matrix*, is shown in Figure 13.22.

Drawing the causality graph based on the correlation matrix of Figure 13.20, we get the correlation graph shown in Figure 13.23.

We will apply this information to a more general situation of the causality graph shown in Figure 13.24 [Kliger S, Yemini S, Yemini Y, Oshie D, & Stolfo S]. Figure 13.24(a) depicts a causality graph of eleven events. Figure 13.24(b) shows the equivalent problem–symptom causality graph. Nodes 1, 2, and 11 show only outgoing directed arrows and hence are identified as problems, the rest of the nodes as symptoms.

We will now reduce the causality graph to a correlation graph. Symptoms 3, 4, and 5 form a cycle of causal equivalence and can be replaced by a single symptom, 3. Symptoms 7 and 10 are caused respectively by symptoms 3 and 5 and hence can be ignored. Likewise, symptom 8 can be eliminated as it is an intermediate symptom node between problem node 1 and symptom node 9, which is also directly related to problem node 11. We thus arrive at the correlation graph shown in Figure 13.25 and the correlation matrix shown in Figure 13.26. Notice that in this example the model is unable to distinguish between problems 1 and 11 because they produce identical symptoms in the correlation graph based on the event model.

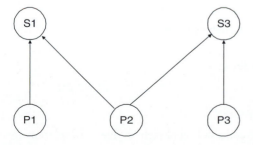

Figure 13.23   A Correlation Graph for Figure 13.20

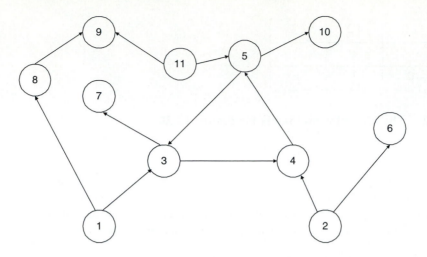

(a) Event Causality Graph

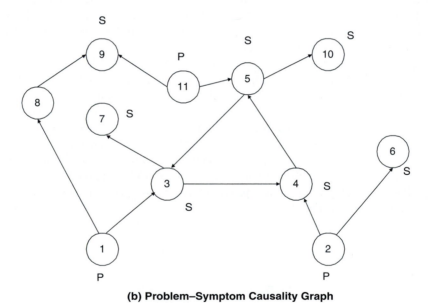

(b) Problem–Symptom Causality Graph

Figure 13.24   A Generalized Causality Graph

Further refinements can be made in the codebook approach to event correlation in terms of tolerance to spurious noises and the probability relationship in the causality graph. We derived the correlation matrix to be the minimal causal matrix. Thus each column in the code matrix is differentiated from other columns by at least one bit (i.e., the value in

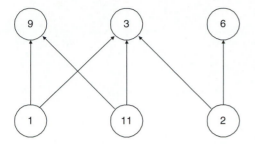

Figure 13.25   The Correlation Graph for Figure 13.24

	P1	P2	P11
S3	1	1	1
S6	0	1	0
S9	1	0	1

Figure 13.26   The Correlation Matrix for Figure 13.24

one cell). From coding theory, this value corresponds to a Hamming distance of 1. Any spurious noise in the event detection could change one of the bits and thus a code word would identify a pair of problems. This situation can be avoided by increasing the Hamming distance to 2 or more, which would increase the number of symptoms in the correlation matrix. Also, the relationship between a problem and symptoms could be defined in terms of probability of occurrence, making the correlation matrix a probabilistic matrix.

The codebook correlation technique has been implemented in the InCharge™ system developed by System Management ARTS (SMARTS) [Yemini SA, Kliger S, Moses E, Yemini Y, & Ohsie D].

13.4.5   State Transition Graph Model

A state transition graph model is used in Seagate's NerveCenter™ correlation system. It can be used as a stand-alone system or integrated with an NMS, which HP has done in OpenView and some other vendors also have done.

A simple state diagram with two states for a ping/response process is shown in Figure 13.27. The two states are *ping node* and *receive response*. When an NMS sends a ping, it transitions from the *ping node* state to the *receive response* state. When it receives a response, it transitions back to the *ping node* state. As you know by now, this method is how the health of all the components is monitored by the NMS.

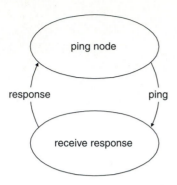

Figure 13.27   The State Transition Diagram for Ping/Response

Let us illustrate with an example of how a state transition diagram can be used to correlate events in a network. We choose the example presented in Figure 13.11. An NMS is pinging the hubs that are accessed via a router. When a hub is working and connectivity to the NMS is good, a response is received for each ping sent—say, every minute—by the NMS. This condition is represented by the top two states, *ping hub* and *receive response*, in Figure 13.28. Let us now consider the situation when a response for a ping is not received before the next ping is ready to be sent. NMS typically expects a response in 300 milliseconds (we are not pinging some obscure host in a foreign country!). An action is taken by the NMS and the state transitions from *receive response* to *pinged twice* (referred to as *ground state* by NerveCenter). A response to the second ping may be received, and in that case the state transitions back to the normal *ping hub* state.

However, if there is no response for the second ping, NMS pings a third time. The state transition is now *pinged three times*. Response for this ping will cause a transition to the *ping hub* state. However, let us consider the situation of no-response for the third ping. We assume that the NMS is configured to ping three times before it declares a communication failure between it and the hub. Without any correlation, an alarm will be triggered and the icon representing the hub will turn red.

However, the hub may actually be working and the workstations on it may all be communicating with each other. From the topology database, the correlator in the NMS is aware that the path to the hub is via the router. Hence, upon failure of the third ping, an action is taken and the system transitions to the *ping router* state. The router is pinged and the system transitions to the *receive response from router* state.

Two outcomes are now possible. The connectivity to the router is lost, and no response is received from the router. The system takes no action, as indicated by the closed loop in the *ping router* state. (How does the router icon turn red in this case?)

The second possibility is that a response is received from the router, which means that the connection to the hub has been lost. Now, the correlator in the NMS triggers an alarm that turns the hub icon red.

In the case of a router connectivity failure, only the router icon turns red. None of the hubs connected to it turn red, thus identifying the root cause of the problem.

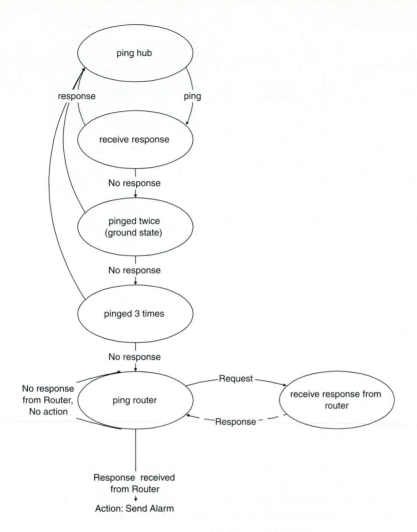

Figure 13.28   A State Transition Graph Example

13.4.6   Finite State Machine Model

Another model-based fault detection scheme uses the communicating finite state machine [Miller, RE]. The main feature of this process is that it is a passive testing system based on the assumption that an observer agent is present in each node and reports abnormalities to a central point. We can visualize the node observer as a Web agent and the central point as the Web server. A failure in a node or a link is indicated by the state machine associated with the component entering an illegal state. An application on the server correlates the events.

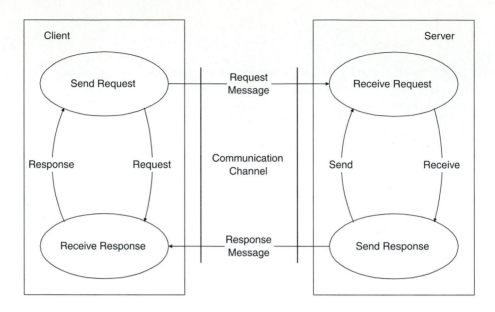

Figure 13.29   A Communicating Finite State Machine

A simple communicating finite state machine for a client/server system is shown in Figure 13.29. It enables communication between a client and server via a communication channel. For simplicity, both client and server are assumed to have two states each. The client, which is in send request state, sends a request message to the server and transitions to the receive response state. The server, currently in the receive request state, receives the request and transitions to the send response state. After processing the request, it sends the response and transitions back to the receive request state. The client then receives the response from the server and transitions to the send request state.

If either client or server enters an illegal state during the transitions, the system has encountered a fault. For example, after sending a response, if the server does not transition to the receive request state, it is in failed state. A message is sent to a central location as a fault condition, either by the component itself or by the one communicating with the failed component. This passive detection scheme is similar to the trap mechanism. No system that implements this technology is commercially available at the present time.

A similarity between the finite state machine model and the state transition graph model is the state transitions. The main difference between them is that the former is a passive system and that the latter is an active system.

13.5   Security Management

Security management is both a technical and an administrative consideration in information management. It involves securing access to the network and information flowing in the network, access to data stored in the network, and manipulating the data stored and flowing through the network. The scope of the network and access to it not only covers an enterprise intranet network, but also the Internet, to which it is connected.

Another area of concern in secure communication is the use of mobile stations. You may be familiar with the embarrassing case of a politician's conversation from a car phone being intercepted by a third party traveling in an automobile. Although that was an analog signal, the same thing could happen in the case of a mobile digital station such as a hand-held stock trading device. An intruder could intercept messages and alter trade transactions either to benefit by them or to hurt the person sending or receiving them.

In Chapter 7 we covered several of the security issues associated with SNMP management as part of SNMPv3 specifications and discussed possible security threats. We identified four types of security threats to network management in Chapter 7: modification of information, masquerade, message stream modification, and disclosure. They are applicable to the implementation of security subsystems in the agent (authoritative engine) and in the manager (nonauthoritative engine). The SNMPv3 security subsystem is the User-Based Security Model (USM). It has two modules—the authentication module and the privacy module. The former addresses data integrity and data origin; the latter is concerned with data confidentiality, message timeliness, and limited message protection. The basic concepts discussed in Chapter 7 are part of generalized security management in data communications.

Security management goes beyond the realm of SNMP management. In this section, we will address needed policies and procedures, resources that can be used to prevent security breaches, and network protection from software attacks. Policies and procedures should cover preventive measures, steps to be taken during the occurrence of a security breach, and postincident measures. Because the Internet is so pervasive and so many networks are part of it, government and private organizations throughout the world are concerned with the security and privacy of information traversing it.

In this introductory book, we will not be able to give security management the attention that it deserves. For additional information, you should pursue any of numerous references available on the subject [Cooper; Kaufman, Perlman, & Speciner; Leinwand & Conroy; Wack & Carnahan; RFC 2196].

13.5.1   Policies and Procedures

The IETF workgroup that generated RFC 2196 defines a security policy as "a formal statement of the rules by which people who are given access to an organization's technology and information assets must abide." An enterprise's policy should address both access and security breaches. Access concerns who is allowed to obtain information and from what source. SNMP management addresses this concern in terms of a community access policy for network management information. An enterprise's network access policy could allow all employees full access to the network. However, in most cases not everyone should have access to all network information, and thus accounts are established for employees to have access only to appropriate hosts and applications in those hosts. The access policy governing these accounts should be written so that all employees are fully aware of it.

However, illegal entry into systems and accessing of networks must be protected against. The policies and procedures covering site security management on the Internet are dealt with in detail elsewhere [RFC 2196, NIST]. The National Computer Security Center (NCSC) has published what is known as the Orange Book, which contains a rating scheme for computers and is a framework for setting security policies and procedures. It is based on the security design features of various types of computers. The issues for enterprise site security for an intranet are the same as those for the Internet and are applicable to them equally.

A basic guide for setting up policies and procedures includes the following:

1. Identify what you are trying to protect.

2. Determine what you are trying to protect it from.

3. Determine how likely the threats are.

4. Implement measures that will protect your assets in a cost-effective manner.

5. Review the process continuously and make improvements if weaknesses are found.

The assets that need to be protected should be listed, including hardware, software, data, documentation, supplies, and the people who have responsibility for them. The classic threats are from unauthorized access to resources and/or information, unintended and/or unauthorized disclosure of information, and denial of service. Denial of service is a serious attack on the network because the network is brought to a state in which it can no longer carry legitimate users' data. Service can be denied either by attacking the routers or by flooding the network with extraneous traffic.

13.5.2   Security Breaches and the Resources Needed to Prevent Them

We addressed the policies and procedures in Section 13.5.1. In this section, we will discuss various security breaches caused by attempts to access data and systems and the resources needed to protect them.

Figure 13.30 shows a secure communication network, which actually is a misnomer. There is no fully secure system in the real world; there are only systems, which are hard and time-consuming to break into, as we will describe. In Figure 13.30, two networks are

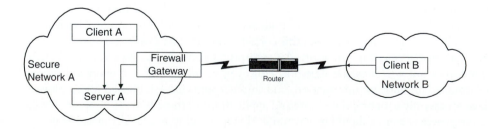

Figure 13.30   A Secure Communication Network

communicating with each other via a WAN which has just one router. Server A and client A shown in network A, are communicating with each other; client B in network B is also communicating (or trying to communicate) with server A in network A.

Let us look at the potential security breach points in this situation. Hosts in network B may not be allowed to access network A. The firewall gateway is used to screen traffic going in and out of the secure network A. Even if network B had access to network A, some intruder—for example, someone who has access to the router in the path—may intercept the message. The contents of the message, as well as the source and destination identifications, can be monitored and manipulated, which are security breaches.

Security breaches can occur in Internet and intranet environments in numerous ways. In most enterprises, authentication is limited to user identification and password. Authorization is limited to establishment of accounts (i.e., who can log onto an application on a host). Besides normal breaches, special situations, as when a disgruntled employee embeds virus programs in an enterprise's programs and products, must be protected against.

13.5.3   Firewalls

The main purpose of a firewall is to protect a network from external attacks. It monitors and controls traffic into and out of a secure network. It can be implemented in a router, gateway, or special host. A firewall is normally located at the gateway to a network, but it may also be located at host access points.

Implementing a firewall to a network yields numerous benefits. It reduces the risk of access to hosts from an external network by filtering insecure services. It can provide controlled access to the network so that only specified hosts or network segments can access some hosts. Because protection from external threats is centralized and transparent, it reduces the annoyance to internal users while controlling the external users. A firewall can also be used to protect the privacy of an enterprise. For example, services such as the utility *finger*, which could provide information about employees to outsiders, can be prevented from accessing the network.

When security policy is implemented in a firewall, it is a concatenation of a higher level access service policy, by which a total service is filtered out. For example, the dial-in service can be totally denied at the service policy level, and the firewall can filter out selected services, such as the utility *finger*. Firewalls involve the use of packet filtering or application-level gateways as the two primary techniques of controlling undesired traffic.

Packet Filters.   Packet filtering is based on protocol-specific criteria. It is done at the OSI data link, network, and transport layers. Packet filters are implemented in some commercial routers, called *screening routers* or *packet filtering routers*. We will use the generic term packet filtering routers here. Although routers do not look at the transport layers, some vendors have implemented this additional feature to sell them as firewall routers. The filtering is done on the following parameters: source IP address, destination IP address, source TCP/UDP port, and destination TCP/IP port. The filtering is implemented in each port of the router and can be programmed independently.

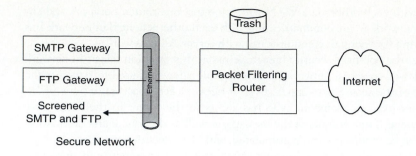

Figure 13.31   A Packet Filtering Router

Packet filtering routers can either drop packets or redirect them to specific hosts for further screening, as shown in Figure 13.31. Some packets never reach the local network because they are trashed. For example, all packets from network segment *a.b.c.0* are programmed to be rejected, as well as FTP packets from *d.e.f.0:21* (note that port 21 is a standard FTP port). The SMTP (e-mail) and FTP packets are redirected to their respective gateways for further screening. The firewall is asymmetric; that is, all the incoming SMTP and FTP packets are parsed to check whether they should be dropped or forwarded. However, the outgoing SMTP and FTP packets have already been screened by the gateways and don't have to be checked by the packet filtering router.

A packet filtering firewall works well when the rules to be implemented are simple. However, the more rules introduced, the more difficult it is to implement. The rules have to be implemented in the right order or they may produce adverse effects. Testing and debugging are also difficult in packet filtering [Chapman DB].

Application-Level Gateway.   An application-level gateway is used to overcome some of the problems identified for packet filtering. Figure 13.32 shows the application gateway

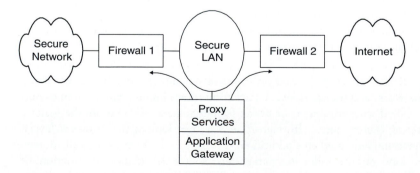

Figure 13.32   An Application-Level Gateway

architecture. Firewalls 1 and 2 will forward data only if it is going to or coming from the application gateway. Thus a secured LAN is a gateway LAN. An application gateway behaves differently for each application, and filtering is handled by the proxy services in the gateway. For example, for FTP service the file is stored first in the application gateway and then forwarded. For TELNET service, the application gateway authenticates the foreign host—its legitimacy to communicate with the local host—and then connects the gateway to the local host. It keeps a log of all transactions.

Firewalls protect a secure site by checking addresses (e.g., IP address), transport parameters (e.g., as FTP and NNTP), and applications. However, how do we protect access from an external source based on a user who is using false identification? Moreover, how do we protect against an intruder manipulating the data while it is traversing the network between source and destination? These concerns are addressed by ensuring secure communication.

13.5.4   Cryptography

For secure communication we need to ensure integrity protection and authentication validation. **Integrity protection** makes sure that information has not been tampered with as it moves between source and destination. **Authentication validation** verifies originator identification. In other words, when someone receives a message that identifies the sender, can the receiver really be sure who sent the message? The two important aspects of secure communication address the four security threats—modification of information, masquerade, message stream modification, and disclosure—mentioned at the beginning of Section 13.5. In addition to the actual message, control and protocol handshakes need to be secure.

Although hardware solutions to authentication problems are available, they are not foolproof. The reason is that information, including user identification and password, can be intercepted and tampered with as it traverses from source to destination.

The technology best suited to achieving secure communication is software based. Its foundation lies in cryptography. Hashing, or message digest, and digital signature, which we will discuss shortly, are built on cryptography to achieve integrity protection and source authentication.

Cryptographic Communication.   Cryptography means secret (crypto) writing (graphy). It deals with techniques of transmitting information from a sender to a receiver without any intermediary being able to decipher it. You may view this approach as information being translated to a special language that only the sender and receiver can interpret. In addition, cryptography should also be able to detect if somebody intercepted the information. Again extending our analogy, if a letter written in a secret language were to be mailed in a sealed (a *really* sealed) envelope—and if somebody tampered with it—the receiver would detect the tampering.

The basic model of cryptographic communication is shown in Figure 13.33. The input message, called **plaintext**, is encrypted with a **secret (encryption) key**. The encrypted message is called **ciphertext**, which moves through an unsecure communication channel, the

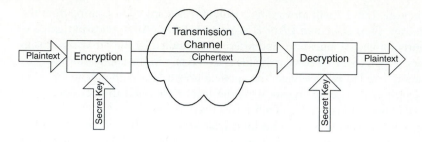

Figure 13.33   Basic Cryptographic Communication

Internet for example. The ciphertext is unintelligible to anyone who does not possess the encryption key. At the receiving end, the message is deciphered with the secret (decryption) key to retrieve the plaintext.

The first known example of cryptography is the Caesar cipher. In this scheme, each letter is replaced with another letter, which is three letters later in the alphabet (i.e., key of 3). Thus the plaintext *network management* will read *qhwzrun pdqdjhphqw* in ciphertext. Of course, the receiver knew ahead of time the secret key (3) for successfully decrypting the message, restoring it to the plaintext *network management* by using the third letter back from each letter transmitted.

Secret Key Cryptography.   The Caesar cipher was later enhanced by the makers of Ovaltine and distributed as Captain Midnight Secret Decoder rings. Each letter was replaced by another letter *n* letters later in the alphabet (i.e., key of *n*). Of course, the sender and the receiver have to agree ahead of time on the secret key for successful communication. It's the same key used for encryption and decryption and is called **secret key cryptography**. The encryption and decryption modules can be implemented in either hardware or software.

An intruder can easily decode the preceding ciphertext. Only a maximum of 26 attempts would be needed to decipher it, as there are 26 letters in the alphabet. In another encryption scheme, the *monoalphabetic cipher,* each letter is replaced uniquely with another letter that is randomly chosen. Now, the maximum number of attempts for the intruder to decipher has been increased to 26! ($26! = 26 \cdot 25 \cdot 24 \cdot \ldots 1$). However, that many attempts really aren't needed because there are patterns in a language.

Obviously, the key is the key (no pun intended) to the security of messages. Another aspect of the key is the convenience of using it. We will illustrate this point with a scenario involving Ian and Rita (Ian for initiator and Rita for responder) as users at the two ends of a secure communication link. Ian and Rita could share a key—their secret key, for secure communication. However, if Ian wants to communicate with Ted (for third party), they also need to share a secret key. Soon, Ian has to remember one secret key for each person with whom he wants to communicate, which, obviously, is impractical. It's hard enough to remember your own passwords, if you have several of them, and which systems they go with.

Two standard algorithms implement secret key cryptography. They are the Data Encryption Standard (DES) and the International Data Encryption Algorithm (IDEA) [Kaufman C, Perlman R & Speciner M]. Both deal with 64-bit message blocks and create the same size ciphertext. DES uses 56-bit key and IDEA uses a 128-bit key. DES is designed for efficient hardware implementation and consequently performs poorly if implemented in software. In contrast, IDEA functions efficiently in software implementations.

Both DES and IDEA are based on the same principle of encryption. The bits in the plaintext block are rearranged several times, using a predetermined algorithm and the secret key. During decryption, the process is repeated in reverse for DES. Decryption is a bit more complicated for IDEA.

A message that is longer than the block length is divided into 64-bit message blocks. Any one of several algorithms is used to break up the message. One of the more popular ones is the cipher block chaining (CBC) method. Recall that we used it with the USM in SNMPv3 in Chapter 7. There, we used CBC to break up the message and then used DES to encrypt it. Performing such an operation on the message, even on identical plaintext blocks, would result in dissimilar ciphertext blocks.

Public Key Cryptography.   In private key cryptography each pair of users must have a secret key. Public key cryptography [Diffe W & Hellman M; Kaufman C, Perlman R, & Speciner M] overcomes the difficulty of having too many cryptography keys. The secret key cryptography is symmetric in that the same key is used for both encryption and decryption, but public key cryptography is asymmetric with a *public key* and a *private key*, which are different. Let us return to our Ian, Rita, and Ted scenario to illustrate. In Figure 13.34, the public key is Ian's; it is the key that Rita, Ted, and everybody else (with whom Ian wants to communicate) knows and uses to encrypt messages that they send to Ian. The private key, which only Ian knows, is the key that he uses to decrypt the messages. This scheme ensures secure communication between Ian and the other communicators on a one-to-one basis. Rita's message to Ian can be read only by Ian and not by anyone else who has his public key because the public key cannot be used to decrypt the message.

We can compare the use of asymmetric public and private keys in cryptography to a mailbox with two openings: a mail slot for dropping off mail and a collection door for

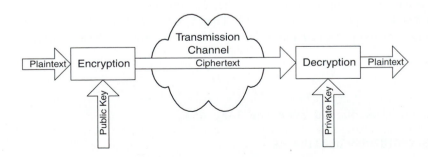

Figure 13.34   Public Key Cryptographic Communication

removing mail. Suppose that it is a private mailbox in a club that restricts access to members only. All members can open the mail slot with a public key provided by the club's administration to drop off their mail, possibly containing comments on a sensitive issue about the club. A member's mail cannot be accessed by other members because only the administrator with a private key can open the collection door and access the mail of all the members. Of course, this asymmetric example has more to do with access than cryptography. But, you get the idea!

The Diffe–Hellman public key algorithm is the oldest public key algorithm. It is a hybrid of secret and public key. The commonly used public key cryptography algorithm is called RSA, after its inventors [Rivest RL, Shamir A, & Adleman L]. It does both encryption and decryption, as well as digital signatures. Both the message length and the key length are variable. The commonly used key length is 512 bits. The block size of the plaintext, which is variable, should be less than the key size. The ciphertext is always the length of the key. RSA is less efficient than either of the secret key algorithms, DES or IDEA. Hence, in practice, RSA is used to encrypt the secret key. The message is then transmitted in one of the secret key algorithms.

Message Digest.   Any telecommunications engineer is familiar with the cyclic redundancy check (CRC) method of detecting errors in digital transmission. It involves calculating a check sum based on the data in the frame or packet at the sending end and transmitting it along with the data. The CRC, also known as *checksum,* is computed at the receiving end and matched against the received checksum to ensure that the packet has not been corrupted. An analogous principle is used in validating the integrity of the message. To ensure that the message has not been tampered with between sender and receiver, a cryptographic CRC is added to the message. It is derived using a cryptographic hash algorithm called *message digest* (MD). There are several versions, one of the most common being MD5. Recall that we covered its use while discussing the authentication protocol in SNMPv3 in Chapter 7. We will look at the use of it in digital signature in the next subsection.

There are different implementations of MD5. In particular, the MD5 utility is used in FreeBSD 2.x (md5sum under LINUX). The utility takes as input a message of arbitrary length producing output consisting of a 128-bit message digest of the input. An example of MD5 utility use is shown in Figure 13.35.

The generated message digest for the string that we entered was based on the data received from standard input (from the screen). The FreeBSD version also has a test mode that can be turned on by specifying "-x" as a parameter, as shown in Figure 13.36.

```
$ md5
The quick brown fox jumped over the lazy dog
^D
d8e8fca2dc0f896fd7cb4cb0031ba249
```

Figure 13.35   Example of an MD5 Message Digest

```
$ md5 -x
MD5 ("") = d41d8cd98f00b204e9800998ecf8427e
MD5 ("a") = 0cc175b9c0f1b6a831c399e269772661
MD5 ("abc") = 900150983cd24fb0d6963f7d28e17f72
MD5 ("message digest") = f96b697d7cb7938d525a2f31aaf161d0
MD5 ("abcdefghijklmnopqrstuvwxyz") = c3fcd3d76192e4007dfb496cca67e13b
MD5 ("ABCDEFGHIJKLMNOPQRSTUVWXYZabcdefghijklmnopqrstuvwxyz0123456789") =
d174ab98d277d9f5a5611c2c9f419d9f
MD5
("12345678901234567890123456789012345678901234567890123456789012345678901234567
890") = 57edf4a22be3c955ac49da2e2107b67a
```

Figure 13.36   MD5 FreeBSD Version Test Mode Output

A second algorithm used to obtain a hash or message digest is the Secure Hash Standard (SHS). This has been proposed by the National Institute for Standards and Technology (NIST). It is similar to MD5, but it can handle a maximum message length of 2^{64} bits in contrast with MD5, which can handle unlimited input length of 32-byte chunks. SHS produces a 160-bit output, whereas MD5 output is 128 bits long.

Some significant features of message digest are worth mentioning. First, there is a one-to-one relationship between the input and output messages. Thus the input is uniquely mapped to an output digest. It is important to observe that even a 1-bit difference in a block of 512 bits could produce a message digest that looks vastly different. In addition, the output messages are completely uncorrelated. Thus any pattern in the input cannot be recognized at the output.

Another feature of message digest is that the output digest is of constant length for a given algorithm with chosen parameters, irrespective of the input message length. In this regard, it is very similar to CRC in that CRC-32 is exactly 32 bits long. Recall that in SNMPv3 the *authKey* generated by MD5 algorithm is exactly 16 octets long.

Finally, generation of a message digest is a one-way function. Given a message, we can generate a unique message digest. However, given a message digest, there is no way that we can generate the original message. Hence transmission of a password from a client to a server would be protected against someone's eavesdropping and deciphering the password. A message digest can also be used for storing a password file in a host without any human being able to decipher it.

We know that generation of a message digest is a one-way function and no two messages can produce identical message digests. Could the combination of these two conditions keep an unauthorized person from tampering with a message in transit? The answer is no. An interceptor who knows which algorithm is being used could modify the message (assuming that the interceptor decrypts the message), generate a new message digest, and send it along with the modified message. Thus, if Ian sent a message to Rita and Ted modified the message in transit, Rita would not know the difference. Additional protection is needed to guard against such a threat, which is achieved by attaching a digital signature to the message.

Digital Signature.   In public key cryptography, or even in secret key cryptography, if Rita receives a message claiming that it is from Ian, there is no guarantee as to who sent the message. For example, somebody other than Ian who knows Rita's public key could use it to send a message identifying himself or herself as Ian. Rita could not be absolutely sure who sent it. To overcome this problem, a digital signature can be used. The use of *signed public key* cryptographic communication is illustrated in Figure 13.37.

The digital signature is the reverse of public key cryptography. Ian can create a digital signature using his private key (marked S for sender in parentheses in Figure 13.37) and Rita could validate it by using Ian's public key. The digital signature depends on the message and the key. Let us suppose that Ian is sending an e-mail message to Rita. A digital signature, which is a message digest, is generated by using any hash algorithm with the combined inputs of the plaintext message and Ian's private key. The digital signature is concatenated with the plaintext message and is encrypted by using Rita's public key (marked R for receiver in parentheses). At the receiving end, Rita uses her private key to decrypt the incoming ciphertext message. She then generates a message digest with the combined input of the plaintext message and Ian's public key, and compares it with the digital signature received. If they match, she concludes that the message has not been tampered with. Furthermore, she is assured that the message is from Ian, as she used Ian's public key to authenticate the source of the message.

Notice that only the originator can create the digital signature with his or her private key. Others can look at it with the originator's public key and validate it, but they cannot create it. A real-world analogy to digital signature is check writing. The bank can validate a person's name from the signature, but actually duplicating the signature (at least manually) of the person who signed the check is extremely difficult.

Digital signature is valuable in electronic commerce. Suppose that Ian wants to place an order with company ABC for its router product. He places the order over the Internet with his digital signature attached to it. The digital signature, making use of a public key,

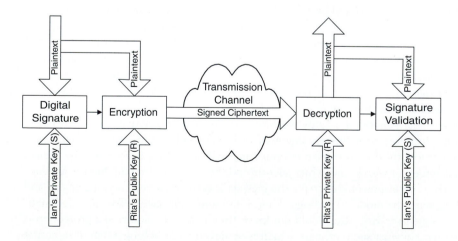

Figure 13.37   Signed Public Key Cryptographic Communication

protects both ABC and Ian regarding the validity of the order and who ordered it. It is even better than using secret key cryptography, because in that case Ian could change his mind and allege that company ABC illegally generated the order, using the secret key that it has been using. In signed public key cryptography, he could not do that.

13.5.5   Authentication and Authorization

Authentication is verification of the user's identification, and **authorization** is the granting of access to the information. On the Internet, without security, a user's identification and password, which are used for authentication, can easily be captured by an intruder snooping on the LAN or WAN. Several secure mechanisms of varying complexity and sensitivity may be used for authentication purposes. Authorization for a particular service could be a simple read, write, read–write, or no-access. The privilege of using the service could be for an indefinite period, a finite period, or just for one-time use.

Two main classes of systems are of interest to us in the implementation of an authentication scheme. The first is the client/server environment in which there is a request–response communication between client and server. The client initiates a request for service to the server, and the server responds with the results of the service performed—essentially two-way communication. In this environment besides authentication (and of course, an integrity check), authorization also is needed.

The second is one-way communication, such as an e-mail or e-commerce transaction. The message transmitted by the source is received by the receiver after a considerable delay—sometimes days if an intermediate server holds up the transaction. In such a case both the authentication and integrity check need to be performed at the receiving end.

We will discuss client/server authentication systems in Section 13.5.6 and one-way message authentication and integrity protection systems in Section 13.5.7.

13.5.6   Client/Server Authentication Systems

We will consider four types of client/server environments and the implementation of authentication in each: a host/user environment, a ticket-granting system, an authentication server system, and authentication using a cryptographic function.

Host/User Authentication.   Both the traditional host and user validations for authentication are not very secure. They are also not convenient to use. Host authentication requires that certain hosts be validated by the server providing the service. The host names are administered by the server administrator. The server recognizes the host by the host address. If server S is authorized to serve a client host C, anyone who has an account in C could access the S. The server maintains the list of users associated with host C and allows access to the user. If John Smith is one of the users in C and wants to access the server from another workstation, W, that workstation has to be authenticated as a client of S. If it can't be, John is out of luck. Moreover, his name has to be added to the list of users in W in order for him to access S. To make the environment flexible, every client with every possible user must be added to the server, negating secure access!

Let's consider user authentication, which is done by the user providing identification and a password. The main problem with a password is that it is detected easily by eavesdropping—possibly with a network probe. To protect against the threat of eavesdropping, security is enhanced by encrypting the password before transmission. Commercial systems are available that generate a one-time password associated with a password server that validates it when presented by the service-providing host. The user uses a unique key each time to obtain the password, such as in the ticket-granting system.

Ticket-Granting System.   We will explain the ticket-granting system by describing the most popular method, Kerberos, a system developed by MIT as part of its Project Athena. As shown in Figure 13.38 Kerberos consists of an authentication server and a ticket-granting server. A user logs onto a client workstation and sends a login request to the authentication server. After verifying that the user is on its access control list, the authentication server grants an encrypted ticket to the client. The client workstation requests a password from the user, which it then uses to decrypt the message from the authentication server. The client then interacts with the ticket-granting server and obtains a service-granting ticket and a session key for use of the application server. The client workstation then requests service from the application server, giving the service-granting ticket and the session key. The application server, after validating the ticket and the session key, provides service to the user. This process, happening in the background, is transparent to the user, whose only interaction is with the client workstation requesting application service.

Authentication Server System.   An authentication server system, depicted in Figure 13.39, is somewhat similar to the ticket-granting system; however, no ticket is granted. No login identification and password pair is sent from the client workstation. The user sends identification to a central authentication server, which has jurisdiction over a

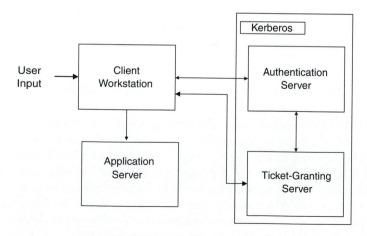

Figure 13.38   A Ticket-Granting System

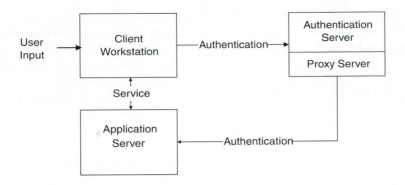

Figure 13.39   An Authentication Server

domain of servers. The central authentication server, after validation of the user, acts as a proxy agent to the client and authenticates the user to the application server. The client proceeds to communicate with the application server. This process is transparent to the user and is the architecture of the Novell LAN.

Authentication Using Cryptographic Functions.   Cryptographic authentication involves the use of cryptographic functions. The sender can encrypt an authentication request to the receiver, who decrypts the message to validate the user's identification. Algorithms and keys are used to encrypt and decrypt messages.

13.5.7   Message Transfer Security

The one-way message transfer system is not interactive. For example if Rita receives an e-mail from a person who claims to be Ian, she needs to authenticate Ian as the originator of the message and ensure that nobody has tampered with the message. This could also be a situation in which Ian sends a sell order for shares of stock from the mobile station in his car. Ted could intercept the message and alter the number of shares or the price. We will treat such situations as ensuring security of mail systems.

There are three secure mail systems: privacy enhanced mail (PEM), pretty good privacy (PGP), and the X.400-based mail system [Kaufman C, Perlman R & Speciner M]. All three are variations of signed public key cryptographic communication discussed previously and shown in Figure 13.37. We will describe PEM and PGP in this section. We will not discuss X-400, which is a set of specifications for an e-mail system defined by the ITU Standards Committee and adopted by OSI; it is actually a framework rather than an implementation-ready system. In addition, we will also review SNMPv3 secure communication, which we covered in Chapter 7 as it bears a close resemblance to message transfer security.

PEM (Privacy Enhanced Mail).   Privacy enhanced mail (PEM) was developed by IETF, and specifications for it are documented in RFCs 1421–1424. It is intended to provide privacy enhanced mail, using end-to-end cryptography between originator and recipient processes [RFC 1421]. The privacy enhanced services provided are (1) confidentiality, (2) authentication, (3) message integrity assurance, and (4) nonrepudiation of origin. The cryptographic key, called the *data encryption key* (DEK), can be either a secret key or a public key, based on the specific implementation, and is thus flexible. However, the originating and terminating ends must have common agreement (obviously!).

Figure 13.40 shows three PEM processes based on message integrity and encryption, as defined by IETF: MIC-CLEAR, MIC-ONLY, and ENCRYPTED. Only the originating end is shown. In all three cases, the processes are to extract the message and validate the originator ID and message integrity. Differences in the three processes depend on the extent of cryptography and message encoding used. The **message integrity code** (MIC) is generated as discussed previously for digital signature and is included as part of e-mail in all three processes.

The specification provides two types of keys: a **data encrypting key** (DEK) and an **interexchange key** (IK). The DEK is a random number generated on a per message basis and is used to encrypt the message text and to generate an MIC, if one is needed. The IK, which is a long-range key agreed upon between sender and receiver, is used to encrypt the DEK for transmission within the message. The IK is either a public or a secret key, depending on the type of cryptographic exchange used.

If an asymmetric public key is used to encrypt the message, the sender cannot repudiate ownership of the message. Legal evidence of message transactions is stored in the data, which are used in applications such as e-commerce. Another common characteristic of these procedures is the first step in converting the user-supplied plaintext to a canonical message text representation, defined as equivalent to the inter-SMTP representation of message text. The final output in each procedure is used as the text portion of an e-mail in the electronic mail system.

Figure 13.40(a) shows the MIC-CLEAR process and is the simplest of the three. The MIC generated is concatenated with encrypted DEK and the SMTP text and inserted as the text portion in the e-mail.

In the MIC-ONLY process, shown in Figure 13.40(b), the SMTP text is encoded as a printable character set. It consists of a limited set of characters that is assured to be present at all sites and thus make the intermediate sites transparent to the message. The MIC is concatenated with encrypted DEK and the encoded message and fed to the e-mail system.

Figure 13.40(c) is the most sophisticated of the three processes. The SMTP text is padded, if necessary, and encrypted. A public key is the best choice here because *it guarantees* the originator ID. The encrypted message, the encrypted MIC, and the encrypted DEK are all encoded in printable code to pass through the e-mail system as ordinary text. They are concatenated and then fed to the e-mail system.

Pretty Good Privacy (PGP).   Pretty good privacy (PGP) is a secure mail package developed by Phil Zimmerman that is available in the public domain. Figure 13.41 shows the various modules in the PGP process at the originating end. The reverse process occurs at the receiving end and is not shown. PGP is a package in the sense that it does not reinvent the wheel. Rather it is a clever process that utilizes various available modules to perform the functions needed to transmit a secure message, such as e-mail.

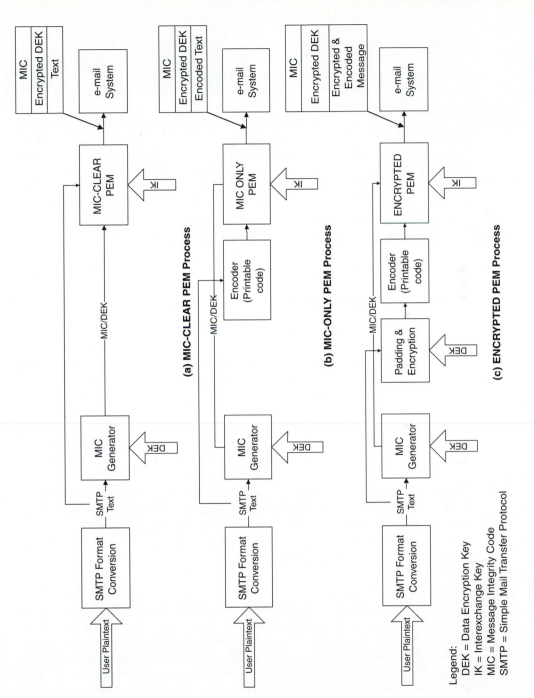

Figure 13.40   PEM Processes

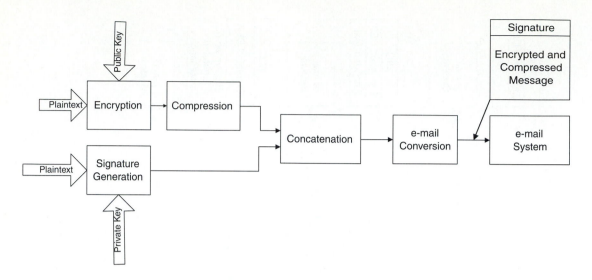

Figure 13.41   The PGP Process

The signature generation module uses MD5 to generate a hash code of the message and encrypts it with the sender's private key, using the RSA algorithm. Either IDEA or RSA is employed to generate the encrypted message. IDEA is more efficient than RSA, but secret key maintenance is necessary in contrast to RSA's use of a public key. The encrypted message is compressed with ZIP. The signature is concatenated with the encrypted message and converted to ASCII format by using the Radix-64 conversion module to make it compatible with the e-mail system.

PGP is similar to ENCRYPTED PEM but has the additional compression capability. The main difference between PGP and PEM is how the public key is administered. In PGP, it is up to the owner. In PEM, it is formally done by a certification authority (the Internet Policy Certification Authority (PCA) Registration Authority). In practice, PGP is used more than PEM. Both PGP and PEM provide more than a secure mail service; they can be used to send any message or file.

SNMPv3 Security.   We dealt with secure transmission in SNMPv3 in Chapter 7. Although a network management system–management agent behaves like a client/server system, the security features are more like message transfer cryptography. We will compare the processes we described in Chapter 7 to message transfer cryptography. Figure 13.42 shows a conceptualized representation of Figure 7.13 for an outgoing message.

In a network management system, the user password and authoritative SNMP engine ID (network management agent ID) are used to generate an authentication key with USM. This key is equivalent to the data encryption key (DEK) in PEM or the private key in PGP.

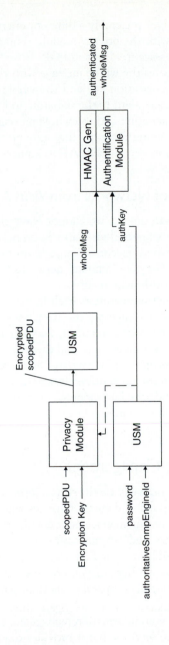

Figure 13.42   SNMP Secure Communication

The authentication key, or preferably a different encryption key, is used to generate an encrypted scoped PDU with the privacy module. This step is similar (but not identical) to encryption of the message in PEM and PGP.

The USM module prepares the whole message with the encrypted scoped PDU and other parameters. The authentication key and the whole message are used as inputs to generate HMAC, which is equivalent to the signature in PEM and PGP. The authentication module combines the signature and the whole message to output the authenticated whole message. For an incoming message, the authentication module is provided the whole message, authentication key, and HMAC as input to validate the authentication.

13.5.8   Protection of Networks from Virus Attacks

In the current Internet environment, we cannot leave the subject of security without mentioning undesired and unexpected virus attacks on networks and hosts. These viruses are usually programs that, when executed, cause harm by making copies and inserting them into other programs. They contaminate networks by importing infected programs from outside sources, either on-line or via disks.

The impact of virus infection manifests itself in many ways. The serious viruses prevent access to your hard disk by infecting the boot track, compromising your processor (an outside source controlling your computer), flooding your network with extraneous traffic that prevents your hosts from using it, and the like.

Generally, viruses are recognized by patterns, and virus checkers look for such patterns. Apart from common sense preventive measures, you should install the latest virus checkers on all your hosts and schedule them to run periodically. They also check inputs into the processor for possible virus infection.

13.6   Accounting Management

Accounting management is probably the least developed network management application. We discussed the gathering of data for statistics with RMON probes in Chapter 8 and in Section 13.3.4. Accounting management could also include the use of individual hosts, administrative segments, and external traffic.

Accounting of individual hosts is useful for identifying some hidden costs. For example, libraries in universities and other large enterprises consume significant resources and may need to be accounted for as a separate function. This task can be done by using RMON statistics on hosts.

The cost of operations for an information management services department is usually apportioned according to the services that it provides to other parts of the organization for planning and budget purposes. The network needs to be configured so that all traffic generated by a department can be gathered from monitoring segments dedicated to that department.

External traffic for an enterprise is handled by service providers. The fee for services negotiated with the service provider is often based on traffic volume and traffic patterns, such as peak traffic and average traffic. Internal verification of the service provider's billing is always good management practice.

13.7   Report Management

We have elected to treat report management as a special category, although it is not assigned a special functionality in the OSI classification. Reports for the various application functions—configuration, fault, performance, security, and accounting—could normally be addressed in sections dealing with those topics. We treat reports as a special category because a well-run network operations center often goes unnoticed. Attention usually is paid to it only when there is a crisis or the quality of service suffers for some reason. Thus generating, analyzing, and distributing various reports to appropriate groups when the network is running smoothly, is important to maintaining a well-funded, well-managed operations center. We can classify such reports as (1) planning and management reports, (2) system reports, and (3) user reports.

Planning and management reports keep upper-level management apprised of the status of network and system operations. They are also helpful for planning purposes and budgeting for capital and operational expenses. Table 13.1 lists some of the planning and management reports under different categories. As the information management services department's main product is service, management also needs to be apprised of how service quality is meeting the terms of any service level agreements (more about this topic in Section 13.9). Reports in this category include network availability, systems availability, problem reports, service response to problem reports, and customer satisfaction. Reports on traffic trends should address traffic patterns and volumes in both the internal network and external networks. Information technology is constantly evolving, and hence management should be apprised of advances in it and the need to plan for adapting to new technology. Finally, for budgeting purposes, the cost of operations by function, use, and personnel needs to be presented.

Table 13.1   Planning and Management Reports

Category	Reports
Quality of service/service level agreement	Network availability
	Systems availability
	Problem reports
	Service response
	Customer satisfaction
Traffic trends	Traffic patterns
	Analysis of internal traffic volume
	Analysis of external traffic volume
Technology trends	Current status
	Technology needs projection
Cost of Operations	Function
	Use
	Personnel

Table 13.2   System Reports

Category	Reports
Traffic	Traffic load—internal
	Traffic load—external
Failures	Network failures
	System failures
Performance	Network
	Servers
	Applications

Table 13.3   User Reports

Category	Reports
Service level agreement	Network availability
	System availability
	Traffic load
	Performance
User-specific reports	User-defined reports

The engineering and operations functions require operation-oriented reports. Traffic, failure, and performance are the important categories, as shown in Table 13.2. Analysis of patterns emerging from these reports is helpful in tuning the network for optimum results.

Users are partners in network services and should be kept informed as to how well any service level agreements are being met. Some service objectives are met by joint efforts of the users and the information management services department. Table 13.3 shows some typical user reports. A service level agreement normally covers network availability, system availability, traffic load, and performance. In addition, users may require special reports. For example, administrators may want periodic payroll or personnel reports.

13.8   Policy-Based Management

We discussed network and system management tools in Chapter 12. In this chapter, we covered the application tools and technology needed in network and system management. For them to be successfully deployed in an operational environment, we need to define a policy and preferably build that into the system (i.e., implement policy management). For example, network operations center personnel may observe an alarm on the network management system, at which time they need to know what action to take. This action will depend on what component failed, the severity or criticality of the failure, when the failure happened, and the like. In addition, they need to know who should be informed and how. That depends on when the failure occurred and what service level agreements are in effect. We illustrated this type of situation with an example of case-based reasoning in Section 13.4, where a policy restraint was used to increase bandwidth as opposed to reducing load in resolving a trouble ticket.

As we mentioned in Section 13.5.1 on security management, policy plays an equally important, if not greater, role as the technical area. Without established policies and their implementation, the technical aspects of security management are not of much use.

However, our focus here is not on administration, although that is important. Rather, it is with the technical aspects of policy implementation in network management. Figure 13.43 is a policy management architecture proposed by [Lewis L5] for network management. It consists of a domain space of objects, a rule space consisting of rules, a policy driver that controls actions to be taken, and action space that implements the actions and attributes of the network being controlled.

Objects in the domain space are events such as alarms in fault management, packet loss in performance, and authentication failure in security management. The objects have attributes. Attributes of alarms include severity, type of device, and location of device. Attributes of packet loss can include the layer at which packets are lost and the percentage loss. Rules in the rule space define actions that can be taken under various object conditions. They are the same as in rule-based reasoning—with if-then, condition-action parameters. The policy driver is the control mechanism, which is similar to the inference engine. Thus the objects in the domain space and the set of rules in the rule space are combined for a policy decision that is made by the policy driver. We need to make clear

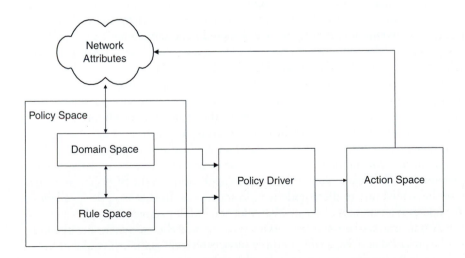

Figure 13.43   Policy Management Architecture

the distinction between a rule and policy here. In an operations center, a rule might be that all network failures are to be reported to the engineering group. A statement that this rule applies to the operations personnel at the network management desk is a policy. Because responsibility is assigned to specific individuals, accountability for failing to do so is properly assigned to the person on duty when a network failure occurs. The action space executes the right-hand side of the rules by changing the attributes of the network and/or executing an external action. In resolving the throughput problem, using the CBR technique, in Section 13.4.3, we considered the options available. Whether network load should be controlled or more bandwidth be allocated is a policy decision. This decision can be implemented as an RBR in the policy rule space. An example of external action would be to page engineering in the case of a severe network failure.

13.9   Service Level Management

The development, establishment, and implementation of enterprise policy does not stop with decisions about the best and consistent use of management tools. The network, systems, and applications that run on them are there to serve customers, and customer satisfaction is essential to the success of the enterprise [Adams EK & Willetts KJ]. Hence policy management should be driven by service level management, which is the second layer from the top in the TMN model shown in Figure 11.11 and in the enhanced version in Figure 13.1.

We illustrated the implementation of service level management in Chapter 11 on TMN with operations systems. An operations system, in general, performs an exclusive or special-purpose function. With the availability of element management and network management systems, generalized service level management should now emerge as a strong management function. Service level management is defined as the process of (1) identifying services and characteristics associated with them; (2) negotiating a service level agreement (SLA); (3) deploying agents to monitor and control network, system, and application component performance; and (4) producing service level reports [Lewis L6]. Lewis compares the definition of service level management to quality of service (QoS) management defined by the Object Modeling Group (OMG).

The characteristics associated with services are service parameters, service levels, component parameters, and component-to-service mappings. A service parameter is an index for the performance of a service—for example, the availability of a business application for a customer. The business application depends on various underlying components—for example, network devices, systems, and applications on the systems. Thus there is a one-to-many mapping between the service parameter and the underlying component parameters. The availability of the business application in the SLA can be defined in terms of the availability of these underlying components. In this case, the availability service parameter is a function of the availability component parameter.

An SLA is a contract between the service provider and the customer, specifying the services to be provided and the quality of those services that the service provider promises to meet. The pricing for the service depends on the QoS commitment.

The objective of service level management is to ensure customer satisfaction by meeting or exceeding the commitments made in the SLA and to guide policy management. In addition, it provides input to a business management system.

Summary

In this chapter we described how to apply all the knowledge that you have gained in the book to practical situations. We dealt with the five categories of OSI application functions—namely, configuration, fault, performance, security, and accounting.

In addition to setting and resetting the parameters of network components, configuration management involves network provisioning and inventory management. Operation systems perform the latter functions. Network topology management is concerned with the discovery and mapping of the network for operations that can be used to monitor them from a centralized operations center.

Fault detection consists of fault detection and fault isolation. Similarly, performance degradation involves detection and isolation. We dealt with these subjects superficially in the early part of the chapter and in more depth in the latter part of the chapter. We discussed the emergence of correlation technology and the various correlation techniques that have been implemented in systems. These techniques correlate events or alarms that arrive from multiple sources and determine the root cause of the problem. A knowledge base built upon heuristic experience, and algorithmic procedures, is used in such systems, either for selection of inputs or for reasoning.

We briefly addressed issues in performance management but emphasized performance metrics and the important role of performance statistics in network management.

Security management played a small part in SNMP management, but it plays an extremely sensitive and crucial role in overall network management. We covered the importance of security policies and procedures. We looked at ways that information can be accessed, tampered with, and destroyed by unauthorized and sometimes vengeful personnel. We also showed how to protect—if not completely, at least partially—against such attacks. In this context, we discussed various authentication and authorization procedures and sophisticated cryptographic methods for transporting information through unsecured channels to ensure secure communication. We introduced secret and public keys in cryptography and how they can be used to accomplish secure message transmission. We briefly addressed the issue of how to protect networks and systems against the growing menace of virus attacks.

From a business management viewpoint, we discussed the use of statistical data gathered from a network to generate accounting applications. We described the three classes of management of information services reports: planning and management, system, and user. We gave examples of the types of reports that are useful in each class.

Many network and service management decisions are policy based. We discussed how they could be built into the system to help personnel who are charged with implementing those policies.

We concluded the chapter by discussing service level management, which is essential in satisfying customer needs. A service level agreement between customer and service provider defines the needs of the customer and the commitments of the service provider.

Exercises

1. You are asked to do a study of the use pattern of 24,000 workstations in an academic institution. Make the following assumptions. You ping each station periodically. The message size in both directions is 128 bytes long. The NMS that you are using to do the study is on a 10-Mbps LAN, which functions at 30 percent efficiency. What would be the frequency of your ping if you were not to exceed 5 percent overhead?

2. List and contrast the tools available to discover network components.

3. The autodiscovery in some NMSs is done by the network management system starting with an *arp* query to the local router.
   a. How would you determine the IP address of the local router?
   b. Determine the local router of your workstation.

4. You are responsible for designing the autodiscovery module of an NMS. Outline the procedure and the software tools that you would use.

5. Redraw Figures 13.4 and 13.5 for VLAN, based on IP address.

6. You are the manager of a NOC. Set up a procedure that would help your operators track the failure of a workstation that is on a virtual LAN.

7. What MIB object would you monitor for measuring the collision rate on an Ethernet LAN?

8. Ethernet performance degrades when the collision ratio reaches 30 to 40 percent. Explain how you would use the 802.3 MIB (RFC 1398) to measure the collision ratio of an Ethernet LAN. The collision ratio of the LAN is the total number of collisions divided by the number of packets offered to the LAN, measured on the Ethernet interface.

9. Repeat Exercise 7, using an RMON MIB.

10. a. The trap alarm thresholds are set at two levels—rising and falling. Explain the reasoning behind these settings.
    b. Define all the RMON parameters to be set for generating and resetting alarms when the collision rate on an Ethernet LAN exceeds 120,000 collisions per second and falls below 100,000 collisions per second. Use *eventIndex* values of 1 and 2 for event generation for the rising and falling thresholds.

11. Download the MRTG tool and measure the following performance statistics on a subnetwork.
    a. current data rate—incoming and outgoing
    b. trend over the past 12 months

12. Review RFC 2064 and write a one- or two-page (maximum) report on the NeTraMet flow meter.

13. For Figure 13.8 network configuration, specify the
   a. RBR rules and
   b. inference engine actions

     to
      • display a red alarm for a failed component.
      • display a yellow alarm for a component that is one layer higher (i.e., one component ahead in its path).
      • display blue alarms on the icons two or more layers higher.

14. Write pseudocode for MBR to detect failure of the components shown in Figure 13.11.

15. Describe three scenarios that require event correlation and explain clearly why each one needs it.

16. a. Describe a scenario (or select one from Exercise 15) that clearly requires event correlation.
    b. Discuss how each method discussed (with the exception of the finite state machine model) could be used to do the task.
    c. Evaluate each method.

17. a. Derive the minimum number of symptoms required to identify n unique problems, using codebook correlation.
    b. Draw a chart with the number of problems on the x-axis and the number of symptoms on the y-axis.

18. The causality graph for a network is shown in Figure 13.44.
    a. Derive a codebook matrix for it.
    b. Derive the correlation matrix, which is a minimal codebook.
    c. Derive the correlation matrix with a Hamming distance of 2.

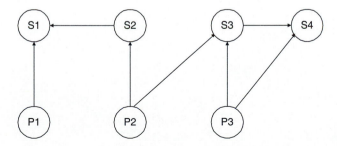

Figure 13.44   Exercise 18

19. a. Assume that in a monoalphabetic cipher encryption scheme, both the alphabet and digits (0–9) can be used interchangeably. Suppose that an intruder who knows the algorithm, but not the key, tries to decipher it. How many attempts would it take, on average, to decipher the message?

    b. If you are given a powerful computer with a nanosecond instruction period to decipher the message, could you do it in your lifetime? How confident are you of your answer?

20. State three important differences in the characteristics of authentication and encryption algorithms.

21. a. You know Ian's public key. What functions of secure e-mail can you perform with it?

    b. Is it safe for you to include the public key with your e-mail address? Draw a comparison to regular mail.

22. Using the md5 utility under FreeBSD 2.x (or md5sum under LINUX), generate a message digest of a file provided by your instructor.

23. Describe the procedure at the originating end when Ian wants to send a secure message, using PEM, simultaneously to Rita and Ted. He communicates with Rita via a secret key and with Ted via a public key.

24. Repeat Exercise 23, using PGP.

CHAPTER 14

Web-Based Management

With the rapid growth of the Internet and World Wide Web, Web technology composed of Web server and Web browsers, has become almost universal in the enterprise environment. In Chapter 12 we discussed the multi router traffic grapher (MRTG) performance tool, which is used to gather traffic statistics and is based on Web technology. Recall that data are gathered by SNMP counters, analyzed, and then stored in Web pages. These Web pages, stored in Web servers, can be accessed locally and remotely via Web browsers. This method illustrates the use of SNMP network management with a Web-user interface.

In Chapter 12 we discussed the use of Web technology in system management and presented the examples of Big Brother and Spong. In both cases, information on the processes running on hosts was gathered by using scripted programs (agents) and then sent to a server, which stored it on Web pages. The Web pages were accessed via Web browsers. This method illustrates use of the Web as a portal in conventional system management.

With the universality of Web technology, marrying the two technologies—network or system management to gather data, and Web technology to display the information at multiple locations on Web browsers—seems logical. We are no longer restricted to displaying information on a centralized monitor associated with an NMS running on a dedicated platform.

However, we can go beyond just displaying the information on a Web browser. We can use Web technology to both gather and display data. This approach takes us into the realm of inserting active Web agents that monitor and control components on networks, systems, and applications and interact with them, using the Web interface.

One of the benefits of using Web technology is the economical means it offers for implementing remote access to network management systems. Network management information needs to be accessed at remote locations for various reasons. For example, a site being managed may have a problem that is being tracked by the network operations center. The personnel at the remote site should be able to look at the same data that the operations center personnel view on their NMS console. Currently, they can do so in a UNIX-based NMS using X-host. The X-host feature in UNIX enables an application to be run on a host from a remote system. However, this method is expensive, both in terms of resource consumption and workstation hardware cost.

Another example is that, during an emergency, a network engineer might need access to a network management system from home. A TELNET access for this purpose is inadequate. It is command driven and does not have the capability of a graphical interface or remote access to NMS. Because a browser is available on any platform, having this information available on a Web server would be convenient. In general, management information can be accessed from any place, using any platform that has a Web browser.

14.1   NMS with Web Interface and Web-Based Management

Based on the preceding discussion, we recognize that we need to distinguish between the Web interface and Web management. The Web interface deals with how information is presented to the user (i.e., with the user interface). For example, Big Brother and Spong use simple UNIX shell or Perl scripts to monitor system conditions and report them periodically to a central server. This communication is based on the TCP/IP protocol. The server converts the information to Web pages and presents it to the user. Thus the collection mechanism has nothing to do with Web technology—only the presentation scheme. A similar approach exists in an SNMP-based management system. For example, a front-end Web interface is available for OpenView Network Node Manager, which makes it appear as a Web-based system. However, it is still a polling-based network management system that uses SNMP queries. Sometimes, the Web interface to an SNMP-based management system is wrongly referred to as Web-based management. We will discuss Web-based portal to SNMP management in Section 14.2.

In its pure implementation, Web-based management is based on Web technology. In this configuration, the agent is embedded in the network element as a Web server and can monitor and/or control the network element. Use of a management application and Web browser allows the information from the Web server agent to be displayed on a Web-based display. This technology is still evolving, but we will cover early implementation of a Web-embedded management system in Section 14.3.

In Section 14.4 we consider the standard for Web-based management of desktops and servers, the Desktop Management Interface (DMI). It was intended to complement the network and system management addressed by SNMP. However, it has created more problems than solutions for those managing information technology, as there are now two standards (SNMP and DMI) for managing systems. However, DMI has been implemented by some vendors including Compaq.

The Desktop Management Task Force (DMTF) is attempting to bring the various management technologies under one umbrella called Web-Based Enterprise Management (WBEM), which we cover in Section 14.5. The purpose of this effort is to integrate, not replace, the different management protocols. We present an implementation infrastructure of WBEM based on Microsoft's Common Information Model (CIM) in Section 14.6.

In parallel with the efforts of the DMTF, a Java-based management system is being developed by Sun Microsystems. It is an extension of the Web-embedded management process discussed in Section 14.3 and makes use of Java applets. Java applets, called Java-Beans, have been extended to manage network and system components; Sun defines them as Java Management Extensions (JMX), which we discuss in Section 14.7. Java technology is also being extended to manage distributed management storage areas. This task is being undertaken by a consortium of Java technology users and is called the Jiro Platform™. We will cover it in Section 14.8.

We will discuss the future directions of management technology in Section 14.9. The challenge is to forecast reasonably accurately what the future holds in terms of the evolution or merger of traditional technologies and active Web-based management of networks, systems, and applications.

14.2   Web Interface to SNMP Management

Two approaches are available to implement a Web interface on existing SNMP-based management systems. The first and short-term approach is to add a Web interface to an existing management system. The second is to have a Web-based system with embedded Web agents in the network components. We will consider the former in this section.

The most common implementation is to establish a Web server on an NMS platform with an interface to the NMS, as shown in Figure 14.1. The SNMP NMS implementation is platform and operating system–specific, and the agents in managed objects are SNMP agents. The protocol between the agents and the manager is the SNMP communication protocol, traversing over UDP/IP. There is a management console for the NMS, and the Web server resides on the same platform. The protocol between the Web server

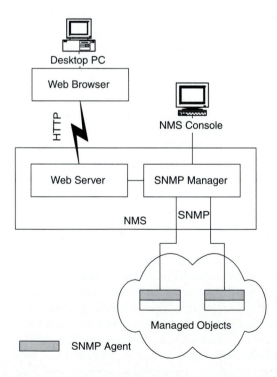

Figure 14.1   An SNMP NMS with a Web Interface

and the Web browser is HTTP, traversing the Internet. The browser can be on any platform (a PC platform is shown).

The SNMP network management systems currently on the market have only text and
tables on the Web interface. However, graphic presentation capabilities may soon be available. When that happens, no console will be required with the NMS. The NMS would
comprise applications and behave as a proxy server [Hyde D], as shown in Figure 14.2.

The basic architecture of the proxy server configuration is the same as that in the
SNMP NMS with a Web interface. The NMS is replaced with the proxy server, and the
NMS console is eliminated, which is an economic advantage. The local Web browser
becomes the NMS console for the operations center.

Other major advantages of this approach are that the proxy server can be implemented on any platform and that the protocol between the proxy server and management
agents can be either SNMP or any proprietary protocol. For example, the Spong server
mentioned previously would fit this architecture. An SNMP proxy server would be one of
the ways to move toward an embedded Web-based management system, which we will
discuss in Sections 14.3 and 14.4. [Hyde D] comments that an SNMP management system would still be used by large enterprises, which have SNMP-based legacy network
components, in combination with Web-based management. Smaller enterprises could
more easily and economically switch to an embedded Web-based management system
[Hyde].

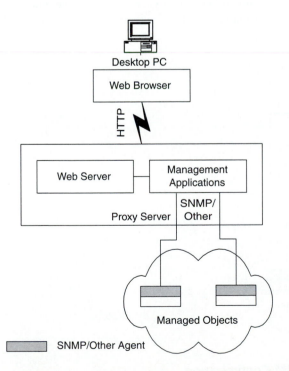

Figure 14.2   A Proxy Server with a Web Interface

14.3   Embedded Web-Based Management

In embedded Web-based management (WBM), Web servers are embedded in the managed objects. Each managed object is assigned a Web address. The management application receives management information from the agents and displays it by means of a Web browser, as shown in Figure 14.3.

Web servers are more intelligent than SNMP agents, which mostly read counters and pass information to the manager or respond to a ping. SNMP agents can send unsolicited basic traps to the manager. However, a Web agent could be sophisticated. For example, it could gather RMON information. Communication between an agent and the manager application is HTTP. For small offices, whose management requirements are minimal, the browser could monitor the Web agents directly, without any management application software. Thus embedded Web agents in network elements greatly simplify network management for network administrators.

Another benefit of embedded WBM is that we can take advantage of portable tools to write the Web agent. For example, the Web agent and server could be written in Java, an interpretive programming language with built-in Web-enabled capabilities. The Java virtual machine (Java interpreter) is available for a variety of platforms. The browser also is portable. The two most popular browsers, Netscape Navigator™ and Microsoft's Internet Explorer™, are also available on multiplatforms. The numerous benefits of using Java for Web-based management applications have been enumerated [Hyde D].

Commercial network products with built-in Web agents are now available, but they are based on proprietary protocols. For example, Hewlett-Packard produces Web-based

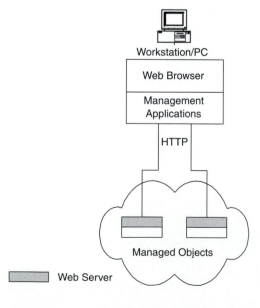

Figure 14.3   An Embedded WBM Configuration

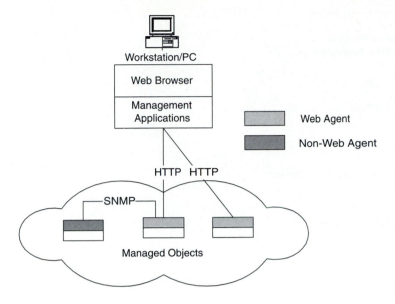

Figure 14.4   The Hewlett-Packard Embedded Agent Configuration

management agents in hubs and switches. Figure 14.4 shows the configuration of both Web and non-Web agents. Web agents function and provide data much the same as RMON does. Communication to the manager application/Web browser, called the HP AdvanceStack Assistant™, is via the HTTP transport protocol. As shown in Figure 14.4, non-Web agents (an SNMP agent is shown) are managed by a Web-agent. This method is especially beneficial for two reasons. First, a network element without a Web agent can be managed in a Web-based management environment. Second, the configuration enables remote probing of switched LANs. As we pointed out in Chapter 8, an expensive means of measuring network statistics is to have a LAN probe in each LAN segment. The Web agent provides an alternative method of measuring statistics. As shown in Figure 14.4, a limited set of statistical data on a non-Web managed device is collected through the Web server and transmitted to the management application. It is limited in that no packet capturing is done.

14.4   Desktop Management Interface

The Desktop Management Interface (DMI) is an industry standard generated by the Desktop Management Task Force (DMTF). The task force was formed in 1992 to develop, support, and maintain management standards for PC systems and products.

The DMI is between computer components and the application software that manages them, as shown in Figure 14.5. Compaq, one of the original founders of DMTF, has implemented DMI [Compaq DMI]. The management application is a desktop-resident

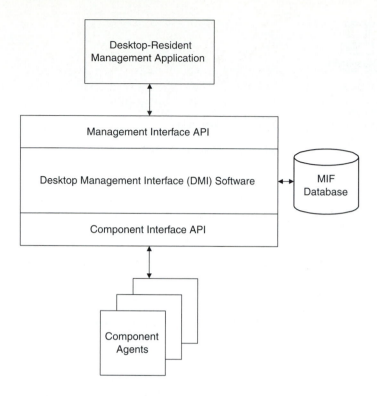

Figure 14.5   DMI Infrastructure

program. The component agents are software agents in the components that go into the desktop. The components can be either software (e.g., a virus checker), hardware (e.g., a network interface card), or firmware (e.g., a Pentium chip). The component agent communicates management information to the management application. To permit multiple vendors' products to be managed by a common application program, two standards are specified in DMI. The first standard is the definition of management information according to a **Management Information Format** (MIF) and stored in a MIF database, which is analogous to MIB in SNMP. Each component's management information is a subset of a MIF database and is compiled into the database when the component is installed. The second standard is the program interface between the component agent and the management application, with DMI software acting as the intermediary between them. It has two standardized application program interfaces (APIs)—one to interface with the component agent and the other to interface with the management program.

As shown in Figure 14.5, the DMI is applicable to local management of desktops and is covered in the DMI 1.0 specifications. The DMI 2.0s specifications extend desktop management to include all the desktops in a network and their management from a centralized remote location. Its design goals are for the system to be independent of a specific computer and operating system, to be usable locally and remotely, and to be mapped to existing management protocols, such as SNMP. Remote accessibility is achieved by using the remote procedure call (RPC).

Figure 14.6 shows the DMI functional block diagram as specified (DMI 2.0s). The left side of the diagram illustrates Version 1.x compatibility with block interfaces. Version 2.0s has user-friendly procedural interfaces, as shown on the right side of the diagram. CI procedural components interface in hardware, software, and firmware with the procedural component interface API in the DMI service provider. Management applications reside in the management interface clients and communicate with the management interface server in the DMI service provider. Events and indications are exchanged between the indication servers at remote stations and the indication client in the DMI service provider. Communication between the DMI service provider and remote stations use RPC. Three RPCs provide support in three different environments. DCE/RPC supports the distributed computing environment used by the IBM operating system and Microsoft. The open network computing/RPC (ONC/RPC) supports the UNIX environment used by Sun workstations. TI/RPC supports the transport independent environment used by Novell networks.

In DMI, managed objects with attributes are defined by ASN.1 syntax. Objects are grouped; and multiple instantiations are defined from tables, as in SNMP management. However, the tables do not have all the capabilities of SNMPv2. DMI-managed objects may be managed by an SNMP manager, using the DMI MIB shown in Figure 14.7. It is a

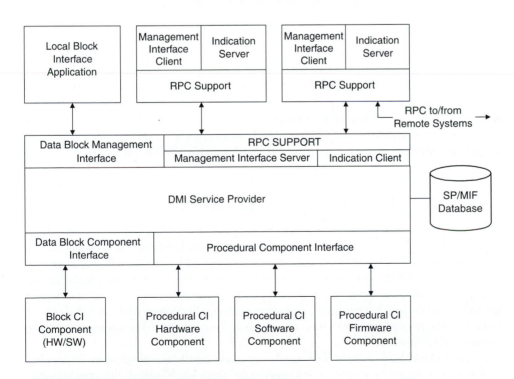

Figure 14.6   DMI Functional Block Diagram

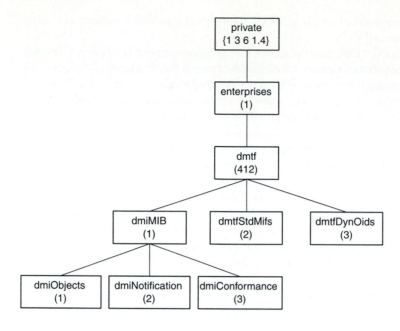

Figure 14.7   Desktop Management Interface MIB

subnode under *dmtf*, which is in the enterprises branch of the Internet MIB. The two MIBs *dmtfStdMifs* and *dmtfDynOids*, are reserved for future use by new standard MIFs and remote SNMP/DMI support. The DMI MIB defines managed objects, notification, and conformance groups.

The role of DMTF has been expanded. In 1996, a consortium of five companies undertook to develop Web-Based Enterprise Management (WBEM) standards, which are designed to integrate existing standards, such as SNMP, CMIP, DMI, and HTTP.

14.5   Web-Based Enterprise Management

There are significant differences between SNMP and DMI. DMTF tried to make them coexist by developing DMI to the SNMP mapping standard (DMI/SNMP), which did not prove successful. DMTF was then assigned in June 1998 a broader Web-Based Enterprise Management (WBEM) task. The goal of the assignment was to unify (not replace) and extend the existing instrumentation and management standards by using object-oriented constructs and design. Then a common management application residing in a Web client could manage network and system components having different management protocol agents via the Internet.

The Desktop Management Task Force has made significant progress in developing WBEM specifications by adopting the **Common Information Model** (CIM), the information-modeling framework developed by Microsoft. The CIM approach is to preserve and extend traditional management information sources, such as SNMP and DMI. The result has been useful for both Internet and intranet services [Hong JWK, Heilbronner S & Wies R]. We will use the name Internet in our description.

CIM is an approach to the management of enterprise systems, software, users, and networks. It uses basic object-oriented structures and concepts. A management model is developed that provides a framework for describing the managed environment. A fundamental taxonomy of objects is defined with respect to both classification and association—and with respect to a basic set of classes—that establishes a common framework.

WBEM consists of five components: Web client, Common Information Model Object Manager (CIMOM), CIM schema, specific management protocol providers, and managed objects with protocol-specific agents. The WBEM architecture is shown in Figure 14.8.

The **Web client** is a Web browser with management applications. The browser uses HTML for presenting management data. The applications could invoke a request to any protocol-specific agent in the managed object, as well as process any data coming from any agent. However, the request is issued against an object in the **CIM schema** and is sent

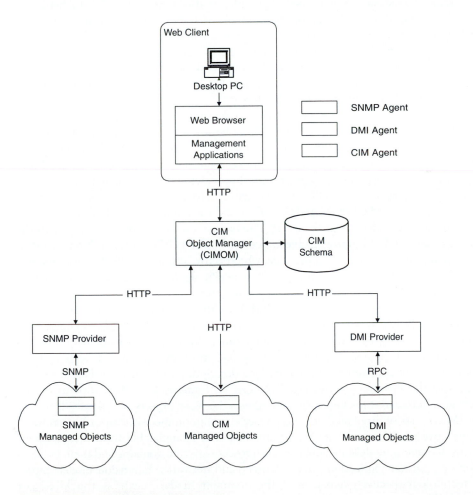

Figure 14.8   WBEM Architecture

to the CIMOM via the HyperText Transport Protocol (HTTP). The management application in the Web client also processes notifications received from CIMOM against objects in the CIM schema. There could be several instances of a Web client on the Internet representing several management systems with manager applications.

The **CIM object manager** forms the heart of WBEM architecture. It mediates all messages among Web client, managed objects, and CIM schema. The messages to and from CIMOM use HTTP as the transport protocol. CIMOM could be implemented as different schemes and in different languages. For example, Microsoft's implementation is Windows Management Instrumentation™ (WMI), which is based on accessing the CIM schema with the Distributed Component Object Model (see Section 14.6). Sun Microsystems has implemented CIMOM with Java Management Extensions, which we will cover in Section 14.7.

CIMOM processes messages from Web clients, as well as those originated by managed objects. When CIMOM receives messages from Web clients, it uses the information from CIM schema to determine which protocol system the managed object belongs to and switches the message to that protocol provider. It also translates the CIM schema format of the managed object to that of the protocol-specific object identification. Thus an SNMP-specific application may send a get request to a managed object, such as a hub, or process a trap received from it. Alternatively, a DMI-specific application may send a set request to a DMI object, such as the hard disk on a desktop or process a disk full notification received from it. These messages pass through CIMOM and the object ID is translated and routed to the appropriate destination.

The **protocol providers** are between CIMOM and the **protocol-specific managed networks**. For example, the SNMP provider is between the CIMOM and the SNMP managed objects network, and the DMI provider is between the CIMOM and the DMI managed objects network. The message between a protocol provider and CIMOM uses HTTP, whereas the message between a protocol provider and a management agent in the managed object uses the specific management protocol. Thus the SNMP provider "speaks" HTTP toward CIMOM and SNMP toward the managed object. You can visualize the protocol provider as a proxy server. The native case is the one associated with the domain containing CIM managed objects accessed using HTTP protocol. No intermediate protocol provider is needed in this case, which is the ultimate WBEM environment.

Each managed domain contains protocol-specific agents and the components that are being managed by that protocol management system.

The common model embodied in CIMOM can be implemented in several ways [Thompson JP]. Two models are actively being implemented now: Java Management Extensions and WBEM. DMTF chose the Common Information Model (CIM) developed by Microsoft for implementation as CIMOM and CIM schema for WBEM. CIM provides a common conceptual framework for a description of the managed environment and defines the taxonomy of managed objects. Its framework is object-oriented. The objects are structured into classes, and associations between objects are identified.

CIM consists of three modules: a core model, common models, and extension models. The **core model** is the high-level framework and is applicable to all management domains. **Common models** are applicable to protocol-specific domains and include information on systems, applications, devices, users, and networks. **Extension models** represent technology-specific extensions of the common models, such as the UNIX or Microsoft Windows operating systems.

A simplified WBEM CIM core model is shown in Figure 14.9 [CIM]. The names are presented as "strings" per model definition. The solid lines indicate the hierarchy or inheritance of the classes; the dashed lines indicate various associations, such as component, system component, realization, and dependency.

In the Core Model, the Managed System Element is at the top level. The Physical and Logical Elements are subclasses of the Managed System Element. A Physical Element is something that occupies physical space and can be touched and felt. Logical Elements are "realized" by installing Physical Elements. Let us illustrate this distinction with an example of a link between two nodes. The Physical Element is the physical medium (e.g., copper wire or optical fiber), and the Logical Element, the circuit identification, is a path connecting the nodes (IP addresses) at the two ends of the link.

Logical Device, System, Service, and Service Access Point are all subclasses of the Logical Element. A Physical Element can have multiple Logical Elements. For example, a physical interface card in a computer can be loaded with either network interface software or modem software. In the former case, it is a network interface card Logical Element, and in the latter case it is a modem Logical Element.

System is an aggregate of an enumerable set of Managed System Elements, as shown by the association, *SystemComponent*. Service is a functionality of a logical device, such as print or file service. Service Access Point represents the management, measurement, and configuration of a Service. For example, using a Service Access Point, a file service can be turned on or off. Dependency relationships exist among the various components shown.

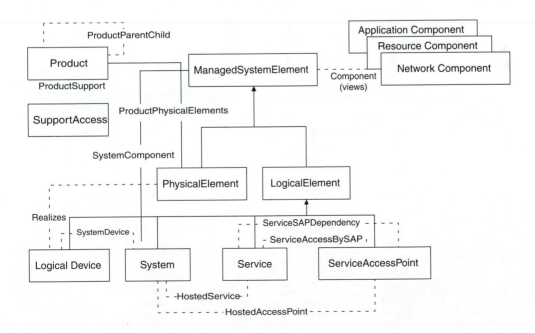

Figure 14.9   Simplified WBEM CIM Core Model

Managed system elements may be viewed as groups of components. We have grouped them into three classifications following the model of [Hong JWK; Heilbronner S & Weiss R]. They are network components, resource components, and application components.

14.6   WBEM: Windows Management Instrumentation

The Windows Management Instrumentation (WMI) is the infrastructure implemented by Microsoft to support the WBEM CIM and Microsoft-specific extensions of it, as shown in Figure 14.10. It comprises a management infrastructure, management applications, and providers of data from managed objects.

The infrastructure includes the CIMOM and the WMI repository. The CIMOM performs, with snap-in management applications, the functions described in Web client in Section 14.5. The communication path in and out of CIMOM uses the *IWbemServices* feature of the COM/DCOM (Component Object Model/Distributed Component Object Model) API. Its services include object creation, deletion, data retrieval, event notification, and query processing.

The WMI repository is the central storage area for management data. The data interchange between CIMOM and the WMI repository uses either the WBEM Managed

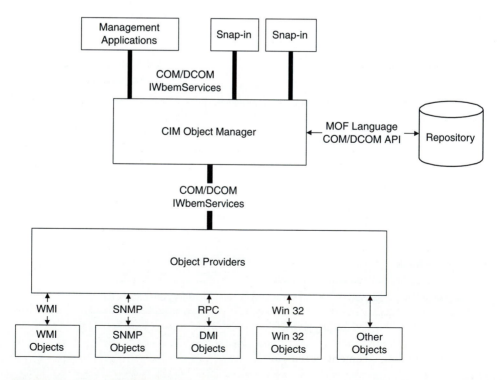

Figure 14.10   WMI Architecture

Object Format (MOF) language or COM/DCOM API. Static data are stored in the repository, and dynamic data are referenced.

The object providers communicate with CIMOM via COM/DCOM API and with the managed objects via their respective protocols. For example, it uses the SNMP protocol with an SNMP-managed object.

14.7   Java Management Extensions

The second approach to developing a common model for total management using Web technology is *Java Management Extensions* (JMX). JMX defines management architecture, APIs, and management services under a single umbrella specification. It evolved from the Java Management API™ (JMAPI) initiative. Sun Microsystems introduced JMAPI as a collection of Java language classes and interfaces designed for network and service management. JMAPI was updated to version 2.0 and then renamed JMX.

The architecture of JMX is vastly different from that of the early version of JMAPI. JMX is based on the *Java Dynamic Management Kit* (JDMK), a key enabling technology in the development of a service driven network, a concept introduced by Sun. We will briefly explain the service-driven network concept in Section 14.7.1 and the role of JDMK in Section 14.7.2. We deal with the architecture and components of JMX in Section 14.7.3. We will also describe how JMX interfaces with the legacy SNMP management system and with the WBEM that is being developed in parallel.

14.7.1   Service-Driven Network

A service-driven network can be considered as a network of services instead of a network of components. (See also Jini technology in Exercises at the end of the chapter.) The service, as a network entity, needs to be provisioned and managed. A good example is the service provided to a residential customer by a telephone company. When a customer requests a service, action is taken at the central office to make the service available to the customer at the telephone jacks in the customer's residence. The customer buys a telephone from a local retail store, plugs it into the telephone jack at home, and hears a dial tone. In the case of a cell phone, the telephone company doesn't need to send an installer to the residence for cable changes. Registration and services are acquired through the hand-held device.

In the Internet environment, the analogy is a *Webphone*. A Webphone is a device with a mini–Web browser—a network-centric device (i.e., a thin client) that can be used as a wired or wireless hand-held device. The wired device may be thought of as a thin client workstation. The wireless device could be any mobile device, such as a pager or palm-computing device. The customer buys a Web-embedded workstation or a hand-held device. The customer then establishes a connection with a service provider by entering the ID of the service provider on the Web page, and transmitting it registers for service. Provisioning is automatic by the service provider; that is, the Webphone is automatically discovered by the management system and included in the topology for operations management. The ultimate goal is for Webphone service to be as reliable and dependable as telephone service. What a dream!

Just as a telephone could be on-hook or off-hook and the switch in the central office automatically recognizes its status, as a service entity the Webphone should be as dynamic as a plug-in module. In the service environment of Java technology, the plug-in module is a **JavaBean**™. A management applet can be added to or be part of the plug-in, which is called JavaBean for Management, or **MBean**™.

14.7.2   Java Dynamic Management Kit

The Java Dynamic Management Kit enables the building of distributed Java-based network management agents. Unlike SNMP network management—wherein the agent mostly responds to queries and operational controls received from the network management system—management intelligence can be built into MBeans. These intelligent agents can be built into systems, applications, and network devices, so long as they are Java compliant. They can generate alarms or notifications (similar to traps in SNMP management) and even take local action to correct problems. Thus we can build an active, distributed network of management agents [Hendricks D].

The Java Dynamic Management Kit has a library of core management services, which are implemented as MBeans. They can be slid in and out of the *JDMK service back plane*. As Java technology has built-in integrity schemes for *push* and *pull* technology, MBeans can be loaded dynamically as they are needed. For example, an MBean can be downloaded to an agent to take a statistical sample on a router that has a congestion problem, and then it can be removed after the problem is solved. In addition, the latest software can be obtained at all times by downloading it from the NMS, without any system or network downtime.

The architecture of a Java Dynamic Management agent is shown in Figure 14.11. It comprises MBeans, a core management framework, also known as an *MBean server* (we will use this terminology), and protocol adaptors to communicate with applications, NMSs, and Web browsers. In addition to MBeans, Figure 14.11 also shows a special Java-Bean, the *C-Bean*™, for *Client Bean*. It is a service entity module built into the agent module and is not associated with any external managed object. For example, a C-Bean could be a collision-monitoring module that the NMS loads on the agent and then invokes as needed. We will use the term MBean rather than C-Bean.

The MBeans and the applications register themselves with the MBean server. It is the interface coordinator between applications and the managed entities. Thus, when an NMS issues a request to perform an operation on a managed object, the MBean server locates the object and performs the operation. Likewise, when a notification is to be sent to an NMS, it directs it to the appropriate protocol adaptor.

The **protocol adaptors** are the interfaces with application programs. Three specific applications are shown—manager, Web browser, and application. The manager is a network management system, and the application could be any specific application program including a proprietary network management system. The protocol adaptor card for the Web browser contains a small Web server that can be used to configure the managed object directly without a management system. This method is equivalent to configuring a managed object via a console interface.

The flow diagram shown in Figure 14.12 [JDMK WP] illustrates how MBeans are accessed and moved around the various components. The components represented in the

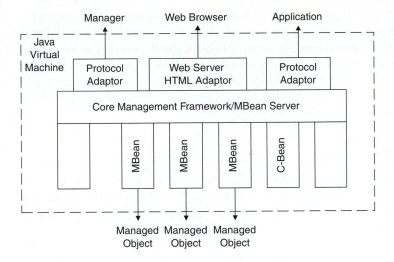

Figure 14.11   Java Dynamic Management Agent Architecture

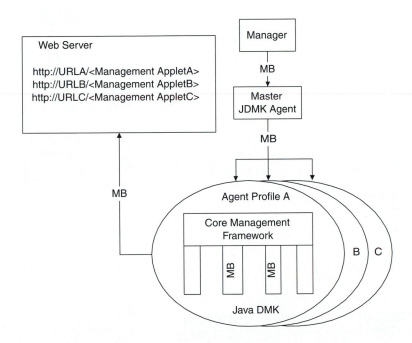

Figure 14.12   Management Bean (MB) Flow Diagram

figure consist of three JDMK agents that are under the control of a master JDMK agent. The manager is an NMS. The Web server stores the management services as applet files with the agents' URLs. Any MBean can be pulled out of the Web server at boot time. The manager pushes the MBean to the master agent, which in turn pushes it to one or more of the three JDMK agents A, B, and C. These agents can be structured hierarchically, which enables services to be cascaded. In the cascade formation, the master agent has an MBean for cascading services.

14.7.3   JMX Architecture

The components of Java Management Extensions (JMX) are presented in Figure 14.13 [JMX WP]. The JMX architecture comprises three main levels: manager, agent, and instrumentation. A fourth level that contains additional management protocol APIs is also defined.

The specifications for implementing JMX-manageable resources are written at the instrumentation level. JMX-manageable resources include all objects developed in Java or

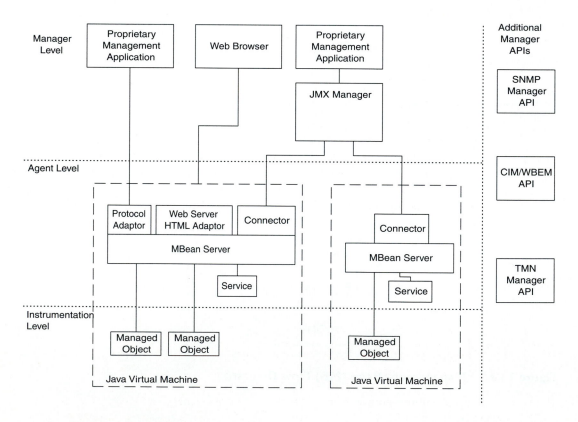

Figure 14.13   JMX Components

have Java wrappers, including network devices, applications, service entities, and systems. The instrumentation of a resource is provided by one or more MBeans. The MBeans can be implemented as either static or dynamic components to be invoked at run time.

The agent level provides specifications for implementing agents. It consists of an MBean server, a set of services for handling MBeans, and protocol adaptors or connectors that interface with the components at the manager level. As we said earlier, every JMAX-manageable resource should be registered with the agent. The interface adaptor to the Web browser also contains a small version of a Web server. The interface to the applications in the manager level is either a *protocol adaptor* or a *connector*. The protocol adaptor gives a representation of MBeans in another protocol. An example is the interface with a non–JMX compliant application, such as an SNMP manager with SNMP protocol. The connector interface is used with a JMX compliant application, such as the JMX manager shown. A variety of protocols that are Java compatible could be used on the connector interface, which include HTTP and the Common Object Request Broker Architecture/Internet Inter-ORB Protocol (CORBA/IIOP).

The manager level components are management applications, network manager, and browser. Multiple agents interface with a JMX manager directly via the connector interface. Proprietary (non–JMX compliant) applications interface with the agent via a protocol adaptor or with the JMX manager via one of the APIs identified in the additional manager APIs.

The modules in the additional manager APIs are the SNMP manager API, CIM/WBEM API, and TMN manager API. They allow the JMX environment to coexist with other management environments. An additional manager API represents a non-Java object as a Java object class to the JMX environment. The SNMP manager API specifies management of SNMP agents by the JMX manager.

The CIM/WBEM APIs are grouped into three categories: CIM, client, and provider. The CIM API represents CIM elements as Java class objects. The client API enables information exchange between the CIMOM and JMX applications. Provider APIs are interfaces between CIMOMs that provide information about Java devices as CIM object classes.

The JMX Manager shown in Figure 14.13 is not a product offered by Sun, similar to its Solstice Enterprise Manager. To implement the JMX manager, Java-based managed applications need to be developed and displayed on a GUI platform, such as a Web browser or a JavaBean display. The JMX Manager can interface with external databases using JDBC (popularly known as Java database connectivity, although Sun Microsystems states that it is not an acronym) API. The JDBC technology provides connectivity to the popular SQL databases.

14.8   Management of a Storage Area Network: The Jiro Platform

So far we have been defining storage areas for each type of management environment. A mixed management environment of networks, systems, applications, hardware, and the like might conceivably contain a network of storage areas. The CIM approach with a

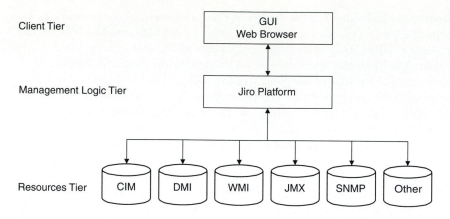

Figure 14.14   Jiro Architecture

CIM schema is a way to address this possibility. Even with CIM schema, we may end up with a distributed network of storage areas, each one being implemented on a different platform supplied by different vendors.

A consortium of Java technology users is developing a solution, called the Jiro (pronounced gyro) platform for managing storage area networks. The objective is to develop a solution for management applications that allows the operation of storage area networks on different vendor platforms. Figure 14.14 shows a three-tier architecture in which the Jiro platform occupies the middle tier. The Jiro platform specification group recommends use of CIM for the resources tier (JMX Supports CIM) and any Java-compatible GUI for the client tier. The client tier is defined as the interface with a human user.

The Jiro Core that specifies the Jiro platform comprises an object model and a component model. The object model is an extension of the Java object model for the support of distributed objects. The component model consists of a set of core components that can be used to build applications, which would run on any platform.

14.9   Future Directions

With fast-moving Web technology and the Internet, the management of networks, systems, and applications is moving toward Web-based management. As we stated in Sections 14.5–14.7, we are offered two options—namely, WBEM and Java-based JMX. Both have merits and a combination of the two (e.g., JMX with Java implementation of WBEM CIM) could be a viable approach. We are not in a position to make a recommendation at this stage because both are still under development. However, the SNMP is a proven and successful management technology that is well entrenched in the enterprise environment and that undoubtedly will continue to be deployed for a long time. Any new technology needs to accommodate the legacy SNMP management.

One important point about Web-based management approaches is the ability to incorporate intelligent distributed agents in a network. As a result, we can implement active network management with local monitoring and control capabilities. This approach would eliminate polling in the traditional systems, such as SNMP and CMIP, and thus reduce network overhead caused by management traffic. In addition, local control would improve the performance of the system as a whole.

WBEM is comprehensive and centralized approach for enterprise management. It builds on the already established management protocol systems and unifies them. It accommodates both scalar and object-oriented schemes. It is being developed as the common integrating standard by DMTF.

JMX is a decentralized management system and uses the new Java technology. Agents in JMX can be embedded in objects and thus can be downloaded from the NMS or a Web server. It is based on JDMK, which is an existing product and runs on a Java virtual machine. A Java virtual machine running on managed objects is platform independent. However, the JMX initiative is still undergoing review.

Summary

In this chapter we reviewed the various stages of development and early implementations of Web-based management systems. We first pointed out how to take advantage of Internet and Web technology to present and distribute management information from a conventional network management system to multiple locations in real time. This result can be achieved by transferring the data to a Web server and accessing it with a Web browser. This method is more economical than today's approach of exporting in the UNIX environment. It also provides the capability to remotely access the network management system.

We then looked at the embedded WBM system. In this simplistic approach, agents are embedded as Web servers in managed objects and given IP addresses. They are then accessed by Web browsers. Web-embedded technology may be considered a precursor to JMX.

The Desktop Management Interface (DMI) system was developed by the Desktop Management Task Force, an industry consortium formed to find ways to manage the assets of desktop systems. The DMI concept is similar to the SNMP concept, yet at the same time much different from it. As the two protocols were managing the same objects from different perspectives, efforts were made to unify them. Those efforts led to a broader objective, WBEM.

The WBEM is an object-oriented approach to integrated network and system management. It does not replace the existing management protocol systems, such as SNMP, DMI, and CMIP, but brings them under a common interface umbrella. The WBEM is based on the Common Information Model (CIM) framework developed by Microsoft. The heart of this framework is a CIM Object Manager (CIMOM) and a database, the CIM schema. The CIMOM mediates between Web-based management applications and the managed objects under various management environments.

The second new approach to network and system management uses Java technology introduced by Sun Microsystems. JMX is an extension to the base Java classes to implement management of networks and systems. It is a distributed architecture based on JDMK, for which some implementations have been completed. It is in competition with WBEM, and at this stage the shape of the Web-based management system that will emerge is unclear. To address the problems created by a multitude of distributed storage area platforms operating on different vendor products, a Java-based management solution, the Jiro platform, is currently under development.

Exercises

1. You have recently joined a small high-technology start-up company as head of its information technology department. The company uses an HP OpenView Network Node Manager as its network management system and Big Brother for system management. You want to integrate them on a common Web interface.

   a. Write the requirements so that one of your engineers can implement it. Be specific in your requirements but do not exceed two pages. (*Hint:* There are several ways that this can be done and the choice is up to your creative imagination.)

   b. Analyze the advantages and limitations of your design.

2. Microsoft has implemented desktop management using DMI specifications on its NT servers. Write a short technical evaluation report on the system.

3. Access Microsoft's Web page and review the white paper on WMI scripting. Write a script for extracting system group information from an SNMP agent.

4. Describe Sun Microsystems' implementation of WBEM on Solaris.

5. a. Describe mandatory group and attribute syntax in DMI MIF.
   b. Write a group MIF for a PC specifying the manufacture and model attributes.

6. Write a brief (less than three pages) report on Sun Microsystems' Jini technology, which could be used to implement a distributed service network.

7. Present an architecture of a JMX-based NMS. Identify all the components and their functions.

8. Imagine that you are working for a company (maybe you are) that has decided to move from an SNMP-based to a Web-based management system. You are asked to prepare an executive summary on the two approaches, WBEM and JMX, and make a recommendation. Present your report, which is not to exceed two pages (executives don't have the time or patience to read longer reports).

APPENDIX A

OSI Network and System Management

In Chapter 3, we introduced OSI management which uses the Common Management Information Protocol (CMIP). Then we discussed its application to the Telecommunications Management Network (TMN) in Chapter 11. We will cover the basic principles of OSI network and system management here. We will describe the management of network resources, including both network elements and the network that connects them. In conjunction with TMN, OSI also addresses management layers above network—namely, service and business management. You may need to review the basic foundations of OSI in Chapter 3 to follow the material in this appendix.

In contrast to the SNMP management standard, which was intentionally kept simple in concept and implementation, the OSI management standard was developed to be broad and flexible and is based on object-oriented technology. Hence it turned out to be complex, difficult to understand, and expensive to implement, which is why it has been sparsely deployed. However, the recent availability of object-oriented technology tools and hardware resources, combined with the need for telecommunication management using TMN, has renewed interest in it.

We will present the complex subject of OSI management by using a simple, easy to follow approach. We will compare OSI management to SNMP management wherever appropriate, which also will help you better understand the former.

A.1   OSI Management Standards

Two standards bodies, the ISO (International Standards Organization) and the ITU (International Telecommunications Union) jointly worked on developing standards for network management. Thus, in the Table A.1 listing of the various standards documents, two numbers are associated with each entry—an ISO designation and an ITU designation (X-series).

Only a partial list is given in Table A.1; for a more complete list see [Raman LG2]. The X.700 series covers the general management framework and a systems management overview. The X.710 series covers the communication protocol and service. The Structure of Management Information (SMI) is specified in the X.720 series. An extensive series of documents ranging from X.730 to X.751 addresses numerous application functions.

A.2   System Overview

The OSI management system concept is similar to that of SNMP management. After introducing the general concept in Chapter 3, we discussed SNMP management in Chapter 4. Figure A.1 shows the OSI management model, defined in ISO 10040/X.701. The managing system consists of an entity playing the manager role and applications that perform the various functions. The managed system comprises the agent role function and managed objects. The managing system performs various operations, such as get and set, which we covered in discussing SNMP management, on a managed system and receives responses. Notification is similar to the trap in SNMP, but it has a broader role in OSI management. The role of the agent is to perform the operations on managed objects and receive notifications from them. This function is similar to SNMP agent operations on network elements. The communication protocol between the managing system and the managed system is the Common Management Information Protocol (CMIP), similar to SNMP in SNMP management.

Table A.1   OSI Systems Management Standards Guide

ISO	ITU	Topic
7498-4	X.700	OSI Basic Reference Model Part 4: Management Framework
10040	X.701	Systems Management Overview
9595	X.710	Common Management Information Service Definition
9596-1		
9596-2	X.711	Common Management Information Protocol
10165-1	X.720	SMI: Management Information Model
10165-2	X.721	SMI: Definition of Management Information
10165-4	X.722	SMI: Guidelines for the Definition of Managed Objects
10165-5	X.723	SMI: Generic Management Information
10165-6	X.724	SMI: Requirements and Guidelines for ICS Proforma associated with Management Information
10165-7	X.725	SMI: General Relationship Model
10165-9	X.727	SMI: System Management Protocol Machine Managed Objects
10164-1 10164-17	X.730-X.751	Systems Management (specifications for various functions and attributes)

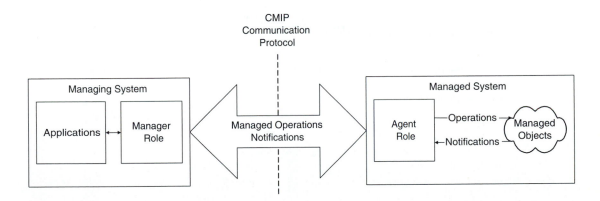

Figure A.1   The OSI Management Model

OSI management differs from SNMP management in the way the managed object is defined. In OSI the managed object is object-oriented, in contrast to the scalar representation of the managed object in SNMP. We observed the difference between the two perspectives in Chapter 3 (Figure 3.9). A managed object representation in OSI is shown in Figure A.2. As OSI is object-oriented, the resources are represented as **managed object classes.** The internal characteristics of a managed object are hidden from the external view, and are specified as **attributes** at the object boundary. The inner **behavior** of the managed object caused by external **operations** is reflected as changes in attributes and is sent out as **notification**s. The operations sent out by the management system as requests requiring responses are part of operations and generate responses by the managed system.

The OSI management system architecture is shown in Figure A.3. It consists of seven messages representing seven services, called **Common Management Information Service Elements** (CMISEs). The communication protocol used by CMISE is the **Common Management Information Protocol** (CMIP).

All but one, **M-EVENT-REPORT,** are generated by the manager and are represented as solid lines in the OSI manager application layer. They are shown as dashed lines in the OSI agent application layer. The M-EVENT-REPORT is shown as a solid line in the agent layer and as a dashed line in the manager layer. All messages are represented by double arrows in both the manager and the agent layers because messages may elicit or require either response(s) or confirmation. Notice that this approach is different from that of SNMP management, in which all messages are unidirectional.

Messages are generated by application processes and are transferred to the presentation layer via an application entity sublayer in the application layer (more about this

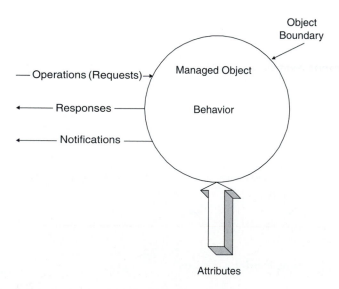

Figure A.2   An OSI Managed Object

OSI Manager   OSI Management Agent

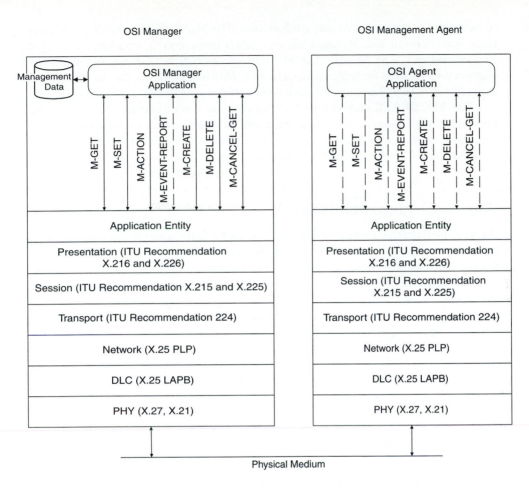

Figure A.3   OSI Management System Architecture

later). The other upper layers of the OSI Reference Model consist of presentation and session layers as described in ITU Recommendations X.216 and X.226 for the former and X.215 and X.225 for the latter.

The lower layers of the model may be either connection-oriented or connectionless. Numerous choices in the set of lower layer protocols are available. Figure A.3 shows an example of a set based on X.25 [ITU Recommendation 224]. Various profiles can be implemented, including the Internet profile [Raman LG2].

The M-GET service comprises *request* and *response* messages. They are equivalent to get-request and get-response messages in SNMP. The get-next-request could also be included in that the OSI get service is for a management object class and thus includes SNMP multiple scalar managed objects. The M-GET requires a confirmation (response) from the agent. The M-SET service enables setting up attribute values in the managed object and may or may not require confirmation. The **M-ACTION** service is used to perform operations in the managed object, and confirmation is optional. An M-GET Request message may be canceled by using the **M-CANCEL-GET** message, which requires confirmation from the agent. The M-EVENT-REPORT is akin to the trap message in SNMP, but it has a much broader effect than the few generic alarms in SNMP.

The **M-CREATE** and **M-DELETE** services are used to create and delete object classes, for which there is no equivalent in SNMP. A close analogy in SNMP for these services is creation and deletion of conceptual rows for tabular objects. Both these OSI messages require confirmation from the agent.

A.3   Organization Model

We explained the OSI organization model in Chapter 3. It comprises the manager system, agent system, and managed objects. A system can perform the dual role of manager and agent, switching from one role to the other dynamically. This approach is significantly different from that of SNMP management, in which the two functions can coexist but are distinct processes.

In the OSI management specifications, managed objects are assigned to groups called *domains*. Such grouping can be done either on an organizational basis or on an administrative basis. When an organizational domain is formed, it consists of a set of managed objects based on functional criteria, such as fault and performance management. The organizational domain may also recognize organizational considerations such as common policies and procedures.

Administrative authority is the basis for an administrative grouping. It determines the creation of and interaction between domains. An administrative grouping may comprise organizational domains.

A.4   Information Model

The OSI information model is based on the abstraction of information on the managed object as seen across the boundary of the managed object by a manager system. (See Figures 3.9(b) and Figure A.2 on perspective of a managed object.) The schema representing the managed object is used by the manager system and the management agent system to communicate with each other as in SNMP management. Again, the OSI management information model is object-oriented and in that regard differs from the SNMP management information model, which is scalar-based. The information model deals with the Structure of Management Information (SMI), managed objects and object classes, and management information trees.

A.4.1   Structure of Management Information

The definition of managed objects, syntax based on ASN.1, and the naming convention in the OSI Structure of Management Information (SMI) are similar in many ways to the

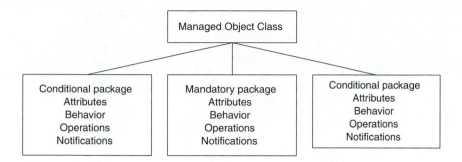

Figure A.4   Structure of a Managed Object Class

SNMP SMI that we covered in Section 4.7.2. However, because of OSI SMI's object-oriented approach, they differ in content from those in the SNMP SMI.

The concept of managed objects in OSI SMI refers to a group of objects having similar properties, defined as a *managed object class*. We can loosely compare this type of grouping to grouping of managed objects in the SNMP model. However, a managed object class is more than a group of SNMP managed objects. It is a collection of objects whose attributes and behavior are similar, and it supports a common set of operations and notifications.

A managed object class can be created from other managed object classes, called **packages,** as shown in Figure A.4. It comprises one **mandatory package** and multiple **conditional packages.** A managed class in this structure has the properties associated with the mandatory package and may include properties of conditional packages. For example, a transport class object class would include an OSI transport class 4, applicable to both connection-oriented and connectionless cases, but would include a transport class 0 or 2, only if it is connection-oriented. We will address the method of defining the properties of an object class and a package in Section A.4.2.

Managed object classes are obtained by using an *inheritance tree,* as we will show in Section A.4.3. There are three types of trees in OSI management. Besides the inheritance tree, there is a *naming tree* and a *registration tree,* which we will discuss in Section A.4.4. We will cover the *template* for specifying managed objects in Section A.4.5.

A.4.2   Managed Object Class and Instance

A **managed object class** is a group of **managed objects** with common attributes and behavior, can be subjected to similar operations, and emit a set of similar notifications, as previously shown in Figure A.1. The properties of a managed object are defined by a template specifying these characteristics. A managed object is an **instance** of a managed object class with defined values in the template. For example, hub can be defined as a managed object class, with each hub having different attribute values (e.g., manufacturer, serial number, number of ports, etc.) as an instance of the hub managed object class. As shown in Figure A.5, the hub is a managed object class having common attributes and two specific hubs as

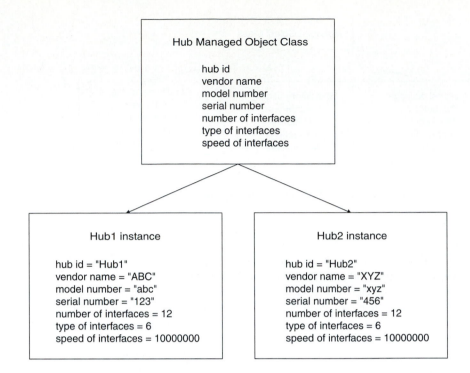

Figure A.5   An Example of a Managed Object Class and Instances

two instances of it. Each instance has different values for hub ID, vendor name, model number, and serial number. They are 10-Mbps Ethernet hubs (ifType=6) with 12 ports.

Let us now look at the properties (or characteristics) associated with the managed object, which we covered briefly in Chapter 3. The properties of a managed object and object class are interdependent, as we will demonstrate shortly.

Attributes and Attribute Group.   **Attributes** of a managed object include the data types and values associated with it. As discussed in Chapter 3, the basic data types could be either simple or constructed. Unlike SNMP, OSI permits the use of a wider range of ASN.1 data types. For example, multiple values can be associated with attributes by using a SET OF construct.

The value associated with an attribute could be either single- or multiple-valued and is specified according to the syntax rule. The syntax is specified in the ASN.1 language described in Chapter 3.

Attributes have access rules (e.g., read, write, and read–write), which are accomplished with *operations*. Attributes can also be created, deleted, or changed with *operations*.

Attributes can be grouped to form an **attribute group**. Because each attribute value may have different syntax requirements, the attribute group does not follow the syntactical rule.

Behavior.   **Behavior** describes the internal actions of a managed object. It is the glue that holds the properties of a managed object together [Raman LG]. Behavior definitions can be specified with attributes and operations and can include notifications. A change in the value of an attribute can generate notification. For example, in an environment with multiple managers performing different functions, such as configuration and performance on a managed system, a change in the configuration made by operations in a configuration management system may affect performance. Hence the performance management system needs to be sent notifications. Another example is a package, in which two attributes may be related in a constrained manner. In such a situation, an operation on one attribute would cause the behavior to affect the other attribute. We can picture the scenario where the **set** command is used to administratively turn off an interface, which would behaviorally effect the **get** command that is gathering data on that interface.

Operations.   **Operations** perform actions on attributes and are also called attribute-oriented operations. The **attribute-oriented operations** are **get**, **set**, **replace**, **add**, and **remove**. We will describe the commands and service entities associated with them when we consider the CMIP service element in Section A.5. The **get** operation is a read function. The **set** operation is used to set a value of attributes. The **replace** operation replaces an attribute in a package with any appropriate value or with a default value. The **add** and **remove** operations perform an addition or removal of a member to or from a set (e.g., addition of a member to a group).

Three **object-oriented operations** are used to perform an operation on an object— **action**, **create**, or **delete**. The **action** operation executes a valid process on the object. Typically, when more than just setting or replacing an attribute value is involved, the **action** operation is used. It could be as complex as running a process that invokes the **behavior**, changes the attributes of a managed class, and invokes multiple **responses** and **notifications**. SNMP management has no equivalent functions.

Notifications.   **Notification**s are similar to traps in SNMP management. They are events generated by the management agent without a command from the management system. However, it is broader in scope than the trap and is generated either by an external or by an internal stimulant. As mentioned under object-oriented operations, notifications may be generated as a side effect. Alarms are also generated and transmitted by managed objects via notifications. Data generated by notifications may also be logged for later utilization and not sent out.

A.4.3   Inheritance

We defined a managed object class as a group of managed objects with common properties. Another way of looking at it is that a managed object is an instantiation of a managed object class, as previously shown in Figure A.5.

We can add attributes to a managed object class and derive a new class, called a *subclass*, which is similar to deriving a data subtype from a data type. The **subclass** is derived from a **superclass** and *inherits* the properties of the *superclass*. All the attributes

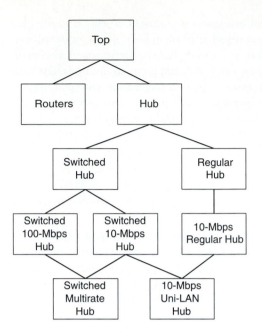

Figure A.6   An Example of Inheritance

of a superclass are maintained by a subclass, and more are added to restrict the class of object instances in the subclass.

The three categories of **inheritance—single inheritance, multiple inheritance (polymorphic)**, and **allomorphic**—are shown in Figure A.6, which represents a network containing routers and hubs. At the top of the managed objects is the ultimate superclass, *top*. Hub is superclass of the switched and (regular) hubs. The 10-Mbps regular (non-switched) hub managed object subclass is derived by single inheritance from the hub superclass. Likewise, the switched 10-Mbps and 100-Mbps hub subclasses are derived by single inheritance from the switched hub superclass. A switched multirate hub that has both 100-Mbps and 10-Mbps port speeds has polymorphic inheritance from its superclasses at the 100-Mbps and 10-Mbps switched hubs. The 10-Mbps uni-LAN hub is the class of hubs that can be configured only as a single LAN. In other words, it behaves as a regular hub and hence is allomorphic with the 10-Mbps regular hub managed object class.

A.4.4   Management Information Trees

Getting lost in OSI terminology and definitions of the various hierarchical structures—literally losing the forest for the trees—is all too easy. So far we have talked about the development of managed object classes, which is done by using the *inheritance tree*. The object instances have to be uniquely identified, which is done by using the *naming tree*. Once a managed object class has been developed and instances have been given names, they have to be registered with a central authority, which is done by using the *registration tree*, so that they can be universally used.

The Inheritance Tree.   The **inheritance tree** defines the relationship between sub-classes and superclasses. Because the properties of a subclass are derived from a superclass, a subclass may be considered a subset or specialization of the superclass. We have discussed three categories of inheritance. *Single inheritance* derives its properties from a single superclass. *Multiple inheritance* of a subclass derives its properties from more than one superclass. Care must be taken in developing multiple inheritance so that no conflict exists between the properties of the superclasses being used to derive the subclass. The third category is a special case, called *allomorphism*, in which a subclass derived from multiple superclasses takes on the properties of one of the superclasses. It may be considered as a pointer to a superclass.

The Naming Tree.   The **naming tree** is used in the naming of a managed object, which is a specific instance of a managed object class, to give it a unique identification. This procedure is very similar to the OBJECT IDENTIFIER and DESCRIPTOR, using MIB, in SNMP management.

Names are uniquely specified in terms of a **superior** or **context object.** Objects named in terms of another object are called **subordinate objects** and are contained in a **superior object.** Because a subordinate object is contained in a superior object, the naming tree is also called a **containment tree.**

An example of contained managed objects is shown in Figure A.7. The top level of the naming tree is the *root*. Here, *system* is the superior object and *log*, *alarmRecord*, and

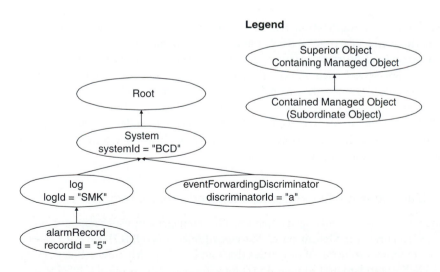

Figure A.7   An Example of Contained Managed Objects (X.720)

Table A.2   Relative Distinguished Names Example

Relative distinguished name	Local distinguished name
systemId = "BDC"	{ }
logId = "SMK"	{logId = "SMK"}
recordId = "5"	{logId = "SMK", recordId = "5"}

eventforwardingDiscriminator are objects subordinate to it. Both *log* and *alarmRecord* are subordinated objects under the context name *system*.

A managed object is identified by a name in the naming tree by either its absolute position in the naming tree with a **global name**, such as OSI or with respect to the context object either with a **relative distinguished** name or a **local distinguished** name. Table A.2 illustrates the naming convention for the example shown in Figure A.7. The local context name *system* is used here for illustration. Figure A.7 and Table A.2 present the name attribute of the managed object and the value of the type of that attribute. Thus the local distinguished name for *alarmRecord* is the sequence of attributes starting with the context name system and is {*logId* = "SMK", *recordId* = "5"}, and the relative distinguished name is *recordId* = "5". The implication is that the relative distinguished name reflects the *system* context name. Notice that the local distinguished name is a sequence of names and hence is bounded by braces, { }.

A subordinate object under a superior object in a naming tree does not imply that the managed object represented by the subordinate object is contained in the superior object class. The inheritance relationship between superclass and subclass is distinct from the name-binding relationship in the naming tree.

Registration Tree.   The **registration tree** is used for officially registering the managed object classes (from the inheritance tree), names of the managed objects (used in the naming tree), attribute definitions, attribute groups, action types, notifications, and packages. The OSI management tree shown in Figure 3.8 has been extended to partially include the registration tree, as shown in Figure A.8. The managed classes, attributes, actions, notifications, and packages developed in the X.700/ISO 10165 series fall under the arc (node) *smi*, structure of management information. It is under the management standard *ms* node. The node *smase* (system management application service entity) and *cmip* are the other two nodes under ms.

A.4.5   Guidelines for Definition of Managed Object Templates

The technique used to specify managed objects in OSI management uses templates and is referred to as **Guidelines for Definition of Managed Objects (GDMO)**. GDMO can be viewed as a set of forms with a list of properties that can be filled with values. See the OSI 10165-4/ITU X.722 standard and [Raman LG2] for a detailed discussion of GDMO.

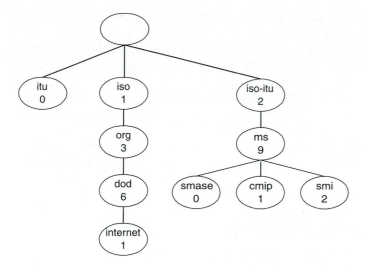

Figure A.8   The OSI Registration Tree

An example of a managed object class using a template for a managed class extracted from X.722 is shown in Figure A.9. The mnemonic name of the managed object class is *lamp*. The MANAGED OBJECT CLASS is the keyword that defines the managed object class.

The DERIVED CLASS identifies the source document and the relationship to either a superclass or subclass. In the example, *lamp* is derived from *top*. It may not always be present, but at least the alternate managed object class in the hierarchy should contain it. Thus, to trace the hierarchy of the managed object class, you may have to trace through a sequence of templates. This procedure is similar to naming of children down the generations in some parts of the world, as in Tamil Nadu, India, where the author was born. The last name of the child (Subramanian in the case of the author) is the given name and the

```
lamp  MANAGED OBJECT CLASS
      DERIVED FROM   "ITU-T Rec. X.721 (1992) | ISO/IEC 1Q165-2 : top;
      CHARACTERIZED BY     lampPackage
      CONDITIONAL PACKAGES      intensityPackage PRESENT IF
         (resourceSupportsIntensity(self ()->lampId);
REGISTERED AS
   {gdmoPlusExamplesModule.lampObjectIdentifier managedObjectClass (3)
   lamp(0)}
```

Figure A.9   An Example of the OSI Managed Object Class Template

first name is the father's given name. Thus to trace a name you have to trace through each generation of the family hierarchy.

The construct CHARACTERIZED BY identifies the mandatory packages and properties. In this example, the *lampPackage* is the mandatory package, and the properties associated with it are part of its template definition.

The CONDITIONAL PACKAGES define the optional packages included in the managed object class. The *intensityPackage* is a conditional package and is present only if the defined condition on *resourceSupportsIntensity* is satisfied.

The REGISTERED AS construct defines the official registered name of the managed object class. Here, *lamp* is defined in the registration tree under *gdmoPlusExamplesModule*.

A.5   The Communication Model

We presented the high-level representation of the OSI communication architecture in Section A.2 and Figure A.3. The manager and agent application processes use seven messages to communicate with each other. The application process interfaces with the application entity sublayer that is above the presentation layer. The communication protocol used for intersystem communication is the Common Management Information Protocol (CMIP). The communication model deals with the application entity layer and the intersystem message protocol.

A.5.1   System Management Application Entity

A management application, the System Management Application Process (SMAP) communicates with another management application by invoking System Management Application Entity (SMAE), as shown in Figure A.10. The SMAE comprises several service entity modules. The System Management Application Service Entity module (SMASE) services the five management applications: configuration, fault, performance, security, and accounting.

The Common Management Information Service Element (CMISE) handles the communications function for SMASE, using the Common Information Management Protocol (CMIP). The Association Control Service Element (ACSE) sets up and coordinates the activities of setting up and releasing an association with the application. Once the association has been set up, the data move from the CMISE to the remote system via the Remote Operation Service Element (ROSE). ROSE issues requests to a remote system and receives responses in an asynchronous mode. In other words, a request may be issued and followed by other requests and the responses correlated with the corresponding requests.

Figure A.11 shows the interoperability of two applications in two remote systems for the OSI network communication model shown in Figure A.10. Communication between SMASE entities exchange management application protocol data units (MA PDU). CMIP PDUs are exchanged between CMISE entities.

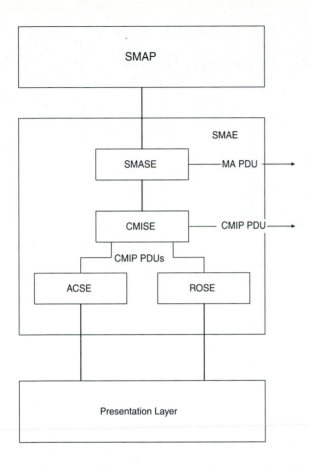

SMAP = Systems Management Application Process
SMAE = Systems Management Application Entity
SMASE = Systems Management Application Service Element
CMISE = Common Management Information Service Entity
CMIP = Common Management Information Protocol
ROSE = Remote Operations Service Element
ACSE = Association Control Service Element

Figure A.10   The OSI Network Communications Model

Common Management Information Service Elements.   We introduced the seven services (or messages) offered by CMISE in Section A.2. The CMISE model consists of two submodels. In the first, the manager sends a command to an agent and may expect one or more responses from the agent, which is called *operations*. The second submodel is concerned with an unsolicited message from an agent, which may expect confirmation from the manager, and is called *notifications*.

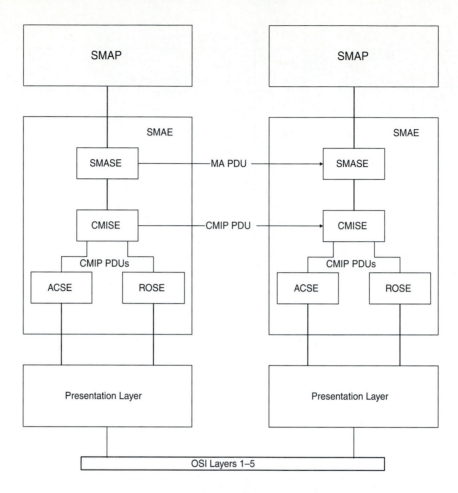

Figure A.11   The OSI Interoperability Communication Model

The commands M-GET, M-SET, M-ACTION, M-CREATE, M-DELETE, and M-CANCEL-GET are operations. The event M-EVENT-REPORT belongs to notifications. The M in all the operation and notification command names stands for *management*. The *get, create, delete,* and *cancel-get* operations expect confirmations or responses, called *confirmed services*. A response may be multiple. For example, the GET command associated with a multiple management object class (called *scope*) could invoke multiple responses.

The operations *set* and *action*, as well as the notifications *event-report*, may or may not require responses or acknowledgements. They can be either confirmed or unconfirmed services. The requirement for confirmation depends on the type of operations or notifications, and the data format should specify it. The CMISE services and CMIP operation values are listed in Table A.3, along with a brief description of each service.

Table A.3   CMISE Services and CMIP Operation Values

Service	Operation Value Confirmed/Unconfirmed	Description
M-EVENT-REPORT	0/1	Send notifications to another open system
Multiple responses	2	Not a CMISE service, but used with scope
M-GET	3	Retrieve attributes and values from managed objects
M-SET	4/5	Set or modify attributes
M-ACTION	6/7	Initiate action in a managed object
M-CREATE	8	Request an open system to create a managed object
M-DELETE	9	Request an open system to delete managed objects
M-CANCEL-GET	10	Command to cancel a previously sent M-GET service

Invoke ID	Operation Value	Managed/ Base Object Class	Managed/ Base Object Instance	Information

Figure A.12   A CMIP PDU

The Common Management Information Protocol.   The Common Management Information Protocol (CMIP) is the communication interface with the CMISE. It generates a protocol data unit (PDU) for a message. The PDU format generated by CMIP is a modification of the generic ROSE PDU format, and is shown in Figure A.12. The invoke ID field is the PDU identifier and is used in correlating the response. The operation value is determined by the appropriate operation/notification from Table A.3. For example, the *get* operation will have an operation value of 3. The next two fields in the CMIP PDU are the managed object class and managed object instance. The term *base object* is used in connection with retrieval of multiple objects associated with the scope clause in which multiple objects could be retrieved using the **get** command by specifying a base object. The information field is a group of fields describing operation-specific data.

A.6   Application Functions Management

OSI management had paid specific attention to the development of management applications (functional model), which motivated development of the rest of the OSI management models. Application functions management can be compartmentalized, as shown in

Figure A.13, as management application functional areas, system management functions, and common management information service elements, which we discussed in Section A.5. Management application functions invoke system management functions, which in turn utilize the common management information services to execute applications.

The five system application functional areas are configuration, fault, performance, security, and accounting. They are represented as clouds in Figure A.13 because the functional areas overlap. For example, packet loss in a network could be classified under both fault and performance management. They may even use common management functions. Hence OSI specifications for system management functions are for primitive service functions.

The system management functions (SMF) are abstract specifications, more like requirements of the functions needed to implement the applications. They are shown

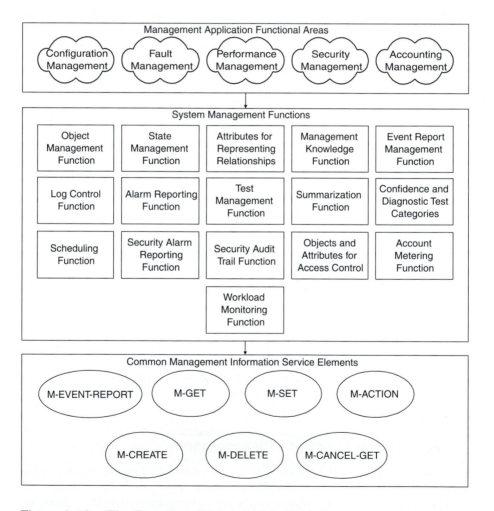

Figure A.13   The Functions Management Model

under system management functions in Figure A.13. The purpose of most of the functions can be inferred from the title. The object management function, state management function, and attributes for representing relationships are concerned with the configuration of managed objects. The Management knowledge function exchanges information between systems.

The event report management function, log control function, alarm reporting function, test management function, and confidence and diagnostic test categories are oriented toward fault administration and notifications. The summarization function could be used for fault management, as in trouble ticket administration, or for performance management, as with statistics. This function preprocesses and compresses the data prior to transmission.

The system management functions related to security management applications are the security alarm reporting function, security audit trail function, and objects and attributes for access control. The account metering function and workload monitoring function are oriented toward accounting management. The scheduling function is a general system management function used to schedule operations.

The third compartment in Figure A.13 identifies the common management service elements invoked by the system management functions to perform the tasks. They are the seven CMISE services: M-EVENT-REPORT, M-GET, M-SET, M-ACTION, M-CRE-ATE, M-DELETE, and M-CANCEL-GET.

Summary

In this appendix we presented an overview of OSI management. We discussed the complexity and flexibility of object-oriented OSI management and compared, where appropriate, it to the simpler scalar-oriented SNMP/Internet management. OSI management is based on the Common Management Information Protocol/Common Management Information Service Elements (CMIP/CMISE). We identified the service elements of a common management information service and explained how they are used.

Our discussion of the information model dealt with managed object classes and instances. They are derived by using the inheritance tree in the OSI management information model. The naming tree is used to name managed objects, and the registration tree registers the names of managed object classes.

The OSI communication model dealt with the CMISE and CMIP. We looked at the lower and upper layer profiles used in OSI management and the role of the Association Control Service Element (ACSE) in establishing and releasing application associations across systems. The Remote Operations Service Element (ROSE) performs the exchange of data after the ACSE has established the associations.

The five management application functional areas of configuration, fault, performance, security, and accounting utilize the system management functions, which in turn invoke the common management information services to execute tasks.

APPENDIX B

Project Suggestions

B.1 Project Structure and Evaluation

Here we are presenting a list of suggested projects to accompany the course. Most have been undertaken by students during the past 3 years, who have found them both challenging and interesting. Each project is expected to take 20 to 30 hours of student time. The projects can be done individually or by a group. If a project is done by a group, each student's contribution should be clearly identified for grading purposes. A group typically comprises two to four students. Each individual or group should present the project and its results to the class upon completion. Presentations should be limited to 10 to 15 minutes. The laboratory or software aspects of projects should be presented to the instructor outside the class presentation.

One way to structure the project is to allow students to pick a project from the list or come up with their own suggestions. Students should select projects and partners (if any) during the first few weeks of the course. An outline of the projects with end products should be expected at midterm. The final report should be due a week before the end of the term. Grading criteria for the project should include creativity, content, report (organization and completeness), and presentation.

B.2   Projects

1. Laboratory setup of a managed LAN with low-end NMS (e.g., SNMPc):

   Students load PCs with the operating system containing the TCP/IP stack and set up multiple LANs, using a hub. The SNMPc is loaded on a PC, which then manages the LANs. Several management applications are practiced.

2. Laboratory setup of a managed virtual LAN with low-end NMS:

   Multiple LANs are set up as VLANs and a network management system is set up to manage them. This project can also be done as a special report on expanding the role of VLANs.

3. LANE management:

   If facilities are available, this can be a laboratory project. If not, a study report can be prepared on the challenges of setting up LANE, using ATM technology, and on the management considerations associated with doing so.

4. ATM network management:

   The use of ATM for SONET and the WAN management associated with it can be researched. Provisioning of an end-to-end configuration is an interesting study. Another area of ATM exploration is multimedia application and the management associated with it.

5. Set up a commercial enterprise NMS:

   Set up an NMS from scratch and perform fault and performance management. This project usually requires the student to have had some prior experience with the UNIX system. This project could be combined with a group that is setting up the LANs.

6. Configuring system management—Big Brother or Spong:

   Big Brother or Spong can be downloaded and configured to manage systems in local networks. Interesting modifications to the original systems can be made as part of this project.

7. Web-based management:

   This popular project may be done by several groups, each implementing a different version of Web-based management. This project can be a software development project or an in-depth theoretical project. A Web interface can be added to an existing SNMP management system. A Web-interface module for the HP OpenView Network Node Manager is available and has been used in this project before. The entire project can be done from scratch, starting with the SNMP tools.

8. Traffic measurement, using MRTG:

   The MRTG freeware can be downloaded and set up on a host to measure the traffic at an interface of a network component.

9. HFC management:

   This new area of network management affords numerous opportunities for hands-on projects if the facilities needed for it exist. Fault localization is a challenge in this project. A theoretical study including QoS management is another opportunity here.

10. ADSL management:

    ADSL management is still in its early stages, and a wealth of projects can be undertaken in this area, both as laboratory and theoretical study projects. In addition, it can be extended to other DSL technologies.

11. Use of Tcl/Tk for network management:

    The scripting tool in general is an area of study for a project in network management. Specifically, Tcl/Tk [Zeltserman D & Puoplo G] is very useful as a management tool.

12. Event correlation:

    We have dealt with several technologies for event correlation. Implementation of any one would be an interesting project.

13. RMON:

    A simple RMON tool, for example *tcpdump*, can be implemented to make statistical measurements and analyze the type of traffic on a network.

14. Software simulation:

    Many of the preceding projects could be simulated with common tools and could be an exciting way to accomplish a laboratory project when needed facilities are lacking.

(Registered) Trademarks

Item	(Registered) Trademark of
AdvanceStack	Hewlett-Packard Company
C-Bean	Sun Microsystems, Inc.
CheetahNet	Superior Electronics Group
CiscoWorks	Cisco Systems, Inc.
CRITTER	Cabletron Systems
HP 9000	Hewlett-Packard Company
HP AdvanceStack Assistant	Hewlett-Packard Company
InCharge	System Management ARTS
Internet Explorer	Microsoft Corporation
Java	Sun Microsystems, Inc.
Java Dynamic Management Kit (JDMK)	Sun Microsystems, Inc.
Java Management API (JMAPI)	Sun Microsystems, Inc.
Java Management Extensions (JMX)	Sun Microsystems, Inc.
JavaBean	Sun Microsystems, Inc.
Jiro Platform	Sun Microsystems, Inc.
MBean	Sun Microsystems, Inc.
MIB Manager	Empire Technologies
Microsoft Windows	Microsoft Corporation
NerveCenter	Seagate Software
NetMetrix	Hewlett-Packard Company
Netscape Navigator	Netscape Communications Corporation
NetView	IBM Corporation
Network Node Manager	Hewlett-Packard Company
OpenView	Hewlett-Packard Company
Real World Interface	Computer Associates, Inc.
RSA	RSA Data Security, Inc.
Sniffer	Network Associates
SNMP Libraries and Utilities	SNMP Research
SNMPc	Allied Telesyn International
Solstice Domain Manager	Sun Microsystems, Inc
Solstice Enterprise Manager	Sun Microsystems, Inc.
Solstice Site Manager	Sun Microsystems, Inc.
SpectroRx	Cabletron Systems
Spectrum	Cabletron Systems
SunNet Manager	Sun Microsystems, Inc.
Sun Solaris	Sun Microsystems, Inc.
Sun Sparc	Sun Microsystems, Inc.
TIRKS	Telcordia Technologies

(Registered) Trademarks *(continued)*

Item	(Registered) Trademark of
TME 10/NetView	Tivoli Systems, Inc.
Transcend	3Com Corporation
Unicenter/TNG	Computer Associates, Inc.
UNIX	AT&T Bell Laboratories
Windows Management Instrumentation (WMI)	Microsoft Corporation
Windows NT	Microsoft Corporation
XNETMON	SNMP Research

SELECTED BIBLIOGRAPHY

Abe, G. Residential Broadband. Cisco, 1997.

Adams, E.K., and K.J. Willets. The Lean Communications Provider: Surviving the Shakeout Through Service Management Excellence. New York: McGraw-Hill, 1996.

ADSL Forum 1. General Introduction to Copper Access Technologies. http://www.adsl.com/genreal_tutorial.html

ADSL Forum 2. ADSL Tutorial: Twisted Pair Access to Information Highway. http://www.adsl.com/genreal_tutorial.html

Ahmed, A., and M.P. Vecchi. Definitions of Managed Objects for HFC RF Spectrum Management Version 2.0. RF Spectrum Management MIB, April 21, 1995.

AT&T. Telecommunications Transmission Engineering, vol. 3, Networks and Services, 2d ed. Winston-Salem, NC: American Telephone and Telegraph Company, 1977.

ATM Forum. Documents: *af-nm-0019.000, af-nm-0020.000, af-nm-0020.001, af-nm-0027.000,af-nm-0058.000,af-nm-0071.000,af-nm-0072.000,af-nm-0073.000, af-nm-0074.000, af-nm-test-0080.000, af-nm-0103.000, af-ilmi-0065.000, af-dxi-0014.000, af-lane-0021.000*, *af-lane-0038.000*, *af-lane-0050.000*, *af-lane-0057.000*, *af-lane-0084.000*, *af-lane-0093.000*, *af-mpoa-0087.000*, *af-mpoa-0092.000*, *af-ini-0010.002*. http://www.atmforum.com/atmforum/specs/approved.html

Autrata, M., and C. Strutt. DME Framework and Design, Network and Distributed Systems Management, ed. M. Sloman. Wokingham, England: Addison-Wesley, 1994.

Azzam, A. High-Speed Cable Modems. New York: McGraw-Hill, 1997.

Black, D.P. Managing Switched Local Area Networks—A Practical Guide. Reading, MA: Addison Wesley Longman, 1998.

Black, U. [1] Network Management Standards, 2d ed. New York: McGraw-Hill, 1995.

———. [2] Emerging Communications Technologies, 2d ed. Upper Saddle River, NJ: Prentice Hall PTR, 1997.

———. [3] Residential Broadband Networks, Xdsl, Hfc, and Fixed Wireless Access. Upper Saddle River, N J: Prentice Hall, 1997.

CA. Unicenter TNG Framework. Computer Associates. 1997. http://www.cai.com/products/unicent/framework/tng_framework_overview.htm

CableLabs [1] Cable Data Modems—A Primer for Non-Technical Readers. Louisville, CO: Cable Television Laboratories, Inc., April 1996.

CableLabs [2] Cable Data Modem Performance Evaluation—A Primer for Non-Technical Readers. Louisville, CO: Cable Television Laboratories, Inc., November 1996.

Cassel, L.N., and R.H. Austing. Computer Networks and Open Systems—A Top-Down Approach. http://www.csc.vill.edu/~cassel/netbook, 1996.

Chadayammuri, P.G. A Platform for Building Integrated Telecommunications Network Management Applications. Hewlett-Packard Journal, October 1996.

Chapman, D.B. Network (In)Security Through IP Filtering. USENIX Security Symposium III Proceedings, September 14 -16, 1992.

CheetahNet. CheetahNet Technical Summary. Superior Electronics Group, Inc., 1996.

Chen, W.Y. DSL Simulations Techniques and Standards Development for Digital Subscriber Line Systems. Indianapolis: Macmillan Technical Publishing, 1998.

Chu, L.C., and M. Subramanian. *Relationship between Physical and Higher Layer Errors in HFC Communication Network*. ICC, June 1999.

CIM. Common Information Model: Core Model White Paper, version 2.0. Desktop Management Task Force, 1999. http:///www.dmtf.org

Cisco/RMON. http://www.cisco.com/warp/public/cc/cisco/mkt/enm/cwsiman/tech/rmon2_wp.html

Clinton, W. The Telecommunications Act of 1996. Signed by President Bill Clinton, February 8, 1996.

Cohen, R.S. The Telecommunications Management Network. Network and Distributed Systems Management, ed. M. Sloman. Wokingham, England: Addison-Wesley, 1994.

Cohen, R., and S. Ramanathan. TCP for High Performance in Hybrid Fiber Coaxial Broad-Band Access Networks. IEEE/ACM Transactions on Networking, February 1998.

Compaq DMI. Intelligent Manageability. Compaq White Paper, May 1998. http://www.compaq.com/im/dmi2.html

Cooper, F.J., et. al. Implementing Internet Security. Indianapolis: New Riders, 1995.

Crank, R., P. Callahan, and L. Berstein. Rulle-Bases Expert Systems for Network Management and Operations: An Introduction. IEEE Network Magazine, September 1988.

Davis, A.W. Cable Modems: A High-Bandwidth Solution to Internet Access. Desktop Video Communications, January-February 1998.

Diffe, W., and M.E. Hellman. New Directions in Cryptography. IEEE Transactions on Information Theory, vol. 22(6), 1976.

DMI 2.0s. Desktop Management Interface Specification version 2.0s. Desktop Management Task Force, June 24, 1998. ftp://ftp.dmtf.org or http://www.dmtf.org

DMI/SNMP. DMI to SNMP Mapping Standard, version 1.0. Desktop Management Task Force, November 1997. ftp://ftp.dmtf.org or http://www.dmtf.org

Feldmeir, J. Network Traffic Management. Unix Review, November 1997.

Forouzan, B., C.A. Coombs, and S.C. Fegan. Introduction to Data Communications and Networking. WCB/McGraw-Hill, 1998.

Glitho, R.H., and S. Hayes [1] Telecommunications Management Network: Vision vs. Reality. IEEE Communications Magazine, March 1995.

———. [2] Approaches for Introducing TMN in Legacy Networks: A Critical Look. IEEE Communications Magazine, September 1996.

Goralski, W. ADSL and DSL technologies. New York: McGraw-Hill, 1998

Greggains, D. ADSL and High Bandwidth Over Copper Lines, International Journal of Network Management 7:277-287, 1997.

Hajela, S. HP OEMF: Alarm Management in Telecommunications Networks. Hewlett-Packard Journal, October 1996.

Halsall, F. Data Communications, Computer Networks and Open Systems. 4th ed. Harlow, England: Addison-Wesley,1996.

Hawley, G.T. Systems Considerations for the Use of xDSL Technology for Data Access. IEEE Communications Magazine, March 1997.

Hegering, H.G., and S. Abeck. Integrated Network and System Management. Wokingham, England: Addison-Wesley, 1995.

Hegering, H.G., and Y. Yemini, eds. Integrated Network Management III. Amsterdam: North-Holland, 1993.

Heilbronner, S., and R. Wies. Managing PC Networks. IEEE Communications Magazine, October 1997.

Hendricks, D. JavaBeans for the Service-Driven Network. Sun Developer News, Spring 1998.

Hill E. Simple System/Network Monitoring—Spong v1.1. http://strobe.weeg.uiowa.edu/~edhill/public/spong/

Hong, J.W.K., S. Heilbronner, and R. Wies. Web-Based Intranet Services and Network Management. IEEE Communications Magazine, October 1997.

HP WBM. HP Proactive Networking: The Networking Management Component. Hewlett-Packard White Paper, January 1998.

Hyde, D. Web-Based Management: The New Paradigm for Network Management, 1977. http://www.3com.com/nsc/500627

IEEE Com. Special Issue on Wireless Broadband Communication Systems, IEEE Communications Magazine, January 1997.

JDMK WP. Java Dynamic Management Kit—A White Paper. http://java.sun.com/products/JavaManagement/, February 1998.

Jiro. Jiro Technical Overview. http://java.sun.com/, July 8, 1999.

JMX WP. Java Management Extensions White Paper http://java.sun.com/products/JavaManagement/, June 15, 1999.

Kaliski, B.S., Jr., A Layman's Guide to a Subset of ASN.1, BER and DER. Public-Key Cryptography Standards (PKCS). RSA Data Security, Inc., http://www.rsa.com/pub/pkcs/ascii/layman.asc

Kaufman, C., R. Perlman, and M. Speciner. Network Security: Private Communication in a Public World. Upper Saddle River, NJ: Prentice Hall PTR, 1995.

Keshav, S. An Engineering Approach to Computer Networking: ATM Networks, the Internet, and the Telephone Network. Reading, MA: Addison-Wesley, 1997.

Kliger, S., S. Yemini, Y. Yemini, D. Ohsie, and S. Stolfo. A Coding Approach to Event Correlations, Proceedings of the 4th International Symposium on Integrated Network Management, 1995.

Kolodner, J. Case-Base Reasoning. San Mateo, CA: Morgan Kaufman, 1997.

Krawczk, H., M. Bellare, and R. Canetti. HMAC: Key-Hashing for Message Authentication. Request for Comments 2104, February 1997.

Larmouth, J. Understanding OSI. University of Salford, Salford, U.K. http://www.salford.ac.uk/iti/books/osi, November 1997.

Lazar, A., R.. Saracco, and R. Stadler, eds. Integrated Network Management V. London: Chapman & Hall, 1997.

Leinwand, A., and K.F. Conroy. Network Management: A Practical Perspective, 2d ed. Addison Wesley Longman, 1996.

Lewis, L. [1] Private communication.

———. [2]A Case-Based Reasoning Approach to the Management of Faults in Communication Networks. Proceedings IEEE Infocom '93, vol. 3. San Francisco March 28-April 1, 1993.

———. [3] A Fuzzy Logic Representation of Knowledge for Detecting/Correcting Network Performance Deficiencies. Network Management and Control—vol. 2, eds. I.T. Frisch, M. Malek, and S.S. Panwar. New York and London: Plenum, 1994.

———. [4] Managing Computer Networks: A Case-Based Reasoning Approach. Norwood, MA: Artech, 1995.

———. [5] Implementing Policy in Enterprise Networks. IEEE Communications Magazine, January 1996.

———. [6] Service Level Management for Enterprise Networks. Norwood, MA: Artech, 1999.

Lewis, L., and J. Frey. Incorporating Business Process Management into Network and Systems Management. Proceedings of the 3rd International Symposium on Automated Decentralized Systems. Berlin, April 9-11, 1997.

Littwin, A. The Great PCS Buildout: A Status Report. Telecommunications, April 1997.

M.3010. Principles of Telecommunications Management Network (TMN). (CCITT) ITU-T Recommendation M.3010, December 1991.

M.3020. TMN Management Services: Overview. (CCITT) ITU-T Recommendation M.3020, 1992.

MacGuire, S. Big Brother: A Web-based Systems and Network Monitoring and Notification System. http://www.maclawran.ca/bb/bb-info.html/

Maurer, H.A. Data Structures and Programming Techniques, Trans. C.C. Price. Englewood Cliffs, NJ: Prentice-Hall, 1977.

Maxwell, Kim, and Kimberly Maxwell. Residential Broadband, An Insider's Guide to the Battle for the Last Mile. John Wiley & Sons, 1998.

Miller, M.A. Managing Internetworks with SNMP. New York: M&T Books, 1995.

Miller, R.E. Passive Testing of Networks Using a CFSM Specification. Proceedings, 1998 IEEE International Performance, Computing, and Communications Conference, February 1998.

Minshall, G. Tracelook. http://www.ipsilon.com/~minshall/

NIST. Keeping Your Site Comfortably Secure: An Introduction to Internet Firewalls. http://csrc.ncsl.nist.gov/nistpubs/800-10.ps, December 1994.

NMF. A Technical Strategy: Implementing TMN using OMNIPoint. Network Management Forum, 1994.

Oetiker, T., and D. Rand. Multi Router Traffic Grapher. http://ee-staff.ethz.ch/~oetiker/webtools/mrtg/mrtg.html

Perkins, D., and E. McGinnis. Understanding SNMP MIBs. Upper Saddle River, NJ: Prentice Hall PTR, 1997.

Perry, E., and S. Ramanathan. Network Management for Residential Broadband Interactive Data Services. IEEE Communications Magazine, November 1996.

Piscitello, D.M., and A.L. Chapin. Open Systems Networking: TCP/IP and OS. Reading, MA: Addison-Wesley, 1993.

Raman, L.G. [1] OSI Systems and Network Management. IEEE Communications Magazine, March 1998.

———. [2] Fundamentals of Telecommunications Network Management. Piscataway, NJ: IEEE Press, 1999.

Rose, M.T., and K. McCloghrie. How to Manage Your Network Using SNMP. Upper Saddle River, NJ: Prentice Hall PTR, 1995.

RFC* 854. Postel, J., and J.K. Reynolds. Telnet Protocol Specifications. May 1, 1983.

RFC 1155. Rose, M., and K. McCloghrie. Structure and Identification of Management Information for TCP/IP-based Internets. May 1990.

RFC 1157. Case, J., M. Fedor, M. Schoffstall, and J. Davin. A Simple Network Management Protocol. May 1990.

RFC 1212. Rose, M., and K. McCloghrie. Concise MIB Definition., March 1991.

RFC 1213. Rose, M. Management Information Base for Network Management of TCP/IP-based Internets: MIB-II. March 1991.

RFC 1215. Rose, M. A Convention for Defining Traps for Use with the SNMP. March 1991.

---

*Request for Comments.

RFC 1244. Holbrook, P., and J .Reynolds. Site Security Handbook. July 1991.

RFC 1284. Cook, J. Definitions of Managed Objects for the Ethernet-like Interface Types. December 1991.

RFC 1285. Case, J. FDDI Management Information Base. January 1992.

RFC 1354. Baker, F. IP Forwarding Table MIB. July 1992.

RFC 1398. Kastenholz, F. Definitions of Manage Objects for the Ethernet-like Interface Types. January 1993

RFC 1406. Definitions of Managed Objects for the DS1 and E1 Interface Types. Baker, F., and J. Watt, eds. January 1993

RFC 1407. Cox, T.A., and K. Tesink. Definitions of Managed Objects for the DS3/E3 Interface Type. January 1994

RFC 1421. Linn, J. Privacy Enhancement for Internet Electronic Mail: Part I—Message Encryption and Authentication Procedures. February 1993.

RFC 1422. Kent, S. Privacy Enhancement for Internet Electronic Mail: Part II—Certificate-Based Key Management. February 1993.

RFC 1423. Balenson, D. Privacy Enhancement for Internet Electronic Mail: Part III—Algorithms, Modes, and Identifiers. February 1993.

RFC 1424. Kaliski, B. Privacy Enhancement for Internet Electronic Mail: Part IV—Key Certification and Related Services. February 1993.

RFC 1445. Glavin, J., and K. McCloghrie. Administrative Model for Version 2 of the Simple Network Management Protocol (SNMPv2). April 1993.

RFC 1446. Glavin, J., and K. McCloghrie. Security Protocol for Version 2 of the Simple Network Management Protocol (SNMPv2). April 1993.

RFC 1470. FYI on a Network Management Tool Catalog: Tools for Monitoring and Debugging TCP/IP Internets and Interconnected Devices. eds. R. Enger and J. Reynolds, June 1993.

RFC 1513. Waldbusser, S. Token Ring Extensions to the Remote Network Monitoring MIB. September 1993.

RFC 1573. McCloghrie, K., and F. Kastenholz. Evolution of the Interfaces Group of MIB-II. January 1994

RFC 1595. Brown, T., and K. Tesink. Definitions of Managed Objects for the SONET/SDH Interface Type. March 1994

RFC 1695. Definitions of Managed Objects for ATM Management Version 8.0 Using SMIv2. Ahmed, M., and K. Tesink, eds., August 1994

RFC 1748. McCloghrie, K., and E. Decker. IEEE 802.5 Token Ring MIB using SMIv2. December 1994.

RFC 1757. Waldbusser, S. Remote Network Monitoring Management Information Base. February 1995.

RFC 1901. Case, J., K. McCloghrie, M. Rose, and S. Waldbusser. Introduction to Community-based SNMPv2. SNMPv2 Working Group, January 1996.

RFC 1902. Case, J., K. McCloghrie, M. Rose, and S. Waldbusser. Structure of Management Information for Version w of the Simple Network Management Protocol (SNMPv2). SNMPv2 Working Group, January 1996.

RFC 1903. Case, J., K. McCloghrie, M. Rose, and S. Waldbusser. Textual Conventions for Version 2 of the Simple Network Management Protocol (SNMPv2). SNMPv2 Working Group, January 1996.

RFC 1904. Case, J., K. McCloghrie, M. Rose, and S. Waldbusser. Conformance Statements for Version 2 of the Simple Network Management Protocol (SNMPv2). SNMPv2 Working Group, January 1996.

RFC 1905. Case, J., K. McCloghrie, M. Rose, and S. Waldbusser. Protocol Operations for Version 2 of the Simple Network Management Protocol (SNMPv2). SNMPv2 Working Group, January 1996.

RFC 1906. Case, J., K. McCloghrie, M. Rose, and S. Waldbusser. Transport Mappings for Version 2 of the Simple Network Management Protocol (SNMPv2). SNMPv2 Working Group, January 1996.

RFC 1907. Case, J., K. McCloghrie, M. Rose, and S. Waldbusser. Management Information Base for Version 2 of the Simple Network Management Protocol (SNMPv2). SNMPv2 Working Group, January 1996.

RFC 1908. Case, J., K. McCloghrie, M. Rose, and S. Waldbusser. Coexistence between Version 1 and Version 2 of the Simple Network Management Protocol (SNMPv2). SNMPv2 Working Group, January 1996.

RFC 2021. Waldbusser, S. Remote Network Monitoring Management Information Base Version 2. January 1997.

RFC 2104. Krawezyk, H., M. Bellare, and R. Canetti. HMAC: Keyed-Hashing for Message Authentication, February 1997.

RFC 2063. Brownlee, N., C. Mills, and G. Ruth. Traffic Flow Measurement: Architecture. January 1997.

RFC 2064. Brownlee, N. Traffic Flow Measurement: Meter MIB. January 1997.

RFC 2074. Bierman, A. Remote Network Monitoring MIB Protocol Identifiers. January 1997.

RFC 2123. Brownlee, N. Traffic Flow Measurement: Experiences with NeTraMet. March 1997.

RFC 2196. Fraser, B. Site Security Management. September 1997.

RFC 2271. Harrington, D., R. Presuhn, and B. Wijnen. An Architecture for Describing SNMP Management Frameworks. January 1998.

RFC 2272. Case, J., D. Harrington, R. Presuhn, and B. Wijnen. Message Processing and Dispatching for the Simple Network Management Protocol (SNMP). January 1998.

RFC 2273. Levi, D., P. Meyer, and B. Stewart. SNMPv3 Applications. January 1998.

RFC 2274. Blumenthal, U., and B. Wijnen. User-based Security Model (USM) for version 3 of the Simple Network Management Protocol (SNMPv3). January 1998.

RFC 2275. Wijnen, B., R. Presuhn, and K. McCloghrie. View-based Access Control Model (VACM) for the Simple Network Management Protocol (SNMP). January 1998.

RFC 2358. Flick, J., and J. Johnson. Definitions of Managed Objects for the Ethernet-like Interface Types. June 1998.

Rivest, R.L., A. Shamir, and L. Adelman, A Method for Obtaining Digital Signatures and Public-key Cryptosystems. Communications of the ACM. February 1978.

Rose, M.T. The Simple Book: An Introduction to Network Management, Upper Saddle River, NJ: Prentice Hall PTR, 1996.

Saadavi, T.N., and M.H. Ammar, with H. El Ahamed. Fundamentals of Telecommunications Networks. New York: John Wiley & Sons, 1994.

Sethi, A.S., Y. Raynaud, and F. Faure-Vincent, eds. Integrated Network Management IV. London: Chapman & Hall, 1995.

Sidor, D.J. [1] Managing Telecommunications Networks Using TMN Interface Standards. IEEE Communications Magazine, March 1995.

————. [2] TMN Standards: Satisfying Today's Needs While Preparing for Tomorrow. IEEE Communications Magazine, March 1998.

Sloman, M. ed. Network and Distributed Systems Management. Workingham, England: Addison-Wesley, 1994.

Sloman, M., S. Mazumdar, and E. Lupu. Integrated Network Management VI. Piscataway, NJ: IEEE, IEEE Communications Society, and IFIP, 1999.

Stallings, W. SNMP, SNMPv2 SNMPv3, and RMON 1 and 2. Reading, MA: Addison-Wesley, 1998.

Strutt, C. and M.W. Sylor. Digital Equipment Corporation's Enterprise Management Architecture. Network and Distributed Systems Management, ed. M. Sloman. Workingham, England: Addison-Wesley, 1994.

Sun Enterprise. Solstice Enterprise Manager 2.1—A Technical White Paper. Palo Alto, CA: Sun Microsystems, Inc., 1994-1998.

Sun Site and Domain. Solstice Site Manager and Solstice Domain Manager 2.3—A Technical White Paper. Palo Alto, CA: Sun Microsystems, Inc., 1994-1998.

Tanenbaum, A.S. Computer Networks, 3d ed. Upper Saddle River, NJ: Prentice Hall PTR, 1996.

Thompson, J.P. Web-Based Enterprise Management Architecture. IEEE Communications Magazine, March 1998.

Tivoli. A series of product and technical documents in http://www.tivoli.com/

Wack, J.P. and L.J. Carnahan. Keeping Your Site Comfortably Secure: An Introduction to Internet Firewalls. NIST Special Publication 800-10. Gaithersburg, MD: U.S. Department of Commerce, National Institute of Standards and Technology, 1994.

WHI. Concepts and Terminology Important to Understanding WMI and CIM. WinHEC 99 White Paper. Windows(Hardware Engineering Conference: Advancing the Platform, 1999.

Wu, C.H., and J.D. Irwin. Emerging Multimedia Computer Communication Technologies. Upper Saddle River, NJ: Prentice Hall PTR, 1998.

X.208. [1988] Specification of Abstract Syntax Notation One (ASN.1). ITU-T Recommendation X.208, 1988.

X.209. [1988] Specification of Basic Encoding Rules for Abstract Syntax Notation One (ASN.1). ITU-T Recommendation X.209, 1988.

Yemini, S.A., S. Kliger, E. Mozes, Y. Yemini, and D. Olsie. High Speed and Robust Event Correlation. IEEE Communications Magazine, May 1996.

ZDNet. Task Masters: Network Monitoring Tools. ZDNet U.K., 1998. http://www.microsite.co.uk/tivoli/tme

Zeltserman, D. and G. Puoplo. Building Network Management Tools with Tcl/Tk. Upper Saddle River, NJ: Prentice Hall PTR, 1998.

GLOSSARY

Abstract Syntax Notation (ASN.1)   A formalized syntax language used to define managed objects.

Access Mode   The MIB access privilege defined in an SNMP agent of a network element, based on the community name. The access mode is read-only or read-write.

Access Policy   A pairing of an SNMP community name with an SNMP community profile.

Accounting Management   Administration of cost allocation based on the use of network resources. Accounting management is one of the OSI system management functional areas.

Agent Module   A management software module in a network component that can be queried for information by another software module in the network manager. Also, the agent module can generate and transmit information in an unsolicited manner. These are called notifications (or traps in SNMPv1).

Aggregate Managed Object   A group of related managed objects. It is represented by a conceptual table of rows, each row comprising a list of scalar managed objects. The columns of the table are columnar objects, with each row being an instance of the entry. This group is distinct from MIB groups.

Amplitude Shift Keying (ASK)   A digital-to-analog modulation scheme in which the carrier is amplitude modulated.

Application Control Service Element (ACSE)   Sets up and coordinates the activities of setting up and releasing an association with an application. This is used in conjunction with ROSE in OSI management.

Asymmetric Digital Subscriber Line (ADSL)   Digital subscriber line that carries multimedia information from the central telephone office to the customer premises. The downstream and upstream frequencies are different, hence the term asymmetric.

Asynchronous Transfer Mode (ATM)   A cell-based technology used to transport digital data. The switch that switches ATM protocol is called an ATM switch.

ATM Forum   An industry-sponsored international organization whose goal is to accelerate cooperation on ATM technology.

ADSL Transmission Unit (ATU)   ATU is an ADSL (asymmetric digital subscriber line) modem. ATU-C is located at the central office and ATU-R is at the customer site.

Authentication Key   A secret key derived from the user's password (SNMPv3). It is used to authenticate the legitimacy of the user accessing a secure system.

Autodiscovery   In a network management system, the process of automatically discovering components of a network, typically using the ping commands. This is done when the system is turned on and during scheduled maintenance.

Basic Encoding Rules (BER)   The rules used to code objects defined in ASN.1 syntax. A SNMP message is encoded in BER using type, length, and value (TLV).

Bit Error Rate / Bit Error Rate Tester (BER/BERT)   Number of bits in error in the received signal normalized to a bit. It is specified as 10^{-n} where n is an integer. BERT is a test system used to measure BER by comparing transmitted bit pattern to the received one.

Bridge   A device that connects two local area networks (LANs) at the data link layer.

Broadband Networks   Multimedia networks that provide integrated services of voice, video, and data over the same medium. It is short form for broadband ISDN (BISDN). The network is made up of a wide area network (WAN), using ATM technology, and a local loop based on cable, digital subscriber line, and wireless technologies. The services offered are called broadband services.

Cable Modem   A device used in broadband networks that modulates and demodulates from the customer equipment to a radio frequency signal carried on the cable.

Case-based Reasoning   A paradigm used in network management that is based on comparing a problem to previously encountered cases to derive the cause of the problem.

Cipher Block Chaining method of Data Encryption Standard (CBC-DES)   A symmetric encryption protocol recommended in SNMPv3 for secure communication.

Codebook   A matrix of problems and symptoms containing problems as columns and symptoms as rows. It is used in network management to isolate the root cause of a problem.

Common Management Information Protocol (CMIP)   An object-oriented OSI standard management protocol.

Common Management Information Service (CMIS)   A service function provided in OSI management that uses CMIP (common management information protocol). A CMIS element is called CMISE.

Community   Pairing of two SNMP entities that can communicate with each other is called a SNMP community. All SNMP entities with the same community name can communicate with each other. Pairing of MIB view with SNMP access mode is called *community profile*.

Compliance   Defined in SNMPv2 as the minimum set of modules and mandatory groups that should be implemented in an SNMP entity for it to be declared compatible with SNMP.

Configuration Management   Setting and changing of configuration of networks and network components.

Conformance   SNMPv2 defines conformance in units of OBJECT-GROUPS. The SNMP conformance of a product is specified including compliance modules and additional OBJECT-GROUPS.

Counter   A SNMP application-wide data type. Its value is monotonically increasing, non-negative integer. It wraps around when it reaches a maximum value.

DESCRIPTOR   Defines a unique mnemonic name for an object type and begins with a lower case letter.

Digital Subscriber Line Access Multiplexer (DSLAM)   A device at the central office that multiplexes several ATU-C modems.

Digital Subscriber Line (DSL)   Transmission link (loop) between the central office and the customer premises that carries information in a digital format. There are several implementations of DSL—Asymmetric DSL, in which the upstream and downstream bands are different (up to 9Mbps downstream and 1.5 Mbps upstream), HDSL, which offers symmetric service at higher data rate (2 Mbps in both directions), and VDSL, an asymmetric link with a very high data rate (2 Mbps upstream and up to 52 Mbps downstream).

Digital Over Cable System Interface Specifications (DOCSIS)   Specifications for cable modem access technology approved by the MCNS industry consortium.

Emulated LAN (ELAN)   An ATM network configured as a LAN and coexists with Ethernet LAN.

Ethernet   A LAN based on bus architecture that uses CSMA/CD medium access protocol and operates at 10 Mbps speed. Fast Ethernet functions at 100 Mbps and Gigabit Ethernet at 1 Gbps.

Fast Channel   In ADSL, the channel that handles audio and real-time video with fast buffers.

Fault Management   Detection and isolation of a problem causing a failure in the network.

Fiber Distributed Data Interface (FDDI)   A LAN based on token ring technology that uses fiber medium and operates at 100 Mbps. It can be implemented in either a single or a dual ring configuration.

Gateway   A router that connects two networks and can perform protocol conversion.

Gauge   A SNMP application-wide data type, whose value is a non-negative integer. Its value can move either up or down and pegs at a maximum value.

Get-Bulk-Request   A SNMP message issued by the manager to an agent, to retrieve a group of managed objects and their values in bulk.

Get-Next-Request   A SNMP message issued by the manager to an agent, to retrieve the object ID and value of the next managed object in the MIB.

Get-Request   A SNMP message issued by the manager to an agent, to retrieve the value of a managed object.

Get-Response   A SNMP message issued by an agent to a manager, in response to either a get- or set-request message. It is simply called response in SNMPv2.

Guidelines for Definition of Managed Objects (GDMO)   Technique adopted to specify managed objects in OSI management. It uses templates.

Half Bridge / Half Router   Provides a method to connect a LAN via a bridge to a router. This configuration is deployed for access to a service provider by a small office or home office customer as required, using a dial-up link.

High Data Rate Digital Subscriber Line (HDSL)   Digital subscriber line that operates in duplex mode at T1 or E1 rate.

HMAC Protocols   Authentication protocols used for the authentication scheme in security management. It is based on a hashing algorithm (H), to derive the message access code (MAC). Two common algorithms used in SNMP security management are HMAC-MD5-96 and HMAC-SHA-96.

Hub   A LAN in a box. It is a hybrid of star topology with either Ethernet or token ring configuration inside the hub.

Hybrid Fiber Coaxial cable (HFC)   Technology Technology based on multimedia services provided over the television cable system. It is also called cable modem technology.

Inform-Request   A SNMPv2 message from a manager to another manager.

Inheritance   In OSI network management, managed object classes are inherited from other managed objects. Inheritance can be single or multiple.

Instructional Scientific and Medical Service (ISM)   A wireless transmission system that operates over two frequency bands, 902-928 MHz and 2400-2483.5 MHz, with a range of 0.5 and 15 miles respectively.

Integrated Local Management Interface (ILMI)   A management interface between two ATM interface management entities (IMFs). It provides a view of configuration and fault parameters across the user network interface (UNI).

Integrated Services Digital Network (ISDN)   Integrated voice and digital services over a single medium. Narrow-band ISDN, referred to as basic rate, carries two channels. Broadband ISDN, or simply, broadband services, is a cell-based technology at a high data rate.

Interleaved Channel   In ADSL, the channel that handles the data signal, which can tolerate latency, and is interleaved between the fast channel signals.

Internet   A worldwide network based on the TCP/IP suite of protocols.

IpAddress   A SNMP application-wide data type that defines four groups of dotted decimal notation of IPv4.

Java Management Extensions (JMX)   A Java-based management architecture proposed by Sun Microsystems.

Local Area Network (LAN)   A shared medium serving many DTEs located in close proximity, as in a building or a campus environment.

Local Multipoint Distribution System (LMDS)   A wireless transmission system operating over two frequency bands (27,500 - 28,350 MHz) and (31,000 to 31,300 MHz), with a range of about 3 miles.

M-ACTION   An OSI management service element that performs operations in managed objects and sends (optional) confirmations.

Managed Object   Commonly, a network element managed remotely by a network management system. Specifically, it is a node in the management information base (MIB), that can be either a physical or a logical entity. In TCP/IP-based network management, it consists of an object type and an object instance.

Managed Object Class   An object-oriented definition of managed objects in OSI network management.

Management Information Base (MIB)   A management information tree containing Internet management objects. A management object holds a unique position and ID in the MIB. The portion of the MIB that a network element permits an SNMP agent to access is called the MIB view.

Management Information Tree   A hierarchical tree structure used to organize managed objects and object classes. It is called MIB in SNMP and naming tree, or containment tree, in OSI.

M-CANCEL-GET   An OSI management service element that cancels a request message.

M-CREATE   An OSI management service element that creates a management object class.

M-DELETE   An OSI management service element that deletes a management object class.

M-EVENT-REPORT   An OSI management service element that generates unsolicited notifications to another open system.

M-GET   An OSI management service element that retrieves attributes and values from managed objects.

MIB Browser   A SNMP tool to browse through the MIB. The process is called MIB walk.

M-interface   Five interfaces, M1-M5, between the network management system and either private or public networks for management of telecommunication networks, including ATM networks.

MODULE-IDENTITY   An ASN.1 macro that describes the semantics of an information module in ASN.1 syntax.

M-SET   An OSI management service element that sets or modifies attributes of managed objects.

Multichannel Multipoint Distribution Service (MMDS)   A wireless transmission system that operates over the frequency band 2500 - 2686 MHz, with a range of up to 35 miles.

Multiple Systems Operator (MSO)   A service provider, who owns and operates several cable television systems and primarily provides cable TV service. MSOs are now providing broadband services over cable.

Network Interface Device / Unit (NID/NIU)   A device at the customer premises that is the demarcation point between the customer network and service provider network.

Network Management System (NMS)   A platform that houses the network manager module. It monitors and controls the network components from a centralized operation.

Network Operations Center (NOC)   A centralized operation to monitor and manage the network using network management tools and systems.

NOTIFICATION-TYPE   An ASN.1 macro of notification, which is an event or alarm generated by a network management agent and sent to a network management system in SNMPv2 and SNMPv3. It is termed as TRAP-TYPE in SNMPv1.

OAM&P   Operations, Administration, Maintenance, and Provisioning functions in the telecommunications industry.

Object   An object type and associated instance.

Object Identifier   Identifies an object type and is a node in the MIB. It is described by a sequence of numbers or DESCRIPTORs, indicating its position in the MIB.

Object Type   The component of the managed object in the MIB that is defined by the structure of management information (SMI). In TCP/IP management, it consists of object identifier defined by ASN.1 syntax OBJECT-TYPE, and encoded using BER. It does not include an object instance.

Operations System   In the telecommunications industry, used to control the network and the network elements. The term is used in ADSL technology and TMN. The operations system does not directly play a role in the information transfer, but helps in the OAM&P of network and information systems.

Optical Carrier (OC)   The data rate unit of SONET (OC-n) digital hierarchy in the United States. The data rate is 51.84 Mbps.

Performance Management   The monitoring and management of performance parameters of a network and the network components.

Phase Shift Keying (PSK)   A digital-to-analog modulation scheme in which the phase of the carrier signal is modulated.

Ping   A network tool to test the connectivity to a remote device.

Protocol Converter   A node in a network, which does protocol conversion at layers above the network layer. It is similar to the gateway, which does protocol conversion at the network layer.

Proxy Server   A SNMP device that converts any protocol to an SNMP compatible MIB and protocol. It is also used to convert SNMPv1 to SNMPv2 protocol.

Quadrature Amplitude Modulation (QAM)   A digital-to-analog modulation scheme in which the carrier is modulated with a combination of amplitude and phase modulation. It is used in HFC and ADSL access technologies.

Quadrature Phase Shift Keying (QPSK)   A digital-to-analog modulation scheme in which the phase of the carrier signal is modulated based on four levels of the signal represented by four phase states. It is used in HFC technology.

Remote Monitoring (RMON)   Remotely monitoring the network with a probe. The monitored information, gathered and analyzed by RMON, is transmitted to a remote network management system. RMON1 deals with the data link control layer and RMON2 covers all the higher layers.

Remote Operation Service Element (ROSE)   Issues a request to the remote system and receives responses in an asynchronous mode. This module is used in conjunction with ACSE in OSI management.

Response   A SNMP message in SNMPv2. (See Get-response.)

Router   A device that routes packets in a network.

Rule-based Reasoning   An *if-then* paradigm used in network management, based on comparing a problem to previously encountered situations to arrive at the cause of the problem.

Security Management   Provides for legal access to network resources and protects the data from modification of information, masquerade, message stream modification, and disclosure, during data transfer. It is one of the OSI systems management functions.

Set-Request   A SNMP message from a manager to an agent, to set the parameters of a network element.

Simple Network Management Protocol (SNMP)   Internet / TCP-IP based network management protocol.

Single-line Digital Subscriber Line (SDSL)   A high data rate digital subscriber line in which 2-way duplex communication occurs over a single twisted pair.

SNMP Framework   Defines a specific version of SNMP and comprises subsystems and models. SNMP Frameworks are specified for SNMPv1, SNMPv2, and SNMPv3.

Source Routing Bridged Network   A network based on token ring bridges, in which the source node determines the path of the packet.

Spectrum Management System   In HFC link management, a system that deals with the management of the RF spectrum allocated to different digital services, both upstream and downstream.

Structure of Management Information (SMI)   A set of definitions for the structure of management information. It defines managed objects and their characteristics, as well as the relationship between the objects.

Switch   A device that switches analog and digital data.

Synchronous Digital Hierarchy (SDH)   The name used in Europe for the digital hierarchy in an ATM network. The data rate is an integral multiple of 51.84 Mbps. The equivalent name in the United States is SONET.

Synchronous Optical Network (SONET)   The name used in United States for the digital hierarchy (OC-n) in an ATM network. The basic SONET rate (OC-3) is 155.52 Mbps and is three times the rate of basic optical carrier (OC-1) of 51.84 Mbps. The equivalent term in Europe is SDH.

Synchronous Transport Signal (STS)   The data rate unit of SDH (STS-n) digital hierarchy in Europe. The data rate is 51.84 Mbps.

System Network Architecture   IBM proprietary network architecture.

Tcpdump   A network tool to monitor IP packets in a network. Another similar tool is called a sniffer.

Telecommunications Management Network (TMN)   Management of the telecommunications network developed by the International Standards Organization as part of ISO management. It is strongly based on ISO network management.

TimeTicks   A SNMP application-wide data type, which measures time in units of hundredths of a second.

Traceroute   A UNIX network tool to test the route to a remote device. A similar tool for Microsoft Windows is *tracert*.

Transparent Bridged Network   A network of Ethernet-based bridges with a tree topology.

Transport Control Protocol / Internet Protocol (TCP/IP)   A suite of transport layer / network layer protocols that forms the basis for the Internet network.

Trap   An alarm or an event generated by a management agent and sent in an unsolicited manner to a network management system.

User-based Security Model (USM)   The security subsystem specified in SNMPv3 based on the traditional concept of a user name.

Very high data rate Digital Subscriber Line (VDSL)   VDSL is similar to ADSL, but operated at a very high data rate over shorter lines.

View-based Access Control Model (VACM)   The access control scheme defined in SNMPv3. It is more secure and flexible than the simple access policy defined in SNMPv1.

Virtual LAN (VLAN)   A LAN based on switched hub technology. It enables stations to be administratively assigned to different LANs; they are not restrained by the physical configuration of LAN networks.

Web-based Enterprise Management (WBEM)   A project of the Desk Top Management Task Force. The goal is to bring different management systems together using the Microsoft object-oriented framework, Common Information Module.

INDEX

MAC	Medium Access Control
MBR	Model-Based Reasoning
MCNS	Multimedia Cable Network System
MD	Message Digest
MF	Mediation Function in TMN
MIB	Management Information Base
MIT	Management Information Tree
MMDS	Multichannel Multipoint Distribution Service
MOM	Manager of Managers
MOTIS	Message Oriented Text Interchange Standard
MSO	Multiple Systems Operator
NID	Network Interface Device
NIU	Network Interface Unit
NMF	Network Management Forum
NMS	Network Management System
NOC	Network Operations Center
OAM	Operation, Administration, and Maintenance
OAMP	Operation, Administration, Maintenance, and Provisioning
OC	Optical Carrier
OS	Operations System
OSF	Operation System Function in TMN
OSF	Open Systems Foundation
OSI	Open System Interface
OSPF	Open Shortest Path First
OSS	Operations Support System
QAF	Q-Adapter Function in TMN
PBX	Private Branch eXchange
PCI	Protocol Control Information
PDU	Packet Data Unit
PEM	Privacy Enhanced Mail
PGP	Pretty Good Privacy
PING	Packet Internet Groper
PPP	Point-to-Point Protocol
RBR	Rule-Based Reasoning
RF	Radio Frequency